T0332112

Programming with *Mathematica*®
An Introduction

Starting from first principles, this book covers all of the foundational material needed to develop a clear understanding of the *Mathematica* language, with a practical emphasis on solving problems. Concrete examples throughout the text demonstrate how *Mathematica* can be used to solve problems in science, engineering, economics/finance, computational linguistics, geoscience, bioinformatics, and a range of other fields.

- Assumes no formal knowledge of programming.
- Over 285 exercises give the reader plenty of practice using the language to solve problems.
- Ideal for self-study, or for anyone wishing to further their understanding of *Mathematica*.
- *Mathematica* notebooks containing examples, programs and solutions to exercises are available from www.cambridge.org/wellin.

Paul Wellin worked for Wolfram Research from the early-1990s through 2011, directing the *Mathematica* training efforts with the Wolfram Education Group. He has taught mathematics at both public schools and at the university level for over 12 years. He has given talks, workshops, and seminars around the world on the integration of technical computing and education and he has served on numerous government advisory panels on these issues. He is the author of several books on *Mathematica*.

Programming with *Mathematica*®

An Introduction

PAUL WELLIN

CAMBRIDGE
UNIVERSITY PRESS

Shaftesbury Road, Cambridge CB2 8EA, United Kingdom

One Liberty Plaza, 20th Floor, New York, NY 10006, USA

477 Williamstown Road, Port Melbourne, VIC 3207, Australia

314–321, 3rd Floor, Plot 3, Splendor Forum, Jasola District Centre, New Delhi – 110025, India

103 Penang Road, #05–06/07, Visioncrest Commercial, Singapore 238467

Cambridge University Press is part of Cambridge University Press & Assessment,
a department of the University of Cambridge.

We share the University's mission to contribute to society through the pursuit of
education, learning and research at the highest international levels of excellence.

www.cambridge.org
Information on this title: www.cambridge.org/9781107009462

Text set in DTL Albertina 11/13 pt; captions set in Syntax LT System Mathematica® .
Designed and typeset by the author.

First published 2013
5th printing 2019 (version 6, September 2022)

Printed in the United Kingdom by TJ Books Limited, Padstow Cornwall

Page 8. Photographs used courtesy of NASA.

Page 343. Quotation from "The Library of Babel" by Jorge Luis Borges. Translated by James E. Irby,
from LABYRINTHS, copyright © 1962, 1964 by New Directions Publishing Corp.
Reprinted by permission of New Directions Publishing Corp.

Page 472. Bottom: Marcel Duchamp, "Roue de bicyclette" © 2012 Artists Rights Society (ARS),
New York / ADAGP, Paris / Succession Marcel Duchamp.

A catalogue record for this publication is available from the British Library

ISBN 978-1-107-00946-2 Hardback

Additional resources for this publication at www.cambridge.org/wellin

Mathematica and Wolfram Mathematica are registered trademarks of Wolfram Research, Inc.

Contents

     3.1   Creating and displaying lists · 58
            List structure and syntax · List construction · Displaying lists · Arrays · Exercises

     3.2   The structure of lists · 67
            Testing a list · Measuring lists · Exercises

     3.3   Operations on lists · 70
            Extracting elements · Rearranging lists · List component assignment · Multiple lists · Exercises

4   Patterns and rules
     4.1   Patterns · 85
            Blanks · Pattern matching by type · Structured patterns · Sequence pattern matching · Conditional pattern
            matching · Alternatives · Repeated patterns · Functions that use patterns · Exercises

     4.2   Transformation rules · 102
            Creating and using replacement rules · Example: counting coins · Example: closed paths · Example: finding
            maxima · Exercises

     4.3   Examples and applications · 109
            Finding subsequences · Sorting a list · Exercises

5   Functional programming
     5.1   Introduction · 116

     5.2   Functions for manipulating expressions · 118
            Map · Apply · Thread and MapThread · The Listable attribute · Inner and Outer · Select and Pick · Exercises

     5.3   Iterating functions · 132
            Nest · FixedPoint · NestWhile · Fold · Exercises

     5.4   Programs as functions · 137
            Building up programs · Example: shuffling cards · Compound functions · Exercises

     5.5   Scoping constructs · 146
            Localizing names: Module · Localizing values: Block · Localizing constants: With · Example: matrix
            manipulation · Exercises

     5.6   Pure functions · 153
            Syntax of pure functions · Using pure functions · Example: searching for attributes and options · Exercises

Solutions to exercises

Preface

Programming with *Mathematica*

Well-designed tools are not simply things of beauty to be admired. They are, above all, a joy to use. They seem to have their own consistent and readily apparent internal logic; using them seems natural – intuitive even – in that it is hard to imagine using any other tool, and, typically, a minimal amount of effort is required to solve the problem for which those tools were designed. You might even begin to think that your problems were designed for the tool rather than the other way around.

Programming with *Mathematica* is, first and foremost, a joy. Having used various programming languages throughout my life (starting with ALGOL and FORTRAN), it is now hard for me to imagine using a tool other than *Mathematica* to solve most of the computational problems that I encounter. Having at my fingertips an extremely well-thought-out language, combined with tools for analysis, modeling, simulation, visualization, interface creation, connections to other technologies, import and export, seems to give me everything I might need.

Ultimately though, no tool can solve every problem you might encounter; what really makes *Mathematica* the indispensable tool for many computational scientists, engineers, and even artists and musicians, is its capability for infinite extension through programming. As a language, built upon the shoulders of such giants as LISP, PROLOG, APL and C++, *Mathematica* has extended some of the best ideas from these languages and created some new ones of its own. A powerful pattern matching language together with a rule-based paradigm for transforming expressions provides for a natural approach to writing programs to solve problems. By "natural" I mean a quick and direct implementation, one that mirrors as closely as possible the statement of the problem to be solved. From there, it is just a short path to prototyping and eventually a program that can be tested for correctness and efficiency.

But there are tools, and there are tools! Some tools are very domain-specific, meaning that they are designed for a narrow set of tasks defined by a certain discipline or framework and are inappropriate for tasks outside of their domain. But *Mathematica* has taken a different approach. It provides broadly useful tools by abstracting the computational tasks (through symbolic expression manipulation) in such a way that it has found wide use in fields as varied as genomics and bioinformatics, astronomy, image processing, social networks, linguistics, and much more.

In addition to the breadth of fields that can be addressed with *Mathematica*, the variety and extent of the computational tasks that now challenge us have greatly expanded since the turn of the millennium. This is due to the explosion in the sheer amount of information and data that people study. This expansion mirrors the rapid growth in computer hardware capabilities of the 1990s and 2000s which saw speed and storage grow exponentially. Now the challenge is to find software solutions that are up to the task of managing this growth in information and data. Given the variety of data objects that people are interested in studying, tools that provide generality and avoid domain-specific solutions will be the most broadly useful across disciplines and across time. *Mathematica* has been around now for over two decades and it continues to find application in surprising places.

Using this book

This book is designed for anyone who wants to learn how to write *Mathematica* programs to solve problems. It does not presuppose a formal knowledge of programming principles as taught in a modern course on a language such as C or JAVA, but there is quite a bit of overlap between this material and what you would expect in such a formal course. You will learn about the basic building blocks of the *Mathematica* language: expressions; the syntax of that language; and how to put these objects together to make more complicated expressions. But it is more than just a primer on the language. The focus is on solving problems and, as such, this is an example-driven book. The approach here is practical. Programming is about solving problems and besides the obvious necessity of learning the rules of the language, many people find it instructive and concrete to see concepts put into action. The book is packed with examples both in the text proper and in the exercises. Some of these examples are quite simple and straightforward and can be understood with a modicum of understanding of *Mathematica*. Other examples and exercises are more involved and may require a bit more study before you feel that you have mastered the underlying concepts and can apply them to related problems. Since this book is written for readers with various backgrounds in programming languages and using *Mathematica*, I think it best to not identify "levels of difficulty" with the examples and exercises.

Becoming a proficient programmer requires not only a clear understanding of the language but also practice using it. As such, one of the aims of this book is to provide the novice with examples of good programming style and practice. Many of the examples in the chapters are, by design, concise, in order to focus on a concept that is being developed. More involved examples drawing together several different conceptual ideas appear in the examples and applications sections at the end of many of the chapters. Depending upon your needs and level of expertise, you can either start with first principles, move on to basic examples, and then to more involved applications of these concepts, or you might find yourself looking at interesting examples and then, as the need arises, jumping back into the discussion of syntax or usage earlier in a chapter.

The exercises (over 290 of them) are designed to extend and expand upon the topics discussed in the chapters in which they occur. You cannot learn how to program by simply reading a book; the old maxim, "you learn by doing" is as true of learning how to speak a foreign (natural) language as it is true of learning a computer programming language. Try to do as many exercises as you can; create and solve problems that interest you; "life is not a spectator sport" and neither is learning how to program.

Due to resource limitations, all the solutions could not be included in the printed book. Fortunately, we live in an age of easily disseminated information, and so you will find an extended set of solutions to most of the exercises in both notebook and PDF format at www.cambridge.org/wellin. In addition, many of the programs developed in the sections and exercises are included as packages at the same website.

Scope of this book

This book evolved from an earlier project, *An Introduction to Programming with Mathematica*, the third edition of which was also published by Cambridge University Press. As a result of several factors, including a long time between editions, much new material due to major upgrades in *Mathematica*, the original authors traveling different paths – it seemed as if a new title was in order, one that both reflects and builds upon this history while incorporating the latest elements of *Mathematica* itself.

The several versions of *Mathematica* that have been released since the third edition of *An Introduction to Programming with Mathematica* was published now include extensive coverage in new application areas, including image processing, control systems, wavelets, graphs and networks, and finance. The present book draws from many of these areas in the never-ending search for good examples that not only help to illustrate conceptual problems, but also serve as interesting and enlightening material on their own. The examples, exercises, and applications draw from a variety of fields, including:

- *textual analysis and natural language processing*: corpus linguistics, word stemming, stop words, comparative textual analysis, scraping websites for data, sorting strings, bigrams and *n*-grams, word games (anagrams, blanagrams, palindromes), filtering text;

- *bioinformatics*: analysis of nucleotide sequences, computing GC ratios, displaying blocks of genetic information, searching for subsequences, protein-protein interaction networks, dot plots;

- *computer science*: hashing (checksums), encoding/encryption, sorting, adjacency structures, triangular numbers, Hamming numbers, Fibonacci numbers, Euler numbers, root finders, random number generation algorithms, sieving;

- *finance and economics*: time-series analysis, trend plots, stock screens;

- *data analysis*: filtering signals, cleaning data, stem plots, statistical tests, lag plots, correlograms, visualizing spread of data;

- *geometry*: convex hull, diameter of pointsets, point-in-polygon problems, traveling salesman-type problems, hypocycloids and epicycloids, Apollonius' circle;

- *image processing*: resizing, filtering, segmentation;

- *graphs and networks*: random graphs, regular graphs, bond percolation, connected components.

Chapter 1 is designed as a brief tour of the current version of *Mathematica* as of the publication of this book. The examples give a sense of the scope of *Mathematica*'s usage in science, engineering, and other analytic fields. Included is a basic introduction to the syntax of *Mathematica* expressions, working with the *Mathematica* interface, and also pointers to the documentation features.

Several important topics are introduced in Chapter 2 that are used throughout the book, in particular, structure of expressions, evaluation of expressions, various aspects of function definitions, predicates, relational and logical operators, and attributes.

Lists are an essential data type in *Mathematica* and an understanding of how to work with them provides a practical framework for the generalization of these ideas to arbitrary expressions. Chapter 3 focuses on structure, syntax, and tools for working with lists. These topics are all extended in later chapters in the context of various programming tasks. Included in this chapter are discussions of functions for creating, displaying, testing, measuring lists, various visualization tools, arrays (sparse and otherwise), list component assignment, and using `Span` to extract ranges of elements.

Patterns and rules are introduced in Chapter 4. Even though pattern-based programming may be new to many, patterns are so essential to all programming in *Mathematica*, that it seems most natural to introduce them at this point and then use them in later chapters on functional and procedural programming. Topics include a discussion of structured patterns, conditional patterns, sequence pattern matching, using data types to match an expression, repeated patterns, replacement rules, and numerous examples of functions and programs that make heavy use of pattern matching.

The chapter on functional programming (Chapter 5) introduces the many functions built into *Mathematica* associated with this programming paradigm: `Map`, `Apply`, `Thread`, `Outer`, `Select`, `Pick`, and many others. Scoping constructs are explicitly called out in a separate section. A section on pure functions includes numerous examples to help understand this important construct in the context of concrete problems. Adding options, error trapping and messaging, so important for well-designed functions and programs, are discussed in this chapter so that they can be used in all that follows. Numerous applied examples are included such as protein interaction networks, Hamming distance, defining new graphics objects, creating palettes for project files, and much more.

Procedural programming may be most familiar to those who learned programming in a more traditional language such as FORTRAN or C. The syntax of procedural programming in *Mathematica* is quite similar to that in C and Chapter 6 is designed to help you transition to using *Mathematica* procedurally but also mixing it with other programming styles when and where appropriate. Looping constructs and their syntax are discussed in terms of basic examples which are then built upon and extended in the remainder of the book. Included are piecewise-defined functions, flow control, and several classical examples such as sieving for primes and sorting algorithms.

The chapter on recursion, Chapter 7, gives a basic introduction to programming recursively-defined functions. The main concepts – base cases, recursion on the tail, recursion with multiple arguments, and so on – are introduced through illustrative examples. The chapter concludes with a discussion of dynamic programming, a technique for greatly speeding up recursive computations by automatically creating definitions at runtime.

Chapter 8 introduces the various types of number you can work with in *Mathematica* – exact, machine-precision, arbitrary-precision as well as different number types and arrays of numbers. It includes an extended discussion of random number generators and functions for sampling and choosing random numbers. The examples and applications section includes a program to compute the radius of gyration tensor of a random walk as well as material on statistical tests, both built-in and user-defined tests for checking the randomness of sequences of numbers.

The chapter on strings, Chapter 9, is included in recognition of the ubiquity of these objects in broad areas of science, engineering, linguistics, and many other fields. Topics include an introduction to the structure and syntax of strings, basic operations on strings including those that mirror similar operations on lists, an extensive discussion on string patterns including regular expressions such as are found in languages like PERL and PYTHON, and many applications and examples drawn from linguistics, computer science, and bioinformatics.

Chapter 10 on visualization is designed to give you a good sense of the symbolic graphics language so that you can both create your own graphics scenes and functions and also make your objects as efficient as possible. Included is a discussion of primitives, directives, and options, all of which is mirrored in the section on sound. A section on efficient graphics structures is included that discusses multi-objects such as multi-points and multi-lines, as well as material on `GraphicsComplex`, a compact way to represent a graphical object with many repeated primitive elements. Many extended examples are included for functions to plot points in space connected by lines, economic or financial trend plots, space-filling molecule plots for proteins and other chemicals, and root plotting functions.

Dynamic objects were introduced in *Mathematica* 6, and there have, sadly, been few resources for learning the ins and outs of dynamic programming. Dynamic objects provide tools to create interactive elements in your documents from as simple as an animation to as complex as…well, as complex as you can imagine. In Chapter 11 we introduce dynamic objects, starting with top-level functions `Animate` and `Manipulate`, moving on to viewers and various control objects that can be used to control changing parameters. The primitive elements that lie underneath all these top-level functions are `Dynamic` and `DynamicModule`, which are the foundations of the entire interactive machinery now built into *Mathematica*. The chapter closes with several applications including building up interfaces to work with multi-dimensional data, extending work earlier in the book on palettes for file openers, event handlers to interact more with your mouse, and a simple geometry demonstration due to Apollonius.

As a result of the many comments and suggestions from people in the broad *Mathematica* community, I have included a chapter on writing efficient programs, Chapter 12. Although there are many approaches you might take to solve a problem, it is often difficult for the novice to tell which is the most appropriate, or the most efficient, or which scales best. Several "good practices" are considered, including choosing the right function, choosing the right algorithm, listability, pure functions, packed arrays, and so on. Sections on parallel computation and on compiling are also included. These issues are discussed through the use of concrete examples drawn from earlier parts of the book.

The chapter on applications, Chapter 13, builds upon much of the work in the rest of the book but extends it for those who wish to turn their code into programs and applications that can be shared with colleagues, students, or clients. The focus is on making your *Mathematica* programs as much like built-in functions as possible, thereby taking advantage of the interface elements that a user of your code would already know and expect from working in *Mathematica*, things like writing modular functions, usage messages, overloading, and creating and working with packages.

In trying to keep this book both introductory and concise, many topics had to be left out. Some of these topics include: creation of new data types; the internals for ordering of rules; upvalues, downvalues and other internal transformation rules; tuning and debugging; connecting to external programs and databases; interacting with web servers. All of these topics are both interesting and important but there was simply not enough room in the present volume to include them.

Colophon

This book was written and developed in *Mathematica*. Stylesheets were created to the page specifications designed by the author while adhering to the constraints of the publisher's production department. Pages were output to PostScript and then distilled to PDF with Adobe Distiller using a configuration file supplied by the publisher to set such parameters as resolution, font embeddings, as well as color and image conversions.

The text for this book, including mathematical formulas, is set in *Albertina*, a humanist font designed by the Dutch calligrapher Chris Brand (1921–1999), and digitized by the Dutch Type Library (DTL). Captions and labels use the fairly animated sans serif *Syntax*, designed by the Swiss typographer Hans Eduard Meier (1922–).

Acknowledgments

Although writing a book may appear to others as a solitary project, authors know better. I consider myself very fortunate to have had wonderful colleagues to work with and have benefited in innumerable ways from their expertise. The following people provided concrete help in discussing various topics and answering my many questions: Darren Glosemeyer on date plotting functions, statistical tests, and statistical plots; Harry Calkins on graphics and general language issues; Charles Pooh on graphs and networks; Dan Lichtblau on internal algorithms and numerous language issues; Michael Kelly for some suggestions on trend lines implementation; Adriano Pascoletti for permission to use and modify his code for computing points in nonconvex polygons; Tom Sherlock and Faisal Whepley for help on front-end related issues; Oyvind Tafjord for various questions and issues with string manipulation and regular expressions; Andre Kuzniarek and Larry Adelston for layout and production questions.

In addition, I am grateful to the reviewers who provided valuable feedback on early drafts of this book: Harry Calkins, Darren Glosemeyer, Mariusz Jankowski, Dan Lichtblau, and Oyvind Tafjord. Any mistakes that remain are mine and mine alone. If you think you have found one, please let me know so that I can update an errata page on the publisher's website as well as in any future printings of this book.

The entire editorial and production stages of this project have been miraculously smooth, in no small part due to the team at Cambridge University Press. In particular, my editor, David Tranah and his team, have been both supportive and encouraging throughout the project, providing all that an author can ask for. Clare Dennison and Abigail Jones were most helpful on the innumerable editorial and production details that accompany a book project such as this.

Loved ones are the unnamed partners in writing a book. Although unrecognized to the reader, they nonetheless play a critical role for the author. They provide nourishment (in its many guises), support, feedback, and that all-too-critical element, time. I have been blessed with a supportive family throughout this project. In particular, my wife Sheri has lovingly provided all these things and more.

Finally, I would like to dedicate this book to the memory of a very special friend, Bob Johnson. Bob was the person most responsible for getting me involved with *Mathematica* when, back in 1989, as chair of the mathematics department at Sonoma State University, he asked me to join him in the basement (computers were always in basements in those days!?) at Sonoma State and we took our first curious look at a strange new program called *Mathematica* running on a strange new computer housed in a strange black magnesium cube. The excitement of realizing that the worlds of mathematics, science, and engineering would be dramatically changed by this new program was matched by the joy Bob and I experienced in learning how to incorporate this tool into our research and teaching. Bob was that unusual person who knew how to keep his eyes on the prize and his encouragement of my efforts made a huge difference in my life and in the lives of others as well. Thanks Bob.

Paul R. Wellin
programmingmathematica@gmail.com

I

An introduction to *Mathematica*

Overview of basic operations · Numerical computation · Symbolic computation · Graphics and visualization · Data import and analysis · Dynamic and interactive computation · Programming · Starting up Mathematica · Notebook interface · Entering input · Mathematical expressions · Syntax of functions · Lists · Dealing with errors · Help and documentation

Mathematica is a very large and seemingly complex system. It contains thousands of functions for performing various tasks in science, mathematics, engineering, and many other disciplines. These tasks include numerical and symbolic computation, programming, data analysis, knowledge representation, and visualization of information. In this introductory chapter, we give a sense of its breadth and depth by looking at some computational and programming examples drawn from a variety of fields. The last part of the chapter covers basic topics in getting started, including how to enter and evaluate expressions, how to deal with errors, and how to get help, with pointers to the documentation system. Users already familiar with *Mathematica* could lightly skim this chapter.

1.1 Overview of basic operations

Numerical and symbolic computation

On a very basic level, *Mathematica* can be thought of as a sophisticated calculator. With it you can enter mathematical expressions and compute their values.

In[1]:= $\sqrt{2.0 \times 10 \, \pi} \left(\frac{10}{e}\right)^{10}$

Out[1]= 3.5987×10^6

You can store values in memory to be used in subsequent computations. For example, the following three inputs compute the Lorentz factor for an object moving at half the speed of light.

In[2]:= $c = 299\,792\,458\,\dfrac{\text{Meter}}{\text{Second}}$;

In[3]:= $v = \dfrac{c}{2}$

Out[3]= $\dfrac{149\,896\,229\;\text{Meter}}{\text{Second}}$

In[4]:= $N\left[\sqrt{1 - \dfrac{v^2}{c^2}}\,\right]$

Out[4]= 0.866025

Yet *Mathematica* differs from calculators and simple computer programs in its ability to calculate exact results and to compute to an arbitrary degree of precision.

In[5]:= $\dfrac{1}{2} + \dfrac{1}{3} + \dfrac{1}{5} + \dfrac{1}{7} + \dfrac{1}{11} + \dfrac{1}{13}$

Out[5]= $\dfrac{40\,361}{30\,030}$

In[6]:= 2^{1024}

Out[6]= 179 769 313 486 231 590 772 930 519 078 902 473 361 797 697 894 230 657 273 ⸞
430 081 157 732 675 805 500 963 132 708 477 322 407 536 021 120 113 879 ⸞
871 393 357 658 789 768 814 416 622 492 847 430 639 474 124 377 767 893 ⸞
424 865 485 276 302 219 601 246 094 119 453 082 952 085 005 768 838 150 ⸞
682 342 462 881 473 913 110 540 827 237 163 350 510 684 586 298 239 947 ⸞
245 938 479 716 304 835 356 329 624 224 137 216

In[7]:= $N\left[\text{Sin}\left[2017 \times 2^{1/5}\right],\, 40\right]$

Out[7]= $-0.9999999999999999785677712610609832590685$

One of the most significant features of *Mathematica* is its ability to manipulate and compute with symbolic expressions. For example, you can factor polynomials and simplify trigonometric expressions.

In[8]:= $\text{Factor}\left[x^7 - 1\right]$

Out[8]= $(-1 + x)\left(1 + x + x^2 + x^3 + x^4 + x^5 + x^6\right)$

In[9]:= **TrigReduce$\left[\text{Sin}[3\,\theta]^5\right]$**

Out[9]= $\dfrac{1}{16}\,(10\,\text{Sin}[3\,\theta] - 5\,\text{Sin}[9\,\theta] + \text{Sin}[15\,\theta])$

You can simplify expressions using assumptions about variables contained in those expressions. For example, if *k* is assumed to be an integer, sin($2\pi k + x$) simplifies to sin(*x*).

In[10]:= **Assuming[k $\in$ Integers, Simplify[Sin[2 π k + x]]]**

Out[10]= **Sin[x]**

Functions are available for solving systems of equations, for example, this solves a symbolic 2×2 linear system.

In[11]:= **LinearSolve$\left[\begin{pmatrix} a_{11} & a_{12} \\ a_{21} & a_{22} \end{pmatrix}, \begin{pmatrix} x_1 \\ x_2 \end{pmatrix}\right]$**

Out[11]= $\left\{\left\{\dfrac{a_{22}\,x_1 - a_{12}\,x_2}{-a_{12}\,a_{21} + a_{11}\,a_{22}}\right\}, \left\{\dfrac{a_{21}\,x_1 - a_{11}\,x_2}{a_{12}\,a_{21} - a_{11}\,a_{22}}\right\}\right\}$

You can solve and plot solutions to differential equations, for example, a system representing a linear damped pendulum.

In[12]:= **soln = DSolve[{y''[x] + 2 y'[x] + 30 y[x] == 0,**
    y[0] == 1, y'[0] == 1 / 2}, y[x], x]

Out[12]= $\left\{\left\{y[x] \rightarrow \dfrac{1}{58}\,e^{-x}\left(58\,\text{Cos}\left[\sqrt{29}\,x\right] + 3\,\sqrt{29}\,\text{Sin}\left[\sqrt{29}\,x\right]\right)\right\}\right\}$

In[13]:= **Plot[y[x] /. soln, {x, 0, 5}, PlotRange $\rightarrow$ All]**

Out[13]=

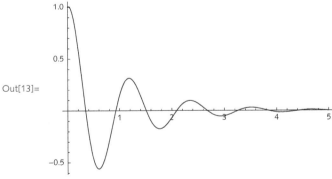

You can create and then operate on functions that are defined piecewise.

In[14]:= **sinc[x_] = Piecewise[{{1, x == 0}}, Sin[x] / x]**

Out[14]= $\begin{cases} 1 & x == 0 \\ \frac{Sin[x]}{x} & True \end{cases}$

In[15]:= **Integrate$\left[\dfrac{sinc\left[x^2\right]}{x}, x\right]$**

Out[15]= $\dfrac{CosIntegral\left[x^2\right]}{2} - \dfrac{Sin\left[x^2\right]}{2\,x^2}$

One of the advantages of working symbolically is that you can quickly see underlying formulas and algorithms at work. For example, this computes a present value for an annuity of 36 payments of $500 using a symbolic effective interest rate.

In[16]:= **presentValue = TimeValue[Annuity[500, 36], r, 0]**

Out[16]= $\dfrac{500\left(-1 + (1 + r)^{36}\right)}{r\,(1 + r)^{36}}$

A plot clearly shows the relationship between the interest rate and the present value of the annuity.

In[17]:= **Plot[presentValue, {r, 0.0, 0.10}]**

Out[17]=

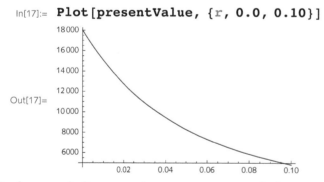

In fact, symbolic expressions are very general objects – you can work with them as you would any expression.

In[18]:= **Factor$\left[^7 - 1\right]$**

Out[18]= $\left(-1 + \right)\left(1 + + ^2 + ^3 + ^4 + ^5 + ^6\right)$

In[19]:= **Rotate[Style["*Mathematica*", "Text"], 45 Degree]**

Out[19]=

Graphics and visualization

Visualizing functions or sets of data often provides greater insight into their structure and properties. *Mathematica* has a wide range of visualization capabilities, including two- and three-dimensional plots of functions or datasets, contour and density plots of functions of two variables, bar charts, histograms and other charting functions for data, and many other functions for specialized areas such as statistical analysis, financial analysis, wavelets, and others. In addition, with the *Mathematica* programming language you can construct graphical images "from the ground up" using primitive elements, as we will see in Chapter 10.

Here is a stream plot of the vector field $\{\cos(1 - x + y^2), \sin(1 + x^2 - y)\}$.

In[20]:= **strm = StreamPlot$\left[\left\{\text{Cos}\left[-1 - x + y^2\right], \text{Sin}\left[1 + x^2 - y\right]\right\},\right.$**
$\left.\{x, -3, 3\}, \{y, -3, 3\}, \text{Frame} \rightarrow \text{None}\right]$

Out[20]=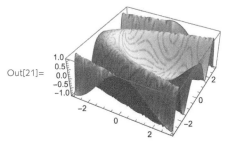

This plot can be thought of as a symbolic expression that can then be used in other expressions, such as a texture on a surface.

In[21]:= **Plot3D$\left[\text{Sin}\left[-1 - x + y^2\right], \{x, -3, 3\},\right.$**
$\left.\{y, -3, 3\}, \text{PlotStyle} \rightarrow \text{Texture}[\text{strm}], \text{Mesh} \rightarrow \text{None}\right]$

Out[21]=

Of course, discrete data, requiring analysis and visualization, are commonly what you will work with. Here we import isotope data and then plot the atomic mass number against the binding energy for all stable isotopes.

```
In[22]:= data = Outer[IsotopeData[#1, #2] &, IsotopeData["Stable"],
          {"MassNumber", "BindingEnergy", "Symbol"}];
```

```
In[23]:= Take[data, 8]
```

$$Out[23]= \{\{1, 0., {}^{1}\mathrm{H}\}, \{2, 1.112283, {}^{2}\mathrm{H}\}, \{3, 2.572681, {}^{3}\mathrm{He}\},$$
$$\{4, 7.073915, {}^{4}\mathrm{He}\}, \{6, 5.332345, {}^{6}\mathrm{Li}\}, \{7, 5.606291, {}^{7}\mathrm{Li}\},$$
$$\{9, 6.462758, {}^{9}\mathrm{Be}\}, \{10, 6.475071, {}^{10}\mathrm{B}\}\}$$

```
In[24]:= ListLinePlot[data[[All, {1, 2}]],
          Mesh → All, PlotRange → {0, 9}, Frame → True,
          FrameLabel → {Style["Atomic mass number", 9],
            Style["Binding energy (MeV)", 9]}]
```

Out[24]=

Data from many possible sources – imported from a collector, a database, an online source – can be used directly. For example, this imports the positions of the atoms on a human protein, grouped by amino acid residue.

```
In[25]:= positions = ProteinData["PAH", "AtomPositions", "Residue"];
          Take[positions[[All, 2]], 8]
```

$$Out[26]= \{\{-2540.6, 3683.2, 1606.4\}, \{-2198.3, 3551.7, 1698.\},$$
$$\{-2103.1, 3212.1, 1554.4\}, \{-2017.6, 2937.4, 1804.2\},$$
$$\{-1649.6, 2912.8, 1901.5\}, \{-1451.6, 2689.9, 2141.6\},$$
$$\{-1397.1, 2827.3, 2492.5\}, \{-1198.3, 2531.6, 2626.9\}\}$$

These data can then be used to visualize the conformation of the protein backbone by running a Bézier curve through the data and wrapping that curve in a tube.

In[27]:= `Graphics3D[Tube[BezierCurve[positions[[All, 2]]], 80]]`

Out[27]=

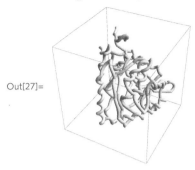

Working with data

A typical workflow with many kinds of data involves: import, cleaning/filtering, analysis, visualization, export of results. The data itself can take many different forms: tabular/numerical data, images, sound files, movies, HTML pages, and many other types. Once the data are in *Mathematica*, the statistical and visualization tools can be applied to analyze and visualize them. For example, this imports some sample data from a spreadsheet.

In[28]:= `data = Import["sampledata.xlsx", {"Data", 1}]`

Out[28]= `{{0., -8.18672}, {0.25, -4.6057},`
`{0.5, -0.709252}, {0.75, 0.300171}, {1., 1.91848},`
`{1.25, 2.2322}, {1.5, 2.7596}, {1.75, 1.94169},`
`{2., 0.748574}, {2.25, -0.852022}, {2.5, -0.368416},`
`{2.75, 0.690119}, {3., 0.488073}, {3.25, 1.83513},`
`{3.5, 2.80307}, {3.75, 7.2199}, {4., 11.6129}}`

A plot of the raw data gives a quick picture of the behavior.

In[29]:= `ListPlot[data]`

Out[29]=

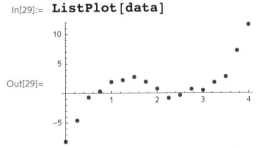

This fits the data with a linear model using the basis functions x, x^2, and x^3.

In[30]:= `model = LinearModelFit[data, {x, x², x³}, x];`

In[31]:= **model["BestFit"]**

Out[31]= $-8.42456 + 19.815\,x - 11.4307\,x^2 + 1.93117\,x^3$

This shows the model together with the raw data.

In[32]:= **Show[**
          Plot[model[x], {x, 0, 4}, PlotRange → All],
          ListPlot[data]
        ]

Out[32]=

Data can be imported directly from the internet; in the following, we import an image from a NASA website and operate on it using built-in image processing tools.

In[33]:= **sun = Import[**
          "http://www.nasa.gov/images/content/491318main_week27-
            transit_946-710.jpg"]

Out[33]=

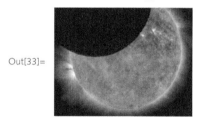

In[34]:= **EdgeDetect[sun]**

Out[34]=

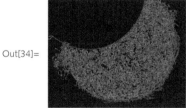

In the following, three-dimensional digital elevation data contained in an archive from the USGS National Elevation Dataset are used to reconstruct a surface.

In[35]:= **Import["NED_40638016.zip"]**

Out[35]=

In[36]:= **Import["NED_40638016.zip", "CoordinateSystemInformation"]**

Out[36]= GEOGCS → {NAD83, DATUM → {North_American_Datum_1983, SPHEROID →
            {GRS 1980, 6 378 137, 298.257, AUTHORITY → {EPSG, 7019}},
          TOWGS84 → {0, 0, 0, 0, 0, 0, 0}, AUTHORITY → {EPSG, 6269}},
        PRIMEM → {Greenwich, 0, AUTHORITY → {EPSG, 8901}},
        UNIT → {degree, 0.0174533, AUTHORITY → {EPSG, 9108}},
        AXIS → {Lat, NORTH}, AXIS → {Long, EAST},
        AUTHORITY → {EPSG, 4269}}

In[37]:= **elevations = Import["NED_40638016.zip", {"ARCGrid", "Data"}];
Dimensions[elevations]**

Out[38]= {575, 799}

In[39]:= **ListPlot3D[elevations, MaxPlotPoints → 300,
  ColorFunction → "Topographic", PlotRange → All,
  PlotLegends → BarLegend[{All, {0, 600}}, LegendLabel →
    Style["Elevation (m)", "Menu"], LegendFunction → "Panel"]]**

Out[39]=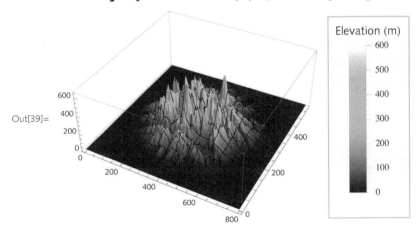

Dynamic interactivity

In addition to the computational tools such as those described above, *Mathematica* also contains tools for creating dynamic interfaces to interact with expressions with which you are working. In this section we will give a few short examples of what is possible, waiting until Chapter 11 for a methodical look at how to program these elements.

Several functions are available to create interfaces in which you manipulate parameters dynamically through controls such as sliders, tabs, checkboxes, pulldown menus, and other mouse-driven interfaces.

In[40]:= `TabView[`
`    Table[TraditionalForm[f[x]] → Plot[f[x], {x, 0, 2 π}],`
`    {f, {Sin, Cos, Tan}}]]`

Out[40]=

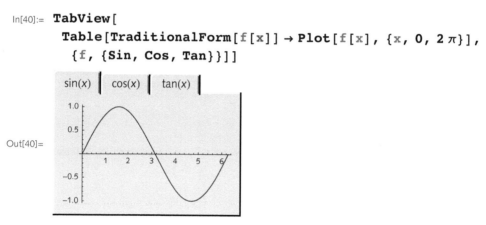

You can interact with plots directly through the use of dynamic `Locator` objects. In the following example, moving the points with your mouse will cause the fitted model and its plot to be dynamically updated.

In[41]:= `Manipulate[`
`    model = LinearModelFit[pts, {x, x², x³}, {x}];`
`    Plot[model[x], {x, 0, 1}, PlotRange → 2],`
`    {{pts, {{.1, .6}, {.2, -.4}, {.45, 0.3},`
`        {0.56, 0.1}, {.92, .25}}}, Locator}]`

Out[41]=

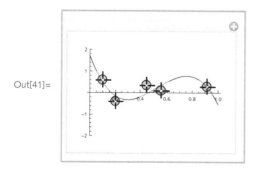

The following fine tunes a segmentation task by using dynamic elements to manually select regions to start the segmentation.

```
In[42]:= DynamicModule[{pts = {{81, 186}, {238, 188}, {89, 281}}},
    LocatorPane[Dynamic[pts], Row[{
        Image[head],
        Dynamic[Image[
            Colorize[ImageForestingComponents[head, pts, 5]]]]}]],
    Initialization :> {head = 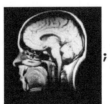 ; }]
```

Out[42]=
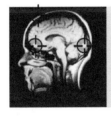

Programming

With the 3000+ functions built into *Mathematica*, it would seem as if a function is available to compute just about anything you might want. But that impression is mistaken. There are simply more kinds of calculations than could possibly be included in a single program. Whether you are interested in simulating a bond percolation computation or finding the mean square distance of a random walk on a torus, *Mathematica* does not have a built-in function to do everything that you could possibly want. What it *does* have – and what really makes it the amazingly useful tool it is – is the capability to define your own functions and use them like the built-in functions. This is called *programming*, and it is what this book is all about.

Sometimes, the programs you create will be succinct and focused on a very specific task. *Mathematica* possesses a rich set of tools that enable you to quickly and naturally translate the statement of a problem into a program. For example, the following program defines a test for perfect numbers, numbers that are equal to the sum of their proper divisors.

```
In[43]:= PerfectQ[n_] := DivisorSigma[1, n] == 2 n
```

Define a second function to select those numbers from a range of integers that pass this `Per‑fectQ` test.

```
In[44]:= PerfectSearch[n_] := Select[Range[n], PerfectQ]
```

This then finds all perfect numbers less than 1 000 000.

```
In[45]:= PerfectSearch[10^6]
```

```
Out[45]= {6, 28, 496, 8128}
```

Sometimes you need to create new objects and operate with them like the built-in expressions. For example, below we create a new graphical object that behaves much like some of the built-in graphics objects. An auxiliary function defines the vertices of a regular *n*-gon, while the second function, `RegularPolygon`, creates a polygon graphics object that will display as a regular polygon like built-in objects such as `Circle`, `Line`, and `Polygon`.

```
In[46]:= vertices[n_] := Table[{Cos[2 π α / n], Sin[2 π α / n]}, {α, 0, n}]
```

```
In[47]:= RegularPolygon /: Graphics[RegularPolygon[n_]] :=
            Graphics[Line[vertices[n]], AspectRatio → Automatic]
```

```
In[48]:= Graphics[RegularPolygon[8]]
```

Out[48]=

Of course, sooner or later the task at hand requires a more involved program, stretching across several lines or even pages of code. More involved programs, especially those intended for others, typically have features such as optional arguments, warning messages issued when the user supplies bad arguments, usage messages, and so on. For example, here is a program – with some of these elements – that generates a network representing a bond percolation problem.

```
In[49]:= Options[BondPercolation] = Options[Graph];
```

```
In[50]:= BondPercolation::baddims =
            "The arguments `1` and `2`, giving the grid
                dimensions, should be positive integers.";
```

```
In[51]:= BondPercolation::usage =
    "BondPercolation[{m,n},prob] simulates a bond
       percolation on an m×n rectangular lattice
       using 0<prob<1 as the probability of a bond
       forming between a site and its neighbors.";
```

```
In[52]:= BondPercolation[{m_, n_}, prob_, opts : OptionsPattern[]] :=
    Module[{gr}, If[! (IntegerQ[m] && IntegerQ[n]),
       Message[BondPercolation::baddims, m, n],
       gr = GridGraph[{m, n}]; Graph[Pick[EdgeList[gr],
          RandomVariate[BernoulliDistribution[prob],
          EdgeCount[gr]], 1], opts]]]
```

This runs a simulation for a 13×21 grid, assuming a 47% probability of a bond between any pair of vertices.

```
In[53]:= gr = BondPercolation[{13, 21}, 0.47];
    HighlightGraph[GridGraph[{13, 21}],
     gr, GraphHighlightStyle → "DehighlightGray"]
```

Out[54]=

Setting up the percolation program to return a `Graph` object enables you to take advantage of all the built-in functions for styling or doing computation on the graph, for example, computing the size of the strongly connected components; or determining if there is a cycle that visits every vertex exactly once; or finding connected paths from one edge to another.

```
In[55]:= Map[Length, ConnectedComponents[gr]]
```

```
Out[55]= {3, 16, 11, 3, 4, 3, 2, 2, 12,
         65, 15, 9, 2, 4, 2, 59, 2, 7, 2, 18, 2}
```

```
In[56]:= HamiltonianGraphQ[gr]
```

```
Out[56]= False
```

```
In[57]:= FindPercolationPath[gr_ , dims : {dimx_ , dimy_}] :=
    Module[{vert, bot, top, spFun},
        vert = VertexList[GridGraph[dims]];
        bot = Select[vert, Mod[#, dimx] == 1 &];
        top = Select[vert, Mod[#, dimx] == 0 &];
        spFun = FindShortestPath[gr, All, All];
        Cases[Outer[spFun, bot, top],
          lis_List /; Length[lis] ≠ 0, {2}]]

In[58]:= path = FindPercolationPath[gr, {13, 21}];
    HighlightGraph[GridGraph[{13, 21}], PathGraph /@ path,
      GraphHighlightStyle → "DehighlightGray"]
```

Out[59]=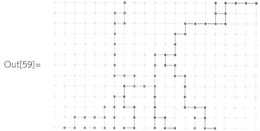

These examples use a variety of programming styles and constructs: functional programming, rule-based programming, pure functions, and more. We do not expect you to understand the different programming examples in this section at this point – that is what this book is all about! What you should understand is that, in many ways, *Mathematica* is designed to be as broadly useful as possible and that there are many computations for which *Mathematica* does not have a built-in function, so, to make full use of its many capabilities, you will sometimes need to program. The main purpose of this book is to show you how.

Another purpose is to teach you the basic principles of programming. These principles – making assignments, defining rules, using conditionals, recursion, and iteration – are applicable (with great differences in detail, to be sure) to all other programming languages.

1.2   Getting started

Before you can really get going using *Mathematica*, you will need to know how to start your *Mathematica* session, how to stop it, and how to get out of trouble when things go wrong. This section provides information about starting *Mathematica*, working with the notebook interface, basic syntax of commands, and several other topics that will be of interest to the novice.

Starting up Mathematica

How you start up *Mathematica* will depend somewhat on the platform you are using.

- Windows: go to the Start menu and choose Programs ▸ Wolfram *Mathematica* ▸ Mathematica X (where X represents the current version, *Mathematica* 8 as of the publication of this book).

- Macintosh OS X: double-click the *Mathematica* icon in the folder in which it was installed, typically, the Applications folder.

- Linux/Unix: type `mathematica` in a shell and then press ENTER.

The computer will then load parts of *Mathematica* into its memory and soon a blank window will appear on the screen. This window, called a notebook, is the visual interface to *Mathematica*.

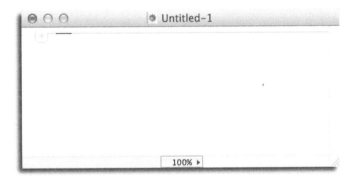

The notebook interface

All your work in *Mathematica* is typically done in what is referred to as a *notebook*. This notebook interface has many of the familiar tools and characteristics of a word processor – menus, toolbars, palettes – but also includes items specific to the work you will do with *Mathematica* including tools for writing text, entering and formatting mathematical formulas, constructing and editing graphics, and balancing brackets in code. In addition, notebooks provide features for outlining material and creating slide shows which you may find useful for giving talks and demonstrations. Of course, notebooks are also the environment in which you perform computations, write and run programs, create graphics, import data and files, and so on.

When a blank notebook first appears on the screen, either from just starting *Mathematica* or from selecting New in the File menu, you can start typing immediately. For example, type

`N[Pi, 200]` and then press SHIFT ENTER (hold down the Shift key while pressing the Enter key) to evaluate an expression. *Mathematica* will evaluate the result and print the 200-decimal digit approximation to π on the screen.

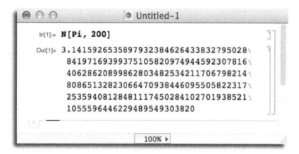

Notice that when you evaluate an expression in a notebook, *Mathematica* adds input and output prompts. In the example notebook above, these are denoted In[1]:= and Out[1]=. These prompts can be thought of as markers (or labels) that you can refer to during your *Mathematica* session.

When you start typing, *Mathematica* places a *bracket* on the far right side of the window that encloses the *cell* in which you are working. These *cell brackets* are helpful for organizational purposes within the notebook. Double-clicking cell brackets will open any collapsed cells, or close any groups of cells. In the notebook displayed below, double-clicking the cell bracket containing "1.1 Overview of basic operations" will open (or close) the cell to display (or hide) its contents:

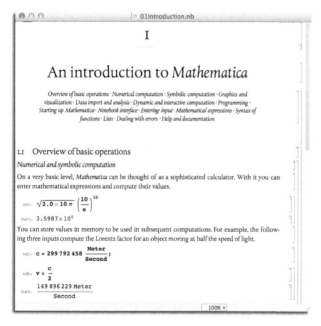

With cell brackets you can organize your work in an orderly manner and create outlines of your material. For a complete description of cell brackets and many other interface features consult the built-in tutorial Working with Cells (WMDC), where WMDC refers to the Wolfram *Mathematica* Documentation Center.

For information on other features such as saving, printing, and editing notebooks, consult the tutorial Using a Notebook Interface (WMDC).

Entering input

New input can be entered whenever there is a horizontal line that runs across the width of the notebook. If one is not present where you wish to place an input cell, move the cursor up and down until it changes to a horizontal bar and then click the mouse once. A horizontal line should appear across the width of the window. You can immediately start typing and an input cell will be created.

Input can be entered exactly as it appears in this book. To get *Mathematica* to evaluate any expression that you have entered, press SHIFT+ENTER, that is, hold down the Shift key and then press the Enter key (on Mac OS X, press SHIFT+RET).

You can enter mathematical expressions in a traditional looking two-dimensional format using either palettes for quick entry of template expressions, or keyboard equivalents. For example, the following expression can be entered by using the Basic Math Assistant palette (under the Palettes menu), or through a series of keystrokes. For details of inputting mathematical expressions, see the tutorial Entering Two-Dimensional Input (WMDC).

In[1]:=
$$\int \frac{1}{1 - x^3} \, dx$$

Out[1]=
$$\frac{\mathrm{ArcTan}\left[\frac{1+2\,x}{\sqrt{3}}\right]}{\sqrt{3}} - \frac{1}{3}\,\mathrm{Log}\,[1 - x] + \frac{1}{6}\,\mathrm{Log}\left[1 + x + x^2\right]$$

As noted previously, *Mathematica* enters the In and Out prompts for you. You do not type these prompts. You will see them *after* you evaluate your input.

To refer to the result of the previous calculation use the symbol %.

In[2]:= 2^{100}

Out[2]= 1 267 650 600 228 229 401 496 703 205 376

In[3]:= % + 1

Out[3]= 1 267 650 600 228 229 401 496 703 205 377

To refer to the result of any earlier calculation use its Out[i] label or, equivalently, % i.

In[4]:= **Out[1]**

$$\text{Out[4]} = \frac{\text{ArcTan}\left[\frac{1+2\,x}{\sqrt{3}}\right]}{\sqrt{3}} - \frac{1}{3}\,\text{Log}\,[\,1\,-\,x\,] + \frac{1}{6}\,\text{Log}\left[\,1\,+\,x\,+\,x^2\,\right]$$

In[5]:= **%2**

Out[5]= 1 267 650 600 228 229 401 496 703 205 376

Mathematical expressions

You can enter mathematical expressions in a linear syntax using arithmetic operators common to almost all computer languages.

In[6]:= **39 / 13**

Out[6]= 3

Enter this expression in the traditional form by typing 39, CTRL[/], then 13.

In[7]:= $\dfrac{39}{13}$

Out[7]= 3

The caret (^) is used for exponentiation.

In[8]:= **2 ^ 5**

Out[8]= 32

To enter this expression in a more traditional typeset form, type 2, CTRL[^], and then 5.

In[9]:= **2^5**

Out[9]= 32

Multiplication can be indicated by putting a space between the two factors, as in mathematics. *Mathematica* will automatically display the traditional multiplication sign, ×, between two numbers. The asterisk (*) is also used for that purpose, as is traditional in most computer languages.

In[10]:= **2 × 5**

Out[10]= 10

In[11]:= **2 * 5**

Out[11]= 10

Operations are given the same precedence as in mathematics. In particular, multiplication and division have a higher precedence than addition and subtraction: $3 + 4 \times 5$ equals 23 and not 35.

In[12]:= **3 + 4 × 5**

Out[12]= 23

You can enter typeset expressions in several different ways: directly from the keyboard as we did above, using a long, functional form, or via palettes available from the Palettes menu. Table 1.1 shows some of the more commonly used typeset expressions and how they are entered through the keyboard. Try to become comfortable entering these inputs so that you can easily enter the kinds of expressions in this book.

TABLE 1.1. *Entering typeset expressions*

Display form	Long (functional) form	Key strokes
x^2	`Superscript[x,2]`	x, CTRL +6, 2
x_i	`Subscript[x,i]`	x, CTRL +_, i
$\frac{x}{y}$	`FractionBox[x,2]`	x, CTRL +/, y
$\sqrt{x}$	`SqrtBox[x]`	CTRL +2, x
$x \geq y$	`GreaterEqual[x,2]`	x, ESC, >=, ESC, y

Syntax of functions

Built-in functions are also written as they are in mathematics books, except that function names are capitalized and their arguments are enclosed in square brackets.

In[13]:= **Factor$\left[x^5 - 1\right]$**

Out[13]= $(-1 + x)\left(1 + x + x^2 + x^3 + x^4\right)$

Almost all the built-in functions are spelled out in full, as in the above example. The exceptions to this rule are well-known abbreviations such as `D` for differentiation, `Sqrt` for square roots, `Log` for logarithms, and `Det` for the determinant of a matrix. The convention of spelling out function names is quite useful when you are not sure whether a function exists to perform a particular task. For example, to compute the conjugate of a complex number, an educated guess would be:

In[14]:= **Conjugate[3 + 4 i]**

Out[14]= 3 − 4 i

Functions of more than one argument separate their arguments with commas, as in traditional mathematical notation. For example, while the following one-argument form of `RandomReal` gives a single random number between 0 and 10, the two-argument form can be used to generate a vector or an array of random numbers.

In[15]:= **RandomReal[10]**

Out[15]= 3.27946

In[16]:= **RandomReal[10, 12]**

Out[16]= {3.47031, 4.01486, 1.3706, 3.326, 0.676231, 8.12965,
          3.40873, 7.27445, 6.34518, 1.39347, 2.04957, 2.45416}

Lists

Lists are a basic data type in *Mathematica* and are used to represent vectors and matrices (and tensors of any dimension), as well as additional arguments to functions such as in Plot and Integrate. Although square brackets [and] are used to enclose the arguments to functions, curly braces { and } are used to indicate a *list* or range of values.

Using lists to represent vectors, the following computes the dot product of two vectors using traditional notation.

In[17]:= **{a, b, c}.{x, y, z}**

Out[17]= a x + b y + c z

Lists are used as the arguments to many built in functions.

In[18]:= $\textbf{Plot}\left[\textbf{Sin}\left[x + \sqrt{2}\ \textbf{Sin}[x]\right], \{x, -2\,\pi, 2\,\pi\}\right]$

Out[18]=

In[19]:= **Integrate[Cos[x], {x, a, b}]**

Out[19]= -Sin[a] + Sin[b]

In[20]:= **RandomReal[{-100, 100}, {5, 5}]**

Out[20]= {{-43.2895, -3.24399, 34.0708, -30.6333, -5.28155},
          {25.1997, 76.4115, 54.9255, 46.6512, -55.571},
          {-40.5392, 20.3037, 36.1977, -78.2481, -93.5398},
          {-27.7766, 67.3532, 59.0608, 80.207, -58.7632},
          {22.7737, -6.28497, -81.3275, 65.8295, -76.538}}

In the `Plot` example, the list $\{\mathbf{x}, -2\,\pi, 2\,\pi\}$ indicates that the function $\sin\!\big(x + \sqrt{2}\,\sin(x)\big)$ is to be plotted over an interval as x takes on values from $-2\,\pi$ to $2\,\pi$. The `Integrate` expression above is equivalent to the integral $\int_a^b \cos(x)\,dx$. In the last example with `RandomReal`, the first list specifies the range from which numbers will be chosen and the second list specifies the dimensions, in this case, a 5×5 array.

Mathematica's list-manipulating capabilities will be explored in detail in Chapter 3.

Semicolons

When you end an expression with a semicolon (`;`), *Mathematica* computes its value but does not display it. This is quite helpful when the result of the expression would be very long and you do not need to see it. In the following example, we first create a list of the integers from 1 to 10 000, suppressing their display with the semicolon; we then compute their sum and average.

```
In[21]:= nums = Range[10 000];
```

```
In[22]:= Total[nums]
```

Out[22]= 50 005 000

```
In[23]:= %
        ─────────────
        Length[nums]
```

$$
\text{Out[23]}= \frac{10\,001}{2}
$$

With the notebook interface, you can input as many lines as you like within an input cell; *Mathematica* will evaluate them all, in order, when you enter ⇧SHIFT⏎ENTER.

Alternative input syntax

There are several different ways to write expressions in *Mathematica*. Usually, you will simply use the traditional notation, *fun*[x], for example. But you should be aware of several alternatives to this syntax that are sometimes used (see Table 1.2).

Here is an example of standard function notation for a function, `N`, of one argument.

```
In[24]:= N[π]
```

Out[24]= 3.14159

This uses a prefix operator.

```
In[25]:= N@π
```

Out[25]= 3.14159

Here is the postfix operator notation.

In[26]:= **π // N**

Out[26]= **3.14159**

For functions with two arguments, you can use an infix notation. The following expression is identical to N[π, 30].

In[27]:= **π ~ N ~ 30**

Out[27]= **3.14159265358979323846264338328**

TABLE 1.2. *Alternative function notation*

Notation	Input
Traditional	N[π]
Prefix	N @ π
Postfix	π // N
Infix	π ~ N ~ 100

Finally, many people prefer to use a more traditional syntax when entering and working with mathematical expressions. For example, this computes an integral using standard *Mathematica* syntax.

In[28]:= **Integrate[1 / Sin[x], x]**

Out[28]= $-\text{Log}\left[\text{Cos}\left[\frac{x}{2}\right]\right] + \text{Log}\left[\text{Sin}\left[\frac{x}{2}\right]\right]$

The same integral, represented in a more traditional manner, can be entered from palettes or using keyboard shortcuts.

In[29]:= $\int \frac{1}{\textbf{Sin[x]}}\, d x$

Out[29]= $-\text{Log}\left[\text{Cos}\left[\frac{x}{2}\right]\right] + \text{Log}\left[\text{Sin}\left[\frac{x}{2}\right]\right]$

Many mathematical functions have traditional symbols associated with their operations and, when available, these can be used instead of the fully spelled-out names. For example, this computes the intersection of two sets using the `Intersection` function.

In[30]:= **Intersection[{a, b, c, d, e}, {b, f, a, z}]**

Out[30]= **{a, b}**

Or you can do the same computation using more traditional notation.

In[31]:= `{a, b, c, d, e} ∩ {b, f, a, z}`

Out[31]= `{a, b}`

To learn how to enter these and other notations quickly, either from palettes or directly from the keyboard using shortcuts, refer to the tutorial Two-Dimensional Expression Input (WMDC).

Comments

Input can include *comments* – text that is not evaluated – by enclosing that text with (* and *). The comment is inert; it will be ignored by the *Mathematica* evaluator.

In[32]:= `D[Sin[x], {x, 1}]` (* first derivative of sin w.r.t. x *)

Out[32]= `Cos[x]`

Errors

Nobody is perfect. In the course of using and programming *Mathematica*, you will encounter various sorts of errors, some obvious, some very subtle, some easily rectified. Perhaps the most frequent error you will make is misspelling the name of a function. *Mathematica* uses syntax-coloring to help you identify misspelled symbol names. For example, in the following input, `Sin` is deliberately misspelled. *Mathematica* colors any symbol it does not know about blue. If you evaluate the input, it is returned unevaluated because *Mathematica* has no built-in rules for a function whose name is `Sine`.

In[33]:= `Sine[30 Degree]`

Out[33]= `Sine[30°]`

Of course it does have rules for the function `Sin`.

In[34]:= `Sin[30 Degree]`

Out[34]= $\dfrac{1}{2}$

Having your original expression returned unevaluated – as if this were perfectly normal – is a problem you will often encounter. Aside from misspelling a function name, or simply using a function that does not exist, another case where this occurs is when you give the wrong number of arguments to a function, especially to a user-defined function. For example, the `Perfec‑tSearch` function defined earlier takes a single argument; if we mistakenly give it two arguments, the input is returned unevaluated because *Mathematica* has no rule for a function `Perfec‑tSearch` with two arguments.

In[35]:= `PerfectSearch[10⁶, 4]`

Out[35]= `PerfectSearch[1 000 000, 4]`

Some kinds of inputs generate genuine error messages. Syntax errors, as shown above, are one example. The built-in functions are designed to usually warn you of such errors in input. In the first example below, we have supplied the `Det` function with a nonsquare matrix. In the second example, `FactorInteger` operates on integers only and so the real number argument causes the error condition.

In[36]:= **Det[{{1, 2, 4}, {2, 8, 4}}]**

Det::matsq : Argument {{1, 2, 4}, {2, 8, 4}} at position 1 is not a non−empty square matrix. ≫

Out[36]= Det[{{1, 2, 4}, {2, 8, 4}}]

In[37]:= **FactorInteger[34.2]**

FactorInteger::exact : Argument 34.2` in FactorInteger[34.2] is not an exact number. ≫

Out[37]= FactorInteger[34.2]

Section 5.7 will introduce the framework for creating and issuing your own messages for the programs you develop in *Mathematica*.

Getting out of trouble

Although it is convenient to have *Mathematica* tell you when you have done something wrong, from time to time, you will evaluate an input which will cause *Mathematica* to misbehave in some way, perhaps by just going silent and not returning a result for a long time or by printing out screen after screen of not terribly useful information. In these cases, you can try to "interrupt" the calculation. How you do this depends on your computer's operating system:

- Macintosh OS X: type ⌘⌊.⌋ (the Command key and the period);
- Windows: type ⌊ALT⌋⌊.⌋ (the Alt key and the period);
- Linux/Unix: type ⌊CTRL⌋⌊.⌋ and then type a and then ⌊RET⌋.

These attempts to stop the computation will sometimes fail. If after waiting a reasonable amount of time (say, a few minutes), *Mathematica* still seems to be stuck, you will have to "kill the kernel". Before attempting to kill the kernel, try to convince yourself that the computation is really in a loop from which it will not return and that it is not just an intensive computation that requires a lot of time. Killing the kernel is accomplished by selecting Quit Kernel from the Evaluation menu. The kernel can then be restarted without killing the front end by first selecting Start Kernel ▸ Local under the Kernel menu, or you can simply evaluate a command in a notebook and a new kernel should start up automatically.

The front end and the kernel

When you work in *Mathematica* you are actually working with two separate programs. They are referred to as the *front end* and the *kernel*. The front end is the user interface. It consists of the notebooks that you work in together with the menu system, palettes (which are really just notebooks), and any element that accepts input from the keyboard or mouse. The kernel is the program that does the calculations. So a typical operation between the user (you) and *Mathematica* consists of the following steps, where the program that is invoked in each step is indicated in parentheses:

- enter input in the notebook (front end);
- send input to the kernel to be evaluated by pressing SHIFT -ENTER (front end);
- compute the result and send it back to the front end (kernel);
- format and display the result in the notebook (front end).

There is one remaining piece that we have not yet mentioned. Since the kernel and front end are two separate programs, a means of communication is necessary for these two programs to "talk" to each other. That communication protocol is called *MathLink* and it comes bundled with *Mathematica*. It operates behind the scenes, completely transparent to the user.

MathLink is a very general communications protocol that is not limited to communication between the front end and the kernel, but can also be used to set up communication between the front end and other programs on your computer, programs like compiled C and Fortran code. It can also be used to connect a kernel to a word processor or spreadsheet or many other programs.

In fact, there are numerous communications protocols that come with *Mathematica*. For example, you can communicate with SQL databases via *DatabaseLink*, JAVA through *J/Link*, .NET via *.NET/Link*. These protocols allow you to extend *Mathematica* into these other domains and work with them in the *Mathematica* interface. These are all beyond the scope of this book, but if you are interested, there is extensive documentation for each in the Documentation Center as well as several books and articles on these protocols (see the bibliography at the end of this book).

1.3 Getting help

Function information

Mathematica contains extensive documentation that you can access in a variety of ways. It is also designed so that you can create new documentation for your own functions and program in such a way that users of your programs can get help in exactly the same way as they would for *Mathematica*'s built-in functions.

If you know the name of a function but are unsure of its syntax or what it does, the easiest way to find out about it is to evaluate ?*function*. For example, here is the usage message for Map.

In[1]:= **? Map**

Map[*f*, *expr*] or *f* /@ *expr* applies *f* to each element on the first level in *expr*.
Map[*f*, *expr*, *levelspec*] applies *f* to parts of *expr* specified by *levelspec*. ≫

Also, if you were not sure of the name of a command, you can use wildcard characters to display all functions that contain certain characters. For example, this displays all functions that start with "Random".

In[2]:= **? Random***

▼ System`

Random	RandomGraph	RandomPermutation	RandomSample
RandomChoice	RandomImage	RandomPrime	RandomSeed
RandomComplex	RandomInteger	RandomReal	RandomVariate

Clicking on one of these links will produce a short usage statement about that function. For example, if you were to click the RandomGraph link, here is what would be displayed in your notebook.

RandomGraph[{*n*, *m*}] gives a pseudorandom graph with *n* vertices and *m* edges.
RandomGraph[{*n*, *m*}, *k*] gives a list of *k* pseudorandom graphs.
RandomGraph[*gdist*, ...] samples from the random graph distribution *gdist*. ≫

Clicking the ≫ hyperlink would take you directly to the Documentation Center where a much more detailed explanation of this function can be found.

You can also get help by highlighting any *Mathematica* function and pressing the F1 key on your keyboard (or CMD + SHIFT +F on Macintosh OS X) to display the documentation for that function.

The Documentation Center

Mathematica contains an extensive set of reference materials called the Documentation Center. The Documentation Center allows you to search for functions easily and it provides extensive documentation, examples, and links to related items.

To open the documentation, select Documentation Center under the Help menu. You should quickly see something like the following:

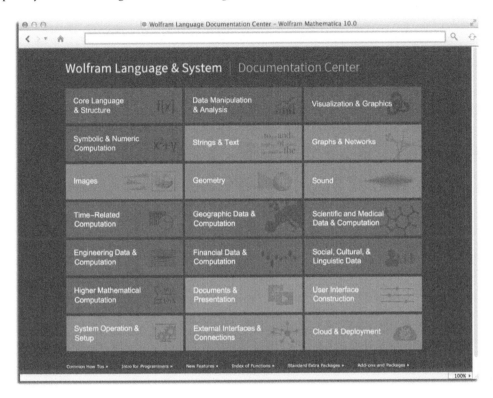

Notice the twenty-one categories: Core Language & Structure, Data Manipulation & Analysis, Visualization & Graphics, Symbolic & Numeric Computation, Strings & Text, Graphs & Networks, Images, Geometry, and so on. Clicking any category will open to an extended list of topics in that area.

Suppose you were looking for information about three-dimensional parametric plots. First click the Visualization & Graphics category, then Function Visualization. The Documentation Center should look like this:

Clicking the `ParametricPlot3D` link will take you to the reference page for that function.

Alternatively, you could have evaluated `?ParametricPlot3D` and then clicked the ≫ link at the end of the usage message.

Many additional features are available in the Documentation Center including dozens of examples showing the usage of each function, applications, and related functions.

2

The *Mathematica* language

Although programming languages are commonly thought to have their early history in the 1940s and 1950s when the first digital computers came about, they in fact go back much earlier to the creation of the Jacquard loom (1801) and also player pianos (~1870s), both of which used physical punch cards to code instructions. Regardless of whether you use punch cards or a more modern means to create and store your programs, programming languages are described by specifying their syntax and semantics. *Syntax* refers to the form, indicating what symbols can be put together in what order to make a meaningful construct in any given language. In other words, the syntax of a programming language is the set of rules that define what is a valid input or program. *Semantics*, on the other hand, refers to the meaning of expressions within a language. Although we will not give a complete, rigorous description of the syntax of the *Mathematica* language here, it is important to understand some of the basic structures and their syntax upon which everything is built. Fortunately, the *Mathematica* language can be understood quickly by learning about just a few basic objects. In this chapter we will focus on the *Mathematica* language with particular emphasis on expressions. We will also look at how to define and name new expressions, how to combine them using logical operators, and how to control properties of expressions through the use of attributes.

2.1 Expressions

All the objects that you work with in *Mathematica* have a similar underlying structure even though they may appear different at first sight. This means that things like a simple computation, a data object, a graphic, the cells in your *Mathematica* notebook, even the notebook itself, all have a similar structure – they are all *expressions*, and an understanding of their structure and syntax is essential to mastering *Mathematica*.

Types of expressions

When doing a simple arithmetic operation such as 3 + 4 × 5, you are usually not concerned with exactly how a system such as *Mathematica* actually performs the additions or multiplications. Yet it is extremely useful to be able to see the internal representation of expressions as this allows you to manipulate them in a consistent and powerful manner.

Internally, *Mathematica* categorizes the objects that it operates on as different types: integers are distinct from real numbers; lists are distinct from numbers. One of the reasons that it is useful to identify these different *data types* is that specialized algorithms can be used on certain classes of objects that will help to speed up the computations involved.

The `Head` function is used to identify types of objects. For numbers, it will report whether the number is an integer, a rational number, a real number, or a complex number.

In[1]:= `{Head[7], Head[1 / 7], Head[7.0], Head[7 + 2 i]}`

Out[1]= `{Integer, Rational, Real, Complex}`

In fact, every *Mathematica* expression has a `Head` that gives some information about that type of expression.

In[2]:= `Head[{1, 2, 3, 4, 5}]`

Out[2]= `List`

In[3]:= `Head[` 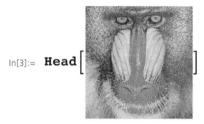 `]`

Out[3]= `Image`

In[4]:= `Head[a + b]`

Out[4]= `Plus`

Atoms

The basic building blocks of *Mathematica* – the *atoms* – from which every expression is ultimately constructed are symbols, numbers, and strings. In addition, graphs and sparse arrays are also atomic (see Table 2.1).

In[5]:= **{AtomQ[x31], AtomQ[1.2345], AtomQ["The rain in Spain"]}**

Out[5]= {True, True, True}

TABLE 2.1. *Atomic expressions*

Atom	Examples
Integer	$-3, 0, 28, \ldots$
Rational	$-\frac{1}{2}, \frac{8}{9}, \ldots$
Real	$0.2348, \ldots$
Complex	$5 - 4\,i, \ldots$
String	"The cat in the hat."
Symbol	Plot, myFun, ...
SparseArray	SparseArray[<4>, {3,3}]
Graph	
Image	

Although you can determine the type of any atomic expression using Head as described above, in general you cannot directly extract parts of an atom.

In[6]:= **Part[1.2345, 1]**

Part::partd : Part specification 1.2345[[1]] is longer than depth of object. »

Out[6]= $1.2345\,[\![1]\!]$

A symbol consists of a sequence of letters and digits, not starting with a digit. This applies to both user-defined symbols and to the built-in symbols.

In[7]:= **Head[x31]**

Out[7]= Symbol

In[8]:= **Head[Integrate]**

Out[8]= Symbol

In *Mathematica*, built-in constants are all symbols.

In[9]:= `{Head[π], Head[e], Head[EulerGamma], Head[Khinchin]}`

Out[9]= `{Symbol, Symbol, Symbol, Symbol}`

Strings are also atomic objects; they are composed of characters and are enclosed in quotes. Strings will be discussed in detail in Chapter 9.

In[10]:= `Head["Mathematica"]`

Out[10]= `String`

Graphs are abstract objects consisting of vertices and edges. They too are atomic.

In[11]:= `Head[`  `]`

Out[11]= `Graph`

In[12]:= `AtomQ[` 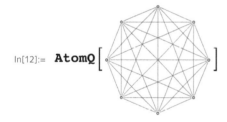 `]`

Out[12]= `True`

Sparse arrays are a special kind of atomic expression. They give a compact and highly efficient means of representing large arrays of numbers, typically with many zero elements. Sparse arrays in *Mathematica* are represented by `SparseArray` whose output form displays the number of nondefault elements and the dimension of the array.

In[13]:= `mat = SparseArray[{i_, i_} → 1, {4, 4}]`

Out[13]= `SparseArray[<4>, {4, 4}]`

In[14]:= `MatrixForm[mat]`

Out[14]//MatrixForm=

$$\begin{pmatrix} 1 & 0 & 0 & 0 \\ 0 & 1 & 0 & 0 \\ 0 & 0 & 1 & 0 \\ 0 & 0 & 0 & 1 \end{pmatrix}$$

In[15]:= **AtomQ[mat]**

Out[15]= **True**

We will have more to say about sparse arrays in Section 8.3.

Structure of expressions

As mentioned earlier, everything in *Mathematica* is an expression. Expressions are either atomic, as described in the previous section, or they are *normal expressions*, built up from atomic expressions and containing a head and zero or more elements. Normal expressions are of the following form, where h is the head of the expression and the e_i are the elements which may themselves be atomic or normal expressions.

$$h[e_1, e_2, ..., e_n]$$

Using **Head** to determine the type of atomic expressions is entirely general. For normal expressions, **Head** simply gives the head of that expression.

In[16]:= **Head[a + b + c]**

Out[16]= **Plus**

To see the full internal representation of an expression, use **FullForm**.

In[17]:= **FullForm[a + b + c]**

Out[17]//FullForm=
        Plus[a, b, c]

In[18]:= **FullForm[{a, b, c}]**

Out[18]//FullForm=
        List[a, b, c]

The important thing to notice is that both of these objects (the sum and the list) have very similar internal representations. Each is made up of a function (**Plus** and **List**, respectively), each encloses its arguments in square brackets, and each separates its arguments with commas. This is the form of every normal expression in *Mathematica*.

Regardless of how an atomic or normal expression may appear in your notebook, its structure is uniquely determined by its head and parts as seen using **FullForm**. This is important for understanding the *Mathematica* evaluation mechanism which depends on the matching of patterns based on their internal representation, a subject we will turn to in detail in Chapter 4.

The number of elements in any expression is given by its length. The internal representation, as returned by **FullForm**, displays this expression as a function with three arguments.

In[19]:= **Length[a + b + c]**

Out[19]= 3

Here is a more complicated expression.

In[20]:= **expr = Sin[x] $\left(a\,x^2 + b\,x + c\right)$**

Out[20]= $\left(c + b\,x + a\,x^2\right)$ Sin[x]

Its head is Times because it is composed of the product of Sin[x] and the quadratic polynomial.

In[21]:= **Head[expr]**

Out[21]= Times

Its length is 2 since it only contains two factors.

In[22]:= **Length[expr]**

Out[22]= 2

Although the FullForm of this expression is a little harder to decipher, if you look carefully you should see that it is composed of the product of Plus [...] and Sin [x]. In other words, its head, Times, has two arguments.

In[23]:= **FullForm[expr]**

Out[23]//FullForm=
       Times [Plus [c, Times [b, x], Times [a, Power [x, 2]]], Sin [x]]

There are several important differences between atomic expressions and nonatomic expressions. While the heads of all expressions are extracted in the same way – using the Head function – the head of an atom provides different information than the head of other expressions. As mentioned above, the head of a symbol or string is the kind of atom that it is.

In[24]:= **Head[Integrate]**

Out[24]= Symbol

In[25]:= **Head["hello"]**

Out[25]= String

The head of a number is the specific kind of number that it is, its data type.

In[26]:= **Head[2]**

Out[26]= Integer

In[27]:= **Head[5.21]**

Out[27]= Real

The FullForm of an atom (except a complex or rational number) is the atom itself.

In[28]:= **FullForm[f]**

Out[28]//FullForm=

     f

In[29]:= **FullForm$\left[\dfrac{5}{7}\right]$**

Out[29]//FullForm=

     Rational[5, 7]

Atoms have no parts (which of course is why they are called atoms). In contrast, nonatomic expressions do have parts. To extract different parts of an expression, use the **Part** function. For example, the first part of the expression a + b is a.

In[30]:= **Part[a + b, 1]**

Out[30]= a

The second part is b.

In[31]:= **Part[a + b, 2]**

Out[31]= b

This should be clearer from looking at the internal representation of this expression.

In[32]:= **FullForm[a + b]**

Out[32]//FullForm=

     Plus[a, b]

So **Part**[a + b, 1] is another way of asking for the first element of **Plus**[a, b], which is simply a. In general, **Part**[*expr*, *n*] gives the *n*th element of *expr*. The zeroth part is the head of the expression.

In[33]:= **Part[a + b, 0]**

Out[33]= **Plus**

As stated above, atomic expressions have no parts.

In[34]:= **Part["vini vidi vici", 1]**

     Part::partd : Part specification vini vidi vici[1] is longer than depth of object. ≫

Out[34]= vini vidi vici⟦1⟧

This error message indicates that the string "vini vidi vici" has no first part, since it is atomic. The expression *expr*[[1]] is shorthand for **Part**[*expr*, 1]. Similarly, complex numbers are atomic and hence have no parts.

In[35]:= **(3 + 4 i)[[1]]**

     Part::partd : Part specification (3 + 4*i*)[1] is longer than depth of object. ≫

Out[35]= (3 + 4 i)⟦1⟧

Because everything in *Mathematica* has the common structure of an expression, most of the built-in functions that are used for list manipulation, such as `Part`, can also be used to manipulate the arguments of any other kind of expression (except atoms).

In[36]:= **Append[w + x y, z]**

Out[36]= w + x y + z

This result can best be understood by looking at the `FullForm` of the following two expressions.

In[37]:= **FullForm[w + x y]**

Out[37]//FullForm=

Plus[w, Times[x, y]]

In[38]:= **FullForm[w + x y + z]**

Out[38]//FullForm=

Plus[w, Times[x, y], z]

Appending z to w + x y is equivalent to adding z as an argument to the `Plus` function. More generally:

In[39]:= **Append[f[a, b], c]**

Out[39]= f[a, b, c]

For more complicated expressions, you might find it useful to display the internal representation with the `TreeForm` function, which shows the "tree structure" of an expression. In the following example, the root node of the tree is `Plus`, which then branches three times at *c*, *bx*, and at *ax*², the latter two branching further.

In[40]:= **TreeForm$\left[a\, x^2 + b\, x + c\right]$**

Out[40]//TreeForm=

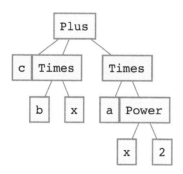

In[41]:= **Head$\left[a\, x^2 + b\, x + c\right]$**

Out[41]= Plus

The second element of this expression is the second term in the sum.

In[42]:= **Part$\left[$a x^2 + b x + c, 2$\right]$**

Out[42]= **b x**

The second element of that is the second factor in the product.

In[43]:= **FullForm[%]**

Out[43]//FullForm=

      Times[b, x]

In[44]:= **Part[b x, 2]**

Out[44]= **x**

You could extract the second part of the second element directly using **Part**.

In[45]:= **Part$\left[$a x^2 + b x + c, 2, 2$\right]$**

Out[45]= **x**

Although parts of atomic expressions cannot, in general, be extracted with the **Part** function, there are *selectors* available that operate on various atomic expressions. Selectors are functions that return some part of a data object. In modern programming languages, they are used to separate functions that operate on data objects from the data objects themselves. For example, here are some of the selectors for rational numbers, real numbers, complex numbers, graphs, and sparse arrays.

In[46]:= **$\left\{$Numerator$\left[\dfrac{3}{4}\right]$, Denominator$\left[\dfrac{3}{4}\right]\right\}$**

Out[46]= **{3, 4}**

In[47]:= **MantissaExponent[3333.14152]**

Out[47]= **{0.333314, 4}**

In[48]:= **{Re[3 - 4 I], Im[3 - 4 I]}**

Out[48]= **{3, -4}**

In[49]:= **{VertexList[CompleteGraph[5]], EdgeList[CompleteGraph[5]]}**

Out[49]= **{{1, 2, 3, 4, 5}, {1 ⟷ 2, 1 ⟷ 3, 1 ⟷ 4,**
      1 ⟷ 5, 2 ⟷ 3, 2 ⟷ 4, 2 ⟷ 5, 3 ⟷ 4, 3 ⟷ 5, 4 ⟷ 5}}

In[50]:= **arr = SparseArray[Band[{1, 1}] → 1, {4, 4}];**
      ArrayRules[arr]

Out[51]= **{{1, 1} → 1, {2, 2} → 1, {3, 3} → 1, {4, 4} → 1, {_, _} → 0}**

Evaluation of expressions

The evaluator, the part of *Mathematica* that evaluates expressions, follows a well-prescribed set of rules to insure correctness and consistency in program evaluation. For example, in a logical expression such as $expr_1$ && $expr_2$ && $expr_3$, *Mathematica* evaluates the expressions $expr_i$ in order until it finds one to be false, at which point, evaluation is terminated. Although there are many such rules built in (some a bit more esoteric than others), it is quite useful to identify a few of the evaluation rules whose consequences you will occasionally encounter.

Briefly, the evaluation sequence involves the following series of steps:

1. When you evaluate an expression (by pressing ⎡SHIFT⎤-⎡RET⎤ or ⎡SHIFT⎤-⎡ENTER⎤), it is left unchanged if that expression is a number or string.

In[52]:= **123.456**

Out[52]= 123.456

2. If the expression is a symbol, it is rewritten if there is an applicable rule, built-in or user-defined. If there is no such rule for the symbol, it is unchanged.

In[53]:= **mysymbol**

Out[53]= mysymbol

If the expression is not a number, string, or symbol, its parts are evaluated in a specific order:

3. The head of the expression is evaluated.

4. The elements of the expression are evaluated in order, except when the head is a symbol with a `Hold` attribute. In this case, some of its arguments are left in their unevaluated forms.

5. After the head and arguments of an expression are each completely evaluated, the expression is rewritten if there is an applicable rule in the global rule base (after making any necessary changes to the arguments based on the attributes of the head). User-defined rules are checked, then the built-in rule base.

6. After carrying out the previous steps, the resulting expression is evaluated in the same way and then the result of that evaluation is evaluated, and so on until there are no more applicable rules.

These steps just give an outline of what happens internally in the standard evaluation procedure. If you are interested in the details, including nonstandard evaluation, see the two tutorials, Evaluation and Evaluation of Expressions (WMDC).

As indicated above, arguments of expressions are evaluated prior to being passed to the calling function (typically given by the head). This principle is common to many modern programming languages but it does cause some surprises occasionally. For example, looking at the internal representation of a simple sum, you might expect something like `Plus[2, 2]`, but that is not what is returned after evaluation.

In[54]:= **FullForm[2 + 2]**

Out[54]//FullForm=

    4

This is a consequence of the fact that arguments to functions are evaluated *before* being passed up to the calling function, in this case, `Plus`. So, how can you see the internal form of an expression before the evaluator gets to it? The answer is to use one of the many `Hold` functions.

In[55]:= **FullForm[HoldForm[2 + 2]]**

Out[55]//FullForm=

    HoldForm[Plus[2, 2]]

Wrapping an expression in `HoldForm` causes that expression to be kept in an unevaluated form as it is passed up to `FullForm`. Many of the built-in functions have one of the `Hold` attributes, thus preventing initial evaluation of their arguments.

In[56]:= **Attributes[Plot]**

Out[56]= {HoldAll, Protected}

In[57]:= **Plot$\left[\text{Table}\left[x^i, \{i, 2, 8, 2\}\right], \{x, -1, 1\}, \text{PlotStyle} \rightarrow \right.$**
$\left.\{\text{Dashing}[.01], \text{Dashing}[.03], \text{Dashing}[.05], \text{Dashing}[.07]\}\right]$

Out[57]=

Ordinarily, `Plot` can handle lists of functions and apply unique styles to each function. In this case, the list structure of the first argument is not explicit – it would be after `Table` is evaluated but the `HoldAll` attribute of `Plot` prevents that. To override any `Hold` attribute, wrap the argument in `Evaluate` (or use the `Evaluated` option to `Plot`).

In[58]:= `Plot[Evaluate@Table[`x^i`, {i, 2, 8, 2}], {x, -1, 1}, PlotStyle →`
`{Dashing[.01], Dashing[.03], Dashing[.05], Dashing[.07]}]`

Out[58]=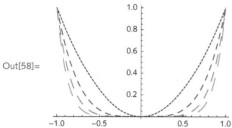

Another approach to preventing the evaluator from initially evaluating an expression is to use `Defer`.

In[59]:= `Defer[2 + 2]`

Out[59]= `2 + 2`

In[60]:= `Defer[FullForm[2 + 2]]`

Out[60]= `Plus[2, 2]`

The advantage of using `Defer` like this is that the output it returns is evaluatable. In other words you can put your cursor in the output cell and evaluate it.

In[61]:= `Plus[2, 2]`

Out[61]= `4`

Exercises

1. Give the full (internal) form of the expression `a (b + c)`.

2. What is the traditional representation of `Times[a, Power[Plus[b, c], -1]]`.

3. What is the part specification of the `b` in the expression $a x^2 + b x + c$?

4. What do you expect to be the result of the following operations? Use the `FullForm` of the expressions to understand what is going on.

   a. `((`x^2`+ y) z / w)[[2, 1, 2]]`.

   b. `(a / b)[[2, 2]]`.

2.2 Definitions

Defining variables and functions

One of the most common tasks in any programming environment is to define functions, constants, and procedures to perform various tasks. Sometimes a particular function that you need is not part of the built-in set of functions. Other times, you may need to use an expression over and over again and so it would be useful to define it once and have it available for future reference. By defining your own functions and constants you essentially expand the range of *Mathematica's* capabilities in such a way that they work with all the built-in functions seamlessly.

For example, you might define a constant a to have a certain numeric value.

In[1]:= **a = N[2 π]**

Out[1]= **6.28319**

Then, whenever a is used in a subsequent computation, *Mathematica* will find the rule associated with a and will substitute that value wherever a occurs.

In[2]:= **Cos[a]**

Out[2]= **1.**

To check what definitions are associated with a, evaluate ? a.

In[3]:= **? a**

Global`a

a = 6.28319

The expression $a = N[2 \pi]$ is called an *assignment* – we are assigning the value of the right-hand side to the symbol on the left-hand side. In this example, we have made an assignment of a constant to the symbol a.

You can also set up assignments to define functions. For example, to define a function f, enclose its arguments in square brackets and use x_ to indicate the variable that will be substituted for x on the right-hand side.

In[4]:= **f[x_] = $\dfrac{1}{1 + x}$**

Out[4]= $\dfrac{1}{1 + x}$

The expression f[x_] on the left-hand side of this assignment is a *pattern*. It indicates the class of expressions for which this definition should be used. We will have much more to say about patterns and pattern matching in *Mathematica* in Chapter 4, but, for now, it is enough to say that the pattern f[x_] matches f[*any expression*].

Once you have defined the rule for f, you can evaluate it at different values by replacing x with any expression: numbers, symbolic expressions, images, anything!

In[5]:= **f[.1]**

Out[5]= **0.909091**

In[6]:= **f[1]**

Out[6]= $\dfrac{1}{2}$

In[7]:= **f$\left[\alpha^2\right]$**

Out[7]= $\dfrac{1}{1 + \alpha^2}$

In[8]:= **f$\left[\right]$**

Out[8]= $\dfrac{1}{1 + \;}$

In this last example, the graph is a symbolic expression that is matched by the pattern **x_** in the definition for **f**. Although it might not make much mathematical sense to add and subtract integers from a graph, symbolically it is entirely consistent.

Clear the symbols that are no longer needed.

In[9]:= **Clear[a, f]**

Immediate vs. delayed assignments

When you make an assignment to a symbol, you are usually only interested in giving that symbol a specific value and then using the symbol name to represent that value in subsequent computations. When you set up definitions for functions, those functions might depend upon the values of previously defined functions or other expressions. In such instances it is useful to delay the assignment until the function is actually used in a computation. This is the basic difference between *immediate* and *delayed* assignments.

An immediate assignment is written **Set**$\left[lhs,\ rhs\right]$ or, more commonly,

   lhs = *rhs*

Here *lhs* is an abbreviation for "left-hand side" and *rhs* abbreviates "right-hand side". Using `Defer`, you can see the internal form of this assignment before *Mathematica* has evaluated it. Assignments are expressions with a head and two elements.

In[10]:= **Defer[FullForm[x = 5]]**

Out[10]= `Set[x, 5]`

As an example, consider defining a symbol `rand1` using an immediate assignment that generates a uniformly distributed random number between 0 and 1.

In[11]:= **rand1 = RandomReal[]**

Out[11]= `0.584973`

Notice that the output of this assignment is the value of the right-hand side and that *Mathematica* evaluates the right-hand side immediately, that is, *when the assignment is made.*

Delayed assignments use `SetDelayed[lhs, rhs]` or, in its standard input form:

> *lhs* **:** = *rhs*

Here is the internal representation of a delayed assignment.

In[12]:= **Defer[FullForm[x := 5]]**

Out[12]= `SetDelayed[x, 5]`

As an example, consider a symbol `rand2` to be defined similarly to `rand1`, but with a delayed assignment.

In[13]:= **rand2 := RandomReal[]**

Notice that the delayed assignment does not return a value when the assignment is made. In fact, the right-hand side will not be evaluated until the symbol `rand2` is used.

Let us call the function `rand1` five times.

In[14]:= **Table[rand1, {5}]**

Out[14]= `{0.584973, 0.584973, 0.584973, 0.584973, 0.584973}`

Because the right-hand side of `rand1` was evaluated when the definition was made, `rand1` was assigned the value `0.584973`. Each subsequent call to `rand1` returns that value.

In[15]:= **? rand1**

   `Global`rand1`

   `rand1 = 0.584973`

On the other hand, creating a table of values using `rand2` produces a very different result.

In[16]:= **Table[rand2, {5}]**

Out[16]= {0.174616, 0.469985, 0.0302229, 0.34487, 0.858773}

Each of the five times that rand2 is called inside Table, *Mathematica* looks up the definition of rand2, and sees that it should evaluate RandomReal[]. It does this each time it is called, generating a new random number each iteration inside Table.

In[17]:= **? rand2**

Global`rand2

rand2 := RandomReal[]

Term rewriting

Rules are used in *Mathematica* to rewrite expressions, that is, to transform an expression to another form. For this reason, these rules are often called *rewrite rules* but we will usually refer to them simply as *rules* when there is no chance of confusing them with other types of rules. Together with pattern matching, rewrite rules are the key to evaluation and transformation of all expressions in *Mathematica*.

In *Mathematica*, you work with two kinds of rules: rules for the built-in functions, which are part of every *Mathematica* session, and user-defined rules, which you enter during a particular session. User-defined rules essentially provide a mechanism for extending the rule base of *Mathematica*.

Information about both kinds of rules is obtained by evaluating *?name*. In the case of a built-in function, the resulting usage message gives information about the syntax for using the function and a brief statement explaining what the function does.

In[18]:= **? Map**

Map[*f*, *expr*] or *f* /@ *expr* applies *f* to each element on the first level in *expr*.

Map[*f*, *expr*, *levelspec*] applies *f* to parts of *expr* specified by *levelspec*. ≫

For user-defined rules, the rule itself is printed. The crucial difference between rules created with the SetDelayed and Set functions becomes apparent by querying *Mathematica* for the rules associated with the symbols rand1 and rand2.

In[19]:= **? rand1**

Global`rand1

rand1 = 0.584973

A rule created using the `Set` function has the same left-hand side as the function that created it but the right-hand side of the rule may differ from the right-hand side of the function. This is because the right-hand side of the rule was evaluated at the moment the definition was made, in this case, returning a number between 0 and 1.

On the other hand, a rule created using the `SetDelayed` function looks exactly like the function that created it. This is because both the left-hand side and right-hand side of a `SetDelayed` function are placed in the rule base *without being evaluated*.

In[20]:= **? rand2**

Global`rand2

rand2 := RandomReal[]

In view of this difference between the `SetDelayed` and `Set` functions, when should you use one or the other function to create a rule? When you define a function, you usually do not want either the left-hand side or the right-hand side to be evaluated; you just want to make it available for use when the appropriate function call is made. This is precisely what occurs when a `SetDelayed` function is entered, so the `SetDelayed` function is commonly used in writing function definitions. When you make a value declaration, you do not want the left-hand side to be evaluated; you just want to make it a nickname to serve as shorthand for a value. This is what happens when a `Set` function is entered and so the `Set` function is commonly used to make value declarations, such as assigning a numeric value to a constant or variable.

A new rule overwrites, or replaces, an older rule with the same left-hand side. However, keep in mind that two rules that only differ in the name of their pattern variables are considered the same by *Mathematica*. `Clear[`*name*`]` is used to remove rules from the global rule base.

Functions with multiple definitions

When you create function definitions, usually the definition is associated with the head of the left-hand side of your definition. So, for example, the following assignment associates the rule $1 + x + x^2$ with the head `f`.

In[21]:= **f[x_] := 1 + x + x^2**

There can be many evaluation rules associated with one symbol. The following assignments associate additional rules with the symbol `f`.

In[22]:= **f[x_, y_] := x + y**

In[23]:= $\mathbf{f[x\_, y\_, z\_]} := \dfrac{1}{\mathbf{x + y - z}}$

To view all the rules associated with $\mathbf{f}$, use ?$\mathbf{f}$.

In[24]:= ? $\mathbf{f}$

Global`f

$f[x\_] := 1 + x + x^2$

$f[x\_, y\_] := x + y$

$f[x\_, y\_, z\_] := \frac{1}{x+y-z}$

The advantage of this structure is that you can use one name for a function that will behave differently depending upon the number or form of arguments you give to that function. Using a different symbol for each of these tasks would require you and those who use your programs to remember multiple function names when one might be sufficient. For example, here are two definitions for a function, one for an arbitrary argument and another for a list of two expressions.

In[25]:= $\mathbf{fun[x\_] := Abs[x]}$

In[26]:= $\mathbf{fun[\{x\_, y\_\}] := Sqrt\left[x^2 + y^2\right]}$

Different rules will be called and evaluated depending upon the pattern match as determined by the argument structure.

In[27]:= $\mathbf{fun[-12]}$

Out[27]= 12

In[28]:= $\mathbf{fun[\{2, 3\}]}$

Out[28]= $\sqrt{13}$

In[29]:= $\mathbf{fun[2 + 3 I]}$

Out[29]= $\sqrt{13}$

This is a very simplistic example, one that would need some modification if we wanted to consider it for, say, a norm computation.

In[30]:= $\mathbf{fun["string"]}$

Out[30]= Abs[string]

In[31]:= **fun[{{a, b}, {c, d}}]**

Out[31]= $\left\{ \sqrt{a^2 + c^2}, \sqrt{b^2 + d^2} \right\}$

Writing more explicit rules for such a computation is straightforward enough but requires a bit more discussion of patterns and predicates to do properly. These topics will be discussed in Chapter 4 on patterns and rules.

Clear symbols that are no longer needed.

In[32]:= **Clear[x, f, g, n, fun]**

Exercises

1. What rules are created by each of the following functions? Check your predictions by evaluating them and then querying *Mathematica* with ?*function_name*.

   a. `randLis1[n_] := RandomReal[1, {n}]`

   b. `randLis2[n_] := (x = RandomReal[]; Table[x, {n}])`

   c. `randLis3[n_] := (x := RandomReal[]; Table[x, {n}])`

   d. `randLis4[n_] = Table[RandomReal[], {n}]`

2. Consider two functions f and g, which are identical except that one is written using an immediate assignment and the other using a delayed assignment.

   In[1]:= **f[$n\_$] = Sum$\left[(1 + x)^j, \{j, 1, n\} \right]$;**

   In[2]:= **g[$n\_$] := Sum$\left[(1 + x)^j, \{j, 1, n\} \right]$**

   Explain why the outputs of these two functions *look* so different. Are they in fact different?

   In[3]:= **f[2]**

   Out[3]= $\dfrac{(1 + x)\left(-1 + (1 + x)^2\right)}{x}$

   In[4]:= **g[2]**

   Out[4]= $1 + x + (1 + x)^2$

3. Write rules for a function `log` (note lowercase) that encapsulate the following identities:

   $\log(a\,b) = \log(a) + \log(b);$
   $\log\left(\frac{a}{b}\right) = \log(a) - \log(b);$
   $\log(a^n) = n\log(a).$

4. Create a piecewise-defined function $g(x)$ based on the following and then plot the function from -2 to 0.

$$g(x) = \begin{cases} -\sqrt{1-(x+2)^2} & -2 \le x \le -1 \\ \sqrt{1-x^2} & x < 0 \end{cases}$$

2.3 Predicates and Boolean operations

Predicates

When working with many kinds of data, you are often presented with the problem of extracting values that meet certain criteria. Similarly, when you write programs, what to do next at any particular point in your program will often depend upon some test or condition being met. Every programming language has constructs for testing data or conditions. Some of the most useful constructs for these sorts of tests are called predicates. A *predicate* is a function that returns a value of true or false depending upon whether its argument passes a test. For example, the predicate `PrimeQ` tests for the primality of its argument.

In[1]:= **PrimeQ$\left[2^{31} - 1\right]$**

Out[1]= True

Other predicates are available for testing numbers to see whether they are even, odd, integral, and so on.

In[2]:= **OddQ[21]**

Out[2]= True

In[3]:= **EvenQ[21]**

Out[3]= False

In[4]:= **IntegerQ$\left[\dfrac{5}{9}\right]$**

Out[4]= False

`NumericQ` tests whether its argument is a numeric quantity. Essentially, `NumericQ[x]` returns a value of `True` whenever `N[x]` evaluates to an explicit number.

In[5]:= **NumericQ$[\pi]$**

Out[5]= True

In[6]:= **NumericQ$[\infty]$**

Out[6]= False

This is distinct from a related function, `NumberQ`, which evaluates to `True` whenever its argument is an explicit number, that is, has head one of `Integer`, `Rational`, `Real`, `Complex`.

In[7]:= **NumberQ[3.2]**

Out[7]= True

In[8]:= **NumberQ[π]**

Out[8]= False

Some predicate functions can take a second argument to test the form of the elements of an expression. For example, this tests whether the argument is a vector and if its elements are all prime.

In[9]:= **VectorQ$\left[\left\{2^3 - 1, 2^7 - 1, 2^{31} - 1\right\},\ \text{PrimeQ}\right]$**

Out[9]= True

Many other predicates are available for testing expressions such as atoms, lists, various matrices, polynomials, and much more.

In[10]:= **AtomQ["string"]**

Out[10]= True

In[11]:= **ListQ[{a, b, c}]**

Out[11]= True

In[12]:= **SymmetricMatrixQ$\left[\begin{pmatrix} 1 & 2 & 3 \\ 2 & 4 & 5 \\ 3 & 5 & 6 \end{pmatrix}\right]$**

Out[12]= True

In[13]:= **PolynomialQ$\left[\dfrac{1}{x} + \dfrac{1}{x^2} + \dfrac{1}{x^3},\ x\right]$**

Out[13]= False

In[14]:= **ConnectedGraphQ$\Big[$**  **$\Big]$**

Out[14]= True

In[15]:= **IntervalMemberQ[Interval[{2, 3}], π]**

Out[15]= False

Relational and logical operators

Another class of commonly-used predicates are the relational operators. They are used to compare two or more expressions and they return a value of `True` or `False`. The relational operators in *Mathematica* are `Equal` (==), `Unequal` (≠), `Greater` (>), `Less` (<), `GreaterEqual`(≥), and `LessEqual` (≤). They can be used to compare numbers or arbitrary expressions.

In[16]:= **7 < 5**

Out[16]= `False`

In[17]:= **3 == 7 - 4 == $\dfrac{6}{2}$**

Out[17]= `True`

In[18]:= **$x^2 - 1 == \dfrac{x^4 - 1}{x^2 + 1}$ // Simplify**

Out[18]= `True`

Note that the relational operators have lower precedence than arithmetic operators. The second example above is interpreted as 3 == (7 - 4) and not as (3 == 7) - 4. Table 2.2 lists the relational operators and their various input forms.

The logical operators (sometimes known as Boolean operators) determine the truth of an expression based on Boolean arithmetic. For example, the conjunction of two true statements is always true.

In[19]:= **4 < 5 && 8 > 1**

Out[19]= `True`

The Boolean operation AND is represented in *Mathematica* by `And`, with shorthand notation `&&` or ∧. Here is a table that gives all the possible values for the `And` operator. (The function `TruthTable` is developed in Exercise 10 in Section 5.8.)

In[20]:= **TruthTable[A ∧ B, {A, B}]**

A	B	A ∧ B
T	T	T
T	F	F
F	T	F
F	F	F

Out[20]=

TABLE 2.2. *Relational operators*

StandardForm	Long (functional) form	Meaning
$x == y$	`Equal[x, y]`	test for equality
$x \neq y$	`Unequal[x, y]`	unequal
$x > y$	`Greater[x, y]`	greater than
$x < y$	`Less[x, y]`	less than
$x \geq y$	`GreaterEqual[x, y]`	greater than or equal
$x \leq y$	`LessEqual[x, y]`	less than or equal

The logical OR operator, represented by `Or` and with shorthand notation `||` (or $\vee$), is true when either of its arguments is true.

In[21]:= **4 == 3 || 3 ==** $\dfrac{6}{2}$

Out[21]= **True**

In[22]:= **0 == 0.0001** $\bigvee$ **π ==** $\dfrac{22}{7}$

Out[22]= **False**

In[23]:= **TruthTable[A $\vee$ B, {A, B}]**

Out[23]=

A	B	$A \vee B$
T	T	T
T	F	T
F	T	T
F	F	F

Note the difference between this Boolean OR and the natural language notion of "or." A phrase such as, "It is cold or it is hot," uses the word "or" in an *exclusive* sense, that is, it excludes the possibility that it is *both* cold and hot. The logical `Or` ($\vee$) is inclusive in the sense that if A and B are both true, then $A \vee B$ is also true.

In[24]:= **True || True**

Out[24]= **True**

Table 2.3 shows the logical operators and their input forms.

TABLE 2.3. *Logical operators*

StandardForm	TraditionalForm	Long form	Meaning
!x	$\neg x$	Not$[x]$	not
x && y	$x \wedge y$	And$[x, y]$	and
x || y	$x \vee y$	Or$[x, y]$	or
(x || y) && !(x && y)	$x \veebar y$	Xor$[x, y]$	exclusive or
!(x || y)	$x \; \overline{\vee} \; y$	Nor$[x, y]$	negation of or
!x || y	$x \Rightarrow y$	Implies$[x, y]$	implication

Mathematica also contains an operator for the exclusive or, Xor.

In[25]:= **Xor[True, True]**

Out[25]= False

In[26]:= **Xor[True, False]**

Out[26]= True

In[27]:= **TruthTable[A $\veebar$ B, {A, B}]**

A	B	$A \veebar B$
T	T	F
T	F	T
F	T	T
F	F	F

Out[27]=

An additional set of useful operators are the *bitwise logical operators* (see Table 2.4). These functions operate on integers as binary bits. For example, BitOr$[x, y]$ gives the integer whose binary representation has 1s wherever the binary representation of x or y has 1s. Here is the bitwise OR of 21 and 19, given in binary form.

In[28]:= **BaseForm[BitOr[2^^10101, 2^^10011], 2]**

Out[28]//BaseForm=

10111_2

In[29]:= **BitOr[21, 19]**

Out[29]= 23

In[30]:= **BaseForm[23, 2]**

Out[30]//BaseForm=

10111_2

Similarly, BitXor$[x, y]$ gives the integer with 1s at positions where either x or y have 1s, but not both.

In[31]:= **BaseForm[BitXor[2^^10101, 2^^10011], 2]**

Out[31]//BaseForm=

110_2

TABLE 2.4. *Bitwise operators*

Long (functional) form	Meaning
BitAnd$[x, y]$	bitwise AND of x and y
BitOr$[x, y]$	bitwise OR of x and y
BitNot$[x]$	bitwise NOT of x
BitXor$[x, y]$	bitwise XOR of x and y

In Section 5.8 we will look at an application of bitwise operators to an example involving error-correcting codes: the computation of Hamming distance.

Exercises

1. Create a predicate function that returns a value of True if its argument is between –1 and 1.

2. Define a predicate function CharacterQ [*str*] that returns true if its argument *str* is a single string character, and returns false otherwise.

3. Write a predicate function NaturalQ [*n*] that returns a value of True if *n* is a natural number and False otherwise, that is, NaturalQ [*n*] is True if *n* is among 0, 1, 2, 3, ...

4. Create a predicate function SubsetQ [lis_1, lis_2] that returns a value of True if lis_1 is a subset of lis_2. Remember, the empty set, { }, is a subset of every set.

5. Create a predicate function CompositeQ that tests whether its argument is a nonprime integer.

2.4 Attributes

All functions in *Mathematica* have certain properties that control various aspects of their behavior. These properties, called *attributes*, can make a function commutative or associative, or they may give the function the ability to be threaded over a list. The attributes of any function are displayed with the Attributes function.

In[1]:= **Attributes[Plus]**

Out[1]= {Flat, Listable, NumericFunction,
        OneIdentity, Orderless, Protected}

The Flat attribute indicates that this function (Plus) is associative. That is, given three elements to add, it does not matter which two are added first. In mathematics, this is known as *associativity* and is written as $a + (b + c) = (a + b) + c$. In *Mathematica* this could be indicated by saying that the two expressions `Plus[a, Plus[b, c]]` and `Plus[Plus[a, b], c]` are equivalent to the flattened form `Plus[a, b, c]`. When *Mathematica* knows that a function has the attribute `Flat`, it writes it in flattened form.

In[2]:= **`Plus[Plus[a, b], c]`**

Out[2]= `a + b + c`

Functions with the attribute `OneIdentity` have the property that repeated application of that function to the same argument will have no effect. For example, `Plus[Plus[a, b]]` is equivalent to `Plus[a, b]`, hence only one addition is performed.

In[3]:= **`FullForm[Plus[Plus[a + b]]]`**

Out[3]//FullForm=

$\qquad$ `Plus[a, b]`

The `Orderless` attribute indicates that the function is commutative, that is, $a + b = b + a$. This allows *Mathematica* to write such an expression in an order that is useful for computation. It does this by sorting the elements into a *canonical order*. For expressions consisting of letters and words, this ordering is alphabetic.

In[4]:= **`t + h + i + n`**

Out[4]= `h + i + n + t`

Sometimes a canonical order is readily apparent.

In[5]:= **`x`^{3}` + x`^{5}` + x`^{4}` + x`^{2}` + 1 + x`**

Out[5]= `1 + x + x`^{2}` + x`^{3}` + x`^{4}` + x`^{5}

Other times, it is not so apparent.

In[6]:= **`x`^{3}` y`^{2}` + y`^{7}` x`^{5}` + y x`^{4}` + y`^{9}` x`^{2}` + 1 + x`**

Out[6]= `1 + x + x`^{4}` y + x`^{3}` y`^{2}` + x`^{5}` y`^{7}` + x`^{2}` y`^{9}

As an aside, note that some formatting functions use ordering rules that are different from those used by the default output formats.

In[7]:= **`TraditionalForm[x`^{3}` + x`^{5}` + x`^{4}` + x`^{2}` + 1 + x]`**

Out[7]//TraditionalForm=

$\qquad x^5 + x^4 + x^3 + x^2 + x + 1$

When a symbol has the attribute `Protected`, the user is prevented from modifying the function in any significant way. All built-in functions have this attribute.

The other attributes for the `Plus` function (`Listable` and `NumericFunction`) will be discussed in later chapters. For a complete list of the attributes that symbols can have, see the tutorial Attributes (WMDC).

Although it is unusual to want to alter the attributes of a built-in function, it is fairly common to change the default attributes of a user-defined function. For example, suppose you had a function that you wanted to inherit the `Orderless` attribute. Without explicitly setting that attribute, the function does not reorder its arguments.

In[8]:= **f[b, e, t, s]**

Out[8]= f[b, e, t, s]

The `SetAttributes` function is used to change the attributes of a function. Explicitly setting f to have the `Orderless` attribute causes its arguments to be automatically sorted.

In[9]:= **SetAttributes[f, Orderless]**

In[10]:= **f[b, e, t, s]**

Out[10]= f[b, e, s, t]

Note: using `Clear` to clear definitions associated with a symbol does *not* clear attributes.

In[11]:= **Clear[f]**

In[12]:= **? f**

Global`f

Attributes[f] = {Orderless}

To clear only attributes, use `ClearAttributes` [*symbol, attribute*]. To clear all values, definitions, attributes and messages associated with a symbol, use `ClearAll` [*sym*].

In[13]:= **ClearAll[f]**

In[14]:= **? f**

Global`f

We will see some applications of `SetAttributes` in Sections 5.2 and 6.2.

Exercises

1. Ordinarily, when you define a function, it has no attributes. *Mathematica* evaluates the arguments before passing them up to the calling function. So, in the following case, 2 + 3 is evaluated before it is passed to f.

In[1]:= **f[x_ + y_] := $x^2 + y^2$**

In[2]:= **f[2 + 3]**

Out[2]= **f[5]**

Use one of the Hold attributes to give f the property that its argument is not evaluated first. The resulting output should look like this:

In[3]:= **f[2 + 3]**

Out[3]= 13

2. Define a function that takes each number, x, in a vector of numbers and returns x if it is within a certain interval, say $-0.5 < x < 0.5$, and returns $\sqrt{x}$ otherwise. Then make your function listable so that it can operate on vectors (lists) directly.

3

Lists

Structure and syntax of lists · Creating lists · Displaying lists · Arrays · Analyzing lists · Testing lists · Measuring lists · Extracting elements of lists · Rearranging lists · List component assignment · Working with multiple lists

Lists are the fundamental data structure used in *Mathematica* to group objects together. They are quite general and they can be used to represent a vast array of objects: vectors, matrices, tensors, iterator and parameter specifications, and much more. An extensive set of built-in functions is available to manipulate lists in a variety of ways, ranging from simple operations, such as rearranging the order of list elements to more sophisticated operations such as partitioning, sorting, or applying a function to a list. For example, this sorts a list numerically.

```
In[1]:= Sort[{4, 16, 1, 77, 23}]
```

```
Out[1]= {1, 4, 16, 23, 77}
```

Fast and efficient linear algebra functions are available for operating on vectors and matrices. A vector is just a flat list of values; a matrix can be thought of as a list of vectors of the same length. For example, this muliplies a symbolic matrix by a vector.

```
In[2]:= {{a, b}, {c, d}}.{x, y}
```

```
Out[2]= {a x + b y, c x + d y}
```

Elements in lists can be rearranged, removed, new elements added, and operations performed on select elements or on the list as a whole or on multiple lists.

```
In[3]:= {a, b, c} ⋃ {c, d, e}
```

```
Out[3]= {a, b, c, d, e}
```

```
In[4]:= {a, b, c} ⋂ {c, d, e}
```

```
Out[4]= {c}
```

Lists are also used to delineate a range of values for some variable or iterator. For example, the second argument to the `Table` function is a list that specifies the iterator variable and the values that it should range over.

In[5]:= **Table$\left[\texttt{i}^2\texttt{, \{i, 1, 5\}}\right]$**

Out[5]= $\{1, 4, 9, 16, 25\}$

Similarly, the plotting functions use lists to specify the range over which a variable should be evaluated.

In[6]:= **Plot[Sin[x], {x, 0, 2 π}]**

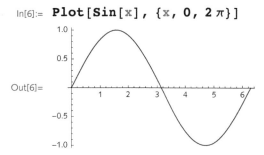

In this chapter, we will demonstrate the use of built-in *Mathematica* functions to manipulate lists in various ways. Almost anything you might wish to do to a list can be accomplished using built-in functions. It is important to have a solid understanding of these functions, since a key to good, efficient programming in *Mathematica* is to use the built-in functions whenever possible to manipulate list structures.

3.1 Creating and displaying lists

List structure and syntax

Lists in *Mathematica* are created using the built-in `List` function which has the standard input form of a sequence of elements separated by commas and enclosed in braces.

$\{e_1, e_2, ..., e_n\}$

Internally, lists are stored in the functional form using the `List` function with an arbitrary number of arguments.

$\texttt{List}[e_1, e_2, ..., e_n]$

`FullForm` gives the internal representation.

In[1]:= **FullForm[{a, b, c}]**

Out[1]//FullForm=

$\texttt{List}[\texttt{a, b, c}]$

The arguments of the `List` function (the *list elements*) can be any type of expression, including numbers, symbols, functions, strings, images, and even other lists.

In[2]:= $\{$ `2.4, Sin, "ossifrage",` `, {5, 3}, {}` $\}$

Out[2]= $\{$ `2.4, Sin, ossifrage,` `, {5, 3}, {}` $\}$

List construction

In addition to using the `List` function to collect various expressions, you can generate lists from scratch by creating the objects and then placing them in a list.

`Range`$\big[$*imin, imax, di*$\big]$ generates a list of ordered numbers starting from *imin* and going up to, but not exceeding, *imax* in increments of *di*.

In[3]:= **Range[0, 30, 3]**

Out[3]= $\{$0, 3, 6, 9, 12, 15, 18, 21, 24, 27, 30$\}$

If *di* is not specified, a value of 1 is used.

In[4]:= **Range[4, 8]**

Out[4]= $\{$4, 5, 6, 7, 8$\}$

If neither *imin* nor *di* is specified, then both are given the value of 1.

In[5]:= **Range[4]**

Out[5]= $\{$1, 2, 3, 4$\}$

It is not necessary for *imin*, *imax*, or *di* to be integers.

In[6]:= **Range[1.5, 6.3, .75]**

Out[6]= $\{$1.5, 2.25, 3., 3.75, 4.5, 5.25, 6.$\}$

`Table`$\big[$*expr*, $\{$*i, imin, imax, di*$\}\big]$ generates a list by evaluating *expr* a number of times as determined by the iterator list.

In[7]:= **Table**$\big[$**2^k, {k, 1, 10, 2}**$\big]$

Out[7]= $\{$2, 8, 32, 128, 512$\}$

The first argument, 2^k in the above example, is the expression that is evaluated to produce the elements in the list. The second argument to the `Table` function, $\{$*i, imin, imax, di*$\}$, is referred to as the *iterator list*. This list specifies the number of times the expression is evaluated and hence the number of elements in the list. The value *imin* is the value of *i* used in the expression to create the first list element. The value *di* is the incremental increase in the value of *i* used in the expression to create additional list elements. The value *imax* is the maximum value of *i* used in the expression to create the last list element. If incrementing *i* by *di* gives a value greater than *imax*, that value is not used.

In[8]:= **Table[i, {i, 1, 10, 2}]**

Out[8]= {1, 3, 5, 7, 9}

Table$\left[i, \left\{i, imin, imax, di\right\}\right]$ is equivalent to **Range**$\left[imin, imax, di\right]$. As with the **Range** function, the arguments to **Table** can be simplified when the iterator increment is 1.

In[9]:= **Table**$\left[2^i, \{i, 1, 10\}\right]$

Out[9]= {2, 4, 8, 16, 32, 64, 128, 256, 512, 1024}

Similarly, both *imin* and *di* can be omitted and are then assumed to be 1.

In[10]:= **Table**$\left[i^2, \{i, 5\}\right]$

Out[10]= {1, 4, 9, 16, 25}

The iterator variable may or may not appear in the expression being evaluated. In this case, the iterator variable may be omitted as well. The expression will then simply be evaluated that many times.

In[11]:= **Table[RandomReal[], {3}]**

Out[11]= {0.765026, 0.623783, 0.596162}

The expression that the **Table** function evaluates can be completely arbitrary. In the following computation, it is used to create a list of plots.

In[12]:= **Table[Plot[BesselJ[n, x], {x, 0, 10}], {n, 2, 5}]**

Out[12]=

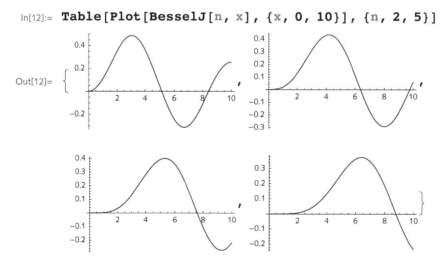

`Table` can be used to create a *nested list*, that is, a list containing other lists as elements. This can be done by using additional iterators.

In[13]:= **Table[i + j, {j, 1, 4}, {i, 1, 3}]**

Out[13]= {{2, 3, 4}, {3, 4, 5}, {4, 5, 6}, {5, 6, 7}}

When there is more than one iterator, their order is important, because the value of the outer iterator is varied for each value of the inner iterator. In the above example, for each value of j (the inner iterator), i was varied from 1 to 3, producing a three-element list for each of the four values of j. If you reverse the iterator order, you will get an entirely different list.

In[14]:= **Table[i + j, {i, 1, 3}, {j, 1, 4}]**

Out[14]= {{2, 3, 4, 5}, {3, 4, 5, 6}, {4, 5, 6, 7}}

The value of the outer iterator may depend on the value of the inner iterator; this can result in a nonrectangular list.

In[15]:= **Table[i + j, {i, 1, 3}, {j, 1, i}]**

Out[15]= {{2}, {3, 4}, {4, 5, 6}}

However, the inner iterator may not depend on the outer iterator because, as we have seen, the inner iterator is fixed as the outer one varies.

In[16]:= **Table[i + j, {i, 1, j}, {j, 1, 3}]**

        Table::iterb : Iterator {i, 1, j} does not have appropriate bounds. ≫

Out[16]= **Table[i + j, {i, 1, j}, {j, 1, 3}]**

Like the function being evaluated, the iterator structure can be quite arbitrary. In fact, it can be almost any expression, for example, a list of primes or a list of image effects.

In[17]:= **Table[$2^p - 1$, {p, {2, 3, 5, 7, 13, 17}}]**

Out[17]= {3, 7, 31, 127, 8191, 131 071}

In[18]:= **Table[ImageEffect[** **, effect],**

      {effect, {"Charcoal", "Posterization", "Solarization"}}]

Out[18]= { , , }

Rather than evaluating the iterator for a *range* of values, these arbitrary iterator specifications cause the function to be evaluated for *each* of the discrete values in the iterator list. So in the first example, the expression $2^p - 1$ is evaluated for each value of p equal to 2, 3, 5, 7, 13, 17; in the second example, `ImageEffect` is evaluated for each of the three different effects, `"Charcoal"`, `"Posterization"`, and `"Solarization"`.

Displaying lists

The default output form of a list, like its input form, uses the curly brace notation.

In[19]:= `{1, 2, 3}`

Out[19]= $\{1, 2, 3\}$

Several formatting functions are available for displaying lists in different forms. For example, `MatrixForm` displays one-dimensional lists as column vectors.

In[20]:= `MatrixForm[{a, b, c}]`

Out[20]//MatrixForm=

$$\begin{pmatrix} a \\ b \\ c \end{pmatrix}$$

It displays rectangular arrays as traditional matrices.

In[21]:= `MatrixForm[{{a, b, c}, {d, e, f}}]`

Out[21]//MatrixForm=

$$\begin{pmatrix} a & b & c \\ d & e & f \end{pmatrix}$$

`TableForm` is useful for displaying nested lists (multi-dimensional data) in a simple rectangular array.

In[22]:= `lis = Table[i + j, {i, 1, 4}, {j, 1, 3}]`

Out[22]= $\{\{2, 3, 4\}, \{3, 4, 5\}, \{4, 5, 6\}, \{5, 6, 7\}\}$

In[23]:= `TableForm[lis]`

Out[23]//TableForm=

2	3	4
3	4	5
4	5	6
5	6	7

Another useful function for displaying nested lists is `Grid`. It contains numerous options specifically for formatting tabular data.

In[24]:= `data = {{"Trial", "Value"}, {1, 0.264084}, {2, 0.185688}, {3, 0.156994}, {4, 0.486455}, {5, 0.334819}, {6, 0.799379}};`

```
In[25]:= Grid[data, Frame → All,
          Background → LightGray, ItemSize → {Automatic, 1.5},
          BaseStyle → {FontFamily → "Helvetica", 8}, FrameStyle → Thin]
```

Out[25]=

Trial	Value
1	0.264084
2	0.185688
3	0.156994
4	0.486455
5	0.334819
6	0.799379

Large arrays of data present a special problem in terms of display. In general you do not want
to look at thousands or millions of rows and columns of numbers in a large array. Functions like
`ArrayPlot` and `MatrixPlot` are useful for visualizing the structure of such expressions. The
correlation between the array of numbers and the "cells" in the plot should be quite apparent for
small arrays.

```
In[26]:= mat = {{1, 0, 1}, {0, 2, 0}, {1, 0, 1}};
         MatrixForm[mat]
```

Out[27]//MatrixForm=

$$\begin{pmatrix} 1 & 0 & 1 \\ 0 & 2 & 0 \\ 1 & 0 & 1 \end{pmatrix}$$

```
In[28]:= ArrayPlot[mat, Mesh → All]
```

Out[28]=

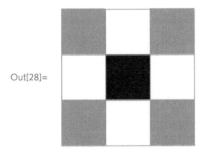

This is particularly useful for large arrays. For example, the following matrix is a representation of
the topology of the US Western States power grid (Watts and Strogatz 1998).

```
In[29]:= grid = Import[
             "http://www.cise.ufl.edu/research/sparse/MM/Newman/power.
                tar.gz", {"TAR", "power/power.mtx"}]
```

Out[29]= SparseArray[<13 188>, {4941, 4941}, Pattern]

`ArrayPlot` shows the structure of the array, in this case giving a visual sense that this matrix is symmetric.

In[30]:= **ArrayPlot[grid]**

Out[30]=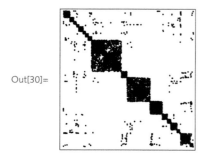

You could also visualize this sparse array as an adjacency graph where the edges represent the transmission lines between power stations (nodes). This representation only gives connectivity information; no geographic information is conveyed.

In[31]:= **AdjacencyGraph[grid]**

Out[31]=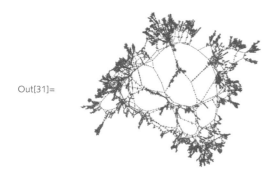

Arrays

In addition to `Table` and `Range`, several other functions are available for constructing lists from scratch, including `Array`, `ConstantArray`, and `SparseArray`. Each of these functions has a similar syntax to `Table` and `Range`.

`Array` is, in some sense, a generalization of `Table` in that you can create arrays of elements wrapped in arbitrary functions. For example, here is a 4×4 array where each element is wrapped in a symbolic function g.

In[32]:= **Array[g, {4, 4}] // MatrixForm**

Out[32]//MatrixForm=

$$\begin{pmatrix} g[1,\ 1] & g[1,\ 2] & g[1,\ 3] & g[1,\ 4] \\ g[2,\ 1] & g[2,\ 2] & g[2,\ 3] & g[2,\ 4] \\ g[3,\ 1] & g[3,\ 2] & g[3,\ 3] & g[3,\ 4] \\ g[4,\ 1] & g[4,\ 2] & g[4,\ 3] & g[4,\ 4] \end{pmatrix}$$

If the function is Greater, we have the following.

In[33]:= **Array[Greater, {4, 4}] // MatrixForm**

Out[33]//MatrixForm=

$$\begin{pmatrix} \text{False} & \text{False} & \text{False} & \text{False} \\ \text{True} & \text{False} & \text{False} & \text{False} \\ \text{True} & \text{True} & \text{False} & \text{False} \\ \text{True} & \text{True} & \text{True} & \text{False} \end{pmatrix}$$

Converting the True/False values to 1s and 0s using Boole, gives a lower triangular matrix.

In[34]:= **Boole[%] // MatrixForm**

Out[34]//MatrixForm=

$$\begin{pmatrix} 0 & 0 & 0 & 0 \\ 1 & 0 & 0 & 0 \\ 1 & 1 & 0 & 0 \\ 1 & 1 & 1 & 0 \end{pmatrix}$$

ConstantArray is useful for quickly creating constant vectors, arrays, and tensors.

In[35]:= **ConstantArray[1, {12}]**

Out[35]= {1, 1, 1, 1, 1, 1, 1, 1, 1, 1, 1, 1}

SparseArray is used to create sparse array objects, that is, arrays where most of the elements are some constant term, typically zero. The first argument to SparseArray is usually a list specifying the nondefault positions and their values. The optional second argument is used to specify the array dimensions. For example, this creates a 3×3 array with symbolic values α, β, and γ on the diagonal.

In[36]:= **array = SparseArray[{{1, 1} → α, {2, 2} → β, {3, 3} → γ}, {3, 3}]**

Out[36]= SparseArray[<3>, {3, 3}]

What is returned by SparseArray is an object whose first argument, <3> in this example, indicates that there are three nondefault elements; the dimensions are given by the second argument, the list {3, 3}.

You can view the array in a traditional matrix form or convert it to a regular list structure.

In[37]:= **MatrixForm[array]**

Out[37]//MatrixForm=

$$\begin{pmatrix} \alpha & 0 & 0 \\ 0 & \beta & 0 \\ 0 & 0 & \gamma \end{pmatrix}$$

In[38]:= **Normal[array]**

Out[38]= $\{\{\alpha, 0, 0\}, \{0, \beta, 0\}, \{0, 0, \gamma\}\}$

Sparse arrays provide a compact representation for what could otherwise be a very large array. For example, this uses a different syntax to create a 1000×1000 array with random numbers on the diagonal.

In[39]:= **bigarray =**
SparseArray[Band[{1, 1}] :→ RandomReal[], {1000, 1000}]

Out[39]= SparseArray[<1000>, {1000, 1000}]

The two big advantages of working with sparse arrays are a compact representation and being able to take advantage of fast linear algebra routines designed explicitly for sparse arrays. So, even though bigarray has 10^6 numbers in it, it only takes about 40 000 bytes to store internally.

In[40]:= **ByteCount[bigarray]**

Out[40]= 40 800

Linear algebra on sparse objects can be quite fast, especially compared with corresponding dense calculations.

In[41]:= **Inverse[bigarray]; // Timing**

Out[41]= {0.36709, Null}

In[42]:= **Det[bigarray]; // Timing**

Out[42]= {0.137751, Null}

Sparse arrays will be discussed in more detail in Section 8.3.

Exercises

1. Generate the list {{0}, {0, 2}, {0, 2, 4}, {0, 2, 4, 6}, {0, 2, 4, 6, 8}} in two different ways using the Table function.

2. A table containing ten random 1s and 0s can be created using RandomInteger[1, {10}]. Create a ten-element list of random 1s, 0s and −1s.

3. Create a ten-element list of random 1s and −1s. This list can be viewed as the steps taken in a random walk along the *x*-axis, where a step can be taken in either the positive *x* direction (corresponding to 1) or the negative *x* direction (corresponding to −1) with equal likelihood.

    The random walk in one, two, three (and even higher) dimensions is used in science and engineering to represent phenomena that are probabilistic in nature. We will use a variety of random walk models throughout this book to illustrate many different programming concepts.

4. Generate both of the following arrays using the `Table` function.

    In[1]:= **`Array[f, 5]`**
    Out[1]= `{f[1], f[2], f[3], f[4], f[5]}`

    In[2]:= **`Array[f, {3, 4}]`**
    Out[2]= `{{f[1, 1], f[1, 2], f[1, 3], f[1, 4]},`
    `{f[2, 1], f[2, 2], f[2, 3], f[2, 4]},`
    `{f[3, 1], f[3, 2], f[3, 3], f[3, 4]}}`

5. Construct an integer lattice graphic like the one below. Start by creating pairs of coordinate points to connect with lines – here we have written the coordinates explicitly but you should generate them programmatically. Once you have your coordinate pairs, you can display the graphic as follows:

    In[3]:= **`coords = {{{-2, -1}, {2, -1}}, {{-2, 0}, {2, 0}},`**
    `{{-2, 1}, {2, 1}}, {{-2, -1}, {-2, 1}}, {{-1, -1}, {-1, 1}},`
    `{{0, -1}, {0, 1}}, {{1, -1}, {1, 1}}, {{2, -1}, {2, 1}}};`
    `Graphics[Line[coords]]`

    Out[4]=

6. Import six images, resize them to the same dimensions, then display them inside a 3 × 2 grid using options for `Grid` to format the output.

3.2 The structure of lists

Testing a list

To find the locations of specific elements in a list, use `Position`. For example, the following result indicates that the number 5 occurs in the first and third positions in the list. The extra braces are used to avoid confusion with the case when elements are *nested* within a list.

In[1]:= **Position[{5, 7, 5, 2, 1, 4}, 5]**

Out[1]= **{{1}, {3}}**

In the following, the expression f occurs once, in the third position within the second inner list.

In[2]:= **Position[{{a, b, c}, {d, e, f}}, f]**

Out[2]= **{{2, 3}}**

Other functions exist to select or count the number of elements in a list that match a certain pattern. For example, Count gives the frequency of an expression or pattern in a list.

In[3]:= **Count[{5, 7, 5, 2, 1, 4}, 5]**

Out[3]= **2**

You can test for membership in a list using MemberQ.

In[4]:= **MemberQ[{5, 7, 5, 2, 1, 4}, 3]**

Out[4]= **False**

Alternatively, you can test whether a list is free of a particular expression.

In[5]:= **FreeQ[{5, 7, 5, 2, 1, 4}, 3]**

Out[5]= **True**

Measuring lists

Recall from Chapter 2 that Length [*expr*] is used to give the number of elements in *expr*. For a simple unnested (linear) list, the Length function tells you how many elements are in the list.

In[6]:= **Length[{a, b, c, d, e, f}]**

Out[6]= **6**

In a nested list, each inner list is an element of the outer list. Therefore, the Length of a nested list indicates the number of inner lists, not their sizes.

In[7]:= **Length[{{{1, 2}, {3, 4}, {5, 6}}, {{a, b}, {c, d}, {e, f}}}]**

Out[7]= **2**

To find out more about the structure of nested lists, use the Dimensions function.

In[8]:= **Dimensions[{{{1, 2}, {3, 4}, {5, 6}}, {{a, b}, {c, d}, {e, f}}}]**

Out[8]= **{2, 3, 2}**

This indicates that there are two inner lists, that each inner list contains three lists, and that the innermost lists each have two elements. MatrixForm helps to see the structure better.

In[9]:= **MatrixForm[{{{1, 2}, {3, 4}, {5, 6}}, {{a, b}, {c, d}, {e, f}}}]**

Out[9]//MatrixForm=

$$\left(\begin{array}{ccc} \left(\begin{array}{c}1\\2\end{array}\right) & \left(\begin{array}{c}3\\4\end{array}\right) & \left(\begin{array}{c}5\\6\end{array}\right) \\ \left(\begin{array}{c}a\\b\end{array}\right) & \left(\begin{array}{c}c\\d\end{array}\right) & \left(\begin{array}{c}e\\f\end{array}\right) \end{array} \right)$$

The number of dimensions of a (possibly nested) list, is given by `ArrayDepth`.

In[10]:= **ArrayDepth[{{{1, 2}, {3, 4}, {5, 6}}, {{a, b}, {c, d}, {e, f}}}]**

Out[10]= 3

This is identical to the number of levels in that expression as displayed by `TreeForm` (remember that the head of an expression is at level 0).

In[11]:= **TreeForm[{{{1, 2}, {3, 4}, {5, 6}}, {{a, b}, {c, d}, {e, f}}}]**

Out[11]//TreeForm=

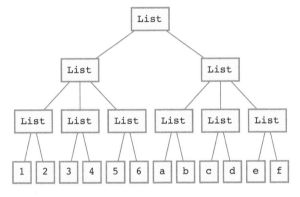

Exercises

1. Given a list of integers such as the following, count the number of 0s. Find a way to count all those elements of the list which are not 1s.

   In[1]:= **ints = RandomInteger[{-5, 5}, 30]**

   Out[1]= {-2, -2, 2, -1, -1, -3, -5, 3, -4, -4, -3, 4, -3,
           4, 2, -2, -3, 1, 2, 3, -2, -4, 1, -1, 1, 1, 5, -2, 0, 3}

2. Given the list {{{1, a}, {2, b}, {3, c}}, {{4, d}, {5, e}, {6, f}}}, determine its dimensions. Use the `Dimensions` function to check your answer.

3. Find the positions of the 9s in the following list. Confirm using `Position`.

   {{2, 1, 10}, {9, 5, 7}, {2, 10, 4}, {10, 1, 9}, {6, 1, 6}}

3.3 Operations on lists

Extracting elements

The `Part` function is designed for extracting elements from expressions by identifying their position within that expression. For example, this extracts the third element in the list `vec`.

In[1]:= **vec = {2, 3, 7, 8, 1, 4};**

In[2]:= **Part[vec, 3]**

Out[2]= 7

The `Part` function is abbreviated using double brackets as shorthand notation.

In[3]:= **vec[[3]]**

Out[3]= 7

To get the elements from more than one location, extract them using a list. For example, this picks out the second and fourth elements of `vec`.

In[4]:= **vec[[{2, 4}]]**

Out[4]= {3, 8}

If you wanted elements in positions 2 through 4, use a list or the `Range` function.

In[5]:= **vec[[{2, 3, 4}]]**

Out[5]= {3, 7, 8}

In[6]:= **vec[[Range[2, 4]]]**

Out[6]= {3, 7, 8}

A shorthand notation for the `Span` function provides a more compact way of doing the same thing.

In[7]:= **vec[[2 ;; 4]]**

Out[7]= {3, 7, 8}

For multi-dimensional lists, you have to specify both the sublist and the position of the element in that sublist that you are interested in. Here is a sample 3×3 matrix that we will work with.

In[8]:= **mat = Table[$a_{i,j}$, {i, 3}, {j, 3}];**

In[9]:= **MatrixForm[mat]**

Out[9]//MatrixForm=

$$\begin{pmatrix} a_{1,1} & a_{1,2} & a_{1,3} \\ a_{2,1} & a_{2,2} & a_{2,3} \\ a_{3,1} & a_{3,2} & a_{3,3} \end{pmatrix}$$

This picks out the first part of the second sublist.

In[10]:= `mat[[2, 1]]`

Out[10]= $a_{2,1}$

For multi-dimensional lists, several options are available to extract different parts. A common operation involves extracting rows or columns from a matrix. The following input extracts the entire second column of `mat`. Think of this as getting all rows, and the second column.

In[11]:= `mat[[All, 2]] // MatrixForm`

Out[11]//MatrixForm=

$$\begin{pmatrix} a_{1,2} \\ a_{2,2} \\ a_{3,2} \end{pmatrix}$$

And here is the third row of this matrix.

In[12]:= `mat[[3, All]]`

Out[12]= $\{a_{3,1},\ a_{3,2},\ a_{3,3}\}$

If you only specify one argument, the second is assumed to be `All`.

In[13]:= `mat[[3]]`

Out[13]= $\{a_{3,1},\ a_{3,2},\ a_{3,3}\}$

In addition to extracting elements from specific locations in a list, you can extract consecutively placed elements within the list using `Take`. Element positions are counted from either the front or the back of a list.

In[14]:= `Take[{1, 9, 7, 17, 33, 57, 107, 197}, 2]`

Out[14]= $\{1,\ 9\}$

In[15]:= `Take[{1, 9, 7, 17, 33, 57, 107, 197}, -2]`

Out[15]= $\{107,\ 197\}$

If you take consecutive elements from a list other than from the front and the back, you need to remember that the numbering of positions is different front-to-back and back-to-front.

In[16]:= `Take[{1, 9, 7, 17, 33, 57, 107, 197}, {2, 4}]`

Out[16]= $\{9,\ 7,\ 17\}$

In[17]:= `Take[{1, 9, 7, 17, 33, 57, 107, 197}, {-5, -3}]`

Out[17]= $\{17,\ 33,\ 57\}$

You can mix positive and negative indices.

In[18]:= **Take[{1, 9, 7, 17, 33, 57, 107, 197}, {-5, 4}]**

Out[18]= {17}

You can also take elements in steps. This takes the first through sixth element in increments of 2, that is, it takes every other element.

In[19]:= **Take[{1, 9, 7, 17, 33, 57, 107, 197}, {1, 6, 2}]**

Out[19]= {1, 7, 33}

Another shorthand notation exists for ranges of this sort.

In[20]:= **Take[{1, 9, 7, 17, 33, 57, 107, 197}, 1 ;; 6 ;; 2]**

Out[20]= {1, 7, 33}

Drop is used to discard elements from a list, keeping the rest. Elements are removed from either end of the list or from consecutive locations.

In[21]:= **Drop[{1, 9, 7, 17, 33, 57, 107, 197}, 2]**

Out[21]= {7, 17, 33, 57, 107, 197}

In[22]:= **Drop[{1, 9, 7, 17, 33, 57, 107, 197}, -1]**

Out[22]= {1, 9, 7, 17, 33, 57, 107}

In[23]:= **Drop[{1, 9, 7, 17, 33, 57, 107, 197}, {3, 5}]**

Out[23]= {1, 9, 57, 107, 197}

Use **Delete** to remove elements at specific locations.

In[24]:= **Delete[{1, 9, 7, 17, 33, 57, 107, 197}, 1]**

Out[24]= {9, 7, 17, 33, 57, 107, 197}

In[25]:= **Delete[{1, 9, 7, 17, 33, 57, 107, 197}, {{3}, {4}}]**

Out[25]= {1, 9, 33, 57, 107, 197}

Certain extractions are used so often that a named function exists for the operation.

In[26]:= **First[{1, 9, 7, 17, 33, 57, 107, 197}]**

Out[26]= 1

In[27]:= **Last[{1, 9, 7, 17, 33, 57, 107, 197}]**

Out[27]= 197

In[28]:= **Rest[{1, 9, 7, 17, 33, 57, 107, 197}]**

Out[28]= {9, 7, 17, 33, 57, 107, 197}

In[29]:= **Most[{1, 9, 7, 17, 33, 57, 107, 197}]**

Out[29]= {1, 9, 7, 17, 33, 57, 107}

Rearranging lists

Every list can be sorted into a canonical order. For lists of numbers or letters, this ordering is usually obvious.

In[30]:= $\mathbf{Sort\left[\left\{3, \frac{223}{71}, \frac{22}{7}, \frac{355}{113}, \frac{25}{8}\right\}\right]}$

Out[30]= $\left\{3, \frac{25}{8}, \frac{223}{71}, \frac{355}{113}, \frac{22}{7}\right\}$

In[31]:= **N[%]**

Out[31]= {3., 3.125, 3.14085, 3.14159, 3.14286}

In[32]:= **Sort[{"s", "p", "a", "m"}]**

Out[32]= {a, m, p, s}

As an aside, note that Sort orders symbols such as π and e by their names, not their values. This is due to the great generality of Sort whereby it can work with any collection of numbers, strings, and symbols.

In[33]:= **Sort[{π, 5, e}]**

Out[33]= {5, e, π}

Convert to explicit numbers to order by the values of these expressions.

In[34]:= **Sort[N[{π, 5, e}]]**

Out[34]= {2.71828, 3.14159, 5.}

Mathematica uses the following canonical orderings: numbers are ordered by numerical value with complex numbers first ordered by real part and then by absolute value of the imaginary part; symbols and strings are ordered alphabetically; powers and products are ordered in a manner corresponding to the terms in a polynomial; expressions are ordered depth-first with shorter expressions first.

In[35]:= $\mathbf{Sort\left[\left\{x^3, x^5, x\right\}\right]}$

Out[35]= $\left\{x, x^3, x^5\right\}$

In[36]:= **Sort[{Expand[(a + b)^2], a (b + c), a b}]**

Out[36]= $\left\{a\,b, a^2 + 2\,a\,b + b^2, a\,(b + c)\right\}$

You can also sort lists according to an ordering function that you can specify as a second argument to Sort.

In[37]:= **Sort** $\left[\left\{3, 1.7, \pi, -4, \frac{22}{7}\right\}, \text{Greater}\right]$

Out[37]= $\left\{\frac{22}{7}, \pi, 3, 1.7, -4\right\}$

When applied to a nested list, Sort will use the first element of each nested list to determine the order.

In[38]:= **Sort[{{2, c}, {7, 9}, {e, f, g}, {1, 4.5}, {x, y, z}}]**

Out[38]= {{1, 4.5}, {2, c}, {7, 9}, {e, f, g}, {x, y, z}}

For multi-dimensional lists, SortBy is also useful. Its second argument is a function that is applied to each element in the list, and the result of that function gives the criterion used for the sort.

In[39]:= **SortBy[{{b, 2}, {a, 3}, {c, 1}, {d, 0}}, Last]**

Out[39]= {{d, 0}, {c, 1}, {b, 2}, {a, 3}}

In addition to sorting, various functions are available to rearrange lists. For example, the order of the elements in a list can be reversed.

In[40]:= **Reverse[{1, 2, 3, 4, 5}]**

Out[40]= {5, 4, 3, 2, 1}

All the elements can be rotated a specified number of positions to the right or the left.

In[41]:= **RotateLeft[{1, 2, 3, 4, 5}]**

Out[41]= {2, 3, 4, 5, 1}

By default RotateLeft (and RotateRight) shifts the list one position to the left (right). This rotates every element two positions to the right.

In[42]:= **RotateRight[{1, 2, 3, 4, 5}, 2]**

Out[42]= {4, 5, 1, 2, 3}

Partition rearranges list elements to form a nested list. It may use all the elements and simply divvy up a list. Here we partition the list into nonoverlapping sublists of length 2.

In[43]:= **Partition[{1, 4, 1, 5, 9, 2}, 2]**

Out[43]= {{1, 4}, {1, 5}, {9, 2}}

You might be interested in only using some of the elements from a list. For example, this takes one-element sublists, with an offset of 2, that is, every other one-element sublist.

In[44]:= **Partition[{1, 4, 1, 5, 9, 2}, 1, 2]**

Out[44]= {{1}, {1}, {9}}

You can also create overlapping inner lists, consisting of ordered pairs (two-element sublists) whose second element is the first element of the next ordered pair.

In[45]:= **Partition[{1, 4, 1, 5, 9, 2}, 2, 1]**

Out[45]= {{1, 4}, {4, 1}, {1, 5}, {5, 9}, {9, 2}}

The **Transpose** function pairs off the corresponding elements of the inner lists. Its argument is a single list consisting of nested lists.

In[46]:= **Transpose[{{x_1, x_2, x_3, x_4}, {y_1, y_2, y_3, y_4}}]**

Out[46]= {{x_1, y_1}, {x_2, y_2}, {x_3, y_3}, {x_4, y_4}}

In[47]:= **mat = {{x_1, x_2, x_3, x_4}, {y_1, y_2, y_3, y_4}, {z_1, z_2, z_3, z_4}};**
Transpose[mat]

Out[48]= {{x_1, y_1, z_1}, {x_2, y_2, z_2}, {x_3, y_3, z_3}, {x_4, y_4, z_4}}

For rectangular lists, you might think of **Transpose** as exchanging the rows and columns of the corresponding matrix.

In[49]:= **MatrixForm[mat]**

Out[49]//MatrixForm=

$$\begin{pmatrix} x_1 & x_2 & x_3 & x_4 \\ y_1 & y_2 & y_3 & y_4 \\ z_1 & z_2 & z_3 & z_4 \end{pmatrix}$$

In[50]:= **Transpose[mat] // MatrixForm**

Out[50]//MatrixForm=

$$\begin{pmatrix} x_1 & y_1 & z_1 \\ x_2 & y_2 & z_2 \\ x_3 & y_3 & z_3 \\ x_4 & y_4 & z_4 \end{pmatrix}$$

Elements can be added to the front, the back, or to any specified position in a given list.

In[51]:= **Append[{1, 2, 3, 4}, 5]**

Out[51]= {1, 2, 3, 4, 5}

In[52]:= **Prepend[{1, 2, 3, 4}, 0]**

Out[52]= {0, 1, 2, 3, 4}

In[53]:= **Insert[{1, 2, 3, 4}, 2.5, 3]**

Out[53]= {1, 2, 2.5, 3, 4}

Elements at specific locations in a list can be replaced with other elements. Here, β replaces the element in the second position of the list.

In[54]:= **ReplacePart[{a, b, c, d, e}, β, 2]**

Out[54]= $\{a, \beta, c, d, e\}$

Some list operations result in deeply nested lists that you may need to flatten. This removes all the inner braces, creating a linear list of elements.

In[55]:= **Flatten[{{{3, 1}, {2, 4}}, {{5, 3}, {7, 4}}}]**

Out[55]= $\{3, 1, 2, 4, 5, 3, 7, 4\}$

You can limit the degree of flattening, removing only some of the inner lists. For example, two inner lists, each having two ordered pairs, can be turned into a single list of four ordered pairs by only flattening down one level deep.

In[56]:= **Flatten[{{{3, 1}, {2, 4}}, {{5, 3}, {7, 4}}}, 1]**

Out[56]= $\{\{3, 1\}, \{2, 4\}, \{5, 3\}, \{7, 4\}\}$

List component assignment

Up until this point, most of the list manipulation functions we have looked at are nondestructive. In other words, operating on a list by, say, reversing its elements, does not change the original list.

In[57]:= **lis = {0, 1, 2, 3, 4};**

In[58]:= **Reverse[lis]**

Out[58]= $\{4, 3, 2, 1, 0\}$

In[59]:= **lis**

Out[59]= $\{0, 1, 2, 3, 4\}$

Sometimes though, it is convenient to modify the list directly. This can be accomplished with list component assignments. The general syntax for modifying a list is:

$$name \left[\left[integer\_valued\_expression \right] \right] = expr$$

The *name* must be the name of a list. The *integer_valued_expression* must evaluate to a legal subscript, that is, a valid position specification for the elements of a list. The assignment returns the value of *expr* (as assignments always do), but has the effect of changing the list to which *name* is bound. In other words, this is a destructive operation, changing the value of the list on which you are operating. For example, this replaces the first element of the above list, lis, with the value 10.

In[60]:= **lis[[1]] = 10**

Out[60]= 10

The value of `lis` itself has changed.

In[61]:= **lis**

Out[61]= $\{10, 1, 2, 3, 4\}$

Components of nested lists can be modified as well.

$$name \,[\, [\, expr_1, \; expr_2 \,] \,] \; = expr$$

$expr_1$ and $expr_2$ are expressions that must evaluate to integers. $expr_1$ chooses the sublist of *name*, and $expr_2$ the element of that sublist.

Here is a 2×3 nested list.

In[62]:= **A = {{1, 2, 3}, {4, 5, 6}};**

This assigns the third element in the second sublist the value 20.

In[63]:= **A⟦2, 3⟧ = 20**

Out[63]= 20

In[64]:= **A**

Out[64]= $\{\{1, 2, 3\}, \{4, 5, 20\}\}$

Note that assigning one array name to another array makes a copy of the first. In this way, component assignments to either one will not affect the other.

In[65]:= **B = A**

Out[65]= $\{\{1, 2, 3\}, \{4, 5, 20\}\}$

In[66]:= **B⟦1, 2⟧ = 30**

Out[66]= 30

In[67]:= **B**

Out[67]= $\{\{1, 30, 3\}, \{4, 5, 20\}\}$

In[68]:= **A**

Out[68]= $\{\{1, 2, 3\}, \{4, 5, 20\}\}$

In[69]:= **A⟦2, 1⟧ = 40**

Out[69]= 40

In[70]:= **B**

Out[70]= $\{\{1, 30, 3\}, \{4, 5, 20\}\}$

This behavior differs from that of languages such as C where aliasing can allow one list to *point* to another; with pointers, changing one array will have an effect on any array that points to it.

As an example of list component assignment, we create a matrix consisting of 1s everywhere except for 0s on the border. Start by creating a matrix of 1s and then replace all elements on the borders with 0s.

```
In[71]:= mat = ConstantArray[1, {5, 5}];
        MatrixForm[mat]
```

Out[72]//MatrixForm=

$$\begin{pmatrix} 1 & 1 & 1 & 1 & 1 \\ 1 & 1 & 1 & 1 & 1 \\ 1 & 1 & 1 & 1 & 1 \\ 1 & 1 & 1 & 1 & 1 \\ 1 & 1 & 1 & 1 & 1 \end{pmatrix}$$

To specify the first and last rows of `mat`, use `mat[[{1, -1}, All]]`, and similarly for the columns.

```
In[73]:= mat[[{1, -1}, All]] = 0;
        mat[[All, {1, -1}]] = 0;
        MatrixForm[mat]
```

Out[75]//MatrixForm=

$$\begin{pmatrix} 0 & 0 & 0 & 0 & 0 \\ 0 & 1 & 1 & 1 & 0 \\ 0 & 1 & 1 & 1 & 0 \\ 0 & 1 & 1 & 1 & 0 \\ 0 & 0 & 0 & 0 & 0 \end{pmatrix}$$

Because *Mathematica* is so efficient at list operations, many computations using list component assignment are often several orders of magnitude faster than other approaches. The reasons behind this are discussed in Chapter 12.

Multiple lists

A number of the functions described earlier in this chapter, such as `Transpose`, work with several lists if they are inside a nested list structure. The following functions, on the other hand, operate on multiple lists as arguments but without the need for the nesting. For example, `Join` concatenates two lists.

```
In[76]:= Join[{2, 5, 7, 3}, {d, a, e, j}]
```

Out[76]= {2, 5, 7, 3, d, a, e, j}

Here is the union of two lists.

```
In[77]:= {4, 1, 2} ∪ {5, 1, 2}
```

Out[77]= {1, 2, 4, 5}

In[78]:= **Union[{4, 1, 2}, {5, 1, 2}]**

Out[78]= {1, 2, 4, 5}

When the Union function is used either on a single list or on a number of lists, a list is formed consisting of the original elements in canonical order with all duplicate elements removed. Complement gives all those elements in the first list that are not in the other list or lists. Intersection$\left[lis_1,\ lis_2,\ ...\right]$ finds all those elements common to the lis_i.

In[79]:= **Complement[{4, 1, 2}, {5, 1, 2}]**

Out[79]= {4}

In[80]:= **{4, 1, 2} ∩ {5, 1, 2}**

Out[80]= {1, 2}

These last three functions, Union, Complement, and Intersection, treat lists somewhat like sets in that there are no duplicates and the order of elements in the lists is not respected. If you simply want to remove duplicates without sorting, use DeleteDuplicates.

In[81]:= **Flatten[{{4, 1, 2}, {5, 1, 2}}]**

Out[81]= {4, 1, 2, 5, 1, 2}

In[82]:= **DeleteDuplicates[%]**

Out[82]= {4, 1, 2, 5}

A common task when working with data that you wish to display in a tabular format is prepending a list of header information.

In[83]:= **header = {"Column A", "Column B"};**
data = RandomReal[1, {5, 2}]

Out[84]= {{0.327946, 0.347031},
{0.401486, 0.13706}, {0.3326, 0.0676231},
{0.812965, 0.340873}, {0.727445, 0.634518}}

When using Prepend$\left[expr,\ elem\right]$, *elem* must have the same structure as the elements of *expr*.

In[85]:= **Prepend[data, header]**

Out[85]= {{Column A, Column B}, {0.327946, 0.347031},
{0.401486, 0.13706}, {0.3326, 0.0676231},
{0.812965, 0.340873}, {0.727445, 0.634518}}

You can do the same with Join, but note that to insure that the two lists have the same structure, header needs to be wrapped in { }.

```
In[86]:=  Join[{header}, data]
```

```
Out[86]=  {{Column A, Column B}, {0.327946, 0.347031},
           {0.401486, 0.13706}, {0.3326, 0.0676231},
           {0.812965, 0.340873}, {0.727445, 0.634518}}
```

We can display this list of headers and data adding some formatting through the use of several options to `Grid`.

```
In[87]:=  Grid[Join[{header}, data],
           Frame → All, Alignment → Left,
           FrameStyle → Thin, ItemStyle → {"Menu", 8}]
```

Out[87]=

Column A	Column B
0.327946	0.347031
0.401486	0.13706
0.3326	0.0676231
0.812965	0.340873
0.727445	0.634518

Using `Join` as follows does not work because the two lists have different structures.

```
In[88]:=  Grid[Join[header, data]]
```

```
Out[88]=  Grid[{Column A, Column B, {0.327946, 0.347031},
               {0.401486, 0.13706}, {0.3326, 0.0676231},
               {0.812965, 0.340873}, {0.727445, 0.634518}}]
```

```
In[89]:=  Dimensions[header]
```

```
Out[89]=  {2}
```

```
In[90]:=  Dimensions[data]
```

```
Out[90]=  {5, 2}
```

Exercises

1. Given a list of data points, $\{\{x_1, y_1\}, \{x_2, y_2\}, \{x_3, y_3\}, \{x_4, y_4\}, \{x_5, y_5\}\}$, separate the x and y components to get:

    $$\{\{x_1, x_2, x_3, x_4, x_5\}, \{y_1, y_2, y_3, y_4, y_5\}\}$$

2. Consider a two-dimensional random walk on a square lattice. (A square lattice can be envisioned as a two-dimensional grid, just like the lines on graph paper.) Each step can be in one of the four directions: $\{1, 0\}, \{0, 1\}, \{-1, 0\}, \{0, -1\}$, corresponding to steps in the compass directions east, north, west and south, respectively. Use the list $\{\{1, 0\}, \{0, 1\}, \{-1, 0\}, \{0, -1\}\}$ to create a list of the steps of a ten-step random walk.

3. Extract elements in the even-numbered locations in the list $\{a, b, c, d, e, f, g\}$.

4. Given a matrix, use list component assignment to swap any two rows.

5. Create a function AddColumn[*mat*, *col*, *pos*] that inserts a column vector *col* into the matrix *mat* at the column position given by *pos*. For example:

   In[1]:= **mat = RandomInteger[9, {4, 4}];**
   MatrixForm[mat]

   Out[2]//MatrixForm=
   $$\begin{pmatrix} 5 & 0 & 9 & 1 \\ 0 & 0 & 0 & 5 \\ 9 & 6 & 2 & 5 \\ 1 & 2 & 2 & 2 \end{pmatrix}$$

   In[3]:= **AddColumn[mat, {a, b, c, d}, 3] // MatrixForm**

   Out[3]//MatrixForm=
   $$\begin{pmatrix} 5 & 0 & a & 9 & 1 \\ 0 & 0 & b & 0 & 5 \\ 9 & 6 & c & 2 & 5 \\ 1 & 2 & d & 2 & 2 \end{pmatrix}$$

6. Suppose you are given a list S of length *n*, and a list P containing *n* different numbers between 1 and *n*, that is, P is a permutation of Range[*n*]. Compute the list T such that for all *k* between 1 and *n*, T[[*k*]] = S[[P[[*k*]]]]. For example, if S = {a, b, c, d} and P = {3, 2, 4, 1}, then T = {c, b, d, a}.

7. Given the lists S and P in the previous exercise, compute the list U such that for all *k* between 1 and *n*, U[[P[[*k*]]]] = S[[*k*]], that is, S[[*i*]] takes the value from position P[[*i*]] in U. Thus, for S = {a, b, c, d} and P = {3, 2, 4, 1}, U = {d, b, a, c}. Think of it as moving S[[1]] to position P[[1]], S[[2]] to position P[[2]], and so on. Hint: start by pairing the elements of P with the elements of S.

8. How would you perform the same task as Prepend[{*x*, *y*}, *z*] using the Join function?

9. Starting with the lists {1, 2, 3, 4} and {a, b, c, d}, create the list {2, 4, b, d}.

10. Starting with the lists {1, 2, 3, 4} and {a, b, c, d}, create the list {1, a, 2, b, 3, c, 4, d}.

11. Given two lists, find all those elements that are not common to the two lists. For example, starting with the lists, {a, b, c, d} and {a, b, e, f}, your answer would return the list {c, d, e, f}.

12. One of the tasks in computational linguistics involves statistical analysis of text using what are called *n*-grams. These are sequences of *n* adjacent letters or words and their frequency distribution in a body of text can be used to predict word usage based on the previous history or usage. Import a file consisting of some text and find the twenty most frequently occurring word combinations. Pairs of words that are grouped like this are called *bigrams*, that is, *n*-grams for *n* = 2.

   Use the following StringSplit code to split long strings into a list of words that can then be operated on with the list manipulation functions. Regular expressions are discussed in detail in Section 9.4.

In[4]:= **words =**
  StringSplit["Use StringSplit to split long strings into words.",
  RegularExpression["\\W+"]]

Out[4]= {Use, StringSplit, to, split, long, strings, into, words}

13. Based on the previous exercise, create a function NGrams[*str*, *n*] that takes a string of text and returns a list of n-grams, that is a list of the *n* adjacent words. For example:

In[5]:= **text = "Use StringSplit to split long strings into words.";**
  NGrams[text, 3]

Out[6]= {{Use, StringSplit, to}, {StringSplit, to, split},
  {to, split, long}, {split, long, strings},
  {long, strings, into}, {strings, into, words}}

4

Patterns and rules

Patterns · Pattern matching by type · Structured patterns · Sequence pattern matching ·
Conditional pattern matching · Alternatives · Repeated patterns · Functions that use patterns ·
Transformation rules · Creating and using replacement rules · Counting coins · Closed paths ·
Finding maxima · Finding subsequences · Sorting lists

The use of rules to transform expressions from one form to another is one of the most powerful tools available in the *Mathematica* programming language. The thousands of rules built in to *Mathematica* can be expanded limitlessly through the creation of user-defined rules. These *rewrite* rules can be used to change the form of expressions and to filter data based on some criteria, and can be set up to apply to broad classes of expressions or they can be limited to certain narrow domains through the use of appropriate pattern matching techniques. Using rules, you can perform many of the tasks normally associated with more traditional programming paradigms such as procedural and functional programming.

When you define a function via an assignment such as the function f below, you are defining a rule that says whenever f is given an argument, it should be replaced with that argument squared. This rule will be applied automatically whenever you evaluate $f[anything]$.

```
In[1]:= f[x_] := x^2
```

```
In[2]:= f[5 i]
Out[2]= -25
```

```
In[3]:= f[LegendreP[5, x]]
```
$$Out[3]= \frac{1}{64}\left(15x - 70x^3 + 63x^5\right)^2$$

In[4]:= $f\left[\right.$$\left.\right]$

Out[4]=

On the other hand, you can set up rules to be applied on demand by using the replacement operator `ReplaceAll`, written in shorthand notation as `/.`. These rules can then be used to transform one expression into another. For example, this rule adds the elements in each ordered pair.

In[5]:= `{{x₁, y₁}, {x₂, y₂}, {x₃, y₃}} /. {x_, y_} :> x + y`

Out[5]= $\{x_1 + y_1,\ x_2 + y_2,\ x_3 + y_3\}$

And here is a rule that interchanges the coordinate points that make up a plot, essentially reflecting in the line $y = x$.

In[6]:= `gr = Plot[Sin[x], {x, 0, π}];`

In[7]:= `Show[{gr, gr /. {x_?NumberQ, y_?NumberQ} :> {y, x},`
`    Graphics[{Dashed, Line[{{0, 0}, {π, π}}]}]},`
`    PlotRange → All, AspectRatio → Automatic]`

Out[7]=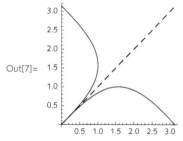

Rules can be used to transform any object in *Mathematica*, such as strings, arrays, or images.

In[8]:= `StringReplace["acgttttccctgagcataaaaacccagcaatacg",`
`    {"ca" → "CA", "tt" → "TT"}]`

Out[8]= `acgTTTTccctgagCAtaaaaaccCAgCAatacg`

$$\text{In[9]:=} \quad \begin{pmatrix} 0.4683 & 0.2699 & \text{"NAN"} \\ 0.8323 & 0.1458 & 0.683 \\ \text{"NAN"} & 0.4935 & 0.4033 \end{pmatrix} \text{ /. (\_String} \rightarrow 0.0) \text{ // MatrixForm}$$

Out[9]//MatrixForm=

$$\begin{pmatrix} 0.4683 & 0.2699 & 0. \\ 0.8323 & 0.1458 & 0.683 \\ 0. & 0.4935 & 0.4033 \end{pmatrix}$$

In[10]:= /. {r_, g_, b_} :> 1 - {r, g, b}

Out[10]=

Rule-based programming has broad application to many different programming tasks and it is essential in learning how to program in *Mathematica*. Although the syntax will be new to anyone brought up on imperative programming common to many procedural languages such as C and FORTRAN, it quickly becomes natural, providing a direct connection between the statement of a problem and its expression in a rule-based program. We start this chapter with a thorough introduction to pattern matching and then proceed to a discussion of transformation rules in which patterns are used to identify the parts of an expression that is to be transformed. Finally, we will conclude the chapter with several concrete examples that make use of pattern matching and transformation rules to show their application to some common programming tasks.

4.1 Patterns

Patterns are objects in *Mathematica* that are used to represent classes of expressions. Pattern matching is the mechanism that *Mathematica* uses to determine if a particular rule should be applied to a given expression. You use patterns to identify the class of expressions for which a user-defined function may apply, that is, for argument checking. They are also used to extract parts of an expression based on a criteria of interest. There are many different types of patterns that you can work with in *Mathematica* and this section introduces their syntax and begins to show some of the great variety of things that are done with them.

Blanks

When you make an assignment to a symbol, like x = 4, you are making a rule that should be applied to the literal expression x. Loosely speaking, the rule says, replace x with the value 4 whenever x is encountered. We have seen that you can also define functions of one or more arguments that allow you to substitute *arbitrary* expressions for those arguments.

In[1]:= **f[x_] :=** x **+ 1**

The left-hand side of the above assignment is a pattern. It contains a pattern object, the blank (underscore), that can stand for any expression, not just the literal expression x.

In[2]:= **f[ζ]**

Out[2]= **1 +** ζ

In[3]:= **f[Bob]**

Out[3]= **1 + Bob**

While any specific expression can be pattern matched (because any object must match itself), we usually want to be able to pattern match large classes of expressions (for example, an expression having Image as its head or a sequence of numbers within a certain range). This is accomplished through patterns and pattern matching. To start, we will define a *pattern* as an expression that may contain *blanks*; specifically, one of the following: a single blank (_), a double blank (__), or a triple blank (___). This is not quite accurate since arbitrary expressions can be used as patterns, but for now, we will only discuss patterns involving blanks.

It is useful to identify the pattern matched by an expression so that it can be referred to by name elsewhere. For example, in the function f defined above, the argument is a pattern named x. The argument is referred to as x on the right-hand side of the definition. Labeled patterns can be used with single, double, and triple blanks.

To see what class of expressions are matched by a given pattern, use MatchQ. For example, the following tests whether the symbol Bob matches any expression because the single underscore can stand for *any Mathematica* expression.

In[4]:= **MatchQ[Bob, _]**

Out[4]= **True**

Clear definitions before continuing.

In[5]:= **Clear[f]**

Pattern matching by type

As stated above, the single blank matches every expression.

In[6]:= {MatchQ[1.2, _], MatchQ["Ciao", _], MatchQ[, _]}

Out[6]= {True, True, True}

Oftentimes you are interested in a more restrictive pattern. For example, you might want to define a function that accepts *only* integers as arguments, or a function that *only* operates on images. One way of restricting the class of expressions matched by a pattern is to match on the head of the expression. This is done with patterns of the form _*head*. For example, the following tests whether the number 3.14 matches any expression with head Real.

In[7]:= MatchQ[3.14, _Real]

Out[7]= True

Of course 3.14 does not match any expression with head Integer.

In[8]:= MatchQ[3.14, _Integer]

Out[8]= False

In[9]:= Head[3.14]

Out[9]= Real

To look at a list of expressions and see which ones are matched by a particular pattern, use Cases. Cases[*expr*, *patt*] returns those elements of *expr* that are matched by the pattern *patt*. For example, the only two elements of the list below that have head Integer are 3 and 17. Notice the fourth element is a string.

In[10]:= Cases[{3, 3.14, 17, "4", 4 + 5 I}, _Integer]

Out[10]= {3, 17}

In[11]:= Cases[{3, 3.14, 17, "4", 4 + 5 I}, _String]

Out[11]= {4}

Remember that the OutputForm of strings is to display without the quote characters. If you want to check the structure of this last output, use InputForm or FullForm.

In[12]:= InputForm[%]

Out[12]//InputForm=
        {"4"}

This next example matches all those expressions with head g.

In[13]:= **Cases[{g[x], f[x], g[h[x]], g[a, 0]}, _g]**

Out[13]= {g[x], g[h[x]], g[a, 0]}

The only expression below that is matched by the pattern _Plus is a + b. The string has head String. But isn't 2 + 3 matched by the pattern _Plus?

In[14]:= **Cases[{a + b, 2 + 3, "3+4"}, _Plus]**

Out[14]= {a + b}

Recall from Section 2.1, that *Mathematica* evaluates the arguments to functions before passing them up to the calling function. So the expression 2 + 3 in this example is evaluated first and returns an expression that does not have head Plus.

In[15]:= **FullForm[2 + 3]**

Out[15]//FullForm=
       5

In practice, pattern matching on heads is extremely useful for restricting the kinds of arguments on which a defined function can operate. For example, the following function sets up a rule for expressions of the form f [*integer*]. Only those expressions matched by this pattern will cause the rule to be invoked.

In[16]:= **f[x_Integer] := x + 1**

In[17]:= **f[5]**

Out[17]= 6

In[18]:= **f[1.25]**

Out[18]= f[1.25]

In[19]:= **Clear[f]**

Structured patterns

Patterns can also be set up to match arbitrary expressions. In the following example, the pattern {p_, q_} matches any list with two elements.

In[20]:= **Cases[{{a, b}, {}, {1, 0}, {c, d, 3}}, {p_, q_}]**

Out[20]= {{a, b}, {1, 0}}

In fact, there is no need to name the patterns in this last example as they are not referred to elsewhere. Hence, the following is equivalent.

In[21]:= **Cases[{{a, b}, {}, {1, 0}, {c, d, 3}}, {_, _}]**

Out[21]= {{a, b}, {1, 0}}

The following result might be a bit surprising. The pattern we are using for matching is a symbolic expression involving a general pattern in both numerator and denominator.

In[22]:= $\textbf{Cases}\left[\left\{2, \dfrac{9}{3}, \dfrac{1}{3}, \dfrac{x}{y+z}\right\}, \dfrac{a\_}{b\_}\right]$

Out[22]= $\left\{\dfrac{x}{y+z}\right\}$

Why doesn't the pattern match 9/3? *Mathematica* evaluates the elements of expressions first and so when 9/3 is evaluated, it reduces to an integer.

In[23]:= $\dfrac{9}{3}$

Out[23]= 3

What is even more mysterious is the fact that the pattern a_ / b_ does not match 1/3. A look at the internal representation of this fraction gives a clue.

In[24]:= $\textbf{FullForm}\left[\dfrac{1}{3}\right]$

Out[24]//FullForm=
     Rational[1, 3]

The pattern matcher is a syntactic tool, not a semantic one. This means that patterns match expressions based on the explicit structure of the expression, not what that expression means or what it might reduce to. This is an important principle to keep in mind when you are creating and using patterns.

In[25]:= $\textbf{MatchQ}\left[\dfrac{1}{3}, \textbf{Rational[a\_, b\_]}\right]$

Out[25]= True

Structured arguments provide a clean mechanism for writing rules that only apply to the kinds of expressions for which you want them to apply. The following function definition is for an argument consisting of a list of two expressions.

In[26]:= $\textbf{f[\{x\_, y\_\}]} := \dfrac{x^2}{y^3}$

In[27]:= **f[{a, b}]**

Out[27]= $\dfrac{a^2}{b^3}$

The pattern does not match in the following case. The function f is expecting a list of two elements as an argument, but here, it is getting a sequence of two elements, not a list.

In[28]:= **f[a, b]**

Out[28]= f[a, b]

The alternative to such a structured pattern on the left-hand side of this definition would be to use a more general pattern matching the head of the expression. But this requires a clumsy right-hand side in which you need to extract the various parts of the list to operate on them.

In[29]:= **ff[*list_List*] := *list*[[1]]² / *list*[[2]]³**

In[30]:= **Clear[f, ff]**

Sequence pattern matching

A *sequence* consists of a number of expressions separated by commas. For example, the elements of expressions are written as sequences. In both the full form and traditional representation for a list, the elements are given as a sequence of expressions.

In[31]:= **FullForm[{a, b, c, d, e}]**

Out[31]//FullForm=

List[a, b, c, d, e]

The double blank (BlankSequence) represents a sequence of one or more expressions. So, the pattern {p__} matches any list consisting of a sequence of one or more elements.

In[32]:= **Cases[{{}, {a}, {b, c}, {d, e, f}}, {p__}]**

Out[32]= {{a}, {b, c}, {d, e, f}}

Using the name p is actually unnecessary here as it is never referred to elsewhere.

In[33]:= **Cases[{{}, {a}, {b, c}, {d, e, f}}, {__}]**

Out[33]= {{a}, {b, c}, {d, e, f}}

Using the triple blank (BlankNullSequence), which represents a sequence of zero or more expressions, this pattern matches any list consisting of a sequence of zero or more elements.

In[34]:= **Cases[{{}, {a}, {b, c}, {d, e, f}}, {___}]**

Out[34]= {{}, {a}, {b, c}, {d, e, f}}

The pattern {___Symbol} matches any list consisting of a sequence of zero or more elements, all of which have head Symbol.

In[35]:= **MatchQ[{a, b, c}, {___Symbol}]**

Out[35]= **True**

In[36]:= **MatchQ[{a, 2, c}, {___Symbol}]**

Out[36]= **False**

In the following examples, the list {a, b, c} is matched by the pattern _, as well as by List[__] and List[___]. However, the list {a, b, c} is not matched by the pattern List[_] because, for the purposes of pattern matching, a sequence is not an expression.

In[37]:= **MatchQ[{a, b, c}, _]**

Out[37]= **True**

In[38]:= **MatchQ[{a, b, c}, {_}]**

Out[38]= **False**

The next two examples return **True** but not for the reason you might think.

In[39]:= **MatchQ[{a, b, c}, __]**

Out[39]= **True**

In[40]:= **MatchQ[{a, b, c}, x__]**

Out[40]= **True**

The pattern __ is matched by a sequence of one or more expressions. In this case the entire list matches that pattern, regardless of the contents of that list.

In[41]:= **MatchQ[{}, __]**

Out[41]= **True**

In the example above where the labeled pattern x__ is used, the label x does not affect the success or failure of the pattern match.

In[42]:= **MatchQ[{a, b, c}, __]**

Out[42]= **True**

Two final notes: first, the discussion about pattern matching on lists applies equally to any expression. For example, the following returns **True**, with x naming the sequence a, b, c.

In[43]:= **MatchQ[Plus[a, b, c], Plus[x__]]**

Out[43]= **True**

Second, sometimes the expression you are working on has a more complicated or nested structure. In such cases, you will often need to coax the pattern matcher to dig a little deeper in its search for a match. For example, using the structured pattern (var_)^n_ to find expressions consisting of a variable raised to a power, this fails initially.

In[44]:= **Cases$\left[a\,x^4 + b\,x^3 + c\,x^2 + d\,x + e,\ (var\_)\,^\wedge n\_\right]$**

Out[44]= $\{\}$

The reason **Cases** did not find any expressions matching the pattern is that the polynomial is deeply nested and **Cases**, by default, only looks at the first level of the expression.

In[45]:= **FullForm$\left[a\,x^4 + b\,x^3 + c\,x^2 + d\,x + e\right]$**

Out[45]//FullForm=

      Plus[e, Times[d, x], Times[c, Power[x, 2]],
         Times[b, Power[x, 3]], Times[a, Power[x, 4]]]

There certainly are some variables raised to powers in there. To get **Cases** to find them, give it a third argument that specifies the level to search down to. Rather than guessing or spending time trying to figure out that level, you can just use **Infinity** as the level specification and this means, go all the way down the expression tree.

In[46]:= **Cases$\left[a\,x^4 + b\,x^3 + c\,x^2 + d\,x + e,\ (var\_)\,^\wedge n\_,\ \text{Infinity}\right]$**

Out[46]= $\left\{x^2,\ x^3,\ x^4\right\}$

Again note that there was no need to name the patterns in this example as they were not referred to elsewhere. You might find it easier though to read such expressions using named patterns; it is your choice.

In[47]:= **Cases$\left[a\,x^4 + b\,x^3 + c\,x^2 + d\,x + e,\ (\_)\,^\wedge\_,\ \text{Infinity}\right]$**

Out[47]= $\left\{x^2,\ x^3,\ x^4\right\}$

Conditional pattern matching

Attaching a condition Conditions are used to place a constraint on the labeled parts of an expression. The general notation for conditional patterns is *expr_* /; *test*. The pattern match is only possible if the predicate *test* returns **True**.

In this first example, the pattern named n must meet the condition that its square root passes the **IntegerQ** test; in other words, that n is a square.

In[48]:= **Cases$\left[\{1,\ 2,\ 3,\ 4,\ 5,\ 6,\ 7,\ 8,\ 9\},\ n\_\ /;\ \text{IntegerQ}\left[\sqrt{n}\right]\right]$**

Out[48]= $\{1,\ 4,\ 9\}$

In the following case, the expressions that are matched by the pattern are powers where the exponent passes the **EvenQ** test.

In[49]:= **Cases[{x, x^2, x^3, x^4, x^5}, _^(n_) /; EvenQ[n]]**

Out[49]= $\left\{x^2,\ x^4\right\}$

Let us try a more applied problem. Given an array, how can we test that it is a square matrix? One way is to check that the dimensions are identical.

```
In[50]:= mat = RandomReal[1, {3, 3}];
         MatrixForm[mat]
```

Out[51]//MatrixForm=
$$\begin{pmatrix} 0.139347 & 0.204957 & 0.245416 \\ 0.283553 & 0.48378 & 0.670354 \\ 0.346834 & 0.473592 & 0.625998 \end{pmatrix}$$

```
In[52]:= Dimensions[mat]
```

Out[52]= {3, 3}

In the definition below, the condition that the expression passes the matrix test is added to the left-hand side. This avoids having to check tensors where the first two dimensions might be identical but the tensor clearly should not be classified as a square matrix.

```
In[53]:= SquareMatrixQ[mat_ /; MatrixQ[mat]] :=
            Dimensions[mat][[1]] == Dimensions[mat][[2]]
```

```
In[54]:= SquareMatrixQ[mat]
```

Out[54]= True

```
In[55]:= mat = RandomReal[1, {3, 4}];
         MatrixForm[mat]
```

Out[56]//MatrixForm=
$$\begin{pmatrix} 0.882058 & 0.774627 & 0.733256 & 0.222145 \\ 0.297304 & 0.601519 & 0.680989 & 0.108759 \\ 0.0323011 & 0.361117 & 0.836766 & 0.795304 \end{pmatrix}$$

```
In[57]:= SquareMatrixQ[mat]
```

Out[57]= False

A 1×1 matrix is also square.

```
In[58]:= SquareMatrixQ[{{1}}]
```

Out[58]= True

We mentioned above that matching a list like {a, b, c} with the pattern x_ is different from matching it with x___ because of the various expressions that can be associated with x.

```
In[59]:= MatchQ[{4, 6, 8}, x_ /; Length[x] > 4]
```

Out[59]= False

In[60]:= **MatchQ[{4, 6, 8}, {x___} /; Length[x] > 4]**

Length::argx : Length called with 3 arguments; 1 argument is expected. ≫

Out[60]= **False**

In[61]:= **MatchQ[{4, 6, 8}, {x___} /; Plus[x] > 10]**

Out[61]= **True**

In the first example, x was associated with the entire list {4, 6, 8}; since the length of the list {4, 6, 8} is not greater than 4, the match failed. In the second example, x became the sequence 4, 6, 8 so that the condition was Length[4, 6, 8] > 4; but Length can only have one argument, hence the error. In the last example, x was again associated with 4, 6, 8, but now the condition was Plus[4, 6, 8] > 10, which is perfectly valid syntax, and true.

Shorthand notation There is a convenient shorthand notation for conditional patterns that is commonly used. The condition *expr_ /; test* can be shortened to *expr_ ? test*.

In[62]:= **MatchQ[** **, _ ? ImageQ]**

Out[62]= **True**

Note the difference in syntax between using a predicate and a head to pattern match: to match a class of expressions that have head *h*, you use _*h*. To match a class of expressions that evaluate to True when the predicate *test* is applied, use _ ? *test*.

In[63]:= **MatchQ[{1, 2, 3}, _List]**

Out[63]= **True**

In[64]:= **MatchQ[{1, 2, 3}, _ ? NumberQ]**

Out[64]= **False**

In the above example, even though the list {1, 2, 3} consists of numbers, it does not match ? NumberQ because its head (List) does not pass the NumberQ test. If you want to match the list consisting of a sequence of numbers, use the double blank as follows.

In[65]:= **MatchQ[{1, 2, 3}, {__ ? NumberQ}]**

Out[65]= **True**

Cases finds all elements of its first argument that match a pattern.

In[66]:= **Cases[{1, 2, 3, a}, _?NumberQ]**

Out[66]= {1, 2, 3}

The pattern _?Negative matches any expression that passes the Negative test, that is, it returns true when Negative is applied to it.

In[67]:= **Cases[{-2, 7, -1.2, 0, -5 - 2 I}, _?Negative]**

Out[67]= {-2, -1.2}

Here is a simple application of attaching a predicate. This definition of the Fibonacci function tests its argument to see that it is an integer.

In[68]:= **f[1] = f[2] = 1;**

In[69]:= **f[n_?IntegerQ] := f[n - 1] + f[n - 2]**

Because of the predicate, f will not evaluate for noninteger arguments; in other words, noninteger arguments do not match the pattern _?IntegerQ.

In[70]:= **f[1.2]**

Out[70]= f[1.2]

In[71]:= **{f[5], f[10], f[20]}**

Out[71]= {5, 55, 6765}

Note that you can test that the argument is both an integer and positive by using a logical connective – in this case, logical AND.

In[72]:= **Clear[f]**
f[1] = f[2] = 1;

In[74]:= **f[n_ /; IntegerQ[n] && Positive[n]] := f[n - 1] + f[n - 2]**

In[75]:= **{f[5], f[10], f[20.0], f[-10]}**

Out[75]= {5, 55, f[20.], f[-10]}

Examples Let us look at a few examples of the use of conditional patterns. We will only scratch the surface here of what can be done with them but we will be using and extending them throughout the rest of this book.

In our first example, we create a predicate function that tests whether a positive integer is composite. The argument is checked to see if it has head Integer and if it is greater than 1.

In[76]:= **CompositeQ[n_Integer /; n > 1] := Not[PrimeQ[n]]**

In[77]:= **CompositeQ[16]**

Out[77]= True

In[78]:= **CompositeQ$\left[2^{31} - 1\right]$**

Out[78]= False

In this next input, the pattern matches all those expressions that are between 2 and 5.

In[79]:= **Cases[{1, 2, 3, 4, 5, 6, 7, 8}, $x\_$ /; 2 < x < 5]**

Out[79]= {3, 4}

This is essentially a filter and we can use this technique to filter all sorts of data. For example, here we remove outliers from a signal.

In[80]:= **sig = Import["signal.dat", "List"];**
        ListPlot[sig, PlotRange → {-1, 1}]

In[82]:= **ListPlot[**
        Cases[sig, $p\_$ /; -0.3 < p < 0.3],
        PlotRange → {-1, 1}]

Stock screens can be thought of similarly. We can use the same technique as above to extract those members of the Dow Jones Industrials that have a large market capitalization.

In[83]:= **Cases$\left[\text{FinancialData}["\texttt{\char`^}DJI", "Members"],\right.$**
        $s\_$ /; FinancialData[s, "MarketCap"] > $10^{11}\left.\right]$

Out[83]= {BAC, CVX, GE, IBM, INTC, JNJ, JPM,
        KO, MRK, MSFT, PFE, PG, T, VZ, WMT, XOM}

In the following screen, two predicates are connected by logical AND to give those members of the Dow Jones Industrials that have a large market capitalization *and* a low price-earnings ratio.

```
In[84]:= Cases[FinancialData["^DJI", "Members"],
           s_ /; (FinancialData[s, "MarketCap"] > 10^11 &&
             FinancialData[s, "PERatio"] < 12)]

Out[84]= {BAC, CVX, INTC, JPM, XOM}
```

Alternatives

Another kind of pattern uses *alternatives*. Alternatives are denoted $p_1 \mid p_2 \mid ... \mid p_n$ where the p_i are independent patterns. This pattern will match an expression whenever any one of those independent patterns match it.

In the following example, x ^ 2 matches "an expression which is either the symbol x raised to a real number or the symbol x raised to an integer."

```
In[85]:= MatchQ[x^2, x^_Real | x^_Integer]

Out[85]= True
```

Here the pattern matches any expression that has head `Integer` or `Rational` or `Real`.

```
In[86]:= Cases[{1, 3.1, 2/3, x, 3 + 4 I, "Hello"},
           _Integer | _Rational | _Real]

Out[86]= {1, 3.1, 2/3}
```

You should think of $p_1 \mid p_2 \mid ... \mid p_n$ as pattern p_1 *or* pattern p_2 *or*.... But note that this is different from the logical OR which requires predicates, not patterns, as its argument.

Repeated patterns

From the discussion of double and triple blanks, we have seen that you can set up a function to have a sequence of arguments the length of which is not known ahead of time. For example, `__List` matches expressions with head `List` with a sequence of one or more elements inside that list.

```
In[87]:= MatchQ[{1, 2, 3, 4, 5}, __List]

Out[87]= True
```

To compute the mean of a list, you could set up the function definition so that the argument has head `List`. Any number of elements can be used inside this list.

```
In[88]:= mean[x_List] := Total[x] / Length[x]
```

You would probably want a separate rule for the special case when the list is empty.

In[89]:= **mean[{}] := 0**

In[90]:= **mean[{a, b, c, d}]**

Out[90]= $\dfrac{1}{4}$ (a + b + c + d)

In[91]:= **mean$\left[\text{Range}\left[10^2\right]\right]$**

Out[91]= $\dfrac{101}{2}$

But what if you wanted to restrict the arguments inside a list, say to numbers only. You could try something like this:

In[92]:= **MatchQ[{1, 2, 3, 4, 5}, {__?NumberQ}]**

Out[92]= True

Or, you could use Repeated[*pattern*] (shorthand notation is *pattern* ..) which stands in for a sequence of one or more expressions all of which match *pattern*; in this case, a sequence of expressions all of which pass the NumberQ test.

In[93]:= **MatchQ[{1, 2, 3, 4, 5}, {_?NumberQ ..}]**

Out[93]= True

Similarly, there is RepeatedNull[*pattern*] (shorthand notation *pattern* ...), a pattern object that will match a sequence of *zero* or more expressions all matching *pattern*.

In[94]:= **MatchQ[{}, {_?NumberQ ...}]**

Out[94]= True

A second argument can be specified for both Repeated and RepeatedNull to limit the number of expressions that are returned. For example, this matches lists of numbers, returning the first three matches.

In[95]:= **Cases[{{1}, {1, 2}, {1, 2, 3}, {1, 2, 3, 4}},**
        {Repeated[_?NumberQ, 3]}]

Out[95]= {{1}, {1, 2}, {1, 2, 3}}

As an example of the use of these repeated pattern objects, let us create two rules for a function that we will use later to display random walks in two and three dimensions. The first pattern, {{_, _} ..}, matches any sequence of one or more two-dimensional coordinates. Similarly, {{_, _, _} ..} matches any sequence of one or more three-dimensional coordinates. We could be a bit more careful and insist that each element in the list pass the NumberQ test, but we will omit that here for purposes of clarity.

In[96]:= **showWalk**[*coords* : {{_, _} ..}] :=
       ListLinePlot[*coords*, **AspectRatio → Automatic**]

In[97]:= **showWalk**[*coords* : {{_, _, _} ..}] :=
       Graphics3D[**Line**[*coords*]]

This is defined and developed further as ShowWalk in Chapter 13. Loading the package from that chapter, we generate a random walk and test one of the showWalk rules written here.

In[98]:= **<< PwM`RandomWalks`**

In[99]:= **RandomWalk**[12, **Dimension → 3**]

Out[99]= {{0, 0, -1}, {0, 1, -1}, {0, 0, -1}, {0, -1, -1},
    {-1, -1, -1}, {-1, -1, -2}, {-1, 0, -2}, {-2, 0, -2},
    {-2, 0, -1}, {-3, 0, -1}, {-2, 0, -1}, {-2, 0, -2}}

In[100]:= **showWalk**[**RandomWalk**[2500, **Dimension → 3**]]

Out[100]=
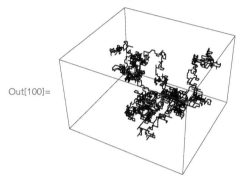

Note that we have not yet written a rule for the one-dimensional case. Hence the following returns unevaluated as there is no rule for showWalk when its argument is a one-dimensional vector.

In[101]:= **showWalk**[**RandomWalk**[5, **Dimension → 1**]]

Out[101]= showWalk[{1, 0, -1, 0, -1}]

We have used one additional construct in these rules for showWalk, *named patterns*. The pattern {{_, _} ..} will be matched by any list of one or more lists of pairs. The pattern is named coords using the construction coords : {{_, _} ..}. We then refer to the entire argument by name inside the body of the function. This really is no different than an ordinary function definition like f below where we name the argument x and refer to the argument by its name on the right-hand side of the function definition. The following two function definitions are equivalent. It is of course more convenient to use the more compact first definition.

In[102]:= **f[x_] := x + 1**

In[103]:= **f[x : _] := x + 1**

Functions that use patterns

We have already seen several functions that make use of patterns: `MatchQ` is used to check if an expression is matched by a pattern; `Cases` returns all those elements in an expression that are matched by a pattern. But there are several other functions that are quite useful and follow on the syntax of these two functions we have already discussed. For example, using `Cases`, this returns all those elements in the list of integers that are divisible by 3.

In[104]:= **ints = RandomInteger[20, {12}]**

Out[104]= {3, 13, 5, 11, 0, 16, 7, 1, 12, 16, 11, 4}

In[105]:= **Cases[ints, x_ /; Mod[x, 3] == 0]**

Out[105]= {3, 0, 12}

But what if you were interested in all those elements that are *not* divisible by 3? `DeleteCases` takes the same syntax as `Cases` but *deletes* those elements that are matched by the pattern.

In[106]:= **DeleteCases[ints, x_ /; Mod[x, 3] == 0]**

Out[106]= {13, 5, 11, 16, 7, 1, 16, 11, 4}

If you were interested in the positions within the list at which the pattern is matched, `Position` is the function to use.

In[107]:= **Position[ints, x_ /; Mod[x, 3] == 0]**

Out[107]= {{1}, {5}, {9}}

And if you wanted a count of the number of elements in the list that are matched by the pattern, use `Count`.

In[108]:= **Count[ints, x_ /; Mod[x, 3] == 0]**

Out[108]= 3

Notice how all four of these functions use the exact same syntax. They are all quite useful in the common task of finding information about the elements within an expression that meet some criteria you are interested in.

As a nontrivial example, suppose you have a collector in the field that gives information about some phenomena that you are studying. Normally, it returns a list of real numbers at specified intervals, but whenever it fails, it inserts a string such as `"NA"`. Using `Count` and `Position` it would be straightforward to find the rate of failure and the positions (times) at which those failures occurred.

```
In[109]:= signal = Import["collectorData.dat", "List"];
```

```
In[110]:= Dimensions[signal]
```

```
Out[110]= {8860}
```

```
In[111]:= badvals = Count[signal, _String]
```

```
Out[111]= 19
```

```
In[112]:= N[badvals / Length[signal]]
```

```
Out[112]= 0.00214447
```

```
In[113]:= Position[signal, _String]
```

```
Out[113]= {{299}, {700}, {1394}, {1488}, {1991}, {2195}, {2360},
          {2628}, {3413}, {3466}, {3553}, {3662}, {5064},
          {5079}, {5505}, {6861}, {6870}, {7118}, {7449}}
```

Exercises

1. Use conditional patterns to find all those numbers in a list of integers that are divisible by 2 or 3 or 5.

2. Write down five conditional patterns that match the expression {4, {a, b}, "g"}.

3. Write a function `Collatz` that takes an integer n as an argument and returns $3n + 1$ if n is an odd integer and returns $n/2$ if n is even.

4. Write the `Collatz` function from the above exercise, but this time you should also check that the argument to `Collatz` is positive.

5. Use alternatives to write a function `abs[x]` that returns x if $x \geq 0$, and $-x$ if $x < 0$, whenever x is an integer or a rational number. Whenever x is complex, `abs[x]` should return $\sqrt{\text{re}(x)^2 + \text{im}(x)^2}$.

6. Create a function `swapTwo[lis]` that returns *lis* with only its first two elements interchanged; for example, the input `swapTwo[{a, b, c, d, e}]` should return {b, a, c, d, e}. If *lis* has fewer than two elements, `swapTwo` just returns *lis*. Write `swapTwo` using three clauses: one for the empty list, one for one-element lists, and one for all other lists. Then write it using two clauses: one for lists of length 0 or 1 and another for all longer lists.

4.2 Transformation rules

Transformation rules are ubiquitous in *Mathematica*. They are used to represent solutions to equations, as a means to specify options for functions, and they form the basis of most of the algebraic manipulation in *Mathematica*. In this section we will look at how to use pattern matching together with replacement rules to transform expressions.

Creating and using replacement rules

A replacement rule is of the form *pattern* → *replacement* or *pattern* :→ *replacement*. Just like traditional function definitions, the left-hand side of each of these rules matches an expression and the right-hand side describes the transformation of that expression.

One of the most common uses for rules is to make substitutions of the form *expr* /. *rule*. Any part of *expr* that is matched by the pattern in *rule* will be rewritten according to that rule.

In[1]:= **x + y /. y → α**

Out[1]= **x + α**

A rule that produces the same output but using assignments would look like this:

In[2]:= **y = α;**

In[3]:= **x + y**

Out[3]= **x + α**

The main difference between the replacement rule and the assignment is that the assignment will automatically be used whenever there is an appropriate pattern match during evaluation. When **x + y** was evaluated, a rule was found for **y** (specifically, **y** = α) and a substitution was automatically made.

Another key difference is that no assignment was made in the first case but one was made in the latter case. Let us clear that value before going on.

In[4]:= **Clear[y]**

Here is the standard input form of the above rule.

In[5]:= **ReplaceAll[x + y, y → α]**

Out[5]= **x + α**

And in general, it is

$$\text{ReplaceAll}\big[\textit{expr, pattern} \rightarrow \textit{replacement}\big]$$

Whether you use the standard form with **ReplaceAll** or use the shorthand notation, there are some important things to note about the evaluation of transformation rules. To start, the expression itself is first evaluated. Then *both* the left-hand side and right-hand side of the rule are evaluated, unless there are parts of the right-hand side that have the `Hold` attribute. Finally, everywhere that the evaluated left-hand side of the rule appears in the evaluated expression, it is replaced by the evaluated right-hand side of the rule.

In[6]:= `{a, a} /. a → RandomReal[]`

Out[6]= `{0.69089, 0.69089}`

`Trace` shows how the transformation rule works. Note in particular, that the right-hand side of the rule (`RandomReal[]`) is evaluated first.

In[7]:= `Trace[{a, a} /. a → RandomReal[]]`

Out[7]= `{{{RandomReal[], 0.833525}, a → 0.833525, a → 0.833525},`
`{a, a} /. a → 0.833525, {0.833525, 0.833525}}`

Just as in the case of assignments, there are immediate and delayed transformation rules. In an immediate rule (*pattern* → *replacement*), the *replacement* will be evaluated immediately. For delayed rules (*pattern* :→ *replacement*), the *replacement* is only evaluated after the substitution is made.

In[8]:= `{a, a} /. a :→ RandomReal[]`

Out[8]= `{0.753241, 0.926807}`

In[9]:= `Trace[{a, a} /. a :→ RandomReal[]]`

Out[9]= `{{a :→ RandomReal[], a :→ RandomReal[]},`
`{a, a} /. a :→ RandomReal[],`
`{RandomReal[], RandomReal[]}, {RandomReal[], 0.228649},`
`{RandomReal[], 0.793173}, {0.228649, 0.793173}}`

In general, it is a good idea to use delayed rules whenever you have global symbols on the right-hand side of your rules to avoid the possibility of values for these symbols being used automatically during evaluation. If there are no global symbols on the right-hand side of your rules, it may be safe to use an immediate rule.

The kinds of patterns that you can use with transformation rules are limitless. For example, using the symbol `List` as the pattern, this changes the following list to a sum.

In[10]:= `{a, b, c} /. List → Plus`

Out[10]= `a + b + c`

Transformation rules can also be written using labeled patterns. In the first example below, a pattern is used to identify the two elements in an ordered pair that we wish to reverse. In the second example, the pattern matches elements on the diagonal of a matrix and this is used to set all elements on the diagonal to 0.

In[11]:= `{{3, 4}, {7, 2}, {1, 5}} /. {x_, y_} :→ {y, x}`

Out[11]= `{{4, 3}, {2, 7}, {5, 1}}`

```
In[12]:= mat = {{a, b, c}, {d, e, f}, {g, h, i}};
         MatrixForm[mat]
```
Out[13]//MatrixForm=

$$\begin{pmatrix} a & b & c \\ d & e & f \\ g & h & i \end{pmatrix}$$

```
In[14]:= ReplacePart[mat, {i_, i_} → 0] // MatrixForm
```
Out[14]//MatrixForm=

$$\begin{pmatrix} 0 & b & c \\ d & 0 & f \\ g & h & 0 \end{pmatrix}$$

ReplacePart$\left[expr, i \to val\right]$ is used to replace the part of *expr* at position *i* with *val*. In the example above, we have used the pattern {i_, i_} to stand in for a two-dimensional position in which the row and column positions are the same, as indicated by the similarly named patterns i_.

To use multiple rules with an expression, enclose them in a list.

```
In[15]:= {a, b, c} /. {c :> b, b :> a}
```
Out[15]= {a, a, b}

A transformation rule is applied only once to each part of an expression (in contrast to a rewrite rule) and multiple transformation rules are used in parallel. Hence, in the above example, the symbol c is transformed into b but it is not further changed into a.

In order to apply one or more transformation rules repeatedly to an expression until the expression no longer changes, ReplaceRepeated is used. For example, the product of x and y below is replaced by the sum of x and y, but this is only done for the first such occurrence that matches.

```
In[16]:= a b c d /. x_ y_ :> x + y
```
Out[16]= a + b c d

Using ReplaceRepeated, the rule is applied repeatedly until the expression no longer changes.

```
In[17]:= a b c d //. x_ y_ :> x + y
```
Out[17]= a + b + c + d

Let us now look at a few problems that can be solved directly using transformation rules.

Example: counting coins

As our first example of the use of transformation rules, we will write a program to perform an operation most of us do every day: calculating how much change you have in your pocket.

Suppose you have the following collection of coins and assume *p*, *n*, *d*, and *q* represent pennies, nickels, dimes, and quarters, respectively (modify as appropriate for different currencies).

In[18]:= **coins = {p, p, q, n, d, d, p, q, q, p};**

Here are the values, given by a list of rules.

In[19]:= **values = {p → .01, n → .05, d → .10, q → .25};**

This replaces each coin by its value.

In[20]:= **coins /. values**

Out[20]= {0.01, 0.01, 0.25, 0.05, 0.1, 0.1, 0.01, 0.25, 0.25, 0.01}

And here is the value of the set of coins.

In[21]:= **Total[coins /. values]**

Out[21]= 1.04

Finally, here is a function that wraps up all these steps.

In[22]:= **CountChange[*coins_List*] :=**
    Total[*coins* /.{p → .01, n → .05, d → .10, q → .25}]

In[23]:= **CountChange[{p, q, q, d, d, p, q, q, d, d}]**

Out[23]= 1.42

Example: closed paths

In this example, we will create a new graphics function for plotting paths through points in the plane. A *path* can be thought of as a sequence of vertices such that for each vertex, there is an edge to the next vertex in the sequence. Path problem arise in visualizing the convex hull of a set of points (see Exercise 3 in Section 10.2) as well as with shortest-tour types of problems (Section 10.4). A path through a set of points typically is closed, meaning that the last point is connected to the first. We will use a rule to deal with that constraint.

Let us start with some data, eighteen pairs of coordinates representing points in the plane.

In[24]:= **data = RandomReal[20, {18, 2}];**

To prototype, we will use the convex hull of this set of data as our path. An intuitive, although naive, description of the convex hull in two dimensions is the smallest convex polygon enclosing a set of points. We will need the `ConvexHull` function defined in the Computational Geometry package.

In[25]:= **<< ComputationalGeometry`**

`ConvexHull` returns the indices of the ordered pairs that make up the convex hull of the entire list. Here are those positions from the list `data`.

In[26]:= **hull = ConvexHull[data]**

Out[26]= {12, 14, 6, 8, 18, 13}

To extract the points in these positions, use **Part**.

In[27]:= **data[[hull]]**

Out[27]= {{19.9831, 13.8968}, {16.0814, 17.2017}, {6.00837, 18.7695},
{1.54244, 16.5229}, {0.628939, 0.311332}, {17.501, 8.018}}

Here is a graphic showing the original points (**ListPlot**) together with a line through the points in the convex hull.

In[28]:= **Show[{ListPlot[data], Graphics[{Line[data[[hull]]],**
PointSize[Medium], Red, Point[data[[hull]]]}]}]

Out[28]=

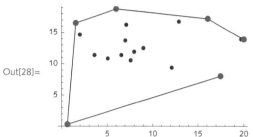

Almost! To close up the figure, we need the last point in the convex hull connected to the first point. A rule does the job nicely. Here, **p1_** represents the first point in the list and **pn__** represents the sequence of remaining points.

In[29]:= **Show[{ListPlot[data],**
Graphics[{Line[data[[hull]]] /. {p1_, pn__} :> {p1, pn, p1}],
PointSize[Medium], Red, Point[data[[hull]]]}]}]

Out[29]=

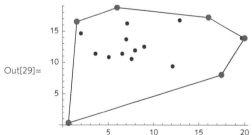

Let us turn this into a reusable function, **PathPlot**, that we will find useful later, specifically in Section 10.4 where we develop algorithms for finding simple closed paths of points in the plane.

```
In[30]:= PathPlot[coords_List] :=
             Graphics[{Line[coords /. {p1_, pn__} :> {p1, pn, p1}],
                PointSize[Medium], Red, Point[coords]}]
```

Here is a more substantial set of points – 1500 points in the plane normally distributed about 0.

```
In[31]:= data = RandomVariate[NormalDistribution[0, 2], {1500, 2}];
```

```
In[32]:= Show[{ListPlot[data], PathPlot[data[[ConvexHull[data]]]]},
             AspectRatio → Automatic]
```

Out[32]=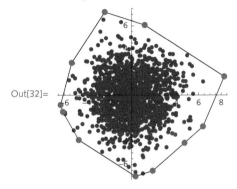

Example: finding maxima

Our next example employs a sophisticated rewrite rule that demonstrates most of the things discussed in this section: the repeated use of a transformation rule with delayed evaluation, sequence patterns, and conditional pattern matching.

The `maxima` function returns the elements in a list of positive numbers that are bigger than all the preceding numbers in the list.

```
In[33]:= maxima[x_List] :=
             x //. {a___, b_, c___, d_, e___} /; d ≤ b :> {a, b, c, e}
```

The transformation rule repeatedly looks through the list for two elements (b and d here), separated by a sequence of zero or more elements, such that the second selected element (d) is less than or equal to the first selected element (b). When that condition is met, the second element is dropped. The process stops when there are no two elements such that the second is less than or equal to the first.

```
In[34]:= maxima[{3, 5, 2, 6, 1, 8, 4, 9, 7}]
```

```
Out[34]= {3, 5, 6, 8, 9}
```

This is actually a variation of a sorting algorithm known as insertion sort. We will look at sorting algorithms in some detail at the end of this chapter, Section 4.3.

Exercises

1. Here is a rule designed to switch the order of each pair of expressions in a list. It works fine on the first example, but fails on the second.

   In[1]:= `{{a, b}, {c, d}, {e, f}} /. {x_, y_} :> {y, x}`

   Out[1]= `{{b, a}, {d, c}, {f, e}}`

   In[2]:= `{{a, b}, {c, d}} /. {x_, y_} :> {y, x}`

   Out[2]= `{{c, d}, {a, b}}`

   Explain what has gone wrong and rewrite this rule to correct the situation, that is, so that the second example returns `{{b, a}, {d, c}}`.

2. The following compound expression returns a value of 14. Describe the evaluation sequence that was followed. Use the **Trace** function to check your answer.

   In[3]:= `z = 11;`
   `a = 9;`
   `z + 3 /. z → a`

   Out[5]= `14`

   Then use the **Hold** function in the compound expression to obtain a value of 12.

3. Create a function to compute the area of any triangle, given its three vertices. The area of a triangle is one-half the base times the altitude. For arbitrary points, the altitude requires a bit of computation that does not generalize. The magnitude of the cross product of two vectors gives the area of the parallelogram that they determine. The cross product is only defined for three-dimensional vectors, so to compute the area of a two-dimensional triangle using the cross product you will need to embed the edges (vectors) in three-dimensional space, say, in the plane $z = 0$. Try a second implementation using determinants instead of cross products.

4. Use pattern matching to extract all negative solutions of the following polynomial:

   $$x^9 + 3.4\, x^6 - 25\, x^5 - 213\, x^4 - 477\, x^3 + 1012\, x^2 + 111\, x - 123$$

   Then extract all real solutions, that is, those which are not complex.

5. Create a rewrite rule that uses a repeated replacement to "unnest" the nested lists within a list.

   In[6]:= `unNest[{{α, α, α}, {α}, {{β, β, β}, {β, β}}, {α, α}}]`

   Out[6]= `{α, α, α, α, β, β, β, β, β, α, α}`

6. Define a function using pattern matching and repeated replacement to sum the elements of a list.

7. Using the built-in function **ReplaceList**, write a function `cartesianProduct` that takes two lists as input and returns the Cartesian product of these lists.

   In[7]:= `cartesianProduct[{x_1, x_2, x_3}, {y_1, y_2}]`

   Out[7]= `{{x_1, y_1}, {x_1, y_2}, {x_2, y_1}, {x_2, y_2}, {x_3, y_1}, {x_3, y_2}}`

8. Write a function to count the total number of multiplications in any polynomial expression. For example, given a power, your function should return one less than the exponent.

In[8]:= **MultiplyCount** $\left[t^5\right]$

Out[8]= 4

In[9]:= **MultiplyCount[a x y t]**

Out[9]= 3

In[10]:= **MultiplyCount** $\left[a\ x\ y\ t^4 + w\ t\right]$

Out[10]= 7

9. Create six graphical objects, one each to represent the faces of a standard six-sided die. Dice [*n*] should display the face of the appropriate die, as below.

In[11]:= **Table[Dice[n], {n, 1, 6}]**

Out[11]=

One way to approach this problem is to think of a die face as a grid of nine elements, some of which are turned on (white) and some turned off (blue above). Then create one set of rules for each die face. Once your rules are defined, you could use something like the following graphics code (a bit incomplete as written here) to create your images.

```
Dice[n_] := GraphicsGrid[
  Map[Graphics, Partition[Range[9], 3] /. rules[[n]], {2}]]
```

4.3 Examples and applications

This next section focuses on two classical problems in computer science: encryption and sorting. Even though we will only scratch the surface of these two very deep problems, they are so important and ubiquitous in modern computing that it is well worthwhile learning about them. At an introductory level, these problems are well suited to a rule-based approach.

Finding subsequences

Consider the problem of finding a particular subsequence within a sequence of numbers. This computation is similar to one involving nucleotide sequence lookups in genes, something that is solved for the specific domain of genes with GenomeLookup.

In[1]:= **GenomeLookup["GCTCTCTAATGGCAT"]**

Out[1]= {{{Chromosome3, 1}, {140 240 043, 140 240 057}},
       {{Chromosome7, -1}, {41 460 946, 41 460 960}},
       {{Chromosome8, 1}, {92 015 447, 92 015 461}},
       {{Chromosome21, 1}, {32 732 065, 32 732 079}}}

We will focus on sequences of digits here and wait to solve the problem involving arbitrary strings – not just gene sequences – until Section 9.5.

To prototype for numeric sequences, assume both the sequence and the subsequence are given as lists of numbers; we will find the positions at which the subsequence 3238 occurs in the digits of π.

Here are the first 50 digits of π, starting from the right of the decimal point. Initially, we only work with a small number of digits so we can easily check on our progress.

```
In[2]:= pidigs = First[RealDigits[π, 10, 50, -1]]
```

```
Out[2]= {1, 4, 1, 5, 9, 2, 6, 5, 3, 5, 8, 9, 7, 9, 3,
         2, 3, 8, 4, 6, 2, 6, 4, 3, 3, 8, 3, 2, 7, 9, 5, 0,
         2, 8, 8, 4, 1, 9, 7, 1, 6, 9, 3, 9, 9, 3, 7, 5, 1, 0}
```

The subsequence is also given as a list of digits.

```
In[3]:= subseq = {3, 2, 3, 8};
```

One approach to this problem is to partition the list of digits in `pidigs` into lists of the same length as the list `subseq`, with overlapping sublists of offset one. This means that we will examine all sublists of length four from `pidigs`.

```
In[4]:= p = Partition[pidigs, Length[subseq], 1]
```

```
Out[4]= {{1, 4, 1, 5}, {4, 1, 5, 9}, {1, 5, 9, 2}, {5, 9, 2, 6},
         {9, 2, 6, 5}, {2, 6, 5, 3}, {6, 5, 3, 5}, {5, 3, 5, 8},
         {3, 5, 8, 9}, {5, 8, 9, 7}, {8, 9, 7, 9}, {9, 7, 9, 3},
         {7, 9, 3, 2}, {9, 3, 2, 3}, {3, 2, 3, 8}, {2, 3, 8, 4}, {3, 8, 4, 6},
         {8, 4, 6, 2}, {4, 6, 2, 6}, {6, 2, 6, 4}, {2, 6, 4, 3}, {6, 4, 3, 3},
         {4, 3, 3, 8}, {3, 3, 8, 3}, {3, 8, 3, 2}, {8, 3, 2, 7}, {3, 2, 7, 9},
         {2, 7, 9, 5}, {7, 9, 5, 0}, {9, 5, 0, 2}, {5, 0, 2, 8}, {0, 2, 8, 8},
         {2, 8, 8, 4}, {8, 8, 4, 1}, {8, 4, 1, 9}, {4, 1, 9, 7}, {1, 9, 7, 1},
         {9, 7, 1, 6}, {7, 1, 6, 9}, {1, 6, 9, 3}, {6, 9, 3, 9}, {9, 3, 9, 9},
         {3, 9, 9, 3}, {9, 9, 3, 7}, {9, 3, 7, 5}, {3, 7, 5, 1}, {7, 5, 1, 0}}
```

Now we are ready for the pattern match. From the list p above, we are looking for the positions of any sublist that matches {3, 2, 3, 8}. The subsequence 3238 occurs starting at the fifteenth digit in `pidigs`.

```
In[5]:= pos = Position[p, subseq]
```

```
Out[5]= {{15}}
```

To mirror the default output of `Position`, we will give the starting and ending positions of this match.

```
In[6]:= pos /. {num_ ? IntegerQ} :> {num, num + Length[subseq] - 1}
```

```
Out[6]= {{15, 18}}
```

Finally, let us turn this into a function and test it on a much larger example. Note that we use the pattern `_List` on both arguments, `digits` and `subseq`, so that `FindSubsequence` will only match arguments that have head `List`.

```
In[7]:= FindSubsequence[digits_List, subseq_List] :=
        Module[{p, len = Length[subseq]},
          p = Partition[digits, len, 1];
          Position[p, subseq] /.
            {num_ ? IntegerQ} :> {num, num + len - 1}]
```

Store the first 10 000 000 digits of π in the symbol pidigs.

```
In[8]:= pidigs = First[RealDigits[π, 10, 10⁷, -1]];
```

The subsequence 314159 occurs seven times in the first 10 000 000 digits of π, starting with the 176 451st digit.

```
In[9]:= FindSubsequence[pidigs, {3, 1, 4, 1, 5, 9}] // Timing
```

```
Out[9]= {8.38962, {{176 451, 176 456}, {1 259 351, 1 259 356},
          {1 761 051, 1 761 056}, {6 467 324, 6 467 329}, {6 518 294, 6 518 299},
          {9 753 731, 9 753 736}, {9 973 760, 9 973 765}}}
```

In Exercise 1 at the end of this section, you are asked to create a version of FindSubse- quence that takes numbers instead of lists as its arguments. In Section 9.5 we will develop a different approach to this problem, one using string-processing functions that gives a substantial speedup compared to the computation in this section.

Sorting a list

The next example, sorting lists, also incorporates several of the concepts discussed in this chapter: using a delayed rule, conditional patterns, and several types of sequence pattern matching.

We will create a rule named listSort that, upon repeated application, will put a list of numbers into numerical order. To account for the first and last elements in the list, we use BlankNullSequence (___).

```
In[10]:= listSort = {{x___, a_ ? NumericQ, b_ ? NumericQ, y___} :>
            {x, b, a, y} /; b < a};
```

The expression that has to match the pattern {x___, a_, b_, y___} is a list of at least two elements since x___ and y___ will match zero or more elements. The condition on the right- hand side of the rule says that whenever b is less than a, switch the order of a and b in the origi- nal list to output {x, b, a, y}.

Here is a list of ten real numbers between 0 and 1.

```
In[11]:= nums = RandomReal[1, {10}]
```

```
Out[11]= {0.0391631, 0.675771, 0.586596, 0.362437, 0.24047,
          0.90963, 0.280937, 0.102957, 0.888019, 0.581504}
```

Note that applying the listSort rule to nums results in only one transformation, in this case only the second and third numbers are sorted (the first two numbers in `nums` were already in numerical order).

```
In[12]:= nums /. listSort
```

```
Out[12]= {0.0391631, 0.586596, 0.675771, 0.362437, 0.24047,
          0.90963, 0.280937, 0.102957, 0.888019, 0.581504}
```

To apply a transformation rule repeatedly until the expression being operated on no longer changes, use `ReplaceRepeated` (`//.`).

```
In[13]:= nums //. listSort
```

```
Out[13]= {0.0391631, 0.102957, 0.24047, 0.280937, 0.362437,
          0.581504, 0.586596, 0.675771, 0.888019, 0.90963}
```

Because we used `?NumericQ` as part of the pattern match, `listSort` will work on expressions that may not be explicit numbers, but are numerical in nature, that is, expressions that return explicit numbers when `N` is applied to them.

```
In[14]:= {e, π, EulerGamma, GoldenRatio, 1} //. listSort
```

```
Out[14]= {EulerGamma, 1, GoldenRatio, e, π}
```

By way of comparison, the built-in `Sort` function, because of its great generality, sorts symbols by their names and so does not return a numerically-sorted list here.

```
In[15]:= Sort[{e, π, EulerGamma, GoldenRatio, 1}]
```

```
Out[15]= {1, e, EulerGamma, GoldenRatio, π}
```

One way around this is to give `Sort` a second argument causing it to sort by numerical value.

```
In[16]:= Sort[{e, π, EulerGamma, GoldenRatio, 1}, Less]
```

```
Out[16]= {EulerGamma, 1, GoldenRatio, e, π}
```

Our `listSort` algorithm is essentially an implementation of the classical bubble sort. It is far less efficient than many other, more commonly used, sorting algorithms, especially those that employ a divide-and-conquer strategy. This is because the pattern matcher generates all possible pairs of adjacent elements and then compares them. The computational complexity of the bubble sort algorithm is known to be $O(n^2)$, meaning running time is proportional to the square of the size of the input.

```
In[17]:= times =
          Table[First[Timing[(RandomReal[1, {n}] //. listSort);]],
           {n, 50, 150, 10}]
```

```
Out[17]= {0.055971, 0.082766, 0.169308, 0.287193, 0.397787,
          0.498622, 0.762439, 1.04713, 1.31721, 1.6914, 2.09163}
```

In[18]:= **model = LinearModelFit$\left[\text{times}, \left\{x, x^2\right\}, x\right]$;**

In[19]:= **model["BestFit"]**

Out[19]= $0.11057 - 0.0514218\, x + 0.0209072\, x^2$

In[20]:= **Show[{Plot[model[t], {t, 1, 10}], ListPlot[times]}]**

Out[20]=

The built-in Sort function uses a classical algorithm called "merge sort" (discussed in Section 7.4), which starts by dividing the list into two parts of approximately equal size. It then sorts each part recursively and finally merges the two sorted sublists. For numerical input it has computational complexity a mere $O(n \log(n))$.

In[21]:= **Timing[Sort[nums];]**

Out[21]= $\{0.000029, \text{Null}\}$

In[22]:= **times = Table[First[Timing[Sort[RandomReal[1, {n}]];]], {n, 500 000, 1 500 000, 100 000}]**

Out[22]= $\{0.153327, 0.183019, 0.211981, 0.250083, 0.285453,$
$0.328241, 0.356609, 0.404033, 0.440554, 0.469802, 0.52071\}$

In[23]:= **model = LinearModelFit[times, {x, Log[x]}, x];**
model["BestFit"]

Out[24]= $0.112765 + 0.0408967\, x - 0.0191854\, \text{Log}[x]$

In[25]:= **Show[{Plot[model[t], {t, 1, 10}], ListPlot[times]}]**

Out[25]=

The above implementation of listSort only works for numerical arguments. It can be overloaded to work on characters of strings. This is implemented in Section 9.1.

For detailed information on the theory and implementation of sorting algorithms, see Sedgewick and Wayne (2011).

Exercises

1. The function `FindSubsequence` defined in this section suffers from the limitation that the arguments `digits` and `subseq` must both be lists of numbers. Write another definition of `FindSubsequence` that takes two integers as arguments. So, for example, the following should work:

    In[1]:= **n = RandomInteger$\left[10^{200}\right]$**

    Out[1]= 99 886 364 225 785 890 637 248 382 678 171 952 235 146 647 070 036 321 273 192
            078 968 865 572 610 676 045 767 583 093 169 497 891 617 017 225 261 830 124
            007 777 401 603 464 795 137 556 513 541 607 966 794 013 354 513 861 062 656
            302 896 471 480 157 720 676 043 512

    In[2]:= **FindSubsequence[n, 22]**

    Out[2]= {{9, 10}, {35, 36}, {105, 106}}

2. Plot the function sin(x) over the interval $[-2\pi, 2\pi]$ and then reverse the x- and y-coordinates of each point by means of a transformation rule to display a reflection in the line $y = x$.

3. Given a two-column array of data,

    In[3]:= **data = RandomReal[{0, 10}, {5, 2}];**
            MatrixForm[data, TableAlignments → "."]

    Out[4]//MatrixForm=
    $$\begin{pmatrix} 2.75703 & 8.36575 \\ 7.99197 & 4.86756 \\ 1.90927 & 5.59835 \\ 7.76051 & 2.29443 \\ 3.87192 & 8.11463 \end{pmatrix}$$

    create a new array that consists of three columns where the first two columns are identical to the original, but the third column consists of the norm of the two numbers from the first two columns.

    $$\begin{pmatrix} 2.75703 & 8.36575 & 8.80835 \\ 7.99197 & 4.86756 & 9.35761 \\ 1.90927 & 5.59835 & 5.91497 \\ 7.76051 & 2.29443 & 8.09258 \\ 3.87192 & 8.11463 & 8.99105 \end{pmatrix}$$

4. Occasionally, when collecting data from an instrument, the collector fails or returns a bad value. In analyzing the data, the analyst has to make a decision about what to use to replace these bad values. One approach is to replace them with a column mean. Given an array of numbers such as the following, create a function to replace each "NAN" with the mean of the numbers that appear in that column.

    $$\text{data} = \begin{pmatrix} 0.9034 & \text{"NAN"} & 0.7163 & 0.8588 \\ 0.3031 & 0.5827 & 0.2699 & 0.8063 \\ 0.0418 & 0.8426 & \text{"NAN"} & 0.8634 \\ \text{"NAN"} & 0.8913 & 0.0662 & 0.8432 \end{pmatrix};$$

5

Functional programming

Higher-order functions · Map · Apply · Thread and MapThread · The Listable attribute · Inner and Outer · Select and Pick · Iterating functions · Nest · FixedPoint · NestWhile · Fold · Defining functions · Compound functions · Scoping constructs · Pure functions · Options · Creating and issuing messages · Hamming distance · Josephus problem · Regular polygons · Protein interaction networks · Palettes for project files · Operating on arrays

Functional programming, the use and evaluation of functions as a programming paradigm, has a long and rich history in programming languages. LISP came about in the search for a convenient language for representing mathematical concepts in programs. It borrowed from the lambda calculus of the logician Alonzo Church. More recent languages have in turn embraced many aspects of LISP – in addition to LISP's offspring such as SCHEME and HASKELL, you will find elements of functional constructs in JAVA, PYTHON, RUBY, and PERL. *Mathematica* itself has clear bloodlines to LISP, including the ability to operate on data structures such as lists as single objects and in its representation of mathematical properties through rules. Being able to express ideas in science, mathematics, and engineering in a language that naturally mirrors those fields is made much easier by the integration of these tools.

Functions not only offer a familiar paradigm to those representing ideas in science, mathematics, and engineering, they provide a consistent and efficient mechanism for computation and programming. In *Mathematica*, unlike many other languages, functions are considered "first class" objects, meaning they can be used as arguments to other functions, they can be returned as values, and they can be part of many other kinds of data objects such as arrays. In addition, you can create and use functions at runtime, that is, when you evaluate an expression. This *functional* style of programming distinguishes *Mathematica* from traditional procedural languages like C and FORTRAN. A solid facility with functional programming is essential for taking full advantage of the *Mathematica* language to solve your computational tasks.

5.1   Introduction

Functions are objects that operate on expressions and output unique expressions for each input. For example, here is a definition for a function that takes a vector of two variables as argument and returns a vector of three elements.

In[1]:= **f[{u_, θ_}] := {Cos[θ] $\sqrt{1 - u^2}$, Sin[θ] $\sqrt{1 - u^2}$, u}**

You can evaluate the function for numeric or symbolic values.

In[2]:= **f[{0, 0.5}]**

Out[2]= {0.877583, 0.479426, 0}

In[3]:= **f[{-1/2, ψ}]**

Out[3]= $\left\{ \frac{1}{2} \sqrt{3} \, \text{Cos}[\psi], \ \frac{1}{2} \sqrt{3} \, \text{Sin}[\psi], \ -\frac{1}{2} \right\}$

Functions can be significantly more complicated objects. Below is a function that operates on functions. It takes two arguments: a function or expression, and a list containing the variable of integration and the integration limits.

In[4]:= **Integrate[Exp[I π x], {x, a, b}]**

Out[4]= $\dfrac{\dot{\imath} \left(e^{i\,a\,\pi} - e^{i\,b\,\pi} \right)}{\pi}$

This particular function can be also be given a different argument structure: a function and a variable.

In[5]:= **Integrate[Exp[I π x], x]**

Out[5]= $- \dfrac{\dot{\imath} \, e^{i\,\pi\,x}}{\pi}$

Whereas procedural programs provide step-by-step sets of instructions, functional programming involves the application of functions to their arguments and typically operates on the entire expression at once. For example, here is a traditional procedural approach to switching the elements in a list of pairs.

In[6]:= **lis = {{α, 1}, {β, 2}, {γ, 3}};**

In[7]:= **temp = Table[0, {Length[lis]}];**

```
In[8]:= Do[temp[[i]] = {lis[[i, 2]], lis[[i, 1]]},
         {i, 1, Length[lis]}];
       temp
```

Out[9]= $\{\{1, \alpha\}, \{2, \beta\}, \{3, \gamma\}\}$

Here is a functional approach to solving the same problem. The `Map` function takes the `Reverse` function as an argument and uses it to operate on the list directly.

```
In[10]:= Map[Reverse, lis]
```

Out[10]= $\{\{1, \alpha\}, \{2, \beta\}, \{3, \gamma\}\}$

This simple example illustrates several of the key features of functional programming. A functional approach often allows for a more direct implementation of the solution to a problem, especially when list manipulations are involved. The procedural approach required first allocating an array, `temp`, of the same size as `lis`; then extracting and putting parts of the list into `temp` one-by-one, looping over `lis`; and finally returning the value of `temp`. The functional approach, although implying an iteration, avoids an explicit looping structure.

In this chapter, we first take a look at some of the most powerful and useful functional programming constructs in *Mathematica* – the so-called *higher-order* functions such as `Map`, `Apply` and `Thread` – and then discuss the creation of functions, using many of the list manipulation constructs discussed earlier. It is well worthwhile to spend time familiarizing yourself with these functions from the chapter on lists. Having a large vocabulary of built-in functions will not only make it easier to follow the programs and do the exercises here, but will enhance your own programming skills as well.

One of the unique features of a functional language such as *Mathematica* (and also LISP, HASKELL, SCHEME, and others) is the ability to create a function at runtime, meaning that you do not need to formally declare such a function. In *Mathematica* this is implemented through pure functions. For example, without creating a formal function definition, we use a pure function below to filter `data` for values in a narrow band around zero.

```
In[11]:= data = RandomReal[{-1, 1}, 10^6];
```

```
In[12]:= Select[data, Function[x, -0.00001 < x < 0.00001]]
```

Out[12]= $\{6.73666 \times 10^{-6}, 2.05057 \times 10^{-6}, -6.53306 \times 10^{-6},$
$6.29973 \times 10^{-6}, -1.50788 \times 10^{-6}, 7.90283 \times 10^{-6},$
$3.94237 \times 10^{-6}, 7.09181 \times 10^{-6}, -8.69555 \times 10^{-6}\}$

We will introduce and explore pure functions in Section 5.6.

Localization of variables, common to many modern programming languages, allows you to isolate symbols and definitions that are local to a function in order to keep them from interfering with, or being interfered by, global symbols. These are discussed in Section 5.5.

Although optional arguments and messaging are not specific to functional constructs, we introduce them in this chapter to start building up the complexity of our examples. Developing your functions so that they behave like built-in functions makes them easier to use for you and users of your programs. Providing options and issuing messages when things goes wrong are common mechanisms for doing this and they are introduced in Section 5.7.

Finally, we put a lot of the pieces together from this chapter and the chapters on lists and on patterns to program more extensive examples and applications, touching on areas as diverse as signal processing, geometry, bioinformatics, and data processing.

5.2   Functions for manipulating expressions

Three of the most powerful functions, and some of those most commonly used by experienced *Mathematica* programmers are `Map`, `Apply`, and `Thread`. They provide efficient and sophisticated ways of manipulating expressions in *Mathematica*. In this section we will discuss their syntax and look at some simple examples of their use. We will also briefly look at some related functions (`Inner` and `Outer`), which will prove useful in manipulating the structure of your expressions; finally, in this section we introduce `Select` and `Pick`, which are used to extract elements of an expression based on some criteria of interest. These higher-order functions are in the toolkit of every experienced *Mathematica* programmer and they will be used throughout the rest of this book.

Map
`Map` applies a function to each element in a list.

In[1]:= $\mathbf{Map}\left[\mathbf{Head,}\ \left\{3,\ \dfrac{22}{7},\ \pi\right\}\right]$

Out[1]= {Integer, Rational, Symbol}

This can be illustrated using an undefined function f and a simple linear list.

In[2]:= **Map[f, {a, b, c}]**

Out[2]= {f[a], f[b], f[c]}

More generally, mapping a function f over the expression g[a, b, c] essentially wraps the function f around each of the *elements* of g.

In[3]:= **Map[f, g[a, b, c]]**

Out[3]= g[f[a], f[b], f[c]]

This symbolic computation is identical to `Map[f, {a, b, c}]`, except in that example `g` is replaced with `List` (remember that `FullForm[{a, b, c}]` is represented internally as `List[a, b, c]`).

The real power of the `Map` function is that you can map any function across any expression for which that function makes sense. For example, to reverse the order of elements in each list of a nested list, use `Reverse` with `Map`,

In[4]:= **Map[Reverse, {{a, b}, {c, d}, {e, f}}]**

Out[4]= {{b, a}, {d, c}, {f, e}}

The elements in each of the inner lists in a nested list can be sorted.

In[5]:= **Map[Sort, {{2, 6, 3, 5}, {7, 4, 1, 3}}]**

Out[5]= {{2, 3, 5, 6}, {1, 3, 4, 7}}

Often, you will need to define your own function to perform a computation on each element of a list. `Map` is expressly designed for this sort of computation. Here is a list of three elements.

In[6]:= **vec = {2, π, γ};**

If you wished to square each element and add 1, you could first define a function that performs this computation on its arguments.

In[7]:= **f[x_] := x^2 + 1**

Mapping this function over `vec`, will then wrap `f` around each element and evaluate `f` of those elements.

In[8]:= **Map[f, vec]**

Out[8]= $\left\{5, 1 + \pi^2, 1 + \gamma^2\right\}$

The `Map` function is such a commonly used construct in *Mathematica* that a shorthand notation exists for it: *fun* /@ *expr* is equivalent to `Map[`*fun, expr*`]`. Hence the above computation can also be written as:

In[9]:= **f /@ vec**

Out[9]= $\left\{5, 1 + \pi^2, 1 + \gamma^2\right\}$

While it does make your code a bit more compact, the use of such shorthand notation comes at the cost of readability. Experienced *Mathematica* programmers and those who prefer such an infix notation tend to use them liberally. We will use the longer form in general in this book but encourage you to become comfortable with either syntax as it will make it easier for you to read programs created by others more readily.

Apply

Whereas `Map` is used to perform the same operation on each element of an expression, `Apply` is used to change the structure of an expression.

In[10]:= **Apply[h, g[a, b, c]]**

Out[10]= h[a, b, c]

The function h was applied to the expression g[a, b, c] and `Apply` replaced the head of g[a, b, c] with h.

If the second argument is a list, applying h to that expression simply replaces its head (`List`) with h.

In[11]:= **Apply[h, {a, b, c}]**

Out[11]= h[a, b, c]

The following computation shows the same thing, except we are using the internal representation of the list {a, b, c} here to better see how the structure is changed.

In[12]:= **Apply[h, List[a, b, c]]**

Out[12]= h[a, b, c]

The elements of `List` are now the arguments of h. Essentially, you should think of Apply[h, *expr*] as replacing the head of *expr* with h.

In the following example, List[1, 2, 3, 4] has been changed to Plus[1, 2, 3, 4] or, in other words, the head `List` has been replaced by `Plus`.

In[13]:= **Apply[Plus, {1, 2, 3, 4}]**

Out[13]= 10

Plus[a, b, c, d] is the internal representation of the sum of these four symbols that you would normally write a + b + c + d.

In[14]:= **Plus[a, b, c, d]**

Out[14]= a + b + c + d

Like `Map`, `Apply` has a shorthand notation: the expression *fun* @@ *expr* is equivalent to Apply[*fun*, *expr*]. So, the above computation could be written as follows:

In[15]:= **Plus @@ {1, 2, 3, 4}**

Out[15]= 10

One important distinction between `Map` and `Apply` concerns the level of the expression at which each operates. By default, `Map` operates at level 1. That is, in Map[*h*, *expr*], h will be applied to each element at the top level of *expr*. So, for example, if *expr* consists of a nested list, h will be applied to each of the sublists, but not deeper, by default.

In[16]:= **Map[h, {{a, b}, {c, d}}]**

Out[16]= {h[{a, b}], h[{c, d}]}

If you wish to apply h at a deeper level, then you have to specify that explicitly using a third argument to Map.

In[17]:= **Map[h, {{a, b}, {c, d}}, {2}]**

Out[17]= {{h[a], h[b]}, {h[c], h[d]}}

Apply, on the other hand, operates at level 0 by default. That is, in Apply[h, *expr*], Apply looks at part 0 of *expr* (that is, its Head) and replaces it with *h*.

In[18]:= **Apply[f, {{a, b}, {c, d}}]**

Out[18]= f[{a, b}, {c, d}]

Again, if you wish to apply h at a different level, then you have to specify that explicitly using a third argument to Apply.

In[19]:= **Apply[h, {{a, b}, {c, d}}, {1}]**

Out[19]= {h[a, b], h[c, d]}

For example, to apply Plus to each of the inner lists, you need to specify that Apply will operate at level 1.

In[20]:= **Apply[Plus, {{1, 2, 3}, {5, 6, 7}}, {1}]**

Out[20]= {6, 18}

If you are a little unsure of what has just happened, consider the following example and, instead of p, think of Plus.

In[21]:= **Apply[p, {{1, 2, 3}, {5, 6, 7}}, {1}]**

Out[21]= {p[1, 2, 3], p[5, 6, 7]}

Applying at the default level 0, is quite different. This is just vector addition, adding element-wise.

In[22]:= **Apply[Plus, {{1, 2, 3}, {5, 6, 7}}]**

Out[22]= {6, 8, 10}

Applying functions at level 1 is also a common task and it too has a shorthand notation: *fun* @@@ *expr* is equivalent to Apply[*fun*, *expr*, {1}].

In[23]:= **p @@@ {{1, 2, 3}, {5, 6, 7}}**

Out[23]= {p[1, 2, 3], p[5, 6, 7]}

Thread and MapThread

The `Thread` function "threads" a function over several lists. You can think of it as extracting the first element from each of the lists, wrapping a function around them, then extracting the next element in each list and wrapping the function around them, and so on.

```
In[24]:= Thread[g[{a, b, c}, {x, y, z}]]
Out[24]= {g[a, x], g[b, y], g[c, z]}
```

You can accomplish the same thing with `MapThread`. It differs from `Thread` in that it takes two arguments – the function that you are mapping and a list of two (or more) lists as arguments of the function. It creates a new list in which the corresponding elements of the old lists are paired (or zipped together).

```
In[25]:= MapThread[g, {{a, b, c}, {x, y, z}}]
Out[25]= {g[a, x], g[b, y], g[c, z]}
```

You could perform this computation manually by first zipping together the two lists using `Transpose`, and then applying g at level one.

```
In[26]:= Transpose[{{a, b, c}, {x, y, z}}]
Out[26]= {{a, x}, {b, y}, {c, z}}
```

```
In[27]:= Apply[g, %, {1}]
Out[27]= {g[a, x], g[b, y], g[c, z]}
```

With `Thread`, you can fundamentally change the structure of the expressions you are using. For example, this threads the `Equal` function over the two lists given as its arguments.

```
In[28]:= Thread[Equal[{a, b, c}, {x, y, z}]]
Out[28]= {a == x, b == y, c == z}
```

```
In[29]:= Map[FullForm, %]
Out[29]= {Equal[a, x], Equal[b, y], Equal[c, z]}
```

Here is another example of the use of `Thread`. We start off with a list of variables and a list of values.

```
In[30]:= vars = {x_1, x_2, x_3, x_4, x_5};
```

```
In[31]:= values = {1.2, 2.5, 5.7, 8.21, 6.66};
```

From these two lists, we create a list of rules.

```
In[32]:= Thread[Rule[vars, values]]
Out[32]= {x_1 → 1.2, x_2 → 2.5, x_3 → 5.7, x_4 → 8.21, x_5 → 6.66}
```

Notice how we started with a *rule of lists* and `Thread` produced a *list of rules*. In this way, you might think of `Thread` as a generalization of `Transpose`.

Here are a few more examples of `MapThread`. `Power` takes two arguments, the base and the exponent, so the following raises each element in the first list to the power given by the corresponding element in the second list.

In[33]:= **MapThread[Power, {{2, 6, 3}, {5, 1, 2}}]**

Out[33]= {32, 6, 9}

Using `Trace`, you can view some of the intermediate steps that *Mathematica* performs in doing this calculation.

In[34]:= **MapThread[Power, {{2, 6, 3}, {5, 1, 2}}] // Trace**

Out[34]= {MapThread[Power, {{2, 6, 3}, {5, 1, 2}}],
  {2^5, 6^1, 3^2}, {2^5, 32}, {6^1, 6}, {3^2, 9}, {32, 6, 9}}

Using the `List` function, the corresponding elements in the three lists are placed in a list structure (note that `Transpose` would do the same thing).

In[35]:= **MapThread[List, {{5, 3, 2}, {6, 4, 9}, {4, 1, 4}}]**

Out[35]= {{5, 6, 4}, {3, 4, 1}, {2, 9, 4}}

The Listable attribute

Many of the built-in functions that take a single argument have the property that, when a list is the argument, the function is automatically applied to all the elements in the list. In other words, these functions are automatically mapped on to the elements of the list. For example, the `Log` function has this attribute.

In[36]:= **Log[{a, E, 1}]**

Out[36]= {Log[a], 1, 0}

You get the same result using `Map`, but it is a bit more to write and, as we will see in Chapter 12, the direct approach is much more efficient for large computations.

In[37]:= **Map[Log, {a, E, 1}]**

Out[37]= {Log[a], 1, 0}

Similarly, many of the built-in functions that take two or more arguments have the property that, when multiple lists are the arguments, the function is automatically applied to all the corresponding elements in the list. In other words, these functions are automatically threaded onto the elements of the lists. For example, this is essentially vector addition.

In[38]:= **{4, 6, 3} + {5, 1, 2}**

Out[38]= {9, 7, 5}

This gives the same result as using the Plus function with MapThread.

In[39]:= **MapThread[Plus, {{4, 6, 3}, {5, 1, 2}}]**

Out[39]= {9, 7, 5}

Functions that are either automatically mapped or threaded onto the elements of list arguments are said to be Listable. Many of *Mathematica*'s built-in functions have this attribute.

In[40]:= **Attributes[Log]**

Out[40]= {Listable, NumericFunction, Protected}

In[41]:= **Attributes[Plus]**

Out[41]= {Flat, Listable, NumericFunction,
          OneIdentity, Orderless, Protected}

By default, user-defined functions do not have any attributes associated with them. So, for example, if you define a function g, it will not automatically thread over a list.

In[42]:= **g[{a, b, c, d}]**

Out[42]= g[{a, b, c, d}]

If you want a function to have the ability to thread over lists, give it the Listable attribute using SetAttributes.

In[43]:= **SetAttributes[g, Listable]**

In[44]:= **g[{a, b, c, d}]**

Out[44]= {g[a], g[b], g[c], g[d]}

Recall from Section 2.4 that clearing a symbol only clears values associated with that symbol. It does not clear any attributes associated with the symbol.

In[45]:= **Clear[g]**

In[46]:= **? g**

Global`g

Attributes[g] = {Listable}

You can use ClearAttributes to clear specific attributes associated with a symbol.

In[47]:= **ClearAttributes[g, Listable]**

In[48]:= **? g**

Global`g

Inner and Outer

The `Outer` function applies a function to all the combinations of the elements in several lists. This is a generalization of the mathematical *outer product*, which produces a matrix from a pair of vectors.

In[49]:= **Outer[f, {x, y}, {2, 3, 4}]**

Out[49]= {{f[x, 2], f[x, 3], f[x, 4]}, {f[y, 2], f[y, 3], f[y, 4]}}

Using the `List` function as an argument, you can create lists of ordered pairs that combine the elements of several lists.

In[50]:= **Outer[List, {x, y}, {2, 3, 4}]**

Out[50]= {{{x, 2}, {x, 3}, {x, 4}}, {{y, 2}, {y, 3}, {y, 4}}}

Here is the classical outer product of two vectors, obtained by wrapping `Times` around each pair of elements.

In[51]:= **Outer[Times, {u_1, u_2, u_3}, {v_1, v_2, v_3, v_4}] // MatrixForm**

Out[51]//MatrixForm=

$$\begin{pmatrix} u_1 v_1 & u_1 v_2 & u_1 v_3 & u_1 v_4 \\ u_2 v_1 & u_2 v_2 & u_2 v_3 & u_2 v_4 \\ u_3 v_1 & u_3 v_2 & u_3 v_3 & u_3 v_4 \end{pmatrix}$$

With `Inner`, you can thread a function onto several lists and then use the result as the argument to another function.

In[52]:= **Inner[f, {a, b, c}, {d, e, f}, g]**

Out[52]= g[f[a, d], f[b, e], f[c, f]]

This function lets you carry out some interesting operations.

In[53]:= **Inner[List, {a, b, c}, {d, e, f}, Plus]**

Out[53]= {a + b + c, d + e + f}

In[54]:= **Inner[Times, {x_1, y_1, z_1}, {x_2, y_2, z_2}, Plus]**

Out[54]= $x_1 x_2 + y_1 y_2 + z_1 z_2$

Looking at these two examples, you can see that `Inner` is really a generalization of the mathematical dot product.

In[55]:= **Dot[{x₁, y₁, z₁}, {x₂, y₂, z₂}]**

Out[55]= $x_1 x_2 + y_1 y_2 + z_1 z_2$

Select and Pick

When working with data, a common task is to extract all those elements that meet some criteria of interest. For example, you might want to filter out all numbers in an array outside of a certain range of values. Or you might need to find all numbers that are of a particular form or pass a particular test. We have already seen how you can use **Cases** with patterns to express the criteria of interest. In this section we will explore two additional functions that can be used for such tasks.

Select[*expr, predicate*] returns all those elements in *expr* that pass the *predicate* test. For example, here we select those elements in this short list of integers that pass the **EvenQ** test.

In[56]:= **Select[{1, 2, 3, 4, 5, 6, 7, 8, 9}, EvenQ]**

Out[56]= {2, 4, 6, 8}

This finds Mersenne numbers (numbers of the form $2^n - 1$) that are prime.

In[57]:= **Select[Table[2ⁿ - 1, {n, 1, 100}], PrimeQ]**

Out[57]= {3, 7, 31, 127, 8191, 131 071, 524 287, 2 147 483 647,
            2 305 843 009 213 693 951, 618 970 019 642 690 137 449 562 111}

You can also create your own predicates to specify the criteria in which you are interested. For example, given an array of numbers, we first create a function, **inRange**, that returns **True** if its argument falls in a certain range, say between 20 and 30.

In[58]:= **data = {24.39001, 29.669, 9.321, 20.8856,
            23.4736, 22.1488, 14.7434, 22.1619, 21.1039,
            24.8177, 27.1331, 25.8705, 39.7676, 24.7762};**

In[59]:= **inRange[x_] := 20 ≤ x ≤ 30**

Then select those elements from **data** that pass the test, **inRange**.

In[60]:= **Select[data, inRange]**

Out[60]= {24.39, 29.669, 20.8856, 23.4736, 22.1488,
            22.1619, 21.1039, 24.8177, 27.1331, 25.8705, 24.7762}

Pick can also be used to extract elements based on predicates, but it is more general than just that. In its simplest form, **Pick**[*expr, selList*] picks those elements from *expr* whose corresponding value in *selList* is **True**.

In[61]:= **Pick[{a, b, c, d, e}, {True, False, True, False, True}]**

Out[61]= {a, c, e}

You can also use binary values in the second argument, but then you need to provide a third argument to `Pick` indicating that the selector value is 1.

In[62]:= **`Pick[{a, b, c, d, e}, {1, 0, 1, 0, 1}, 1]`**

Out[62]= `{a, c, e}`

Let us work through an example that is a bit more interesting – creating random graphs. We will start with a set of edges, assigning a probability to each. Then, using `Pick`, we will include only those edges whose corresponding probability is less than some threshold value. We begin with the edges in a complete graph, that is, a graph in which there is an edge between every pair of vertices.

In[63]:= **`CompleteGraph[11]`**

Out[63]=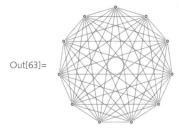

Here are the edges.

In[64]:= **`edges = EdgeRules[CompleteGraph[11]]`**

Out[64]= $\{1 \to 2, 1 \to 3, 1 \to 4, 1 \to 5, 1 \to 6, 1 \to 7, 1 \to 8, 1 \to 9, 1 \to 10, 1 \to 11,$
$2 \to 3, 2 \to 4, 2 \to 5, 2 \to 6, 2 \to 7, 2 \to 8, 2 \to 9, 2 \to 10, 2 \to 11, 3 \to 4,$
$3 \to 5, 3 \to 6, 3 \to 7, 3 \to 8, 3 \to 9, 3 \to 10, 3 \to 11, 4 \to 5, 4 \to 6,$
$4 \to 7, 4 \to 8, 4 \to 9, 4 \to 10, 4 \to 11, 5 \to 6, 5 \to 7, 5 \to 8, 5 \to 9,$
$5 \to 10, 5 \to 11, 6 \to 7, 6 \to 8, 6 \to 9, 6 \to 10, 6 \to 11, 7 \to 8, 7 \to 9,$
$7 \to 10, 7 \to 11, 8 \to 9, 8 \to 10, 8 \to 11, 9 \to 10, 9 \to 11, 10 \to 11\}$

The number of edges in the complete graph grows quickly with n. It is the same as the number of 2-element subsets of a list of length n which is given by the binomial coefficient $\binom{n}{2}$.

In[65]:= **`Length[edges] == Binomial[11, 2]`**

Out[65]= `True`

We start by creating a list of probabilities consisting of random real numbers between 0 and 1. For `Pick`, this list and the list of edges must be the same length. This list is then used to choose those edges whose corresponding probability is less than .3 (you could choose any threshold between 0 and 1). Essentially we have a probability for each edge and we are choosing those edges whose corresponding probability value is below the threshold.

In[66]:= **probs = RandomReal[1, Binomial[11, 2]];**
         Short[probs, 6]
Out[67]//Short=
         {0.100506, 0.71338, 0.140067, 0.247101, 0.737098,
          ≪46≫, 0.467768, 0.692795, 0.439899, 0.940476}

The third argument to Pick below is the pattern that the corresponding element of probs must match.

In[68]:= **includedEdges = Pick[edges, probs, *pr_* /; *pr* < .3]**

Out[68]= {1 → 2, 1 → 4, 1 → 5, 1 → 7, 1 → 10, 2 → 8, 2 → 9, 2 → 11, 3 → 4,
          4 → 5, 4 → 7, 4 → 9, 5 → 6, 5 → 7, 6 → 7, 6 → 9, 7 → 8, 8 → 10}

Finally, we turn this list of included edges into a graph.

In[69]:= **Graph[includedEdges, GraphLayout → "CircularEmbedding"]**

Out[69]=

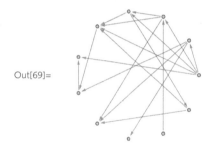

Let us try this out with more vertices and a lower probability of an edge connecting any two.

In[70]:= **n = 100;**
         p = .03;
         edges = EdgeRules[CompleteGraph[n]];
         probs = RandomReal[1, Binomial[n, 2]];
         includedEdges = Pick[edges, probs, *pr_* /; *pr* < p];
         Graph[includedEdges, GraphLayout → "CircularEmbedding"]

Out[75]=

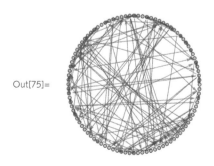

In fact, this functionality is built into `BernoulliGraphDistribution`[n, pr] which constructs an n-vertex graph, starting with an edge connecting every pair of vertices and then selects edges independently via a Bernoulli trial with probability pr.

```
In[76]:= RandomGraph[BernoulliGraphDistribution[100, 0.03],
          GraphLayout → "CircularEmbedding"]
```

Out[76]=

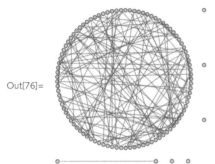

This mirrors the construction of our random graph above, although we used a uniform probability distribution (the default for `RandomReal`) rather than running Bernoulli trials via a Bernoulli distribution. In addition, a bit more work is needed to insure that our simple `randomGraph` always returns a graph with n vertices.

As an aside, it does not take a very large probability threshold to significantly increase the likelihood that any two vertices will be connected; in this next computation, it is only .08.

```
In[77]:= n = 100;
         p = .08;
         edges = EdgeRules[CompleteGraph[n]];
         probs = RandomReal[1, Binomial[n, 2]];
         includedEdges = Pick[edges, probs, pr_ /; pr < p];
         Graph[includedEdges, GraphLayout → "CircularEmbedding"]
```

Out[82]=

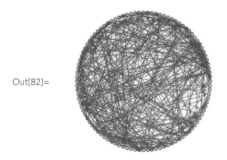

Exercises

1. Rewrite the definition of `SquareMatrixQ` given in Section 4.1 to use `Apply`.

2. Given a set of points in the plane (or 3-space), find the maximum distance between any pair of these points. This is often called the *diameter* of the pointset.

3. An adjacency matrix can be thought of as representing a graph of vertices and edges where a value of 1 in position a_{ij} indicates an edge between vertex i and vertex j, whereas $a_{ij} = 0$ indicates no such edge between vertices i and j.

   In[1]:= **mat = RandomInteger[1, {5, 5}];**
           MatrixForm[mat]

   Out[2]//MatrixForm=
   $$\begin{pmatrix} 0 & 0 & 0 & 1 & 1 \\ 0 & 0 & 1 & 1 & 0 \\ 1 & 1 & 1 & 0 & 1 \\ 0 & 1 & 1 & 0 & 0 \\ 0 & 0 & 0 & 1 & 1 \end{pmatrix}$$

   In[3]:= **AdjacencyGraph[mat, VertexLabels → "Name"]**

   Out[3]=
   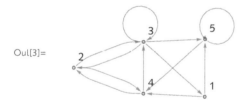

   Compute the total number of edges for each vertex in both the adjacency matrix and graph representations. For example, you should get the following edge counts for the five vertices represented in the above adjacency matrix. Note: self-loops count as two edges each.

   {3, 4, 7, 5, 5}

4. Create a function `ToGraph[lis]` that takes a list of pairs of elements and transforms it into a list of graph (directed) edges. For example:

   In[4]:= **lis = RandomInteger[9, {12, 2}]**

   Out[4]= {{4, 3}, {6, 4}, {0, 1}, {6, 0}, {5, 2}, {4, 7},
            {6, 4}, {7, 1}, {7, 6}, {7, 8}, {4, 0}, {3, 4}}

   In[5]:= **ToGraph[lis]**

   Out[5]= {4 ↦ 3, 6 ↦ 4, 0 ↦ 1, 6 ↦ 0, 5 ↦ 2,
            4 ↦ 7, 6 ↦ 4, 7 ↦ 1, 7 ↦ 6, 7 ↦ 8, 4 ↦ 0, 3 ↦ 4}

   Make sure that your function also works in the case where its argument is a single list of a pair of elements.

In[6]:= **ToGraph[{3, 6}]**

Out[6]= 3 ⟷ 6

5. Create a function `RandomColor[]` that generates a random RGB color. Add a rule for `RandomColor[n]` to create a list of *n* random colors.

6. Create a graphic that consists of *n* circles in the plane with random centers and random radii. Consider using `Thread` or `MapThread` to thread `Circle[…]` across the lists of centers and radii. Use `RandomColor` from the previous exercise to give each circle a random color.

7. Use `MapThread` and `Apply` to mirror the behavior of `Inner`.

8. While matrices can easily be added using `Plus`, matrix multiplication is a bit more involved. The `Dot` function, written as a single period, is used.

In[7]:= **{{1, 2}, {3, 4}}.{x, y}**

Out[7]= {x + 2 y, 3 x + 4 y}

Perform matrix multiplication on `{{1, 2}, {3, 4}}` and `{x, y}` without using `Dot`.

9. `FactorInteger[n]` returns a nested list of prime factors and their exponents for the number *n*.

In[8]:= **FactorInteger[3 628 800]**

Out[8]= {{2, 8}, {3, 4}, {5, 2}, {7, 1}}

Use `Apply` to reconstruct the original number from this nested list.

10. Repeat the above exercise but instead use `Inner` to reconstruct the original number *n* from the factorization given by `FactorInteger[n]`.

11. Create a function `PrimeFactorForm[n]` that formats its argument *n* in prime factorization form. For example:

In[9]:= **PrimeFactorForm[12]**

Out[9]= $2^2 \cdot 3^1$

You will need to use `Superscript` and `CenterDot` to format the factored integer.

12. The Vandermonde matrix arises in Lagrange interpolation and in reconstructing statistical distributions from their moments. Construct the Vandermonde matrix of order *n*, which should look like the following:

$$\begin{pmatrix} 1 & x_1 & x_1^2 & \cdots & x_1^{n-1} \\ 1 & x_2 & x_2^2 & \cdots & x_2^{n-1} \\ \vdots & \vdots & \vdots & \ddots & \vdots \\ 1 & x_n & x_n^2 & \cdots & x_n^{n-1} \end{pmatrix}$$

13. Using `Inner`, write a function `div[vecs, vars]` that computes the divergence of an *n*-dimensional vector field, *vecs* = $\{e_1, e_2, \ldots, e_n\}$ dependent upon *n* variables, *vars* = $\{v_1, v_2, \ldots, v_n\}$. The divergence is given by the sum of the pairwise partial derivatives.

$$\frac{\partial e_1}{\partial v_1} + \frac{\partial e_2}{\partial v_2} + \cdots + \frac{\partial e_n}{\partial v_n}$$

14. The example in the section on `Select` and `Pick` found those Mersenne numbers $2^n - 1$ that are prime doing the computation for all exponents n from 1 to 100. Modify that example to only use prime exponents (since a basic theorem in number theory states that a Mersenne number with composite exponent must be composite).

5.3 Iterating functions

A common task in computer science, mathematics, and many sciences is to repeatedly apply a function to some expression. Iterating functions has a long and rich tradition in the history of computing with perhaps the most famous example being Newton's method for root finding. Another area, chaos theory, rests on studying how iterated functions behave under small perturbations of their initial conditions or starting values. In this section, we will introduce several functions available in *Mathematica* for function iteration. In later chapters we will apply these and other programming constructs to look at some applications of iteration, including Newton's method, the visualization of Julia sets, and several types of numerical computation.

Nest

The `Nest` function is used to iterate functions. Here, `g` is iterated four times starting with initial value `a`.

```
In[1]:= Nest[g, a, 4]
```

```
Out[1]= g[g[g[g[a]]]]
```

`NestList` performs the same iteration but displays all the intermediate values.

```
In[2]:= NestList[g, a, 4]
```

```
Out[2]= {a, g[a], g[g[a]], g[g[g[a]]], g[g[g[g[a]]]]}
```

Using a starting value of 0.85, this generates a list of ten iterates of the `Cos` function.

```
In[3]:= NestList[Cos, 0.85, 10]
```

```
Out[3]= {0.85, 0.659983, 0.790003, 0.703843, 0.76236, 0.723208,
          0.749687, 0.731902, 0.743904, 0.73583, 0.741274}
```

The list elements above are the values of $0.85, \text{Cos}[0.85], \text{Cos}[\text{Cos}[0.85]]$, and so on.

```
In[4]:= {0.85, Cos[0.85], Cos[Cos[0.85]], Cos[Cos[Cos[0.85]]]}
```

```
Out[4]= {0.85, 0.659983, 0.790003, 0.703843}
```

Using a lowercase symbol `cos`, you can see the symbolic computation clearly. Although this is a useful tip for helping you to see the structure of such computations, be careful to keep the iteration count manageable; otherwise you can easily generate many pages of symbolic output on your screen.

In[5]:= **NestList[cos, 0.85, 3]**

Out[5]= {0.85, cos[0.85], cos[cos[0.85]], cos[cos[cos[0.85]]]}

The objects that you can iterate are entirely general – they could be graphics. For example, suppose we had a triangle in the plane that we wanted to rotate iteratively. Starting with a set of vertices, here is a display of the starting triangle. To close up the figure, the rule {a_, b__} :→ {a, b, a} is used to copy the first point in `vertices` to the end of the list.

In[6]:= **vertices = $\left\{\{0, 0\}, \{1, 0\}, \left\{1/2, \sqrt{3}/2\right\}\right\}$;**

In[7]:= **tri = Line[vertices /. {a_, b__} :→ {a, b, a}];**
Graphics[tri]

Out[8]=

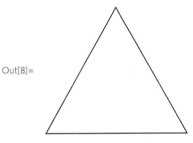

This creates a function that we will iterate inside `Nest`. `rotation` takes a graphical object and rotates it $\pi/13$ radians about the point {1, 1}.

In[9]:= **rotation[gr_] := Rotate[gr, π/13, {1, 1}]**

Here are eighteen steps of this iteration.

In[10]:= **Graphics[NestList[rotation, tri, 18]]**

Out[10]=

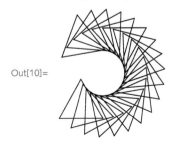

Or you can iterate a translation. First, create some translation vectors.

In[11]:= **vecs = 1 / 2 vertices**

Out[11]= $\left\{ \{0, 0\}, \left\{ \frac{1}{2}, 0 \right\}, \left\{ \frac{1}{4}, \frac{\sqrt{3}}{4} \right\} \right\}$

The **translation** function creates three objects translated by the vectors **vecs**.

In[12]:= **translation[*gr_*] := Translate[*gr*, vecs]**

In[13]:= **Graphics[{Blue, NestList[translation, tri, 3]}]**

Out[13]=

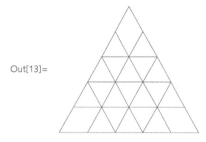

The exercises at the end of this section build upon these ideas to create a more interesting and well-known object, the Sierpinski triangle.

FixedPoint

In the example of the cosine function from the previous section, the iterates converge to a fixed point, that is, a point x such that $x = \cos(x)$. To apply a function repeatedly to an expression until it no longer changes, use **FixedPoint**. This function is particularly useful when you do not know how many iterations to perform on a function whose iterations eventually converge. For example, here is a function that, when iterated, gives a fixed point for the Golden ratio.

In[14]:= **golden[*ϕ_*] := 1 + $\dfrac{1}{ϕ}$**

In[15]:= **FixedPoint[golden, 1.0]**

Out[15]= **1.61803**

Using **FixedPointList**, you can see all the intermediate results. **FullForm** shows all digits computed, making it easier to see the convergence. Here we display every third element in the list.

In[16]:= **phi = FixedPointList[golden, 1.0];**

```
In[17]:= phi[[1 ;; -1 ;; 3]] // FullForm
```
Out[17]//FullForm=
```
        List[1.`, 1.6666666666666665`, 1.6153846153846154`,
            1.6181818181818182`, 1.6180257510729614`,
            1.618034447821682`, 1.6180339631667064`,
            1.6180339901755971`, 1.6180339886704433`,
            1.6180339887543225`, 1.6180339887496482`,
            1.6180339887499087`, 1.618033988749894`]
```

Sometimes, the iteration does not converge quickly and you need to relax the constraint on the closeness of successive iterates. For example, the cosine function has a fixed point but there is some difficulty converging using the default values for `FixedPoint`.

```
In[18]:= TimeConstrained[
            FixedPoint[Cos, 0.85],
            5]
```
Out[18]= $Aborted

In such cases, either you can give an optional third argument to indicate the maximum number of iterations to perform or you can specify a looser tolerance for the comparison of successive iterates.

```
In[19]:= FixedPoint[Cos, 0.85, 100]
```
Out[19]= 0.739085

In the following computation, we stop the iteration when two successive iterates differ by less than 10^{-10}. (We will discuss the odd notation involving # and & in Section 5.6, on pure functions.)

```
In[20]:= FixedPoint[Cos, 0.85, SameTest → (Abs[#1 - #2] < 10^-10 &)]
```
Out[20]= 0.739085

NestWhile

The `Nest` function iterates a fixed number of times, whereas `FixedPoint` iterates until a fixed point is reached. Sometimes you want to iterate until a condition is met. `NestWhile` (or `NestWhileList`) is perfect for this. For example, here we find the next prime after a given number, using `CompositeQ` from Exercise 5 of Section 2.3.

```
In[21]:= addOne[n_] := n + 1
```

```
In[22]:= CompositeQ[n_Integer /; n > 1] := Not[PrimeQ[n]]
```

```
In[23]:= NestWhile[addOne, 2^100, CompositeQ]
```
```
Out[23]= 1 267 650 600 228 229 401 496 703 205 653
```

```
In[24]:= PrimeQ[%]
```
```
Out[24]= True
```

Verify with the built-in function that computes the next prime after a given number.

```
In[25]:= NextPrime[2^100]
```
```
Out[25]= 1 267 650 600 228 229 401 496 703 205 653
```

Fold

Whereas `Nest` and `NestList` operate on functions of one variable, `Fold` and `FoldList` generalize this notion by iterating a function of two arguments. In the following example, the function `f` is first applied to a starting value `x` and the first element from a list, then this result is used as the first argument of the next iteration, with the second argument coming from the second element in the list, and so on.

```
In[26]:= Fold[f, x, {a, b, c}]
```
```
Out[26]= f[f[f[x, a], b], c]
```

Use `FoldList` to see all the intermediate values.

```
In[27]:= FoldList[f, x, {a, b, c}]
```
```
Out[27]= {x, f[x, a], f[f[x, a], b], f[f[f[x, a], b], c]}
```

It is easier to see what is going on with `FoldList` by working with an arithmetic operator. This generates "running sums."

```
In[28]:= FoldList[Plus, 0, {a, b, c, d, e}]
```
```
Out[28]= {0, a, a + b, a + b + c, a + b + c + d, a + b + c + d + e}
```

```
In[29]:= FoldList[Plus, 0, {1, 2, 3, 4, 5}]
```
```
Out[29]= {0, 1, 3, 6, 10, 15}
```

The built-in `Accumulate` function also creates running sums but it does not return the initial value 0 as in `FoldList`.

```
In[30]:= Accumulate[{1, 2, 3, 4, 5}]
```
```
Out[30]= {1, 3, 6, 10, 15}
```

Exercises

1. Determine the locations after each step of a ten-step one-dimensional random walk. (Recall that you have already generated the step *directions* in Exercise 3 at the end of Section 3.1.)

2. Create a list of the step locations of a ten-step random walk on a square lattice.

3. Using `Fold`, create a function `fac[n]` that takes an integer n as argument and returns the factorial of n, that is, $n(n-1)(n-2)\cdots3\cdot2\cdot1$.

4. The Sierpinski triangle is a classic iteration example. It is constructed by starting with an equilateral triangle (other objects can be used) and removing the inner triangle formed by connecting the midpoints of each side of the original triangle.

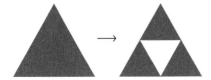

The process is iterated by repeating the same computation on each of the resulting smaller triangles.

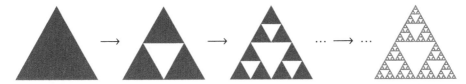

One approach is to take the starting equilateral triangle and, at each iteration, perform the appropriate transformations using `Scale` and `Translate`, then iterate. Implement this algorithm, but be careful about nesting large graphical structures too deeply.

5.4   Programs as functions

A computer program is a set of instructions (a recipe) for carrying out a computation. When a program is evaluated with appropriate inputs, the computation is performed and the result is returned. In a certain sense, a program is a mathematical function and the inputs to a program are the arguments of the function. Executing a program is equivalent to applying a function to its arguments or, as it is often referred to, making a function call.

Building up programs

Using the output of one function as the input of another is one of the keys to functional programming. This nesting of functions is commonly referred to by mathematicians as "composition of functions." In *Mathematica*, this sequential application of several functions is sometimes referred to as a *nested function call*. Nested function calls are not limited to using a single function repeatedly, such as with the built-in `Nest` and `Fold` functions.

As an example, consider the following expression involving three nested functions.

In[1]:= **Total[Sqrt[Range[2, 8, 2]]]**

Out[1]= $2 + 3\sqrt{2} + \sqrt{6}$

This use of functions as arguments to other functions is a key part of functional programming, but if you are new to it, it is instructive to step through the computation working from the inside out. In this computation, the *Mathematica* evaluator does the computation from the most deeply nested expression outward. The inner-most function is **Range** and it produces a list of numbers from 2 through 8 in steps of 2. Moving outwards, **Sqrt** is then applied to the result of the **Range** function to produce a list of the square roots. Finally, **Total** adds up the elements in the list produced by **Sqrt**.

In[2]:= **Range[2, 8, 2]**

Out[2]= {2, 4, 6, 8}

In[3]:= **Sqrt[%]**

Out[3]= $\left\{\sqrt{2}, 2, \sqrt{6}, 2\sqrt{2}\right\}$

In[4]:= **Total[%]**

Out[4]= $2 + 3\sqrt{2} + \sqrt{6}$

Wrapping **Trace** around the computation shows all the intermediate expressions that are used in this evaluation.

In[5]:= **Trace[Total[Sqrt[Range[2, 8, 2]]]]**

Out[5]= $\left\{\left\{\{\text{Range}[2, 8, 2], \{2, 4, 6, 8\}\}, \sqrt{\{2, 4, 6, 8\}},\right.\right.$
$\left\{\sqrt{2}, \sqrt{4}, \sqrt{6}, \sqrt{8}\right\}, \left\{\sqrt{2}, \sqrt{2}\right\}, \left\{\sqrt{4}, 2\right\},$
$\left\{\sqrt{6}, \sqrt{6}\right\}, \left\{\sqrt{8}, 2\sqrt{2}\right\}, \left\{\sqrt{2}, 2, \sqrt{6}, 2\sqrt{2}\right\}\right\},$
$\left.\text{Total}\left[\left\{\sqrt{2}, 2, \sqrt{6}, 2\sqrt{2}\right\}\right], 2 + 3\sqrt{2} + \sqrt{6}\right\}$

You can read nested functions in much the same way that they are created, starting with the innermost functions and working towards the outermost functions.

listEvenQ As another example, the following expression determines whether all the elements in a list are even numbers.

In[6]:= **Apply[And, Map[EvenQ, {2, 4, 6, 7, 8}]]**

Out[6]= False

Let us step through the computation much the same as *Mathematica* does, from the inside out. Start by mapping the predicate **EvenQ** to every element in the list {2, 4, 6, 7, 8}.

In[7]:= **Map[EvenQ, {2, 4, 6, 7, 8}]**

Out[7]= {True, True, True, False, True}

Apply the logical function And to the result of the previous step.

In[8]:= **Apply[And, %]**

Out[8]= False

Actually, EvenQ has the Listable attribute – it automatically maps across lists and so this computation can be shortened a bit.

In[9]:= **Attributes[EvenQ]**

Out[9]= {Listable, Protected}

Finally, here is a definition that can be used on arbitrary lists.

In[10]:= **listEvenQ[*lis_*] := Apply[And, EvenQ[*lis*]]**

In[11]:= **listEvenQ[{11, 5, 1, 18, 16, 6, 17, 6}]**

Out[11]= False

maxima In the next example, we return to a computation done with rules in Chapter 4 – returning the elements in a list of positive numbers that are bigger than all the preceding numbers in the list.

In[12]:= **Rest[DeleteDuplicates[FoldList[Max, 0, {3, 1, 6, 5, 4, 8, 7}]]]**

Out[12]= {3, 6, 8}

Tracing the evaluation shows the intermediate steps of the computation.

In[13]:= **Trace[Rest[**
          DeleteDuplicates[FoldList[Max, 0, {3, 1, 6, 5, 4, 8, 7}]]]]

Out[13]= {{{FoldList[Max, 0, {3, 1, 6, 5, 4, 8, 7}],
          {Max[0, 3], 3}, {Max[3, 1], Max[1, 3], 3},
          {Max[3, 6], 6}, {Max[6, 5], Max[5, 6], 6},
          {Max[6, 4], Max[4, 6], 6}, {Max[6, 8], 8},
          {Max[8, 7], Max[7, 8], 8}, {0, 3, 3, 6, 6, 6, 8, 8}},
        DeleteDuplicates[{0, 3, 3, 6, 6, 6, 8, 8}], {0, 3, 6, 8}},
      Rest[{0, 3, 6, 8}], {3, 6, 8}}

FoldList is first applied to the Max, 0, and the list {3, 1, 6, 5, 4, 8, 7}. Look at the Trace of this computation to see what FoldList is doing here.

In[14]:= **FoldList[Max, 0, {3, 1, 6, 5, 4, 8, 7}]**

Out[14]= {0, 3, 3, 6, 6, 6, 8, 8}

`DeleteDuplicates` is then applied to the result of the previous step to remove the duplicates.

In[15]:= **DeleteDuplicates[%]**

Out[15]= {0, 3, 6, 8}

Finally, `Rest` is applied to the result of the previous step to drop the first element, 0.

In[16]:= **Rest[%]**

Out[16]= {3, 6, 8}

Here is the function definition.

In[17]:= **maxima[*lis_*] := Rest[DeleteDuplicates[FoldList[Max, 0, *lis*]]]**

Applying `maxima` to a list of numbers produces a list of all those numbers that are larger than any number that comes before it.

In[18]:= **maxima[{4, 2, 7, 3, 4, 9, 14, 11, 17}]**

Out[18]= {4, 7, 9, 14, 17}

Example: *shuffling cards*

Here is an interesting application of building up a program with nested functions – the creation and shuffling of a deck of cards.

In[19]:= **cardDeck = Flatten[Outer[List,**
   {♣, ♢, ♡, ♠}, Join[Range[2, 10], {𝒥, 𝒬, 𝒦, 𝒜}]], 1]

Out[19]= {{♣, 2}, {♣, 3}, {♣, 4}, {♣, 5}, {♣, 6}, {♣, 7}, {♣, 8}, {♣, 9}, {♣, 10},
   {♣, 𝒥}, {♣, 𝒬}, {♣, 𝒦}, {♣, 𝒜}, {♢, 2}, {♢, 3}, {♢, 4}, {♢, 5}, {♢, 6},
   {♢, 7}, {♢, 8}, {♢, 9}, {♢, 10}, {♢, 𝒥}, {♢, 𝒬}, {♢, 𝒦}, {♢, 𝒜},
   {♡, 2}, {♡, 3}, {♡, 4}, {♡, 5}, {♡, 6}, {♡, 7}, {♡, 8}, {♡, 9}, {♡, 10},
   {♡, 𝒥}, {♡, 𝒬}, {♡, 𝒦}, {♡, 𝒜}, {♠, 2}, {♠, 3}, {♠, 4}, {♠, 5}, {♠, 6},
   {♠, 7}, {♠, 8}, {♠, 9}, {♠, 10}, {♠, 𝒥}, {♠, 𝒬}, {♠, 𝒦}, {♠, 𝒜}}

The suit icons are entered by typing in \[ClubSuit], \[DiamondSuit], etc., or by using one of the character palettes built into *Mathematica*. We have used special characters to represent the jack, queen, king, and ace rather than the plain symbols J, Q, K, and A. This is to avoid the possibility that these symbols may have rules associated with them that would interfere with our intent here. In fact, K already has meaning – it is a built-in symbol.

In[20]:= **? K**

K is a default generic name for a summation index in a symbolic sum.

You might think of `cardDeck` as a name for the expression given on the right-hand side of the immediate definition, or you might think of `cardDeck` as defining a function with zero arguments.

To understand what is going on here, we will build up this program from scratch, working from the inside out. First, we form a list of the number and face cards in a suit by combining a list of the numbers 2 through 10, with a four-element list representing the jack, queen, king, and ace, $\{J, Q, K, A\}$.

In[21]:= **Join[Range[2, 10], {J, Q, K, A}]**

Out[21]= $\{2, 3, 4, 5, 6, 7, 8, 9, 10, J, Q, K, A\}$

Next we pair each of the 13 elements in this list with each of the four elements in the list representing the card suits $\{\clubsuit, \diamondsuit, \heartsuit, \spadesuit\}$. This produces a list of 52 ordered pairs representing the cards in a deck, where the king of clubs, for example, is represented by $\{\clubsuit, K\}$).

In[22]:= **Outer[List, {$\clubsuit$, $\diamondsuit$, $\heartsuit$, $\spadesuit$}, %]**

Out[22]= $\{\{\{\clubsuit, 2\}, \{\clubsuit, 3\}, \{\clubsuit, 4\}, \{\clubsuit, 5\}, \{\clubsuit, 6\}, \{\clubsuit, 7\},$
$\{\clubsuit, 8\}, \{\clubsuit, 9\}, \{\clubsuit, 10\}, \{\clubsuit, J\}, \{\clubsuit, Q\}, \{\clubsuit, K\}, \{\clubsuit, A\}\},$
$\{\{\diamondsuit, 2\}, \{\diamondsuit, 3\}, \{\diamondsuit, 4\}, \{\diamondsuit, 5\}, \{\diamondsuit, 6\}, \{\diamondsuit, 7\}, \{\diamondsuit, 8\},$
$\{\diamondsuit, 9\}, \{\diamondsuit, 10\}, \{\diamondsuit, J\}, \{\diamondsuit, Q\}, \{\diamondsuit, K\}, \{\diamondsuit, A\}\},$
$\{\{\heartsuit, 2\}, \{\heartsuit, 3\}, \{\heartsuit, 4\}, \{\heartsuit, 5\}, \{\heartsuit, 6\}, \{\heartsuit, 7\}, \{\heartsuit, 8\},$
$\{\heartsuit, 9\}, \{\heartsuit, 10\}, \{\heartsuit, J\}, \{\heartsuit, Q\}, \{\heartsuit, K\}, \{\heartsuit, A\}\},$
$\{\{\spadesuit, 2\}, \{\spadesuit, 3\}, \{\spadesuit, 4\}, \{\spadesuit, 5\}, \{\spadesuit, 6\}, \{\spadesuit, 7\}, \{\spadesuit, 8\},$
$\{\spadesuit, 9\}, \{\spadesuit, 10\}, \{\spadesuit, J\}, \{\spadesuit, Q\}, \{\spadesuit, K\}, \{\spadesuit, A\}\}\}$

While we now have all the cards in the deck, they are grouped by suit in a nested list. We therefore unnest the list.

In[23]:= **Flatten[%, 1]**

Out[23]= $\{\{\clubsuit, 2\}, \{\clubsuit, 3\}, \{\clubsuit, 4\}, \{\clubsuit, 5\}, \{\clubsuit, 6\}, \{\clubsuit, 7\}, \{\clubsuit, 8\}, \{\clubsuit, 9\},$
$\{\clubsuit, 10\}, \{\clubsuit, J\}, \{\clubsuit, Q\}, \{\clubsuit, K\}, \{\clubsuit, A\}, \{\diamondsuit, 2\}, \{\diamondsuit, 3\},$
$\{\diamondsuit, 4\}, \{\diamondsuit, 5\}, \{\diamondsuit, 6\}, \{\diamondsuit, 7\}, \{\diamondsuit, 8\}, \{\diamondsuit, 9\}, \{\diamondsuit, 10\},$
$\{\diamondsuit, J\}, \{\diamondsuit, Q\}, \{\diamondsuit, K\}, \{\diamondsuit, A\}, \{\heartsuit, 2\}, \{\heartsuit, 3\}, \{\heartsuit, 4\}, \{\heartsuit, 5\},$
$\{\heartsuit, 6\}, \{\heartsuit, 7\}, \{\heartsuit, 8\}, \{\heartsuit, 9\}, \{\heartsuit, 10\}, \{\heartsuit, J\}, \{\heartsuit, Q\},$
$\{\heartsuit, K\}, \{\heartsuit, A\}, \{\spadesuit, 2\}, \{\spadesuit, 3\}, \{\spadesuit, 4\}, \{\spadesuit, 5\}, \{\spadesuit, 6\}, \{\spadesuit, 7\},$
$\{\spadesuit, 8\}, \{\spadesuit, 9\}, \{\spadesuit, 10\}, \{\spadesuit, J\}, \{\spadesuit, Q\}, \{\spadesuit, K\}, \{\spadesuit, A\}\}$

Voila!

The step-by-step construction used here, applying one function at a time, checking each function call separately, is a very efficient way to *prototype* your programs in *Mathematica*. We will use this technique again in many subsequent examples.

Next, let us perform what is called a *perfect shuffle*, consisting of cutting the deck in half and then interleaving the cards from the two halves. Rather than working with the large list of 52 ordered pairs during the prototyping, we will use a short list of an even number of ordered integers.

In[24]:= **lis = Range[6]**

Out[24]= {1, 2, 3, 4, 5, 6}

First divide the list into two equal-sized lists and then apply the built-in **Riffle** function which interleaves two lists. Notice that even with this simple prototype, we are using code that will generalize to arbitrary inputs. That is, rather than give 3 as the second argument to **Partition** here, we let *Mathematica* compute the length.

In[25]:= **Partition[lis, Length[lis] / 2]**

Out[25]= {{1, 2, 3}, {4, 5, 6}}

In[26]:= **Apply[Riffle, %]**

Out[26]= {1, 4, 2, 5, 3, 6}

That does the job. Given this prototype, here is a function to perform a perfect shuffle on a deck of cards.

In[27]:= **shuffle[*lis*_] := Apply[Riffle, Partition[*lis*, Length[*lis*] / 2]]**

In[28]:= **shuffle[{1, 2, 3, 4, 5, 6}]**

Out[28]= {1, 4, 2, 5, 3, 6}

In[29]:= **shuffle[cardDeck]**

Out[29]= {{♣, 2}, {♡, 2}, {♣, 3}, {♡, 3}, {♣, 4}, {♡, 4}, {♣, 5}, {♡, 5},
       {♣, 6}, {♡, 6}, {♣, 7}, {♡, 7}, {♣, 8}, {♡, 8}, {♣, 9}, {♡, 9},
       {♣, 10}, {♡, 10}, {♣, J}, {♡, J}, {♣, Q}, {♡, Q}, {♣, K},
       {♡, K}, {♣, A}, {♡, A}, {♢, 2}, {♠, 2}, {♢, 3}, {♠, 3},
       {♢, 4}, {♠, 4}, {♢, 5}, {♠, 5}, {♢, 6}, {♠, 6}, {♢, 7}, {♠, 7},
       {♢, 8}, {♠, 8}, {♢, 9}, {♠, 9}, {♢, 10}, {♠, 10}, {♢, J},
       {♠, J}, {♢, Q}, {♠, Q}, {♢, K}, {♠, K}, {♢, A}, {♠, A}}

Unfortunately, this definition for **shuffle** does not properly handle lists of odd length.

In[30]:= **shuffle[{a, b, c, d, e}]**

Partition::ilsmp : Single or list of positive machine–sized

integers expected at position 2 of Partition$\left[\{a, b, c, d, e\}, \frac{5}{2} \right]$. $\gg$

Out[30]= $\left\{ a, \frac{5}{2}, b, \frac{5}{2}, c, \frac{5}{2}, d, \frac{5}{2}, e \right\}$

This is not an uncommon situation when writing programs: after some prototyping and writing of code to solve the problem, you try it out on various inputs and, if you are thorough, you cover all the possible situations that your program was designed to take into account. In this case, one of those scenarios pointed up a deficiency in our program. Fortunately, this can be corrected by making a few minor modifications including the use of a different argument structure for `Partition`.

$$\texttt{Partition}\big[\textit{list}, \, n, \, d, \, 1, \, \{\} \big]$$

The first argument given to `Partition`, *lis*, is the list on which we are operating. The second argument, *n*, gives the size of the sublists. The third argument, *d*, gives the offset: in this case no overlap by setting this argument to the same value as the size of the sublists. The fourth argument, 1, treats the lists as cyclic. And the fifth argument, { }, allows for no padding so the lists can be of unequal length. Since we want to take into account lists of odd length, we also use `Ceiling` to get an integer value for `len`.

In[31]:= **`Clear[shuffle]`**

In[32]:= **`shuffle[`***`lis`***`_]` `:= Module[{len = Ceiling[Length[`***`lis`***`] / 2]},`**
   `Apply[Riffle, Partition[`*`lis`***`, len, len, 1, {}]]]`**

In[33]:= **`shuffle[{1, 2, 3, 4, 5}]`**

Out[33]= {1, 4, 2, 5, 3}

In[34]:= **`shuffle[{1, 2, 3, 4, 5, 6}]`**

Out[34]= {1, 4, 2, 5, 3, 6}

An obvious thing to do with a deck of cards is to deal them! Simply use `RandomSample`, which randomly chooses without replacement.

In[35]:= **`deal[`***`n`***`_]` `:= RandomSample[cardDeck, `***`n`***`]`**

In[36]:= **`deal[5]`**

Out[36]= {{♠, 3}, {♢, 5}, {♢, Q}, {♡, K}, {♡, Q}}

Compound functions

There are several major drawbacks to the above approach to dealing cards. To use `deal`, the definition of `cardDeck` must be entered before calling `deal`. It would be much more convenient if we could incorporate this function within the `deal` function definition itself. This can be done using compound function definitions, or simply, *compound functions*. The left-hand side of a compound function is the same as that of a user-defined function. The right-hand side consists of expressions enclosed in parentheses, separated by semicolons.

$$\textit{name}[\textit{arg}_1 \_, \, \textit{arg}_2 \_, \, ..., \, \textit{arg}_n \_] \texttt{:=} (\textit{expr}_1 ; \, \textit{expr}_2 ; \, ...; \, \textit{expr}_m)$$

The expressions $\textit{expr}_i$ can be any expression: a simple value assignment or a user-defined function, for example. When a compound function is evaluated with particular argument values, the expressions on the right-hand side are evaluated in order and the result of the evaluation of the last expression is returned (by adding a semicolon after *expr*$_m$, the display of the final evaluation result can also be suppressed).

We will work with the `deal` function to illustrate how a compound function is created. Here is a compound expression consisting of two inputs, separated by a semicolon.

```
In[37]:=  cardDeck = Flatten[Outer[List, {♣, ◇, ♡, ♠},
              Join[Range[2, 10], {J, Q, K, A}]], 1];
          deal[n_] := RandomSample[cardDeck, n]
```

To convert to a compound function, first remove the old definitions.

```
In[39]:=  Clear[deal, cardDeck]
```

Now create and enter the new definition.

```
In[40]:=  deal[n_] := (
              cardDeck = Flatten[Outer[List, {♣, ◇, ♡, ♠},
                  Join[Range[2, 10], {J, Q, K, A}]], 1];
              RandomSample[cardDeck, n]
          )
```

Let us check that this works.

```
In[41]:-  deal[5]
```

```
Out[41]=  {{♠, A}, {♣, 8}, {♡, 4}, {♡, Q}, {♣, J}}
```

Several things should be pointed out about the right-hand side of a compound function definition. Since the expressions on the right-hand side are evaluated in order, value declarations and (auxiliary) function definitions should be given *before* they are used and the argument names used on the left-hand side of auxiliary function definitions *must* differ from the argument names used by the compound function itself.

Secondly, note the use of parentheses wrapped around the compound expressions (those separated by semicolons). If you omitted the parentheses, *Mathematica* would think the function definition ended at the first semicolon. This is a bit of an inconvenience that we will deal with more effectively in the next section on scoping constructs.

Finally, when you evaluate a compound function definition, you are creating not only the function but also the auxiliary functions and the value declarations. If you then remove the function definition using `Clear`, the auxiliary function definitions and value declarations remain. This can cause a problem if you subsequently try to use the names of these auxiliary functions and values elsewhere. Again, this issue will be addressed in the next section on scoping constructs.

How does the global rule base treat compound functions? When a compound function definition is entered, a rewrite rule corresponding to the entire definition is created. Each time the compound function is subsequently called, rewrite rules are created from the auxiliary function definitions and value declarations within the compound function.

In[42]:= **? cardDeck**

Global`cardDeck

cardDeck = {{♣, 2}, {♣, 3}, {♣, 4}, {♣, 5}, {♣, 6}, {♣, 7}, {♣, 8}, {♣, 9},
{♣, 10}, {♣, 𝒥}, {♣, 𝒬}, {♣, 𝒦}, {♣, 𝒜}, {◇, 2}, {◇, 3}, {◇, 4}, {◇, 5},
{◇, 6}, {◇, 7}, {◇, 8}, {◇, 9}, {◇, 10}, {◇, 𝒥}, {◇, 𝒬}, {◇, 𝒦}, {◇, 𝒜},
{♡, 2}, {♡, 3}, {♡, 4}, {♡, 5}, {♡, 6}, {♡, 7}, {♡, 8}, {♡, 9}, {♡, 10},
{♡, 𝒥}, {♡, 𝒬}, {♡, 𝒦}, {♡, 𝒜}, {♠, 2}, {♠, 3}, {♠, 4}, {♠, 5}, {♠, 6},
{♠, 7}, {♠, 8}, {♠, 9}, {♠, 10}, {♠, 𝒥}, {♠, 𝒬}, {♠, 𝒦}, {♠, 𝒜}}

It is considered bad programming practice to leave auxiliary definitions in the global rule base if they are not explicitly needed by the user of your function. In fact, it could interfere with a user's workspace and cause unintended problems. To prevent these additional rewrite rules from being placed in the global rule base, you can localize their names by using the `Module` construct in the compound function definition. This is discussed in the next section.

Exercises

1. Using `Total`, create a function to sum the first *n* positive integers.

2. Rewrite the `listEvenQ` function from this section using `MemberQ`.

3. Using the `shuffle` function developed in this section, how many shuffles of a deck of cards (or any list, for that matter) are needed to return the deck to its original order?

4. Many lotteries include games that require you to pick several numbers and match them against the "house." The numbers are independent, so this is essentially random sampling with replacement. The built-in `RandomChoice` does this. For example, here are five random samples from the integers 0 through 9.

   In[1]:= **RandomChoice[Range[0, 9], 5]**

   Out[1]= {4, 1, 8, 7, 4}

   Write your own function `randomChoice`[*lis, n*] that performs a random sampling with replacement, where *n* is the number of elements being chosen from the list *lis*. Here is a typical result using a list of symbols.

   In[2]:= **randomChoice[{a, b, c, d, e, f, g, h}, 12]**

   Out[2]= {g, c, a, a, d, h, c, a, c, f, c, a}

5. Use `Trace` on the rule-based `maxima` from Section 4.2 and `maxima` developed in this section to explain why the functional version is much faster than the pattern matching version.

6. Write your own user-defined functions using the `Characters` and `StringJoin` functions to perform the same operations as `StringInsert` and `StringDrop`.

7. Write a function `interleave` that interleaves the elements of two lists of unequal length. (You have already seen how to interleave lists of equal length using `Partition` earlier in this section with the `shuffle` function.) Your function should take the lists {a, b, c, d} and {1, 2, 3} as inputs and return {a, 1, b, 2, c, 3, d}.

8. Write nested function calls using `ToCharacterCode` and `FromCharacterCode` to perform the same operations as the built-in `StringJoin` and `StringReverse` functions.

5.5   Scoping constructs

Localizing names: Module

When you define functions using assignments, it is generally a good idea to isolate the *names* of values and functions defined on the right-hand side from the outside world in order to avoid any conflict with the use of a name elsewhere in the session (for example, `cardDeck` from the previous section might be used elsewhere to represent a pinochle deck). This localization of the variable names is done by wrapping the right-hand side of the function definition with the `Module` function.

$$name\,[arg_1\,\_,\ arg_2\,\_,\ ...,\ arg_n\,\_]\ := \texttt{Module}\Big[\big\{name_1,\ name_2 = value,\ ...\big\},$$
$$\quad body\_of\_function$$
$$\Big]$$

The first argument of `Module` is a list of the symbols to be localized. If you wish, you can assign values to these names, as is shown with $name_2$ above; the assigned value is only an initial value and can be changed subsequently. The list of variables to be localized is separated from the right-hand side by a comma and so the parentheses enclosing the right-hand side of a compound function are not needed.

Let us use `Module` to rewrite the `deal` function from the previous section, localizing the auxiliary symbol `cardDeck`.

```
In[1]:= Clear[deal, cardDeck]
```

```
In[2]:= deal[n_] := Module[{cardDeck},
           cardDeck = Flatten[Outer[List, {♣, ◇, ♡, ♠},
             Join[Range[2, 10], {J, Q, K, A}]], 1];
           RandomSample[cardDeck, n]]
```

In[3]:= **deal[5]**

Out[3]= {{◊, 7}, {♠, 8}, {◊, 5}, {◊, 𝒥}, {◊, 10}}

Briefly, when Module is encountered, the symbols that are being localized (cardDeck in the above example) are temporarily given new and unique names, and all occurrences of those symbols in the body of the Module are given those new names as well. In this way, these unique and temporary names, which are local to the function, will not interfere with any names of functions or values outside of the Module.

To see how Module works we'll trace a computation involving a simple function, showing some of the internals.

In[4]:= **f[*n*_] := Module[{tmp = Range[*n*]},**
   tmp = N[tmp];
   tmp.tmp]

In[5]:= **f[5]**

Out[5]= **55.**

In[6]:= **Trace[f[5]]**

Out[6]= {f[5], Module[{tmp = Range[5]}, tmp = N[tmp]; tmp.tmp],
   {Range[5], {1, 2, 3, 4, 5}}, {tmp$1532 = {1, 2, 3, 4, 5}, {1, 2, 3, 4, 5}},
   {tmp$1532 = N[tmp$1532]; tmp$1532.tmp$1532,
    {{{tmp$1532, {1, 2, 3, 4, 5}}, N[{1, 2, 3, 4, 5}], {1., 2., 3., 4., 5.}},
     tmp$1532 = {1., 2., 3., 4., 5.}, {1., 2., 3., 4., 5.}},
    {{tmp$1532, {1., 2., 3., 4., 5.}}, {tmp$1532, {1., 2., 3., 4., 5.}},
     {1., 2., 3., 4., 5.}.{1., 2., 3., 4., 5.}, 55.}, 55.}, 55.}

Looking at the trace, the local variable tmp has been *renamed* tmp$1532, a unique and new name. In this way, the local variable will not interfere with any global variable whose name is tmp.

It is generally a good idea to wrap the right-hand side of all compound function definitions in the Module function. Another way to avoid conflicts between the names of auxiliary function definitions is to use a function that can be applied without being given a name. Such functions are called *pure functions* and are discussed in Section 5.6.

Localizing values: Block

Occasionally, you will need to localize a *value* associated with a symbol without localizing the symbol *name* itself. For example, you may have a recursive computation that requires you to temporarily reset the system variable $RecursionLimit. You can do this with Block, thereby only localizing the *value* of $RecursionLimit during the evaluation inside Block. Block has the same syntax as Module.

```
In[7]:= Block[{$RecursionLimit = 20},
           x = g[x]]
```

$RecursionLimit::reclim : Recursion depth of 20 exceeded. ≫

```
Out[7]= g[g[g[g[
            g[g[g[g[g[g[g[g[g[g[g[g[g[g[Hold[g[x]]]]]]]]]]]]]]]]]]]]]
```

Notice the global value of $RecursionLimit is unchanged.

```
In[8]:= $RecursionLimit
```

```
Out[8]= 256
```

Module, on the other hand, creates an entirely new symbol, $RecursionLimit$*nn* that has nothing to do with the global variable $RecursionLimit, and so Module would be inappropriate for this particular task. Block only affects the *values* of these symbols, not their names.

As another example, we will do a computation with fixed ten-digit precision by setting the two system variables $MaxPrecision and $MinPrecision to 10. In general you would not want to set these variables globally.

```
In[9]:= Block[{$MaxPrecision = 10, $MinPrecision = 10},
           Log[1000000`10]]
```

```
Out[9]= 13.81551056
```

```
In[10]:= Precision[%]
```

```
Out[10]= 10.
```

In fact, Block is used to localize the iterators in Table, Do, Sum, and Product.

Localizing constants: With

Another scoping construct is available when you simply need to localize constants. If, in the body of your function, you use a variable that is assigned a constant once and never changes, then With is the preferred means to localize that constant.

This sets the global variable y to have the value 5.

```
In[11]:= y = 5;
```

Here is a simple function that initializes y as a local constant.

```
In[12]:= f[x_] := With[{y = x + 1}, y]
```

We see the global symbol is unchanged and it does not interfere with the local symbol y inside of With.

```
In[13]:= y
```

```
Out[13]= 5
```

In[14]:= **f[2]**

Out[14]= 3

With is particularly handy when you want to perform a computation and experiment with some values of your parameters without setting them globally. For example, suppose you are prototyping code for a function that returns an upper triangular matrix, that is, a matrix with os below the diagonal. In the following example, the matrix will have 1s on and above the diagonal. **With** is used here to temporarily set the value of n, the size of the matrix.

In[15]:= **With[{n = 5},**
      Table[If[j ≥ i, 1, 0], {i, n}, {j, n}]
    ] // MatrixForm

Out[15]//MatrixForm=
$$\begin{pmatrix} 1 & 1 & 1 & 1 & 1 \\ 0 & 1 & 1 & 1 & 1 \\ 0 & 0 & 1 & 1 & 1 \\ 0 & 0 & 0 & 1 & 1 \\ 0 & 0 & 0 & 0 & 1 \end{pmatrix}$$

The advantage of this approach is that it is extremely easy to turn this into a reusable function. Copying and pasting the line of code starting with **Table[…]** essentially gives the right-hand side of the function definition without the need to modify any parameters.

In[16]:= **UpperTriangularMatrix[*n*_] :=**
      Table[If[j ≥ i, 1, 0], {i, *n*}, {j, *n*}]

In[17]:= **UpperTriangularMatrix[6] // MatrixForm**

Out[17]//MatrixForm=
$$\begin{pmatrix} 1 & 1 & 1 & 1 & 1 & 1 \\ 0 & 1 & 1 & 1 & 1 & 1 \\ 0 & 0 & 1 & 1 & 1 & 1 \\ 0 & 0 & 0 & 1 & 1 & 1 \\ 0 & 0 & 0 & 0 & 1 & 1 \\ 0 & 0 & 0 & 0 & 0 & 1 \end{pmatrix}$$

Finally, it should be noted that **With** is generally faster than **Module**, so if you are really working with local constants – that is, symbols whose values do not change in the body of your functions – you will see some speed improvements.

In[18]:= **f1[*n*_] := Module[{tmp = N@Range[*n*]},**
      tmp.tmp]

```
In[19]:= Timing[
           Do[f1[100], {10^5}]
         ]
```

Out[19]= {0.882004, Null}

```
In[20]:= f2[n_] := With[{tmp = N@Range[n]},
            tmp.tmp]
```

```
In[21]:= Timing[
           Do[f2[100], {10^5}]
         ]
```

Out[21]= {0.513982, Null}

Example: matrix manipulation

In this example we will create functions to switch rows or columns of a matrix. As seen in the solution to Exercise 4 in Section 3.3, the need for localization becomes apparent quickly.

Let us prototype with a small 5×5 matrix.

```
In[22]:= SeedRandom[123];
         mat = RandomInteger[9, {5, 5}];
```

```
In[23]:= MatrixForm[mat]
```

Out[24]//MatrixForm=

$$\begin{pmatrix} 7 & 4 & 0 & 2 & 6 \\ 7 & 9 & 8 & 3 & 9 \\ 8 & 5 & 2 & 6 & 2 \\ 6 & 2 & 0 & 4 & 1 \\ 7 & 6 & 8 & 3 & 6 \end{pmatrix}$$

We could use a parallel assignment to switch two rows, say rows 2 and 3.

```
In[25]:= {mat[[2]], mat[[3]]} = {mat[[3]], mat[[2]]}
```

Out[25]= {{8, 5, 2, 6, 2}, {7, 9, 8, 3, 9}}

The problem with this approach is that mat is changed by the assignment. List component assignment is a destructive operation.

In[26]:= **mat // MatrixForm**

Out[26]//MatrixForm=

$$\begin{pmatrix} 7 & 4 & 0 & 2 & 6 \\ 8 & 5 & 2 & 6 & 2 \\ 7 & 9 & 8 & 3 & 9 \\ 6 & 2 & 0 & 4 & 1 \\ 7 & 6 & 8 & 3 & 6 \end{pmatrix}$$

We can avoid this problem by using a local variable, lmat, and only operating on that expression, not the original matrix. When the computation is done, we return the value of lmat.

In[27]:= **switchRows[*mat_*, {*r1_*, *r2_*}] := Module[{lmat = *mat*},**
    {lmat[[*r1*]], lmat[[*r2*]]} = {lmat[[*r2*]], lmat[[*r1*]]};
    lmat]

This can be written a bit more compactly using list component assignment on the correct parts.

In[28]:= **switchRows[*mat_*, {*r1_*, *r2_*}] := Module[{lmat = *mat*},**
    lmat[[{*r1*, *r2*}]] = lmat[[{*r2*, *r1*}]];
    lmat]

In[29]:= **SeedRandom[123];**
    mat = RandomInteger[9, {5, 5}];

In[31]:= **switchRows[mat, {2, 3}] // MatrixForm**

Out[31]//MatrixForm=

$$\begin{pmatrix} 7 & 4 & 0 & 2 & 6 \\ 8 & 5 & 2 & 6 & 2 \\ 7 & 9 & 8 & 3 & 9 \\ 6 & 2 & 0 & 4 & 1 \\ 7 & 6 & 8 & 3 & 6 \end{pmatrix}$$

Using local variables in this situation is preferable as the original matrix is left unchanged.

In[32]:= **mat // MatrixForm**

Out[32]//MatrixForm=

$$\begin{pmatrix} 7 & 4 & 0 & 2 & 6 \\ 7 & 9 & 8 & 3 & 9 \\ 8 & 5 & 2 & 6 & 2 \\ 6 & 2 & 0 & 4 & 1 \\ 7 & 6 & 8 & 3 & 6 \end{pmatrix}$$

You can even use negative indices to count rows from the end. For example, this switches the first and the last row.

In[33]:= **switchRows[mat, {1, -1}] // MatrixForm**

Out[33]//MatrixForm=

$$\begin{pmatrix} 7 & 6 & 8 & 3 & 6 \\ 7 & 9 & 8 & 3 & 9 \\ 8 & 5 & 2 & 6 & 2 \\ 6 & 2 & 0 & 4 & 1 \\ 7 & 4 & 0 & 2 & 6 \end{pmatrix}$$

Switching columns is basically switching rows of the transposed matrix and then transposing back.

In[34]:= **switchColumns[*mat_*, {*c1_*, *c2_*}] :=**
    Transpose@switchRows[Transpose[*mat*], {*c1*, *c2*}]

In[35]:= **switchColumns[mat, {3, 4}] // MatrixForm**

Out[35]//MatrixForm=

$$\begin{pmatrix} 7 & 4 & 2 & 0 & 6 \\ 7 & 9 & 3 & 8 & 9 \\ 8 & 5 & 6 & 2 & 2 \\ 6 & 2 & 4 & 0 & 1 \\ 7 & 6 & 3 & 8 & 6 \end{pmatrix}$$

These are fairly simplistic functions and will fail if you are not careful with the row or column numbers.

In[36]:= **switchRows[mat, {1, 6}]**

Part::partw :
Part 6 of {{7, 4, 0, 2, 6}, {7, 9, 8, 3, 9}, {8, 5, 2, 6, 2}, {6, 2, 0, 4, 1}, {7, 6, 8, 3, 6}} does not exist. ≫

Out[36]= {{7, 4, 0, 2, 6}, {7, 9, 8, 3, 9}, {8, 5, 2, 6, 2}, {6, 2, 0, 4, 1}, {7, 6, 8, 3, 6}}

In Exercise 1 of Section 5.7 we will do some argument checking and issue an appropriate message when bad arguments are passed to these functions.

Exercises

1. Write a compound function definition for the location of steps taken in an n-step random walk on a square lattice. The step directions can be taken to be the compass directions with north represented by {1, 0}, south by {-1, 0}, and so on. Hint: consider using the Accumulate function.

2. The PerfectSearch function defined in Section 1.1 is impractical for checking large numbers because it has to check all numbers from 1 through n. If you already know the perfect numbers below 500, say, it is inefficient to check all numbers from 1 to 1000 if you are only looking for perfect numbers in the range 500 to 1000. Modify PerfectSearch so that it accepts two num-

bers as input and finds all perfect numbers between the inputs. For example, PerfectSearch$[a, b]$ will produce a list of all perfect numbers in the range from a to b.

3. A number, n, is k-perfect if the sum of its proper divisors equals $k\,n$. Redefine PerfectSearch from the previous exercise so that it accepts as input two numbers a and b, a positive integer k, and computes all k-perfect numbers in the range from a to b. Use your rule to find the only three 4-perfect numbers less than 2 200 000.

4. Often in processing files you are presented with expressions that need to be converted into a format that can be more easily manipulated inside *Mathematica*. For example, a file may contain dates in the form 20120515 to represent May 15, 2012. *Mathematica* represents its dates as a list in the form $\{year, month, day, hour, minutes, seconds\}$. Write a function convertToDate$[n]$ to convert a number consisting of eight digits such as 20120515 into a list of the form {2012, 5, 15}.

In[2]:= **convertToDate[20 120 515]**

Out[2]= {2012, 5, 15}

5. Create a function zeroColumns$[mat, m ;; n]$ that zeros out columns m through n in matrix mat. Include rules to handle the cases of zeroing out one column or a list of nonconsecutive columns.

5.6 Pure functions

Many computations that you perform involve creating and using a function quickly to perform some transformation on an expression. Typically, you introduce a formal function definition and then use that function explicitly.

In[1]:= **f[x_] := x^2**

In[2]:= **Map[f, {a, b, c, c, e}]**

Out[2]= $\{a^2, b^2, c^2, c^2, e^2\}$

But what if you could use a function "on the fly" without creating an explicit definition? That is what you can do with pure functions. A *pure function* is a function that does not have a name and that can be used "on the spot", at the moment it is created. This is often convenient, especially if the function is only going to be used once or if it will be used as an argument to a higher-order function, such as Map, Fold, or Nest. The built-in function Function is used to create pure functions.

Syntax of pure functions
The basic form of a pure function is Function$[x, body]$ for a pure function with a single variable x (any symbol can be used for the variable), and Function$[\{x, y, \ldots\}, body]$ for a pure function with more than one variable. The body looks like the right-hand side of a user-

defined function definition, with the variables *x*, *y*, ..., where argument names would be. As an example, here is a pure function that squares its argument.

In[3]:= **Function$\left[z, z^2\right]$**

Out[3]= Function$\left[z, z^2\right]$

There is also a standard input form that can be used in writing a pure function which is easier to write than the **Function** notation but can be a bit cryptic to read. The right-hand side of the function definition is rewritten by replacing the variable by the number sign, or, hash symbol (#) and ending the expression with the ampersand symbol (&) to indicate that this is a pure function.

$\#^2$ **&**

If there is more than one variable, #1, #2, and so on are used.

A pure function can be used exactly like more conventional looking functions, by following the function with the argument values enclosed in square brackets. First we show the pure function using **Function**.

In[4]:= **Function$\left[z, z^2\right]$[6]**

Out[4]= 36

Here is the same thing, but using the more cryptic shorthand notation; the parentheses in the following example are purely for readability and can be omitted if you wish.

In[5]:= $\left(\#^2 \text{ \&}\right)$ **[6]**

Out[5]= 36

In fact, you can do anything with a pure function that you can do with a formally-defined function. You can evaluate it at a value, plot it, integrate it, and so on.

In[6]:= $\#^2$ **& [10]**

Out[6]= 100

In[7]:= **Plot$\left[\#^2 \text{ \& [x]}, \{x, -2, 2\}\right]$**

Out[7]=

In[8]:= $\texttt{Integrate}\big[\#^2\,\texttt{\&[x], x}\big]$

Out[8]= $\dfrac{x^3}{3}$

If you prefer, you can give a pure function a name and then use that name to call the function later. This has the same effect as defining the function in the more traditional manner (although, as we will see later, working with pure functions can give significant speed increases on many types of computations).

In[9]:= $\texttt{squared = }\#^2\texttt{ \&;}$

In[10]:= $\texttt{squared[6]}$

Out[10]= 36

Pure functions are very commonly used with higher-order functions like Map and Apply, so, before going further, let us first look at a few basic examples of the use of pure functions.

Here is a list of numbers.

In[11]:= $\texttt{lis = \{2, -5, 6.1\};}$

Now suppose we wished to square each number and then add 1 to it. The pure function that does this is $\#^2 + 1$ &. So that is what we need to map across this list.

In[12]:= $\texttt{Map}\big[\#^2\texttt{ + 1 \&, lis}\big]$

Out[12]= $\{5,\ 26,\ 38.21\}$

In the next example we will create a set of data and then use the Select function to filter out outliers.

In[13]:= $\texttt{data = \{24.39001, 29.669, 9.321, 20.8856,}$
$\texttt{23.4736, 22.1488, 14.7434, 22.1619, 21.1039,}$
$\texttt{24.8177, 27.1331, 25.8705, 39.7676, 24.7762\};}$

A plot of the data shows there are two outliers.

In[14]:= $\texttt{ListPlot[data]}$

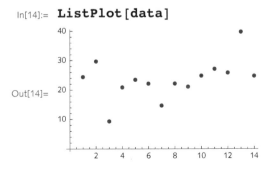

Out[14]=

We introduced the `Select` function in Section 5.2. Recall `Select`[*expr*, *test*] returns those elements from *expr* that return `True` when *test* is applied to them. We will use a pure function as the test, in this case excluding all data points that lie outside of the range 20 to 30.

```
In[15]:= Select[data, 20 ≤ # ≤ 30 &]
```
```
Out[15]= {24.39, 29.669, 20.8856, 23.4736, 22.1488,
          22.1619, 21.1039, 24.8177, 27.1331, 25.8705, 24.7762}
```

Using pure functions

A good way to become comfortable with pure functions is to see them in action, so we will convert some of the functions we defined earlier into pure functions, showing both the short-hand notation and the `Function` form so that you can decide which you prefer to use.

listEvenQ This function tests whether all the elements of a list are even.

```
In[16]:= listEvenQ[lis_] := Apply[And, EvenQ[lis]]
```

```
In[17]:= listEvenQ[{2, 4, 5, 8}]
```
```
Out[17]= False
```

Here it is written using pure functions.

```
In[18]:= Function[lis, Apply[And, EvenQ[lis]]][{2, 4, 5, 8}]
```
```
Out[18]= False
```

```
In[19]:= (Apply[And, EvenQ[#]]) &[{2, 4, 5, 8}]
```
```
Out[19]= False
```

maxima This function returns each element in the list greater than all previous elements.

```
In[20]:= maxima[x_] := Union[Rest[FoldList[Max, 0, x]]]
```

```
In[21]:= maxima[{2, 6, 3, 7, 9, 2}]
```
```
Out[21]= {2, 6, 7, 9}
```

Here it is written using pure functions.

```
In[22]:= Function[x, Union[Rest[FoldList[Max, 0, x]]]][
          {2, 6, 3, 7, 9, 2}]
```
```
Out[22]= {2, 6, 7, 9}
```

```
In[23]:= Union[Rest[FoldList[Max, 0, #]]] &[{2, 6, 3, 7, 9, 2}]
```
```
Out[23]= {2, 6, 7, 9}
```

Pure predicate functions The following examples use a pure function as a predicate to check various criteria. In the first example, we are testing if {a, b, c} has head `List` and if the length of {a, b, c} is greater than 2. Since it passes both of these conditions, `MatchQ` returns `True`.

In[24]:= **MatchQ[{a, b, c}, _List? (Length[#] > 2 &)]**

Out[24]= True

Even though the head of {a, b, c} is `List`, the condition below fails since the list has length less than 4.

In[25]:= **MatchQ[{a, b, c}, _List? (Length[#] > 4 &)]**

Out[25]= False

Note that when using a pure function as in `? ` *test*, because of the precedence *Mathematica* gives to evaluating various quantities, it is necessary to enclose the entire function, including the `&`, in parentheses.

In Exercise 1 in Section 5.4, you were asked to create a function to sum the integers 1 through *n*. The following works fine if *n* is a positive integer, but is not well-defined otherwise.

In[26]:= **sumInts[n_] := Total[Range[n]]**

In[27]:= **sumInts[1.3]**

Out[27]= 1

In[28]:= **sumInts[-3]**

Out[28]= 0

Some argument checking, using pure function predicates can rectify this.

In[29]:= **Clear[sumInts]**

In[30]:= **sumInts[n_? (IntegerQ[#] && Positive[#] &)] := Total[Range[n]]**

In[31]:= **sumInts[-1.3]**

Out[31]= sumInts[-1.3]

In[32]:= **sumInts[100]**

Out[32]= 5050

Indexing with pure functions Oftentimes it is necessary to index parts of an expression by the position of each element. `MapIndexed` is designed for this purpose and it is often used with pure functions.

Given an expression to index, the default behavior of `MapIndexed` is to create pairs (e_i, i), where e_i is the *i*th element in the expression, and then to pass them as arguments to a function given as the first argument to `MapIndexed`.

In[33]:= **expr = {a, b, c, d, e};**
MapIndexed[f, expr]

Out[34]= {f[a, {1}], f[b, {2}], f[c, {3}], f[d, {4}], f[e, {5}]}

If instead of a symbolic function f, we use `List`, we get pairs of the form {e_i, {i}}.

In[35]:= **MapIndexed[List, expr]**

Out[35]= {{a, {1}}, {b, {2}}, {c, {3}}, {d, {4}}, {e, {5}}}

Using pure functions you can modify this quite a bit by operating on either the index or the subexpression. With `MapIndexed`, #2 refers to the index and #1 to the element itself. For example, the following pure function is a list consisting of the first part of the index (strip away one set of braces) followed by the element in that position.

In[36]:= **MapIndexed[{First@#2, #1} &, expr]**

Out[36]= {{1, a}, {2, b}, {3, c}, {4, d}, {5, e}}

Nested pure functions You can also create nested pure functions; the key is to keep the variables straight. For example, the following pure function is mapped over the list to square each element.

In[37]:= **Map$\left[\#^2 \ \&, \ \{3, \ 2, \ 7\}\right]$**

Out[37]= {9, 4, 49}

When dealing with nested pure functions, the shorthand notation can be used for each of the pure functions but care needs to be taken to avoid confusion as to which # variable belongs to which pure function. This can be avoided by using `Function`, in which case different variable names can be used. Note the order in which the arguments are slotted into these two pure functions – the outer function gets the arguments first.

In[38]:= **Function$\left[y, \ \text{Map}\left[\text{Function}\left[x, \ x^2\right], \ y + 1\right]\right]$[{3, 2, 7}]**

Out[38]= {16, 9, 64}

In[39]:= **Function$\left[x, \ \text{Map}\left[\text{Function}[y, \ y + 1], \ x^2\right]\right]$[{3, 2, 7}]**

Out[39]= {10, 5, 50}

Example: searching for attributes and options

As described in Section 2.4, many built-in functions have a set of properties, or, attributes, that govern their behavior in various ways. For example, functions that have the `Listable` attribute automatically map or thread across lists of arguments.

In[40]:= **Attributes[Sin]**

Out[40]= {Listable, NumericFunction, Protected}

In[41]:= **Sin$\left[\left\{\dfrac{\pi}{6}, \dfrac{\pi}{3}, \dfrac{\pi}{2}, \pi\right\}\right]$**

Out[41]= $\left\{\dfrac{1}{2}, \dfrac{\sqrt{3}}{2}, 1, 0\right\}$

In this section we will create a function that searches the entire built-in symbol list for functions with a given attribute or option.

It is easy to check one function. MemberQ$\left[list, form\right]$ returns true if an element of *list* matches the pattern *form*.

In[42]:= **MemberQ[Attributes[Sin], Listable]**

Out[42]= True

A list of all the built-in functions is given by the following.

In[43]:= **names = Names["System`*"];**

In[44]:= **RandomSample[names, 8]**

Out[44]= {FindCurvePath, EdgeLabeling, SucceedsTilde, TriangleWave, Prism, SetProperty, StyleNames, ConfidenceTransform}

One minor point to note: the output of Names is a list of strings.

In[45]:= **InputForm[%]**

Out[45]//InputForm=
```
{"FindCurvePath", "EdgeLabeling",
  "SucceedsTilde", "TriangleWave", "Prism",
  "SetProperty", "StyleNames",
  "ConfidenceTransform"}
```

Fortunately, Attributes can take either a symbol or a string as an argument so we do not need to worry about the distinction here (but we will need to worry about this when we do something similar for options).

In[46]:= **Attributes["Sin"]**

Out[46]= {Listable, NumericFunction, Protected}

Hopefully it is clear how we should proceed. We want to select all those System` symbols that have a given attribute. For example, this selects all those System` symbols that have the Constant attribute.

In[47]:= **Select[names, MemberQ[Attributes[#], Constant] &]**

Out[47]= {Catalan, ChampernowneNumber, Degree, E, EulerGamma,
          Glaisher, GoldenRatio, Khinchin, MachinePrecision, Pi}

Let us turn this into a function that takes the attribute as an argument. Note, this function is "self-contained"; the user does not need to evaluate Names["System`"] prior to using it as we did above.

In[48]:= **FunctionsWithAttribute[*attrib_Symbol*] :=**
          Select[Names["System`*"], MemberQ[Attributes[#], *attrib*] &]

In[49]:= **FunctionsWithAttribute[Constant]**

Out[49]= {Catalan, ChampernowneNumber, Degree, E, EulerGamma,
          Glaisher, GoldenRatio, Khinchin, MachinePrecision, Pi}

In[50]:= **FunctionsWithAttribute[Orderless]**

Out[50]= {ArithmeticGeometricMean, BitAnd, BitOr, BitXor, CoprimeQ,
          DiracComb, DiracDelta, DiscreteDelta, Equivalent,
          GCD, HeavisideLambda, HeavisidePi, HeavisideTheta,
          KroneckerDelta, LCM, Majority, Max, Min, Multinomial,
          Plus, Times, UnitBox, UnitStep, UnitTriangle, Xnor, Xor}

Attempting to mimic this function for options instead of attributes requires several adjustments. First, note that Options, unlike Attributes, does not take a string as an argument.

In[51]:= **Options["Integrate"]**

Out[51]= { }

We can work around this by converting strings to symbols.

In[52]:= **Options[Symbol["Integrate"]]**

Out[52]= {Assumptions :→ $Assumptions,
          GenerateConditions → Automatic, PrincipalValue → False}

The second issue is that options are given as a list of rules which is a more deeply nested expression structure than the list of attributes.

In[53]:= **MemberQ[Options[Integrate], Assumptions]**

Out[53]= False

The tree structure shows that the option names occur down at level 2.

In[54]:= **TreeForm[Options[Integrate]]**

Out[54]//TreeForm=

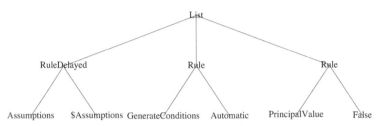

We will map **First** across the list of option rules to extract the option names only.

In[55]:= **MemberQ[Map[First, Options[Integrate]], Assumptions]**

Out[55]= **True**

Finally, note that warning messages are issued for some of the symbols.

In[56]:= **Select[Names["System`*"], MemberQ[**
　　　　Map[First, Options[Symbol[#]]], InterpolationOrder] &];

Options::opmix : Cannot mix streams and non−streams in {Courier, 10.}. ≫

ToExpression::notstrbox :
　　FEPrivate`FrontEndResourceString[GetFEKernelInit] is not a string or a box.
　　　　ToExpression can only interpret strings or boxes as Mathematica input. ≫

Since the computation is correct, we can simply turn off the display of the warning messages by using **Quiet**. Here then is our function.

In[57]:= **FunctionsWithOption[*opt_Symbol*] := Select[Names["System`*"],**
　　　　Quiet[MemberQ[First /@ Options[Symbol[#]], *opt*]] &]

In[58]:= **FunctionsWithOption[StepMonitor]**

Out[58]= {FindArgMax, FindArgMin, FindFit, FindMaximum,
　　FindMaxValue, FindMinimum, FindMinValue, FindRoot,
　　NArgMax, NArgMin, NDSolve, NMaximize, NMaxValue,
　　NMinimize, NMinValue, NonlinearModelFit, NRoots}

Exercises

1. Write a function to sum the squares of the elements of a numeric list.

2. In Exercise 2 from Section 5.2 you were asked to create a function to compute the diameter of a set of points in n-dimensional space. Modify that solution by instead using the `Norm` function and pure functions to find the diameter.

3. Rewrite the code from Section 5.3 for finding the next prime after a given integer so that it uses pure functions instead of relying upon auxiliary definitions `addOne` and `CompositeQ`.

4. Create a function `RepUnit[n]` that generates integers of length n consisting entirely of ones. For example `RepUnit[7]` should produce 1111111.

5. Given a set of numerical data, extract all those data points that are within one standard deviation of the mean of the data.

   In[1]:= **data = RandomVariate[NormalDistribution[0, 1], {2500}];**

6. Write a pure function that moves a random walker from one location on a square lattice to one of the four adjoining locations with equal probability. For example, starting at {0, 0}, the function should return {0, 1}, {0, -1}, {1, 0}, or {-1, 0} with equal likelihood. Now, use this pure function with `NestList` to generate the list of step locations for an n-step random walk starting at {0, 0}.

7. Find all words in the dictionary that start with the letter q and are of length five. Here is the list of words in the dictionary that comes with *Mathematica*.

   In[2]:= **words = DictionaryLookup[];**
   RandomSample[words, 24]

   Out[3]= {leafage, uncorrupted, cocci, disadvantaged, inflicter, Moira,
            interpolates, squander, archer, tricking, lithosphere,
            deforested, throb, soapboxes, monopolies, advisedly, silencer,
            tames, satanists, individuals, snorter, huh, noised, WWW}

8. A naive approach to polynomial arithmetic would require three additions and six multiplications to carry out the arithmetic in the expression $a x^3 + b x^2 + c x + d$. Using Horner's method for fast polynomial multiplication, this expression can be represented as $d + x(c + x(b + a x))$, where there are now half as many multiplications. You can see this using the `MultiplyCount` function developed in Exercise 8 of Section 4.2.

   In[4]:= **MultiplyCount$\left[a x^3 + b x^2 + c x + d\right]$**

   Out[4]= 6

   In[5]:= **MultiplyCount[d + x (c + x (b + a x))]**

   Out[5]= 3

   In general, the number of multiplications in an n-degree polynomial is given by:

   In[6]:= **Binomial[n + 1, 2]**

   Out[6]= $\dfrac{1}{2}$ n (1 + n)

This, of course, grows quadratically with n, whereas Horner's method grows linearly. Create a function Horner$[lis, var]$ that gives a representation of a polynomial in Horner form. Here is some sample output that your function should generate.

In[7]:= **Horner[{a, b, c, d}, x]**

Out[7]= d + x (c + x (b + a x))

In[8]:= **Expand[%]**

Out[8]= $d + c x + b x^2 + a x^3$

9. Graphs that are not too dense are often represented using *adjacency structures* which consist of a list for each vertex v_i that includes those other vertices that v_i is connected to. Create an adjacency structure for any graph, directed or undirected. For example, consider the graph gr below.

In[9]:= **gr = RandomGraph[{8, 12}, VertexLabels → "Name"]**

Out[9]=

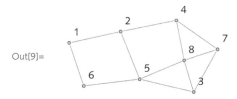

Start by creating an adjacency list for any given vertex; that is, a list of those vertices to which the given vertex is connected. For example, the adjacency list for vertex 8 in the above graph would be:

{3, 4, 5, 7}

The adjacency structure is then the list of adjacency lists for every vertex in that graph. It is common to prepend each adjacency list with its vertex; typically the adjacency structure takes the following form where this syntax indicates that vertex 1 is connected to vertices 2 and 6; vertex 2 is connected to vertices 1, 4, and 5; and so on.

{{1, {2, 6}}, {2, {1, 4, 5}}, {3, {5, 7, 8}}, {4, {2, 7, 8}}, {5, {2, 3, 6, 8}}, {6, {1, 5}}, {7, {3, 4, 8}}, {8, {3, 4, 5, 7}}}

10. Use FoldList to compute an exponential moving average of a list $\{x_1, x_2, x_3\}$. You can check your result against the built-in ExponentialMovingAverage.

In[10]:= **ExponentialMovingAverage[{x_1, x_2, x_3}, α]**

Out[10]= {x_1, $x_1 + \alpha (-x_1 + x_2)$, $x_1 + \alpha (-x_1 + x_2) + \alpha (-x_1 - \alpha (-x_1 + x_2) + x_3)$}

11. A well-known programming exercise in many languages is to generate Hamming numbers, sometimes referred to as *regular numbers*. These are numbers that divide powers of 60 (the choice of that number goes back to the Babylonians who used 60 as a number base). Generate a sorted sequence of all Hamming numbers less than 1000. The key observation is that these numbers have only 2, 3, and 5 as prime factors.

5.7   Options and messages

When developing programs that will be used by your colleagues, students, or customers, it is always a good idea to think about the user interface to your code. That is, how will the user figure out the correct syntax, how will they get helpful information, and so on. The easier it is for a user (including yourself!) to actually use your code, the more likely it is to be used for its intended purpose. One of the hallmarks of modern languages is that they provide a framework for you to apply standard design principles making it easier to develop programs that look and behave in a consistent manner. One of the pieces of this framework is a mechanism for passing messages when a bad argument is given or a certain condition occurs. Another piece is using optional arguments, or options, to modify the default behavior of your functions. In this section we discuss how you can set up your functions so that they inherit this framework, making them behave just like built-in *Mathematica* functions in terms of argument structure and messaging.

Options

When writing your own programs, it is often difficult to predict how a user will interact with them. You might, for example, write separate functions to handle special cases, but the problem with having a separate function for each special case is that the user can soon become overloaded with the variety of functions to learn. A cleaner approach, one used by the built-in functions in *Mathematica*, is to use optional arguments to specify some variant or special case rather than to have a separate function for each such case. In this section, we will show how to write options for your functions so that they behave like the built-in options in *Mathematica*.

When you create a function, generally you design the argument structure in such a way that it covers the most common cases for which you intended to use this function. For example, given the required arguments, the `Plot` function returns a basic plot.

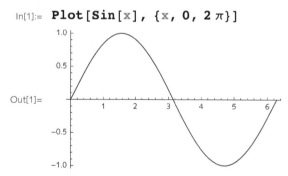

```
In[1]:= Plot[Sin[x], {x, 0, 2 π}]
```

But there is also a mechanism for overriding the default behavior by specifying optional arguments, or simply, *options*. Options are specified following any required arguments and are generally given as a rule: *optionname* → *value*.

In[2]:= `Plot[Sin[x], {x, 0, 2 π},`
`GridLines → Automatic,`
`Frame → True]`

Out[2]=

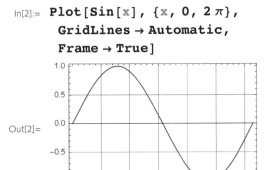

This provides a consistent framework for modifying the default behavior of the built-in functions. Below we will outline this framework and then start to put it into action at the end of this chapter in Section 5.8 and then again repeatedly in later chapters.

The first part of the framework is to declare that a function will have optional arguments and identify their names and default values. For example, the following indicates that a function named `myFun` will have two optional arguments, `opt1` and `opt2` and declares their default values to be α and β, respectively.

In[3]:= `Options[myFun] = {opt1 → α, opt2 → β}`

Out[3]= $\{opt1 \rightarrow \alpha, opt2 \rightarrow \beta\}$

The second piece of the options framework is to set up the argument structure to allow for optional arguments. This is done by using `OptionsPattern` following any required arguments. So in the example below, the required argument is `x` and this statement indicates that some number (possibly zero) of optional arguments will follow that required argument.

`myFun[x_, OptionsPattern[]] := …`

The third piece of the framework is using `OptionsValue` to extract the value of a given option in the function definition.

In[4]:= `myFun[x_, OptionsPattern[]] :=`
`2 x + 3 OptionValue[opt1] + 4 OptionValue[opt2]`

Let us try it out, first with default values for the options.

In[5]:= `myFun[a]`

Out[5]= $2 a + 3 \alpha + 4 \beta$

Now exercise the options.

In[6]:= `myFun[a, opt1 → x, opt2 → y]`

Out[6]= $2 a + 3 x + 4 y$

So far, so good, but let us use the options framework to do something a bit more interesting. There are many times when it would be useful to use, or inherit, some or all the options from a built-in function. This saves time and effort in that the structure already is in place, you just need to borrow it. Fortunately, this is quite straightforward using `Options`. We will create a function `StemPlot` that inherits options from `ListPlot` and displays discrete data as stems; that is, points of height specified by the values of the data with lines drawn to the axis.

```
In[7]:= Options[StemPlot] = Options[ListPlot];
        StemPlot[lis_, opts : OptionsPattern[]] :=
         ListPlot[lis, opts, Filling → Axis]
```

We named the optional arguments `opts` so that we can slot whatever options are given into `ListPlot`. This is done by having `opts` precede any other options we wish to use. This way the user-passed options, appearing first, will override any similarly named options that come later.

```
In[9]:= StemPlot[Range[12]]
```

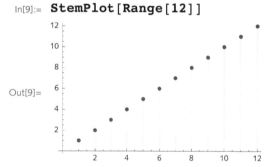

Here we exercise some of the options, all inherited from `ListPlot`.

```
In[10]:= StemPlot[Range[8], Filling → 4,
          FillingStyle → {{Purple, Dashed}}, Frame → True,
          PlotLabel → Style["A stem plot", "Menu"]]
```

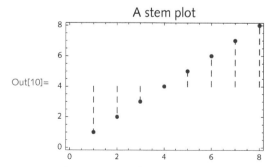

As an alternative to how we set up the options for `StemPlot`, you could also set up the inheritance of the options directly in the definition for your function, rather than using a separate `Options[...] = ...` statement.

```
In[11]:= StemPlot[lis_, opts : OptionsPattern[ListPlot]] :=
         ListPlot[lis, opts, Filling → Axis]
```

At the end of Section 9.5 in the example on displaying DNA sequences and again in the visualization functions in Section 10.4 we will look at some variations of this options framework in which you can mix options from different functions.

Messages

When you give an invalid argument to a *Mathematica* function, it returns a warning message.

```
In[12]:= Inverse[{1.2, 2.3, 4.5}]
```

Inverse::matsq : Argument {1.2, 2.3, 4.5} at position 1 is not a non−empty square matrix. ≫

```
Out[12]= Inverse[{1.2, 2.3, 4.5}]
```

You can set up your own functions to do likewise. The basic framework is: define the message and then use a rule to issue the message under the appropriate conditions.

Let us set up a message for the simple function `CompositeQ` discussed in Section 5.3. Here is the original definition.

```
In[13]:= CompositeQ[n_Integer /; n > 1] := Not[PrimeQ[n]]
```

As written, this function returns unevaluated for any argument that does not match the pattern `n_Integer /; n > 1`. It is a good candidate for a warning message when it is given arguments that do not match this pattern.

```
In[14]:= CompositeQ[π]
```

```
Out[14]= CompositeQ[π]
```

We would like to set up a message that is issued whenever a bad argument is passed to `CompositeQ`. Messages have names of the form *symbol::tag*, where *symbol* is the symbol with which you want to associate the message. The *tag* should be chosen to reflect the purpose of the message. So in our case we will create a message `CompositeQ::badarg`.

```
In[15]:= CompositeQ::badarg =
         "Bad argument to CompositeQ. It should be
            an integer greater than 1.";
```

To issue this message, we create a general rule that covers all arguments other than integers greater than 1 which is covered by the rule we wrote above.

```
In[16]:= CompositeQ[n_] := Message[CompositeQ::badarg]
```

```
In[17]:= CompositeQ[π]
```

CompositeQ::badarg : Bad argument to CompositeQ. It should be an integer greater than 1.

So far, so good. We could go a bit further and pass the bad argument itself into the message. Built-in functions do this automatically.

In[18]:= **FactorInteger[π]**

> FactorInteger::exact : Argument π in FactorInteger[π] is not an exact number. ≫

Out[18]= FactorInteger[π]

This is accomplished by using `` `1` `` to indicate the position in the string to slot in a value. Then use a two-argument form of **Message** to issue the warning with a value slotted into the string.

In[19]:= **CompositeQ::badarg =**
        "Argument `1` in CompositeQ[`1`] is not an
            integer greater than 1.";

In[20]:= **CompositeQ[$n\_$] := Message[CompositeQ::badarg, n]**

In[21]:= **CompositeQ[π]**

> CompositeQ::badarg : Argument π in CompositeQ[π] is not an integer greater than 1.

We can go one step further and create a more general rule, one that could cover more than one argument or more complicated argument structures and, in addition to issuing the warning, also return the input unevaluated. The **If** statement below checks to see if the argument, n, is an integer greater than 1. If it is, the **If** statement returns **True**, the conditional is satisfied, and the right-hand side of the definition will be invoked. If the argument is not an integer greater than 1, then the message is issued and **False** is returned to the condition, making the pattern match fail (which causes the input to be returned), and so the right-hand side is not evaluated.

In[22]:= **Clear[CompositeQ]**

In[23]:= **CompositeQ[$n\_$] /; If[TrueQ[Head[n] == Integer && n > 1], True,**
            Message[CompositeQ::badarg, n]; False] := Not@PrimeQ[n]

In[24]:= **CompositeQ[π]**

> CompositeQ::badarg : Argument π in CompositeQ[π] is not an integer greater than 1.

Out[24]= CompositeQ[π]

In[25]:= **CompositeQ[{a, b, c}]**

> CompositeQ::badarg :
>   Argument {a, b, c} in CompositeQ[{a, b, c}] is not an integer greater than 1.

Out[25]= CompositeQ[{a, b, c}]

Of course, you could have multiple messages associated with any symbol by writing another *symbol* **::** *tag* and modifying your code appropriately. This is what functions like `Inverse` do for the various arguments that could be given.

In[26]:= **Inverse[{a, b, c}]**

  Inverse::matsq : Argument {a, b, c} at position 1 is not a non−empty square matrix. ≫

Out[26]= **Inverse** [{a, b, c}]

In[27]:= **Inverse[{{a, b}, {a, b}}]**

  Inverse::sing : Matrix {{a, b}, {a, b}} is singular. ≫

Out[27]= **Inverse** [{{a, b}, {a, b}}]

Exercises

1. In Section 5.5 we developed a function `switchRows` that interchanged two rows in a matrix. Create a message for this function that is issued whenever a row index greater than the size of the matrix is used as an argument. For example,

In[1]:= **mat = RandomInteger[{0, 9}, {4, 4}];**
       MatrixForm[mat]

Out[2]//MatrixForm=
$$\begin{pmatrix} 5 & 7 & 5 & 9 \\ 3 & 5 & 2 & 6 \\ 4 & 4 & 5 & 8 \\ 5 & 6 & 7 & 1 \end{pmatrix}$$

In[3]:= **switchRows[mat, {5, 2}]**

  switchRows::badargs :
      The absolute value of the row indices 5 and 2 in switchRows[*mat*,{5,2}] must
          be between 1 and 4, the size of the matrix.

Out[3]= {{5, 7, 5, 9}, {3, 5, 2, 6}, {4, 4, 5, 8}, {5, 6, 7, 1}}

You should also trap for a row index of 0.

In[4]:= **switchRows[mat, {0, 2}]**

  switchRows::badargs :
      The absolute value of the row indices 0 and 2 in switchRows[*mat*,{0,2}] must
          be between 1 and 4, the size of the matrix.

Out[4]= {{5, 7, 5, 9}, {3, 5, 2, 6}, {4, 4, 5, 8}, {5, 6, 7, 1}}

2. Create an error message for `StemPlot`, developed in this section, so that an appropriate message is issued if the argument is not a list of numbers.

5.8 Examples and applications

In this section we will put several of the concepts we have explored to work in solving concrete, real-world problems. Some of these solutions are short and avoid the use of auxiliary function definitions – so-called *one-liners*. Others require localization constructs and auxiliary function definitions. The examples include a problem from signal processing on computing Hamming distance; one from ancient history, the Josephus problem; a graphical problem on the creation and display of regular polygons; a practical problem involving the creation of a palette to open files from a project directory; and a data processing problem on cleaning/filtering arrays of data in which the notion of modular programs is discussed.

Hamming distance

When a signal is transmitted over a channel in the presence of noise, errors often occur. A major concern in telecommunications is measuring (and of course, trying to minimize) that error. For two lists of binary symbols, the Hamming distance is defined as the number of nonmatching elements and so gives a measure of how well these two lists of binary digits match up. In this first example, we will create a function to compute the Hamming distance of a binary signal.

Let us first think about how we might determine if two binary numbers are identical. Various tests of equality are available. SameQ $[x, y]$ will return True if x and y are identical. It differs from Equal (==) in that, for numbers, Equal tests for numerical equality within a certain tolerance, but SameQ is testing for identical structures.

```
In[1]:=  SameQ[0, 0.0]
Out[1]=  False
```

```
In[2]:=  Equal[0, 0.0]
Out[2]=  True
```

Here is what SameQ returns for the different pairings of binary numbers.

```
In[3]:=  {SameQ[0, 0], SameQ[1, 0], SameQ[1, 1]}
Out[3]=  {True, False, True}
```

So we need to thread SameQ over the two lists of binary numbers,

```
In[4]:=  MapThread[SameQ, {{1, 0, 0, 1, 1}, {0, 1, 0, 1, 0}}]
Out[4]=  {False, False, True, True, False}
```

and then count up the occurrences of False.

```
In[5]:=  Count[%, False]
Out[5]=  3
```

Putting these last two pieces together, we have our first definition for Hamming distance.

```
In[6]:= HammingDistance1[lis1_, lis2_] :=
          Count[MapThread[SameQ, {lis1, lis2}], False]
```

```
In[7]:= HammingDistance1[{1, 0, 0, 1, 1}, {0, 1, 0, 1, 0}]
```

Out[7]= 3

We might also try to solve this problem by a more direct approach. Since we are dealing with binary information, we will use some of the logical binary operators built into *Mathematica*. BitXor [*x*, *y*] returns the bitwise XOR of *x* and *y*. So if *x* and *y* can only be among the binary integers 0 or 1, BitXor will return 0 whenever they are the same and will return 1 whenever they are different. Note that BitXor is listable and so automatically threads over lists.

```
In[8]:= BitXor[{1, 0, 0, 1, 1}, {0, 1, 0, 1, 0}]
```

Out[8]= {1, 1, 0, 0, 1}

And here are the number of 1s that occur in that list.

```
In[9]:= Total[%]
```

Out[9]= 3

Here then is our bit-operator based version for the Hamming distance computation.

```
In[10]:= HammingDistance2[lis1_, lis2_] := Total[BitXor[lis1, lis2]]
```

```
In[11]:= HammingDistance2[{1, 0, 0, 1, 1}, {0, 1, 0, 1, 0}]
```

Out[11]= 3

Let us compare the running times of these implementations using a large data set, in this case two lists consisting of one million 0s and 1s.

```
In[12]:= sig1 = RandomInteger[1, {10^6}];
```

```
In[13]:= sig2 = RandomInteger[1, {10^6}];
```

```
In[14]:= Timing[HammingDistance1[sig1, sig2]]
```

Out[14]= {0.497098, 499 922}

```
In[15]:= Timing[HammingDistance2[sig1, sig2]]
```

Out[15]= {0.007763, 499 922}

That is quite a difference in the efficiency of these two approaches! Using bit operators gives a speedup of almost two orders of magnitude. We will leave a discussion of the causes of this difference until Chapter 12. There are numerous other approaches that you might consider – the exercises ask you to write implementations of `HammingDistance` that use `Select` and `Cases` and also one using modular arithmetic.

As an aside, the above computations are not a bad check on the built-in random number generator – we would expect that about one-half of the paired-up lists would contain different elements.

The Josephus problem

Flavius Josephus (37 – *ca*. 100 AD) was a Jewish historian who fought in the Roman–Jewish war of the first century AD. Through his writings comes the following story; see Herstein and Kaplansky (1978) or Graham, Knuth, and Patashnik (1994):

> *The Romans had chased a group of ten Jews into a cave and were about to attack. Rather than die at the hands of their enemy, the group chose to commit suicide one by one. Legend has it though, that they decided to go around their circle of ten individuals and eliminate every other person until only one was left.*

The Josephus problem is stated simply: who was the last to survive? Although a bit macabre, this problem has a definite mathematical interpretation that lends itself well to a functional style of programming. We will start by changing the problem a bit (the importance of rewording a problem can hardly be overstated; the key to most problem-solving resides in turning something we cannot work with into something we can). We will restate the problem as follows: n people are lined up; the first person is moved to the end of the line; the second person is removed from the line; the third person is moved to the end of the line; and so on until only one person remains in the line.

The statement of the problem indicates that there is a repetitive action, performed over and over again. It can be encoded with the `RotateLeft` function (move the person at the front of the line to the back of the line) followed by the use of the `Rest` function (remove the next person from the line).

In[16]:= **`Rest[RotateLeft[{a, b, c, d}]]`**

Out[16]= `{c, d, a}`

At this point it should be fairly clear where this computation is headed. We want to take a list and, using the `Nest` function, iterate the pure function `Rest[RotateLeft[#]]` & until only one element remains. A list of n elements will need $n - 1$ iterations. We will create the list of n elements using `Range[n]`. Here then is the function `survivor`.

In[17]:= **`survivor[n_] := Nest[Rest[RotateLeft[#]] &, Range[n], n - 1]`**

Trying out the `survivor` function on a list of ten, we see that the survivor is the fifth starting position.

```
In[18]:= survivor[10]
```

Out[18]= {5}

Tracing the applications of `RotateLeft` in this example gives a clear picture of what is happening. Using `TracePrint` with a second argument shows only the results of the applications of `RotateLeft` that occur during evaluation of the expression `survivor[6]`.

```
In[19]:= TracePrint[survivor[6], RotateLeft]
            RotateLeft
            {2, 3, 4, 5, 6, 1}
            RotateLeft
            {4, 5, 6, 1, 3}
            RotateLeft
            {6, 1, 3, 5}
            RotateLeft
            {3, 5, 1}
            RotateLeft
            {1, 5}
```

Out[19]= {5}

And, of course, you could generate the list of survivors at each round by using `NestList` instead of `Nest`.

```
In[20]:= With[{n = 6}, NestList[Rest[RotateLeft[#]] &, Range[n], n - 1]]
```

Out[20]= {{1, 2, 3, 4, 5, 6}, {3, 4, 5, 6, 1},
            {5, 6, 1, 3}, {1, 3, 5}, {5, 1}, {5}}

Regular graphs/polygons

Section 1.1 included some brief code to create and display regular polygons from points equally spaced on a circle. Here we will use some of the built-in graph machinery together with several functional programming constructs to create an alternative implementation. The advantage of this approach is that we can then take advantage of the style and formatting functionality built into `Graph` objects.

Let us start by creating a regular pentagon. Whereas the code in Section 1.1 identified the vertices spatially as coordinates in the plane, graphs identify the vertices by their index; a graph with five vertices labels them 1, 2, 3, 4, 5.

In[21]:= **Range[5]**

Out[21]= {1, 2, 3, 4, 5}

We need to connect vertex 1 to vertex 2, vertex 2 to vertex 3, and so on. This is done by partitioning this list of five vertices into overlapping pairs. The last argument to **Partition** indicates that the list is cyclic.

In[22]:= **pairs = Partition[Range[5], 2, 1, 1]**

Out[22]= {{1, 2}, {2, 3}, {3, 4}, {4, 5}, {5, 1}}

We next turn each pair of vertices into an (undirected) edge. Note the need to apply **UndirectedEdge** at level 1.

In[23]:= **Apply[UndirectedEdge, pairs, {1}]**

Out[23]= {1 ↔ 2, 2 ↔ 3, 3 ↔ 4, 4 ↔ 5, 5 ↔ 1}

Then, we turn the rules into a graph object that will display as a polygon.

In[24]:= **Graph[%]**

Out[24]=

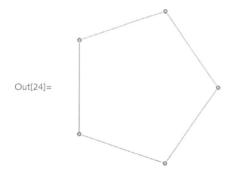

Finally, we put all the above pieces together to create a reusable function, adding several **Graph** options to stylize the graph.

In[25]:= **RegularGraph[*n_Integer*] := Graph[**
        Apply[UndirectedEdge, Partition[Range[*n*], 2, 1, 1], {1}],
        VertexSize → 0.002, EdgeStyle → Thick]

In[26]:= **RegularGraph[5]**

Out[26]=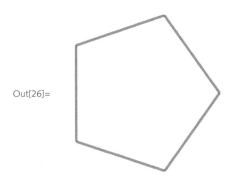

In the above implementation, we have hard-coded the two options, `VertexSize` and `EdgeStyle`. That is fine for the default representation, but let us take advantage of all the rich formatting and stylistic functionality built into `Graph` objects. This is done by passing the options for `Graph` to our `RegularGraph` function.

Let us also try a different approach to constructing the vertex rules, using `MapThread`. First, we rotate the original list one position to the left.

In[27]:= **lis = Range[5];**
        pairs = {lis, RotateLeft[lis]}

Out[28]= {{1, 2, 3, 4, 5}, {2, 3, 4, 5, 1}}

Then we thread `UndirectedEdge` over these paired vertices.

In[29]:= **MapThread[UndirectedEdge, pairs]**

Out[29]= {1 ⟷ 2, 2 ⟷ 3, 3 ⟷ 4, 4 ⟷ 5, 5 ⟷ 1}

Using the options framework introduced in Section 5.7, set up `RegularGraph` to inherit all the options of `Graph`.

In[30]:= **Options[RegularGraph] = Options[Graph];**

In[31]:= **RandomSample[Options[RegularGraph], 8]**

Out[31]= {AspectRatio → Automatic, AxesOrigin → Automatic,
        VertexLabels → Automatic, FrameTicksStyle → {},
        Properties → {}, GraphLayout → Automatic,
        BaselinePosition → Automatic, EdgeStyle → Automatic}

We use the localization construct `With` here as the list of vertices, `verts`, is really a constant, an expression that does not change in the body of the function.

```
In[32]:= RegularGraph[n_Integer, opts : OptionsPattern[]] :=
     With[{verts = Range[n]},
       Graph[
         MapThread[UndirectedEdge, {verts, RotateLeft[verts]}],
         opts,
         VertexSize → 0.002, EdgeStyle → Thick]]
```

Here then is a regular pentagon, displayed as a graph, using a variety of options to stylize the output.

```
In[33]:= RegularGraph[5, VertexSize → Small,
     VertexStyle → Red, VertexLabels → "Name",
     VertexLabelStyle → Directive["Menu", 8]]
```

Out[33]=

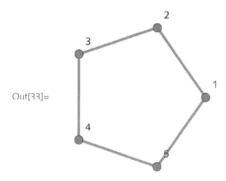

Representing these objects as graphs provides not only styling and labeling options, but also gives access to functions for operating on and measuring graphs. For example, a quick check shows that regular graphs are *2-regular*, meaning that every vertex has two edges.

```
In[34]:= VertexDegree[RegularGraph[5]]
```

```
Out[34]= {2, 2, 2, 2, 2}
```

Or you can determine if another graph is isomorphic to a regular graph.

```
In[35]:= IsomorphicGraphQ[RegularGraph[4], HypercubeGraph[2]]
```

```
Out[35]= True
```

As an aside, the built-in `CycleGraph[n]` returns a similar object.

In[36]:= **CycleGraph[5, VertexLabels → "Name"]**

Out[36]=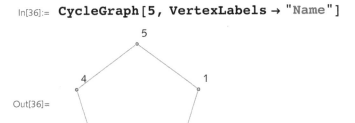

Protein interaction networks

Proteins interact with other proteins in biological processes as varied as DNA replication, signal transduction, movement of molecules into and between cells, and essentially all processes in living cells. In fact, signal transduction, a process in which proteins control the signaling into and out of the cell, is key to the study of diseases including many cancers. Their importance in all cellular activity has given rise to active work in the visualization of these protein-protein interactions (PPIs). In this section, we will combine some of the functional constructs, pattern matching, and graph tools to visualize proteins within networks that have a high level of interaction.

We will work with proteins from the worm *Caenorhabditis elegans*, a heavily studied organism (Worm Interactome Database). The data, courtesy of Dana-Farber Cancer Institute and Harvard Medical School, are in the form of a text file. This imports that file from the internet and displays the first twelve entries.

In[37]:= **data = Import[
        "http://interactome.dfci.harvard.edu/C_elegans/graphs/
        sequence_edges/wi2007.txt", "TSV"];**

In[38]:= **Take[data, 12]**

Out[38]= {{#IDA, IDB}, {AC3.3, F29G6.3}, {AC3.3, R05F9.10},
        {AC3.3, Y69H2.3}, {AC3.7, Y40B10A.2}, {B0001.4, F19B6.1},
        {B0001.7, B0281.5}, {B0001.7, F37H8.1},
        {B0024.10, C06A1.1}, {B0024.12, C06E2.1},
        {B0024.14, B0228.1}, {B0024.14, C05G6.1}}

The data are of the form {*protein*$_1$, *protein*$_2$} indicating an interaction between these two named proteins. Using the function **ToGraph**, developed in Exercise 4 of Section 5.2, we turn these lists into edges, where each edge represents an interaction between two proteins (vertices).

In[39]:= **ToGraph[*lis* : {{_, _} ..}] := Apply[DirectedEdge, *lis*, {1}]**

In[40]:= **ToGraph[*lis* : {_, _}] := Apply[DirectedEdge, *lis*]**

In[41]:= **ToGraph[Take[data, 12]]**

Out[41]= {♯IDA ↦ IDB, AC3.3 ↦ F29G6.3, AC3.3 ↦ R05F9.10,
          AC3.3 ↦ Y69H2.3, AC3.7 ↦ Y40B10A.2, B0001.4 ↦ F19B6.1,
          B0001.7 ↦ B0281.5, B0001.7 ↦ F37H8.1, B0024.10 ↦ C06A1.1,
          B0024.12 ↦ C06E2.1, B0024.14 ↦ B0228.1, B0024.14 ↦ C05G6.1}

We need to delete the first entry ("♯IDA" ↦ "IDB") which is meant as a comment. So we use ToGraph on Rest[data] and then visualize the result with Graph.

In[42]:= **edgerules = ToGraph[Rest[data]];**
         gr = Graph[edgerules]

Out[43]=

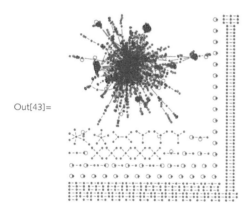

It is a fairly dense graph showing all the protein interactions, and, as a result, it is a bit difficult to discern detail. Many of the interactions involve only two proteins as seen in the small components on the right and bottom of the above output. Our task in this example is to find the subgraph consisting of all those proteins with at least *n* interactions with other proteins. We will take *n* = 12; that is, proteins that have at least 12 interactions with other proteins.

The vertices (the proteins) are strings.

In[44]:= **vertices = VertexList[gr];**
         Take[vertices, 5] // FullForm

Out[45]//FullForm=
         List["AC3.3", "F29G6.3", "R05F9.10", "Y69H2.3", "AC3.7"]

VertexDegree[gr, *vertex*] gives the number of edges incident to *vertex* in graph *gr*. So in our protein network, the vertex degree for vertex v_i gives the number of interactions between that protein represented by v_i and all other proteins.

In[46]:= **VertexDegree[gr, "R05F9.10"]**

Out[46]= 86

A slightly different syntax for `VertexDegree` gives the degree for every vertex in the graph. So from the tally below, vertices with one edge occur 933 times in this network, vertices with two edges occur 246 times, and so on. There is only one vertex with 86 edges.

In[47]:= **SortBy[Tally@VertexDegree[gr], First]**

Out[47]= {{1, 933}, {2, 246}, {3, 107}, {4, 64}, {5, 40}, {6, 21},
{7, 19}, {8, 6}, {9, 10}, {10, 6}, {11, 2}, {12, 11}, {13, 2},
{14, 1}, {15, 2}, {16, 3}, {17, 2}, {18, 2}, {19, 3},
{21, 2}, {23, 1}, {24, 2}, {28, 1}, {30, 1}, {31, 3},
{39, 1}, {44, 1}, {45, 1}, {47, 1}, {49, 1}, {86, 1}}

To extract all those vertices that have a vertex degree greater than 12, use `Select` with the appropriate predicate.

In[48]:= **Select[VertexList[gr], (VertexDegree[gr, #] > 12 &)]**

Out[48]= {R05F9.10, Y69H2.3, Y40B10A.2, DH11.4, K09B11.9, R02F2.5,
ZK1053.5, W05H7.4, C18G1.2, T11B7.1, F52E1.7, F46A9.5,
Y54E2A.3, ZK858.4, C50F4.1, K12C11.2, C06G1.5, Y65B4BR.4,
F32B4.4, ZK849.2, C36C9.1, ZK1055.7, C06A5.9, W09C2.1, F44G3.9,
ZK121.2, M04G12.1, T21G5.5, W10C8.2, F01G10.2, Y55F3C.6}

Or, we thread the inequality over the list of vertex degrees and pick those vertices for which this inequality is true.

In[49]:= **proteins = Pick[VertexList[gr], Thread[VertexDegree[gr] > 12]]**

Out[49]= {R05F9.10, Y69H2.3, Y40B10A.2, DH11.4, K09B11.9, R02F2.5,
ZK1053.5, W05H7.4, C18G1.2, T11B7.1, F52E1.7, F46A9.5,
Y54E2A.3, ZK858.4, C50F4.1, K12C11.2, C06G1.5, Y65B4BR.4,
F32B4.4, ZK849.2, C36C9.1, ZK1055.7, C06A5.9, W09C2.1, F44G3.9,
ZK121.2, M04G12.1, T21G5.5, W10C8.2, F01G10.2, Y55F3C.6}

`Thread` is needed here because `Greater` (>) is not listable.

In[50]:= **{1, 2, 3, 4} > 3**

Out[50]= {1, 2, 3, 4} > 3

In[51]:= **Attributes[Greater]**

Out[51]= {Protected}

Note that `Thread` can thread over two expressions that are not the same structurally, as in our example here.

In[52]:= **Thread[{1, 2, 3, 4} > 3]**

Out[52]= {False, False, False, True}

Now we get all those interactions that involve `proteins` as defined above.

```
In[53]:= edges = Cases[EdgeList[gr], (p1_ ⇸ p2_) /;
             MemberQ[proteins, p1] && MemberQ[proteins, p2], Infinity];
```

```
In[54]:= Take[edges, 12]
```

```
Out[54]= {C06A5.9 ⇸ C36C9.1, C06A5.9 ⇸ DH11.4, C06A5.9 ⇸ F44G3.9,
          C06G1.5 ⇸ DH11.4, C06G1.5 ⇸ F32B4.4, C06G1.5 ⇸ K09B11.9,
          C06G1.5 ⇸ W05H7.4, C06G1.5 ⇸ Y54E2A.3, C06G1.5 ⇸ ZK121.2,
          C06G1.5 ⇸ ZK849.2, C36C9.1 ⇸ K09B11.9, C36C9.1 ⇸ Y54E2A.3}
```

We delete self-loops (although proteins certainly can interact with themselves).

```
In[55]:= gr1 = DeleteCases[edges, x_ ⇸ x_];
         Take[gr1, 12]
```

```
Out[56]= {C06A5.9 ⇸ C36C9.1, C06A5.9 ⇸ DH11.4, C06A5.9 ⇸ F44G3.9,
          C06G1.5 ⇸ DH11.4, C06G1.5 ⇸ F32B4.4, C06G1.5 ⇸ K09B11.9,
          C06G1.5 ⇸ W05H7.4, C06G1.5 ⇸ Y54E2A.3, C06G1.5 ⇸ ZK121.2,
          C06G1.5 ⇸ ZK849.2, C36C9.1 ⇸ K09B11.9, C36C9.1 ⇸ Y54E2A.3}
```

Finally, we use `Graph` and several options to visualize this PPI.

```
In[57]:= Graph[gr1, VertexStyle → Red, VertexSize → Large,
         VertexLabels → "Name", VertexStyle → Directive[Orange],
         GraphLayout → "CircularEmbedding",
         EdgeShapeFunction → "CarvedArrow"]
```

Out[57]=
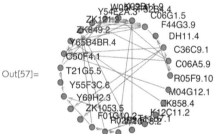

The exercises include an extension of this PPI visualization in which you are asked to color the vertices according to that protein's biological processes.

Palettes for project files

In this next example we will use the functional constructs developed in this chapter to create a palette of hyperlinks to files in a given directory. This is particularly useful if you are working on a project consisting of numerous files, all of which live in the same location.

Let us start by getting a list of files from a project directory. We will use the notebook files (`"*.nb"`) from the directory PwM. You could choose any directory containing your project notebooks. In this case we will only work with the first nine files in this directory. The palette will consist of a column of buttons, one for each file.

```
In[58]:= dir = FileNameJoin[{$BaseDirectory, "Applications", "PwM"}];
         files = Take[FileNames["*.nb", dir], 9]
```

```
Out[59]= {/Library/Mathematica/Applications/PwM/01Introduction.nb,
          /Library/Mathematica/Applications/PwM/02Language.nb,
          /Library/Mathematica/Applications/PwM/03Lists.nb,
          /Library/Mathematica/Applications/PwM/04PatternsAndRules.nb,
          /Library/Mathematica/Applications/PwM/05Functions.nb,
          /Library/Mathematica/Applications/PwM/06Procedural.nb,
          /Library/Mathematica/Applications/PwM/07Recursion.nb,
          /Library/Mathematica/Applications/PwM/08Numerics.nb,
          /Library/Mathematica/Applications/PwM/09Strings.nb}
```

Hyperlink has a two-argument form: the first argument is the label, the second argument is the target file for that label.

```
In[60]:= ? Hyperlink
```

> Hyperlink[*uri*] represents a hyperlink that jumps to the specified URI when clicked.
>
> Hyperlink[*label*, *uri*] represents a hyperlink to be displayed as *label*. ≫

So we will need to create a list of labels corresponding to our list of files. As a label for each button, we will use the basic file name, as given by FileBaseName.

```
In[61]:= labels = Map[FileBaseName, files]
```

```
Out[61]= {01Introduction, 02Language, 03Lists, 04PatternsAndRules,
          05Functions, 06Procedural, 07Recursion, 08Numerics, 09Strings}
```

Now, we thread Hyperlink over the labels and files. Note the use of a pure function to slot in each label and file in the correct location.

```
In[62]:= MapThread[Hyperlink[#1, #2] &, {labels, files}]
```

```
Out[62]= {01Introduction, 02Language, 03Lists, 04PatternsAndRules,
          05Functions, 06Procedural, 07Recursion, 08Numerics, 09Strings}
```

Although it is not obvious in print, the above list consists of hyperlinks to each of the files. Clicking any of these links will open the corresponding file.

Now let us create a palette of these links. We wrap the list of links in Column to give a vertical list of buttons.

```
In[63]:= CreatePalette[
           Column[MapThread[Hyperlink[#1, #2] &, {labels, files}]]];
```

Here is a screenshot of this palette.

With a little more work, we can add some styles to the links as well as options to `Hyperlink`, `Column`, and `CreatePalette`.

```
In[64]:= linkStyles = {FontSize → 14, FontColor → White};
        linkOpts = {ImageSize → {Automatic, 16}};
        colOpts = {Background → Darker@Gray, Dividers → All};
        palOpts = {WindowTitle → "File Palette",
            WindowElements → "MagnificationPopUp"};
```

```
In[68]:= CreatePalette[Column[
            MapThread[Hyperlink[Style[#1, linkStyles], #2, linkOpts] &,
                {labels, files}], colOpts], palOpts];
```

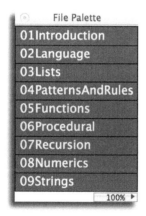

Operating on arrays

Up to this point, many of the examples we have worked through resulted in short programs, either what are often called "one-liners" or simply short, self-contained programs. One of the advantages of such an approach is that everything you might need to run the program is contained in the body of your function. Although it may seem convenient to put all auxiliary definitions into the body of a function, there are several good reasons not to do so. One large chunk of code with many definitions embedded is often difficult to debug. Running the program may fail with several warning or error messages displayed and no clear indication at which line in your program the problem lies. The same holds for a program that returns an incorrect result. Another issue has to do with efficiency. If your program takes longer than you think it should to run, how do you locate the bottleneck?

Modern programming design uses a modular concept to break up computational or programmatic tasks into small separate chunks and then put the pieces together in one program in such a way that you can isolate each part and diagnose errors or inefficient code more readily. Although we have been trying to adhere to this approach implicitly up to this point, in this section we will explicitly look at how a modular approach is implemented in *Mathematica*, using a matrix-processing example: replacing "bad" entries in a matrix with the column mean.

In working with tabular data collected by an instrument or by some other means, you occasionally find nonnumeric values (strings, for example) in the matrix where either the instrument has failed to collect a datum point for some reason or the value is "out of range." If an analysis of the matrix depends upon numeric values, what should be used to replace the nonnumeric values? One solution is to replace them with the column mean; that is, take the column in which the nonnumeric value occurs, compute the column mean using only the numeric values, and then replace the nonnumeric value with this mean.

To prototype, we will use a small matrix of integers, making it easier to check our work along the way.

$$
\text{In[69]:= } \mathbf{mat} = \begin{pmatrix} 44 & 72 & 6 & \texttt{"NAN"} \\ \texttt{"NAN"} & 46 & 28 & 75 \\ 19 & 10 & 40 & 2 \\ 99 & 98 & \texttt{"NAN"} & 47 \end{pmatrix};
$$

First, extract and work on the first column and then later extend this to all the other columns.

```
In[70]:= col1 = mat[[All, 1]];
         MatrixForm[col1]
```

Out[71]//MatrixForm=

$$
\begin{pmatrix} 44 \\ \text{NAN} \\ 19 \\ 99 \end{pmatrix}
$$

We need to extract just the numeric values. `Cases`, with the appropriate pattern, will do that. Several approaches using different patterns could be used.

In[72]:= **Cases[col1, _?NumberQ]**

Out[72]= {44, 19, 99}

In[73]:= **Cases[col1, Except[_String]]**

Out[73]= {44, 19, 99}

Then compute the mean of these numeric values.

In[74]:= **Mean[Cases[col1, _?NumberQ]]**

Out[74]= 54

Replace the string "NAN" with the mean.

In[75]:= **col1 /. "NAN" → Mean[Cases[col1, _?NumberQ]] // MatrixForm**

Out[75]//MatrixForm=

$$\begin{pmatrix} 44 \\ 54 \\ 19 \\ 99 \end{pmatrix}$$

This operation needs to be performed on each column so we write a function that will be mapped across the columns of a matrix.

In[76]:= **colMean[*col_*] := *col* /. "NAN" ⧴ Mean[Cases[*col*, _?NumberQ]]**

In[77]:= **Map[colMean, Transpose[mat]]**

Out[77]= $\Big\{ \{44, 54, 19, 99\}, \{72, 46, 10, 98\},$

$\Big\{6, 28, 40, \dfrac{74}{3}\Big\}, \Big\{\dfrac{124}{3}, 75, 2, 47\Big\}\Big\}$

Since we operated on the columns, the above array is a list of the column vectors. We need to transpose back.

In[78]:= **MatrixForm[Transpose[%]]**

Out[78]//MatrixForm=

$$\begin{pmatrix} 44 & 72 & 6 & \frac{124}{3} \\ 54 & 46 & 28 & 75 \\ 19 & 10 & 40 & 2 \\ 99 & 98 & \frac{74}{3} & 47 \end{pmatrix}$$

Finally, let us put these pieces together:

In[79]:= **ReplaceElement[*mat_*] :=**
     Transpose[Map[colMean, Transpose[*mat*]]]

In[80]:= **ReplaceElement[mat] // MatrixForm**

Out[80]//MatrixForm=

$$\begin{pmatrix} 44 & 72 & 6 & \frac{124}{3} \\ 54 & 46 & 28 & 75 \\ 19 & 10 & 40 & 2 \\ 99 & 98 & \frac{74}{3} & 47 \end{pmatrix}$$

and try it out on a larger matrix of approximate numbers.

In[81]:= **mat =**
$$\begin{pmatrix} 0.737 & "NAN" & -0.2648 & -0.5882 & 0.49 \\ 0.1984 & -0.3382 & -0.5793 & 0.9473 & 0.8809 \\ -0.5538 & 0.5038 & -0.9728 & 0.4061 & "NAN" \\ -0.0839 & 0.8139 & "NAN" & -0.7658 & 0.5081 \\ 0.9343 & 0.6257 & -0.3668 & 0.0851 & -0.8783 \end{pmatrix};$$

In[82]:= **ReplaceElement[mat] // MatrixForm**

Out[82]//MatrixForm=

$$\begin{pmatrix} 0.737 & 0.4013 & -0.2648 & -0.5882 & 0.49 \\ 0.1984 & -0.3382 & -0.5793 & 0.9473 & 0.8809 \\ -0.5538 & 0.5038 & -0.9728 & 0.4061 & 0.250175 \\ -0.0839 & 0.8139 & -0.545925 & -0.7658 & 0.5081 \\ 0.9343 & 0.6257 & -0.3668 & 0.0851 & -0.8783 \end{pmatrix}$$

Perform a quick, manual check on the second column.

In[83]:= **Mean[{-0.3382, 0.5038, 0.8139, 0.6257}]**

Out[83]= 0.4013

With just a few small adjustments, ReplaceElement can work with arbitrary strings, not just "NAN" as above. Instead of the "hard-coded" string "NAN" in columnMean, we introduce a second argument str and use that wherever "NAN" appeared in the previous version.

In[84]:= **colMean[*col_*, *str_String*] :=**
  ***col* /. *str* :→ Mean[Cases[*col*, _?NumberQ]]**

In[85]:= **ReplaceElement[*mat_*, *str_String*] :=**
  Transpose[Map[colMean[#, *str*] &, Transpose[*mat*]]]

Here you can see the real advantage of using modular code. Rather than rewrite the entire program, we make one change to colMean, writing a new rule to accommodate an arbitrary string, and then create a second rule for ReplaceElement with a second argument to specify the string, and replacing colMean with the pure function colMean[#, str] &.

Let us try out the new code.

```
In[86]:= mat2 = {{-0.4444, "N/A", 0.3319, 0.4242, 0.},
         {-0.5088, -0.6955, 0.8398, 0.4287, -0.9319},
         {"N/A", 0.8287, 0.5286, 0.2591, -0.6978},
         {0.6499, 0.4035, -0.099, 0.6052, 0.5332},
         {0.2575, -0.0589, -0.4938, "N/A", -0.5924}};
      MatrixForm[mat2]
```

Out[87]//MatrixForm=

$$
\begin{pmatrix}
-0.4444 & \text{N/A} & 0.3319 & 0.4242 & 0. \\
-0.5088 & -0.6955 & 0.8398 & 0.4287 & -0.9319 \\
\text{N/A} & 0.8287 & 0.5286 & 0.2591 & -0.6978 \\
0.6499 & 0.4035 & -0.099 & 0.6052 & 0.5332 \\
0.2575 & -0.0589 & -0.4938 & \text{N/A} & -0.5924
\end{pmatrix}
$$

```
In[88]:= ReplaceElement[mat2, "N/A"] // MatrixForm
```

Out[88]//MatrixForm=

$$
\begin{pmatrix}
-0.4444 & 0.11945 & 0.3319 & 0.4242 & 0. \\
-0.5088 & -0.6955 & 0.8398 & 0.4287 & -0.9319 \\
-0.01145 & 0.8287 & 0.5286 & 0.2591 & -0.6978 \\
0.6499 & 0.4035 & -0.099 & 0.6052 & 0.5332 \\
0.2575 & -0.0589 & -0.4938 & 0.4293 & -0.5924
\end{pmatrix}
$$

Of course, we should check that this code is reasonably efficient. This creates a random matrix, then inserts strings here and there, and finally runs `ReplaceElement`.

```
In[89]:= With[{size = 1000},
         mat = RandomReal[1, {size, size}];
         rmat = ReplacePart[mat,
            RandomInteger[{1, size}, {size, 2}] :> "NAN"]
         ];
      ReplaceElement[rmat, "NAN"]; // Timing
```

Out[90]= {0.877081, Null}

That is not too bad – processing a 1000×1000 matrix in under a second. That is on the same order of magnitude as some of the highly optimized built-in linear algebra functions.

```
In[91]:= mat = RandomReal[1, {1000, 1000}];
      {Timing[Inverse[mat];], Timing[Det[mat];]}
```

Out[92]= {{0.403233, Null}, {0.140302, Null}}

In the exercises you are asked to go a bit further and rewrite `ReplaceElement` to accept an arbitrary list of strings that should be used as the nonnumeric values to be replaced with the column means.

Exercises

1. Write a version of the function that computes Hamming distance by using `Count` to find the number of nonidentical pairs of corresponding numbers in two binary signals.

2. Write an implementation of Hamming distance using the `Total` function and then compare running times with the other versions discussed in this chapter.

3. Extend the survivor function developed in this section to a function of two arguments, so that `survivor[n, m]` returns the survivor starting from a list of n people and executing every mth person.

4. Create a function `median[lis]` that computes the median of a one-dimensional list. Create one rule for the case when *lis* has an odd number of elements and another rule for the case when the length of *lis* is even. In the latter case, the median is given by the average of the middle two elements of *lis*.

5. One of the best ways to learn how to write programs is to practice reading code. We list below a number of one-liner function definitions along with a very brief explanation of what these user-defined functions do and a typical input and output. Deconstruct these programs to see what they do and then reconstruct them as compound functions without any pure functions.

   a. Tally the frequencies with which distinct elements appear in a list.

   ```
   In[1]:= tally[lis_] := Map[({#, Count[lis, #]}) &, Union[lis]]

   In[2]:= tally[{a, a, b, b, b, a, c, c}]

   Out[2]= {{a, 3}, {b, 3}, {c, 2}}

   In[3]:= Tally[{a, a, b, b, b, a, c, c}]

   Out[3]= {{a, 3}, {b, 3}, {c, 2}}
   ```

   b. Divide up a list such that the length of each part is given by the second argument.

   ```
   In[4]:= split1[lis_, parts_] :=
            (Inner[Take[lis, {#1, #2}] &, Drop[#1, -1] + 1, Rest[#1], List] &) [
             FoldList[Plus, 0, parts]]

   In[5]:= split1[Range[10], {2, 5, 0, 3}]

   Out[5]= {{1, 2}, {3, 4, 5, 6, 7}, {}, {8, 9, 10}}
   ```

   This is the same as the previous program, done in a different way.

   ```
   In[6]:= split2[lis_, parts_] :=
            Map[Take[lis, #1 + {1, 0}] &, Partition[FoldList[Plus, 0, parts], 2, 1]]
   ```

6. In Section 4.2 we created a function `CountChange[lis]` that took a list of coins and, using transformation rules, returned the monetary value of that list of coins. Rewrite `CountChange` to use a purely functional approach. Consider using `Dot`, or `Inner`, or `Tally`.

7. Write a function that generates a one-dimensional off-lattice, random walk, that is, a walk with step positions any real number between -1 and 1. Then do the same for two- and three-dimensional off-lattice walks.

8. Extend the range of `ReplaceElement` developed in this section to accept a list of strings considered as nonnumeric matrix entries, each of which should be replaced by a column mean.

9. Extend the visualization of PPI networks from this section by coloring vertices according to the biological process in which they are involved. The built-in `ProteinData` contains this information, for example:

    In[7]:= **`ProteinData["KLKB1", "BiologicalProcesses"]`**

    Out[7]= {BloodCoagulation, Fibrinolysis,
              InflammatoryResponse, Proteolysis}

10. Create a function `TruthTable`[*expr*, *vars*] that takes a logical expression such as $A \wedge B$ and outputs a truth table similar to those in Section 2.3. You can create a list of truth values using `Tuples`. For example,

    In[8]:= **`Tuples[{True, False}, 2]`**

    Out[8]= {{True, True}, {True, False}, {False, True}, {False, False}}

    You will also find it helpful to consider threading rules over the tuples using `MapThread` or `Thread`.

11. Given a list of expressions, *lis*, create a function `NearTo`[*lis*, *elem*, *n*] that returns all elements of *lis* that are exactly *n* positions away from *elem*. For example:

    In[9]:= **`chars = CharacterRange["a", "z"]`**

    Out[9]= {a, b, c, d, e, f, g, h, i, j, k,
              l, m, n, o, p, q, r, s, t, u, v, w, x, y, z}

    In[10]:= **`NearTo[chars, "q", 3]`**

    Out[10]= {{n}, {t}}

    Write a second rule, `NearTo`[*lis*, *elem*, {*n*}] that returns all elements in *lis* that are within *n* positions of *elem*.

    In[11]:= **`NearTo[chars, "q", {4}]`**

    Out[11]= {{m, n, o, p, q, r, s, t, u}}

    Finally, create you own distance function (`DistanceFunction`) and use it with the built-in `Nearest` to do the same computation.

    Two useful functions for these tasks are `Position` and `Extract`. `Extract`[*expr*, *pos*] returns elements from *expr* whose positions *pos* are given by `Position`.

12. A *Smith number* is a composite number such that the sum of its digits is equal to the sum of the digits of its prime factors. For example, the prime factorization of 852 is $2^2 \cdot 3^1 \cdot 71^1$, and so the sum of the digits of its prime factors is $2 + 2 + 3 + 7 + 1 = 15$ which is equal to the sum of its digits, $8 + 5 + 2 = 15$. Write a program to find all Smith numbers less than 10 000.

6

Procedural programming

Conventional programming languages like C and FORTRAN embody a style of programming that has roots in the early days of computing when resource constraints forced programmers to write their code in a step-by-step manner. These procedures, as they came to be known, typically involved certain basic elements: looping over an array, conditional statements that controlled the flow of execution, logical constructs to build up tests, and functions to jump from one place in a program to another. Although newer languages have introduced many new programming paradigms, procedural programming continues to be used and remains an appropriate style for certain kinds of problems.

A *procedure* is a series of instructions that are evaluated in a definite order. The following program is a procedure.

```
In[1]:= mat = {{a, b, c}, {d, e, f}, {g, h, k}};
```

```
In[2]:= newmat = mat;
```

```
In[3]:= Do[newmat[[i, j]] = mat[[j, i]],
    {i, Length[mat]}, {j, Length[mat]}]
```

```
In[4]:= newmat
Out[4]= {{a, d, g}, {b, e, h}, {c, f, k}}
```

In[5]:= **MatrixForm[%]**

Out[5]//MatrixForm=

$$\begin{pmatrix} a & d & g \\ b & e & h \\ c & f & k \end{pmatrix}$$

This procedure is a compound expression consisting of a sequence of four expressions: the first assigns the symbolic 3×3 matrix to the symbol mat; the second is also an assignment, copying the matrix to another symbol, newmat; the third expression loops through the matrix, interchanging columns and rows of the original and putting them into the new matrix – essentially performing a transpose operation; the final expression simply outputs the new matrix.

Procedural programs also typically involve some *flow control*. What this means is that, depending upon a certain condition, different steps in the procedure will be followed. Perhaps the simplest example of this is an If statement.

In[6]:= **f[x_] := If[20 ≤ x ≤ 30, x²,**
       Print["The number ", x, " is outside the range."]]

In[7]:= **f[25]**

Out[7]= 625

In[8]:= **f[-67]**

The number -67 is outside the range.

The value of the first argument of the If function determines the direction of the rest of the evaluation. This is a control structure. Procedural programs typically contain a series of expressions to evaluate in some order and functions to control the flow of execution.

In this chapter we will explore these topics in addition to conditional definitions which are another form of flow control. All these features will greatly expand what you can do with *Mathematica* and many applications of these techniques will be explored in later chapters on recursion and numerics.

6.1 Loops and iteration

Newton's method
One of the most famous of all numerical algorithms is Newton's method for finding the roots of a function. Even though *Mathematica* includes a built-in function, **FindRoot**, that implements this method, this is a classical use of iteration and so central to numerical analysis that it is well worth your time learning how to implement it.

Throughout this section we will work with the function $x^2 - 2$, whose root is, of course, the square root of 2. Here is the computation using the built-in `FindRoot`. The number 1 in the list `{x, 1}` is the initial guess of the root.

In[1]:= **FindRoot$\left[x^2 - 2 == 0, \{x, 1\}\right]$**

Out[1]= $\{x \to 1.41421\}$

So why should you learn how to program Newton's method? The underlying algorithm is the basis of many more advanced root-finding techniques in numerical analysis. But also, with many numerical problems, the built-in operations are designed to work for the broadest possible set of situations, and might therefore have occasional trouble with certain exceptional cases. An understanding of these issues can help in such situations. An example is the following piecewise function.

In[2]:= **f[x_] := Piecewise$\left[\left\{\{0, x == 0\}, \left\{x + x^2 \text{ Sin}[2 / x], x \neq 0\right\}\right\}\right]$;**
Plot[f[x], {x, -.2, .2}]

Out[3]=

In[4]:= **FindRoot[f[x] == 0, {x, 1}]**

FindRoot::lstol :
  The line search decreased the step size to within tolerance specified by AccuracyGoal
    and PrecisionGoal but was unable to find a sufficient decrease in
    the merit function. You may need more than MachinePrecision
    digits of working precision to meet these tolerances. ≫

Out[4]= $\left\{x \to 1.81096 \times 10^{-9}\right\}$

This particular function is discontinuous at the root with its derivative changing sign as x gets closer and closer to zero. Although this is a somewhat pathological example, you can still better approximate this function's root by using some options to `FindRoot` to help speed convergence and increase the precision.

In[5]:= **FindRoot[f[x] == 0, {x, 1},**
   WorkingPrecision → 90, MaxIterations → 200]

Out[5]= $\{$ x →
   7.0064923216240853546186479164495806564013097093825788587 ⠆
   853414194489554134293030074331909 × 10^{-46} $\}$

Although finding roots of functions such as this are the exception rather than the norm, it is instructive to program your own root-finding functions and learn about algorithm implementation, numerical issues, and, in the process, the structure of iterative programming.

Do loops and For loops

Suppose you are given a function f and can compute its derivative, f'. Then Newton's algorithm works as follows:

- give an initial estimate of the root, say x_0;

- keep generating better estimates, $x_1, x_2, \ldots$, using the following rule until you are done (we will discuss this later):

$$x_{i+1} = x_i - \frac{f(x_i)}{f'(x_i)}.$$

The method is illustrated in Figure 6.1. The basic idea, as learned in a first-year calculus course, is to choose an initial estimate x_0, draw the tangent to the function at $f(x_0)$, and set x_1 to the point where that tangent line intersects the x-axis. Under favorable circumstances, the estimates get closer and closer to the root. "Unfavorable conditions" include a poor choice for the initial estimate and the function not being continuously differentiable in a neighborhood of the root.

FIGURE 6.1. *Illustration of Newton's method.*

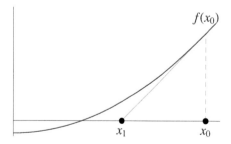

We will discuss in a moment when to stop the iteration, but first let us look at an example. For the function $f(x) = x^2 - 2$, the derivative is $f'(x) = 2x$. This specific case is shown in Figure 6.2, with 2 itself as the initial estimate. Let us see what happens after five iterations of this procedure.

In[6]:= $\mathbf{f[x\_] := x^2 - 2}$

In[7]:= $\mathbf{x_0 = 1;}$

In[8]:= $\mathbf{x_1 = N\left[x_0 - \dfrac{f[x_0]}{f'[x_0]}\right]}$

Out[8]= 1.5

In[9]:= $\mathbf{x_2 = N\left[x_1 - \dfrac{f[x_1]}{f'[x_1]}\right]}$

Out[9]= 1.41667

In[10]:= $\mathbf{x_3 = N\left[x_2 - \dfrac{f[x_2]}{f'[x_2]}\right]}$

Out[10]= 1.41422

In[11]:= $\mathbf{x_4 = N\left[x_3 - \dfrac{f[x_3]}{f'[x_3]}\right]}$

Out[11]= 1.41421

In[12]:= $\mathbf{x_5 = N\left[x_4 - \dfrac{f[x_4]}{f'[x_4]}\right]}$

Out[12]= 1.41421

As you can see, these values are getting closer and closer to the real square root of 2, which is approximately 1.4142135.

FIGURE 6.2. *Newton's method for* $f(x) = x^2 - 2$.

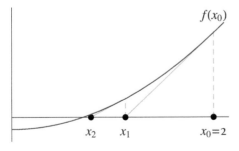

We need to discuss how to decide when we are confident that the answer we have computed is accurate enough. First, though, note one thing: wherever we decide to stop, say at the fifth iteration, all the previous values we computed are of no interest. So we could have avoided introducing those new names by instead just writing the following:

In[13]:= **a = 2;**

In[14]:= $\mathbf{a = N\left[a - \dfrac{f[a]}{f'[a]}\right]}$

Out[14]= **1.5**

In[15]:= $\mathbf{a = N\left[a - \dfrac{f[a]}{f'[a]}\right]}$

Out[15]= **1.41667**

In[16]:= $\mathbf{a = N\left[a - \dfrac{f[a]}{f'[a]}\right]}$

Out[16]= **1.41422**

In[17]:= $\mathbf{a = N\left[a - \dfrac{f[a]}{f'[a]}\right]}$

Out[17]= **1.41421**

In[18]:= $\mathbf{a = N\left[a - \dfrac{f[a]}{f'[a]}\right]}$

Out[18]= **1.41421**

After each iteration, the symbol a is assigned the new value computed, thus overwriting the old values of a.

To return to the question of when to terminate the computation, one simple answer is: repeat it ten times.

In[19]:= **Do[a = N[a - f[a] / f'[a]], {10}]**

In general, Do [*expr*, {*n*}], evaluates *expr n* times. So, in this case, we can initialize a and perform the ten evaluations as follows:

In[20]:= **a = 1;**

$\mathbf{Do\left[a = N\left[a - \dfrac{f[a]}{f'[a]}\right], \ \{10\}\right]}$

In[22]:= **a**

Out[22]= **1.41421**

The Do loop itself yields no value (or rather, it yields the special value Null, which is a symbol *Mathematica* uses when there is no result from an evaluation; nothing is printed). But, more importantly, at the end of the iteration the value assigned to a is very close to the square root of 2.

The arguments of the `Do` function are the same as those of `Table` (see Section 3.2 and also Exercise 2 at the end of this section).

$$\mathrm{Do}\big[\mathit{expr},\ \{i,\ i_{min},\ i_{max},\ di\}\big]$$

This loop repeatedly evaluates *expr* with the variable i taking the values i_{min}, $i_{min} + di$, and so on, as long as the value of i_{max} is not exceeded. The loop is repeated a total of $\lfloor (i_{max} - i_{min}) / di \rfloor$ times, where $\lfloor expr \rfloor$ gives the floor of *expr* (more precisely, the loop is actually repeated a total of $\max(0, \lfloor (i_{max} - i_{min}) / di \rfloor + 1)$ times). Furthermore, if *di* is omitted, it is assumed to be one; if only i and i_{max} are given, both i_{min} and *di* are assumed to be one.

To print each approximation and label it with a number, we could use a compound expression inside the body of the `Do` loop, in this case, adding a `Print` statement.

```
In[23]:= a = 1;
        Do[a = N[a - f[a] / f'[a]];
          Print["iteration ", i, ": ", a], {i, 1, 5}]
        iteration 1: 1.5

        iteration 2: 1.41667

        iteration 3: 1.41422

        iteration 4: 1.41421

        iteration 5: 1.41421
```

Another commonly used control structure in procedural code is the `For` loop. Its function is similar to that of a `Do` loop, but instead of an iterator list, you explicitly specify a starting value and increment for the iterator. The `For` function in *Mathematica* has the following syntax:

$$\mathrm{For}\big[\mathit{start},\ \mathit{test},\ \mathit{increment},\ \mathit{body}\big]$$

`Do` loops and `For` loops are quite similar and in fact you can often cast a problem using either construction. For example, here is a `For` implementation of the `Do` loop given above for Newton's method.

```
In[25]:= For[a = 1; i = 0, i < 10, i++, a = N[a - f[a]/f'[a]]]

In[26]:= a

Out[26]= 1.41421
```

In this example, the *start* conditions are a = 1 and i = 0; the *test* is i < 10; increment is i++ which is shorthand for increasing the value of i by one; the body of the function is the same as for the `Do` loop, namely, Newton's formula.

We will return to this problem repeatedly throughout this book: in some of the exercises later in this chapter we will explore some efficiencies that can be gained from a more careful look at the evaluations done within the iterations; we will use a different loop structure, `While`, later in this section; and in Chapter 8 we will explore mechanisms for gaining finer control over the precision and accuracy of the Newton iteration.

Example: random permutations

Let us look at another example of a `Do` loop. We will create a function that takes a list as an argument and generates a random permutation of its elements.

To build this function up step-by-step, start with a small list of ten elements.

```
In[27]:= lis = Range[10]
```
```
Out[27]= {1, 2, 3, 4, 5, 6, 7, 8, 9, 10}
```

The idea is to choose a position within the list at random and remove the element in that position and put it into a new list `lis2`.

```
In[28]:= rand := RandomInteger[{1, Length[lis]}]
```

```
In[29]:= x = Part[lis, rand]
```
```
Out[29]= 2
```

```
In[30]:= lis2 = {};
         lis2 = Append[lis2, x]
```
```
Out[31]= {2}
```

We then repeat the above process on the remaining elements of the list. Note that `lis` is assigned the value of this new list, thus overwriting the previous value.

```
In[32]:= lis = Complement[lis, {x}]
```
```
Out[32]= {1, 3, 4, 5, 6, 7, 8, 9, 10}
```

```
In[33]:= x = lis[[rand]]
         lis2 = Append[lis2, x]
         lis = Complement[lis, {x}]
```
```
Out[33]= 6
```
```
Out[34]= {2, 6}
```
```
Out[35]= {1, 3, 4, 5, 7, 8, 9, 10}
```

In this example we know explicitly how many iterations to perform in our `Do` loop: *n* iterations, where *n* is the length of the list, `lis`.

Before proceeding, we should clear some symbols.

```
In[36]:= Clear[lis, lis2, x, rand];
```

Now we just put the pieces of the previous computations together in one input.

```
In[37]:= lis = Range[10];
        lis2 = {};
        Do[
          x = Part[lis, RandomInteger[{1, Length[lis]}]];
          lis2 = Append[lis2, x];
          lis = Complement[lis, {x}],
          {i, 1, 10}]
```

When we are done, the result is left in the new list `lis2`.

```
In[40]:= lis2
```

```
Out[40]= {2, 6, 8, 4, 3, 10, 9, 7, 1, 5}
```

Here then is our function `randomPermutation` that takes a list as an argument and generates a random permutation of that list's elements.

```
In[41]:= randomPermutation[arg_List] :=
        Module[{lis = arg, x, lis2 = {}},
          Do[
            x = Part[lis, RandomInteger[{1, Length[lis]}]];
            lis2 = Append[lis2, x];
            lis = Complement[lis, {x}],
            {i, 1, Length[lis]}];
          lis2]
```

Here is a permutation of the list consisting of the first 20 integers.

```
In[42]:= randomPermutation[Range[20]]
```

```
Out[42]= {8, 14, 7, 10, 16, 13, 11, 6,
          17, 12, 2, 19, 18, 5, 9, 15, 4, 1, 20, 3}
```

And here is a random permutation of the lowercase letters of the English alphabet.

```
In[43]:= alphabet = CharacterRange["a", "z"]
```

```
Out[43]= {a, b, c, d, e, f, g, h, i, j, k,
          l, m, n, o, p, q, r, s, t, u, v, w, x, y, z}
```

```
In[44]:= randomPermutation[alphabet]
```

```
Out[44]= {n, k, b, v, d, r, o, y, x, j, h,
          f, c, t, p, q, i, e, u, w, s, g, a, z, m, l}
```

This functionality is built into *Mathematica* via the `RandomSample` function.

In[45]:= **RandomSample[CharacterRange["a", "z"]]**

Out[45]= {x, b, e, a, p, l, o, r, m, t, y,
            s, u, w, f, q, g, z, j, h, i, n, d, v, c, k}

Nonetheless, it is useful to program these functions yourself to give you a better understanding (and appreciation) of the underlying algorithms as well as some practical facility at using the programming constructs such as the Do loop in this example.

In[46]:= **Clear[x, lis, lis2]**

While loops

Let us return to Newton's method for finding roots and see how we can use a different control structure to improve the procedure by fine-tuning the number of iterations that are performed. In the previous section on Do loops, we explicitly stopped the iteration after ten times through the loop. Ten times is okay for $f(x) = x^2 - 2$, but not always. Consider the function $x - \sin(x)$.

In[47]:= **g[x_] := x - Sin[x]**

It has a root at 0.

In[48]:= **g[0]**

Out[48]= 0

However, ten iterations of Newton's algorithm does not get very close to it.

In[49]:= $x_i = 1.0;$
$$\text{Do}\left[x_i = N\left[x_i - \frac{g[x_i]}{g'[x_i]}\right], \{10\}\right]$$

In[51]:= x_i

Out[51]= 0.0168228

Twenty-five iterations does a bit better.

In[52]:= $x_i = 1.0;$
$$\text{Do}\left[x_i = N\left[x_i - \frac{g[x_i]}{g'[x_i]}\right], \{25\}\right]$$

In[54]:= x_i

Out[54]= 0.0000384172

In practice, no fixed number of iterations is going to do the trick for all functions. We need to iterate repeatedly until our estimate is close enough to stop. When is that? When $f(x_i)$ is very close to zero. So, choose ϵ to be a very small number, and iterate until $|f(x_i)| < \epsilon$.

But how can we write a loop that will test some condition and stop when the condition is no longer met? The looping construct Do iterates a fixed number of times. We need a new kind of iterative function. It is While, and it has the following form.

> While[*test*, *expr*]

The first argument is the test or condition, the second is the body, *expr*. It works like this: evaluate the test; if it is true, then evaluate the body and then the test again. If it is true, then again evaluate the body and the test. Continue this way until the test evaluates to False. Note that the body may not be evaluated at all (if the test is false the first time), or it may be evaluated once, or a thousand times.

This is just what we want: if the estimate is not yet close enough, compute a new estimate and try again. Newton's method insures, under suitable conditions, that the iteration will converge to the root. Those conditions are that the initial guess is near the root and not near a local minimum or maximum, and also that the function is continuously differentiable near the root.

In[55]:= $f[x\_] := x^2 - 2$

In[56]:= $\epsilon = .0001;$
$x_i = 50;$
$\text{While}\Big[\text{Abs}[f[x_i]] > \epsilon,$

$\qquad x_i = N\Big[x_i - \dfrac{f[x_i]}{f'[x_i]}\Big]\Big]$

In[59]:= x_i

Out[59]= 1.41422

To finish, let us put all these pieces into a reusable function. And instead of simply returning the value of x_i, we will return a rule of the form $\{x \to value\}$ similar to the built-in functions such as Solve, DSolve, FindRoot, and others.

In[60]:= $\textbf{findRoot}[fun\_Symbol, \{var\_, init\_\}, \epsilon\_] := \text{Module}\Big[\{xi = init\},$

$\qquad \text{While}\Big[\text{Abs}[fun[xi]] > \epsilon,$

$\qquad\qquad xi = N\Big[xi - \dfrac{fun[xi]}{fun'[xi]}\Big]\Big];$

$\qquad \{var \to xi\}\Big]$

In[61]:= $\textbf{findRoot}[f, \{x, 2\}, .0001]$

Out[61]= $\{x \to 1.41422\}$

As written, this function only accepts a symbol such as f for its first argument. Users might want to provide an expression like $x^2 - 2$, or even an equation such as $x^2 - 2 == 0$. The best way to accommodate these different kinds of arguments is to overload `findRoot` by giving additional rules that cover these cases. In both of the rules below we are setting up a local variable, `fun`, using a pure function. In the first case, the value on the right-hand side of the equation is subtracted from the expression on the left-hand side; in the second rule, we are just passing the expression to the pure function directly and then using that in the body of the function.

```
In[62]:= findRoot[expr_ == val_, {var_, init_}, ε_] :=
    Module[{xi = init, fun = Function[var, expr - val]},
        While[Abs[fun[xi]] > ε,
            xi = N[xi - fun[xi]/fun'[xi]]];
        {var → xi}]
```

```
In[63]:= findRoot[expr_, {var_, init_}, ε_] :=
    Module[{xi = init, fun = Function[var, expr]},
        While[Abs[fun[xi]] > ε,
            xi = N[xi - fun[xi]/fun'[xi]]];
        {var → xi}]
```

Let us see how these additional rules work for various kinds of expressions that could be used to represent this problem.

```
In[64]:= findRoot[f, {x, 2.0}, 0.0001]
```
```
Out[64]= {x → 1.41422}
```

```
In[65]:= findRoot[x^2 - 2, {x, 2.0}, 0.0001]
```
```
Out[65]= {x → 1.41422}
```

```
In[66]:= findRoot[x^2 - 2 == 0, {x, 2.0}, 0.0001]
```
```
Out[66]= {x → 1.41422}
```

```
In[67]:= findRoot[f[x] == 0, {x, 2.0}, 0.0001]
```
```
Out[67]= {x → 1.41422}
```

Let us work with this example a little more. Suppose you would like to know how many iterations were needed to find the answer. Built-in numerics functions and many visualization functions use the option `EvaluationMonitor` to keep track of and display information derived from the numerical operations these functions are performing internally. For example, `EvaluationMonitor` is used here first to display intermediate values of `x` and, in the second example, to count and display the number of iterations performed.

```
In[68]:= FindRoot[f[x], {x, 1}, EvaluationMonitor :→ Print[x]]

        1.

        1.5

        1.41667

        1.41422

        1.41421

        1.41421

Out[68]= {x → 1.41421}
```

```
In[69]:= Block[{count = 0},
          {FindRoot[f[x], {x, 1}, EvaluationMonitor :→ count++],
           StringForm["Number of iterations → `1`", count]}]

Out[69]= {{x → 1.41421}, Number of iterations → 6}
```

We can mirror this functionality in our `findRoot` function in several different ways. One possibility is to insert a `Print` expression to show the value of `xi` each time through the loop.

```
In[70]:= findRoot[fun_Symbol, {var_, init_}, ε_] := Module[{xi = init},
          While[Abs[fun[xi]] > ε,
            Print["x = ", xi];
            xi = N[xi - fun[xi]/fun'[xi]]];
          {var → xi}]
```

```
In[71]:= findRoot[f, {x, 2.0}, 0.0001]

        x = 2.

        x = 1.5

        x = 1.41667

Out[71]= {x → 1.41422}
```

Counting the lines shows that the function converged after three iterations (we were seeing the value of `xi` at the *beginning* of each execution of the body). Alternatively, insert a counter that keeps track of the number of iterations and return that as part of the answer.

```
In[72]:= findRoot[fun_Symbol, {var_, init_}, ∈_] :=
         Module[{xi = init, count = 0},
          While[Abs[fun[xi]] > ∈,
           count = count + 1;
           xi = N[xi - fun[xi]/fun'[xi]]];
          {{var → xi},
           StringForm["Number of iterations → `1`", count]}]

In[73]:= findRoot[f, {x, 2}, 0.0001]

Out[73]= {{x → 1.41422}, Number of iterations → 3}
```

Here is another question: in all these versions of findRoot, fun[xi] is computed two times at each iteration, once in the condition and once in the body. In some circumstances, calls to functions can be very time consuming, and should be minimized. Can we set things up so that fun[xi] is only computed once in each iteration?

The solution to this is to create a new local variable, funxi, which *always* contains the value of fun[xi] for the current value of xi. We can ensure that it does so by recomputing it whenever xi is reassigned.

```
In[74]:= Clear[findRoot]

In[75]:= findRoot[fun_, {var_, init_}, ∈_] :=
         Module[{xi = init, funxi = fun[init]},
          While[Abs[funxi] > ∈,
           xi = N[xi - funxi/fun'[xi]];
           funxi = fun[xi]];
          {var → xi}]

In[76]:= findRoot[f, {x, 2.0}, 0.0001]

Out[76]= {x → 1.41422}
```

In all our examples, we used Module to introduce a local variable to which we assigned values in the body of the While loop. We did this to avoid a common error in the use of iteration: *attempting to assign a value to a function's argument.*

For example, the following version of `findRoot` does not work. (Wrapping the input in `TimeConstrained[…, 2]` restricts the computation to two seconds regardless of the outcome.)

In[77]:= **Clear[findRoot]**

In[78]:= **findRoot[*fun_*, *x_*, *ϵ_*] :=**

$$\left(\text{While}\left[\text{Abs}[fun[x]] > \epsilon, \right.\right.$$

$$\left.\left. x = N\left[x - \frac{fun[x]}{fun'[x]}\right]\right];\right.$$

$$\left. x\right)$$

In[79]:= **TimeConstrained[**
      findRoot[Sin, 0.1, .01],
      2]

   Set::setraw : Cannot assign to raw object 0.1`. ≫

   General::stop : Further output of Set::setraw will be suppressed during this calculation. ≫

Out[79]= **$Aborted**

What happened can be seen from the trace, of which we have only shown some of the output.

In[80]:= **TimeConstrained[**
      TracePrint[findRoot[Sin, 0.1, .01], findRoot],
      2]

   findRoot

$$\text{While}\left[\text{Abs}[\text{Sin}[0.1]] > 0.01, 0.1 = N\left[0.1 - \frac{\text{Sin}[0.1]}{\text{Sin}'[0.1]}\right]\right]; 0.1$$

   Set::setraw : Cannot assign to raw object 0.1`. ≫

   General::stop : Further output of Set::setraw will be suppressed during this calculation. ≫

Out[80]= **$Aborted**

The symbol x in the body of `findRoot` is replaced by the argument 0.1, leaving an expression of the form 0.1 = *something*, which is not possible. It is, of course, bad programming practice and leads to wrong results to call a function and find, when it is done, that your global variables have changed values. There is a way around this, using the `HoldFirst` attribute, but introducing local variables is a bit cleaner and a more direct approach.

NestWhile and NestWhileList

Let us look again at the last version of the `findRoot` function we just created.

```
In[81]:= findRoot[fun_, {var_, init_}, ε_] :=
            Module[{xi = init, funxi = fun[init]},
              While[Abs[funxi] > ε,
                xi = N[xi - funxi/fun'[xi]];
                funxi = fun[xi]];
              {var → xi}]
```

The `While` loop evaluates the body of this function (the two assignments, one to `xi` and the other to `funxi`) until the test fails. There is another function we could use to simplify this calculation – it is `NestWhile`.

$$\text{NestWhile}\big[f,\ init,\ test\big]$$

This function iterates f with initial value *init*, while *test* continues to be true.

Let us rewrite `findRoot` using `NestWhile`. The first argument is the function we are iterating. Here we will use a pure function that represents the Newton iteration. The second argument to `NestWhile` is the initial guess, the initial value for the iteration. The third argument to `NestWhile` is the test that will be performed each time through the loop until it returns `False`. We are going to add one new construct here: a default value for ϵ. The syntax is `ε_: 0.0001` and what this means is that this is an optional argument that, when omitted, takes the value 0.0001.

```
In[82]:= f[x_] := x^2 - 2
```

```
In[83]:= findRoot[fun_, {var_, init_}, ε_: 0.0001] := Module[{result},
            result =
              NestWhile[# - fun[#]/fun'[#] &, N[init], Abs[fun[#]] > ε &];
            {var → result}]
```

This computes the square root of 2 with an initial guess of 2.0.

```
In[84]:= findRoot[f, {x, 2.0}]
```

```
Out[84]= {x → 1.41422}
```

Try it with a nondefault value for ϵ, a wider tolerance.

In[85]:= **findRoot[f, {x, 2.0}, 0.1]**

Out[85]= $\{x \to 1.41667\}$

Exercise 6 asks you to create a variation of this `findRoot` function that returns a list of all intermediate values computed during the iteration.

Before going on, we should mention that the functions introduced in this section are rather simplistic implementations of Newton's algorithm. At this stage, we are only interested in learning about how to use some of *Mathematica*'s procedural functions to implement the iterations here. In their current form, they have some serious limitations regarding accuracy and precision that we will address in Chapter 8, where we will discuss numerical issues in detail. The exercises at the end of this section also walk you through several improvements to these functions.

Exercises

1. Compare the use of a `Do` loop with using the function `Nest` (see Section 5.3). In particular, compute the square root of 2 using `Nest`.

2. `Do` is closely related to `Table`, the main difference being that `Do` does not return any value, whereas `Table` does. Use `Table` instead of `Do` to rewrite one of the `findRoot` functions given in this section. Compare the efficiency of the two approaches.

3. Compute Fibonacci numbers iteratively. Fibonacci numbers consist of the sequence 1, 1, 2, 3, 5, 8, 13, …, where, after the first two 1s, each Fibonacci number is the sum of the previous two numbers in the sequence. You will need to have two variables, say `this` and `prev`, giving the two most recent Fibonacci numbers, so that after the *i*th iteration, `this` and `prev` have the values F_i and F_{i-1}, respectively.

4. One additional improvement can be made to the `findRoot` program developed in this section. Notice that the derivative of the function `fun` is recomputed each time through the loop. This is quite inefficient. Rewrite `findRoot` so that the derivative is computed only once and that result is used in the body of the loop.

5. Another termination criterion for root-finding is to stop when $|x_i - x_{i+1}| < \epsilon$, that is, when two successive estimates are very close. The idea is that if you are not getting much improvement, you must be very near the root. The difficulty in programming this is that you need to remember the *two* most recent estimates computed. (It is similar to computing Fibonacci numbers iteratively, as in Exercise 3.) Program `findRoot` this way.

6. The built-in `FindRoot` function is set up so that you can monitor intermediate computations using the option `EvaluationMonitor` and `Reap` and `Sow`. For example, the following sows the values of x and $f(x)$ and when `FindRoot` is done, `Reap` displays the sown expressions.

In[1]:= **f[x_] := x^2 - 2**

```
In[2]:=  Reap[
           FindRoot[f[x], {x, 1}, EvaluationMonitor :> Sow[{x, f[x]}]]
         ]
```
$$\text{Out[2]}= \ \{\{x \to 1.41421\}, \{\{\{1., -1.\}, \{1.5, 0.25\},$$
$$\{1.41667, 0.00694444\}, \{1.41422, 6.0073 \times 10^{-6}\},$$
$$\{1.41421, 4.51061 \times 10^{-12}\}, \{1.41421, 4.44089 \times 10^{-16}\}\}\}\}$$

Modify each of the versions of `findRoot` presented in the text that uses a `Do` or `While` loop to produce a similar output to that above.

7. To guard against starting with a poor choice of initial value, modify your solution to the previous exercise to take, as an argument, a *list* of initial values, and simultaneously compute approximations for each until one converges; then return that one.

8. The *bisection method* is quite useful for finding roots of functions. If a continuous function $f(x)$ is such that $f(a) < 0$ and $f(b) > 0$ for two real numbers a and b, then, as a consequence of the Intermediate Value Theorem of calculus, a root of f must occur between a and b. If f is now evaluated at the midpoint of a and b, and if $f(a + b)/2 < 0$, then the root must occur between $(a + b)/2$ and b; if not, then it occurs between a and $(a + b)/2$. This bisection can be repeated until a root is found to a specified tolerance.

   Define `bisect[f, {x, a, b}, ∈]` to compute a root of f, within ϵ, using the bisection method. You should give it two initial values a and b and assume that $f(a) \cdot f(b) < 0$, that is, $f(a)$ and $f(b)$ differ in sign.

9. Using a `While` loop, write a function `gcd[m, n]` that computes the greatest common divisor (gcd) of m and n. The Euclidean algorithm for computing the gcd of two positive integers m and n, sets $m = n$ and $n = m$ mod n. It iterates this process until $n = 0$, at which point the gcd of m and n is left in the value of m.

10. Create a procedural definition for each of the following functions. For each function, create a definition using a `Do` loop and another using `Table`.

    For example, the following function first creates an array consisting of 0s of the same dimension as `mat`. Then inside the `Do` loop it assigns the element in position {j, i} in `mat` to position {i, j} in `matA`, effectively performing a transpose operation. Finally, it returns `matA`, since the `Do` loop itself does not return a value.

```
In[3]:=  transposeDo[mat_] :=
           Module[{matA, rows = Length[mat], cols = Length[mat[[1]]], i, j},
             matA = ConstantArray[0, {rows, cols}];
             Do[matA[[i, j]] = mat[[j, i]],
               {i, 1, rows},
               {j, 1, cols}];
             matA]
In[4]:=  mat1 = {{a, b, c}, {d, e, f}, {g, h, i}};
```

In[5]:= `MatrixForm[mat1]`

Out[5]//MatrixForm=

$$\begin{pmatrix} a & b & c \\ d & e & f \\ g & h & i \end{pmatrix}$$

In[6]:= `MatrixForm[transposeDo[mat1]]`

Out[6]//MatrixForm=

$$\begin{pmatrix} a & d & g \\ b & e & h \\ c & f & i \end{pmatrix}$$

This same computation could be performed with a *structured iteration* using `Table`.

In[7]:= `transposeTable[mat_?MatrixQ] := Module[{matA, rows, cols},`
    `{rows, cols} = Dimensions[mat];`
    `matA = ConstantArray[0, {rows, cols}];`
    `Table[matA[[i, j]] = mat[[j, i]], {i, rows}, {j, cols}]`
    `]`

In[8]:= `transposeTable[mat1] // MatrixForm`

Out[8]//MatrixForm=

$$\begin{pmatrix} a & d & g \\ b & e & h \\ c & f & i \end{pmatrix}$$

a. Create the function `reverse[vec]` that reverses the elements in the list *vec*.

b. Create a function `rotateRight[vec, n]`, where *vec* is a vector and *n* is a (positive or negative) integer.

c. Create a procedural implementation of `rotateRows`, which could be defined in this functional way:

In[9]:= `rotateRows[mat_] :=`
    `Map[rotateRight[mat[[#]], # - 1] &, Range[1, Length[mat]]]`

That is, it rotates the *i*th row of `mat` by $i - 1$ places to the right.

d. Create a procedural function `rotateRowsByS`, which could be defined in this functional way:

In[10]:= `rotateRowsByS[mat_, S_] /; Length[mat] == Length[S] :=`
    `Map[(rotateRight[mat[[#1]], S[[#1]]] &), Range[1, Length[mat]]]`

That is, it rotates the *i*th row of `matA` by the amount `S[[i]]`.

e. Create a function $pick[lis_a, lis_b]$, where lis_a and lis_b are lists of equal length, and lis_b contains only Boolean values (`False` and `True`). This function selects those elements from lis_a corresponding to `True` in lis_b. For example, the result of the following should be {a, b, e}.

`pick[{a, b, c, d, e}, {True, True, False, False, True}]`

6.2 Flow control

Conditional functions

In this section we will look at functions that control the flow of execution of an evaluation. Perhaps the simplest and easiest to understand is `If`. Here is a rather simplistic implementation of the absolute value function, using `If`.

In[1]:= **abs[$x\_$] := If[$x \geq 0$, x, $-x$]**

In[2]:= **abs[-4]**

Out[2]= 4

The `If` function takes three arguments: $If\left[test,\ then,\ else\right]$. If *test* evaluates to `True`, the second argument, *then*, is evaluated; if the test evaluates to `False`, the third argument, *else*, is evaluated.

Once defined, these functions can be used with any other computations. For example, `abs` can now be mapped over a list of numbers.

In[3]:= **Map[abs, {-2, -1, 0, 1, 2}]**

Out[3]= {2, 1, 0, 1, 2}

By default, this function will not *automatically* map across lists.

In[4]:= **abs[{-2, -1, 0, 1, 2}]**

Out[4]= If[{-2, -1, 0, 1, 2} $\geq$ 0, {-2, -1, 0, 1, 2}, $-$ {-2, -1, 0, 1, 2}]

If you want `abs` to behave like many of the built-in functions and automatically map across lists when they are given as the argument to `abs`, you need to make the function `Listable` as described in Sections 2.4 and 5.2.

In[5]:= **SetAttributes[abs, Listable]**

In[6]:= **abs[{-2, -1, 0, 1, 2}]**

Out[6]= {2, 1, 0, 1, 2}

Here are some additional examples using `If`. Given a list, the following function divides each element of the list by 100 unless an element is nonnumeric.

In[7]:= **divideBy100[$lis\_$] := Map$\left[$If$\left[$NumericQ[#], $\dfrac{\#}{100}$, # $\right]$ &, lis $\right]$**

In[8]:= **divideBy100[{5, π, 0, α}]**

Out[8]= $\left\{\dfrac{1}{20}, \dfrac{\pi}{100}, 0, \alpha\right\}$

The following function resizes large images and leaves them alone if they are smaller than some threshold size.

In[9]:= `img =` 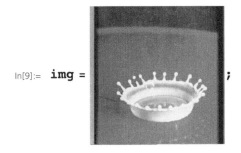 `;`

In[10]:= `ResizeImage[img_Image, target_ : 100] :=`
`    If[First@ImageDimensions[img] > target,`
`      ImageResize[img, target], img]`

In[11]:= `ResizeImage[img, 75]`

Out[11]=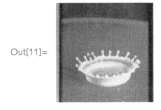

In[12]:= `ImageDimensions[%]`
Out[12]= `{75, 75}`

As an aside, *Mathematica* automatically resizes images when used inline such as the input where `img` is defined above. The full size of the original image is quite a bit larger.

In[13]:= `ImageDimensions[img]`
Out[13]= `{512, 512}`

Oftentimes you will find yourself using nested If/Then/Else chains to deal with multiple conditions that need to be checked. In the following example, we create plot labels that are determined by the interpolation order chosen. The parameter `order` will be manipulated inside the dynamic interface. To start, create a static plot.

```
In[14]:= data = Table[Sin[x y], {x, 0, 4, 0.5}, {y, 0, 4, 0.5}];
        ListPlot3D[data, InterpolationOrder → 0,
         PlotLabel → "Voronoi cells"]
```

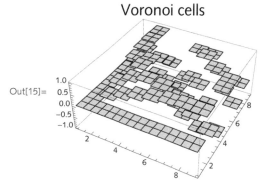

The labels of this dynamic interface will change depending upon the value of the parameter, `order`. Figure 6.3 displays the four panes from the dynamic interface.

```
In[16]:= Manipulate[
          ListPlot3D[data, InterpolationOrder → order,
           PlotLabel →
            If[order == "None", "Linear",
             If[order == 0, "Voronoi cells",
              If[order == 1, "Baricentric",
               If[order == 2, "Natural neighbor"
               ]
              ]
             ]
            ]
          ],
          {{order, "None", "InterpolationOrder"}, {"None", 0, 1, 2}}];
```

This code contains several nested `If`s, each occurring in the false clause of the previous one. The structure of the computation is a sequence of tests of predicates $cond_i$ until one is found to be true, at which point a result can be computed.

$$
\text{If}\left[cond_1,\ result_1,\right.
$$
$$
\text{If}\left[cond_2,\ result_2,\right.
$$
$$
\vdots
$$
$$
\text{If}\left[cond_n,\ result_n,\right.
$$
$$
\left.\left.\cdots,\ result_{n+1}\right]\ \cdots\right]\right]
$$

Such a sequence of *cascading* `If` statements, although common to most procedural code, can be quite long, somewhat difficult to read, and hard to debug. An alternative is to use a `Which` statement that essentially collapses the nested structure to a more manageable object. We will explore Which later in this section.

FIGURE 6.3. *Manipulate showing different interpolation orders used to construct a surface.*

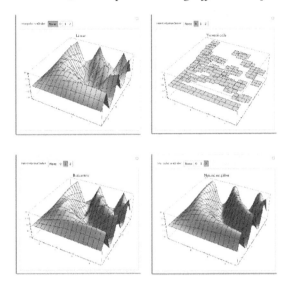

Conditional definitions can be written using another construct in *Mathematica*, the Condition operator /; that has already been introduced in the context of conditional patterns in Section 4.1. For example, the abs function can be entered (using several definitions) as follows:

In[17]:= **Clear[abs]**

In[18]:= **abs[x_] := x /; x ≥ 0**

In[19]:= **abs[x_] := -x /; x < 0**

The first definition should be interpreted as "abs[x] is equal to x whenever (or under the condition that) x is greater than or equal to zero" and the second definition as "abs[x] is equal to the opposite of x whenever x is less than zero."

The conditions on the right-hand side of the rules can also be entered on the left-hand side of these definitions as follows:

In[20]:= **Clear[abs]**

In[21]:= **abs[x_ /; x ≥ 0] := x**

In[22]:= **abs[x_ /; x < 0] := -x**

This last notation has the advantage of preventing the right-hand side of the definitions from being evaluated whenever the pattern on the left does not match.

In[23]:= **abs[-4]**

Out[23]= 4

In[24]:= **abs[z]**

Out[24]= abs[z]

The **abs** function defined above is fine for integers and real number arguments, but, since the complex numbers cannot be ordered, the tests comparing the argument x with zero will fail.

In[25]:= **abs[3 + 4 I]**

        GreaterEqual::nord : Invalid comparison with $3 + 4i$ attempted. $\gg$

        Less::nord : Invalid comparison with $3 + 4i$ attempted. $\gg$

Out[25]= abs[3 + 4 i]

Exercise 3 at the end of this section walks through a solution to this problem through the use of several more specific rules.

Piecewise-defined functions

The last absolute value function given in the previous section is defined piecewise. This means that for different intervals, or under different conditions, the values will be computed differently. **Piecewise** is designed specifically for such problems. The syntax is:

$$\texttt{Piecewise}[\{\{e_1, c_1\}, \ldots, \{e_n, c_n\}\}]$$

Piecewise outputs e_1 if c_1 is true, e_2 if c_2 is true, ... , e_n if c_n is true, and zero otherwise (the default). So, for example, here is the definition for the absolute value function given as a piecewise object.

In[26]:= **abspw[x_] := Piecewise[{{x, x ≥ 0}, {-x, x < 0}}]**

Piecewise objects display as you would expect in traditional mathematical notation.

In[27]:= **abspw[x]**

$$\text{Out[27]}= \begin{cases} x & x \geq 0 \\ -x & x < 0 \\ 0 & \text{True} \end{cases}$$

One of the advantages to using **Piecewise** compared with the previous approaches is that the earlier implementations given in terms of conditionals are not fully supported by many of the built-in functions.

In[28]:= **Clear[abs]**

In[29]:= **abs[*x_*] := *x* /; *x* ≥ 0**

In[30]:= **abs[*x_*] := -*x* /; *x* < 0**

In[31]:= **Integrate[abs[x], {x, -1, 1}]**

Out[31]= $\int_{-1}^{1}$ abs[x] dx

In[32]:= **D[abs[x], x]**

Out[32]= abs′[x]

Piecewise, on the other hand, is fully integrated with the algebraic, symbolic, and graphical functions in *Mathematica* and so is preferable to other approaches.

In[33]:= **Integrate[abspw[x], {x, -1, 1}]**

Out[33]= 1

In[34]:= **D[abspw[x], x]**

Out[34]= $\begin{cases} -1 & x < 0 \\ 1 & x > 0 \\ \text{Indeterminate} & \text{True} \end{cases}$

In[35]:= **Plot[abspw[x], {x, -2, 2}]**

Out[35]=

Which and Switch

Recall the earlier plot of some three-dimensional data using cascading If s to specify different plot labels.

```
In[36]:= Manipulate[
          ListPlot3D[data, InterpolationOrder → order,
           PlotLabel →
            If[order == "None", "Linear",
             If[order == 0, "Voronoi cells",
              If[order == 1, "Baricentric",
               If[order == 2, "Natural neighbor"
               ]
              ]
             ]
            ]
          ],
          {order, {"None", 0, 1, 2}}];
```

It can be a little difficult to read these nested If statements and figure out which clause goes with which If. Fortunately, cascaded If s are so common that there is a more direct way of writing them, using the function Which.

$$\text{Which}\left[cond_1, \; result_1, \right.$$
$$cond_2, \; result_2,$$
$$\vdots$$
$$cond_n, \; result_n,$$
$$\left. \text{True}, \; result_{n+1} \right]$$

This has exactly the same effect as the cascaded If expression above: it tests each condition in turn, and, when it finds an i such that $cond_i$ is true, it returns $result_i$ as the result of the Which expression itself. If none of the conditions turns out to be true, then it will test the final condition, namely the expression True, which always evaluates to true, and it will then return $result_{n+1}$.

In[37]:= `Manipulate[`
    `ListPlot3D[data, InterpolationOrder → order,`
     `PlotLabel →`
      `Which[`
        `order == "None", "Linear",`
        `order == 0, "Voronoi cells",`
        `order == 1, "Baricentric",`
        `order == 2, "Natural neighbor"]],`
      `{{order, "None", "Interpolation order"}, {"None", 0, 1, 2}}]`

Out[37]=

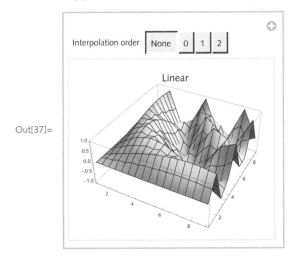

One additional function deserves mention. Our use of `Which` is still quite special in that it consists of a simple sequence of comparisons between a variable and a constant. Since this is also a common form, *Mathematica* provides a special function for it, called `Switch`. Where `Which` compares values to determine which result to evaluate, `Switch` does pattern matching.

$$\mathtt{Switch}\big[expr,$$
$$pattern_1, \ result_1,$$
$$pattern_2, \ result_2,$$
$$\vdots$$
$$pattern_n, \ result_n,$$
$$\_, \ result_{n+1}\big]$$

This evaluates *expr* and then checks each pattern sequentially to see whether *expr* matches; as soon as *expr* matches one, say *pattern*$_i$, it returns the value of *result*$_i$. Of course, if none of the patterns *pattern*$_1$, ..., *pattern*$_n$ matches, the general pattern _ certainly will.

Here is a toy example showing how Switch works. If the expression expr matches the pattern _Integer, that is, if it has head Integer, then "I am an integer" will be returned. If not, but expr has head Rational, then "I am rational" is returned, and so on.

```
In[38]:= WhatAmI[expr_] := Switch[expr,
        _Integer, "I am an integer",
        _Rational, "I am rational",
        _Real, "I am real",
        _Complex, "I am complex",
        _, "I am not a number"]
```

```
In[39]:= WhatAmI[3 + 4 I]
```

```
Out[39]= I am complex
```

```
In[40]:= WhatAmI[fun]
```

```
Out[40]= I am not a number
```

Notice that Switch uses the blank character, _, for the final, or *default* case, just as Which often uses the always-true expression True.

Here then is the version of the Manipulate example using Switch instead of Which.

```
In[41]:= Manipulate[
        ListPlot3D[data, InterpolationOrder → order,
         PlotLabel →
          Switch[order,
            "None", "Linear",
            0, "Voronoi cells",
            1, "Baricentric",
            2, "Natural neighbor"]],
         {{order, "None", "Interpolation order"},
          {"None", 0, 1, 2}}];
```

If all the patterns happen to be constants, the Switch expression is equivalent to the following Which expression.

$$
\texttt{Which}\Big[\\
\quad expr == pattern_1,\ result_1, \\
\quad expr == pattern_2,\ result_2, \\
\quad \vdots \\
\quad expr == pattern_n,\ result_n, \\
\quad \texttt{True},\ result_{n+1}\Big]
$$

Argument checking

When you write functions, you often know ahead of time that their definitions are valid only for certain kinds of inputs. For example, the following recursive definition for the factorial function only makes sense for positive integers.

```
In[42]:= factorial[0] = 1;
         factorial[n_] := n factorial[n - 1]
```

```
In[44]:= factorial[5]
```

```
Out[44]= 120
```

If you were to give `factorial` an argument that was not a positive integer, the recursion could run away from you.

```
In[45]:= factorial[3.4] // Short
```

> $RecursionLimit::reclim : Recursion depth of 256 exceeded. ≫

Conditionals are a convenient way of checking that the arguments to a function pass some test. For example, there are several ways that you could make the `factorial` function valid only under the condition that its argument is a positive integer. Here is how you might approach it using the `If` construct to test that *n* passes the appropriate criteria.

```
In[46]:= Clear[factorial]
```

```
In[47]:= factorial[0] = 1;
```

```
In[48]:= factorial[n_] := If[IntegerQ[n] && n > 0, n factorial[n - 1]]
```

```
In[49]:= {factorial[5], factorial[-3], factorial[2.4]}
```

```
Out[49]= {120, Null, Null}
```

The function works fine for positive integers, but since we did not give an alternative condition to the `If` function, nothing is returned (technically, `Null` is returned) when the test condition fails.

Let us define a message that will be output in the case that the argument to `factorial` fails the positive integer test.

```
In[50]:= factorial::noint =
         "The argument `1` is not a positive integer.";
```

`Message[messname, e_1, e_2, …]` prints using `StringForm[messname, e_1, e_2, …]`, where *messname* is the value of the message name and the e_i are substituted for any expressions of the form `\`i\``. We will use `Message` as the third argument to the `If` function; when the condition fails, the message will be triggered. In the above example, the message name is `noint` and its value is the string beginning with `"The argument..."`. In this example, the value of n will be substituted into the string where the `\`1\`` occurs.

```
In[51]:= factorial[n_] := If[IntegerQ[n] && n > 0,
            n factorial[n - 1],
            Message[factorial::noint, n]]
```

```
In[52]:= factorial[-4]
```

       factorial::noint : The argument −4 is not a positive integer.

Exercises

1. Create a function UpperTriangularMatrix[{m, n}] that generates an $m \times n$ upper triangular matrix, that is, a matrix containing 1s on and above the diagonal and 0s below the diagonal. Create an alternative rule that defaults to 1 for the upper values, but allows the user to specify a nondefault upper value.

   ```
   In[1]:= UpperTriangularMatrix[{3, 3}] // MatrixForm
   ```
   Out[1]//MatrixForm=
   $$\begin{pmatrix} 1 & 1 & 1 \\ 0 & 1 & 1 \\ 0 & 0 & 1 \end{pmatrix}$$

   ```
   In[2]:= UpperTriangularMatrix[{4, 4}, ξ] // MatrixForm
   ```
   Out[2]//MatrixForm=
   $$\begin{pmatrix} \xi & \xi & \xi & \xi \\ 0 & \xi & \xi & \xi \\ 0 & 0 & \xi & \xi \\ 0 & 0 & 0 & \xi \end{pmatrix}$$

2. Write a function signum[x] which, when applied to an integer x, returns −1, 0, or 1, if x is less than, equal to, or greater than 0, respectively. Write it in four ways: using three clauses, using a single clause with If, using a single clause with Which, and using Piecewise.

3. The definition of the absolute value function in this section does not handle complex numbers properly.

   ```
   In[3]:= abs[3 + 4 I]
   ```
          GreaterEqual::nord : Invalid comparison with $3 + 4i$ attempted. ≫

          Less::nord : Invalid comparison with $3 + 4i$ attempted. ≫
   Out[3]= abs[3 + 4 I]

   Correct this problem by rewriting abs to include a specific rule for the case where its argument is complex.

4. Use If in conjunction with Map or Fold to define the following functions:

   a. In a list of numbers, double all the positive numbers, but leave the negative numbers alone.

b. `remove3Repetitions` alters three or more consecutive occurrences in a list, changing them to two occurrences; if there are only two occurrences to begin with, they are left alone. For example, `remove3Repetitions[{0, 1, 1, 2, 2, 2, 1}]` will return `{0, 1, 1, 2, 2, 1}`.

c. Add the elements of a list in consecutive order, but never let the sum go below 0.

In[4]:= **`positiveSum[{5, 3, -13, 7, -3, 2}]`**

Out[4]= 6

Since the −13 caused the sum to go below 0, it was instead put back to 0 and the summation continued from there.

5. Rewrite the `median` function from Exercise 4 in Section 5.8 using an `If` control structure.

6. Using `NestWhileList`, write a function `CollatzSequence[n]` that produces the Collatz sequence for any positive integer n. The Collatz sequence is generated as follows: starting with a number n, if it is even, then output $n/2$; if n is odd, then output $3n + 1$. Iterate this process while the value of the iterate is not equal to 1.

6.3 Examples and applications

Classifying points

Quadrants in the Euclidean plane are traditionally numbered counterclockwise from quadrant I (x and y positive) to quadrant IV (x positive, y negative) with some convention adopted for points that lie on either of the axes. In this section we will create a function that classifies any point in the plane according to this scheme (see Table 6.1). We will give a number of different solutions: using multi-clause function definitions with predicates, single-clause definitions with `If` and its relatives, and combinations of the two.

TABLE 6.1. *Quadrant classification*

Point	Classification
(0, 0)	0
$y = 0$ (on the x-axis)	−1
$x = 0$ (on the y-axis)	−2
Quadrant I	1
Quadrant II	2
Quadrant III	3
Quadrant IV	4

Perhaps the first solution that suggests itself is one that uses a clause for each of the cases above.

```
In[1]:= quadrant[{0, 0}] := 0
        quadrant[{x_, 0}] := -1
        quadrant[{0, y_}] := -2
        quadrant[{x_, y_}] := 1 /; x > 0 && y > 0
        quadrant[{x_, y_}] := 2 /; x < 0 && y > 0
        quadrant[{x_, y_}] := 3 /; x < 0 && y < 0
        quadrant[{x_, y_}] := 4  (* x > 0 && y < 0 *)
```

It is not a bad idea to include the last condition as a comment to yourself; it is not needed as an actual condition like the three rules preceding it because this rule will apply to any argument $\{x, y\}$ without condition. Evaluating the rule last will cause it to be checked last by the pattern matcher.

Here is a list of points that we will use as our test cases.

```
In[8]:= pts = {{0, 0}, {4, 0}, {0, 1.3},
        {2, 4}, {-2, 4}, {-2, -4}, {2, -4}};
```

```
In[9]:= Map[quadrant, pts]
```

```
Out[9]= {0, -1, -2, 1, 2, 3, 4}
```

Translated directly to a one-clause definition using If, this becomes:

```
In[10]:= quadrant[{x_, y_}] :=
         If[x == 0 && y == 0, 0,
          If[y == 0, -1,
           If[x == 0, -2,
            If[x > 0 && y > 0, 1,
             If[x < 0 && y > 0, 2,
              If[x < 0 && y < 0, 3, 4]]]]]]
```

```
In[11]:= Map[quadrant, pts]
```

```
Out[11]= {0, -1, -2, 1, 2, 3, 4}
```

Actually, a more likely solution here uses Which.

```
In[12]:= quadrant[{x_, y_}] := Which[
         x == 0 && y == 0, 0,
         y == 0, -1,
         x == 0, -2,
         x > 0 && y > 0, 1,
         x < 0 && y > 0, 2,
         x < 0 && y < 0, 3,
```

True, 4 (* x > 0 && y < 0 *)]

In[13]:= **Map[quadrant, pts]**

Out[13]= {0, -1, -2, 1, 2, 3, 4}

Each of our solutions so far suffers from a certain degree of inefficiency, because of repeated comparisons of a single value with 0. Take the last solution as an example, and suppose the argument is $(-5, -9)$. It will require five comparisons of -5 with 0 and three comparisons of -9 with 0 to obtain this result.

In[14]:= **quadrant[{-5, -9}]**

Out[14]= 3

The steps to perform this computation are:

1. evaluate x == 0; since it is false, the associated y == 0 will not be evaluated, and we next

2. evaluate y == 0 on the following line; since it is false, we

3. evaluate x == 0 on the third line; since it is false, we

4. evaluate x > 0 on next line; since it is false, the associated y > 0 will not be evaluated, and we next,

5. evaluate x < 0 on the next line; since it is true, we do,

6. the y > 0 comparison, which is false, so we next,

7. evaluate x < 0 on the next line; since it is true, we then evaluate y < 0, which is also true, so we return the answer 3.

How can we improve this? By nesting conditional expressions inside other conditional expressions. In particular, as soon as we discover that x is less than, greater than, or equal to 0, we should make maximum use of that fact without rechecking it. That is what the following quadrant function does.

In[15]:= **quadrant[{x_, y_}] :=**
   Which[
    x == 0, If[y == 0, 0, -2],
    x > 0, Which[y > 0, 1, y < 0, 4, True, -1],
    True, Which[y < 0, 3, y > 0, 2, True, -1]
   ]

In[16]:= **Map[quadrant, pts]**

Out[16]= {0, -1, -2, 1, 2, 3, 4}

Let us count up the comparisons for $(-5, -9)$ this time: (*i*) evaluate x == 0; since it is false, we next, (*ii*) evaluate x > 0; since it is false, we go to the third branch of the Which, evaluate True, which is, of course, true, then we (*iii*) evaluate $y < 0$, which is true, and we return 3. Thus, we made only three comparisons, a substantial improvement.

When pattern matching is used, as in our first, multi-clause solution, efficiency calculations can be more difficult. It would be inaccurate to say that *Mathematica* has to compare x and y to 0 to tell whether the first clause applies; what actually happens is more complex. What is true, however, is that it will do the comparisons indicated in the last four clauses. So, even if we discount the first three clauses with argument $(-5, -9)$, some extra comparisons are done. Specifically: (*i*) the comparison $x > 0$ is done; then, (*ii*) $x < 0$ and (*iii*) $y > 0$; then, (*iv*) $x < 0$ and (*v*) $y < 0$. This can be avoided by using conditional expressions within clauses.

```
In[17]:=  quadrant[{0, 0}] := 0
          quadrant[{x_, 0}] := -1
          quadrant[{0, y_}] := -2
          quadrant[{x_, y_}] := If[x < 0, 2, 1] /; y > 0
          quadrant[{x_, y_}] := If[x < 0, 3, 4]  (* /; y<0 *)
```

```
In[22]:=  Map[quadrant, pts]
Out[22]=  {0, -1, -2, 1, 2, 3, 4}
```

Now, no redundant comparisons are done. For $(-5, -9)$, since $y > 0$ fails, the fourth clause is not used, so the $x > 0$ comparison in it is not done. Only the single $x < 0$ comparison in the final clause is done, for a total of two comparisons.

Having implemented all these versions of quadrant, you should still be mindful of a basic fact of life in programming: your time is more valuable than your computer's time. You should not spend your time worrying about how slow a function is until there is a demonstrated need to worry. Far more important is the clarity and simplicity of the code, since this will determine how much time you (or another programmer) will have to spend when it comes time to modify it. In the case of quadrant, we would argue that we were lucky and found a version (the final one) that wins on both counts (if only programming were always like that!).

Finally, a technical, but potentially important, point: not all the versions of quadrant work exactly the same way. The integer 0, as a pattern, does not match the real number 0.0, since they have different heads. Thus, using the last version as an example, quadrant[{0.0, 0.0}] returns 4.

```
In[23]:=  quadrant[{0.0, 0.0}]
Out[23]=  4
```

Exercise 4 walks through the use of alternatives to deal more efficiently with these various cases.

Sieve of Eratosthenes

One of the oldest algorithms in the history of computing is the Sieve of Eratosthenes. Named after the famous Greek astronomer Eratosthenes (*ca.* 276 – *ca.* 194 BC), this method is used to find all prime numbers below a given number n. The great feature of this algorithm is that it finds prime numbers without doing any division, an operation that took considerable skill and concentration before the introduction of the Arabic numeral system. In fact, in our implementation its only operations are addition and component assignment.

The algorithm can be summarized as follows. To find all the prime numbers less than an integer n:

1. create a list of the integers 1 through n;

2. starting with $p = 2$, cross out all multiples of p;

3. increment p (that is, add 1 to p) and cross out all multiples of p;

4. repeat the previous two steps until $p > \sqrt{n}$.

You should convince yourself that the numbers that are left after all the crossings out are in fact the primes less than n. This algorithm lends itself very well to a procedural approach, so let us walk through the steps.

We will use a For structure for this problem. The syntax is For$\left[\textit{start, test, incr, body}\right]$, where *start* will first be evaluated (initializing values), and then *incr* and *body* will be repeatedly evaluated until *test* fails.

1. Let lis be a list containing all the integers between 1 and n.

```
In[24]:= n = 20;
         lis = Range[n]
```

```
Out[25]= {1, 2, 3, 4, 5, 6, 7, 8, 9, 10,
          11, 12, 13, 14, 15, 16, 17, 18, 19, 20}
```

Let $p = 2$. Repeat the following two steps:

2. Starting at position $2p$, "cross out" every pth value in lis. We will assign 1 to lis at positions $2p$, $3p$, and the 1 will represent a crossed-out value.

```
In[26]:= p = 2;
         Do[lis[[i]] = 1, {i, 2 p, n, p}]
```

```
In[28]:= lis
```

```
Out[28]= {1, 2, 3, 1, 5, 1, 7, 1, 9, 1, 11, 1, 13, 1, 15, 1, 17, 1, 19, 1}
```

3. While $p \le \sqrt{n}$, increment p by 1, until lis[[p]] is not 1, or until $p > \sqrt{n}$.

```
In[29]:= n = 20;
         lis = Range[n];
         For[p = 2,
           p ≠ 1 && p ≤ Floor[Sqrt[n]],
           p++,
           Do[lis[[i]] = 1, {i, 2 p, n, p}]]
```

The numbers other than 1 in `lis` are all the prime numbers less than or equal to *n*.

```
In[32]:= DeleteCases[lis, 1]

Out[32]= {2, 3, 5, 7, 11, 13, 17, 19}
```

Let us put these steps together in the function `Sieve`.

```
In[33]:= Clear[n, p, lis]
```

```
In[34]:= Sieve[n_Integer] := Module[{lis = Range[n], p},
           For[p = 2,
             p ≠ 1 && p ≤ Floor[Sqrt[n]],
             p++,
             Do[lis[[i]] = 1, {i, 2 p, n, p}]];
           DeleteCases[lis, 1]]
```

Here are a few simple tests to check the correctness of our function. First a basic check that `Sieve` returns the same list of primes as the built-in functions. The built-in `PrimePi[x]` gives the number of primes $\pi(x)$ less than or equal to *x*.

```
In[35]:= Map[Prime, Range@PrimePi[100]]

Out[35]= {2, 3, 5, 7, 11, 13, 17, 19, 23, 29, 31, 37,
          41, 43, 47, 53, 59, 61, 67, 71, 73, 79, 83, 89, 97}
```

```
In[36]:= Sieve[100]

Out[36]= {2, 3, 5, 7, 11, 13, 17, 19, 23, 29, 31, 37,
          41, 43, 47, 53, 59, 61, 67, 71, 73, 79, 83, 89, 97}
```

We should check that the list of primes less than 10 000 is the same as that produced by the built-in functions.

```
In[37]:= With[{n = 10^4}, Sieve[n] == Map[Prime, Range@PrimePi[n]]]

Out[37]= True
```

Next, we check that `Sieve` produces the correct *number* of primes less than a large integer.

```
In[38]:= Length[Sieve[10^5]]

Out[38]= 9592
```

In[39]:= **PrimePi$\left[10^5\right]$**

Out[39]= 9592

Finally, we do some simple timing tests to check the efficiency of this algorithm against the built-in functions that are optimized for this task.

In[40]:= **Sieve$\left[10^5\right]$; // Timing**

Out[40]= {1.03762, Null}

In[41]:= **Map$\left[$Prime, Range@PrimePi$\left[10^5\right]\right]$; // Timing**

Out[41]= {0.009463, Null}

For numbers in this range (less than about 10^5), sieving is fairly efficient. But, beyond this range, it gets slower and slower. The implementation here is quite basic and there are a number of things that we could do to optimize it. In Section 12.2 we will make several improvements to this sieving algorithm reducing the overall number of computations performed by carefully structuring the Do loop. Ultimately, if you are interested in working on very large numbers, it would be best to consider specialized algorithms that are asymptotically fast. For large integers, PrimePi uses an algorithm due to Lagarias, Miller, and Odlyzko (Lagarias and Odlyzko 1987) that is based on estimates of the density of primes.

Sorting algorithms

In Section 4.3 we developed a sorting routine in which the pattern matcher was invoked to check every pair of adjacent elements in a list to see if they were out of order. Although that code is quite compact, it is not terribly efficient due to the large number of pattern matches needed. In this section we will develop two well-known sorting algorithms – *selection sort* and *bubble sort* – that lend themselves to procedural approaches quite well. Although these two algorithms are still slow for larger input, it is instructive to work through them as they are good exercises in procedural programming and provide useful insights into the issues involved in sorting lists of numbers.

We will start with the selection sort algorithm, as it is fairly simple to understand and implement. After developing the algorithm, we will look at its computational complexity as well as create a quick visualization of the algorithm at work.

The selection sort algorithm works by finding (selecting) the smallest number in a list and exchanging it with the element in the first position in the list. It then finds the next smallest element in the list and exchanges it with the element in the second position. It continues like this to the end of the list at which point the entire list is sorted.

We already have developed some of the pieces needed here; in particular, the solution to Exercise 4 from Section 3.3 has code for swapping two elements in a list, say elements in positions i and j:

$$\texttt{lis}[[\{i,\ j\}]] = \texttt{lis}[[\{j,\ i\}]]$$

We will create a local variable `slist` that is a copy of the list that we wish to sort and then operate only on `slist`. If two elements are out of order, we swap them:

```
If[slist[[i]] > slist[[j]],
  slist[[{i, j}]] = slist[[{j, i}]]]
```

The only real difficulty is determining the correct starting and ending values for the iterators `i` and `j`. We will use a `Do` loop, fix `i` and then have `j` vary; then increment `i` and have `j` vary through its values again, and so on. Here is the code.

```
In[42]:= selectionSort[lis_] := Module[{slist = lis, len = Length[lis]},
           Do[
             If[slist[[i]] > slist[[j]],
               slist[[{i, j}]] = slist[[{j, i}]]],
             {i, len - 1}, {j, i + 1, len}];
           slist]
```

Let us try it out on a small vector containing some repeated values (one of the things you want to test for in sorting algorithms).

```
In[43]:= vec = RandomInteger[10, 50]
```

```
Out[43]= {0, 6, 1, 8, 7, 9, 7, 4, 7, 4, 6, 5, 0, 4, 10, 5,
          6, 1, 8, 2, 3, 10, 10, 5, 6, 7, 1, 3, 5, 2, 2, 7, 8,
          1, 6, 4, 0, 4, 7, 1, 7, 10, 1, 0, 2, 10, 7, 2, 4, 6}
```

```
In[44]:= selectionSort[vec]
```

```
Out[44]= {0, 0, 0, 0, 1, 1, 1, 1, 1, 1, 2, 2, 2, 2, 2, 3,
          3, 4, 4, 4, 4, 4, 4, 5, 5, 5, 5, 6, 6, 6, 6, 6, 6, 7,
          7, 7, 7, 7, 7, 7, 8, 8, 8, 9, 10, 10, 10, 10, 10}
```

Let us try it out on a larger vector of random reals.

```
In[45]:= vec = RandomReal[1, {1500}];
```

```
In[46]:= selectionSort[vec]; // Timing
```

```
Out[46]= {3.479029, Null}
```

As a quick check, we compare it with the built-in `Sort` function, first for correctness, then for speed.

In[47]:= **selectionSort[vec] == Sort[vec]**

Out[47]= True

In[48]:= **Timing[Sort[vec];]**

Out[48]= {0.000241, Null}

Obviously, our naive implementation of selection sort is not going to compare with the efficiency of the built-in Sort, which uses a much more efficient algorithm known as merge sort. In fact, selection sort is known to have computational complexity $O(n^2)$, meaning we would expect the time to do selection sort to be proportional to the square of the size of the input. To get a basic confirmation of the complexity, average several trials of increasing size and then plot the timings. We will choose three trials for each size of the input from 100 to 2000 in steps of 100.

In[49]:= **times = Table[**
        vec = RandomReal[1, {size}];
        mean = Mean@Table[First@Timing[selectionSort[vec]], {3}];
        {size, mean},
        {size, 100, 2000, 100}]

Out[49]= {{100, 0.0144407}, {200, 0.058554},
        {300, 0.133603}, {400, 0.219965}, {500, 0.350014},
        {600, 0.517022}, {700, 0.69728}, {800, 0.932},
        {900, 1.1802}, {1000, 1.45561}, {1100, 1.73962},
        {1200, 2.06994}, {1300, 2.39579}, {1400, 2.82256},
        {1500, 3.18691}, {1600, 3.80523}, {1700, 4.16283},
        {1800, 4.76077}, {1900, 5.37576}, {2000, 5.73151}}

Here is a plot of the times with the size of the input on the horizontal axis and average time (in seconds) for the three trials on the vertical axis.

In[50]:= **dataplot = ListPlot[times, Mesh → All, DataRange → {100, 2000}]**

Out[50]=

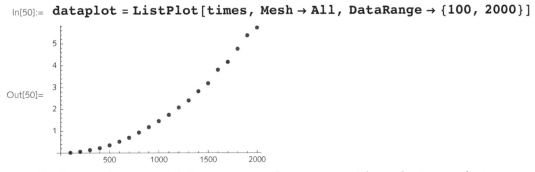

Fitting the data to a linear model shows very good agreement with quadratic complexity.

```
In[51]:= lm = LinearModelFit[times, {x, x^2}, x];
         lm["BestFit"] // TraditionalForm
```

Out[52]//TraditionalForm=

$$1.48606 \times 10^{-6} x^2 - 0.0000615729 x + 0.0126375$$

```
In[53]:= Show[dataplot,
           Plot[lm["BestFit"], {x, 100, 2000}, PlotStyle → Red]]
```

Out[53]=

Finally, let us create an animation that shows the selection sort algorithm at work. To do so, we will convert the Do loop to a For loop and insert one line of code to "record" the sort after each pass, that is, for each value of i. Start by converting from the Do loop implementation. For readability purposes, we will convert the double loop – iterators i and j in the Do loop – and write this using two (nested) For loops.

```
In[54]:= selectionSortFor[lis_] :=
           Module[{slist = lis, len = Length[lis]},
             For[i = 1, i ≤ len, i++,
               For[j = i + 1, j ≤ len, j++,
                 If[slist[[i]] > slist[[j]], slist[[{i, j}]] = slist[[{j, i}]]]
               ]];
             slist]
```

Let us perform a quick check.

```
In[55]:= selectionSortFor[RandomInteger[100, {20}]]
```

```
Out[55]= {3, 3, 9, 18, 20, 31, 41, 43, 45,
          47, 53, 53, 56, 57, 60, 60, 63, 85, 97, 98}
```

For the animation, we want the value of slist before each increment of the iterator i. We will simply append that value to a temporary list and when done with the sort, return that temporary list of lists to animate. Because of inclusion of AppendTo, this code is going to be slower than the previous implementations. But since the AppendTo is not part of the actual sort, it should not slow things down too much. Nonetheless, we only use it here for purposes of creating the visualization. Figure 6.4 shows several frames from the animation.

```
In[56]:= selectionSortList[lis_] :=
           Module[{slist = lis, len = Length[lis], temp = {}},
             For[i = 1, i ≤ len, i++,
               AppendTo[temp, slist];
               For[j = i + 1, j ≤ len, j++,
                 If[slist[[i]] > slist[[j]], slist[[{i, j}]] = slist[[{j, i}]]]
               ]];
             temp]

In[57]:= vec = RandomReal[1, 500];
         sort = selectionSortList[vec];

In[59]:= ListAnimate[ListPlot /@ sort]
```

FIGURE 6.4.   *Frames from selection sort animation: after 1, 50, 100, 150, 200, 300, 400, and 500 steps.*

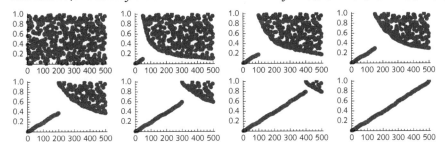

Bubble sort Another elementary sorting algorithm somewhat similar to selection sort is bubble sort. It operates on adjacent elements, exchanging them if they are out of order. After numerous passes, but specifically when no more swaps are needed, the list is sorted.

Note, in this implementation, the iterator i starts at n, equal to the length of the list, and then decrements *down* to 1.

```
In[60]:= bubbleSort[lis_] := Module[{slist = lis, n = Length[lis]},
           For[i = n, i > 0, i--,
             For[j = 2, j ≤ i, j++,
               If[slist[[j - 1]] > slist[[j]],
                 slist[[{j - 1, j}]] = slist[[{j, j - 1}]]]
             ]];
           slist]

In[61]:= vec = RandomReal[1, {1500}];
```

Bubble sort has computational complexity similar to that of selection sort, that is $O(n^2)$, which is too slow for serious sorting work.

```
In[62]:= bubbleSort[vec]; // Timing
Out[62]= {5.66688, Null}
```

```
In[63]:= bubbleSort[vec] == Sort[vec]
Out[63]= True
```

For a more detailed discussion of sorting algorithms, including their computational complexity, see Knuth (1998) or Sedgewick and Wayne (2011).

Exercises

1. Using an `If` function, write a function `gcd[m, n]` that implements the Euclidean algorithm (see Exercise 9 of Section 6.1) for finding the greatest common divisor of *m* and *n*.

2. The *digit sum* of a number is given by adding the digits of that number. For example, the digit sum of 7763 is $7 + 7 + 6 + 3 = 23$. If you iterate the digit sum until the resulting number has only one digit, this is called the *digit root* of the original number. So the digit root of 7763 is $7763 \rightarrow 7 + 7 + 6 + 3 = 23 \rightarrow 2 + 3 = 5$. Create a function to compute the digit root of any positive integer.

3. Use `Piecewise` to define the `quadrant` function given in this section.

4. In the version of `quadrant` using `If` and `Which` developed in this section, the point {0.0, 0.0} is not handled properly because of how *Mathematica* treats the real number 0.0 compared with the integer 0. Write another version of `quadrant` using alternatives (discussed in Section 4.1) to handle this situation and correctly return the 0.

5. Extend `quadrant` to three dimensions, following this rule: for point (x, y, z), if z ≥ 0, then give the same classification as (x, y), with the exception that 0 is treated as a positive number (so the only classifications are 1, 2, 3, and 4); if z < 0, add 4 to the classification of (x, y) (with the same exception). For example, (1, 0, 1) is in octant 1, and (0, −3, −3) is in octant 8. `quadrant` should work for points in two or three dimensions.

6. Consider a sequence of numbers generated by the following iterative process: starting with the list of odd integers 1, 3, 5, 7, …, the first odd number greater than 1 is 3, so delete every third number from the list; from the list of remaining numbers, the next number is 7, so delete every seventh number; and so on. The numbers that remain after this process has been carried out completely are referred to as *lucky numbers* (Weisstein, Lucky numbers). Use a sieving method to find all lucky numbers less than 1000.

7. Create an animation for bubble sort similar to the animation in the text for selection sort.

7

Recursion

*Fibonacci numbers · Thinking recursively · List length · Recursion with multiple arguments ·
Multiplying pairwise elements · Dealing cards, recursively · Finding maxima · Higher-order
functions · Dynamic programming · Merge sort · Run-length encoding*

Many important and classical problems in mathematics and computer science are defined, or
have solutions in terms of recursive definitions: the factorial function, the natural numbers, many
divide-and-conquer algorithms, and parsers for programming languages all use recursion in
fundamental ways. A function is defined using recursion if in its definition, it makes calls to itself.
The great advantage of recursive definitions is their simplicity and directness. Their one major
drawback however, is how quickly the depth and complexity can increase to the point of making
your computations intractable.

This programming paradigm is easily implemented in *Mathematica* in a manner that is both
natural and quite efficient. In fact, many of the built-in operations of *Mathematica* could be written
in *Mathematica* itself using recursion. In this chapter, we will present several examples of recursion
and explain how recursive functions are written and what you can do to work around some of
their potential inefficiencies.

7.1 Fibonacci numbers

Recursive definitions of mathematical quantities were used by mathematicians for centuries
before computers even existed. One famous example is the definition of a special sequence of
numbers first studied in the Middle Ages by the Italian mathematician Leonardo Fibonacci
(*ca.* 1170 – *ca.* 1250). The *Fibonacci numbers* have since been studied extensively, finding application
in such diverse areas as random number generation, compression algorithms, musical tunings,
phyllotaxy in plants, population generation, and much more. See Knuth (1997) for a detailed
discussion.

The Fibonacci numbers are generated as follows: start with two 1s, then add them to generate the third number in the sequence; and generally, each new number in the sequence is created by adding the previous two numbers you have written down.

$$
\begin{array}{cccccccc}
1 & 1 & 2 & 3 & 5 & 8 & 13 & 21 & \ldots \\
F_1 & F_2 & F_3 & F_4 & F_5 & F_6 & F_7 & F_8 & \ldots
\end{array}
$$

The simplest way to define these numbers is with recursion.

$$F_1 = 1$$
$$F_2 = 1$$
$$F_n = F_{n-2} + F_{n-1}, \quad \text{for } n > 2$$

If we think of this sequence as a function, we would just change this to a functional definition.

$$F(1) = 1$$
$$F(2) = 1$$
$$F(n) = F(n-2) + F(n-1), \quad \text{for } n > 2$$

In this form, we can translate the definition directly into *Mathematica*.

```
In[1]:= F[1] = 1;
```

```
In[2]:= F[2] = 1;
```

```
In[3]:= F[n_] := F[n - 2] + F[n - 1] /; n > 2
```

As it turns out, the condition n > 2 is unnecessary because *Mathematica* looks up specific rules such as F[1] = 1 before more general rules like that for F[n].

Here is a list of the first twenty-six Fibonacci numbers.

```
In[4]:= Table[F[i], {i, 1, 26}]
```

```
Out[4]= {1, 1, 2, 3, 5, 8, 13, 21, 34, 55, 89, 144,
         233, 377, 610, 987, 1597, 2584, 4181, 6765,
         10 946, 17 711, 28 657, 46 368, 75 025, 121 393}
```

It is somewhat amazing that this works, but note that whenever you want to compute F[n] for some n > 2, you only apply F to numbers smaller than n. Let us trace the evaluation of F[4] only looking at expressions that involve an F[*integer*] or a sum of two Fs.

In[5]:= **TracePrint[F[4], F[_Integer] | F[_] + F[_]]**

    F[4]

    F[4 - 2] + F[4 - 1]

      F[2]

      F[3]

      F[3 - 2] + F[3 - 1]

        F[1]

        F[2]

Out[5]= 3

The first two lines indicate that F[4] is rewritten to F[4 - 2] + F[4 - 1], and the lines that are indented show the calls of F[2] and F[3]. The lines showing calls to F[1] and F[2] do not have any indented lines under them, since those values are computed directly by a single rule, without making any recursive calls.

There are two key things to understand about recursion:

- You can always apply a function within its own definition, so long as you apply it only to *smaller* values.

- You can apply the function to smaller and smaller values, but you must eventually reach a value that can be computed *without* recursion. In the case of the Fibonacci numbers, the numbers that can be computed without recursion – the *base cases* – are F[1] and F[2].

These principles are applied repeatedly in this chapter and more generally in any recursive function definitions. In terms of the Fibonacci numbers, we will return to them later in Section 7.3, where we will see what can be done about a serious inefficiency in our implementation (also, see Exercise 2 below).

Exercises

1. For each of the following sequences of numbers, see if you can deduce the pattern and write a *Mathematica* function to compute the general term.

   a.
   $$2, \quad 3, \quad 6, \quad 18, \quad 108, \quad 1944, \quad 209\,952, \quad \ldots$$
   $$A_1 \quad A_2 \quad A_3 \quad A_4 \quad A_5 \quad A_6 \quad A_7 \quad \ldots$$

   b.
   $$0, \quad 1, \quad -1, \quad 2, \quad -3, \quad 5, \quad -8, \quad 13, \quad -21, \quad \ldots$$
   $$B_1 \quad B_2 \quad B_3 \quad B_4 \quad B_5 \quad B_6 \quad B_7 \quad B_8 \quad B_9 \quad \ldots$$

   c.
   $$0, \quad 1, \quad 2, \quad 3, \quad 6, \quad 11, \quad 20, \quad 37, \quad 68, \quad \ldots$$
   $$C_1 \quad C_2 \quad C_3 \quad C_4 \quad C_5 \quad C_6 \quad C_7 \quad C_8 \quad C_9 \quad \ldots$$

2. The numbers FA_n represent the number of additions that are done in the course of evaluating the Fibonacci function `F[n]` defined in this section.

$$
\begin{array}{ccccccccc}
0 & 0 & 1 & 2 & 4 & 7 & 12 & 20 & 33 & \ldots \\
FA_1 & FA_2 & FA_3 & FA_4 & FA_5 & FA_6 & FA_7 & FA_8 & FA_9 & \ldots
\end{array}
$$

    Write a function `FA` such that `FA[n]` $= FA_n$.

3. A faster approach to computing Fibonacci numbers uses various identities associated with these numbers (The Fibonacci Sequence 2011). We start the base case at 0 instead of 1 here. The notation $\lfloor number \rfloor$ represents the floor of *number*. You can use `IntegerPart`.

$$f_0 = 0$$
$$f_1 = 1$$

$$
f_n = \begin{cases}
f[k]\,(f[k] + 2\,f[k-1]) & n \text{ even, } k = \lfloor n/2 \rfloor \\
(2\,f[k] + f[k-1])\,(2\,f[k] - f[k-1]) + 2 & n \bmod 4 = 1, \; k = \lfloor n/2 \rfloor \\
(2\,f[k] + f[k-1])\,(2\,f[k] - f[k-1]) - 2 & \text{otherwise}
\end{cases}
$$

    Implement this algorithm. Consider using `Which` for the different conditions.

4. The Fibonacci sequence can also be defined for negative integers using the following formula (Graham, Knuth, and Patashnik 1994):

$$F_{-n} = (-1)^{n-1}\, F_n$$

    The first few terms are

$$
\begin{array}{ccccccccc}
0 & 1 & -1 & 2 & -3 & 5 & -8 & 13 & -21 & \ldots \\
F_0 & F_{-1} & F_{-2} & F_{-3} & F_{-4} & F_{-5} & F_{-6} & F_{-7} & F_{-8} & \ldots
\end{array}
$$

    Write the definitions for Fibonacci numbers with negative integer arguments.

7.2   Thinking recursively

The procedure by which expressions are rewritten during *Mathematica*'s evaluation process – as seen using `Trace` or `TracePrint` – provides insight into how recursion works. But that knowledge is of only limited usefulness in writing recursive functions.

Indeed, the real trick is to *forget* the evaluation process and simply *assume* that the function you are defining will return the correct answer when applied to smaller values. Suspend disbelief – you will begin to see how simple recursion really is. In this section, we will start with some relatively simple recursive programs of some common computational tasks, gradually building up the complexity of the examples.

Length of a list

In Chapter 5, we looked at functional implementations of some list-oriented functions in *Mathematica*. Although most of these functions have more efficient implementations in terms of functional constructs, they provide a convenient vehicle for discussing recursion, and so in this section we will use them to give you some practice with the basic concepts of recursive programming.

As noted in our discussion of Fibonacci numbers, recursion works if the arguments of recursive calls are smaller than the original argument. The same principle applies to functions on lists. One common case is when the argument in the recursive call is the "tail" (think, `Rest`) of the original argument. An example is a recursively defined version of the built-in `Length` function. The idea is that the length of a list is always one greater than the length of its tail.

In[1]:= **length[*lis_*] := length[Rest[*lis*]] + 1**

Applying `length` to a list, however, leads to trouble.

In[2]:= **length[{a, b, c}]**

Rest::norest : Cannot take the rest of expression {} with length zero. ≫

Rest::argx : Rest called with 0 arguments; 1 argument is expected. ≫

$RecursionLimit::reclim : Recursion depth of 256 exceeded. ≫

Well, perhaps it is already obvious, but what we are experiencing is one of the most common errors in defining functions recursively – we forgot the base cases. For `length`, there is just one base case, the empty list.

In[3]:= **length[{}] := 0**

Now `length` works as intended.

In[4]:= **length[{a, b, c}]**

Out[4]= 3

Recursion with multiple arguments

Recursion is of course used for functions with multiple arguments as well. The following function `addPairs[*lis_1*, *lis_2*]` takes two lists of numbers of equal length and returns a list containing the pairwise sums; think vector addition.

The idea is to apply `addPairs` recursively to the tails of both lists. The base case consists of the two empty lists.

In[5]:= **addPairs[{}, {}] := {}**

```
In[6]:=  addPairs[{x1_, r1___}, {x2_, r2___}] :=
           Join[{x1 + x2}, addPairs[{r1}, {r2}]]

In[7]:=  addPairs[{1, 2, 3}, {4, 5, 6}]

Out[7]=  {5, 7, 9}

In[8]:=  addPairs[{x₁, y₁, z₁}, {x₂, y₂, z₂}]

Out[8]=  {x₁ + x₂, y₁ + y₂, z₁ + z₂}
```

Multiplying pairwise elements

Recursive calls do not always have to be on the tail of the original argument. Any smaller list will do. The function `multPairwise` multiplies together successive pairs of elements in a list. The trick is to make the recursive call on the tail of the tail.

```
In[9]:=  multPairwise[{}] := {}
           multPairwise[{x_, y_, r___}] :=
             Join[{x y}, multPairwise[{r}]]

In[11]:=  multPairwise[{3, 9, 17, 2, 6, 60}]

Out[11]=  {27, 34, 360}
```

Note, we are doing no argument checking in these basic examples as we are focused on how recursion works at this point. So, for example, the `multPairwise` function above fails for lists containing an odd number of elements.

```
In[12]:=  multPairwise[{3, 9, 17, 2, 6, 60, 12}]

         Join::heads : Heads List and multPairwise at positions 1 and 2 are expected to be the same. ≫
         Join::heads : Heads List and multPairwise at positions 1 and 3 are expected to be the same. ≫
         Join::heads : Heads List and multPairwise at positions 1 and 4 are expected to be the same. ≫
         General::stop : Further output of Join::heads will be suppressed during this calculation. ≫

Out[12]=  Join[{27}, {34}, {360}, multPairwise[{12}]]
```

Some of the exercises extend these examples asking you to create additional rules to deal with unintended arguments as well as exceptional or pathological cases.

Dealing cards, recursively

Recall the `deal` function defined in Chapter 5: `deal[n]` produces a list of n playing cards randomly chosen from a 52-card deck. Here is how we might write this function recursively.

First, dealing zero cards is easy.

```
In[13]:=  deal[0] := {}
```

Now, suppose we have dealt $n − 1$ cards; how do we deal n? Just randomly deal a card from the remaining $52 - (n - 1) = 53 - n$. To do this, take the complement of the card deck with the dealt cards and add it to the list of cards already dealt.

```
In[14]:= deal[n_] := Module[{dealt = deal[n - 1]},
            Append[dealt, RandomChoice[Complement[cardDeck, dealt]]]
         ]
```

Here again is the cardDeck function defined earlier in Chapter 5.

```
In[15]:= cardDeck = Flatten[Outer[List, {♣, ♦, ♡, ♠},
            Join[Range[2, 10], {J, Q, K, A}]], 1];
```

And here is the recursive deal.

```
In[16]:= deal[5]
```
```
Out[16]= {{♠, Q}, {♡, 2}, {♠, A}, {♡, 4}, {♣, 9}}
```

Finding maxima

Given a list of numbers, the function maxima from Section 5.4 produces a list of those numbers greater than all those that precede them.

```
In[17]:= maxima[{9, 2, 10, 3, 14, 9}]
```
```
Out[17]= {9, 10, 14}
```

To program this using a recursive definition we start by assuming that we can easily compute $\mathtt{maxima}\big[\mathtt{Rest}\big[lis\big]\big]$ for any list, *lis*, and then ask ourselves: how can we compute $\mathtt{maxima}\big[lis\big]$ starting from $\mathtt{maxima}\big[\mathtt{Rest}\big[lis\big]\big]$?

```
In[18]:= maxima[Rest[{9, 2, 10, 3, 14, 9}]]
```
```
Out[18]= {2, 10, 14}
```

The answer is to remove any values not greater than $\mathtt{First}\big[lis\big]$, then put $\mathtt{First}\big[lis\big]$ at the beginning of the result.

```
In[19]:= Select[%, # > 9 &]
```
```
Out[19]= {10, 14}
```

```
In[20]:= Join[{9}, %]
```
```
Out[20]= {9, 10, 14}
```

Again, the base case needs to be accounted for, and we end up with the following:

```
In[21]:= Clear[maxima]
         maxima[{}] := {}
```

```
In[23]:= maxima[{x_, r___}] := Join[{x}, Select[maxima[{r}], # > x &]]
```

In[24]:= **maxima[{3, 6, 2, 1, 8, 7, 12}]**

Out[24]= {3, 6, 8, 12}

The lesson of this section – and it is an important one – is not to worry about how the recursive cases are computed; *assume* that they work, and just think about how to compute the value you want from the result of the recursive call.

Higher-order functions

Many of the built-in functions discussed in Chapter 5 could be written as user-defined functions using recursion. Although they may not be as efficient as the built-in functions, creating them will give you good practice with recursion and should also give you some insight into how these functions operate.

We start with Map. We will call our version map. map$[f, lis]$ applies f to each element of the list *lis*. This is a simple recursion on the tail of *lis*: if we assume that map$[f, \text{Rest}[lis]]$ works, then map$[f, lis]$ is easily obtained from it by joining $f[\text{First}[lis]]$ to the beginning.

In[25]:= **map[f_, {}] := {}**
       map[f_, {x_, y___}] := Join[{f[x]}, map[f, {y}]]

We can quickly check that our map does what was intended.

In[27]:= **map[f, {1, 2, 3}]**

Out[27]= {f[1], f[2], f[3]}

We give one more example of a built-in function that can be defined using recursion, and leave the rest as exercises. Nest$[f, x, n]$ applies f to x, n times. The recursion is, obviously, on n.

In[28]:= **nest[f_, x_, 0] := x**
       nest[f_, x_, n_] := f[nest[f, x, n - 1]]

This iterates the Sin function four times starting with initial value θ.

In[30]:= **nest[Sin, θ, 4]**

Out[30]= Sin[Sin[Sin[Sin[θ]]]]

Exercises

1. Create a recursive function to reverse the elements in a flat list.

2. Create a recursive function to transpose the elements of two lists. Write an additional rule to transpose the elements of three lists.

3. Write a recursive function sumOddElements$[lis]$ that adds up only the elements of the list *lis* that are odd integers. *lis* may contain even integers and nonintegers.

4. Write a recursive function `sumEveryOtherElement`⌈*lis*⌉ that adds up *lis*[[1]], *lis*[[3]], *lis*[[5]], etc. Each of these elements is a number. *lis* may have any number of elements.

5. Write a function `addTriples`⌈*lis₁*, *lis₂*, *lis₃*⌉ that is like `addPairs` in that it adds up the corresponding elements of the three equal-length lists of numbers.

6. Write a function `multAllPairs`⌈*lis*⌉ that multiplies every consecutive pair of integers in the numerical list *lis*. Add a rule that issues an appropriate warning message if the user supplies a list with an odd number of elements.

   In[1]:= **multAllPairs[{3, 9, 17, 2, 6, 60}]**

   Out[1]= {27, 153, 34, 12, 360}

7. Write the function `maxPairs`⌈*lis₁*, *lis₂*⌉ which, for numerical lists of equal length, returns a list of the larger value in each corresponding pair.

8. The function `riffle`⌈*lis₁*, *lis₂*⌉, which merges two lists of equal length, can be defined as follows:

   In[2]:= **riffle[*lis1_*, *lis2_*] := Flatten[Transpose[{*lis1*, *lis2*}]]**

   In[3]:= **riffle[{a, b, c}, {x, y, z}]**

   Out[3]= {a, x, b, y, c, z}

   Rewrite `riffle` using recursion.

9. `maxima` can also be computed more efficiently with an auxiliary function.

   ```
   maxima[{}] := {}
   maxima[{x_, r___}] := maxima[x, {r}]
   ```

   The two-argument version has this meaning: `maxima`⌈*x*, *lis*⌉ gives the maxima of the list `Join`⌈{*x*}, *lis*⌉. Define it. (Hint: the key point about this is that `maxima`⌈*x*, *lis*⌉ is equal to `maxima`⌈*x*, `Rest`⌈*lis*⌉⌉ if *x* ≥ `First`⌈*lis*⌉.) Compare its efficiency with the version in the text.

10. Write recursive definitions for `Fold`, `FoldList`, and `NestList`.

7.3 Dynamic programming

The function `F` defined in Section 7.1 is simple, but quite "expensive" to execute. The reason for this excessive cost is easy to see – in the course of computing `F`[*n*], there are numbers *m* < *n* for which `F`[*m*] is computed many times. For instance, `F`[*n* - 2] is computed twice – it is called from `F`[*n*] and also from `F`[*n* - 1]; `F`[*n* - 3] is computed three times; and `F`[*n* - 4] five times. The number of calls to the Fibonacci function to compute `F`[*n*] is `F`[*n*] itself! This grows exponentially and is therefore quite impractical for large *n*. Even computing the first thirty Fibonacci numbers using this approach will be slow.

This continual recalculation can be eliminated by memorizing these values as they are computed using a technique known as *dynamic programming*. The idea is to dynamically create rules *during* evaluation. Using dynamic programming, a delayed assignment whose right-hand side is an immediate assignment of the same name is defined.

$$f[x\_] := f[x] = \text{right-hand side}$$

When an expression matches this rule, term rewriting creates a `Set` function (immediate assignment) with the specific argument value which, upon evaluation of the right-hand side, becomes a new rule. Since the global rule base is always consulted during evaluation, storing results as rules can cut down on computation time, especially in recursive computations. It is like caching values, but in this case we are caching rules.

In this way, dynamic programming can be described as a method in which rewrite rules are added to the global rule base *dynamically*, that is, during the running of a program. A well-known application of this is to speed up the computation of Fibonacci numbers.

The following definition of `fibD` (D for *dynamic*) is just like the definition of F, but it adds a rule `fibD[n] = fibD[n - 2] + fibD[n - 1]` to the global rule base the first time the value is computed. Since *Mathematica* always chooses the most specific rule to apply when rewriting, whenever a future request for `fibD[n]` is made, the new rule will be used instead of the more general rule in the program. Thus, for every *n*, `fibD[n]` will be computed just once; after that, its value will be found in the rule base.

```
In[1]:= Clear[fibD]
```

```
In[2]:= fibD[1] = 1;
        fibD[2] = 1;
        fibD[n_] := fibD[n] = fibD[n - 2] + fibD[n - 1]
```

We can see the change in the trace of `fibD[4]` as compared with that for F in Section 7.1. Specifically, there is only one evaluation of `fibD[3]` now, since the second evaluation of it is just a use of a global rule. Only those expressions in the following computation that match the pattern given by the second argument to `TracePrint` will be shown: either `fibD` with an integer argument or an assignment for `fibD`.

```
In[5]:= TracePrint[fibD[4],
          fibD[_Integer] | (fibD[_] = fibD[_] + fibD[_])]
        fibD[4]
        fibD[4] = fibD[4 - 2] + fibD[4 - 1]
         fibD[2]
         fibD[3]
```

```
fibD[3] = fibD[3 - 2] + fibD[3 - 1]
  fibD[1]
  fibD[2]
  fibD[3]
 fibD[4]
```

Out[5]= 3

Another way to understand what is going on is to look at the global rule base *after* evaluating fibD[4].

In[6]:= **? fibD**

```
Global`fibD

fibD[1] = 1

fibD[2] = 1

fibD[3] = 2

fibD[4] = 3

fibD[n_] := fibD[n] = fibD[n - 2] + fibD[n - 1]
```

The cost of executing fibD is dramatically lower (see Table 7.1). It is linear in n, rather than in $F[n]$ which grows exponentially.

Furthermore, these costs are only for the first time fibD[n] is computed; in the future, we can find fibD[n] for free, or rather, for the cost of looking it up in the global rule base.

In[7]:= **Timing[fibD[100]]**

Out[7]= {0.000543, 354 224 848 179 261 915 075}

TABLE 7.1. *Number of additions in Fibonacci algorithm using dynamic programming*

n	5	10	15	20	25
additions of fibD[n]	3	8	13	18	23

Dynamic programming can be a useful technique, but needs to be used with care. It will entail some increased cost in memory, as the global rule base is expanded to include the new rules. Furthermore, you could still bump up against the built-in limits with a large computation.

In[8]:= **fibD[1000]**

$RecursionLimit::reclim : Recursion depth of 256 exceeded. ≫

In such cases, if you know that the algorithm is correct, you can temporarily increase the recursion limit. But you first need to clear out the values to `fibD` that were assigned during the previous, failed computation.

In[9]:= **Clear[fibD]**

In[10]:= **fibD[1] = 1;**
       fibD[2] = 1;
       fibD[n_] := fibD[n] = fibD[n - 2] + fibD[n - 1]

In[13]:= **Block[{$RecursionLimit = ∞},**
        fibD[1000]
       ]

Out[13]= 43 466 557 686 937 456 435 688 527 675 040 625 802 564 660 517 371 780 ⋅
         402 481 729 089 536 555 417 949 051 890 403 879 840 079 255 169 295 ⋅
         922 593 080 322 634 775 209 689 623 239 873 322 471 161 642 996 440 ⋅
         906 533 187 938 298 969 649 928 516 003 704 476 137 795 166 849 228 ⋅
         875

Exercises

1. An Eulerian number, denoted $\left\langle {n \atop k} \right\rangle$, gives the number of permutations with k increasing runs of elements. For example, for $n = 3$ the permutations of {1,2,3} contain four increasing runs of length 1, namely {1,3,2}, {2,1,3}, {2,3,1}, and {3,1,2}. Hence, $\left\langle {3 \atop 1} \right\rangle = 4$.

   In[1]:= **Permutations[{1, 2, 3}]**
   Out[1]= {{1, 2, 3}, {1, 3, 2}, {2, 1, 3}, {2, 3, 1}, {3, 1, 2}, {3, 2, 1}}

   This can be programmed using the following recursive definition (Graham, Knuth, and Patashnik 1994), where n and k are assumed to be integers:

   $$\left\langle {n \atop k} \right\rangle = (k+1)\left\langle {n-1 \atop k} \right\rangle + (n-k)\left\langle {n-1 \atop k-1} \right\rangle, \text{ for } n > 0,$$

   $$\left\langle {0 \atop k} \right\rangle = \begin{cases} 1 & k = 0 \\ 0 & k \neq 0. \end{cases}$$

   Create a function `EulerianNumber[n, k]`. You can check your work against Table 7.2 which displays the first few Eulerian numbers.

TABLE 7.2. *Eulerian number triangle*

	$\left\langle{n\atop0}\right\rangle$	$\left\langle{n\atop1}\right\rangle$	$\left\langle{n\atop2}\right\rangle$	$\left\langle{n\atop3}\right\rangle$	$\left\langle{n\atop4}\right\rangle$	$\left\langle{n\atop5}\right\rangle$	$\left\langle{n\atop6}\right\rangle$	$\left\langle{n\atop7}\right\rangle$	$\left\langle{n\atop8}\right\rangle$
0	1								
1	1	0							
2	1	1	0						
3	1	4	1	0					
4	1	11	11	1	0				
5	1	26	66	26	1	0			
6	1	57	302	302	57	1	0		
7	1	120	1191	2416	1191	120	1	0	
8	1	247	4293	15 619	15 619	4293	247	1	0

Because of the triple recursion, you will find it necessary to use a dynamic programming implementation to compute any Eulerian numbers of even modest size.

Hint: Although the above formulas will compute it, you can add the following rule to simplify some of the computation:

$$\left\langle{n\atop k}\right\rangle = 0, \ \ \text{for } k \ge n$$

2. Using dynamic programming is one way to speed up the computation of the Fibonacci numbers, but another is to use a different algorithm. A much more efficient algorithm is based on the following identities.

$$F_1 = 1$$
$$F_2 = 1$$
$$F_{2n} = 2F_{n-1}F_n + F_n^2, \ \ \text{for } n \ge 1$$
$$F_{2n+1} = F_{n+1}^2 + F_n^2, \ \ \ \ \ \ \text{for } n \ge 1$$

Program a Fibonacci number generating function using these identities.

3. You can still speed up the code for generating Fibonacci numbers in the previous exercise by using dynamic programming. Do so, and construct tables like those in this section, giving the number of additions performed for various n by the two programs you have just written.

4. Calculation of the Collatz numbers, as described in Exercise 6 from Section 6.2, can be implemented using recursion and sped up by using dynamic programming. Using recursion and dynamic programming, create the function `collatz[n, i]`, which computes the ith iterate of the Collatz sequence starting with integer n. Compare its speed with that of your original solution.

7.4 Classical examples

Merge sort

Sorting the elements of a list is one of the most common and important tasks in computer science. There are quite a few well-studied algorithms that have been developed for performing various types of sorting. These include selection sort, insertion sort, bubble sort, quick sort, heap sort, merge sort, and many others. We have already looked at a rather primitive list sorting algorithm in Section 4.3 and some elementary sorting algorithms in Section 6.3. In this section, we will develop an algorithm for merge sort, which is a classical divide-and-conquer algorithm.

The procedure for merge sort consists of three basic steps:

1. split the original list into two parts of roughly equal size;

2. sort each part recursively;

3. finally, merge the two sorted sublists.

We will start with the last step first – creating a function `merge` that takes two lists, each assumed to be sorted, and, using recursion, produces a single merged, sorted list. First we deal with the cases of when either of the two lists is empty.

```
In[1]:= merge[lis_List, {}] := lis
        merge[{}, lis_List] := lis
```

The recursion then is on the tail of the sublists. We use the triple blank to pattern match `ra` and `rb` here so that they can represent zero, one, or more arguments.

```
In[3]:= merge[{a_, ra___}, {b_, rb___}] :=
          If[a ≤ b,
            Join[{a}, merge[{ra}, {b, rb}]],
            Join[{b}, merge[{a, ra}, {rb}]]
          ]
```

Here are several test cases.

```
In[4]:= merge[{1, 4, 7}, {2, 6, 9, 14}]
Out[4]= {1, 2, 4, 6, 7, 9, 14}
```

```
In[5]:= merge[{14}, {2, 5, 7, 8}]
Out[5]= {2, 5, 7, 8, 14}
```

Now we turn to the sorting function. This too will be defined recursively by first dividing the list into two sublists, performing the sort on each sublist and then merging these two sorted sublists using the above `merge` function. Here are the two base cases: the empty list and a list with a single element in it.

```
In[6]:= MergeSort[{}] := {};
       MergeSort[{x_}] := {x};
```

Here is the recursion.

$$
In[8]:= \texttt{MergeSort[lis\_List] := Module}\left[\left\{\texttt{div = Floor}\left[\frac{\texttt{Length[lis]}}{2}\right]\right\}\right,
$$

```
       merge[
         MergeSort[Take[lis, div]], MergeSort[Drop[lis, div]]]]
```

Let us look at a few test cases to check for correctness and get a sense of the efficiency of our program.

```
In[9]:= vecI = RandomInteger[{1, 20}, 20]
Out[9]= {6, 20, 5, 5, 4, 2, 18, 19, 20,
         11, 7, 11, 5, 10, 15, 6, 9, 10, 6, 2}
```

```
In[10]:= MergeSort[vecI]
Out[10]= {2, 2, 4, 5, 5, 5, 6, 6, 6, 7,
          9, 10, 10, 11, 11, 15, 18, 19, 20, 20}
```

```
In[11]:= vecR = RandomReal[{0, 1}, 1000];
```

```
In[12]:= Timing[
         Block[{$RecursionLimit = ∞},
           MergeSort[vecR];
         ]]
Out[12]= {0.083562, Null}
```

Notice the need to increase the built-in recursion limit for larger computations. This limitation in our current definitions is due to the facts that both `merge` and `MergeSort` use recursion and that `MergeSort` has a double recursive call in it. In comparison, the built-in `Sort` function, which uses a modified merge sort, is optimized for dealing with large arrays of numbers and is much, much faster.

```
In[13]:= Timing[Sort[vecR];]
Out[13]= {0.000125, Null}
```

Not surprisingly, `Sort` can perform this computation about three orders of magnitude faster than our `MergeSort` for lists of this size. The double recursion of `MergeSort` together with the recursion in the auxiliary `merge` function has come at a fairly steep cost. The exercises will give you a chance to refine the `MergeSort` and improve its efficiency.

Run-length encoding

We now turn to another, somewhat more involved example – programming run-length encoding. `runEncode` implements a method commonly used to compress large amounts of data in those cases where the data are likely to contain long sequences ("runs") of the same value. A good example is the representation of video images in a computer as collections of color values for the individual dots, or pixels, in the image. Since video images often contain large areas of a single color, this representation may lead to lists of hundreds, or even thousands of occurrences of identical color values, one after another. Such a sequence can be represented very compactly using just two numbers, the color value and the length of the run.

`runEncode` compresses a list by dividing it into runs of occurrences of a single element, and returns a list of the runs, each represented as a pair containing the element and the length of its run. So the following list,

```
{9, 9, 9, 9, 9, 4, 3, 3, 3, 3, 5, 5, 5, 5, 5, 5}
```

should produce the following encoding.

```
{{9, 5}, {4, 1}, {3, 4}, {5, 6}}
```

Given a list, *lis*, we just assume that $\texttt{runEncode}\big[\texttt{Rest}\big[\textit{lis}\big]\big]$ gives the compressed form of the tail of *lis* (call it *res*), and ask ourselves: how can we compute $\texttt{runEncode}\big[\textit{lis}\big]$? Let x be $\textit{lis}[[1]]$, and consider the cases:

1. We define what `runEncode` should do in the two base cases: when the list is empty and when the list consists of only one element.

In[14]:= `runEncode[{}] := {}`
        `runEncode[{x_}] := {{x, 1}}`

2. `res` might be `{ }`, if *lis* has one element. In this case, $\textit{lis} = \{\texttt{x}\}$ and $\texttt{runEncode}\big[\textit{lis}\big] = \{\{\texttt{x}, \texttt{1}\}\}$.

3. If the length of *lis* is greater than one, `res` has the form $\{\{y, k\}, ...\}$, and there are two cases:

- $y = x$: $\texttt{runEncode}\big[\textit{lis}\big] = \{\{y, k+1\}, ...\}$

- $y \neq x$: $\texttt{runEncode}\big[\textit{lis}\big] = \{\{x, 1\}, \{y, k\}, ...\}$

In[16]:= `runEncode[{x_, res__}] := Module[{R = runEncode[{res}], p},`
        `p = First[R];`
        `If[x == First[p],`
        `  Join[{{x, p[[2]] + 1}}, Rest[R]],`
        `  Join[{{x, 1}}, R]]]`

```
In[17]:= runEncode[{9, 9, 9, 9, 9, 4, 3, 3, 3, 3, 5, 5, 5, 5, 5, 5}]
Out[17]= {{9, 5}, {4, 1}, {3, 4}, {5, 6}}
```

This can be made a lot clearer by replacing the last clause above with a transformation rule.

```
In[18]:= runEncodeT[{x_, res__}] :=
           runEncodeT[{res}] /. {{y_, k_}, s___} →
             If[x == y, {{x, k + 1}, s}, {{x, 1}, {y, k}, s}]
```

```
In[19]:= runEncodeT[{}] := {}
         runEncodeT[{x_}] := {{x, 1}}
```

```
In[21]:= runEncodeT[{9, 9, 9, 9, 9, 4, 3, 3, 3, 3, 5, 5, 5, 5, 5, 5}]
Out[21]= {{9, 5}, {4, 1}, {3, 4}, {5, 6}}
```

Mathematica contains a function `Split` which effectively does run-length encoding, although it represents the output in a slightly different form from our `runEncode` functions.

```
In[22]:= Split[{9, 9, 9, 9, 9, 4, 3, 3, 3, 3, 5, 5, 5, 5, 5, 5}]
Out[22]= {{9, 9, 9, 9, 9}, {4}, {3, 3, 3, 3}, {5, 5, 5, 5, 5, 5}}
```

You could easily convert the output of `Split` to that produced by our `runEncode` functions by mapping the appropriate pure function.

```
In[23]:= Map[First[Tally[#]] &, %]
Out[23]= {{9, 5}, {4, 1}, {3, 4}, {5, 6}}
```

We leave it as an exercise to go in the other direction, that is, convert the output of our `runEncode` function to that produced by `Split`.

Finally, we should mention some efficiency issues. Each of the run-length encoding implementations presented in this section is reasonably fast for relatively small inputs, vectors of length less than a few hundred. But for larger vectors and for certain cases, they get quite bogged down, mostly due to the deep recursion needed in these cases. This can be seen quite plainly as follows:

```
In[24]:= data = Range[300];
```

```
In[25]:= runEncode[data]
```

$RecursionLimit::reclim : Recursion depth of 256 exceeded. ≫

Join::heads : Heads List and If at positions 1 and 2 are expected to be the same. ≫

```
Out[25]= If[1 == {2, 1}, Join[{{1, p$191261[[2]] + 1}}, Rest[R$191261]],
           Join[{{1, 1}}, R$191261]]
```

A possible solution would be to acknowledge the deep recursion here and increase the built-in recursion limit.

```
In[26]:= Block[{$RecursionLimit = ∞},
          Timing[runEncode[data];]]

Out[26]= {0.005932, Null}
```

But trying larger examples shows that the underlying algorithm, although mostly linear in the size of the input, is quite slow for input as small as about 10 000 in length.

```
In[27]:= Block[{$RecursionLimit = ∞},
          Table[Timing[runEncode[Range[2^k 10^3]];][[1]], {k, 0, 3}]]

Out[27]= {0.041358, 0.10847, 0.393503, 1.55499}
```

In such cases it is best to rethink your algorithm and either try to refine it or find a different and better implementation. In the case of run-length encoding, a more direct, functional approach proves to be much more efficient. Although the following code does not use recursion, we present it here anyway so the reader can compare it with the recursive functions and perform some efficiency tests on the various implementations.

Here is an example list we will use to prototype the code.

```
In[28]:= vec = {9, 9, 9, 9, 9, 4, 3, 3, 3, 3, 5, 5, 5, 5, 5, 5};
```

First take overlapping pairs from vec.

```
In[29]:= Partition[vec, 2, 1]

Out[29]= {{9, 9}, {9, 9}, {9, 9}, {9, 9}, {9, 4}, {4, 3}, {3, 3}, {3, 3},
          {3, 3}, {3, 5}, {5, 5}, {5, 5}, {5, 5}, {5, 5}, {5, 5}}
```

Each run ends at the position at which a pair from the above partition contains different elements.

```
In[30]:= end = Flatten[Position[%, {a_, b_} /; a ≠ b]]

Out[30]= {5, 6, 10}
```

We have to add the positions at the beginning and at the end of the list.

```
In[31]:= end = Join[{0}, end, {Length[vec]}]

Out[31]= {0, 5, 6, 10, 16}
```

Here is the ending position paired up with the next ending position for each run.

```
In[32]:= Partition[end, 2, 1]

Out[32]= {{0, 5}, {5, 6}, {6, 10}, {10, 16}}
```

To indicate where the run starts, not where the previous run ended, we add 1 to each first coordinate.

```
In[33]:= runs = Map[# + {1, 0} &, %]

Out[33]= {{1, 5}, {6, 6}, {7, 10}, {11, 16}}
```

Now each pair from `runs` consists of the starting position and the run length. We can use these pairs as the second argument to `Take` as in the following example.

In[34]:= **Take[{a, b, c, d, e}, {3, 5}]**

Out[34]= **{c, d, e}**

So, finally, here is the list of runs.

In[35]:= **Map[Take[vec, #] &, runs]**

Out[35]= **{{9, 9, 9, 9, 9}, {4}, {3, 3, 3, 3}, {5, 5, 5, 5, 5, 5}}**

Here then is the function `split` that produces output identical to the built-in `Split`.

In[36]:= **split[*lis_*] := Module[{end, t, runs},**
    end =
      Flatten[Position[Partition[*lis*, 2, 1], {*a_*, *b_*} /; *a* ≠ *b*]];
    t = Partition[Join[{0}, end, {Length[*lis*]}], 2, 1];
    runs = Map[# + {1, 0} &, t];
    Map[Take[*lis*, #] &, runs]]

In[37]:= **split[vec]**

Out[37]= **{{9, 9, 9, 9, 9}, {4}, {3, 3, 3, 3}, {5, 5, 5, 5, 5, 5}}**

This implementation is extremely efficient. For example, here is a binary vector weighted more heavily with ones.

In[38]:= **data = RandomChoice$\left[\{.25, .75\} \to \{0, 1\}, 10^5\right]$;**

In[39]:= **Timing[split[data];][[1]]**

Out[39]= **0.386471**

By comparison, we see that our `split` is only about one order of magnitude slower than the built-in function, which is optimized for such tasks.

In[40]:= **Timing[Split[data];][[1]]**

Out[40]= **0.01539**

And here is a quick check to make sure our result is consistent with the built-in function.

In[41]:= **split[data] == Split[data]**

Out[41]= **True**

Exercises

1. Modify one of the `runEncode` functions so that it produces output in the same form as the built-in `Split` function.

   In[1]:= **Split[{9, 9, 9, 9, 9, 4, 3, 3, 3, 3, 5, 5, 5, 5, 5, 5}]**

   Out[1]= {{9, 9, 9, 9, 9}, {4}, {3, 3, 3, 3}, {5, 5, 5, 5, 5, 5}}

2. A slightly more efficient version of `runEncode` uses a three-argument auxiliary function.

   $$\textbf{runEncode[\{\}] := \{\}}$$
   $$\textbf{runEncode[\{}x\_\textbf{, }r\_\_\_\textbf{\}] := runEncode[}x\textbf{, 1, \{}r\textbf{\}]}$$

   $\text{runEncode}\left[x,\ k,\ \{r\}\right]$ computes the compressed version of $\{x,\ x,\ x,\ \dots,\ x,\ r\}$, where the xs are given k times. Define this three-argument function. Using the `Timing` function, compare the efficiency of this version with our earlier version; be sure to try a variety of examples, including lists that have many short runs and ones that have fewer, but longer runs. Use `Table` to generate lists long enough to see any difference in speed.

3. Write the function `runDecode`, which takes an encoded list produced by `runEncode` and returns its unencoded form.

   In[2]:= **runDecode[{{9, 5}, {4, 1}, {3, 4}, {5, 6}}]**

   Out[2]= {9, 9, 9, 9, 9, 4, 3, 3, 3, 3, 5, 5, 5, 5, 5, 5}

4. The `MergeSort` function defined in this section becomes quite slow for moderately sized lists. Perform some experiments to determine if the bottleneck is caused mostly by the auxiliary `merge` function or the double recursion inside `MergeSort` itself. Once you have identified the cause of the problem, try to rewrite `MergeSort` to overcome the bottleneck issues.

8

Numerics

*Types of numbers · Digits and number bases · Random numbers · Precision and accuracy ·
Representation of approximate numbers · Exact vs. approximate numbers · High precision vs.
machine precision · Computations with mixed number types · Working with precision and
accuracy · Arrays of numbers · Sparse arrays · Packed arrays · Newton's method revisited ·
Radius of gyration of a random walk · Statistical tests*

Of the many data types that are used in programming – numbers, strings, symbols, lists – numbers are perhaps the most familiar. You can work with all kinds of numbers in *Mathematica*, but what distinguishes it from traditional programming languages and other computational systems is that with it you can operate on numbers of any size and to any degree of precision. In this chapter we will explore some of the issues related to working with numerical quantities and show how you can incorporate these ideas into programs that involve numerical computations to gain greater control over the precision and accuracy of your results as well as to improve the efficiency of your numerical computations and programs.

8.1   Numbers in *Mathematica*

One of the first things you will notice as you start using *Mathematica* is the manner in which it treats numbers compared with other systems such as calculators, traditional programming languages, and other technical computing software. In most traditional programming languages, you must declare the type of number your functions can take as an argument. Although *Mathematica* automatically handles such details for you an understanding of the different number types and how they invoke different algorithms is helpful for taking full advantage of *Mathematica*'s numerical capabilities and for writing efficient programs.

Mathematica operates differently depending upon the type of input you give it. For example, the following two inputs each compute $\sin(\pi/3)$ but something quite different results.

In[1]:= $\mathbf{Sin}\left[\dfrac{\pi}{3}\right]$

Out[1]= $\dfrac{\sqrt{3}}{2}$

In[2]:= $\mathbf{Sin}\left[\dfrac{\pi}{3.0}\right]$

Out[2]= 0.866025

Not only are different kinds of output returned, but *Mathematica* uses entirely different algorithms for these two computations. In the first case, it looks up identities involving the sine function and multiples of $\pi/3$ and applies the appropriate transformation rule to give an algebraic result. In the second example, because a floating-point number is involved in the input, a numerical routine (a series expansion for sine) is used and the computation is carried out to insure a result with the same precision as the input. In the first case, the exact computation is performed in software; in the second case, most of the computation is done in the hardware of your computer.

Another important numerical feature involves computations with high-precision numbers. When you need to, you can raise the number of digits of precision of the numbers with which you are working. For example, this computes π to 200-digit precision.

In[3]:= $\mathbf{N[\pi, 200]}$

Out[3]= 3.14159265358979323846264338327950288419716939937510582097419445923078164062862089986280348253421170679821480865132823066470938446095505822317253594081284811174502841027019385211055596446229489549303820

You can extend such arbitrary-precision computations to *Mathematica*'s built-in functions. Consider the numerical solution of the van der Pol equation $x''(t) - \frac{1}{5}\big(1 - x^2(t)\big)x'(t) + x(t) = 0$ with the given initial conditions.

In[4]:= $\mathbf{soln = NDSolve\big[\{x''[t] - 1/5\ (1 - x[t]^2)\ x'[t] + x[t] == 0,}$
$\qquad\mathbf{x[0] == 1,\ x'[0] == 0\},\ x,\ \{t, 0, 30\}\big]}$

Out[4]= $\{\{x \to \text{InterpolatingFunction}[\{\{0., 30.\}\}, <>]\}\}$

The solution is represented as an interpolating function, one that passes through the solution over the range for t from 0 to 30. Here is a plot of the original function evaluated at this numerical solution, essentially giving a visual picture of the error in the solution.

In[5]:= $\texttt{Plot}\Big[\texttt{x''[t]} - \dfrac{1}{5}\left(1 - \texttt{x[t]}^2\right)\texttt{x'[t]} + \texttt{x[t]} \texttt{ /.soln,}$

$\{\texttt{t, 0, 30}\}, \texttt{PlotRange} \rightarrow \left\{-10^{-5}, 10^{-5}\right\}\Big]$

Out[5]=

By increasing the precision of the internal algorithms used to solve this differential equation, we can get a more precise solution.

In[6]:= $\texttt{soln24 = NDSolve}\Big[$

$\left\{(\texttt{x'})\texttt{'[t]} - \dfrac{1}{5}\left(1 - \texttt{x[t]}^2\right)\texttt{x'[t]} + \texttt{x[t]} == 0, \texttt{x[0]} == 1, \texttt{x'[0]} == 0\right\},$

$\texttt{x, }\{\texttt{t, 0, 30}\}, \texttt{WorkingPrecision} \rightarrow 26, \texttt{PrecisionGoal} \rightarrow 24\Big]$

Out[6]= $\{\{\texttt{x} \rightarrow \texttt{InterpolatingFunction}[$
$\{\{0, 30.000000000000000000000000\}\}, <>]\}\}$

The plot of the original function evaluated at this higher-precision solution clearly shows much smaller error obtained with soln24. Note the scale on the vertical axis.

In[7]:= $\texttt{Plot}\Big[\texttt{x''[t]} - \dfrac{1}{5}\left(1 - \texttt{x[t]}^2\right)\texttt{x'[t]} + \texttt{x[t]} \texttt{ /.soln24,}$

$\{\texttt{t, 0, 30}\}, \texttt{PlotRange} \rightarrow \left\{-10^{-7}, 10^{-7}\right\}\Big]$

Out[7]=

Working with numbers and understanding issues of precision and accuracy and the interplay between your machine's hardware and software are essential to working with any computational system or programming language. In this chapter we will discuss all these issues to help you to perform efficient computations and write fast code.

Types of numbers

There are four kinds of numbers represented in *Mathematica* – integer, rational, real, and complex. In addition, mathematical constants like π and e are symbols but with numerical properties. Integers are considered to be exact and are represented without a decimal point; rational numbers are quotients of integers and are also considered to be exact.

As discussed in Section 2.1, numbers are atomic expressions, meaning they cannot be broken down into smaller parts. Use the `Head` function to identify the type of number you are working with.

In[8]:= $\mathbf{Map}\left[\mathbf{Head},\ \left\{3,\ \frac{22}{7},\ 3.14,\ 2.34 + 2.09618\ \mathbf{I},\ \pi\right\}\right]$

Out[8]= {Integer, Rational, Real, Complex, Symbol}

Use `FullForm` to see how *Mathematica* represents these objects internally.

In[9]:= $\mathbf{Map}\left[\mathbf{FullForm},\ \left\{3,\ \frac{22}{7},\ 3.14,\ 2.34 + 2.09618\ \mathbf{I},\ \pi\right\}\right]$

Out[9]= {3, Rational[22, 7], 3.14`, Complex[2.34`, 2.09618`], Pi}

Rational numbers As can be seen in the above example, *Mathematica* simplifies rational numbers to lowest terms and leaves them as exact numbers.

This representation of rational numbers as a pair of integers has one more consequence. If you need to pattern match with rational numbers it is important to be aware of their internal representation. For example, trying to pattern match with x_ / y_ will not work.

In[10]:= $\frac{3}{4}\ /.\ \frac{x\_}{y\_} \to \{\mathbf{x},\ \mathbf{y}\}$

Out[10]= $\frac{3}{4}$

But pattern matching instead with `Rational` works fine.

In[11]:= $\frac{3}{4}\ /.\mathbf{Rational}[x\_,\ y\_] \to \{\mathbf{x},\ \mathbf{y}\}$

Out[11]= {3, 4}

The pattern matcher works on the internal form of expressions. So although two expressions may be semantically equivalent, if their underlying structure is different, the pattern matcher will distinguish between them. In other words, the pattern matcher is syntactic, not semantic.

Real numbers Any number containing a decimal point is classified as a real number in *Mathematica*. These numbers are not considered exact and hence are often referred to as *approximate num-*

bers. This often leads to confusion for new users of *Mathematica*. You may know that the number 6.0 is identical to the number 6, *from a mathematical perspective*, but from the perspective of the floating-point unit (FPU) of your computer they are quite different both in terms of their representation and in terms of the algorithms that are used to do arithmetic with them.

One way to see that these numbers are different is to compare them using Equal (==) and SameQ(===).

In[12]:= **6 == 6.0**

Out[12]= True

In[13]:= **6 === 6.0**

Out[13]= False

Equal effectively converts the integer 6 to an approximate number and then compares the last seven binary digits (roughly the last two decimal digits) of the two numbers. SameQ, on the other hand, checks to see if they are identical expressions. Since one is an exact integer and the other is an approximate real number, SameQ returns False.

We will have much more to say about approximate numbers including a full discussion of precision and accuracy in Section 8.2.

Complex numbers Complex numbers are of the form $a + bi$, where a and b are any numbers – integer, rational, or real. *Mathematica* represents $\sqrt{-1}$ by the symbols I or i.

In[14]:= **z = 3 + 4 i**

Out[14]= 3 + 4 i

In[15]:= **Head[z]**

Out[15]= Complex

In[16]:= **FullForm[z]**

Out[16]//FullForm=
            Complex[3, 4]

You can add and subtract complex numbers.

In[17]:= **z + (2 - i)**

Out[17]= 5 + 3 i

You can find the real and imaginary parts of any complex number.

In[18]:= **{Re[z], Im[z]}**

Out[18]= {3, 4}

The absolute value of any number is its distance to the origin in the complex plane. The conjugate can be thought of as the reflection of the complex number in the real axis of the complex plane.

In[19]:= **{Conjugate[z], Abs[z]}**

Out[19]= $\{3 - 4\,\dot{\imath},\ 5\}$

The phase angle is given by the argument.

In[20]:= **Arg[4 $\dot{\imath}$]**

Out[20]= $\dfrac{\pi}{2}$

Each of these properties of complex numbers can be visualized geometrically, as shown in Figure 8.1.

FIGURE 8.1.   *Geometric representation of complex numbers in the plane.*

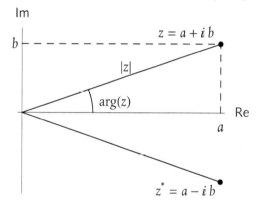

For purposes of pattern matching, complex numbers are quite similar to rational numbers. A complex number $z = a + b\,i$ is treated as a single object for many operations, and is stored as **Complex$\left[a,\ b\right]$**, hence $x\_ + i\ y\_$ will not match with a complex number.

In[21]:= **MatchQ[2 - 3 I, a_ + I b_]**

Out[21]= **False**

In[22]:= **FullForm[2 - 3 I]**

Out[22]//FullForm=

         Complex[2, -3]

To match a complex number z, use the pattern `Complex[x_, y_]` (or `z_Complex`) and use `Re[z]` and `Im[z]` to extract the real and imaginary parts. This is particularly important if you need to plot complex numbers in the plane. For example, here are the roots of a cyclotomic polynomial.

```
In[23]:= Clear[z];
        roots = NSolve[Cyclotomic[11, z], z]
```

Out[24]= {{z → -0.959493 - 0.281733 i}, {z → -0.959493 + 0.281733 i},
          {z → -0.654861 - 0.75575 i}, {z → -0.654861 + 0.75575 i},
          {z → -0.142315 - 0.989821 i}, {z → -0.142315 + 0.989821 i},
          {z → 0.415415 - 0.909632 i}, {z → 0.415415 + 0.909632 i},
          {z → 0.841254 - 0.540641 i}, {z → 0.841254 + 0.540641 i}}

Using a replacement rule, the values of each root are substituted into the list `{Re[z], Im[z]}` to create coordinate points in the plane.

```
In[25]:= pts = {Re[z], Im[z]} /. roots
```

Out[25]= {{-0.959493, -0.281733}, {-0.959493, 0.281733},
          {-0.654861, -0.75575}, {-0.654861, 0.75575},
          {-0.142315, -0.989821}, {-0.142315, 0.989821},
          {0.415415, -0.909632}, {0.415415, 0.909632},
          {0.841254, -0.540641}, {0.841254, 0.540641}}

```
In[26]:= Graphics[{PointSize[Medium], Point[pts]}, Axes → Automatic]
```

Out[26]=

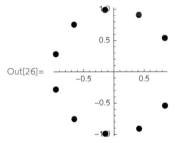

Mathematical constants Built-in constants such as π, e, i, and `Degree` are not treated as explicit numbers by *Mathematica*.

```
In[27]:= {Head[π], NumberQ[π]}
```

Out[27]= {Symbol, False}

These mathematical constants have an attribute that essentially alerts *Mathematica* to the fact that they are numeric in nature. Here is a list of all those built-in symbols that have the `Constant` attribute; this uses `FunctionsWithAttribute` defined in Section 5.6.

In[28]:= **FunctionsWithAttribute[Constant]**

Out[28]= {Catalan, ChampernowneNumber, Degree, E, EulerGamma,
        Glaisher, GoldenRatio, Khinchin, MachinePrecision, Pi}

All mathematical constants and any expressions that are explicit numbers are considered numeric and will return a value of True when NumericQ is applied to them.

In[29]:= **Map[NumericQ, {Catalan, E, Pi}]**

Out[29]= {True, True, True}

For purposes of comparison, *Mathematica* converts any symbol with this attribute to a real number, using what it perceives to be necessary precision.

In[30]:= **RandomReal[{ϕ, e}]**

Out[30]= 1.73228

In[31]:= $e^{\pi} > \pi^{e}$

Out[31]= True

In[32]:= **NumericQ[π^{e}]**

Out[32]= True

Note, in particular, that the symbol ∞ is not numeric.

In[33]:= **NumericQ[∞]**

Out[33]= False

If you have to distinguish between explicit numbers and symbols that represent numbers, then use NumberQ.

In[34]:= **Map[NumberQ, {3.14, π}]**

Out[34]= {True, False}

Digits and number bases

To extract a list of the digits of a number use either IntegerDigits or RealDigits.

In[35]:= **IntegerDigits[1293]**

Out[35]= {1, 2, 9, 3}

In[36]:= **RealDigits[N[EulerGamma]]**

Out[36]= {{5, 7, 7, 2, 1, 5, 6, 6, 4, 9, 0, 1, 5, 3, 2, 9}, 0}

Numbers in base 10 can be displayed in other bases by means of the BaseForm function. For example, the following displays 18 in base 2.

In[37]:= **BaseForm[18, 2]**

Out[37]//BaseForm=
10010_2

The operator $b\,\hat{}\,\hat{}\,n$ takes the number n in base b and converts it to base 10.

In[38]:= **2^^10010**

Out[38]= 18

The letters of the alphabet are used for numbers in bases larger than 10. For example, here are the numbers 1 through 20 in base 16.

In[39]:= **Table[BaseForm[j, 16], {j, 1, 20}]**

Out[39]= $\{1_{16},\ 2_{16},\ 3_{16},\ 4_{16},\ 5_{16},\ 6_{16},\ 7_{16},\ 8_{16},\ 9_{16},\ a_{16},$
$b_{16},\ c_{16},\ d_{16},\ e_{16},\ f_{16},\ 10_{16},\ 11_{16},\ 12_{16},\ 13_{16},\ 14_{16}\}$

Numbers other than integers can be represented in bases different from 10. Here are the first few digits of π in base 2.

In[40]:= **BaseForm[N[π], 2]**

Out[40]//BaseForm=
11.00100100001111111_2

Recall that *Mathematica* is only displaying six significant *decimal* digits while storing quite a few more. In the exercises you are asked to convert the base 2 representation back to base 10. You will need the digits from the base 2 representation, which are obtained with the `RealDigits` function.

In[41]:= **RealDigits[N[π], 2]**

Out[41]= $\{\{1,\ 1,\ 0,\ 0,\ 1,\ 0,\ 0,\ 1,\ 0,\ 0,\ 0,\ 0,\ 1,\ 1,\ 1,\ 1,\ 1,$
$1,\ 0,\ 1,\ 1,\ 0,\ 1,\ 0,\ 1,\ 0,\ 1,\ 0,\ 0,\ 0,\ 1,\ 0,\ 0,\ 0,\ 1,\ 0,$
$0,\ 0,\ 0,\ 1,\ 0,\ 1,\ 1,\ 0,\ 1,\ 0,\ 0,\ 0,\ 1,\ 1,\ 0,\ 0,\ 0\},\ 2\}$

The 2 in this last result indicates where the binary point is placed and can be stripped off this list by wrapping `First` around the expression `RealDigits[N[$\pi$], 2]`.

You are not restricted to integral bases such as in the previous examples. The base can be any real number greater than one. For example:

In[42]:= **RealDigits[N[π], N[GoldenRatio]]**

Out[42]= $\{\{1,\ 0,\ 0,\ 0,\ 1,\ 0,\ 0,\ 1,\ 0,\ 1,\ 0,\ 1,\ 0,\ 0,\ 1,\ 0,\ 0,\ 0,$
$1,\ 0,\ 1,\ 0,\ 1,\ 0,\ 1,\ 0,\ 0,\ 0,\ 0,\ 0,\ 1,\ 0,\ 1,\ 0,\ 0,\ 1,\ 0,$
$0,\ 0,\ 0,\ 1,\ 0,\ 0,\ 1,\ 0,\ 1,\ 0,\ 0,\ 0,\ 1,\ 0,\ 0,\ 0,\ 0,\ 0,\ 1,$
$0,\ 1,\ 0,\ 1,\ 0,\ 1,\ 0,\ 1,\ 0,\ 1,\ 0,\ 0,\ 0,\ 0,\ 0,\ 0,\ 1,\ 0\},\ 3\}$

Random numbers

Statistical work and numerical experimentation often require random numbers to test hypotheses. Several different random number functions are used to generate random numbers in various ranges, domains, and distributions.

Using `RandomReal` without any arguments will generate a uniformly distributed random real number between 0 and 1.

```
In[43]:= RandomReal[]
```

```
Out[43]= 0.225009
```

`RandomReal` can be given a range of numbers. For example, this generates a random real in the range 0 to 100.

```
In[44]:= RandomReal[{0, 100}]
```

```
Out[44]= 41.6008
```

Use a second argument to create vectors or arrays of random numbers.

```
In[45]:= RandomReal[{-10, 10}, {12}]
```

```
Out[45]= {3.48021, 7.14373, -4.43218, 2.47535, 4.67863, -4.43861,
          4.85942, 9.88515, 6.85049, -0.90122, -1.10244, -2.11616}
```

```
In[46]:= RandomReal[1, {5, 5}] // MatrixForm
```

Out[46]//MatrixForm=

$$
\begin{pmatrix}
0.830433 & 0.144071 & 0.161864 & 0.177618 & 0.541445 \\
0.993166 & 0.786002 & 0.550678 & 0.62231 & 0.790748 \\
0.683565 & 0.853041 & 0.481592 & 0.0215971 & 0.584457 \\
0.481247 & 0.41259 & 0.567719 & 0.639649 & 0.231998 \\
0.224393 & 0.266376 & 0.83076 & 0.526745 & 0.716633
\end{pmatrix}
$$

Similar functions are available for generating random integers and complex numbers; they have the same syntax as `RandomReal`.

```
In[47]:= RandomInteger[{-100, 100}, {8}]
```

```
Out[47]= {-26, 66, -31, 26, 82, -54, 17, 7}
```

```
In[48]:= RandomComplex[]
```

```
Out[48]= 0.273891 + 0.242711 i
```

A good random number generator will distribute random numbers evenly over many trials. For example, this generates a list of 10 000 integers between 0 and 9.

```
In[49]:= numbers = RandomInteger[{0, 9}, {10 000}];
```

To plot of the frequency with which each of the digits 0 through 9 occur start by tallying the frequency of each integer and sorting on the first number in each pair.

In[50]:= **snumbers = Sort[Tally[numbers]]**

Out[50]= {{0, 1004}, {1, 983}, {2, 1051}, {3, 959}, {4, 954},
{5, 964}, {6, 1024}, {7, 1023}, {8, 1041}, {9, 997}}

In[51]:= **BarChart[Map[Last, snumbers], ChartLabels → Range[0, 9],
ChartElementFunction → "FadingRectangle"]**

Out[51]=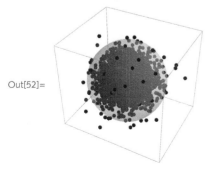

Each of the numbers 0 through 9 occurs *roughly* one-tenth of the time. You would not want these numbers to occur exactly one-tenth of the time, as there would be no randomness in this. In fact, for a uniform distribution of the numbers 0 through 9, any sequence of 10 000 digits is equally as likely to occur as any other sequence of 10 000 digits. A sequence of 10 000 numbers that contains exactly 1000 occurrences of the digit 0 followed by 1000 occurrences of the digit 1, followed by 1000 occurrences of the digit 2, etc., is no more likely than the sequence that contains ten thousand 7s, for example.

In addition to working with uniformly distributed random numbers (the default for RandomReal), you can also work with any of the built-in distributions or even your own, user-defined distribution. RandomVariate is designed for generating numbers for any distribution, continuous or discrete, univariate or multivariate. For example, suppose you wished to work with the normal (or Gaussian) distribution. Here are 2500 points in 3-space, normally distributed about the origin with standard deviation one.

In[52]:= **Graphics3D[{{Opacity[0.4], Sphere[{0, 0, 0}, 3]},
Point[RandomVariate[NormalDistribution[0, 1], {2500, 3}]]}]**

Out[52]=

This gives ten random numbers using the χ^2 distribution with four degrees of freedom.

In[53]:= **RandomVariate[ChiSquareDistribution[4], 10]**

Out[53]= {3.46865, 6.37075, 8.29378, 5.57685, 1.89799,
          2.03538, 1.71713, 8.30217, 1.99303, 0.351816}

Additional functions are available for generating random samples from lists, with or without replacement. For example, `RandomChoice` selects elements from a list with replacement. That can be a list of numbers or any arbitrary expressions.

In[54]:= **RandomChoice[{"red", "blue", "green"}, 20]**

Out[54]= {red, blue, blue, blue, green, blue, red, red, red, red, green,
          blue, red, green, green, blue, green, green, green, green}

Randomly choosing from the list {1, -1} can be used to create step directions in a one-dimensional random walk. A value of 1 indicates a step of unit length to the right and a value of -1 indicates a step to the left.

In[55]:= **RandomChoice[{1, -1}, {12}]**

Out[55]= {1, 1, -1, 1, 1, -1, 1, 1, 1, 1, -1, -1}

The random walk is then created by generating running sums, or accumulating the step directions.

In[56]:= **Accumulate[%]**

Out[56]= {1, 2, 1, 2, 3, 2, 3, 4, 5, 6, 5, 4}

In[57]:= **walk1D[*steps*_] := Accumulate[RandomChoice[{1, -1}, {*steps*}]]**

Visualizing with `ListLinePlot` shows the displacement from the origin on the vertical axis and the number of steps on the horizontal axis.

In[58]:= **ListLinePlot[walk1D[20 000]]**

Out[58]=

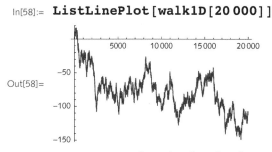

`RandomSample`, on the other hand, selects without replacement and so its output is limited by the size of the list from which you are selecting. For example, this generates a random permutation on the first twenty integers.

In[59]:= **RandomSample[Range[20], 20]**

Out[59]= {17, 3, 19, 9, 15, 20, 13, 2,
10, 11, 8, 6, 16, 5, 4, 12, 1, 7, 18, 14}

Weights can be assigned in both `RandomChoice` and `RandomSample`. This chooses ten 0s and 1s, with a 25% chance of a 0 being chosen and a 75% chance of a 1.

In[60]:= **RandomChoice[{0.25, 0.75} → {0, 1}, 10]**

Out[60]= {0, 1, 1, 1, 1, 0, 1, 1, 1, 1}

Using a similar syntax to `RandomReal` and `RandomInteger`, you can create vectors, arrays, and tensors of random numbers.

In[61]:= **RandomChoice[{0, 1}, {4, 4}] // MatrixForm**

Out[61]//MatrixForm=

$$\begin{pmatrix} 0 & 0 & 1 & 1 \\ 0 & 0 & 1 & 1 \\ 1 & 0 & 0 & 1 \\ 0 & 1 & 0 & 1 \end{pmatrix}$$

Exercises

1. Define a function `complexToPolar` that converts complex numbers to their polar representations. Then, convert the numbers $3 + 3i$ and $e^{\pi i/3}$ to polar form.

2. Using the built-in `Fold` function, write a function `convert[lis, b]` that accepts a list of digits in any base b (less than 20) and converts it to a base 10 number. For example, 1101_2 is 13 in base 10, so your function should handle this as follows:

   In[1]:= **convert[{1, 1, 0, 1}, 2]**

   Out[1]= 13

3. Create a function to compute the sum of the digits of any integer. Write an additional rule to give the sum of the base-b digits of an integer. Then use your function to compute the *Hamming weight* of any integer: the Hamming weight of an integer is given by the number of 1s in the binary representation of that number.

4. Write a function `sumsOfCubes[n]` that takes a positive integer argument n and computes the sums of cubes of the digits of n (Hayes 1992).

5. Use `NestList` to iterate the process of summing cubes of digits, that is, generate a list starting with an initial integer of the successive sums of cubes of digits. For example, starting with 4, the list should look like: {4, 64, 280, 520, 133, …}. Note, $64 = 4^3$, $280 = 6^3 + 4^3$, etc. Extend the list for at least 15 values and make an observation about any patterns you notice. Experiment with other starting values.

6. Binary shifts arise in the study of computer algorithms because they often allow you to speed up calculations by operating in base 2 or in bases that are powers of 2. Try to discover what a binary shift does by performing the following shift on 24 (base 10). First get the integer digits of 24 in base 2.

In[2]:= **IntegerDigits[24, 2]**

Out[2]= {1, 1, 0, 0, 0}

Then, do a binary shift, one place to the right.

In[3]:= **RotateRight[%]**

Out[3]= {0, 1, 1, 0, 0}

Finally, construct an integer from these binary digits and convert back to base 10.

In[4]:= **FromDigits[%, 2]**

Out[4]= 12

Experiment with other numbers (including both odd and even integers) and make some conjectures.

7. The `survivor[n]` function from Section 5.8 can be programmed using binary shifts. This can be done by rotating the base 2 digits of the number n by one unit to the left and then converting this rotated list back to base 10. For example, if $n = 10$, the base 2 representation is 1010_2; the binary shift gives 0101_2; converting this number back to base 10 gives 5, which is the output to `survivor[5]`. Program a new `survivor` function using the binary shift.

8. Using the `Dice` function from Exercise 9 in Section 4.2, create a function `RollDice[]` that "rolls" two dice and displays them side-by-side. Then create an additional rule, `RollDice[n]`, that rolls a pair of dice n times and displays the result in a list or row.

9. Create functions `walk2D` and `walk3D` that generate two-dimensional and three-dimensional lattice walks, respectively. For example, the two-dimensional case can use compass directions north, south, east, west that are represented by the list {{0, 1}, {0, -1}, {1, 0}, {-1, 0}}.

10. A surprisingly simple pseudorandom number algorithm is the *linear congruential* method. It is quite easy to implement and has been studied extensively. Sequences of random numbers are generated by a formula such as the following:

$$x_{n+1} = x_n \, b + 1 \pmod{m}.$$

The starting value x_0 is the *seed*, b is the *multiplier*, and m is the *modulus*. Recall that 7 mod 5 is the remainder upon dividing 7 by 5.

In[5]:= **Mod[7, 5]**

Out[5]= 2

Implement the linear congruential method and test it with a variety of numbers m and b. If you find that the generator gets in a loop easily, try a large value for the modulus m. See Knuth (1997) for a full treatment of random number generating algorithms.

11. Implement a *quadratic congruential* random number generator. The iteration is given by the following, where a, b, and c are the parameters, m is the modulus, and x_0 is the starting value:

$$x_{n+1} = \left(a \, x_n^2 + b \, x_n + c\right) \bmod m$$

12. John von Neumann, considered by many to be the "father of computer science," suggested a random number generator known as the *middle-square* method. Starting with a ten-digit integer, square the initial integer and then extract its middle ten digits to get the next number in the sequence. For example, starting with 1234567890, squaring it produces 1524157875019052100. The middle digits are 1578750190, so the sequence starts out 1234567890, 1578750190, 4521624250, ... Implement a middle square random number generator and then test it on a 1000-number sequence. Was the "father of computer science" a good random number generator?

13. Information theory, as conceived by Claude Shannon in the 1940s and 1950s, was originally interested in maximizing the amount of data that can be stored and retrieved over some channel such as a telephone line. Shannon devised a measure, now called the *entropy*, that gives the theoretical maxima for such a signal. Entropy can be thought of as the average uncertainty of a single random variable and is computed by the following, where $p(x)$ is the probability of event x over a domain X:

$$H(X) = -\sum_{x \in X} p(x) \log_2 p(x)$$

Generate a plot of the entropy (built into *Mathematica* as `Entropy`) as a function of success probability. You can simulate n trials of a coin toss with probability p using:

```
RandomVariate[BernoulliDistribution[p], n]
```

See Manning and Schütze (1999) for a discussion of entropy in the context of information theory generally and in natural language processing in particular. Also, see Claude Shannon's very readable original paper on the mathematical theory of communication (Shannon 1948).

8.2 Numerical computation

Precision and accuracy

When working with real numbers in any programming language, you are working with inexact, or approximate quantities. In *Mathematica*, any number that contains a decimal point is considered to be an approximate number. An approximate number can be specified explicitly, such as 1.57, or you can use N to get approximations to exact quantities.

```
In[1]:= e = N[e]
```
```
Out[1]= 2.71828
```

The *precision* of an approximate number provides a measure of the relative uncertainty in the value of that number. This can be represented as the number of significant decimal digits in that number. *Accuracy* gives a measure of the absolute size of the uncertainty in the value of a number. It can be thought of as the number of these digits to the right of the decimal point.

```
In[2]:= {Precision[e], Accuracy[e]}
```
```
Out[2]= {MachinePrecision, 15.5203}
```

For an exact number, these are both infinite.

In[3]:= **{Precision[3 / 4], Accuracy[3 / 4]}**

Out[3]= $\{\infty, \infty\}$

For arbitrary-precision numbers, you are measuring the size of the relative and absolute errors.

In[4]:= **a = 22.111111111111111111;**
{Precision[a], Accuracy[a]}

Out[5]= $\{19.3446, 18.\}$

The symbol `MachinePrecision` is used to indicate a machine-precision number. There is no measure of the uncertainty of machine-precision numbers since machine-precision arithmetic does not keep track of significance. As we will see, this is in contrast to arbitrary-precision numbers for which *Mathematica* is able to track the uncertainty.

To see the effective number of digits in the representation of a machine number on your computer, evaluate `$MachinePrecision`.

In[6]:= **$MachinePrecision**

Out[6]= **15.9546**

Numbers that can be operated with on your computer's hardware (typically the FPU) are called *machine numbers*. Typically, 64 binary digits (IEEE double floats) are needed to specify a machine number: one for the sign, eleven for the exponent, and fifty-two for the mantissa (actually fifty-three, since the leading digit is implicitly taken as zero). The value of `$MachinePrecision` is $(64 - 11) \log_{10} 2$, giving machine numbers of about 16 decimal digits.

In[7]:= **53 Log[10, 2] // N**

Out[7]= **15.9546**

The reason we refer to these numbers as "approximate" is that there is some uncertainty about their value. To be more precise about this, an approximate number x is one in which the value of x lies somewhere inside of an interval $x - \frac{\delta}{2}$ to $x + \frac{\delta}{2}$ for some uncertainty δ. A number with precision p is then defined to have uncertainty $|x| 10^{-p}$.

In[8]:= **p /. Solve[δ == Abs[x] 10^{-p}, p]**

> Solve::ifun : Inverse functions are being used by Solve, so some solutions
> may not be found; use Reduce for complete solution information. ≫

Out[8]= $\left\{ -\dfrac{\text{Log}\left[\frac{\delta}{\text{Abs}[x]}\right]}{\text{Log}[10]} \right\}$

In other words, the precision of a real number x is given by $-\log_{10}(\delta/|x|)$ for some uncertainty δ. So we could manually compute the precision of e above using an uncertainty of 10^{-15}, which is approximately what *Mathematica* assumes for machine-precision numbers.

In[9]:= $-\textbf{Log}\left[\textbf{10, }\dfrac{\textbf{10}^{-15}}{\textbf{Abs[e]}}\right]$

Out[9]= 15.4343

On the other hand, a number with accuracy *a* will have uncertainty $\delta = 10^{-a}$ and hence accuracy can be expressed as $-\log_{10}(\delta)$.

Another way to think about precision and accuracy involves the notion of scale (Knapp 2001). If the scale of a number is defined as $\log_{10}|n|$, then you can think of the precision of a number as being equal to *scale + accuracy*. The scale is essentially a measure of the size of the logarithm of the number itself.

In[10]:= `scale[x_] := Log[10, Abs[x]]`

Looking at a few examples will help to make this more concrete. In this first example, the scale is zero so precision and accuracy are the same.

In[11]:= `x = 1.0;`
`{InputForm[x], scale[x], Accuracy[x], Precision[x]}`

Out[12]= `{1., 0., 15.9546, MachinePrecision}`

The number 0.01 is a machine-precision number; because of the two digits to the right of the decimal point, its accuracy is increased and its scale is −2.

In[13]:= `x = 0.01;`
`{InputForm[x], scale[x], Accuracy[x], Precision[x]}`

Out[14]= `{0.01, -2., 17.9546, MachinePrecision}`

And going in the other direction, for the number 1000.0, scale is increased and accuracy decreased. Each addition of a digit to the left of the decimal point has the effect of reducing the number of significant digits to the right of the decimal point by one.

In[15]:= `x = 1000.0;`
`{InputForm[x], scale[x], Accuracy[x], Precision[x]}`

Out[16]= `{1000., 3., 12.9546, MachinePrecision}`

Representation of approximate numbers

When *Mathematica* displays numbers in output, the default is to print six digits.

In[17]:= $\textbf{pi = N}[\pi]$

Out[17]= 3.14159

Do not assume that typing in what is displayed will result in the same value.

In[18]:= **pi - 3.14159**

Out[18]= 2.65359×10^{-6}

This seemingly strange behavior – the fact that `pi` does not appear to be equal to 3.14159 – can be explained by looking at the internal representation of this expression.

In[19]:= **FullForm[pi]**

Out[19]//FullForm=

   3.141592653589793`

The command N[π] causes *Mathematica* to first convert π to a machine-precision number, and then to display the number of digits determined by the built-in output formatting rules, which, by default, specify six digits to display in the output. Any computations with this number occur using the number's full precision.

Note that a number mark `` ` `` was printed at the end of the above number. This is a machine-independent mark used to indicate that this is a machine-precision number. When you work with numbers that are not at machine precision, this will be indicated by a number following the number mark. For example, here is a high-precision number.

In[20]:= **N[π, 18]**

Out[20]= 3.14159265358979324

The following shows the full internal representation of this number with the precision indicated by the 18 following the number mark. The extra digits are a result of the adaptive procedure that N uses to increase the working precision of internal computations so that the requested precision can be achieved.

In[21]:= **FullForm[%]**

Out[21]//FullForm=

   3.14159265358979323846264338327950288442`18.

You can use this number mark to set the precision of a number.

In[22]:= **x = 1.23`25**

Out[22]= 1.230000000000000000000000

In[23]:= **{Precision[x], Accuracy[x]}**

Out[23]= {25., 24.9101}

Similarly, you can set the accuracy using the double number mark.

In[24]:= **y = 1.23``25**

Out[24]= 1.230000000000000000000000

In[25]:= `{Precision[y], Accuracy[y]}`

Out[25]= `{25.0899, 25.}`

In a sense, *Mathematica* treats all machine real numbers as having the same precision. And, most significantly, there is no real measure of how uncertain a machine number is since the hardware-dependent machine-precision arithmetic does not keep track of significance. Explicitly setting the precision with N or using number marks forces *Mathematica* to use significance arithmetic and thus track precision throughout a computation. This is not possible with machine-precision numbers. So, even a number with three digits of precision is considered more precise than a machine-precision number since *Mathematica* is able to track its precision using significance arithmetic.

Exact vs. approximate numbers

As described above, all integers and rational numbers are considered exact. For complex numbers, if both the real and imaginary parts are exact, then the complex number is treated as exact.

In[26]:= $\left\{\texttt{Precision[7], Precision}\left[\frac{1}{9}\right]\texttt{, Precision[3 + 4 I]}\right\}$

Out[26]= $\{\infty, \infty, \infty\}$

Exact numbers have more precision than any approximate number. Representing a number with infinite precision is another way of saying that it is exact.

As we saw in the example at the beginning of this chapter, this distinction between exact and approximate numbers allows *Mathematica* to operate on expressions involving such numbers differently.

In[27]:= $\left\{\texttt{Cos}\left[\frac{\pi}{4}\right]\texttt{, Cos}\left[\frac{\pi}{4.0}\right]\right\}$

Out[27]= $\left\{\frac{1}{\sqrt{2}}, 0.707107\right\}$

But, in fact, more is true. As far as *Mathematica* is concerned, all integers are not created equal. In stark contrast to programming languages, such as C or PASCAL that typically restrict computations with integers to 16 or 32 bits (this restricts integers to a magnitude of 2^{16} in the case of 16-bit integers, or to a magnitude of 2^{32} in the case of 32-bit integers), *Mathematica* allows you to compute with integers and rational numbers of arbitrary size. A machine integer is an integer whose magnitude is small enough to fit into your machine's natural word size, and to be operated on by the machine's instructions, generally on its floating-point processor. Word size means the number of bits used to represent integers.

If two integers are to be added, *Mathematica* first checks to see if the numbers can be added as machine integers. On most computers, machine integers typically have a word size of $\pm 2^{31}$. You can see this using a function defined in the `Developer` context.

In[28]:= **Developer`MachineIntegerQ$\left[2^{31}\right]$**

Out[28]= **False**

In[29]:= **Developer`MachineIntegerQ$\left[2^{31} - 1\right]$**

Out[29]= **True**

You could also see how this is dealt with outside of *Mathematica* by compiling a C program and giving it an input that causes an overflow.

In[30]:= **cAdd = Compile[{{n, _Integer}}, n + 1, CompilationTarget → "C"]**

Out[30]= CompiledFunction[{n}, n + 1, –CompiledCode–]

The hardware of the machine that this C function is using to do this computation cannot handle numbers of this size.

In[31]:= **cAdd[2^31 - 1]**

CompiledFunction::cfne :
   Numerical error encountered; proceeding with uncompiled evaluation. ≫

Out[31]= 2 147 483 648

This number is within range.

In[32]:= **cAdd[2^31 - 2]**

Out[32]= 2 147 483 647

We will have more to say about compiling functions in Section 12.4.

Arithmetic operations on integers within the word-size range can be performed using the machine's own instructions (typically on the machine's FPU), whereas operations on integers out of that range must be done by software, which can be less efficient.

If the two numbers to be added are machine integers and *Mathematica* can determine that their sum is a machine integer, then the addition is performed at this low level.

If, on the other hand, either of the integers or their sum is larger than the size of a machine integer, then *Mathematica* performs the arithmetic using special algorithms. Integers in this range are referred to as extended-precision integers. For example, the following computation, although impossible to execute on most machine FPUs, is handled by *Mathematica*'s arithmetic algorithms for operating on extended-precision integers.

In[33]:= **$2^{256} + 2^{1024}$**

Out[33]= 179 769 313 486 231 590 772 930 519 078 902 473 361 797 697 894 230 657 273 ⸴
430 081 157 732 675 805 500 963 132 708 477 322 407 536 021 120 113 879 ⸴
871 393 357 658 789 768 814 416 622 492 847 430 639 474 124 377 767 893 ⸴
424 865 485 276 302 219 601 246 094 119 453 082 952 085 005 768 838 150 ⸴
682 342 462 881 589 705 199 778 143 432 586 921 495 693 274 206 093 217 ⸴
230 604 120 280 344 292 940 337 537 353 777 152

Rational numbers are treated somewhat similarly to integers in *Mathematica* since the rational number a/b can be thought of as a pair of integers, and, in fact, as we saw earlier, it is represented as `Rational[a, b]`. In this way, algorithms for exact rational arithmetic will use integer arithmetic (either machine or extended) to perform many of the necessary computations.

High precision vs. machine precision

Real numbers (often referred to as "floating-point numbers") contain decimal points; they are not considered exact.

In[34]:= **{Head[1.61803], Precision[1.61803]}**

Out[34]= {Real, MachinePrecision}

In[35]:= **{Head[1.4987349873487454511],**
      Precision[1.4987349873487454511]}

Out[35]= {Real, 19.1757}

In a manner similar to how integers are treated, *Mathematica* uses different internal algorithms to do arithmetic on real numbers, depending upon whether you are using high-precision reals or not. Whenever possible, arithmetic operations on real numbers are performed using machine-precision (fixed) reals. Real numbers that can be computed at the hardware level of the machine are referred to as fixed-precision reals. This is seen from the computation of the precision of the number 1.61803 above; `MachinePrecision` was returned.

The number of digits that each machine uses for fixed-precision real numbers is given by the system variable `$MachinePrecision`.

In[36]:= **$MachinePrecision**

Out[36]= 15.9546

Here are the limits on the size of *machine* numbers with which you can work.

In[37]:= **{$MinMachineNumber, $MaxMachineNumber}**

Out[37]= $\{2.22507 \times 10^{-308}, 1.79769 \times 10^{308}\}$

Creating a compiled C function that simply divides its argument by 10, shows that the hardware is restricted to the numbers given above.

```
In[38]:= div10 = Compile[{{x, _Real}}, x / 10, CompilationTarget → "C"]
```

$$Out[38]= \text{CompiledFunction}\left[\{x\}, \frac{x}{10}, -\text{CompiledCode}-\right]$$

```
In[39]:= div10[10^-308]
```

CompiledFunction::cfsa :
Argument 1/(10000000000000000000000000000000000000000000000000000 ≪211≫
000000000000000000000000000000000000000000000000000)
at position 1 should be a machine–size real number. ≫

Out[39]= 1 /
1 000 000 000 000 000 000 000 000 000 000 000 000 000 000 000 000 000 000 000 .
000 000 000 000 000 000 000 000 000 000 000 000 000 000 000 000 000 000 000 .
000 000 000 000 000 000 000 000 000 000 000 000 000 000 000 000 000 000 000 .
000 000 000 000 000 000 000 000 000 000 000 000 000 000 000 000 000 000 000 .
000 000 000 000 000 000 000 000 000 000 000 000 000 000 000 000 000 000 000 .
000 000 000 000 000 000 000 000

The limit imposed by $MaxMachineNumber is essentially given by $2^{1023} * 1.1111\ldots11$ (53 total binary digits), a number just smaller than 2^{1024}. The number 53 comes from the number of binary digits that are used to specify the mantissa for any floating-point number.

```
In[40]:= n = N[2^1024]
```

Out[40]= $1.797693134862316 \times 10^{308}$

```
In[41]:= MantissaExponent[n]
```

Out[41]= {0.1797693134862316, 309}

```
In[42]:= Length[First@RealDigits[First[%], 2]]
```

Out[42]= 53

```
In[43]:= $MaxMachineNumber
```

Out[43]= 1.79769×10^{308}

As with machine integers discussed above, although there is a limit to the magnitude of the machine-precision numbers on any given computer, you can still compute with numbers outside of this range. Real numbers larger than machine-precision reals are referred to as multiple-, or extended-precision reals and arithmetic on such numbers is called multiple-precision arithmetic or arbitrary-precision floating-point arithmetic. On a machine whose $MachinePrecision is 16 decimal digits, computations involving real numbers with greater than 16 significant digits will be performed using arbitrary-precision algorithms.

When doing computations on inexact numbers, *Mathematica* uses two different types of arithmetic, depending upon the precision of the numbers involved. Machine-precision floating-point arithmetic is used whenever the numbers can be handled in the machine's hardware routines. For example:

In[44]:= **{Precision[1.23], Accuracy[1.23]}**

Out[44]= {MachinePrecision, 15.8647}

In[45]:= **{Sin[1.23], Precision[Sin[1.23]], Accuracy[Sin[1.23]]}**

Out[45]= {0.942489, MachinePrecision, 15.9803}

Mathematica represents 1.23 as a machine floating-point number and will use machine arithmetic on it whenever possible. The accuracy of the sine of this number is a reflection of the fact that this number is a machine number a bit smaller than 1.

In the following example, n has smaller accuracy due to the fact that there is an explicit number of digits to the right of the decimal point and roughly speaking, for machine-precision numbers, the number of digits to the right of the decimal plus the number of digits to the left of the decimal should add up to the number of decimal digits given by $MachinePrecision.

In[46]:= **n = 12 345.6789101112**

Out[46]= 12 345.7

In[47]:= **{Precision[n], Accuracy[n], scale[n]}**

Out[47]= {MachinePrecision, 11.8631, 4.09151}

You can adjust the precision of numbers with **SetPrecision**, although you should note that this function will not make an inexact number more exact.

In[48]:= **SetPrecision$\left[\frac{1}{3}, 30\right]$**

Out[48]= 0.333333333333333333333333333333

Using **SetPrecision** on an approximate number returns a number that might look odd at first sight. This happens because **SetPrecision** is adding digits that are zero *in base* 2.

In[49]:= **SetPrecision[0.6000000000, 20]**

Out[49]= 0.59999999999999997780

In fact, *Mathematica* has created more digits than are displayed.

In[50]:= **FullForm[%]**

Out[50]//FullForm=
0.59999999999999997779553950749686919152736663818359375`20.

As an aside, you can effectively do fixed-precision computation by setting $MaxPrecision and $MinPrecision to the same value. As their names imply, these two global variables limit the number of digits of precision in arbitrary-precision numbers.

```
In[51]:= Block[{$MaxPrexision = 4, $MinPrecision = 4},
            Exp[2`4]] // FullForm
```

Out[51]//FullForm=

7.3890560989306502272304274465767803601`4.

Using an infamous function, the logistic map, you can see the effect of using fixed precision on unstable computations.

```
In[52]:= f[x_] := 4 x (1 - x)
```

First, using extended precision, you can see that iterating this function causes such a loss of precision that the results have no significant digits after about 50 iterations. This is indicated below by the last few iterates framed with an error box. Hovering your mouse over these boxes displays a message, "No significant digits are available to display."

```
In[53]:= NestList[f, N[3 / 10, 30], 60]
```

Out[53]= {0.300000000000000000000000000000, 0.840000000000000000000000000000,
          0.537600000000000000000000000000, 0.994344960000000000000000000000,
          0.0224924242090393600000000000000, 0.0879453645445629061557063688,
          0.320843909598747375414539001, 0.871612381088552788772233283,
          0.447616952886784854529917, 0.989024065500538729658560,
          0.0434218534452992248573233, 0.16614558345469672277398,
          0.55416491661653231340733, 0.988264647231696406743, 0.046390537054828249786,
          0.17695382050637142753, 0.58256466365828124158, 0.9727323052599795713,
          0.1060966702543419638, 0.3793606672611335716, 0.941784605585284283,
          0.21930544907141921, 0.68484227631600947, 0.8633333315452640,
          0.4719555607528770, 0.996854037709258, 0.01254426084803,
          0.04954760947123, 0.1883705754677, 0.6115484070626, 0.950227811527,
          0.18917967091, 0.61356289210, 0.9484138782, 0.1956999755, 0.629605980,
          0.93280916, 0.25070493, 0.7514079, 0.7471763, 0.755615, 0.73864,
          0.77220, 0.7036, 0.8341, 0.553, 0.99, 0.05, 0.2, 0.6, 0.×10□, 0.×10□, 0.×10□,
          0.×10², 0.×10⁵, 0.×10¹¹, 0.×10²⁴, 0.×10⁴⁹, 0.×10⁹⁸, 0.×10¹⁹⁷, 0.×10³⁹⁶}
```

Trying the same computation but with 30-digit fixed precision, *Mathematica* essentially is using SetPrecision[..., 30] at every step in this computation and hence there is no loss of precision.

```
In[54]:= Block[{$MinPrecision = 30, $MaxPrecision = 30},
            values = NestList[f, N[3 / 10, 30], 60]];
```
```

In[55]:= **ListPlot[Map[Precision, values]]**

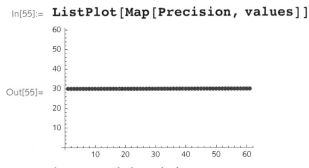

Out[55]=

Let us clear unneeded symbols.

In[56]:= **Clear[a, b, n, x, f, values]**

Computations with mixed number types

When doing computations with numbers, *Mathematica* tries to work with the most general type of number in the expression at hand. For example, when adding two rational numbers, the sum is a rational number, unless of course it can be reduced to an integer.

In[57]:= $\dfrac{34}{21} + \dfrac{2}{11}$

Out[57]= $\dfrac{416}{231}$

In[58]:= $\dfrac{3}{4} + \dfrac{9}{4}$

Out[58]= 3

But, if one of the terms is a real number, then all computations are done using real-number arithmetic – *Mathematica* works at the lowest precision of the numbers in the expression.

Here the machine-precision number 2.0 is raised to an exact integer power. A machine-precision result is returned.

In[59]:= 2.0^{100}

Out[59]= 1.26765×10^{30}

In[60]:= **Precision[%]**

Out[60]= MachinePrecision

Similarly, if a machine-precision number is added to a high-precision number, *Mathematica* will perform the computation at the lower machine precision.

In[61]:= **2.1 + 3.0`30**

Out[61]= **5.1**

In[62]:= **Precision[%]**

Out[62]= MachinePrecision

Because *Mathematica* keeps track of the precision for arbitrary-precision numbers, doing arithmetic with two such numbers causes significance arithmetic to be used allowing for a result with precision close to that of the summands themselves.

In[63]:= **2.1`35 + 3.0`45**

Out[63]= **5.1000000000000000000000000000000000**

In[64]:= **Precision[%]**

Out[64]= **35.3854**

And similarly when one number has machine precision and another has arbitrary precision.

In[65]:= **a = N[2];**

In[66]:= **b = N[2^{99}, 30];**

In[67]:= **{Precision[a], Precision[b], Precision[a b]}**

Out[67]= {MachinePrecision, 30., MachinePrecision}

When a symbol such as π is present in the expression to be computed, *Mathematica* does not necessarily convert the symbol to a machine number.

In[68]:= **Simplify[Sin[k π], k $\in$ Integers]**

Out[68]= 0

In[69]:= **Simplify[Sin[k N[π]], k $\in$ Integers]**

Out[69]= Sin[3.14159 k]

It will convert symbolic constants for purposes of comparison and whenever an approximate number is present in the input.

In[70]:= **π < 4**

Out[70]= True

In[71]:= **{π^2, $\pi^{2.0}$}**

Out[71]= {π^2, 9.8696}

For addition of real numbers, it is their accuracy that counts most. Recall, Accuracy[x] measures the absolute error in the number x, essentially given by the number of digits to the right of the decimal point.

In[72]:= **{Accuracy[1.23], Accuracy[12.5]}**

Out[72]= {15.8647, 14.8577}

In[73]:= **Accuracy[1.23 + 12.5]**

Out[73]= 14.8169

For machine-precision numbers, which have a fixed number of digits, you can think of adding a digit to the left of the decimal point as essentially removing one digit from the right of the decimal point.

This is not the case though for extended-precision numbers, where all the digits to the right of the decimal can be considered significant.

In[74]:= **Accuracy[123.44444444444444444444444444]**

Out[74]= 28.

In[75]:= **Accuracy[12321.44444444444444444444444444]**

Out[75]= 28.

In an analogous manner to the use of **Precision** with multiplication, the **Accuracy** of an addition will be the minimum of the accuracies of the summands.

In[76]:= **Accuracy[1.1111111111111111 + 1.1111111111111111111]**

Out[76]= 15.6078

In[77]:= **Accuracy[1.1111111111111111]**

Out[77]= 15.9088

Adding a machine number to an extended-precision or an exact number can lead to some unexpected results.

In[78]:= **1.0 + 10^{-25}**

Out[78]= 1.

In[79]:= **Accuracy[%]**

Out[79]= 15.9546

In[80]:= **Accuracy$\left[10^{-25}\right]$**

Out[80]= ∞

Working with precision and accuracy

In this section we will put the notions of precision and accuracy discussed above into practice and see how they are controlled and modified with the built-in numerical functions. In Section 8.4 we will implement these ideas in several user-defined examples.

When you do computations with *Mathematica*'s numerical functions, results are returned at the default machine precision.

In[81]:= **NIntegrate$\left[\text{Sin}\left[x^2\right], \left\{x, 0, \sqrt{\pi}\right\}\right]$**

Out[81]= 0.894831

In[82]:= **Precision[%]**

Out[82]= MachinePrecision

If you need results with higher precision change the option **PrecisionGoal**, which sets the desired precision of the result (similarly for accuracy, with **AccuracyGoal**).

Here is the same computation as above, but asking for 30 digits of precision in the result.

In[83]:= **NIntegrate$\left[\text{Sin}\left[x^2\right], \left\{x, 0, \sqrt{\pi}\right\}, \text{PrecisionGoal} \rightarrow 30\right]$**

NIntegrate::slwcon :
Numerical integration converging too slowly; suspect one of the following: singularity, value of the integration is 0, highly oscillatory integrand, or WorkingPrecision too small. ≫

NIntegrate::ncvb :
NIntegrate failed to converge to prescribed accuracy after 9 recursive bisections in x near {x} = {3.1415805607065542416335380757064221768359857378527522087097167 9687}. NIntegrate obtained 0.894831469484146` and 1.6524379533168436`*^-16 for the integral and error estimates. ≫

Out[83]= 0.894831

Mathematica is complaining that it is unable to produce a result with the requested precision. If you look at the default value for the option **WorkingPrecision**, you will see that it is set to **MachinePrecision**. This means that the internal algorithms will work at machine precision, essentially on the hardware of your machine which is fast. But, in this example, that was not sufficient to guarantee a result with much higher precision.

In[84]:= **Options[NIntegrate]**

Out[84]= {AccuracyGoal → ∞,
          Compiled → Automatic, EvaluationMonitor → None,
          Exclusions → None, MaxPoints → Automatic,
          MaxRecursion → Automatic, Method → Automatic,
          MinRecursion → 0, PrecisionGoal → Automatic,
          WorkingPrecision → MachinePrecision}

To insure that the `PrecisionGoal` is met, we need to increase the `WorkingPrecision` a bit above the `PrecisionGoal`.

In[85]:= **NIntegrate$\left[\mathbf{Sin}\left[x^2\right],\ \left\{x,\ 0,\ \sqrt{\pi}\right\},\right.$**

   $\left.\mathbf{PrecisionGoal} \to 30,\ \mathbf{WorkingPrecision} \to 32\right]$

Out[85]= 0.89483146948414495880102201341651

In[86]:= **Precision[%]**

Out[86]= 32.

How much to increase the value of `WorkingPrecision` above that of `PrecisionGoal` is a bit dependent upon the problem at hand, but a simple rule of thumb is to start by setting `WorkingPrecision` about 10–15% higher than your `PrecisionGoal`.

Another option to numerical functions that is important to understand is `MaxIterations`. As its name implies, this is the maximum number of iterations that a given iterative function will perform in doing its computation. For example, the default value of `MaxIterations` in `FindRoot` is 100.

In[87]:= **Options[FindRoot]**

Out[87]= {AccuracyGoal → Automatic, Compiled → Automatic,
    DampingFactor → 1, Evaluated → True, EvaluationMonitor → None,
    Jacobian → Automatic, MaxIterations → 100,
    Method → Automatic, PrecisionGoal → Automatic,
    StepMonitor → None, WorkingPrecision → MachinePrecision}

For many computations, this limit will be sufficient. But with root finding, for example, a function that is very flat near the desired zero may need a higher number of iterations to find that zero. For example, the function $x^{11} - x^8$ has a root at zero of course, but `FindRoot` has difficulty locating it and is unable to guarantee its precision and accuracy using the default settings.

In[88]:= **FindRoot$\left[x^{11} - x^8,\ \{x,\ 0.5\}\right]$**

   FindRoot::cvmit :
      Failed to converge to the requested accuracy or precision within 100 iterations. ≫

Out[88]= $\left\{x \to 7.76534 \times 10^{-7}\right\}$

In[89]:= **Plot$\left[x^{11} - x^8, \{x, -1, 1\}\right]$**

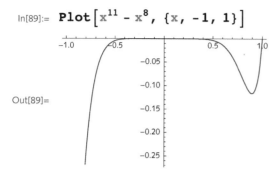

Out[89]=

If you increase the value of MaxIterations, you will get a more accurate result.

In[90]:= **FindRoot$\left[x^{11} - x^8, \{x, 0.5\}, \text{MaxIterations} \to 200\right]$**

Out[90]= $\left\{x \to 7.01949 \times 10^{-8}\right\}$

To get even more accuracy, try increasing AccuracyGoal. As discussed above, you should increase the value of the WorkingPrecision option as well.

In[91]:= **FindRoot$\left[x^{11} - x^8, \{x, 0.5\}, \text{AccuracyGoal} \to 30,\right.$**
        $\text{WorkingPrecision} \to 32, \text{MaxIterations} \to 700\right]$

Out[91]= $\left\{x \to 6.4471177850662807136865275894714 \times 10^{-30}\right\}$

One additional option to *Mathematica*'s numerical functions that we will explore is EvaluationMonitor. This option can be used to evaluate an expression during the computation of the function. For example, suppose you would like to see all the intermediate values that FindRoot comes up with during its computation. You could simply print the values that x takes on throughout the computation using a Print statement. InputForm shows all the digits present in the internal representation of the number.

In[92]:= **FindRoot[Sin[x], {x, 2.0},**
        EvaluationMonitor :> Print[InputForm[x]]]

    2.

    4.185039863261519

    2.467893674514666

    3.266186277569106

    3.1409439123176353

    3.1415926536808043

    3.141592653589793

Out[92]= $\{x \to 3.14159\}$

This approach suffers from the fact that the `Print` expression produces no output and so there is no direct way to access these intermediate values. A different and more useful approach was introduced in Exercise 6 in Section 6.1; it sows the intermediate values of x during the computation and then reaps them at the end.

```
In[93]:= Reap[
          FindRoot[Sin[x], {x, 2.0},
            EvaluationMonitor :> Sow[InputForm[x]]]
        ]
Out[93]= {{x → 3.14159},
          {{2., 4.185039863261519, 2.467893674514666, 3.266186277569106,
            3.1409439123176353, 3.1415926536808043, 3.141592653589793}}}
```

Note the use of the delayed rule above with `EvaluationMonitor`. This ensures that the right-hand side of the rule is not evaluated before `FindRoot` starts its computation. We have also wrapped x with `InputForm` to display all digits.

A similar approach can be used to extract the explicit values computed during the numerical computation of the solution of a differential equation. For example, this computes the solution of the differential equation, reaping the triple {x, f[x], f'[x]} from the solution.

```
In[94]:= soln = Reap[
          NDSolve[{f''[x] + f'[x] + f[x] == 0, f[0] == 1, f'[0] == 1}, f,
            {x, 0, 10}, EvaluationMonitor :> Sow[{x, f[x], f'[x]}]]];
```

Here are the first six values from the solution.

```
In[95]:= Take[soln[[2, 1]], 6]
Out[95]= {{0., 1., 1.}, {0.000102139, 1.0001, 0.999796},
          {0.000102139, 1.0001, 0.999796},
          {0.000204278, 1.0002, 0.999591},
          {0.000204278, 1.0002, 0.999591}, {0.00472055, 1.0047, 0.99057}}
```

Exercises

1. Explain why *Mathematica* is unable to produce a number with 100 digits of precision in the following example.

```
In[1]:= N[1.23, 100]
Out[1]= 1.23
```

```
In[2]:= Precision[%]
Out[2]= MachinePrecision
```

2. Determine what level of precision is necessary when computing $N\left[\sqrt{2}, prec\right]^{200}$ to produce accuracy in the output of at least 100 digits.

3. Explain why the following computation produces an unexpected result (that is, why the value 0.000000000001 is not returned).

    In[3]:= **1.0 - 0.999999999999**

    Out[3]= **9.99978 × 10^{-13}**

4. How close is the number $e^{\pi\sqrt{163}}$ to an integer? Use N, but mind the precision of your computations.

8.3   Arrays of numbers

Scientists, engineers, and everyone who works with numbers typically use arrays to store and represent their data. In many applications these arrays can become quite large and hence pose special problems when computing with them. The main issues with these arrays are representing and storing such large objects and finding efficient algorithms for computing with them. *Mathematica* uses two special data types to make computations with arrays faster and more efficient — sparse arrays and packed arrays. In this section we will introduce each of these data types and see how a working knowledge of them can help your work with very large sets of data.

Sparse arrays

In the sciences, engineering, and many other disciplines it is not uncommon to work with very large matrices that have mostly zeros as elements. These matrices, or arrays, are referred to as *sparse* and many optimized algorithms have been developed by the linear algebra community for working with such objects. Using these algorithms, you can work with arrays that are often several orders of magnitude larger than dense arrays and at speeds much faster than those for dense arithmetic.

There are two main sources for sparse arrays: either you import them from an external file or source or you can create them in *Mathematica* from scratch. We will start by importing a sample sparse matrix from a well-known test suite from the US National Institute of Standards and Technology (Sparse Matrix Collection, NIST).

```
In[1]:= mat = Import[
           "http://phase.hpcc.jp/mirrors/MatrixMarket/data/Harwell-
             Boeing/bcspwr/bcspwr09.psa.gz"]
```

Out[1]= **SparseArray[<6511>, {1723, 1723}, Pattern]**

```
In[2]:= Head[mat]
```

Out[2]= **SparseArray**

The data in this matrix represent the US western power grid and are in the Harwell-Boeing format. The compact representation given in the output indicates that this matrix has 6511 nonzero elements and that its dimensions are 1723 × 1723. Even though the matrix has this special representation internally, it can still be operated on directly as an ordinary matrix. For example, here we find the dimensions, test for symmetry, and visualize the matrix structure.

In[3]:= **Dimensions[mat]**

Out[3]= {1723, 1723}

In[4]:= **SymmetricMatrixQ[mat]**

Out[4]= True

In[5]:= **ArrayPlot[mat]**

Out[5]=

The two great advantages of working with sparse arrays are their compact representation and the speed with which you can perform linear algebra operations on them.

In[6]:= **ByteCount[mat]**

Out[6]= 33 696

In[7]:= **Timing[mat.mat;]**

Out[7]= {0.000618, Null}

A dense matrix of the same size is many orders of magnitude larger in terms of the number of bytes used internally to store it.

In[8]:= **densemat = RandomReal[1, {1723, 1723}];**

In[9]:= **ByteCount[densemat]**

Out[9]= 23 750 000

And linear algebra on the dense matrix is also much slower than the corresponding sparse computation.

In[10]:= **Timing[densemat.densemat;]**

Out[10]= {1.43976, Null}

The other way to work with sparse arrays in *Mathematica* is to create them from scratch with the **SparseArray** function. The first argument to **SparseArray** specifies the rules to be used to create the nonzero elements and the second argument specifies the dimensions of the array. For example, this creates a 5×5 sparse array object with elements on the diagonal equal to 1.

In[11]:= **spmat = SparseArray[{i_, i_} → 1, {5, 5}]**

Out[11]= SparseArray[<5>, {5, 5}]

Wrapping Normal around a sparse array object converts it into a list of lists.

In[12]:= **Normal[spmat]**

Out[12]= {{1, 0, 0, 0, 0}, {0, 1, 0, 0, 0},
          {0, 0, 1, 0, 0}, {0, 0, 0, 1, 0}, {0, 0, 0, 0, 1}}

Using MatrixForm, you can view the array in a more traditional form. This use of Normal and MatrixForm makes sense only for small to moderate-sized matrices.

In[13]:= **MatrixForm[spmat]**

Out[13]//MatrixForm=

$$\begin{pmatrix} 1 & 0 & 0 & 0 & 0 \\ 0 & 1 & 0 & 0 & 0 \\ 0 & 0 & 1 & 0 & 0 \\ 0 & 0 & 0 & 1 & 0 \\ 0 & 0 & 0 & 0 & 1 \end{pmatrix}$$

Here are the rules associated with this sparse array object. Notice that in addition to the explicit rules we specified, *Mathematica* uses the rule {_, _} → 0 for the default cases, that is, any element not explicitly specified by a rule should be set to 0.

In[14]:= **ArrayRules[spmat]**

Out[14]= {{1, 1} → 1, {2, 2} → 1, {3, 3} → 1,
          {4, 4} → 1, {5, 5} → 1, {_, _} → 0}

Using a third argument to SparseArray, you can specify that the implicit elements are other than 0.

In[15]:= **spmat2 = SparseArray[{i_, i_} → 1, {5, 5}, 13]**

Out[15]= SparseArray[<5>, {5, 5}, 13]

In[16]:= **MatrixForm[spmat2]**

Out[16]//MatrixForm=

$$\begin{pmatrix} 1 & 13 & 13 & 13 & 13 \\ 13 & 1 & 13 & 13 & 13 \\ 13 & 13 & 1 & 13 & 13 \\ 13 & 13 & 13 & 1 & 13 \\ 13 & 13 & 13 & 13 & 1 \end{pmatrix}$$

Here is a slightly more complicated specification for the rules associated with a sparse array. In this example, the diagonal elements are 1, and the elements whose vertical and horizontal positions differ by one will be 6. Band is a convenient function for representing elements on and off the diagonal of a matrix. Band[{1, 1}] gives the diagonal; Band[{1, 2}] gives the off-diagonal just above the main diagonal; and so on.

In[17]:= **spmat3 = SparseArray[**
{Band[{1, 1}] → 1, Band[{1, 2}] → 6, Band[{2, 1}] → 6}, {8, 8}]

Out[17]= SparseArray[<22>, {8, 8}]

In[18]:= **MatrixForm[spmat3]**

Out[18]//MatrixForm=

$$\begin{pmatrix} 1 & 6 & 0 & 0 & 0 & 0 & 0 & 0 \\ 6 & 1 & 6 & 0 & 0 & 0 & 0 & 0 \\ 0 & 6 & 1 & 6 & 0 & 0 & 0 & 0 \\ 0 & 0 & 6 & 1 & 6 & 0 & 0 & 0 \\ 0 & 0 & 0 & 6 & 1 & 6 & 0 & 0 \\ 0 & 0 & 0 & 0 & 6 & 1 & 6 & 0 \\ 0 & 0 & 0 & 0 & 0 & 6 & 1 & 6 \\ 0 & 0 & 0 & 0 & 0 & 0 & 6 & 1 \end{pmatrix}$$

Here is a simple pictorial representation of a sparse array using ArrayPlot.

In[19]:= **ArrayPlot[spmat3]**

Out[19]=

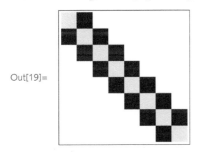

Using a larger array, you can clearly see the nature of the "sparseness" of values.

In[20]:= **ArrayPlot[SparseArray[**
{i_, j_} /; Abs[i - j] ≤ 8 :→ RandomInteger[4], {100, 100}]]

Out[20]=

Let us take a look at some computations on some large sparse arrays to see how speed and memory issues are affected. First we create a 100 000×100 000 sparse array with random numbers on and just off the diagonal, and zeros everywhere else.

In[21]:= **mat = SparseArray[**

     {{$i\_$, $j\_$} /; Abs[i - j] ≤ 2 :→ RandomReal[]}, {10^5, 10^5}]

Out[21]= SparseArray[<499 994>, {100 000, 100 000}]

Here is a vector consisting of 100 000 random numbers.

In[22]:= **b = RandomReal[1, Length[mat]];**

First, note the difference in size of this sparse array compared with a dense array. The sparse array takes up approximately six megabytes.

In[23]:= **N[ByteCount[mat]] Byte**

Out[23]= 6.40088×10^6 Byte

The corresponding dense array would require 80 gigabytes to store (assuming 8 bytes per double float).

In[24]:= **N[10^5 10^5 8] Byte**

Out[24]= $8. \times 10^{10}$ Byte

Computations involving this sparse linear system are extremely fast.

In[25]:= **Timing[LinearSolve[mat, b];]**

Out[25]= {0.037164, Null}

In[26]:= **Timing[mat.mat;]**

Out[26]= {0.080528, Null}

Packed arrays

One of the great advantages of the *Mathematica* programming language is that it seamlessly handles the administrative tasks of dealing with a wide variety of data types. So, for example, when you perform computations with floating-point numbers, *Mathematica* determines the type of numbers you are working with and then either it performs the computation on your machine's floating-point processor (if working with numbers that fit there) or it does the computation using extended-precision software routines. Similarly, computations involving integers will be done in hardware or using special software routines depending upon the size of the integers relative to your machine's hardware constraints.

However, all this comes at a cost, and the cost involves the administrative overhead necessary to determine the appropriate routine and whether to perform the computation in hardware or software. For small computations, this overhead is not noticeable, but for large computations involving tens of thousands of rows and columns of a matrix, say, this overhead could cause your computations to slow down considerably.

Fortunately, there is a way to bypass some of this overhead and get significant speed improvements together with a smaller memory footprint. The technology that does this is referred to as *packed arrays* and they are fairly simple to understand. Whenever possible *Mathematica* will automatically represent a list of a single type of machine numbers (integer, real, or complex) as an array, in fact, a packed array object. So a matrix consisting of all machine real numbers will be represented internally as a packed array. This internal representation is transparent to the user.

Here is a 1000×1000 array consisting of random real numbers.

```
In[27]:= mat = RandomReal[1, {1000, 1000}];
```

Mathematica recognizes that this array consists entirely of machine numbers and so it *packs* the array automatically.

```
In[28]:= Developer`PackedArrayQ[mat]
```

```
Out[28]= True
```

Let us also create an array that is not packed. We can do this by replacing one of the elements in mat with a number that is not a machine floating-point number. Here we replace the element in the first row, second column of mat with the integer 1.

```
In[29]:= mat2 = ReplacePart[mat, 1, {1, 2}];
```

```
In[30]:= Developer`PackedArrayQ[mat2]
```

```
Out[30]= False
```

The first thing to notice is the memory saving obtained by using packed arrays.

```
In[31]:= Map[ByteCount, {mat, mat2}]
```

```
Out[31]= {8 000 168, 32 048 040}
```

In this example, it takes 75% less memory to store the packed array over the similar unpacked array.

$$In[32]:= \frac{32\,048\,040 - 8\,000\,168}{32\,048\,040} \; // \; N$$

```
Out[32]= 0.75037
```

The time to compute the minimum value is roughly an order of magnitude faster for the packed array.

```
In[33]:= Map[Timing[Min[#];] &, {mat, mat2}]
```

```
Out[33]= {{0.002753, Null}, {0.010015, Null}}
```

Simple arithmetic on such objects is also significantly sped up with packed arrays.

```
In[34]:= Timing[Do[mat + mat, {100}];]
Out[34]= {0.98052, Null}
```

```
In[35]:= Timing[Do[mat2 + mat2, {100}];]
Out[35]= {8.62979, Null}
```

When packed arrays are used in *Mathematica*, the compiler is invoked, thus generally improving the time it takes for the computation to take place. Many of the built-in functions are designed to take advantage of the packed array technology. But they do *not* invoke the compiler whenever the time it takes to compile is close to the running time of the computation itself. There are length limits on many common *Mathematica* functions that determine whether the compiler will be used or not. For example, the length limit for Table is 250.

```
In[36]:= m1 = Table[i², {i, 1.0, 249}];
         Developer`PackedArrayQ[m1]
Out[37]= False
```

```
In[38]:= m2 = Table[i², {i, 1.0, 250}];
         Developer`PackedArrayQ[m2]
Out[39]= True
```

For NestList, it is 100 (remember that NestList[f, *init*, n] produces a list of $n+1$ elements because it prepends the initial value to the list of iterates).

```
In[40]:= n1 = NestList[Sin, .5, 98];
         Developer`PackedArrayQ[n1]
Out[41]= False
```

```
In[42]:= n2 = NestList[Sin, .5, 99];
         Developer`PackedArrayQ[n2]
Out[43]= True
```

These length limits are system parameters that can be displayed and set with SystemOptions.

```
In[44]:= SystemOptions["CompileOptions"]
```

```
Out[44]= {CompileOptions → {ApplyCompileLength → ∞,
        ArrayCompileLength → 250, AutoCompileAllowCoercion → False,
        AutoCompileProtectValues → False, AutomaticCompile → False,
        BinaryTensorArithmetic → False, CompileAllowCoercion → True,
        CompileConfirmInitializedVariables → True,
        CompiledFunctionArgumentCoercionTolerance → 2.10721,
        CompiledFunctionMaxFailures → 3, CompileDynamicScoping → False,
        CompileEvaluateConstants → True, CompileOptimizeRegisters → False,
        CompileReportCoercion → False, CompileReportExternal → False,
        CompileReportFailure → False, CompileValuesLast → True,
        FoldCompileLength → 100, InternalCompileMessages → False,
        ListableFunctionCompileLength → 250,
        MapCompileLength → 100, NestCompileLength → 100,
        NumericalAllowExternal → False, ProductCompileLength → 250,
        ReuseTensorRegisters → True, SumCompileLength → 250,
        SystemCompileOptimizations → All, TableCompileLength → 250}}
```

So how do you best take advantage of packed arrays when you write your code? First, whenever possible, it is important that you insure that your lists and arrays consist of machine numbers *all of the same type* – integer, real, or complex. In addition, whenever possible, try to operate on lists and arrays all at once instead of looping through your arrays. Listable operations with packed array input will use the compiler and will produce packed array output. Fortunately, many of the commonly used functions have this attribute (FunctionsWithAttribute is defined in Section 5.6).

```
In[45]:= names = FunctionsWithAttribute[Listable];
        Length[names]
```

```
Out[46]= 363
```

Here is a sample of the symbols that have this attribute.

```
In[47]:= RandomSample[names, 30]
```

```
Out[47]= {BesselI, SpheroidalRadialFactor, PrimePowerQ, PolynomialGCD,
        InverseJacobiDC, ArcCot, CreateDirectory, JacobiNS, ZernikeR,
        StopScheduledTask, IntegerPart, PolyLog, ChebyshevT, IntegerString,
        InverseJacobiCD, HarmonicNumber, AiryAi, PrimeOmega, NevilleThetaD,
        Floor, LegendreQ, Divide, GCD, StirlingS2, FractionalPart, JacobiCS,
        SpheroidalS1Prime, NumberFieldRootsOfUnity, SinhIntegral, In}
```

Exercises

1. Create a function `RandomSparseArray[n]` that generates an $n \times n$ sparse array with random numbers along the diagonal.

2. Write a function `TridiagonalMatrix[n, p, q]` that creates an $n \times n$ matrix with the integer p on the diagonal, the integer q on the upper and lower subdiagonals, and 0s everywhere else.

3. Create a vector `vec` consisting of 100 000 random real numbers between 0 and 1. Check that it is indeed a packed array by using `Developer`PackedArrayQ`. Then replace one element in `vec` with an integer. Check that this new vector is not a packed array. Finally, perform some memory and timing tests on these two vectors, using functions such as `Max`, `Norm`, `RootMeanSquare`.

4. An interesting computation of the Fibonacci numbers can be obtained using the determinant of a certain tridiagonal matrix: 1s on the diagonal and $i = \sqrt{-1}$ running along each subdiagonal. For example, the following 4×4 matrix has determinant equal to the fifth Fibonacci number.

    $$\text{In[1]:=} \quad \left| \begin{pmatrix} 1 & i & 0 & 0 \\ i & 1 & i & 0 \\ 0 & i & 1 & i \\ 0 & 0 & i & 1 \end{pmatrix} \right|$$

    Out[1]= 5

    Create a function that computes the nth Fibonacci number using a sparse array implementation of this tri-diagonal matrix. You will need special rules for $n = 1$ and $n = 2$.

5. An efficient approach to computing large Fibonacci numbers relies upon the observation that a certain matrix has its characteristic polynomial equal to the characteristic equation for the Fibonacci numbers.

    $$\text{In[2]:=} \quad \mathbf{mat} = \begin{pmatrix} 1 & 1 \\ 1 & 0 \end{pmatrix};$$

    $$\mathbf{poly} = \mathbf{CharacteristicPolynomial[mat, x]}$$

    Out[3]= $-1 - x + x^2$

    In[4]:= `Solve[poly == 0, x]`

    Out[4]= $\left\{ \left\{ x \to \frac{1}{2} \left(1 - \sqrt{5} \right) \right\}, \left\{ x \to \frac{1}{2} \left(1 + \sqrt{5} \right) \right\} \right\}$

    The Fibonacci numbers F_n can be generated from successive powers of this matrix.

    $$\begin{pmatrix} 1 & 1 \\ 1 & 0 \end{pmatrix}^n = \begin{pmatrix} F_{n+1} & F_n \\ F_n & F_{n-1} \end{pmatrix}$$

    Use these facts to implement an algorithm for computing the Fibonacci numbers using the built-in `MatrixPower` function with sparse arrays.

8.4 Examples and applications

Mathematica's built-in numerical functions are designed to guarantee the accuracy of their results as much as possible and they are optimized to minimize the work done to generate those results. Functions such as `FindRoot`, `NDSolve`, `NMinimize`, and `NIntegrate` use options to allow you to adjust their behavior and get finer control over precision, accuracy, and other internal aspects of the underlying numerical routines.

In this section we will first discuss how to incorporate the ideas on controlling precision and accuracy discussed earlier in this chapter into your own numerical programs using the Newton's method root finder as an example. The last two examples are a bit more advanced. The first, computing the radius of gyration of a random walk, is a purely numerical computation involving some linear algebra and eigenvector/eigenvalue computation. The computation is then interpreted visually, thus providing a nice marriage of numerics and visualization. The final set of examples in this section involve the creation of statistical tests that can be used on various datasets. Although many such tests are built into *Mathematica*, it is not only instructive but also sometimes necessary to construct your own tests for special purposes.

Newton's method revisited

In Section 6.1 we wrote a program to implement Newton's method for finding roots of equations.

```
findRoot[fun_, {var_, init_}, ε_] :=
  Module[{xi = init, funxi = fun[init]},
    While[Abs[funxi] > ε,
      xi = N[xi - funxi/fun'[xi]];
      funxi = fun[xi]];
    {var → xi}]
```

One of the limitations of this implementation is that the user has little control over the precision or accuracy of the results. In addition, although the loop will continue until values are within ϵ of the root, there is no mechanism for automatically adjusting this tolerance, nor for controlling the number of iterations that are performed. In this section we will rewrite this root-finding function to take advantage of the options for numerical functions that control precision and accuracy.

First we will change the iterative structure from a `While` loop to a fixed point iteration. The first argument to `FixedPoint` is the function that we are iterating, so that will be the same as the function above, namely, $x_i - f(x_i)/f'(x_i)$. The second argument to `FixedPoint` is the initial value for the iteration. The third argument is the maximum number of iterations. So, using a pure function for the first argument, the Newton iteration will look like this:

$$\texttt{FixedPoint}\left[\texttt{\#} - \frac{\texttt{fun}[\texttt{\#}]}{\texttt{fun'}[\texttt{\#}]} \texttt{ \&, initx, maxIterations}\right]$$

Let us set up the needed options with some default values.

```
In[1]:= Options[findRoot] = {
          MaxIterations :> $IterationLimit,
          PrecisionGoal -> Automatic,
          WorkingPrecision -> Automatic
        };
```

The default value of `MaxIterations` is set to `$IterationLimit` (normally 4096) using a delayed rule so that `$IterationLimit` is not evaluated until the option is called. The two options `PrecisionGoal` and `WorkingPrecision` are set to `Automatic`, which, at the moment, has no value associated with it. In the body of our function, we will take a value of `Automatic` for `PrecisionGoal` to mean a precision that is equal to the precision of the initial value passed to `findRoot`.

```
If[precisionGoal === Automatic,
  precisionGoal = Precision[init]]
```

As we saw in the previous section, we will need to bump up the value of `WorkingPrecision` to something a little bigger than `PrecisionGoal`. We will set it to be ten more digits than the precision goal.

```
If[workingPrecision === Automatic,
  workingPrecision = precisionGoal + 10];
initx = SetPrecision[init, workingPrecision]
```

Here then is the definition of `findRoot` with these added pieces.

```
In[2]:= findRoot[fun_, {var_, init_?NumericQ},
          opts : OptionsPattern[]] :=
        Module[{maxIterations, precisionGoal,
          workingPrecision, initx, df = fun', result},
          {maxIterations, precisionGoal, workingPrecision} =
          OptionValue[
            {MaxIterations, PrecisionGoal, WorkingPrecision}];
          If[precisionGoal === Automatic, precisionGoal =
            Precision[init]]; If[workingPrecision === Automatic,
            workingPrecision = precisionGoal + 10];
          initx = SetPrecision[init, workingPrecision];
```

$$result = \texttt{SetPrecision}\left[\texttt{FixedPoint}\left[\#1 - \frac{fun[\#1]}{df[\#1]} \&,\right.\right.$$

$$\left.\left.initx, \, maxIterations\right], precisionGoal\right];$$

$$\left.\{var \rightarrow result\}\right]$$

Let us use `findRoot` to find the roots of various functions.

In[3]:= $f[x\_] := x^2 - 2$

In[4]:= `findRoot[f, {x, 1.0}]`

Out[4]= $\{x \rightarrow 1.41421\}$

The precision of this result is the same as the precision of the initial guess.

In[5]:= `Precision[%]`

Out[5]= `MachinePrecision`

Setting `PrecisionGoal` higher generates a high-precision result.

In[6]:= $\texttt{findRoot}\left[\texttt{Sin}, \, \left\{x, \, \frac{14}{10}\right\}, \, \texttt{PrecisionGoal} \rightarrow 40\right]$

Out[6]= $\{x \rightarrow 3.1415926535897932384626433832795028841997\}$

In[7]:= $(x \, / . \, \%) - \pi$

Out[7]= $0. \times 10^{-40}$

There are still a number of problems that can arise with this implementation of Newton's method. First is the possibility that the derivative of the function we are working with might be equal to zero. This will produce a division-by-zero error. Another type of difficulty that can arise in root finding occurs when the derivative of the function in question is either difficult or impossible to compute. As a very simple example, consider the function $|x + 3|$, which has a root at $x = -3$. Both the built-in function `FindRoot` and our user-defined root finder will fail with this function since a symbolic derivative cannot be computed.

In[8]:= `D[Abs[x + 3], x]`

Out[8]= $\texttt{Abs}'[3 + x]$

One way around such problems is to use a numerical derivative (as opposed to an analytic derivative). The *secant method* approximates $f'(x_k)$ using the difference quotient:

$$\frac{f(x_k) - f(x_{k-1})}{x_k - x_{k-1}}$$

To implement this method, we overload `findRoot` by adding a rule for the case when two initial values are given.

```
In[9]:= findRoot[f_, {var_, a_, b_}] := Module[{x1 = a, x2 = b, df},

    While[Abs[f[x2]] > 1/10^10,

      df = (f[x2] - f[x1])/(x2 - x1);

      {x1, x2} = {x2, x2 - f[x2]/df}];

    {var → x2}]
```

```
In[10]:= f[x_] := Abs[x + 3]
```

```
In[11]:= findRoot[f, {x, -3.1, -1.8}]
```

```
Out[11]= {x → -3.}
```

In the exercises, you are asked to refine this last implementation by writing it in a functional style and including mechanisms to gain finer control over precision and accuracy in a manner similar to what we did with the `findRoot` function earlier in this section.

Radius of gyration of a random walk

In this next example we will work through the computation and visualization of a certain way of measuring the extent of a dataset. In particular we will compute the radius of gyration of a random walk. Given some masses distributed about an axis, the radius of gyration gives the root mean square distance from the masses to the their center of gravity or to the axis. It has application in: structural engineering in determining where columns may buckle; polymer physics to describe certain properties of a polymer chain; and other theoretical areas.

One means of characterizing the shape of random walks focuses on their asphericity, a measure of how far the distribution of walk locations is from being spherically symmetric. As it turns out, this really is another way of measuring the anisotropic (not uniform in each dimension) nature of random walks. To get a sense of this, consider a two-dimensional off-lattice random walk. It is hard to tell much from one such walk – one might be severely elongated along the horizontal axis, another might be elongated along a different axis (Figure 8.2).

FIGURE 8.2. *Two 2500-step, off-lattice walks.*

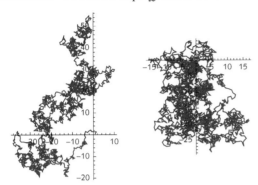

There are several measures one could use to characterize the shape of individual random walks; see for example, Costa and Cesar (2001). Using a quantity called the *radius of gyration tensor*, we can get a good sense of the extent of these random walks in the sense of length and direction of certain orthogonal vectors that span the walk (Figure 8.3).

FIGURE 8.3. *A 10 000-step off-lattice walk. The two thick lines are in the direction of greatest and smallest extent of the walk. The center of mass is located at the intersection of these two lines.*

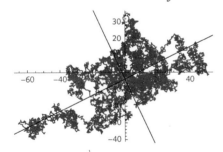

The radius of gyration tensor for a two-dimensional random walk is given by the following (Rudnick and Gaspari 2004):

$$
\mathcal{T} =
\begin{pmatrix}
\frac{1}{n} \sum_{i=1}^{n} (x_i - \langle x \rangle)^2 & \frac{1}{n} \sum_{i=1}^{n} (x_i - \langle x \rangle)(y_i - \langle y \rangle) \\
\frac{1}{n} \sum_{i=1}^{n} (x_i - \langle x \rangle)(y_i - \langle y \rangle) & \frac{1}{n} \sum_{i=1}^{n} (y_i - \langle y \rangle)^2
\end{pmatrix}
$$

The quantities $\frac{1}{n} \sum_{i=1}^{n} (x_i - \langle x \rangle)^2$ and $\frac{1}{n} \sum_{i=1}^{n} (y_i - \langle y \rangle)^2$ are the sums of the squares of the distances of the step locations from the center of mass divided by the number of step locations. The *center of mass* is the sum of the step locations divided by the number of step locations and is denoted by $(\langle x \rangle, \langle y \rangle)$. For example, for a 10 000-step off-lattice walk, this computes the center of mass coordinates which we will label cmx and cmy.

In[12]:= **Needs["PwM`RandomWalks`"]**

```
In[13]:= coords = RandomWalk[10 000, Dimension → 2, LatticeWalk → False];
```

```
In[14]:= {cmx, cmy} = Mean[coords]
```

```
Out[14]= {70.6457, 58.1533}
```

This gives a quick visual check, showing the center of mass as a red point.

```
In[15]:= Show[{
          ListLinePlot[coords, PlotStyle → LightGray],
          Graphics[{PointSize[Medium], Red, Point[Mean[coords]]}]
          }]
```

The radius of gyration tensor $\mathcal{T}$ defined above can be computed as follows. First, separate the *x*- and *y*-coordinates.

```
In[16]:= {xcoords, ycoords} = Transpose[coords];
```

Then compute the off-diagonal elements of the matrix $\mathcal{T}$.

```
In[17]:= xy = (xcoords - cmx) . (ycoords - cmy) / Length[coords]
```

```
Out[17]= 513.817
```

This gives the computation for the tensor $\mathcal{T}$ itself.

```
In[18]:= T = {{Mean[(xcoords - cmx)^2], xy}, {xy, Mean[(ycoords - cmy)^2]}};
```

```
In[19]:= MatrixForm[T]
```

```
Out[19]//MatrixForm=
```

$$\begin{pmatrix} 930.16 & 513.817 \\ 513.817 & 438.695 \end{pmatrix}$$

These computations are bundled up in the function RadiusOfGyrationTensor defined in the package PwM`RandomWalks`.

```
In[20]:= RadiusOfGyrationTensor[lis_] :=
          Module[{cmx, cmy, xcoords, ycoords, xy},
            {cmx, cmy} = Mean[lis];
            {xcoords, ycoords} = Transpose[lis];
            xy = (xcoords - cmx) . (ycoords - cmy) / Length[lis];
```

$$\{\{\texttt{Mean}\big[(\texttt{xcoords - cmx})^2\big],\ \texttt{xy}\},\ \{\texttt{xy},\ \texttt{Mean}\big[(\texttt{ycoords - cmy})^2\big]\}\}\big]$$

In[21]:= **RadiusOfGyrationTensor[coords]**

Out[21]= {{930.16, 513.817}, {513.817, 438.695}}

This function is quite efficient, computing the radius of gyration tensor for a one-million step random walk in under a second.

In[22]:= **walk = RandomWalk$\big[10^6$, LatticeWalk → False$\big]$;**

In[23]:= **($\mathcal{T}$ = RadiusOfGyrationTensor[walk]) // Timing**

Out[23]= {0.337405, {{49 173., -19 009.3}, {-19 009.3, 18 798.5}}}

Next we will try to visualize this system. The eigenvectors of $\mathcal{T}$ point in the directions of greatest and smallest spans of the walk. The eigenvalues give a measure of how elongated the walk is in these directions. This can be seen by creating lines along each eigenvector of a length proportional to the corresponding eigenvalues. In the computation below, the slope of the line is given by the *y*-coordinate of the eigenvector divided by the corresponding *x*-coordinate.

In[24]:= **{v1x, v1y} = First@Eigenvectors[$\mathcal{T}$]**

Out[24]= {-0.901163, 0.43348}

In[25]:= **{v2x, v2y} = Last@Eigenvectors[$\mathcal{T}$]**

Out[25]= {-0.43348, -0.901163}

In[26]:= **ev1 = $\dfrac{\texttt{v1y}}{\texttt{v1x}}$ (x - cmx) + cmy // Expand**

Out[26]= 92.1355 - 0.481023 x

In[27]:= **ev2 = $\dfrac{\texttt{v2y}}{\texttt{v2x}}$ (x - cmx) + cmy // Expand**

Out[27]= -88.7124 + 2.0789 x

Putting all these pieces together, we create the function `EigenvectorPlot` that returns a plot of the original data set together with plots of the orthogonal lines ev1 and ev2, and puts a large red point at their intersection, the center of mass.

In[28]:= **EigenvectorPlot[*data* : {{_, _} ..}, *tensor*_] := Module$\big[$**

    {T = *tensor*, cmx, cmy, x, λ1, λ2, v1x, v1y, v2x, v2y, l1, l2},
    {λ1, λ2} = Eigenvalues[T];
    {cmx, cmy} = Mean[*data*];
    {{v1x, v1y}, {v2x, v2y}} = Eigenvectors[T];

```
      v1y
11 = ──── (x - cmx) + cmy;
      v1x

      v2y
12 = ──── (x - cmx) + cmy;
      v2x

Show[{
  ListLinePlot[data, PlotStyle → LightGray],
  Plot[11, {x, cmx - λ1, cmx + λ1},
    PlotStyle → {Gray, Thick}],
  Plot[12, {x, cmx - λ2, cmx + λ2},
    PlotStyle → {Gray, Thick}],
  Graphics[{PointSize[Large], Red, Point[Mean[data]]}]
  }, AspectRatio → Automatic]
```

In[29]:= 𝒯 = RadiusOfGyrationTensor[coords];
EigenvectorPlot[coords, 𝒯]

Out[30]=

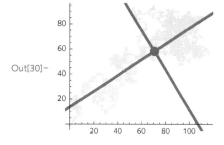

Statistical tests

Working with data often involves checks for randomness or goodness-of-fit to a distribution. Numerous tools are built in to perform certain tests, but there are so many situations where you need to construct your own tests that it is useful to study what tools can be used for these tasks. In this section, we will explore several statistical tests for randomness of a sequence.

Built-in tests Mathematica has numerous built-in tests for answering such questions as how good the fit is between a dataset and a distribution, or even between several datasets. These tests are automatically chosen by functions such as `DistributionFitTest` and, in fact, you can see various test statistics and p-values for many different tests.

In[31]:= **data = RandomVariate[NormalDistribution[], {10⁴}];**

`DistributionFitTest` creates a `HypothesisTestData` object from which you can get various test results and properties. In the following example, we have also set the significance level to a smaller value than the default of .05.

In[32]:= **𝒟 = DistributionFitTest[data, Automatic,
        "HypothesisTestData", SignificanceLevel → .01]**

Out[32]= HypothesisTestData[≪DistributionFitTest≫]

With *p*-values significantly larger than zero, we can be reasonably confident that the random number generator is doing a fine job.

In[33]:= **𝒟["TestDataTable", All]**

Out[33]=

	Statistic	P-Value
Anderson-Darling	0.451966	0.276274
Cramér-von Mises	0.0589674	0.397779
Jarque-Bera ALM	1.87111	0.391968
Kolmogorov-Smirnov	0.00595404	0.561924
Kuiper	0.0100215	0.648128
Pearson χ^2	80.176	0.379777
Watson U^2	0.0536632	0.40886

Comparing the data created from a normal distribution with a uniform distribution gives very low *p*-values as might be expected.

In[34]:= **DistributionFitTest[data, UniformDistribution[],
        {"TestDataTable", "PearsonChiSquare"}]**

Out[34]=

	Statistic	P-Value
Pearson χ^2	10 000.	$2.683064656446425 \times 10^{-2075}$

In[35]:= **DistributionFitTest[data,
        UniformDistribution[], "TestConclusion"]**

Out[35]= The null hypothesis that the data is distributed according
        to the UniformDistribution[{0,1}] is rejected at the
        5. percent level based on the Cramér-von Mises test.

Let us now turn to the creation of tests of randomness where the data we will be working with consist of sequences of random numbers. We will look at three different kinds of tests: those involving frequencies, fixed ranges of values, and also probability or *p*-values. In all cases, we will consider binary sequences, that is, sequences of numbers consisting entirely of 0s and 1s. Finally, we will create one function for testing for autocorrelation and another function for visualizing correlations in time-series data, correlograms.

Frequency tests In a frequency test on binary sequences, we are interested in the proportion of 0s and 1s in the sequence. Obviously, in a random binary sequence, these would be about the same. The test first computes an observed test statistic s_{obs} and uses that to compute a *p*-value which is finally compared with a threshold, typically .01. A large *p*-value would indicate a greater likelihood of randomness. A *p*-value near or less than .01 would suggest nonrandomness.

The steps in computing the test statistic (the *p*-value) are as follows:

1. Convert 0s to -1, then add the bits. If the converted individual bits are denoted ε_i, and the length of the sequence is *n*, then the sum is given by $S_n = \varepsilon_1 + \varepsilon_2 + \cdots + \varepsilon_n$.

2. Compute the statistic $S_{obs} = \frac{|S_n|}{\sqrt{n}}$.

3. The *p*-value is given by $\mathrm{erfc}\left(\frac{S_{obs}}{\sqrt{2}}\right)$ where erfc is the complementary error function. If the *p*-value is greater than or equal to .01, then conclude the sequence is random.

We start by creating a sequence of values ±1.

In[36]:= **data = 2 RandomInteger[1, {100}] - 1**

Out[36]= {-1, 1, 1, 1, 1, -1, 1, -1, 1, 1, 1, -1, -1, -1, -1, 1, 1, -1, 1, 1, 1, 1,
          -1, -1, -1, 1, -1, -1, -1, 1, 1, 1, -1, 1, 1, -1, 1, -1, -1, 1, -1, 1,
          1, 1, -1, 1, 1, -1, -1, 1, -1, -1, 1, -1, -1, 1, -1, -1, -1, -1, 1, 1,
          -1, 1, -1, -1, 1, -1, -1, 1, -1, 1, 1, -1, -1, -1, -1, -1, 1, 1, -1,
          1, -1, 1, -1, -1, -1, 1, -1, 1, -1, 1, -1, -1, 1, -1, -1, -1, 1, 1}

The test statistic is given by the following formula, where the e_i are the elements (±1) of the sequence and *n* is the length of the sequence.

$$S_{obs} = \frac{|e_1 + e_2 + \cdots + e_n|}{\sqrt{n}}$$

In[37]:= **Sobs[seq_List] := Abs[Total[seq]] / $\sqrt{\text{Length[seq]}}$**

In[38]:= **Sobs[data] // N**

Out[38]= **0.6**

Finally, the *p*-value is given by the error function:

In[39]:= **Erfc$\left[$Sobs[data] / $\sqrt{2}$$\right]$ // N**

Out[39]= **0.548506**

The large *p*-value, compared with .01, would suggest a sufficiently random sequence. This was a very short sequence, so let us repeat with a much longer sequence.

In[40]:= **data = 2 RandomInteger$\left[$1, $\left\{10^6\right\}\right]$ - 1;**

Erfc$\left[$Sobs[data] / $\sqrt{2}$$\right]$ // N

Out[41]= **0.841481**

Let us now try this test on a random number generator known to be problematic – a linear congruential generator. **BlockRandom** is used here and in what follows to keep the random seeds local to the block in which they are called. In this way, seeding will not affect other (global) random computations.

```
In[42]:= BlockRandom[SeedRandom[0,
            Method → {"Congruential", "Multiplier" → 15, "Increment" → 1,
              "Modulus" → 381}]; 2 RandomInteger[1, 20] - 1]

Out[42]= {-1, -1, -1, -1, -1, -1, -1, 1,
         -1, -1, -1, 1, -1, -1, -1, -1, 1, 1, 1, 1}
```

```
In[43]:= data = BlockRandom[SeedRandom[0, Method →
            {"Congruential", "Multiplier" → 15, "Increment" → 1,
              "Modulus" → 381}]; 2 RandomInteger[1, 10^6] - 1];
```

$$N\left[\text{Erfc}\left[\frac{\text{Sobs[data]}}{\sqrt{2}}\right]\right]$$

Out[44]= 1.98947×10^{-15}

Clearly, with such a small *p*-value, the linear congruential generator with these parameter values is not a good choice for generating sequences of random numbers.

Fixed range tests With fixed range tests, a test statistic is computed and the test is said to fail if the statistic is outside of the range of values. The frequency (monobit) test above is an example of a fixed range test. In this section we will run a simulation for a relatively large number of trials and tally the number of trials that pass or fail the test.

Assuming a sequence of one million zeros and ones, we would expect about 500 000 ones. So at a .01 significance level, the test will be passed if the number of ones is in the range $500\,000 \pm x$, where *x* is given by the following:

```
In[45]:= With[{significance = 0.01, n = 10^6},
```

$$\frac{1}{2}\sqrt{n}\ \text{InverseCDF}\left[\text{NormalDistribution}[0, 1], 1 - \frac{\text{significance}}{2}\right]\right]$$

Out[45]= 1287.91

Here is a function that encodes the statistic and returns `$Pass` if the total number of ones in the sequence is within the prescribed range, and returns `$Fail` otherwise. No special significance is attached to these expressions – any suitable string would do.

```
In[46]:= test[data_, expect_, significance_] :=
          Module[{n = Length[data], ran},
```

$$\text{ran} = \frac{1}{2}\sqrt{n}\ \text{InverseCDF}\left[\right.$$

$$\text{NormalDistribution[0, 1], } 1 - \frac{significance}{2}\Big];$$
$$\text{If[}(expect - ran) < \text{Total[}data\text{]} < (expect + ran),$$
$$\text{"\$Pass", "\$Fail"]}\Big]$$

Let us simulate 100 tests, each with a significance level of .01. Note the need for a delayed assignment in defining data.

In[47]:= **data := RandomInteger$\Big[$1, $\{10^6\}\Big]$;**

In[48]:= **Table$\Big[$test$\Big[$data, $\dfrac{\text{Length[data]}}{2}$, 0.01$\Big]$, {100}$\Big]$;**

In[49]:= **Tally[%]**

Out[49]= {{\$Pass, 99}, {\$Fail, 1}}

Although frequency tests such as the one above are fairly basic, they can be good at detecting an abundance of zeros or ones in a binary sequence. For example, if we were to weight the generator, the test is quite good at finding failures even with a very small weight factor.

In[50]:= **With$\Big[$ {ε = 0.0015, trials = 100},**
Table$\Big[$test$\Big[$RandomChoice$\Big[$ {0.5 + ε, 0.5 - ε} → {0, 1}, $\{10^6\}\Big]$,
5 × 10^5, 0.01$\Big]$, {trials}$\Big]$
$\Big]$ //
Tally

Out[50]= {{\$Fail, 70}, {\$Pass, 30}}

Runs tests A runs test is primarily concerned with detecting an unusual (nonrandom) number of runs of zeros or ones in a binary sequence.

The steps in computing the test statistic (the *p*-value) are as follows:

1. Compute the proportion of ones in the sequence: $\pi = (\varepsilon_1 + \varepsilon_2 + \cdots + \varepsilon_n)/n$.

2. Compute the statistic $Vn_{obs} = \sum_{k=1}^{n-1} r(k) + 1$, where $r(k) = 0$ if $\varepsilon_k = \varepsilon_{k+1}$ and $r(k) = 1$ otherwise; this is computing the number of runs in the sequence.

3. The *p*-value is given by $\operatorname{erfc}\left(\dfrac{Vn_{obs} - 2n\,\pi(1-\pi)}{2\sqrt{2n}\,\pi(1-\pi)}\right)$. If the *p*-value is greater than or equal to .01, then we conclude the sequence is random.

Let us generate some binary data.

```
In[51]:= data = RandomInteger[1, {100}]
```

```
Out[51]= {1, 0, 1, 1, 1, 0, 1, 1, 1, 1, 1, 0, 1, 1, 1, 0, 0, 1, 0, 1, 1, 1, 1, 0, 0, 1,
         0, 1, 1, 0, 1, 0, 1, 0, 0, 1, 1, 0, 0, 0, 0, 1, 1, 1, 1, 1, 1, 1, 0, 1, 0,
         1, 0, 0, 0, 1, 0, 1, 0, 1, 1, 1, 0, 0, 0, 0, 1, 1, 1, 1, 1, 0, 1, 0, 0, 1,
         1, 1, 1, 1, 1, 1, 1, 1, 1, 0, 0, 0, 0, 0, 0, 1, 1, 1, 0, 0, 1, 0, 1, 1}
```

Then we compute the proportion of 1s:

```
In[52]:= pi = Total[data] / Length[data] // N
```

```
Out[52]= 0.6
```

To compute Vn_{obs} we use `Split` to partition by runs of the same number and then count the number of runs present.

```
In[53]:= Vn = Length[Split[data]]
```

```
Out[53]= 45
```

Here is the function using the above pieces of code with one modification – using `Mean` to compute `pi`.

```
In[54]:= RunsTest[data_] :=
           Module[{n = Length[data], pi = Mean[data], Vn},
             Vn = Length[Split[data]];
             N[Erfc[Abs[Vn - 2 n pi (1 - pi)] / (2 √(2 n) pi (1 - pi))]]
           ]
```

For the small sequence of 0s and 1s, the statistic is far enough from 0 that we can conclude the sequence exhibits randomness.

```
In[55]:= RunsTest[data]
```

```
Out[55]= 0.531971
```

The following example is part of the NIST test suite for testing randomness in binary sequences.

```
In[56]:= seq =
           1 100 100 100 001 111 110 110 101 010 001 000 100 001 011 010 001 100 ⸲
           001 000 110 100 110 001 001 100 011 001 100 010 100 010 111 000;
         data = IntegerDigits[seq];
```

```
In[57]:= Length[data]
```

```
Out[57]= 100
```

In[58]:= **RunsTest[data]**

Out[58]= 0.500798

Since this *p*-value is significantly greater than .01, we can conclude the sequence passes our test for randomness.

The runs test is commonly used to detect runs of 0s or 1s in a binary sequence. A very small (or large) number of oscillations would have fewer (or more) runs than expected. For example, a sequence of 100 bits consisting of fifty 1s followed by fifty 0s would have only two runs, which is quite a lot fewer than the expected fifty runs. See Rukhin et al. (2010) for further information on runs tests.

Autocorrelation tests and correlograms Sometimes a quick visualization can give a good sense of statistical information at a glance. One commonly used visualization in time-series analysis, for example, is an autocorrelation plot, or, more broadly, correlograms. These plots provide visual information showing correlations for data at various time or position lags.

For testing randomness in sequences of numbers, the autocorrelation statistic should be near zero. For time series, the statistic can help determine if one datum point is related to a subsequent value in a list or if the values are unrelated and essentially represent uncorrelated data, or white noise.

We will use the built-in statistical functions to create a visualization of autocorrelation statistics for a range of time lags. We will start with a small dataset consisting of a sequence of 1000 random integers between one and one hundred.

In[59]:= **data = RandomInteger[{1, 100}, {1000}];**

Assuming a lag of 1, we need to pair up the second element with the first, the third element with the second, and in general, create a list $\{x_{i-1}, x_i\}$ for each element in the dataset. Finally we run `Correlation` on these two vectors.

In[60]:= **Correlation[Drop[data, 1], Drop[data, -1]] // N**

Out[60]= 0.019673

The computed autocorrelation values will generally be in the range $[-1, 1]$ with values close to 0 being more closely associated with randomness.

Here then is a function to compute the autocorrelation for arbitrary time lags, with a default time lag of 1.

In[61]:= **AutoCorrelation[*data_*, *lag_* : 1] :=**
            Correlation[Drop[*data*, *lag*], Drop[*data*, -*lag*]]

Let us create a set of autocorrelation statistics for time lags from 1 to 40.

```
In[62]:= correlations =
           N@Table[AutoCorrelation[data, lag], {lag, 1, 40, 1}];
```

Typically, autocorrelation data like the above are visualized over the range of time lags that are being used. Here is a plot with dashed lines set at the constant values 0.1 and −0.1 to highlight the range of the autocorrelation values.

```
In[63]:= ListPlot[correlations, AspectRatio → .35,
           Frame → True, Axes → False, PlotRange → {-0.25, 0.25},
           FrameTicks → {{Automatic, False}, {Automatic, False}},
           Epilog → {Thin, Dashed, Line[{{0, 0.1}, {40, 0.1}}],
             Line[{{0, -0.1}, {40, -0.1}}]}]
```

Out[63]=

With a bit more work, we could turn all the work above into a function that takes three arguments: the data that are being studied, a list indicating the range of time lags, and a scalar value for the dashed lines range. (See Section 10.1 for more information on working with graphics functions and their many options.) These types of plots are commonly referred to as correlograms.

```
In[64]:= Correlogram[data_, {lagmin_, lagmax_, incr_:1}, coeff_] :=
           Module[{corrs, len},
             len = (lagmax - lagmin + 1) / incr;
             corrs = Table[{lag, AutoCorrelation[data, lag]},
               {lag, lagmin, lagmax, incr}];
             ListPlot[corrs,
               AspectRatio → .35, Frame → True, Axes → False,
               FrameLabel → {"Lag", "Autocorrelation"},
               FrameTicks → {{Automatic, False}, {Automatic, False}},
               Epilog → {Thin, Dashed, Line[{{0, coeff}, {len, coeff}}],
                 Line[{{0, -coeff}, {len, -coeff}}]}]]
```

In[65]:= **Correlogram[data, {1, 100}, 0.05]**

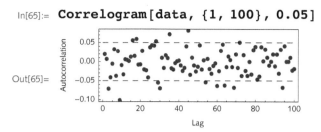

Out[65]=

Interestingly, if the data exhibit periodicity, the correlogram will follow this fluctuation at the same frequency. For example, mean monthly air temperatures taken over a twenty-year period show this phenomenon quite clearly.

In[66]:= **temps = WeatherData["Chicago", "MeanTemperature",**
{{1992, 1}, {2012, 1}, "Month"}, "Value"];

In[67]:= **Correlogram[temps, {1, 40}, 0.35]**

Out[67]=

Several improvements to this function such as adding options to indicate the autocorrelation range and options to be passed to `ListPlot` are discussed in Exercise 8 below.

See Chatfield (2004) or Box, Jenkins, and Reinsel (2008) for more information on the analysis and visualization of time-series statistics.

Exercises

1. Write a functional implementation of the secant method. Your function should accept as arguments the name of a function and two initial guesses. It should maintain the precision of the inputs and it should output the root at the precision of the initial guess, and the number of iterations required to compute the root. Consider using the built-in functions `FixedPoint` or `Nest`.

2. The `findRoot` function developed in this section suffers from several inefficiencies. One of them is that if the precision goal is no more than machine precision, all intermediate computations should be done at the more efficient machine precision as well. Modify `findRoot` so that it will operate at machine precision if the precision goal is at most machine precision.

3. In the `findRoot` program, we added $\text{SetPrecision}\big[result,\ precisionGoal\big]$ at the very end to return the final result at the precision goal, but we have done no test to insure that the result meets the required precision. Add a test to the end of the `findRoot` function so that, if this condition is not met, an error message is generated and the current result is output.

4. Some functions tend to cause root-finding methods to converge rather slowly. For example, the function $f(x) = \sin(x) - x$ requires over ten iterations of Newton's method with an initial guess of $x_0 = 0.1$ to get three-place accuracy.

```
In[1]:= FindRoot[Sin[x] - x, {x, 0.1},
          MaxIterations → 12, EvaluationMonitor :> Sow[x]] // Reap
        FindRoot::cvmit :
          Failed to converge to the requested accuracy or precision within 12 iterations. ≫
Out[1]= {{x → 0.000770503},
          {{0.1, 0.0666556, 0.0444337, 0.0296215, 0.0197474, 0.0131648,
            0.00877654, 0.00585102, 0.00390068, 0.00260045,
            0.00173363, 0.00115576, 0.000770503}}}
```

Implement the following acceleration of Newton's method and determine how many iterations of the function $f(x) = \sin(x) - x$, starting with $x_0 = 0.1$, are necessary for six-place accuracy.

$$\text{accelNewton}(x) = \frac{f(x)\, f'(x)}{[f'(x)]^2 - f(x)\, f''(x)}$$

This accelerated method is particularly useful for functions with multiple roots.

5. The *norm* of a matrix gives some measure of the size of that matrix. The norm of a matrix A is indicated by $\|A\|$. There are numerous matrix norms, but all share certain properties. For $n \times n$ matrices A and B:

   (i.) $\|A\| \geq 0$;

   (ii.) $\|A\| = 0$ if and only if A is the zero matrix;

   (iii.) $\|c\,A\| = |c|\, \|A\|$ for any scalar c;

   (iv.) $\|A + B\| = \|A\| + \|B\|$;

   (v.) $\|A\,B\| \leq \|A\|\, \|B\|$.

   One particularly useful norm is the l_∞ norm, sometimes referred to as the *max norm*. For a vector, this is defined as

   $$\|\vec{x}\|_\infty = \max_{1 \leq i \leq n} |x_i|\,.$$

   The corresponding matrix norm is defined similarly. Hence, for a matrix $A = a_{ij}$, we have

   $$\|A\|_\infty = \max_{1 \leq i \leq n} \sum_{j=1}^{n} |a_{ij}|\,.$$

   This computes the sum of the absolute values of the elements in each row, and then takes the maximum of these sums, that is, the l_∞ matrix norm is the max of the l_∞ norms of the rows.

   Write a function norm[*mat*, ∞] that takes a square matrix as an argument and outputs its $\|\cdot\|_\infty$ norm. Compare your function with the built-in Norm function. Include rules for the l_2 and l_1 norms.

6. If a matrix A is nonsingular (invertible), then its *condition number* is defined as $\|A\| \cdot \|A^{-1}\|$. A matrix is called *well-conditioned* if its condition number is close to 1, the condition number of the identity matrix. A matrix is called *ill-conditioned* if its condition number is significantly larger than 1.

Write a function `conditionNumber`[*mat*] that uses `norm` defined in the previous exercise or the built-in `Norm` function and outputs the condition number of *mat*. Use `conditionNumber` to compute the condition number of the first ten Hilbert matrices.

7. Create a function `LagPlot`[*data, lag*] that plots *data* (a one-dimensional vector) against the data lagged by a displacement, *lag*. For example, if *lag* = 1, then `LagPlot` would display values $\{x_{i-1}, x_i\}$. Use NIST's lew.dat which consists of 200 observations of beam deflection data and whose lag plot indicates a lack of randomness in the sequence of numbers. You can import and post-process the data using the following:

```
In[2]:=  data = Import[
             "http://itl.nist.gov/div898/education/eda/lew.dat", "Data"];
         Short[lewdata = Cases[data, {x_ ? NumberQ} :> x]]
```
Out[3]//Short=
```
             {-213, -564, -35, -15, 141, <<190>>, -385, 198, -218, -536, 96}
```

Or, if you have the files associated with this book, use something like the following:

```
In[4]:=  lewdata = Import[
             FileNameJoin[{NotebookDirectory[], "Data", "lew.dat"}], "List"];
```

8. Modify the `Correlogram` function developed in this section to provide for an option, `Coefficient`, that sets the range of values for the dashed lines within which the autocorrelation coefficients are hoped to lie. In addition, set things up so `Correlogram` inherits all the options of `ListPlot`.

Then use your function to look at some time-series data, such as that below; the plot here shows a high degree of autocorrelation for small time lags, but less so for larger lags, suggesting a serial dependence in the data. In finance, autocorrelation analysis (usually referred to as serial correlation) is used to predict how price movements may be affected by each other.

```
In[5]:=  data = FinancialData["^DJI", {{2011, 1, 1}, {2011, 12, 31}}, "Value"];
In[6]:=  Correlogram[data, {1, 150}, Coefficient -> 0.5,
             Filling -> Axis, PlotRange -> {-1, 1},
             PlotLabel -> Style["Dow Jones 2011: autocorrelation plot", 8],
             FrameLabel -> {{"Autocorrelation", None}, {"Lag", None}}]
```

Out[6]=

9. Create random walks on the binary digits of π. For a one-dimensional walk, use `RealDigits`[*num*, 2] to get the base 2 digits and then convert each 0 to −1 so that you have a vector of ±1s for the step directions; then use `Accumulate`. For the two-dimensional walk, use `Partition` to pair up digits and then use an appropriate transformation to have the four pairs, $\{0, 0\}, \{0, 1\}, \{1, 0\},$ and $\{1, 1\}$ map to the compass directions; then use `Accumulate`. See Bailey et al. (2012) for more on visualizing digits of π.

9

Strings

Structure and syntax · Character codes · Sorting lists of characters · Ordered words · Operations on strings · Strings vs. lists · Encoding text · Indexed symbols · Anagrams · String patterns· Finding subsequences with strings · Alternatives · Regular expressions · Word stemming · Random strings · Partitioning strings · Adler checksum · Substring searches · DNA sequence analysis · Displaying DNA sequences · Blanagrams

Strings are used across many disciplines to represent filenames, data, and other objects: linguists working with text data study representation, classification, and patterns involved in audio and text usage; biologists dealing with genomic data as strings are interested in sequence structure and assembly and perform extensive statistical analysis of their data; programmers operate on string data for such tasks as text search, file manipulation, and text processing. Strings are so ubiquitous that almost every modern programming language has a string datatype and dozens of functions for operating on and with strings.

In *Mathematica*, strings are represented by any concatenation of characters enclosed in double quotes.

In[1]:= **StringQ["The magic words are squeamish ossifrage."]**

Out[1]= True

Strings are also used to represent file names that you import and export.

In[2]:= **Import["ExampleData/ocelot.jpg"]**

Out[2]=

Strings are used as arguments, option values, and as the output to many functions.

In[3]:= **GenomeData["SNORD107"]**

Out[3]= GGTTCATGATGACACAGGACCTTGTCTGAACATAATGATTTCAAAATTTGAGCTTAAAA⸱
ATGACACTCTGAAATC

In[4]:= **StringQ[%]**

Out[4]= True

In this chapter we will introduce the tools available for working with strings in *Mathematica*. We will begin with a look at the structure and syntax of strings, then move on to a discussion of the many high-level functions that are optimized for string manipulation. String patterns follow on the discussion of patterns in Chapter 4 and we will introduce an alternative syntax (regular expressions) that provides a very compact mechanism for working with strings. The chapter closes with several applied examples drawn from computer science (checksums) as well as bioinformatics (working with DNA sequences) and also word games (anagrams, blanagrams).

9.1   Structure and syntax

Strings are expressions consisting of a number of characters enclosed in quotes. The characters can be anything you can type from your keyboard, including uppercase and lowercase letters, numbers, punctuation marks, and spaces. For example, here is the standard set of printable Ascii characters.

In[1]:= **CharacterRange[" ", "~"]**

Out[1]= { , !, ", #, $, %, &, ', (,), *, +, ,, -, ., /, 0, 1, 2,
3, 4, 5, 6, 7, 8, 9, :, ;, <, =, >, ?, @, A, B, C, D, E,
F, G, H, I, J, K, L, M, N, O, P, Q, R, S, T, U, V, W, X,
Y, Z, [, \,], ^, _, `, a, b, c, d, e, f, g, h, i, j, k,
l, m, n, o, p, q, r, s, t, u, v, w, x, y, z, {, |, }, ~}

Other character sets are available as well. For example, here are the lowercase Greek letters. These are typically entered from one of *Mathematica*'s many built-in character palettes, or using a keyboard shortcut such as ESC-a-ESC for α.

In[2]:= **CharacterRange["α", "ω"]**

Out[2]= {α, β, γ, δ, ε, ζ, η, θ, ι, κ, λ,
μ, ν, ξ, ο, π, ρ, ς, σ, τ, υ, φ, χ, ψ, ω}

When *Mathematica* displays a string in output, it appears without the quotes. This is the default behavior of the formatting rules for OutputForm.

In[3]:= `"The magic words are squeamish ossifrage."`

Out[3]= `The magic words are squeamish ossifrage.`

Use `InputForm` or `FullForm` to display these quotes in output.

In[4]:= `FullForm["The magic words are squeamish ossifrage."]`

Out[4]//FullForm=
`"The magic words are squeamish ossifrage."`

Various predicates test whether a string consists entirely of letters, or uppercase and lowercase letters.

In[5]:= `LetterQ["ossifrage"]`

Out[5]= `True`

In[6]:= `LetterQ["x1"]`

Out[6]= `False`

In[7]:= `LowerCaseQ["strings"]`

Out[7]= `True`

Use `===` (`SameQ`) to test for equality of strings.

In[8]:= `"sty" === "sty "`

Out[8]= `False`

Several functions are available for working with the structure of strings.

In[9]:= `Head["The magic words are squeamish ossifrage."]`

Out[9]= `String`

In[10]:= `StringLength["The magic words are squeamish ossifrage."]`

Out[10]= `40`

`StringLength` also works with lists of strings. In other words, it has the `Listable` attribute.

In[11]:= `StringLength[`
`    {"How", "I", "wish", "I", "could", "calculate", "pi"}]`

Out[11]= `{3, 1, 4, 1, 5, 9, 2}`

Character codes

One way to work with strings is to convert them to a list of character codes and then operate on the codes using mathematical functions. Each character in a computer's character set is assigned a number, called its *character code*. By general agreement, almost all computers use the same character codes, called the *Ascii code*. In this code, the uppercase letters A, B, ..., Z are assigned the numbers 65, 66, ..., 90 while the lowercase letters *a*, *b*, ..., *z* have the numbers 97, 98, ..., 122 (note that the number of an uppercase letter is 32 less than its lowercase version). The numbers 0, 1, ..., 9 are coded as 48, 49, ..., 57 while the punctuation marks period, comma, and exclamation point have the codes 46, 44, and 33, respectively. The space character is represented by the code 32. Table 9.1 shows the characters and their codes.

TABLE 9.1. *Ascii character codes*

Characters	Ascii codes
A, B, ..., Z	65, 66, ..., 90
a, b, ..., z	97, 98, ..., 122
0, 1, ..., 9	48, 49, ..., 57
. (period)	46
, (comma)	44
? (question mark)	63
␣ (space)	32

Here are the printable Ascii characters.

In[12]:= **FromCharacterCode[Range[32, 126]]**

Out[12]=

```
 !"#$%&'()*+,-./0123456789:;<=>?@ABCDEFGHIJKLMNOPQRSTUVWXYZ
[\]^_`abcdefghijklmnopqrstuvwxyz{|}~
```

ToCharacterCode[*char*] converts any string character *char* to its Ascii code.

In[13]:= **ToCharacterCode[%]**

Out[13]= {32, 33, 34, 35, 36, 37, 38, 39, 40, 41, 42, 43, 44, 45, 46,
47, 48, 49, 50, 51, 52, 53, 54, 55, 56, 57, 58, 59, 60, 61,
62, 63, 64, 65, 66, 67, 68, 69, 70, 71, 72, 73, 74, 75, 76,
77, 78, 79, 80, 81, 82, 83, 84, 85, 86, 87, 88, 89, 90, 91,
92, 93, 94, 95, 96, 97, 98, 99, 100, 101, 102, 103, 104,
105, 106, 107, 108, 109, 110, 111, 112, 113, 114, 115,
116, 117, 118, 119, 120, 121, 122, 123, 124, 125, 126}

You can also get a list of the characters in a range if you know how they are ordered by their character codes.

```
In[14]:= CharacterRange["a", "z"]
```

```
Out[14]= {a, b, c, d, e, f, g, h, i, j, k,
         l, m, n, o, p, q, r, s, t, u, v, w, x, y, z}
```

```
In[15]:= Flatten[ToCharacterCode[%]]
```

```
Out[15]= {97, 98, 99, 100, 101, 102, 103, 104, 105, 106, 107, 108, 109,
         110, 111, 112, 113, 114, 115, 116, 117, 118, 119, 120, 121, 122}
```

Characters from other languages can also be used, for example, Greek and Japanese.

```
In[16]:= FromCharacterCode[Range[913, 1009]]
```

Out[16]= ΑΒΓΔΕΖΗΘΙΚΛΜΝΞΟΠΡ ΣΤΥΦΧΨΩΪΫάέήίΰαβγδεζηθικλμνξοπρςστυφχψωϊϋό᾽
        ύώϐ ϑϒϓϔφϖϗϘϙϚϛϜϝϞϟϠϡϢϣϤϥϦϧϨϩϪϫϬϭϮϯϰϱ

```
In[17]:= FromCharacterCode[Range[30010, 30030]]
```

Out[17]= 町画甲刪甾甿畀畁畂畃畄畅畆畇畈畉畊畋界畍畎畏

Unicode charts for many languages are available online (for example, www.unicode.org/charts). With these charts you can find the hexadecimal code for characters in many different languages. For Gujarati, the first character in its code table has hex value 0A90. Here we convert from base 16 and then display the character.

```
In[18]:= 16^^0A90
```

```
Out[18]= 2704
```

```
In[19]:= FromCharacterCode[%]
```

Out[19]= એ

Using the character code representation of characters, the following series of computations changes a word from lowercase to uppercase.

```
In[20]:= ToCharacterCode["mathematica"]
```

```
Out[20]= {109, 97, 116, 104, 101, 109, 97, 116, 105, 99, 97}
```

```
In[21]:= % - 32
```

```
Out[21]= {77, 65, 84, 72, 69, 77, 65, 84, 73, 67, 65}
```

```
In[22]:= FromCharacterCode[%]
```

Out[22]= MATHEMATICA

Or, simply use a built-in function that is designed specifically for this task.

```
In[23]:= ToUpperCase["mathematica"]
```

Out[23]= MATHEMATICA

Sorting lists of characters

As a practical example of the use of character codes, we will extend the simple sorting function from Chapter 4 to work with lists of string characters. Although written to operate on numbers, this rule can be overloaded to work on characters by making only a few small changes. Here is the original rule from Section 4.3.

```
In[24]:= listSort = {{x___ , a_ ?NumericQ, b_ ?NumericQ, y___} :>
            {x, b, a, y} /; b < a};
```

The first change is to check that the patterns a and b have head `String` instead of testing for numbers with the predicate `NumericQ`. Second, instead of the numerical comparison b < a, we need to compare their character codes.

```
In[25]:= ToCharacterCode[{"q", "t"}]
```

```
Out[25]= {{113}, {116}}
```

```
In[26]:= charSort = {x___ , a_String, b_String, y___} :> {x, b, a, y} /;
            First[ToCharacterCode[b]] < First[ToCharacterCode[a]]
```

```
Out[26]= {x___ , a_String, b_String, y___} :> {x, b, a, y} /;
            First[ToCharacterCode[b]] < First[ToCharacterCode[a]]
```

Here is a list of characters.

```
In[27]:= chars = {"d", "h", "c", "m", "r", "l", "c", "h", "t", "d", "j"};
```

Here is the sort.

```
In[28]:= chars //. charSort
```

```
Out[28]= {c, c, d, d, h, h, j, l, m, r, t}
```

Section 9.5 explores the use of character codes to create hash tables, or checksums.

Ordered words

When studying word or language structure, a common task is to find all words within a corpus that meet some criteria you are interested in. In this brief example, we will use character codes to search for words whose letters are "in order" when read from the first letter to the last. We will create a Boolean function `OrderedWordQ` that returns `True` or `False` depending upon whether its argument is in alphabetic order. So `OrderedWordQ["best"]` would return `True` but `OrderedWordQ["brag"]` would return `False`. Then we will use this predicate to find all words in a dictionary that are ordered in this sense.

Start by getting a list of all words in the dictionary using `DictionaryLookup`.

```
In[29]:= words = DictionaryLookup[];
         Short[words, 4]
```
Out[30]//Short=
>   {a, Aachen, aah, Aaliyah, aardvark, aardvarks,
>   Aaron, abaci, aback, abacus, abacuses, abaft,
>   ≪92 495≫, Zürich, zwieback, Zwingli, Zworykin, zydeco,
>   zygote, zygotes, zygotic, zymurgy, Zyrtec, Zyuganov}

Alternatively, you can use the data in WordData, which contains phrases in addition to words. You could use any similar resource for your list of words.

```
In[31]:= Short[WordData[All], 4]
```
Out[31]//Short=
>   {0, 1, 10, 100, 1000, 10000, 100000, 1000000,
>   1000000000, 1000000000000, 1000th, 100th, ≪149 168≫,
>   Zyloprim, zymase, zymogen, zymoid, zymology, zymolysis,
>   zymolytic, zymosis, zymotic, zymurgy, Zyrian}

First, consider the character code of a string.

```
In[32]:= ToCharacterCode["best"]
```
Out[32]= {98, 101, 115, 116}

Then we only need to know if this list of codes is in order.

```
In[33]:= OrderedQ[%]
```
Out[33]= True

Here is a predicate that returns True if its argument is ordered in this alphabetic sense.

```
In[34]:= OrderedWordQ[word_String] := OrderedQ[ToCharacterCode[word]]
```

Now we will find all the words in the dictionary file that comes with *Mathematica* that are ordered in this way; we will use Select to return those words that pass the test. Finally, we randomly sample 40 of them.

```
In[35]:= orderedwords = Select[words, OrderedWordQ];
```

```
In[36]:= RandomSample[orderedwords, 40]
```
Out[36]= {Tabor, dot, loos, first, Phipps, Gap, I, Kent, Milo, Dior,
>   bells, or, ABS, Kass, ens, Nader, been, adds, a, Hiss, access,
>   Lajos, Kerr, allow, cellos, Babel, Rh, his, ah, almost, abbes,
>   chippy, Cam, ABC, ally, Igor, cent, Odell, floppy, Tory}

Almost correct! In the English character code set, capitals appear before lowercase letters. So, although our words are ordered in the sense of character codes, they are not ordered in the commonly-used sense.

In[37]:= **ToCharacterCode["A"]**

Out[37]= {65}

In[38]:= **ToCharacterCode["a"]**

Out[38]= {97}

One approach to resolving this issue is to only work with words of the same case. We could either convert words of the form uppercase/lowercase to lowercase/lowercase or we could select only words from the dictionary that match a pattern that codes for this. We will wait until the discussion of string patterns in Section 9.3 to correct this issue.

Exercises

1. Convert the first character in a string (which you may assume to be a lowercase letter) to uppercase.

2. Given a string of digits of arbitrary length, convert it to its integer value. (Hint: you may find that the Dot function is helpful.)

3. Create a function UniqueCharacters[*str*] that takes a string as its argument and returns a list of the unique characters in that string. For example, UniqueCharacters["Mississippi"] should return {M, i, s, p}.

9.2 Operations on strings

Strings are expressions and, like other expressions (such as numbers and lists), there are built-in functions available to operate on them. Many of these functions are very similar to those for operating on lists. In this section we will first look at some of these basic functions for operating on strings and then use them on some nontrivial examples: analyzing a large piece of text, encoding strings, creating index variables, and finally, a word game for creating anagrams.

Basic string operations

StringTake, which has a similar syntax to Take, is used to extract parts of a string. The second argument specifies the positions of the characters to extract. So, for example, this takes the first twelve characters in this string.

In[1]:= **StringTake["Three quarks for Muster Mark!", 12]**

Out[1]= Three quarks

And this takes the last twelve characters from the string.

In[2]:= **StringTake["Three quarks for Muster Mark!", -12]**

Out[2]= Muster Mark!

A list of the individual characters is returned by `Characters`.

In[3]:= **Characters**["Three quarks for Muster Mark!"]

Out[3]= {T, h, r, e, e, , q, u, a, r, k, s, ,
        f, o, r, , M, u, s, t, e, r, , M, a, r, k, !}

`StringJoin` concatenates strings.

In[4]:= **StringJoin**["q", "u", "a", "r", "k", "s"]

Out[4]= quarks

The shorthand notation for `StringJoin` is $str_1 <> str_2$.

In[5]:= "x" <> "22"

Out[5]= x22

The following functions mirror those for list operations.

In[6]:= **StringReverse**["abcde"]

Out[6]= edcba

In[7]:= **StringDrop**["abcde", -1]

Out[7]= abcd

In[8]:= **StringPosition**["abcde", "bc"]

Out[8]= {{2, 3}}

In[9]:= **StringCount**["When you wish upon a star", "o"]

Out[9]= 2

In[10]:= **StringInsert**["abcde", "T", 3]

Out[10]= abTcde

In[11]:= **StringReplace**["abcde", "cd" → "CD"]

Out[11]= abCDe

Some functions are quite specific to strings and do not have analogs with lists. For example, conversion to uppercase and lowercase.

In[12]:= **ToUpperCase**["words"]

Out[12]= WORDS

This trims substrings from a string using alternative patterns (discussed further in Section 9.3). So if either "http://" or "/" is found, they will be trimmed.

In[13]:= **StringTrim**["http://www.google.com/", "http://" | "/"]

Out[13]= www.google.com

Strings vs. lists

For some computations, you might be tempted to convert a string to a list of characters and then operate on the list using some list manipulation functions. For example, this first constructs a list of the individual characters and then uses `Count` to get the number of occurrences of the letter *B* in the list of characters from the text of Charles Darwin's *On the Origin of Species*.

```
In[14]:= text = ExampleData[{"Text", "OriginOfSpecies"}];
         StringTake[text, 200]

Out[15]= INTRODUCTION. When on board H.M.S. 'Beagle,' as
            naturalist, I was much struck with certain facts
            in the distribution of the inhabitants of South
            America, and in the geological relations of the present

In[16]:= Count[Characters[text], "B"] // Timing

Out[16]= {0.167993, 427}
```

Since the string functions in *Mathematica* are optimized for working on strings directly you will often find that they are much faster than the more general list manipulation functions.

```
In[17]:= StringCount[text, "B"] // Timing

Out[17]= {0.001424, 427}
```

This speedup results from the fact that the string pattern matching algorithms are operating only on a well-defined finite alphabet and string expressions are essentially flat structures, whereas the algorithms for more general expression matching are designed to operate on arbitrary expressions with potentially much more complicated structures.

Converting to lists and using list manipulation functions will often be more cumbersome than working with the string functions directly. For example, counting the occurrences of a word within a chunk of text by first converting to a list of characters would be quite indirect and computationally more taxing than simply using `StringCount` directly.

```
In[18]:= StringCount[text, "selection"] // Timing

Out[18]= {0.005508, 351}
```

In fact, sometimes you will even find it more efficient to convert a numerical problem to one involving strings, do the work with string manipulation functions, and then convert back to numbers as in the subsequence example in Section 9.5.

Encoding text

In this example, we will develop functions for coding and decoding strings of text. The particular coding that we will use is quite simplistic compared with contemporary commercial-grade ciphers, but it will give us a chance to see how to combine string manipulation, the use of functional programming constructs, and rule-based programming all in a very practical example that should be accessible to anyone.

The problem in encryption is to develop an algorithm that can be used to encode a string of text and then a dual algorithm that can be used to decode the encrypted message. Typically, the input string is referred to as the *plaintext* and the encoded output as the *ciphertext*.

To start, we will limit ourselves to the 26 lowercase letters of the alphabet.

In[19]:= **alphabet = CharacterRange["a", "z"]**

Out[19]= {a, b, c, d, e, f, g, h, i, j, k,
l, m, n, o, p, q, r, s, t, u, v, w, x, y, z}

One of the simplest encryption schemes is attributed to Julius Caesar who is said to have used this cipher to encode communications with his generals. The scheme is simply to shift each letter of the alphabet some fixed number of places to the left and is commonly referred to as a substitution cipher. Using Thread, we can set up rules that implement this shift, here just shifting one place to the left.

In[20]:= **CaesarCodeRules = Thread[alphabet → RotateLeft[alphabet]]**

Out[20]= {a → b, b → c, c → d, d → e, e → f, f → g, g → h, h → i,
i → j, j → k, k → l, l → m, m → n, n → o, o → p, p → q, q → r,
r → s, s → t, t → u, u → v, v → w, w → x, x → y, y → z, z → a}

The decoding rules are simply to reverse the encoding rules.

In[21]:= **CaesarDecodeRules = Map[Reverse, CaesarCodeRules]**

Out[21]= {b → a, c → b, d → c, e → d, f → e, g → f, h → g, i → h,
j → i, k → j, l → k, m → l, n → m, o → n, p → o, q → p, r → q,
s → r, t → s, u → t, v → u, w → v, x → w, y → x, z → y, a → z}

To code a string, we will decompose the string into individual characters, apply the code rules, and then join up the resulting characters in a "word."

In[22]:= **Characters["hello"]**

Out[22]= {h, e, l, l, o}

In[23]:= **% /. CaesarCodeRules**

Out[23]= {i, f, m, m, p}

In[24]:= **StringJoin[%]**

Out[24]= ifmmp

Here is the function to accomplish this.

```
In[25]:= encode[str_String, coderules_] :=
           StringJoin[Characters[str] /. coderules]
```

Similarly, here is the decoding function.

```
In[26]:= decode[str_String, decoderules_] :=
           StringJoin[Characters[str] /. decoderules]
```

Let us try it out on a phrase.

```
In[27]:= encode["squeamish ossifrage", CaesarCodeRules]

Out[27]= trvfbnjti pttjgsbhf
```

```
In[28]:= decode[%, CaesarDecodeRules]

Out[28]= squeamish ossifrage
```

In this example, we have shifted one position for each letter to encode (and decode). It is thought that Caesar (or his cryptographers) used a shift of length three to encode his military messages. In the exercises, you are asked to implement a different shift length in the encoding and decoding functions.

Even with longer shifts, the Caesar cipher is terribly insecure and highly prone to cracking since there are only 26 possible shifts with this simple cipher. A slightly more secure cipher involves permuting the letters of the alphabet.

```
In[29]:= p = RandomSample[alphabet]

Out[29]= {a, m, j, c, d, k, p, u, x, z, b,
          w, n, e, t, s, g, l, y, h, v, i, f, o, q, r}
```

Using `Thread`, we create a rule for each letter paired up with the corresponding letter from the permutation p.

```
In[30]:= PermutationCodeRules = Thread[alphabet → p]

Out[30]= {a → a, b → m, c → j, d → c, e → d, f → k, g → p, h → u,
          i → x, j → z, k → b, l → w, m → n, n → e, o → t, p → s, q → g,
          r → l, s → y, t → h, u → v, v → i, w → f, x → o, y → q, z → r}
```

Again, the decoding rules are obtained by simply reversing the above rules.

```
In[31]:= PermutationDecodeRules = Thread[p → alphabet]

Out[31]= {a → a, m → b, j → c, c → d, d → e, k → f, p → g, u → h,
          x → i, z → j, b → k, w → l, n → m, e → n, t → o, s → p, g → q,
          l → r, y → s, h → t, v → u, i → v, f → w, o → x, q → y, r → z}
```

```
In[32]:= encode["squeamish ossifrage", PermutationCodeRules]
```

```
Out[32]= ygvdanxyu tyyxklapd
```

```
In[33]:= decode[%, PermutationDecodeRules]
```

```
Out[33]= squeamish ossifrage
```

Although these substitution ciphers are not terribly difficult to crack, they should give you some good practice in working with strings and the various *Mathematica* programming constructs. Modern commercial-grade ciphers such as public-key ciphers are often based on the difficulty of factoring large integers. For a basic introduction to the history of ciphers, see Sinkov (1966). A more thorough treatment can be found in Paar and Pelzl (2010).

Indexed symbols

When developing algorithms that operate on large structures (for example, large systems of equations), it is often helpful to be able to create a set of unique symbols with which to work. As an example of operations on strings, we will use some of the functions discussed in this section to develop a little utility function that creates unique symbols. Although there is a built-in function, `Unique`, that does this, it has some limitations for this particular task.

```
In[34]:= Table[Unique["x"], {8}]
```

```
Out[34]= {x3, x4, x5, x6, x7, x8, x9, x10}
```

One potential limitation of `Unique` is that it uses the first *unused* symbol of a particular form. It does this to avoid overwriting existing symbols.

```
In[35]:= Table[Unique["x"], {8}]
```

```
Out[35]= {x11, x12, x13, x14, x15, x16, x17, x18}
```

However, if you want to explicitly create a list of indexed symbols with a set of specific indices, it is useful to create a different function. First, note that a string can be converted to a symbol using `ToExpression` or by wrapping the string in `Symbol`.

```
In[36]:= Head["x1"]
```

```
Out[36]= String
```

```
In[37]:= ToExpression["x1"] // Head
```

```
Out[37]= Symbol
```

```
In[38]:= Symbol["x1"] // Head
```

```
Out[38]= Symbol
```

`StringJoin` is used to concatenate strings. So, let us concatenate the variable with the index, first with one number and then with a range of numbers.

```
In[39]:= StringJoin["x", "8"] // FullForm
```

Out[39]//FullForm=
```
       "x8"
```

```
In[40]:= ToExpression[Map["x" <> ToString[#] &, Range[12]]]
```

Out[40]= {x1, x2, x3, x4, x5, x6, x7, x8, x9, x10, x11, x12}

We put all the pieces of code together.

```
In[41]:= MakeVarList[x_Symbol, n_Integer] :=
          ToExpression[Map[ToString[x] <> ToString[#] &, Range[n]]]
```

```
In[42]:= MakeVarList[tmp, 20]
```

Out[42]= {tmp1, tmp2, tmp3, tmp4, tmp5, tmp6,
          tmp7, tmp8, tmp9, tmp10, tmp11, tmp12, tmp13,
          tmp14, tmp15, tmp16, tmp17, tmp18, tmp19, tmp20}

Let us create an additional rule for this function that takes a range specification as its second argument.

```
In[43]:= MakeVarList[x_Symbol, {n_Integer, m_Integer}] :=
          ToExpression[Map[ToString[x] <> ToString[#] &, Range[n, m]]]
```

```
In[44]:= MakeVarList[tmp, {20, 30}]
```

Out[44]= {tmp20, tmp21, tmp22, tmp23, tmp24,
          tmp25, tmp26, tmp27, tmp28, tmp29, tmp30}

Note that we have not been too careful about argument checking.

```
In[45]:= MakeVarList[tmp, {-2, 2}]
```

Out[45]= {-2 + tmp, -1 + tmp, tmp0, tmp1, tmp2}

In the exercises you are asked to correct this.

Anagrams

Anagrams are words that have the same set of letters but in a different order. Good Scrabble players are adept at anagram creation. Anagrams can be created by taking a word, extracting and permuting its characters, and then finding which permutations are real words.

Start by getting the characters in a word.

```
In[46]:= chars = Characters["tame"]
```

Out[46]= {t, a, m, e}

Permute the characters.

```
In[47]:= p = Permutations[chars]

Out[47]= {{t, a, m, e}, {t, a, e, m}, {t, m, a, e}, {t, m, e, a},
         {t, e, a, m}, {t, e, m, a}, {a, t, m, e}, {a, t, e, m},
         {a, m, t, e}, {a, m, e, t}, {a, e, t, m}, {a, e, m, t},
         {m, t, a, e}, {m, t, e, a}, {m, a, t, e}, {m, a, e, t},
         {m, e, t, a}, {m, e, a, t}, {e, t, a, m}, {e, t, m, a},
         {e, a, t, m}, {e, a, m, t}, {e, m, t, a}, {e, m, a, t}}
```

Concatenate the characters in each list.

```
In[48]:= words = Map[StringJoin, p]

Out[48]= {tame, taem, tmae, tmea, team, tema, atme, atem,
         amte, amet, aetm, aemt, mtae, mtea, mate, maet,
         meta, meat, etam, etma, eatm, eamt, emta, emat}
```

Now, which of these "words" are really words? One way to check is to select those that are in the dictionary. Those elements in words that are not in the dictionary will return {} when run against DictionaryLookup, so we omit those using ≠.

```
In[49]:= Select[words, DictionaryLookup[#, IgnoreCase → True] ≠ {} &]

Out[49]= {tame, team, mate, meta, meat}
```

Putting all the pieces together, we have the function Anagrams.

```
In[50]:= Anagrams[word_String] :=
          Module[{chars = Characters[word], words},
            words = Map[StringJoin, Permutations[chars]];
            Select[words, DictionaryLookup[#, IgnoreCase → True] ≠ {} &]
          ]

In[51]:= Anagrams["parsley"] // Timing

Out[51]= {0.300797, {parsley, parleys, players, replays, sparely}}

In[52]:= Anagrams["elvis"]

Out[52]= {elvis, evils, levis, lives, veils}

In[53]:= Anagrams["instance"]

Out[53]= {instance, ancients, canniest}
```

Other than extracting the characters of a word and joining the permuted list of characters, the operations here are essentially those on lists (of strings) and pattern matching. Exercise 2 in Section 9.5 discusses a more direct approach to this problem, one that avoids the creation of permutations of the characters in the word.

Exercises

1. Create a function `PalindromeQ[str]` that returns a value of `True` if its argument *str* is a palindrome, that is, if the string *str* is the same forward and backward. For example, *refer* is a palindrome.

2. Create a function `StringRotateLeft[str, n]` that takes a string *str*, and returns a string with the characters rotated to the left *n* places. For example:

    In[1]:= **StringRotateLeft**["a quark for Muster Mark ", 8]

    Out[1]= for Muster Mark a quark

3. In creating the function `MakeVarList` in this section, we were not careful about the arguments that might be passed. Correct this problem using pattern matching on the arguments to this function to insure that the indices are positive integers only.

4. Create a function `StringPad[str, {n}]` that pads the end of a string with *n* whitespace characters. Then create a second rule `StringPad[str, n]` that pads the string out to length *n*. If the input string has length greater than *n*, issue a warning message. Finally, mirroring the argument structure for the built-in `PadLeft`, create a third rule `StringPad[str, n, m]` that pads with *n* whitespaces at the front and *m* whitespaces at the end of the string.

5. Modify the Caesar cipher so that it encodes by shifting five places to the right. Include the space character in the alphabet.

6. A mixed-alphabet cipher is created by first writing a keyword followed by the remaining letters of the alphabet and then using this as the substitution (or cipher) text. For example, if the keyword is *django*, the cipher text alphabet would be:

        djangobcefhiklmpqrstuvwxyz

    So, *a* is replaced with *d*, *b* is replaced with *j*, *c* is replaced with *a*, and so on. As an example, the piece of text

    > *the sheik of araby*

    would then be encoded as

    > *tcg scgeh mo drdjy*

    Implement this cipher and go one step further to output the cipher text in blocks of length five, omitting spaces and punctuation.

7. Modify the alphabet permutation cipher so that instead of being based on single letters, it is instead based on adjacent pairs of letters. The single letter cipher will have
    $26! = 403\,291\,461\,126\,605\,635\,584\,000\,000$ permutations; the adjacent pairs cipher will have
    $26^2! = 1.883707684133810 \times 10^{1621}$ permutations.

9.3 String patterns

Most of the string operations we have looked at up until this point have involved literal strings. For example, in string replacement, we have specified both the explicit string that we are operating on as well as the replacement string.

```
In[1]:= StringReplace["11/28/1986", "/" → "-"]

Out[1]= 11-28-1986
```

But the real power of programming with strings comes with the use of patterns to represent different classes of strings. A string pattern is a string expression that contains symbolic patterns. Much of the pattern matching discussed in the previous chapters extends to strings in a very powerful manner. For example, this uses patterns to change the first letter in a string to uppercase.

```
In[2]:= str = "colorless green ideas sleep furiously";

In[3]:= StringReplace[str, f_ ~~ rest__ :> ToUpperCase[f] <> rest]

Out[3]= Colorless green ideas sleep furiously
```

Or, use a conditional pattern to check if a word begins with an uppercase character.

```
In[4]:= StringMatchQ["Jekyll", f_?UpperCaseQ ~~ rest__]

Out[4]= True
```

To get started, you might find it helpful to think of strings as a sequence of characters and use the same general principles on these expressions as you do with lists.

For example, the expression {a, b, c, c, d, e} matches the pattern {__, s_, s_, __} because it is a list that starts with a sequence of one or more elements, it contains an element repeated once, and then ends with a sequence of one or more elements.

```
In[5]:= MatchQ[{a, b, c, c, d, e}, {__, s_, s_, __}]

Out[5]= True
```

If we now use a string instead of a list and `StringMatchQ` instead of `MatchQ`, we get a similar result using the shorthand notation ~~ for `StringExpression`.

```
In[6]:= StringMatchQ["abccde", __ ~~ s_ ~~ s_ ~~ __]

Out[6]= True
```

str_1 ~~ str_2 is shorthand notation for `StringExpression`[str_1, str_2], which, for the purpose of pattern matching, represents a sequence of strings.

```
In[7]:= "a" ~~ "b"

Out[7]= ab
```

In[8]:= **Defer[FullForm["a" ~~ "b"]]**

Out[8]= StringExpression["a", "b"]

StringExpression is quite similar to StringJoin (both can be used to concatenate strings) except that with StringExpression, you can concatenate nonstrings.

The next example also shows the similarity between the general expression pattern matching that we explored earlier in Chapter 4 and string patterns. Using Cases, the following returns all those expressions that match the pattern _Symbol, that is, pick out all symbols from the list.

In[9]:= **Cases[{1, f, g, 6, x, t, 2, 5}, _Symbol]**

Out[9]= {f, g, x, t}

With strings we use StringCases whose second argument is a pattern that represents a class of characters to match. StringCases returns those substrings that match a given pattern. Many named patterns are available for various purposes. For example, LetterCharacter matches a single letter.

In[10]:= **StringCases["1fg6xt25", LetterCharacter]**

Out[10]= {f, g, x, t}

Match single digits with DigitCharacter and one or more digits with NumberString.

In[11]:= **StringCases["1fg6xt25", DigitCharacter]**

Out[11]= {1, 6, 2, 5}

In[12]:= **StringCases["1fg6xt25", NumberString]**

Out[12]= {1, 6, 25}

To see the generality and power of working with string patterns, suppose we were looking for a nucleotide sequence in a gene consisting of a repetition of A followed by any character, followed by T. Using a gene from the human genome, the following string pattern neatly does the job.

In[13]:= **gene = GenomeData["IGHV357"]**

Out[13]= AAGTCCTGTGTGAAGTTTATTGATGGAGTCAGAGGCAGAAAATTGTACAGCCCAGTGGTTCA ⋮
        CTGAGACTCTCCTGCAAAGCCTCTGATTTCACCTTTACTGGCTACAGCATGAGCTTGGT ⋮
        CCAGCAGGCTTCATGACAGGGATTGGTGTGGGTGGAAACAGTGAGTGATCAAGTGGGAG ⋮
        TTCTCAGAGTTACTCTCCATGAGTACAAATAAATTAACAGTCCCAAGCGACACCTTTTC ⋮
        ATGTGCAGTCTACCTTACAATGACCAACCTGAAAGCCAAGGACAAGGCTGTGTATTACT ⋮
        GTGAGGGA

In[14]:= **StringCases[gene, "AA" ~~ _ ~~ "T"]**

Out[14]= {AAGT, AAGT, AAAT, AAGT, AAAT, AAAT}

Here are the starting and ending positions of these substrings. `StringPosition` takes the same syntax as `StringCases`, analogous to `Position` and `Cases`.

In[15]:= **StringPosition[gene, "AA" ~~ _ ~~ "T"]**

Out[15]= {{1, 4}, {13, 16}, {40, 43}, {41, 44},
         {172, 175}, {207, 210}, {211, 214}, {212, 215}}

And if you wanted to return those characters that follow all occurrences of the string "GTC", you can name the pattern and use a rule to return it.

In[16]:= **StringCases[gene, *pat* : "GTC" ~~ *x_* :→ *pat* <> *x*]**

Out[16]= {GTCC, GTCA, GTCC, GTCC, GTCT}

In this example, the pattern is `pat : "GTC" ~~ x_`. This pattern is named `pat` and it consists of the string GTC which is then followed by any character. That character is named x so that we can refer to it in the replacement expression on the right-hand side of the rule. The replacement expression is the pattern `pat` concatenated with the character named x.

As another example of the use of string patterns, suppose you were interested in scraping phone numbers off of a web page; you need to construct a pattern that matches the form of the phone numbers you are looking for. In this case we use the form *n-nnn-nnn-nnnn* which matches the form of North American phone numbers. `NumberString` comes in handy as it picks up strings of numbers of any length. Otherwise you would have to use `DigitCharacter ..` which matches repeating digits.

In[17]:= **webpage = Import[**
           "http://www.wolfram.com/company/contact.cgi", "HTML"];

In[18]:= **StringCases[webpage,**
           NumberString ~~ "-" ~~ NumberString ~~
           "-" ~~ NumberString ~~ "-" ~~ NumberString]

Out[18]= {+1-217-398-0700, +1-217-398-0747,
         +1-217-398-5151, +1-217-398-0747, +1-217-398-6500}

Finding subsequences with strings

In this section we will explore a related problem to the one in Section 4.3, where we searched for subsequences within a sequence of numbers. Here we will transform the problem from working with lists of digits to one where we work with strings.

Using pattern matching it is not too difficult to construct the pattern of interest. For example, suppose we were looking for the substring *are* within a larger string. Using the special named string pattern `WordBoundary` which matches the beginning or end of a word, we concatenate (`StringJoin`) the patterns we need. See Table 9.3 in the next section for a listing of other named patterns.

```
In[19]:= StringCases["The magic words are squeamish ossifrage.",
           WordBoundary ~~ "are" ~~ WordBoundary]

Out[19]= {are}
```

```
In[20]:= StringPosition["The magic words are squeamish ossifrage.",
           WordBoundary ~~ "are" ~~ WordBoundary]

Out[20]= {{17, 19}}
```

To start, we will prototype with a short sequence of digits of π, converted to a string.

```
In[21]:= num = ToString[N[π, 50]]

Out[21]= 3.1415926535897932384626433832795028841971693993751
```

Check that the output is in fact a string.

```
In[22]:= {Head[num], InputForm[num]}

Out[22]= {String,
          "3.1415926535897932384626433832795028841971693993751"}
```

For our purposes here, we are only interested in the digits following the decimal point. We can extract them by splitting the string of digits on the decimal point and then taking the second part of that expression. This will generalize for numbers with an arbitrary number of digits before the decimal point.

```
In[23]:= StringSplit[num, "."]

Out[23]= {3, 1415926535897932384626433832795028841971693993751}
```

```
In[24]:= Part[%, 2]

Out[24]= 1415926535897932384626433832795028841971693993751
```

The subsequence 3238 occurs starting 15 positions to the right of the decimal point.

```
In[25]:= StringPosition[%, "3238"]

Out[25]= {{15, 18}}
```

Collecting the code fragments, we turn this into a function.

```
In[26]:= FindSubsequence[num_?NumberQ, subseq_?NumberQ] :=
           With[{n = ToString[num], s = ToString[subseq]},
            StringPosition[Part[StringSplit[n, "."], 2], s]
           ]
```

Let us try it out on a more challenging example: finding occurrences of the sequence 314159 in the decimal expansion of π.

```
In[27]:= pi = N[π, 10^7];
```

In[28]:= **FindSubsequence[pi, 314 159] // Timing**

Out[28]= {4.39282,
  {{176 451, 176 456}, {1 259 351, 1 259 356}, {1 761 051, 1 761 056},
  {6 467 324, 6 467 329}, {6 518 294, 6 518 299},
  {9 753 731, 9 753 736}, {9 973 760, 9 973 765}}}

Comparing with the function that takes lists of digits developed in Section 4.3, our string implementation is about twice as fast.

In[29]:= **pidigs = First[RealDigits[π, 10, 10^7, -1]];**
  Timing[
   FindSubsequence[pidigs, {3, 1, 4, 1, 5, 9}]
  ]

Out[30]= {9.08731,
  {{176 451, 176 456}, {1 259 351, 1 259 356}, {1 761 051, 1 761 056},
  {6 467 324, 6 467 329}, {6 518 294, 6 518 299},
  {9 753 731, 9 753 736}, {9 973 760, 9 973 765}}}

Alternatives

We have already seen general patterns with alternatives discussed in Chapter 4. Here we will use alternatives with string patterns. The idea is quite similar. For example, a common task in genome analysis is determining the GC content or ratios of the nucleobases guanine (G) and cytosine (C) to all four bases in a given fragment of genetic material.

In[31]:= **gene = GenomeData["MRPS35P1"];**

You could count the occurrences of G and the occurrences of C and add them together.

In[32]:= **StringCount[gene, "G"] + StringCount[gene, "C"]**

Out[32]= 41

But it is much easier to use alternatives to indicate that you want to count all occurrences of either G or C. The syntax for using alternative string patterns is identical to that for general expressions that we introduced in Section 4.1.

In[33]:= **StringCount[gene, "G" | "C"]**

Out[33]= 41

We will return to the computation of GC content in Section 9.5.

As a slightly more involved example, suppose you are interested in tallying the lengths of words in a corpus. You might start by using `StringSplit` to split the large string into a list of words.

In[34]:= **text = ExampleData[{"Text", "OriginOfSpecies"}];**

In[35]:= **sstext = StringSplit[text];**
       Short[sstext, 6]

Out[36]//Short=
       {INTRODUCTION., When, on, board, H.M.S.,
        'Beagle,', as, naturalist,, I, was, much, struck,
        ≪149 839≫, forms, most, beautiful, and, most,
        wonderful, have, been,, and, are, being,, evolved.}

Looking at the result, you will see that some elements of this list include various types of punctuation. For example, StringSplit, with default delimiters, missed certain hyphenated words and some punctuation.

In[37]:= **sstext[[{53, 362}]]**

Out[37]= {species--that, statements;}

There are 149863 elements in this split list.

In[38]:= **Length[sstext]**

Out[38]= 149 863

Fortunately, StringSplit takes a second argument that specifies the delimiters to match. The pattern is given as a set of alternatives followed by the repeated operator to catch one or more repetitions of any of these delimiters. Searching through the text will help to come up with this list of alternatives.

In[39]:= **splitText = StringSplit[text,**
       (" " | "." | "," | ";" | ":" | "'" | "\"" | "?" | "!" | "-") ..];

In[40]:= **Short[splitText, 5]**

Out[40]//Short=
       {INTRODUCTION, When, on, board, H, M, S, Beagle,
        as, naturalist, I, ≪151 181≫, beautiful, and, most,
        wonderful, have, been, and, are, being, evolved}

Notice that this list contains many more elements than the initial approach given above.

In[41]:= **Length[splitText]**

Out[41]= 151 202

Finally, here is a histogram showing the distribution of word lengths in the text, *On the Origin of Species*.

```
In[42]:= Histogram[StringLength[splitText], Frame → True,
           FrameLabel → {"Word length", "Frequency"},
           FrameTicks → {{Automatic, None}, {Automatic, None}}]
```

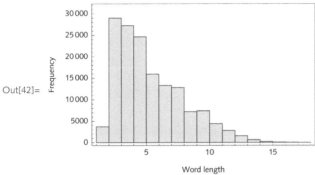

Out[42]=

Let us compare this with a different text: *A Portrait of the Artist as a Young Man,* by James Joyce (available online at Project Gutenberg). We are postprocessing here by removing metadata at the beginning and at the end of the file.

```
In[43]:= joyce = StringTake[Import[
           "http://www.gutenberg.org/cache/epub/4217/pg4217.txt",
           "Text"], 688 ;; -18843];
         StringTake[joyce, {75, 164}]
```

```
Out[44]= Once upon a time and a very good time it
         was there was a moocow coming down along the road
```

An alternative syntax uses a list of delimiters as given by Characters. The repeated pattern, .., helps to catch such constructions as "--", "::" and double-spaces.

```
In[45]:= words = StringSplit[joyce, Characters[":,;.!?'\- "] ..];
         Histogram[StringLength[words], Frame → True,
           FrameLabel → {"Word length", "Frequency"},
           FrameTicks → {{Automatic, None}, {Automatic, None}}]
```

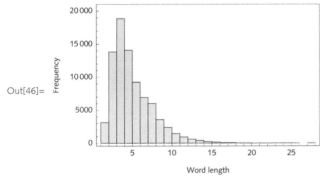

Out[46]=

In the next section, on regular expressions, we will see that there are more compact ways of accomplishing some of these tasks.

Exercises

1. At the end of Section 9.1 we created a predicate `OrderedWordQ` to find all words in a dictionary whose letters are in alphabetic order. This predicate used character codes and returned incorrect results for words that started with a capital letter. Correct this error by only selecting words from the dictionary that start with a lowercase letter. Consider using a conditional string pattern involving the built-in function `LowerCaseQ`.

2. Given a list of words, some of which start with uppercase characters, convert them all to words in which the first character is lowercase. You can use the words in the dictionary as a good sample set.

3. Create a function `Palindromes[n]` that finds all palindromic words of length *n* in the dictionary. For example, *kayak* is a five-letter palindrome.

4. Find the number of unique words in a body of text such as *Alice in Wonderland*.

    ```
    In[1]:= text = ExampleData[{"Text", "AliceInWonderland"}];
    ```

    After splitting the text into words, convert all uppercase characters to lowercase so that you count words such as *hare* and *Hare* as the same word.

    Such computations are important in information retrieval systems, for example, in building term-document incidence matrices used to compare the occurrence of certain terms across a set of documents (Manning, Raghavan, and Schütze 2008).

9.4 Regular expressions

In addition to the use of string patterns discussed up to this point, you can also specify string patterns using what are known as *regular expressions*. Regular expressions in *Mathematica* follow a syntax very close to that of the PERL programming language. This syntax is quite compact and powerful but it comes at the cost of readability – regular expressions tend to be quite cryptic to humans. As a result, we will only cover a few examples of their use here and refer the interested reader to the *Mathematica* documentation on string patterns (Working with String Patterns, WMDC).

You should think of regular expressions as an alternative syntax for string pattens. To indicate that you are using a regular expression, wrap the expression in `RegularExpression`. For example, the regular expression . is a wildcard character. It matches any single character except a newline. To use it as a string pattern, write `RegularExpression["."]`.

```
In[1]:= StringMatchQ["a", RegularExpression["."]]
Out[1]= True
```

The string `"abc"` does not match the pattern because it does not consist of a single character.

In[2]:= **StringMatchQ["abc", RegularExpression["."]]**

Out[2]= False

You can also match a set or range of characters. For example, this matches any of the characters *a* through *z*.

In[3]:= **StringMatchQ["a", RegularExpression["[a-z]"]]**

Out[3]= True

Certain constructs give patterns with repeating elements. For example, `"c*"` is a pattern matched by a string with character *c* repeated zero or more times; `"c+"` stands in for the character *c* repeated one or more times.

In[4]:= **StringMatchQ["aa", RegularExpression["a*"]]**

Out[4]= True

In[5]:= **StringMatchQ["aaab", RegularExpression["a+"]]**

Out[5]= False

You can also match on concatenated characters using the syntax $c_1 \; c_2$ ....

In[6]:= **StringPosition["ACAACTGGAGATCATGACTG",**
RegularExpression["ACT"]]

Out[6]= {{4, 6}, {17, 19}}

Several constructs are available for classes of characters. The named classes in the last two entries of Table 9.2 include *alpha, ascii, blank, digit, space, word,* and several more.

TABLE 9.2. *Regular expressions classes of characters*

Regular expression	Meaning
\\d	digit 0–9
\\D	nondigit
\\s	space, newline, tab, whitespace
\\S	non–whitespace character
\\w	word character, e.g. letter, digit
\\W	nonword character
[[:*class*:]]	characters in a named class
[^[:*class*:]]	characters not in a named class

The regular expression a.* matches any expression beginning with the character *a* followed by any sequence of characters.

```
In[7]:= StringMatchQ["all in good time", RegularExpression["a.*"]]

Out[7]= True
```

The regular expression \\d represents any digit 0 through 9.

```
In[8]:= StringCases["1a2b3c4d", RegularExpression["\\d"]]

Out[8]= {1, 2, 3, 4}
```

The regular expression a.+\\d matches any expression beginning with an *a*, followed by any character repeated one or more times, followed by a digit.

```
In[9]:= StringCases["abc1, abd2, abc", RegularExpression["a.+\\d"]]

Out[9]= {abc1, abd2}
```

Let us try something more ambitious. This finds all words in text that are of length 16 to 18.

```
In[10]:= text = ExampleData[{"Text", "OriginOfSpecies"}];
        StringCases[text, RegularExpression["\\b\\w{16,18}\\b"]] //
        DeleteDuplicates

Out[11]= {agriculturalists, disproportionably,
         malconformations, experimentalists, palaeontological,
         incomprehensibly, PALAEONTOLOGICAL, palaeontologists,
         intercommunication, incomprehensible}
```

The regular expression \\b matches any word boundary (typically whitespace, period, comma, etc.) and \\w {16, 18} matches any word of length 16 to 18.

Various shortcuts exist for some commonly used patterns (Table 9.3).

TABLE 9.3. *Patterns for special locations within strings*

Pattern	Matches
StartOfString	beginning of entire string
EndOfString	end of entire string
StartOfLine	beginning of a line
EndOfLine	end of a line
WordBoundary	boundary between words

Conveniently, you can mix regular expressions and other string patterns in various ways. This accomplishes the same thing as the previous computation, but using WordBoundary, instead of the regular expression \\b.

In[12]:= **StringCases[text,**
      WordBoundary ~~ RegularExpression["\\w{16,18}"] ~~
      WordBoundary] // DeleteDuplicates

Out[12]= {agriculturalists, disproportionably,
     malconformations, experimentalists, palaeontological,
     incomprehensibly, PALAEONTOLOGICAL, palaeontologists,
     intercommunication, incomprehensible}

Sometimes you will need to refer to the pattern by name in order to perform some operation on it. This is similar to the situation with regular named patterns. For example, given a list of words, some of which are uppercase/lowercase, this uses string patterns to transform the list to all lowercase words, naming the pattern that is matched by the first character after a word boundary, a.

In[13]:= **words = {"festively", "frolicking",**
      "subcategories", "retreated", "recompiling",
      "Barbary", "Herefords", "geldings", "Norbert",
      "incalculably", "proselytizers", "topmast"};

In[14]:= **StringReplace[words, WordBoundary ~~ a_ :> ToLowerCase[a]]**

Out[14]= {festively, frolicking, subcategories, retreated,
     recompiling, barbary, herefords, geldings,
     norbert, incalculably, proselytizers, topmast}

So how do we name a pattern with regular expressions so that we can refer to it on the right-hand side of a rule? The syntax using regular expressions is to wrap the pattern in parentheses and then refer to it using "$n", where n is the nth occurrence of such patterns. For example, \\b(\\w) is a named pattern that is matched by an expression consisting of a word boundary followed by a word character. The subexpression matching (\\w) is referenced by "$1" on the right-hand side of the rule.

In[15]:= **StringReplace[words,**
      RegularExpression["\\b(\\w)"] :> ToLowerCase["$1"]]

Out[15]= {festively, frolicking, subcategories, retreated,
     recompiling, barbary, herefords, geldings,
     norbert, incalculably, proselytizers, topmast}

To change the second character after the word boundary to uppercase, use "$2" to refer to the expression that matches the second (\\w).

In[16]:= **StringReplace[words, RegularExpression["\\b(\\w)(\\w)"] :→**
    ToLowerCase["$1"] ~~ ToUpperCase["$2"]]

Out[16]= {fEstively, fRolicking, sUbcategories, rEtreated,
    rEcompiling, bArbary, hErefords, gEldings,
    nOrbert, iNcalculably, pRoselytizers, tOpmast}

A particularly useful construct in many situations is the lookahead/lookbehind construct.
(? = *patt*) is used when the following text must match *patt* and (? < = *patt*) is used when the
preceding text must match *patt*. For example, this finds all those words in some example text that
follow "Raven, ".

In[17]:= **text = ExampleData[{"Text", "TheRaven"}];**

In[18]:= **StringCases[text,**
    RegularExpression["(?<=Raven,)\\w+"]]

Out[18]= {sitting, never}

There are many more constructs available for doing quite sophisticated things with regular
expressions. We will explore some of these in the examples and exercises below as well as in the
applications in Section 9.5. For a more detailed discussion, see the tutorials Regular Expressions
(WMDC) and Working with String Patterns (WMDC).

Word stemming

Many aspects of linguistic analysis include a study of the words used in a piece of text or in a
speech. For example, you might be interested in comparing the complexity of articles written in
two different newspapers. The length and frequency of certain words might be a useful measure
for such an analysis. Patterns in usage of certain word combinations can be used to identify
authenticity or the identity of an author of a work.

There are some basic issues that arise again and again in such analyses. For example, what
should be done with contractions such as *shouldn't*? What about sets of words such as *run, runs,
ran, running*. Are they considered distinct? One approach in language processing is to strip suf-
fixes and reduce alternate forms to some *stem*. This process, known as word stemming, is extensively used in many online search systems to try to distill user's queries to some basic form that
can be processed and operated on. It is a bit tricky, as natural languages are notorious for exceptions to almost any rule. For example, although the word *entertainment* can sensibly be stemmed
to *entertain*, the stem of *comment* is certainly not *com*. In other words, a rule that dropped the suffix
ment is too broad and returns nonwords in many cases. In most word stemming algorithms, there
are numerous rules for the many cases that need to be examined; and there are many special
cases. In this section, we will create a set of rules for word stemming to show how these rules are
described and how the string pattern constructs in *Mathematica* provide a good set of tools to

implement these concepts. A full-fledged stemming application would include hundreds of rules for each language, so we will only give a small set here to indicate the general process.

Words ending in ...xes The first set of stemming rules we will create involves a relatively small set of words in the English language – those ending in *xes*, such as *boxes* or *complexes*. The rule is to strip off the *es*.

To prototype, we collect all the words in the dictionary that end in *xes*. We will also restrict ourselves to words that are all lowercase. `Quiet` is used here to suppress the error messages that arise when `StringTake` operates on words of length less than three. Alternatively, you could put an extra clause (`StringLength[w]` $\geq$ 3) in the conjunction.

```
In[19]:= words = DictionaryLookup[
          w__ /; StringTake[w, -3] === "xes" && LowerCaseQ[w]] // Quiet
```

```
Out[19]= {admixes, affixes, annexes, anticlimaxes, apexes, appendixes,
          aviatrixes, axes, bandboxes, bollixes, boxes, breadboxes,
          calyxes, chatterboxes, circumflexes, climaxes, coaxes,
          complexes, convexes, coxes, crucifixes, cruxes, detoxes,
          duplexes, equinoxes, exes, faxes, fireboxes, fixes,
          flexes, flummoxes, fluxes, foxes, gearboxes, hatboxes,
          hexes, hoaxes, horseboxes, hotboxes, ibexes, iceboxes,
          indexes, influxes, intermixes, jinxes, jukeboxes,
          laxes, letterboxes, loxes, lummoxes, lunchboxes, lynxes,
          mailboxes, matchboxes, maxes, minxes, mixes, moneyboxes,
          multiplexes, nixes, onyxes, orthodoxes, outboxes, outfoxes,
          overtaxes, oxes, paintboxes, paradoxes, parallaxes,
          perplexes, phalanxes, phoenixes, pickaxes, pillboxes,
          pixes, poleaxes, postboxes, postfixes, poxes, prefixes,
          premixes, prophylaxes, pyxes, reflexes, relaxes, remixes,
          saltboxes, sandboxes, saxes, sexes, shadowboxes, simplexes,
          sixes, snuffboxes, soapboxes, sphinxes, squeezeboxes,
          strongboxes, suffixes, surtaxes, taxes, telexes, thoraxes,
          tinderboxes, tippexes, toolboxes, transfixes, triplexes,
          tuxes, unfixes, vertexes, vexes, vortexes, waxes, xeroxes}
```

Here is the replacement rule. The regular expression `"(\\w)(x)es"` will be matched by any word character followed by *xes*. It is replaced by that word character followed only by *x*. On the right-hand side of the rule, `$1` refers to the first pattern on the left, `(\\w)`; and `$2` refers to the second pattern on the left, `(x)`.

```
In[20]:= rule1 = RegularExpression["(\\w)(x)es"] :> "$1$2";
```

In[21]:= **stemmed = StringReplace[words, rule1]**

Out[21]= {admix, affix, annex, anticlimax, apex, appendix, aviatrix, ax,
bandbox, bollix, box, breadbox, calyx, chatterbox, circumflex,
climax, coax, complex, convex, cox, crucifix, crux, detox,
duplex, equinox, ex, fax, firebox, fix, flex, flummox, flux,
fox, gearbox, hatbox, hex, hoax, horsebox, hotbox, ibex,
icebox, index, influx, intermix, jinx, jukebox, lax, letterbox,
lox, lummox, lunchbox, lynx, mailbox, matchbox, max, minx,
mix, moneybox, multiplex, nix, onyx, orthodox, outbox,
outfox, overtax, ox, paintbox, paradox, parallax, perplex,
phalanx, phoenix, pickax, pillbox, pix, poleax, postbox,
postfix, pox, prefix, premix, prophylax, pyx, reflex, relax,
remix, saltbox, sandbox, sax, sex, shadowbox, simplex, six,
snuffbox, soapbox, sphinx, squeezebox, strongbox, suffix,
surtax, tax, telex, thorax, tinderbox, tippex, toolbox,
transfix, triplex, tux, unfix, vertex, vex, vortex, wax, xerox}

In[22]:= **Select[stemmed, Not@MemberQ[DictionaryLookup[], #] &]**

Out[22]= {max, poleax, postfix, prophylax}

This is pretty good; it appears only four stemmed words are not in the dictionary; although *max* might be considered an abbreviation, *postfix* is certainly a word! Nonetheless, these sorts of exceptions are common and will need to be dealt with separately.

Plural nouns ending …mming A word such as *programming* has a stem of *program*; so the rule for words ending in …*mming* could be: drop the *ming*. Start by gathering all the words in the dictionary that end with …*mming*.

In[23]:= **words =
DictionaryLookup[w__ /; StringTake[w, -5] === "mming"] // Quiet**

Out[23]= {bedimming, brimming, bumming, chumming, clamming, cramming,
damming, deprogramming, diagramming, dimming, drumming,
flimflamming, gumming, hamming, hemming, humming, jamming,
lamming, lemming, monogramming, multiprogramming, programming,
ramming, reprogramming, rimming, scamming, scramming, scrumming,
scumming, shamming, shimming, skimming, slamming, slimming,
slumming, spamming, stemming, strumming, summing, swimming,
thrumming, tramming, trimming, unjamming, whamming, whimming}

Recall the regular expression \\ w + represents a word character repeated some number of times; \\ b represents a word boundary; the $1 refers to the first expression (\\ w +), that is, the characters up to the *mming*. These characters will be joined with a single *m*.

In[24]:= **rule2 = RegularExpression["(\\w+)mming\\b"] :→ "$1" ~~ "m";**

In[25]:= **StringReplace[words, rule2]**

Out[25]= {bedim, brim, bum, chum, clam, cram, dam, deprogram, diagram, dim,
drum, flimflam, gum, ham, hem, hum, jam, lam, lem, monogram,
multiprogram, program, ram, reprogram, rim, scam, scram,
scrum, scum, sham, shim, skim, slam, slim, slum, spam, stem,
strum, sum, swim, thrum, tram, trim, unjam, wham, whim}

Again, this is quite good although the word *lemming* has been stemmed to the nonword *lem*, something that will need to be dealt with as a special case. The way to do that is to order the rules so that the special cases are caught first.

In[26]:= **rule2 = {"lemming" :→ "lemming",**
        RegularExpression["(\\w+)mming\\b"] :→ "$1" ~~ "m"
      };

In[27]:= **StringReplace[words, rule2]**

Out[27]= {bedim, brim, bum, chum, clam, cram, dam, deprogram, diagram,
dim, drum, flimflam, gum, ham, hem, hum, jam, lam, lemming,
monogram, multiprogram, program, ram, reprogram, rim, scam,
scram, scrum, scum, sham, shim, skim, slam, slim, slum, spam,
stem, strum, sum, swim, thrum, tram, trim, unjam, wham, whim}

Words ending in …otes Numerous rules are needed for turning plural words into their singular stems. To see this, consider a naive rule that simply drops the *s* for any such words.

In[28]:= **StringReplace[{"possess", "thrushes", "oasis"},**
        RegularExpression["(\\w+)s"] :→ "$1"]

Out[28]= {posses, thrushe, oasi}

This is clearly too general a rule. In fact, several different rules are needed for words that end in *s*, depending upon the preceding characters. Here, we will only deal with words that end in …*otes*. First gather the words in the dictionary that match this pattern.

In[29]:= **words = DictionaryLookup[w__ /;**
         StringTake[w, -4] === "otes" && LowerCaseQ[w]] // Quiet

Out[29]= {anecdotes, antidotes, asymptotes, banknotes, compotes, connotes,
          cotes, coyotes, creosotes, demotes, denotes, devotes,
          dotes, dovecotes, emotes, footnotes, garrotes, keynotes,
          litotes, misquotes, motes, notes, outvotes, promotes,
          quotes, remotes, rotes, totes, unquotes, votes, zygotes}

Here is the replacement rule.

In[30]:= **rule3 = RegularExpression["(\\w+)(ote)s"] :→ "$1$2";**

In[31]:= **StringReplace[words, rule3]**

Out[31]= {anecdote, antidote, asymptote, banknote, compote,
          connote, cote, coyote, creosote, demote, denote,
          devote, dote, dovecote, emote, footnote, garrote,
          keynote, litote, misquote, mote, note, outvote, promote,
          quote, remote, rote, tote, unquote, vote, zygote}

Stemming *litotes* gives the nonword *litote*. This can again be resolved by adding some specific rules for these not uncommon situations.

Plural to singular Let us try to deal with the general problem of stemming plural forms to singular. This is a more difficult scenario to deal with as there are many rules and even more exceptions. We will begin by showing how the order of the replacement rules matters in the stemming process.

You might imagine the rules given in Table 9.4 being used to stem plurals (these are not complete, but they will get us started). In fact, these are step 1a of the commonly-used Porter's algorithm for word stemming in the English language.

TABLE 9.4. *Stemming rules, plural to singular*

Rule	Example
... *sses* → ... *ss*	posseses → possess
... *shes* → ... *sh*	churches → church
... *ies* → ... *y*	theories → theory
... *ss* → ... *ss*	pass → pass
... *us* → ... *us*	abacus → abacus
... *s* → ...	cats → cat

The order in which such rules are used is important. You do not want the last rule being used before any of the others. As we saw with the previous set of rules, *Mathematica* will apply rules in the order in which they are given, assuming that they have roughly the same level of specificity. Note also that some of these rules are designed to leave certain words unchanged. For example neither *pass* nor *abacus* are plural and they should not be stemmed.

Here then is a rough attempt at stemming plural words. First we gather the words from the dictionary that end in *s* and display a random sample of them.

```
In[32]:= words = DictionaryLookup[
          w__ /; StringTake[w, -1] == "s" && LowerCaseQ[w]];
       randwords = RandomSample[words, 30]
```

```
Out[33]= {preses, mentalities, hazes, celestas, pluperfects,
         booksellers, loganberries, drillers, commits, outgoes,
         assumings, clotures, factories, coses, sportswriters,
         illustrates, lampreys, tormentors, dichotomous, jobless,
         whees, heinous, flowerings, outargues, sunfishes,
         recrudesces, almanacks, kills, reconvenes, users}
```

```
In[34]:= rules = {
          RegularExpression["(\\w+)(ss)(es)"] :> "$1$2",
          RegularExpression["(\\w+)(sh)(es)"] :> "$1$2",
          RegularExpression["(\\w+)(ies)"] :> "$1" ~~ "y",
          RegularExpression["(\\w+)(ss)"] :> "$1$2",
          RegularExpression["(\\w+)(us)"] :> "$1$2",
          RegularExpression["(\\w+)(s)"] :> "$1"
        };
```

```
In[35]:= StringReplace[randwords, rules]
```

```
Out[35]= {prese, mentality, haze, celesta, pluperfect, bookseller,
         loganberry, driller, commit, outgoe, assuming, cloture,
         factory, cose, sportswriter, illustrate, lamprey, tormentor,
         dichotomous, jobless, whee, heinous, flowering, outargue,
         sunfish, recrudesce, almanack, kill, reconvene, user}
```

This process of word stemming requires a lot of trial and error and the creation of many rules for the exceptions. Another approach, called *lemmatization*, does a more careful and thorough job by working with vocabularies and performing morphological analysis of the words to better understand how to reduce them to a root. For more information, see Manning, Raghavan, and Schütze (2008).

Exercises

1. Rewrite the genomic example in Section 9.3 to use regular expressions instead of string patterns to find all occurrences of the sequence AA*anything*T. Here is the example using general string patterns.

   ```
   In[1]:= gene = GenomeData["IGHV357"];
   In[2]:= StringCases[gene, "AA" ~~ _ ~~ "T"]
   Out[2]= {AAGT, AAGT, AAAT, AAGT, AAAT, AAAT}
   ```

2. Rewrite the web page example in Section 9.3 to use regular expressions to find all phone numbers on the page, that is, expressions of the form *nnn–nnn–nnnn*. Modify accordingly for other web pages and phone numbers formatted for other regions.

3. Create a function UcLc⁢[*word*] that takes its argument *word* and returns the word with the first letter uppercase and the rest of the letters lowercase.

4. Use a regular expression to find all words given by DictionaryLookup that consist only of the letters *a, e, i, o, u*, and *y* in any order with any number of repetitions of the letters.

5. The basic rules for pluralizing words in the English language are roughly, as follows: if a noun ends in *ch, s, sh, j, x*, or *z*, it is made plural by adding *es* to the end. If the noun ends in *y* and is preceded by a consonant, replace the *y* with *ies*. If the word ends in *ium*, replace with *ia* (*Chicago Manual of Style* 2010). Of course, there are many more rules and even more exceptions, but you can implement a basic set of rules to convert singular words to plural based on these rules and then try them out on the following list of words.

   ```
   In[3]:= words = {"building", "finch", "fix", "ratio",
               "envy", "boy", "baby", "faculty", "honorarium"};
   ```

6. A common task in transcribing audio is cleaning up text, removing certain phrases such as *um, er*, and so on, and other tags that are used to make a note of some sort. For example, the following transcription of a lecture from the University of Warwick, Centre for Applied Linguistics (BASE Corpus), contains quite a few fragments that should be removed, including newline characters, parenthetical remarks, and nonwords. Use StringReplace with the appropriate rules to "clean" this text and then apply your code to a larger corpus.

   ```
   In[4]:= text = "okay well er today we're er going to be carrying on with the er
           French \nRevolution you may have noticed i was sort of getting
           rather er enthusiastic \nand carried away at the end of the
           last one i was sort of almost er like i sort \nof started at
           the beginning about someone standing on a coffee table and
           s-, \nshouting to arms citizens as if i was going to sort
           of leap up on the desk and \nsay to arms let's storm the
           Rootes Social Building [laughter] or er let's go \nout arm
           in arm singing the Marseillaise or something er like that";
   ```

7. Find the distribution of sentence lengths for any given piece of text. ExampleData["Text"] contains several well-known books and documents that you can use. You will need to think about and identify sentence delimiters carefully. Take care to deal properly with words such as *Mr., Dr.*, and so on that might incorrectly trigger a sentence-ending detector.

8. In web searches and certain problems in natural language processing (NLP), it is often useful to filter out certain words prior to performing the search or processing of the text to help with the performance of the algorithms. Words such as *the, and, is*, and so on are commonly referred to as *stop words*

for this purpose. Lists of stop words are almost always created manually based on the constraints of a particular application. We will assume you can import a list of stop words as they are commonly available across the internet. For our purposes here, we will use one such list that comes with the materials for this book.

```
In[5]:=  stopwords = Rest@Import["StopWords.dat", "List"];
         RandomSample[stopwords, 12]
```

```
Out[6]=  {what, look, taken, specify, wants, thorough,
          they, hello, whose, them, mightn't, particular}
```

Using the above list of stop words, or any other that you are interested in, first filter some sample "search phrases" and then remove all stop words from a larger piece of text.

```
In[7]:=  searchPhrases = {"Find my favorite phone",
             "How deep is the ocean?", "What is the meaning of life?"};
```

9. Modify the previous exercise so that the user can supply a list of punctuation in addition to the list of stop words to be used to filter the text.

9.5 Examples and applications

This section puts together many of the concepts and techniques developed earlier in the chapter to solve several nontrivial applied problems. The first example creates a function to generate random strings, mirroring the syntax of the built-in random number functions. People who work with large strings, such as those in genomic research, often partition their strings into small blocks and then perform some analysis on those substrings. We develop functions for partitioning strings as well as several examples for analyzing sequences of genetic code. An additional example covers checksums, which are used to verify stored and transmitted data. Finally, a word game is included in which we create blanagrams, a variant of anagrams.

Random strings

> *A blasphemous sect suggested ... that all men should juggle letters and symbols until they constructed, by an improbable gift of chance, these canonical books.*

— JORGE L. BORGES, *The Library of Babel*

Those who work with genomic data often need to test their algorithms on strings. While it may be sensible to test against real data – for example, using genes on the human genome – random data might be more appropriate to quickly test and measure the efficiency of an algorithm. Although *Mathematica* has a variety of functions for creating random numbers, random variates, and so on, it does not have a function to create random sequences of strings. In this section we will create one.

To start, we will choose the characters A, C, T, and G – representing the nucleotide, or DNA, bases – as our alphabet, that is, the letters in the random strings we will create.

In[1]:= **chars = {"A", "C", "T", "G"};**

The key observation is that we want to choose one character at random from this list. Since we need to repeat this *n* times, we need to randomly choose with replacement. That is the purpose of RandomChoice.

In[2]:= **RandomChoice[chars, 10]**

Out[2]= {C, A, C, G, G, G, C, G, A, T}

This expression is a list of strings.

In[3]:= **FullForm[%]**

Out[3]//FullForm=

List["C", "A", "C", "G", "G", "G", "C", "G", "A", "T"]

Finally, we concatenate the strings.

In[4]:= **StringJoin[%] // FullForm**

Out[4]//FullForm=

"CACGGGCGAT"

So a first attempt at putting these pieces together would look like this. Note the use of a default value of 1 for the optional argument n (see Section 6.1 for a discussion of default values for arguments to functions).

In[5]:= **RandomString[*chars_List*, *n_Integer: 1*] :=**
      StringJoin[RandomChoice[*chars*, *n*]]

In[6]:= **RandomString[{"A", "C", "T", "G"}, 500]**

Out[6]= TACTGACCCTTCGACTAAGGTACCAACCCGGGCACTCTCCACAGGCAGAACGTTTACCGCCCCTCCTGGC·
      AACTGGCGGAACCATACTGGTTATACGCGTCGGCCACGCGATACCTATATAAGCAAACGCCCGACC·
      GATGTAAGATGTTATTTAAGGTCGCTGATGATTGACTCGACGGGCACACCACGATGTCGCTGATCA·
      CCTACATTAAACCTACGCGCATTCCCGGGCCCTCTATATTGGAGAGGGTAAGTGGTTGAGAAACTT·
      ATGGCAACTATTCTAGCTTACAAACTCACACACAAGGTCACCTAATGCCAACAACGGAGAGACGTC·
      CCCTGCGTACCATCAGACCGACAAGATCGAATGGGCTTGAGGCACTTGGCTAATAGCTATGCGTAG·
      TACTGGCGGTAGGATCGTGAAGACTATCGACGCCAATGCGAGGGCTGGATAAGAACACTGCACCGA·
      GGTATACAGTCTGCGAAAGGCGCCTCAATGCACT

The default value of the second argument gives one choice.

In[7]:= **RandomString[{"A", "C", "T", "G"}]**

Out[7]= G

We can make the arguments a bit more general using structured patterns. The first argument in this next version must be a list consisting of a sequence of one or more strings.

In[8]:= **Clear[RandomString]**

```
In[9]:= RandomString[{ch__String}, n_Integer: 1] :=
           StringJoin[RandomChoice[{ch}, n]]
```

```
In[10]:= RandomString[{"a", "b", "d"}, 12]
```

```
Out[10]= dbbdbaaabdbd
```

Here is a ten-character password generator.

```
In[11]:= RandomString[
           CharacterRange["A", "z"] ⋃ CharacterRange["0", "9"], 10]
```

```
Out[11]= 9SZ1zkMPDI
```

It is not hard to extend this function to create *n* random strings of a given length. We essentially pass that argument structure to RandomChoice.

```
In[12]:= RandomString[{ch__String}, {n_Integer, len_Integer}] :=
           Map[StringJoin, RandomChoice[{ch}, {n, len}]]
```

```
In[13]:= RandomString[{"A", "C", "T", "G"}, {4, 12}]
```

```
Out[13]= {TCCAACTAACTC, GTACTACCCTGG, GGTAAGCTATTT, GCACTCTCGCTT}
```

```
In[14]:= RandomString[{"A", "C", "T", "G"}, {50, 1}]
```

```
Out[14]= {G, T, C, A, A, C, G, A, A, T, G, G, G, A, A, T,
         G, G, T, G, G, G, T, G, A, T, T, C, G, G, G, A, G,
         A, C, G, C, A, C, A, A, T, T, G, C, G, C, T, C, T}
```

The exercises at the end of this section include a problem that asks you to add an option that provides a mechanism to weight the individual characters in the random string.

Partitioning strings

Some string analysis requires strings to be broken up into blocks of a certain size and then computations are performed on those blocks. Although there is no built-in function for partitioning strings, we can easily create one, taking advantage of the syntax and speed of the built-in Partition function.

The Partition function requires a list as its first argument. To start, we will give it a list of the characters in a prototype string, a gene on the human genome.

```
In[15]:= GenomeData["IGHVII671", "Name"]
```

```
Out[15]= immunoglobulin heavy variable (II)-67-1
```

In[16]:= **str = GenomeData["IGHVII671"]**

Out[16]= ATGTCCTATTCAGGAGCAGCTACAGCAGTCATGCCTAGGTGTGAAGATCACACACTGAC⁚
         CTCACCCATGCTGTCTCTGGCCACTTCATCACAACCAATGCTTAATATTGGACGTG⁚
         GATCTGCCAGTCCCCGGGGAATGGGTTGAATGGAT

In[17]:= **Characters[str]**

Out[17]= {A, T, G, T, C, C, T, A, T, T, C, A, G, G, A, G, C, A, G, C, T, A, C, A, G, C,
         A, G, T, C, A, T, G, C, C, T, A, G, G, T, G, T, G, A, A, G, A, T, C, A, C,
         A, C, A, C, T, G, A, C, C, T, C, A, C, C, C, A, T, G, C, T, G, T, C, T, C,
         T, G, G, C, C, A, C, T, T, C, A, T, C, A, C, A, A, C, C, A, A, T, G, C, T,
         T, A, A, T, A, T, T, G, G, A, C, G, T, G, G, A, T, C, T, G, C, C, A, G, T,
         C, C, C, C, G, G, G, G, A, A, T, G, G, G, T, T, G, A, A, T, G, G, A, T}

Now, partition this list of characters into lists of length 4 with offset 1.

In[18]:= **Partition[Characters[str], 4, 4, 1]**

Out[18]= {{A, T, G, T}, {C, C, T, A}, {T, T, C, A}, {G, G, A, G},
         {C, A, G, C}, {T, A, C, A}, {G, C, A, G}, {T, C, A, T},
         {G, C, C, T}, {A, G, G, T}, {G, T, G, A}, {A, G, A, T}, {C, A, C, A},
         {C, A, C, T}, {G, A, C, C}, {T, C, A, C}, {C, C, A, T}, {G, C, T, G},
         {T, C, T, C}, {T, G, G, C}, {C, A, C, T}, {T, C, A, T}, {C, A, C, A},
         {A, C, C, A}, {A, T, G, C}, {T, T, A, A}, {T, A, T, T}, {G, G, A, C},
         {G, T, G, G}, {A, T, C, T}, {G, C, C, A}, {G, T, C, C}, {C, C, G, G},
         {G, G, A, A}, {T, G, G, G}, {T, T, G, A}, {A, T, G, G}, {A, T, A, T}}

Because the number of characters in str is not a multiple of 4, this use of Partition has padded the last sublist with the first two characters from the original string; in other words, this has treated the list cyclically; not quite what we want here.

In[19]:= **Mod[StringLength[str], 4] == 0**

Out[19]= False

A slightly different syntax for Partition gives an uneven subset at the end. We will need to use this form so as not to lose or introduce any spurious information.

In[20]:= **parts = Partition[Characters[str], 4, 4, 1, {}]**

Out[20]= {{A, T, G, T}, {C, C, T, A}, {T, T, C, A}, {G, G, A, G},
         {C, A, G, C}, {T, A, C, A}, {G, C, A, G}, {T, C, A, T},
         {G, C, C, T}, {A, G, G, T}, {G, T, G, A}, {A, G, A, T}, {C, A, C, A},
         {C, A, C, T}, {G, A, C, C}, {T, C, A, C}, {C, C, A, T}, {G, C, T, G},
         {T, C, T, C}, {T, G, G, C}, {C, A, C, T}, {T, C, A, T}, {C, A, C, A},
         {A, C, C, A}, {A, T, G, C}, {T, T, A, A}, {T, A, T, T}, {G, G, A, C},
         {G, T, G, G}, {A, T, C, T}, {G, C, C, A}, {G, T, C, C}, {C, C, G, G},
         {G, G, A, A}, {T, G, G, G}, {T, T, G, A}, {A, T, G, G}, {A, T}}

Finally, convert each sublist into a contiguous string.

```
In[21]:= Map[StringJoin, parts]
```

```
Out[21]= {ATGT, CCTA, TTCA, GGAG, CAGC, TACA, GCAG, TCAT,
         GCCT, AGGT, GTGA, AGAT, CACA, CACT, GACC, TCAC, CCAT, GCTG,
         TCTC, TGGC, CACT, TCAT, CACA, ACCA, ATGC, TTAA, TATT, GGAC,
         GTGG, ATCT, GCCA, GTCC, CCGG, GGAA, TGGG, TTGA, ATGG, AT}
```

This puts everything together in a function.

```
In[22]:= StringPartition[str_String, blocksize_] := Map[StringJoin,
           Partition[Characters[str], blocksize, blocksize, 1, {}]]
```

This partitions the string into nonoverlapping blocks of length 12.

```
In[23]:= StringPartition[str, 12]
```

```
Out[23]= {ATGTCCTATTCA, GGAGCAGCTACA, GCAGTCATGCCT, AGGTGTGAAGAT,
         CACACACTGACC, TCACCCATGCTG, TCTCTGGCCACT, TCATCACAACCA,
         ATGCTTAATATT, GGACGTGGATCT, GCCAGTCCCCGG, GGAATGGGTTGA, ATGGAT}
```

This function operates on large strings fairly fast. Here we partition a random string of length ten million into nonoverlapping blocks of length ten.

```
In[24]:= data = RandomString[{"A", "T", "C", "G"}, 10^7];
```

```
In[25]:= Timing[StringPartition[data, 10];]
```

```
Out[25]= {2.91544, Null}
```

Adler checksum

Checksums, or hashes, are commonly used to check the integrity of data when that data are either stored or transmitted. A checksum might be created, for example, when some data are stored on a disk. To check the integrity of that data, the checksum can be recomputed and if it differs from the stored value, there is a very high probability that the data was tampered with. Hash functions are used to create hash tables which are used for record lookup in large arrays of data. As an example of the use of character codes, we will implement a basic checksum algorithm, the Adler checksum.

Mathematica has a built-in function, `Hash`, that can be used to create hash codes, or checksums.

```
In[26]:= Hash["Mathematica"]
```

```
Out[26]= 1 089 499 110
```

If the string is changed, its checksum changes accordingly.

```
In[27]:= Hash["mathematica"]
```

```
Out[27]= 1 007 196 870
```

We will implement a basic hash code, known as the Adler-32 checksum algorithm. Given a string $c_1 c_2 \cdots c_n$ consisting of concatenated characters c_i, we form two 16-bit sums m and n as follows:

$$m = 1 + cc_1 + cc_2 + \cdots + cc_n \bmod 65\,521,$$

$$n = (1 + cc_1) + (1 + cc_1 + cc_2) + \cdots + (1 + cc_1 + cc_2 + \cdots + cc_n) \bmod 65\,521,$$

where cc_i is the character code for the character c_i. The number 65521 is chosen as it is the largest prime smaller than 2^{16}. Choosing primes for this task seems to reduce the probability that an interchange of two bytes will not be detected. Finally, the Adler checksum is given by

$$m + 65\,536\,n$$

Let us take *Mathematica* as our test word. We start by getting the Ascii character codes for each character.

```
In[28]:= str = "Mathematica";
         codes = ToCharacterCode[str]
```

```
Out[29]= {77, 97, 116, 104, 101, 109, 97, 116, 105, 99, 97}
```

The number m above is given by the cumulative sums of the character codes, with 1 prepended to that list. (This step could also be done using `FoldList`.)

```
In[30]:= mList = Accumulate[Join[{1}, codes]]
```

```
Out[30]= {1, 78, 175, 291, 395, 496, 605, 702, 818, 923, 1022, 1119}
```

```
In[31]:= m = Last[mList]
```

```
Out[31]= 1119
```

The number n is given by the cumulative sums from this last list, omitting the 1 at the beginning as it is already part of the cumulative sums.

```
In[32]:= nList = Accumulate[Rest[mList]]
```

```
Out[32]= {78, 253, 544, 939, 1435, 2040, 2742, 3560, 4483, 5505, 6624}
```

```
In[33]:= n = Last[nList]
```

```
Out[33]= 6624
```

```
In[34]:= m + 65 536 n
```

```
Out[34]= 434 111 583
```

We can check our result against the algorithm implemented in the `Hash` function.

```
In[35]:= Hash["Mathematica", "Adler32"]
```

```
Out[35]= 434 111 583
```

Finally, this puts these steps together in a reusable function. Our prototype worked with small numbers and so the need to work mod 65521 was not necessary. For general inputs, the arithmetic will be done using this modulus.

```
In[36]:= AdlerChecksum[str_String] := Module[{codes, n, m},
          codes = ToCharacterCode[str];
          m = Mod[Accumulate[Join[{1}, codes]], 65521];
          n = Mod[Accumulate[Rest[m]], 65521];
          Last[m] + Last[n] 65536
        ]
```

```
In[37]:= AdlerChecksum["Mathematica"]
```

```
Out[37]= 434 111 583
```

As an aside, here is its hash code in hexadecimal.

```
In[38]:= IntegerString[%, 16]
```

```
Out[38]= 19e0045f
```

And here is a lengthier example.

```
In[39]:= AdlerChecksum[
          "Lorem ipsum dolor sit amet, consectetur adipiscing
           elit. Fusce ultrices ornare odio. Proin adipiscing,
           mi non pharetra eleifend, nibh libero laoreet
           metus, at imperdiet urna ante in lectus."]
```

```
Out[39]= 3 747 169 622
```

Search for substrings

As we have seen in this chapter, string patterns provide a powerful and compact mechanism for operating on text data. In this example, we will create a function that searches the dictionary for words containing a specified substring.

If our test substring is *cite*, here is how we would find all words that end in *cite*. Note the triple blank pattern to match any sequence of zero or more characters.

```
In[40]:= DictionaryLookup[___ ~~ "cite"]
```

```
Out[40]= {anthracite, calcite, cite, excite,
          incite, Lucite, overexcite, plebiscite, recite}
```

Here are all words that begin with *cite*.

```
In[41]:= DictionaryLookup["cite" ~~ ___]
```

```
Out[41]= {cite, cited, cites}
```

And this gives all words that have *cite* somewhere in them, at the beginning, middle, or end.

In[42]:= **DictionaryLookup[___ ~~ "cite" ~~ ___]**

Out[42]= {anthracite, calcite, cite, cited, cites, elicited, excite,
        excited, excitedly, excitement, excitements, exciter, exciters,
        excites, incite, incited, incitement, incitements, inciter,
        inciters, incites, Lucite, Lucites, overexcite, overexcited,
        overexcites, plebiscite, plebiscites, recite, recited,
        reciter, reciters, recites, solicited, unexcited, unsolicited}

Using the double blank gives words that have *cite* in them but not beginning or ending with *cite*.

In[43]:= **DictionaryLookup[__ ~~ "cite" ~~ __]**

Out[43]= {elicited, excited, excitedly, excitement, excitements, exciter,
        exciters, excites, incited, incitement, incitements, inciter, inciters,
        incites, Lucites, overexcited, overexcites, plebiscites, recited,
        reciter, reciters, recites, solicited, unexcited, unsolicited}

Let us put these pieces together in a reusable function FindWordsContaining. We will include one option, WordPosition that identifies where in the word the substring is expected to occur.

In[44]:= **Options[FindWordsContaining] = {WordPosition → "Start"};**

Depending upon the value of the option WordPosition, Which directs which expression will be evaluated.

In[45]:= **FindWordsContaining[*str_String*, OptionsPattern[]] :=**
        Module[{wp = OptionValue[WordPosition]},
          Which[
            wp == "Start", DictionaryLookup[*str* ~~ ___],
            wp == "Middle", DictionaryLookup[__ ~~ *str* ~~ __],
            wp == "End", DictionaryLookup[___ ~~ *str*],
            wp == "Anywhere", DictionaryLookup[___ ~~ *str* ~~ ___]
          ]]

Using the default value for WordPosition, this finds all words in the dictionary that start with the string *cite*.

In[46]:= **FindWordsContaining["cite"]**

Out[46]= {cite, cited, cites}

And this finds all words that have *cite* anywhere in the word.

In[47]:= **FindWordsContaining["cite", WordPosition → "Anywhere"]**

Out[47]= {anthracite, calcite, cite, cited, cites, elicited, excite,
    excited, excitedly, excitement, excitements, exciter, exciters,
    excites, incite, incited, incitement, incitements, inciter,
    inciters, incites, Lucite, Lucites, overexcite, overexcited,
    overexcites, plebiscite, plebiscites, recite, recited,
    reciter, reciters, recites, solicited, unexcited, unsolicited}

Finally, here is a dynamic interface that includes a text field in which you can enter an input string; tabs are used to specify in which part of the word you expect the string to occur.

In[48]:= **Framed[Labeled[Manipulate[**
    FindWordsContaining[ToString@string, WordPosition → pos],
    {string, bobs}, {{pos, "Anywhere", "Position"},
     {"Start", "Middle", "End", "Anywhere"}},
    ContentSize → {300, 80}, SaveDefinitions → True],
   "Find words containing a string", Top],
  Background → LightGray]

Out[48]=

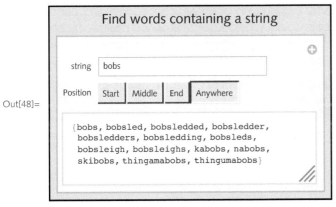

For more on the creation of these sorts of dynamic interfaces, see Chapter 11.

DNA *sequence analysis*

DNA molecules are composed of sequences of the nitrogenous bases guanine, cytosine, thymine, and adenine. Guanine and cytosine bond with three hydrogen bonds and thymine and adenine bond with two. Research has indicated that high GC content (guanine and cytosine) DNA is more stable than that with lower GC. The exact reasons for this are not completely understood and determining the GC content of various DNA materials is an active area of biomolecular research. GC content is often described as a percentage of the guanine and cytosine nucleotides compared to the entire nucleotide content (Cristianini and Hahn 2007). In this section we will create a function to compute the ratio of GC in any given DNA sequence or fragment.

We will start by importing a FASTA file consisting of human mitochondrial DNA, displaying some information about the contents of this file.

```
In[49]:= hsMito = Import["ExampleData/mitochondrion.fa.gz"];
```

```
In[50]:= Import["ExampleData/mitochondrion.fa.gz",
          {"FASTA", "Header"}]
```

```
Out[50]= {gi|17981852|ref|NC_001807.4|
              Homo sapiens mitochondrion, complete genome}
```

```
In[51]:= StringLength[hsMito]
```

```
Out[51]= {16 571}
```

```
In[52]:= StringTake[hsMito, 500]
```

```
Out[52]= {GATCACAGGTCTATCACCCTATTAACCACTCACGGGAGCTCTCCATGCATTTGGTATTTTCGTCTGGGG ⋮
           GGTGTGCACGCGATAGCATTGCGAGACGCTGGAGCCGGAGCACCCTATGTCGCAGTATCTGTCT ⋮
           TTGATTCCTGCCTCATTCTATTATTTATCGCACCTACGTTCAATATTACAGGCGAACATACCTA ⋮
           CTAAAGTGTGTTAATTAATTAATGCTTGTAGGACATAATAATAACAATTGAATGTCTGCACAGC ⋮
           CGCTTTCCACACAGACATCATAACAAAAAATTTCCACCAAACCCCCCCCTCCCCCCGCTTCTGG ⋮
           CCACAGCACTTAAACACATCTCTGCCAAACCCCAAAAACAAAGAACCCTAACACCAGCCTAACC ⋮
           AGATTTCAAATTTTATCTTTAGGCGGTATGCACTTTTAACAGTCACCCCCCAACTAACACATTA ⋮
           TTTTCCCCTCCCACTCCCATACTACTAATCTCATCAATACAACCCCC}
```

We use `StringCount` to count the number of occurrences of G or C in this sequence.

```
In[53]:= gc = StringCount[hsMito, "G" | "C"]
```

```
Out[53]= {7372}
```

And here is the number of occurrences of A or T.

```
In[54]:= at = StringCount[hsMito, "A" | "T"]
```

```
Out[54]= {9199}
```

The GC percentage is given by the following ratio.

```
In[55]:= N[ gc / (gc + at) ]
```

```
Out[55]= {0.444874}
```

Here then is an auxiliary function we will use in what follows.

```
In[56]:= gcRatio[ls_String] := Module[{gc, at},
          gc = StringCount[ls, "G" | "C"];
          at = StringCount[ls, "A" | "T"];
          N[gc / (gc + at)]
         ]
```

Note that `gcRatio` expects a string as an argument, but this fails with `hsMito`, imported from an external source.

```
In[57]:= Short[gcRatio[hsMito], 8]
```

Out[57]//Short=

```
gcRatio[
    {GATCACAGGTCTATCACCCTATTAACCACTCACGGGAGCTCTCCATGCATTTGGTATTTTCGTCTGGG ⋮
        GGGTGTGCACGCGATAGCATTGCGAGACGCTGGAGCCGGAGCACCCTATGTCGCAGTATC ⋮
        TGTCTTTGATTCCTGCCTCATTCTATTATTTATCGCACCTACGTTCAATATTACAGGCGA ⋮
        ACATACCTACTAAAGTGTGTTAATT ...
    TCTCGTCCCCATGGATGACCCCCCTCAGATAGGGGTCCCTTGACCACCATCCTCCGTGAAATCAAT ⋮
        ATCCCGCACAAGAGTGCTACTCTCCTCGCTCCGGGCCCATAACACTTGGGGGTAGCTAAA ⋮
        GTGAACTGTATCCGACATCTGGTTCCTACTTCAGGGCCATAAAGCCTAAATAGCCCACAC ⋮
        GTTCCCCTTAAATAAGACATCACGATG}]
```

It fails because `Import` returns a list consisting of a string, not a raw string. We can remedy this by writing a rule to deal with this argument structure and then call the first rule.

```
In[58]:= gcRatio[{str_String}] := gcRatio[str]
```

```
In[59]:= gcRatio[hsMito]
```

```
Out[59]= 0.444874
```

Typically, researchers are interested in studying the GC ratio on particular fragments of DNA and comparing it with similar fragments on another molecule. One common way of doing this is to compute the GC ratio for blocks of nucleotides of some given length. We will use the function `StringPartition`, developed earlier to partition the sequence into blocks of a given size. We will work with a small random sequence to prototype.

```
In[60]:= blocksize = 10;
        str = RandomString[{"A", "C", "T", "G"}, 125];
        lis = StringPartition[str, blocksize]
```

```
Out[62]= {GAGCTCTGAA, GTCCGCCCAG, TAAGGCCCCT, AATGCTGTGA,
    TACCGCAGGG, ACACATGGAA, TACAAGAAGC, CCTAGCATTG,
    TGATCTCCGC, CGGTAGCTTT, AGAGGGTCAG, GCTTAAGGCT, CTAGG}
```

Here are the GC ratios for each of the blocks given by `lis`.

```
In[63]:= Map[gcRatio, lis]
```

```
Out[63]= {0.5, 0.8, 0.6, 0.4, 0.7, 0.4, 0.4, 0.5, 0.6, 0.5, 0.6, 0.5, 0.6}
```

Finally, it is helpful to be able to identify each block by its starting position. So we first create a list of the starting positions for each block and then transpose that with the ratios.

```
In[64]:= Table[i, {i, 1, StringLength[str], blocksize}]
```

```
Out[64]= {1, 11, 21, 31, 41, 51, 61, 71, 81, 91, 101, 111, 121}
```

```
In[65]:= Transpose[{Table[i, {i, 1, StringLength[str], blocksize}],
           Map[gcRatio, lis]}]
```

```
Out[65]= {{1, 0.5}, {11, 0.8}, {21, 0.6}, {31, 0.4},
         {41, 0.7}, {51, 0.4}, {61, 0.4}, {71, 0.5}, {81, 0.6},
         {91, 0.5}, {101, 0.6}, {111, 0.5}, {121, 0.6}}
```

Here are all the pieces in one function, GCRatio.

```
In[66]:= GCRatio[str_String, blocksize_Integer] :=
           Module[{lis, blocks},
             lis = StringPartition[str, blocksize];
             blocks = Table[i, {i, 1, StringLength[str], blocksize}];
             Transpose[{blocks, Map[gcRatio, lis]}]
           ]
```

And again, a second rule in case the string is wrapped in a list.

```
In[67]:= GCRatio[{str_String}, blocksize_Integer] :=
           GCRatio[str, blocksize]
```

Let us try it out first on our prototype sequence.

```
In[68]:= GCRatio[str, 10]
```

```
Out[68]= {{1, 0.5}, {11, 0.8}, {21, 0.6}, {31, 0.4},
         {41, 0.7}, {51, 0.4}, {61, 0.4}, {71, 0.5}, {81, 0.6},
         {91, 0.5}, {101, 0.6}, {111, 0.5}, {121, 0.6}}
```

And then on the human mitochondrial DNA with block size 1000.

```
In[69]:= gcdata = GCRatio[hsMito, 1000]
```

```
Out[69]= {{1, 0.46}, {1001, 0.441}, {2001, 0.43}, {3001, 0.478},
         {4001, 0.427}, {5001, 0.439}, {6001, 0.474}, {7001, 0.438},
         {8001, 0.434}, {9001, 0.461}, {10 001, 0.396},
         {11 001, 0.448}, {12 001, 0.429}, {13 001, 0.471},
         {14 001, 0.435}, {15 001, 0.446}, {16 001, 0.464098}}
```

Various types of analysis can then be performed on these blocks. For example, using Select, this quickly finds regions of high GC content.

```
In[70]:= Select[gcdata, Last[#] > 0.47 &]
```

```
Out[70]= {{3001, 0.478}, {6001, 0.474}, {13 001, 0.471}}
```

Here is a quick visualization of the GC content across the blocks.

In[71]:= **ListLinePlot[gcdata, Mesh → All]**

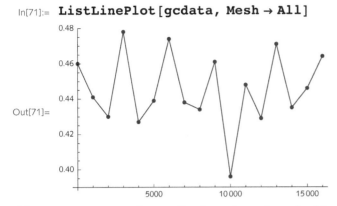

Out[71]=

Numerous comparative studies have been done looking at the GC content for different organisms. One much-studied organism is *Thermoplasma volcanium,* a bacterium-like organism that exists in very high-acid and high-temperature environments. To accommodate the extreme conditions, organisms in such environments often have high GC content which has a higher thermal stability. The following sequence is in the public domain and was obtained courtesy of the National Center for Biotechnology Information (NCBI Nucleotide Database).

In[73]:= **thermoVolc =**
  Import["638154522.tar.gz", "638154522/638154522.fna"];
StringTake[thermoVolc, 250]

Out[74]= {TTTGTATAAGAAAAAATAGGAAAGGTTAATATCCATGCTCATATGGCTGTCCGAAAAA`.
ATCAATAACGAATATTAACCACGATAAAATAAGGTAAGGAAAGAATCCTGCATG`.
AGCACAATAGAAGAACGCATTAAGGAAATAGAAGACGAAATCAAGAGAACTCAG`.
TACAATAAAGCCACTGAACACCACATCGGGCTTCTAAAAGCCAAGATTGCAAGG`.
CTCCAGATGGAGGCTAGAGCCCATAAAGGA}

In[75]:= **StringLength[First@thermoVolc]**

Out[75]= 1 584 804

Here is the GC ratio for the entire sequence.

In[76]:= **gcRatio[thermoVolc]**

Out[76]= 0.399185

And here are the ratios for block sizes of 100 000.

In[77]:= **tVratios = GCRatio[thermoVolc, 10^5]**

Out[77]= {{1, 0.4094}, {100 001, 0.39122}, {200 001, 0.39003},
{300 001, 0.40184}, {400 001, 0.40104}, {500 001, 0.40368},
{600 001, 0.39334}, {700 001, 0.39086}, {800 001, 0.41034},
{900 001, 0.37086}, {1 000 001, 0.40323}, {1 100 001, 0.39508},
{1 200 001, 0.39598}, {1 300 001, 0.40744},
{1 400 001, 0.40825}, {1 500 001, 0.417091}}

In[78]:= **BarChart[Map[Last, tVratios], BarSpacing → Medium,
ChartElementFunction → "GlassRectangle", ChartLabels →
Placed[Map[Last, tVratios], Top, (Rotate[#, 90 Degree] &)]]**

Out[78]=

Displaying DNA sequences

DNA sequences are typically long strings of nucleotides that are difficult to visualize simply by looking at the string of characters. Various visualization tools have been used to work with these sequences and in this section we will look at a common way of viewing them in a formatted table.

As before, we will prototype with a short random string consisting of nucleotide characters G, C, A, and T.

In[79]:= **str = RandomString[{"G", "C", "A", "T"}, 125]**

Out[79]= TGGACCACTGAAATCTTTGACCTGGTTAAACAAATTATTTAGCTAGTCTGTAGGCACAGACA ⦂
GTCCAACGGGTGTCCAGGAACGTTACCATGTCAAACTCGTTGCTCCGCCTCGGCCTTAA ⦂
GGCG

Using **StringPartition** developed earlier in this chapter, we split the string into blocks of a desired size.

In[80]:= **str1 = StringPartition[str, 10]**

Out[80]= {TGGACCACTG, AAATCTTTGA, CCTGGTTAAA, CAAATTATTT,
AGCTAGTCTG, TAGGCACAGA, CAGTCCAACG, GGTGTCCAGG,
AACGTTACCA, TGTCAAACTC, GTTGCTCCGC, CTCGGCCTTA, AGGCG}

We have 13 blocks here, but for readability purposes, we will put five blocks on each line of output. We use the blank string " " to pad out any string shorter than the blocksize, in this case 10.

In[81]:= **str2 = Partition[str1, 5, 5, 1, " "]**

Out[81]= {{TGGACCACTG, AAATCTTTGA, CCTGGTTAAA, CAAATTATTT, AGCTAGTCTG},
{TAGGCACAGA, CAGTCCAACG, GGTGTCCAGG, AACGTTACCA, TGTCAAACTC},
{GTTGCTCCGC, CTCGGCCTTA, AGGCG,   ,   }}

The following code gives the starting positions for each line once we have set the block length and row length.

In[82]:= **blocklength = 10;**
rowlength = 5;
ind = Select[Range[StringLength[str]],
Mod[#, rowlength * blocklength] == 1 &]

Out[84]= {1, 51, 101}

We prepend the starting position of each row at the head of the row. Recall, the second argument to Prepend is the expression you wish to put in front (the indices) of your target expression (the rows).

In[85]:= **MapThread[Prepend[#1, #2] &, {str2, ind}]**

Out[85]= {{1, TGGACCACTG, AAATCTTTGA, CCTGGTTAAA, CAAATTATTT, AGCTAGTCTG},
{51, TAGGCACAGA, CAGTCCAACG, GGTGTCCAGG, AACGTTACCA,
TGTCAAACTC}, {101, GTTGCTCCGC, CTCGGCCTTA, AGGCG,   ,   }}

This is what the formatted output should look like.

In[86]:= **Grid[%, Alignment → {{Right, {Left}}, Automatic}]**

Out[86]=
```
  1  TGGACCACTG  AAATCTTTGA  CCTGGTTAAA  CAAATTATTT  AGCTAGTCTG
 51  TAGGCACAGA  CAGTCCAACG  GGTGTCCAGG  AACGTTACCA  TGTCAAACTC
101  GTTGCTCCGC  CTCGGCCTTA  AGGCG
```

Finally, let us put this all together, setting up an option, BlockSize that is combined with the inherited options from Grid.

```
In[87]:= Options[SequenceTable] = Join[{BlockSize → 10}, Options[Grid]]

Out[87]= {BlockSize → 10, Alignment → {Center, Baseline},
    AllowedDimensions → Automatic, AllowScriptLevelChange → True,
    AutoDelete → False, Background → None,
    BaselinePosition → Automatic, BaseStyle → {},
    DefaultBaseStyle → Grid, DefaultElement → □,
    DeleteWithContents → True, Dividers → None, Editable → Automatic,
    Frame → None, FrameStyle → Automatic, ItemSize → Automatic,
    ItemStyle → None, Selectable → Automatic, Spacings → Automatic}
```

```
In[88]:= SequenceTable[lis_String, opts : OptionsPattern[]] :=
    Module[{n = OptionValue[BlockSize],
      len = StringLength[lis], rowlength = 5, str, blocks, ind},
     str = StringPartition[lis, n];
     blocks = Partition[str, 5, 5, 1, " "];
     ind = Select[Range[len], Mod[#, rowlength * n] == 1 &];
     Grid[MapThread[Prepend[#1, #2] &, {blocks, ind}],
      FilterRules[{opts}, Options[Grid]],
      Alignment → {{Right, {Left}}, Automatic},
      Frame → True, Dividers → {{True, False}, All}]
    ]
```

```
In[89]:= str = RandomString[{"C", "A", "T", "G"}, 178]

Out[89]= GTCACGTTTGACTGTCAGGAAGGATTCACGCTGATGAATCCGGGGCTGTAAGCCCATCTGCA
    AAGACATGAGGAGGGCTCGGGAGTCGAGAGATATTTCGTGCCCACGTTTAGACCTGCAT
    ACAACCAAAGATCCTCGGTGCATACTACACGTCGCCTTCCTCGACCAGTAAGTGCGG
```

```
In[90]:= SequenceTable[str]
```

1	GTCACGTTTG	ACTGTCAGGA	AGGATTCACG	CTGATGAATC	CGGGGCTGTA
51	AGCCCATCTG	CAAAGACATG	AGGAGGGCTC	GGGAGTCGAG	AGATATTTCG
101	TGCCCACGTT	TAGACCTGCA	TACAACCAAA	GATCCTCGGT	GCATACTACA
151	CGTCGCCTTC	CTCGACCAGT	AAGTGCGG		

Out[90]=

Let us exercise some of the options.

```
In[91]:= SequenceTable[str, BlockSize → 12,
    Background → LightYellow, BaseStyle → Directive[FontSize → 8]]
```

1	GTCACGTTTGAC	TGTCAGGAAGGA	TTCACGCTGATG	AATCCGGGGCTG	TAAGCCCATCTG
61	CAAAGACATGAG	GAGGGCTCGGGA	GTCGAGAGATAT	TTCGTGCCCACG	TTTAGACCTGCA
121	TACAACCAAAGA	TCCTCGGTGCAT	ACTACACGTCGC	CTTCCTCGACCA	GTAAGTGCGG

Out[91]=

Blanagrams

A blanagram is an anagram for another word except for the substitution of one letter. Think of Scrabble with a blank square (blank + anagram = blanagram). For example, *phyla* is a blanagram of *glyph*: replace the *g* with an *a* and find anagrams. In this section we will create a function that finds all blanagrams of a given word.

We will prototype with a simple word, *glyph*.

In[92]:= **Characters["glyph"]**

Out[92]= {g, l, y, p, h}

Start by replacing the first letter in *glyph* with an *a* and then finding all anagrams (using `Anagrams` from Section 9.2). The third argument to `StringReplacePart` is a list of beginning and ending positions for the replacement.

In[93]:= **StringReplacePart["glyph", "a", {1, 1}]**

Out[93]= alyph

In[94]:= **Anagrams[%]**

Out[94]= {phyla, haply}

Now do the same for each character position in the word.

In[95]:= **Map[StringReplacePart["glyph", "a", {#, #}] &,**
        Range[StringLength["glyph"]]]

Out[95]= {alyph, gayph, glaph, glyah, glypa}

Running `Anagrams` on each of these strings, only two appear as words in the dictionary.

In[96]:= **Flatten[Map[Anagrams, %]]**

Out[96]= {phyla, haply}

Having done this for the letter *a*, we now repeat for all other single characters.

In[97]:= **CharacterRange["a", "z"]**

Out[97]= {a, b, c, d, e, f, g, h, i, j, k,
        l, m, n, o, p, q, r, s, t, u, v, w, x, y, z}

```
In[98]:= blana = Table[
          Map[StringReplacePart["glyph", ch, {#, #}] &,
           Range[StringLength["glyph"]]],
          {ch, CharacterRange["a", "z"]}]
```

```
Out[98]= {{alyph, gayph, glaph, glyah, glypa}, {blyph, gbyph, glbph, glybh, glypb},
          {clyph, gcyph, glcph, glych, glypc}, {dlyph, gdyph, gldph, glydh, glypd},
          {elyph, geyph, gleph, glyeh, glype}, {flyph, gfyph, glfph, glyfh, glypf},
          {glyph, ggyph, glgph, glygh, glypg}, {hlyph, ghyph, glhph, glyhh, glyph},
          {ilyph, giyph, gliph, glyih, glypi}, {jlyph, gjyph, gljph, glyjh, glypj},
          {klyph, gkyph, glkph, glykh, glypk}, {llyph, glyph, gllph, glylh, glypl},
          {mlyph, gmyph, glmph, glymh, glypm}, {nlyph, gnyph, glnph, glynh, glypn},
          {olyph, goyph, gloph, glyoh, glypo}, {plyph, gpyph, glpph, glyph, glypp},
          {qlyph, gqyph, glqph, glyqh, glypq}, {rlyph, gryph, glrph, glyrh, glypr},
          {slyph, gsyph, glsph, glysh, glyps}, {tlyph, gtyph, gltph, glyth, glypt},
          {ulyph, guyph, gluph, glyuh, glypu}, {vlyph, gvyph, glvph, glyvh, glypv},
          {wlyph, gwyph, glwph, glywh, glypw}, {xlyph, gxyph, glxph, glyxh, glypx},
          {ylyph, gyyph, glyph, glyyh, glypy}, {zlyph, gzyph, glzph, glyzh, glypz}}
```

Because of the extra nesting (Table[Map[…]]) we need to flatten the output at a deeper level; and delete duplicates.

```
In[99]:= Flatten[Map[Anagrams, blana, {2}]] // DeleteDuplicates
```

```
Out[99]= {phyla, haply, glyph, lymph, sylph}
```

Finally, put all the pieces together to create the function Blanagrams.

```
In[100]:= Blanagrams[word_String] := Module[{blana},
           blana = Table[
             Map[StringReplacePart[word, ch, {#, #}] &,
              Range[StringLength[word]]],
             {ch, CharacterRange["a", "z"]}];
           DeleteDuplicates[Flatten[Map[Anagrams, blana, {2}]]]
          ]
```

This turns out to be fairly quick for small words, but it bogs down for larger words.

```
In[101]:= Blanagrams["glyph"] // Timing
```

```
Out[101]= {1.09503, {phyla, haply, glyph, lymph, sylph}}
```

```
In[102]:= Blanagrams["zydeco"] // Timing
```

```
Out[102]= {7.82883, {zydeco, cloyed, comedy, decoys}}
```

We will wait until Section 12.3 to optimize this code by profiling (identifying slow computational chunks) and taking advantage of parallel processing built into *Mathematica*.

Exercises

1. Generalize the `RandomString` function to allow for a `Weights` option so that you can provide a weight for each character in the generated string. Include a rule to generate a message if the number of weights does not match the number of characters. For example:

    In[1]:= **RandomString[{"A", "T", "C", "G"}, 30, Weights → {.1, .2, .3, .4}]**

    Out[1]= AAGGCTCGCGGCGTGGCCATGGGTTTGGCC

    In[2]:= **RandomString[{"A", "T", "C", "G"}, {5, 10}, Weights → {.1, .4, .4, .1}]**

    Out[2]= {GATTGTCGCC, TTCGTCTGTC, CTTCTACTAT, TATCTTCCCC, TTTCTCTCCT}

    In[3]:= **RandomString[{"A", "T", "C", "G"}, {5, 10}, Weights → {.1, .4}]**

    RandomString::badwt :
        The length of the list of weights must be the same as the length of the list of characters.

2. Write the function `Anagrams` developed in Section 9.2 without resorting to the use of `Permutations`. Consider using the `Sort` function to sort the characters. Note the difference in speed of the two approaches: one involving string functions and the other list functions that operate on lists of characters. Increase the efficiency of your search by only searching for words of the same length as your source word.

3. Rewrite the function `FindWordsContaining` using regular expressions instead of the patterns used in this section.

4. Using the text from several different sources, compute and then compare the number of punctuation characters per 1000 characters of text. `ExampleData["Text"]` gives a listing of many different texts that you can use.

5. The function `StringPartition` was developed specifically to deal with genomic data where one often needs uniformly-sized blocks to work with. Generalize `StringPartition` to fully accept the same argument structure as the built-in `Partition`.

6. Rewrite the text encoding example from Section 9.2 using `StringReplace` and regular expressions. First create an auxiliary function to encode a single character based on a key list of the form $\{\{pt_1, ct_1\}, ...\}$ where pt_i is a plaintext character and ct_i is its ciphertext encoding. For example, the pair $\{z, a\}$ would indicate the character z in the plaintext will be encoded as an a in the ciphertext. Then create an encoding function $encode[str, key]$ using regular expressions to encode any string str using the key consisting of the plaintext/ciphertext character pairs.

7. Word collocation refers to expressions of two or more words that create a customary phrase such as *black coffee*, or *sharp as a tack*. They are important in many linguistic applications: natural language translation and corpus research involving social phenomena, for example. In this exercise you will create functions for extracting pairs of words of a predetermined form involving parts of speech such as {*adjective, noun*}.

    Start by creating some functions to preprocess your text: split the text into pairs of words and, for simplicity, convert all words to lowercase. Next, filter out words that are not contained in the dictionary. Then, find all remaining pairs that are of a certain form involving the parts of speech. This information is contained in WordData:

```
In[4]:= WordData["split", "PartsOfSpeech"]

Out[4]= {Noun, Adjective, Verb}
```

Finally, create a function Collocation[*expr*, {*PoS*₁, *PoS*₂}] that returns all pairs in *expr* that consist of the part of speech PoS_1 followed by the part of speech PoS_2. For example:

```
In[5]:= sentence =
         "Alice was beginning to get very tired of sitting by her sister
             on the bank, and of having nothing to do. Once or twice
             she had peeped into the book her sister was reading, but ";
```

```
In[6]:= PreProcessString[sentence]

Out[6]= {{was, beginning}, {beginning, to}, {to, get}, {get, very},
         {very, tired}, {tired, of}, {of, sitting}, {sitting, by},
         {by, her}, {her, sister}, {sister, on}, {on, the}, {the, bank},
         {bank, and}, {and, of}, {of, having}, {having, nothing},
         {nothing, to}, {to, do}, {do, once}, {once, or},
         {or, twice}, {twice, she}, {she, had}, {had, peeped},
         {peeped, into}, {into, the}, {the, book}, {book, her},
         {her, sister}, {sister, was}, {was, reading}, {reading, but}}
```

```
In[7]:= Collocation[%, {"Verb", "Noun"}]

Out[7]= {{was, beginning}, {having, nothing}, {was, reading}}
```

10

Graphics and visualization

Structure of graphics · Primitives and directives · Options · Structure of built-in graphics functions · Bézier curves · Hypocycloids · Efficient structures · Multi-objects · GraphicsComplex · Numeric vs. symbolic expressions · Sounds of mathematics · Sound primitives and directives · Space-filling plots · Plotting lines in space · Visualizing standard deviations · Simple closed paths · Points in a polygon · Root plotting · Trend plots · Brownian music

Visualization is a means to organize, represent, and make sense of information. The visual representation may involve functions, numerical or abstract data, text, and many other objects of study. Sometimes the representation is fixed spatially as in much scientific visualization; other times, as with information visualization, a spatial representation is not given and must be created. In either domain, the idea is to find a representation that best conveys the information and relationships under study.

Mathematica contains a rich set of tools for visualizing functions, data, and many kinds of expressions. Generally the built-in graphics functions provide what you need for your visualizations, but, like the rest of the *Mathematica* programming language, you will periodically find yourself needing to create your own customized visualizations. Sometimes it is most efficient to build upon existing visualization functions, modifying them as needed.

```
In[1]:= ProteinDotPlot[p1_, p2_, {name1_String, name2_String}] :=
    ArrayPlot[
      Outer[Boole[#1 == #2] &, Characters[p1], Characters[p2]],
      Frame → True, FrameLabel → {name1, name2}]

In[2]:= seq1 = ProteinData["SCNN1A"];
    seq2 = First@Import["NP_001030.2.fasta", "FASTA"];
```

In[4]:= **ProteinDotPlot[seq1, seq2, {"SCNN1A", "SCNN1G"}]**

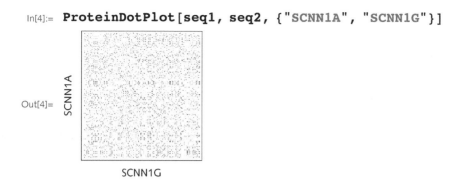

Out[4]=

Other times you will find it best to create such visualizations from scratch, using the graphics building blocks.

In[5]:= **pts= RandomInteger[{-100, 100}, {24, 3}];**
      Graphics3D[{
          {Opacity[.3], Line[Subsets[pts, {2}]]},
          {Red, Point[pts]}}, PlotLabel→
          StringForm["`1` vertices, `2` edges", Length[pts],
          Binomial[Length[pts], 2]]]

Out[6]=

24 vertices, 276 edges

In this chapter we will discuss how to construct functions for visualizing many different kinds of data and objects. We will start with the basic building blocks of graphical expressions in *Mathematica* – primitives, directives, and options. We then discuss ways to make your graphics more efficient by looking at the internal representation of graphics objects as well as using multi-objects and a different representation that results in a compressed graphics object, GraphicsComplex. Finally, we will develop several different programs for visualizing functions, data, and other objects: space-filling plots for representing proteins and other chemical structures; a plotting function for displaying points in 3-space that is particularly useful for visualizing phenomena such as random walks; a geometric computation that finds and displays simple closed paths for a set of points in the plane; a standard computational geometry problem, determining if a point is inside a polygon, convex or nonconvex; creating a visualization that finds and displays the roots of a function; creation of trend plots for visualizing trends in time-series data such as financial data; and finally we develop a set of functions for creating and exploring random music compositions.

Throughout this chapter we will use and build upon the different constructs and programming paradigms developed earlier. For many of the functions that are developed here we also include usage messages, an options structure, and error checking, issuing appropriate warnings when something goes wrong or an incorrect input is supplied as an argument. Although the code for these examples starts to become a bit lengthier, we try to break down the major concepts to make it easier for you to parse these programs.

10.1 Structure of graphics

A line is a dot that went for a walk.

— Paul Klee

Cultivate your curves… they may be dangerous but they won't be avoided.

— Mae West

All *Mathematica* graphics are constructed from objects called *graphics primitives* such as `Point`, `Line`, `Polygon`, `Circle`. Primitives are the basic building blocks of all graphics in *Mathematica*. They are used by built-in functions such as `Plot` to create graphics. You too can create graphics scenes from scratch using these building blocks by putting them together according to the rules governing the structure of the language and the nature of the problem at hand. This section introduces the building blocks of graphics programming and discusses how to put them together to make graphical objects.

The three graphics elements we will discuss are primitives, directives, and options. The two-dimensional graphics primitives include the following: `Point`, `Line`, `Polygon`, `Disk`, `Circle`, `Rectangle`, `BezierCurve`, `Arrow`, `Text` (see Table 10.1 or consult the documentation for a complete listing).

For example, here is a circle centered at the origin of radius 1. Evaluating this input simply returns the primitive circle object.

```
In[1]:= Circle[{0, 0}, 1]
Out[1]= Circle[{0, 0}, 1]
```

To display two-dimensional graphics primitives, wrap them in `Graphics`.

In[2]:= **Graphics[Circle[{0, 0}, 1]]**

Out[2]=

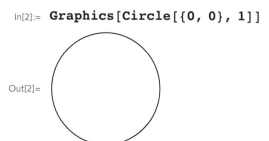

To display more than one graphics primitive, put them in a list.

In[3]:= **Graphics[{Circle[{0, 0}, 1], Circle[{1, 0}, 1]}]**

Out[3]=

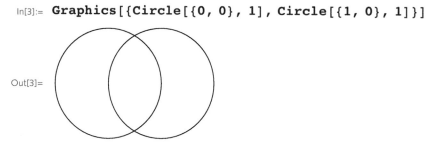

Graphics directives are used to modify primitives. For example, in the following input the first circle is modified with the Thick directive and the second circle with the Dashed directive. Note the use of lists to *scope* the directive with the primitive element it is modifying.

In[4]:= **Graphics[{**
        {Thick, Circle[{0, 0}, 1]},
        {Dashed, Circle[{1, 0}, 1]}
        }]

Out[4]=

Entire graphics are customized through the use of options. Options to Graphics should follow any elements or list of elements given as arguments to Graphics. For example, this adds axes and a frame around the graphic. Axes and Frame are options to the Graphics function.

In[5]:= `Graphics[{`
    `{Thick, Circle[{0, 0}, 1]},`
    `{Dashed, Circle[{1, 0}, 1]}`
    `},`
    `Axes → True, Frame → True]`

Out[5]=

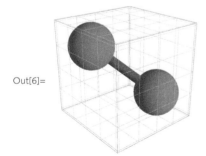

For three-dimensional graphics, a different wrapper is used to display the primitives, `Graphics3D`. In the following, the two sphere primitives are within the scope of the `Red` directive and the cylinder is within the scope of the `Blue` directive. Two options to `Graphics3D` are used here: `FaceGrids` adds a grid to each of the box faces and `ViewVertical` is used to change the vertical direction in the image. Note an identical structure to that for `Graphics`.

In[6]:= `Graphics3D[{`
    `{Red, Sphere[{0, 0, 0}], Sphere[{2, 2, 2}]},`
    `{Blue, Cylinder[{{0, 0, 0}, {2, 2, 2}}, .2]}`
    `},`
    `FaceGrids → All, ViewVertical → {1, 0, 0}]`

Out[6]=

This is the basic syntax for creating graphics objects from scratch: directives modify primitives in their scope and options are used to modify the entire graphic. In the following sections, we will look at graphics primitives, directives, and options in some detail.

Graphics primitives

We will start to explore these graphics elements by constructing a graphic using *only* primitive elements. In Section 8.1, we displayed a graphic that demonstrated some of the properties of complex numbers. Let us show how this graphic was created, using some of *Mathematica*'s graphics primitives.

Table 10.1 lists some of the two-dimensional graphics primitives that we will use in this example in addition to several other two-dimensional elements that are available.

Three-dimensional versions of `Point`, `Line`, `Polygon`, and `Text` are also available for constructing three-dimensional graphics. For a full listing of `Graphics3D` primitives, see the tutorial Three-Dimensional Graphics Primitives (WMDC).

The graphic we will create will contain the following elements:

- points in the plane at a complex number $a + b\,i$ and at its conjugate $a - b\,i$;

- lines drawn from the origin to each of these points;

- an arc, indicating the polar angle of the complex number;

- dashed lines indicating the real and imaginary values;

- a set of axes in the coordinate plane;

- labels for each of the above elements.

TABLE 10.1. *Basic two-dimensional graphics primitives*

Graphics primitive	Usage
`Point[{x, y}]`	point at position $\{x, y\}$
`Line[{{x_1, y_1}, {x_2, y_1}, ...}]`	line through the points $\{x_i, y_i\}$
`Rectangle[{{x_min, y_min}, {x_max, y_max}}]`	filled rectangle
`Polygon[{{x_1, y_1}, {x_2, y_2}, ...}]`	filled polygon
`Circle[{x, y}, r, {θ_1, θ_2}]`	circular arc of radius r
`Disk[{x, y}, r]`	filled disk of radius r
`Raster[{{x_{11}, x_{12}, ...}, {x_{21}, x_{22}, ...}, ...}]`	rectangular array of gray levels
`Text[expr, {x, y}]`	text centered at $\{x, y\}$
`Arrow[{pt_1, pt_2}]`	arrow from pt_1 to pt_2

First we choose a point in the first quadrant and then construct a line from the origin to this point.

In[7]:= **z = 8 + 3 i;**

`Line[{{`x_1`,` y_1`}, {`x_2`,` y_2`}, …, {`x_n`,` y_n`}}]` is a graphics primitive that creates a polygonal line from the point whose coordinates are (x_1, y_1) to the point (x_2, y_2), etc. The points need not be collinear.

In[8]:= `line1 = Line[{{0, 0}, {Re[z], Im[z]}}];`

Let us also create a point at the coordinates of the complex number.

In[9]:= `pt1 = Point[{Re[z], Im[z]}];`

To display what we have created so far, wrap the `Graphics` function around the points and lines to display them as a two-dimensional *graphics image*.

In[10]:= `Graphics[{`
            `line1, pt1`
         `}]`

Out[10]=

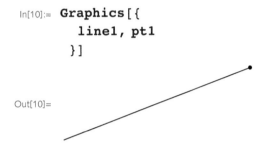

Graphics directives

The default behavior of graphics primitives is modified by using *graphics directives*. Graphics directives work by changing only those objects within their scope. The directive *dir* will affect each of the primitives *prim$_i$* occurring within its scope. That scope is delineated using curly braces.

$$\{dir, prim_1, prim_2, …, prim_n\}$$

A partial list of the two-dimensional graphics directives, together with usage statements, is given in Table 10.2. For a complete listing of the three-dimensional directives, see the tutorial Three-Dimensional Graphics Directives (WMDC).

Use the `PointSize` graphics primitive to increase the size of the point.

In[11]:= `pt1 = {PointSize[.025], Point[{Re[z], Im[z]}]};`

In[12]:= `Graphics[{`
            `line1, pt1`
         `}]`

Out[12]=

Admittedly this is not too exciting, but it is a start. Let us add a line and a point for the conjugate.

```
In[13]:=  cz = Conjugate[z];
          line2 = Line[{{0, 0}, {Re[cz], Im[cz]}}];
          pt2 = {PointSize[.025], Point[{Re[cz], Im[cz]}]};
```

```
In[16]:=  Graphics[{
              line1, pt1, line2, pt2
          }]
```

Out[16]=

TABLE 10.2. *Two-dimensional graphics directives*

Graphics directive	Usage
AbsoluteDashing[$\{d_1, d_2, …\}$]	dashed line segments using absolute units
AbsoluteThickness[d]	lines of thickness d measured in absolute units
CMYKColor[$\{c, m, y, b\}$]	cyan, magenta, yellow, black values between 0 and 1
Dashing[$\{d_1, d_2, …\}$]	dashed line segments of lengths $d_1, d_2, …$
GrayLevel[g]	gray between 0 (black) and 1 (white)
Hue[h, s, b]	hue, saturation, and brightness between 0 and 1
PointSize[r]	point of radius r given as a fraction of width of plot
RGBColor[r, g, b]	red, green, blue values between 0 and 1
Thickness[d]	lines of thickness d given as fraction of width of plot

Graphics options

Whereas directives are used to modify the primitives that are within their scope, options are used to modify the entire graphic. Options to functions are placed after any required arguments and are separated by commas. All of *Mathematica*'s graphics functions have options that allow you to modify some attribute of the entire graphic. Here is a list of some of those options relevant to Graphics objects.

In[17]:= **Options[Graphics] // Short**

Out[17]//Short=

> {AlignmentPoint → Center, AspectRatio → Automatic,
> Axes → False, AxesLabel → None, AxesOrigin → Automatic,
> AxesStyle → {}, ≪28≫, PlotRegion → Automatic,
> RotateLabel → True, Ticks → Automatic, TicksStyle → {}}

Each option is specified as a rule with its default value given on the right-hand side of the rule. For example, Axes is one of the options for graphics types; it is set to False by default.

Since Axes is an option to the Graphics function, it is placed after the graphics elements {line1, pt1, …}. Using the value Automatic for the Axes option lets *Mathematica* figure out the best arrangement for the axes placement and labels, given the elements present in the graphic.

In[18]:= **Graphics[{line1, pt1, line2, pt2}, Axes → Automatic]**

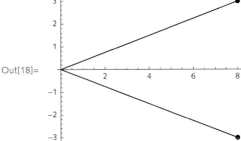

Out[18]=

Combining graphics elements

We have the basic structure of the graphic object so now let us add some additional elements. We start with dashed lines indicating the real and imaginary components of our complex number. The Dashing directive with Line gives the desired effect.

In[19]:= **hline =**
{Dashing[{0.04, 0.04}], Line[{{0, Im[z]}, {Re[z], Im[z]}}]};

In[20]:= **vline =**
{Dashing[{0.04, 0.04}], Line[{{Re[z], 0}, {Re[z], Im[z]}}]};

Since we were using this graphic to display an arbitrary complex number, we are not interested in the units on the axes, so we suppress the default value and add our own with the Ticks option. Ticks → {{{Re[z], "a"}}, {{Im[z], "b"}}} places tick marks at Re[z] on the horizontal axis and at Im[z] on the vertical axis and labels them a and b, respectively. In addition, let us add labels on the axes. And, to make reading the input a bit easier, we will append new elements as we go.

In[21]:= **elements = {line1, pt1, line2, pt2, hline, vline};**

```
In[22]:= Graphics[elements,
         Axes → Automatic, AxesLabel → {"Re", "Im"},
         Ticks → {{{Re[z], "a"}}, {{Im[z], "b"}}}]
```

Out[22]=

We next put labels at the two complex numbers and along the line representing the length Abs[z]. We will use another graphics primitive, Text, to annotate these primitives. Text[*expr*, {*x*, *y*}] creates a text object of the expression *expr* and centers it at (*x*, *y*). So, to create "*z* = *a* + *bi*" as a piece of text centered at a point a little bit above and to the left of *z*, we use:

$$\text{Text}["z = a + b i", \{\text{Re}[z] - 0.5, \text{Im}[z] + 0.35\}]$$

Here then are the labels for the complex number and the length given by the absolute value of the complex number. Defer is needed here to prevent the expression z = a + bi from being evaluated and thus overwriting the value of z. You could also use HoldForm for this purpose.

```
In[23]:= text1 = Text[Defer[z = a + b i], {Re[z] - .5, Im[z] + .35}];
         text2 = Text[Defer[Abs[z]], {4.2, 2}];
```

```
In[25]:= Graphics[AppendTo[elements, {text1, text2}], Axes → Automatic,
         AxesLabel → {Re, Im}, Ticks → {{{Re[z], "a"}}, {{Im[z], "b"}}}]
```

Out[25]=

Lastly, we need to add the arc representing the polar angle and label it. The arc can be generated with another graphics primitive. Circle[{*x*, *y*}, *r*, {*a*, *b*}] will draw an arc of a circle centered at (*x*, *y*), of radius *r*, counterclockwise from an angle of *a* radians to an angle of *b* radians. The arc that we are interested in will have a radius smaller than Abs[z] and will be drawn from the real (horizontal) axis to the line connecting the origin and z. Here is the code for the arc and its label, as well as the graphic containing all the above elements (we also add the text to label the conjugate).

```
In[26]:= arc = Circle[{0, 0}, Abs[z]/3, {0, Arg[z]}];

       text3 = Text[Defer[Arg[z]], {3.6, .6}];
       text4 = Text[Defer[Conjugate[z] = a - b i],
           {Re[cz] - .5, Im[cz] - .35}];

In[29]:= Graphics[AppendTo[elements, {text3, text4, arc}],
         Axes → True, AxesLabel → {Re, Im},
         Ticks → {{{Re[z], "a"}}, {{Im[z], "b"}}}]
```

Out[29]=

An important point about options to keep in mind is that if you happen to give one option multiple times, *Mathematica* will only use the first occurrence and ignore all others.

```
In[30]:= Graphics[elements,
         Axes → True,
         Axes → False,
         AxesLabel → {Re, Im},
         Ticks → {{{Re[z], "a"}}, {{Im[z], "b"}}}]
```

Out[30]=

We have made assignments to many different symbols in this section. Before going on, it would be a good idea to clear the values associated with all these symbols. In Chapter 13 we will talk about contexts in detail, but for now, you can clear the values associated with all symbols in the Global` context by evaluating the following.

In[31]:= **Clear["Global`*"]**

Structure of built-in graphics functions

Graphics created with functions such as **Plot** and **ListPlot** are constructed using the same syntax as described above for creating graphics from primitive elements: primitives such as lines connecting points, and options governing the overall display. It is useful to get some insight into this structure for the built-in functions for those situations where you need to transform or modify a graphic created with **Plot** or **Plot3D** say.

Let us start by looking at the internal representation of a plot of the sine function.

In[32]:= **sinplot = Plot[Sin[x], {x, 0, 2π}]**

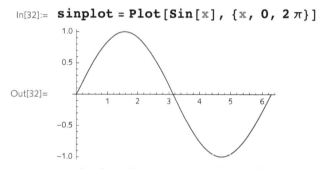

Out[32]=

InputForm displays the expression that could have been entered manually to get the same plot. **Short** is used here to display an abbreviated listing of that expression. (Note: The formatted output from **Short** will vary slightly depending upon the width of your notebook.)

In[33]:= **Short[InputForm[sinplot], 8]**

Out[33]//Short=

    Graphics[
        {{{}, {}, {Hue[0.67, 0.6, 0.6], Line[{{1.28228 × 10⁻⁷, 1.28228 × 10⁻⁷},
            {0.0019271655319089223, 0.001927164339004283},
            {0.0038542028355462695, 0.00385419329326691}, << 426 >>,
            {<< 2 >>}, {6.283185178951315, -1.28228 × 10⁻⁷}}]]}}}, {<< 7 >>}]

This graphic consists of a series of coordinates, or points, in the plane connected by lines of a certain hue. There are several hundred points that are sampled to make this plot, some of which are explicitly displayed above and the rest implicitly indicated by the notation <<*n*>>. The following shows that there are precisely 431 points in this plot.

```
In[34]:= Cases[InputForm[sinplot],
           Line[coords_List] :→ Length[coords], Infinity]
```

```
Out[34]= {431}
```

Numerous options are used to display this plot. `AbsoluteOptions[gr]` is useful for displaying what values were used with which options for any graphic *gr*.

```
In[35]:= RandomSample[AbsoluteOptions[sinplot], 5]
```

```
Out[35]= {LabelStyle → {}, ImageMargins → 0.,
           FormatType → TraditionalForm,
           DisplayFunction → Identity, BaseStyle → {}}
```

To see how an understanding of this internal structure can be used to perform some transformations, here we use a geometric transformation on the coordinates of the lines to essentially perform a reflection in the line $y = x$.

```
In[36]:= Show[{
           sinplot,
           Graphics[{Dashed, Line[{{-1, -1}, {6, 6}}]}],
           sinplot /. line_Line :→ GeometricTransformation[
               line, ReflectionTransform[{-1, 1}]]
           }, PlotRange → All, AspectRatio → 1]
```

Out[36]=

There are three graphical elements present in this plot: the original `sinplot`, a dashed line, and the transformed `sinplot`. For the transformation rule operating on `sinplot`, the pattern `line_Line` will match any expression in `sinplot` that has head `Line`. It will be transformed into a line that is reflected according to `ReflectionTransform`.

```
           sinplot /. line_Line :→ GeometricTransformation[
               line, ReflectionTransform[{-1, 1}]]
```

Example: Bézier curves

The representation and visualization of information is a common task in almost any area of research or analytic activity. The variety of data that people study can give rise to a vast set of representations. If the data consist of interrelated objects, their relationships are often represented in a graph where vertices represent the objects under study and an edge connecting any two vertices indicates a "relationship" of some kind – interactions amongst proteins, friends in a group of individuals, or airline routes between a set of hubs.

If you were studying friendship networks, the objects of study would be people: each person would be represented by a vertex; a relationship between two people would be represented by an edge between two vertices. For example, in Figure 10.1, which represents a friendship network, you can see at a glance that Mara has six friends, Luigi has three, and so on.

FIGURE 10.1.   *Friendship network for ten people.*

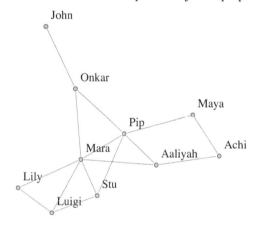

The use of graphs to represent such information is convenient from a computational point of view since you can take advantage of all the built-in functions to measure and query graphs, such as vertex edge counts (how many friends any given person has), shortest paths (how many degrees of separation between any two people), or centrality measures (measures of the influence or importance of a particular individual). Using graphs in *Mathematica* to represent such data also gives you immediate access to the formatting and styling functionality of `Graph` objects.

In this example we will work through the creation of a function to use Bézier curves instead of lines as the graphical object for edges. Table 10.3 lists the various curve graphics primitives that can be used for such purposes. Let us start with a simple undirected graph with only three edges and vertices.

In[37]:= **Graph[{1 ⟷ 2, 2 ⟷ 3, 3 ⟷ 1}]**

Out[37]=

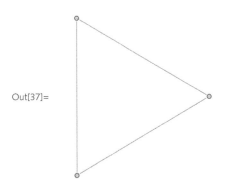

The Graph option that controls the edges is called EdgeShapeFunction and it is its value with which we will work. To begin, there are numerous named styles built in to *Mathematica* that can be given (GraphElementData["Edge"] gives a complete list).

In[38]:= **Graph[{1 ⟷ 2, 2 ⟷ 3, 3 ⟷ 1}, EdgeShapeFunction → "DottedLine"]**

Out[38]=

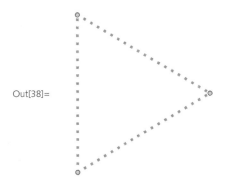

As of the writing of this book, there are no values for EdgeShapeFunction that produce curves or other objects that are not essentially stylized lines and arrows. So we will create one.

The documentation for EdgeShapeFunction indicates that the function it expects needs to be of the following form: $\mathit{fun}\big[\{\{x_1,\ y_1\},\ \{x_2,\ y_2\},\ \dots\},\ v_i \leftrightarrow v_j\big]$. The $\{x_i,\ y_i\}$ are the coordinates of the vertices used to create line segments for the edge connecting vertex v_i to vertex v_j. In fact, you can see precisely what form this takes using the following. The notation ## is a sequence of arguments passed to a pure function; in this example, that is a sequence of lists of vertices and rules as printed here.

```
In[39]:=  Graph[{1 ⟷ 2, 2 ⟷ 3, 3 ⟷ 1},
           EdgeShapeFunction → ((Print[{##}]; Line[#1]) &)]
```

$\{\{\{0.866025, 0.5\}, \{3.88578 \times 10^{-16}, 1.\}\}, 1 \leftrightarrow 2\}$

$\{\{\{0.866025, 0.5\}, \{0., 0.\}\}, 1 \leftrightarrow 3\}$

$\{\{\{3.88578 \times 10^{-16}, 1.\}, \{0., 0.\}\}, 2 \leftrightarrow 3\}$

Out[39]=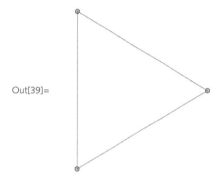

We would like to replace `Line` with `BezierCurve`, but a Bézier curve with two control points is just a straight line.

```
In[40]:=  Graphics@BezierCurve[{{0.866025, 0.5}, {0., 0.}}]
```

Out[40]=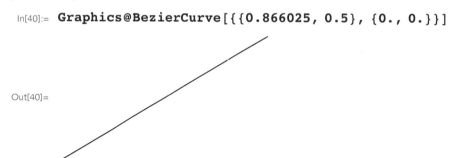

We will use a rule to introduce additional points that can be used to create higher-order Bézier curves. First, we will naively add a random point between any pair of existing points (represented by the patterns a and b in this code). The function `edgeFun` expects two arguments: a list of the coordinates and an edge. Although we do not use the edge information here, we do return a Bézier curve that uses the control points given on the right-hand side of the delayed rule. The various curve primitives, including Bézier curves, are listed in Table 10.3.

```
In[41]:=  edgeFun[pts_, e_] := Module[{controlPts},
           controlPts = pts /. {a_, b_} ⧴ {a, RandomReal[{0, 1}, 2], b};
           BezierCurve[controlPts]]
```

In[42]:= `Graph[{1 ⟷ 2, 2 ⟷ 3, 3 ⟷ 1}, EdgeShapeFunction → edgeFun]`

Out[42]=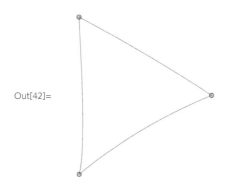

That works, but rather than use an arbitrary, random coordinate as the additional control point, we really should get a little more control over the control points. So, instead let us add two new control points that are dependent upon the positions of a and b.

In[43]:= `edgeFun[pts_, e_] := Module[{controlPts},`
`    controlPts =`
`      pts /. {a_, b_} :> {a, {a[[1]] + 2 b[[1]] / 3, a[[2]]},`
`        {a[[1]] + 2 b[[1]] / 3, b[[2]]}, b};`
`    BezierCurve[controlPts]]`

Let us try it out on some different graphs.

In[44]:= `CompleteGraph[5, EdgeShapeFunction → edgeFun]`

Out[44]=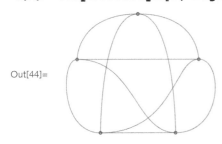

In[45]:= `WheelGraph[13, EdgeShapeFunction → edgeFun]`

Out[45]=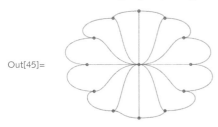

Here is a slight variation on the creation of the additional control points from the two points a and b.

```
In[46]:= edgeFun[pts_, e_] := Module[{controlPts},
            controlPts = pts /. {a_, b_} :> {a, {a[[1]] + .1 b[[1]], a[[2]]},
                {a[[1]] + .1 b[[1]], b[[2]]}, b};
            BezierCurve[controlPts]]
```

```
In[47]:= RandomGraph[UniformGraphDistribution[30, 50],
            GraphLayout → "CircularEmbedding",
            EdgeShapeFunction → edgeFun]
```

Out[47]=

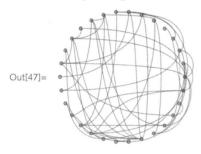

```
In[48]:= TreeGraph[EdgeList@CompleteKaryTree[3, 5],
            GraphLayout → "SpringElectricalEmbedding",
            EdgeShapeFunction → edgeFun]
```

Out[48]=

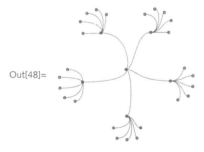

TABLE 10.3. *Curve primitives*

Graphics primitive	Usage
BezierCurve[{pt_1, pt_2, ...}]	Bézier curve with control points pt_i
BSplineCurve[{pt_1, pt_2, ...}]	nonuniform B-spline curve with control points pt_i
JoinedCurve[{$segmt_1$, $segmt_2$, ... }]	curve with $segmt_1$ followed by $segmt_2$, etc.
FilledCurve[{$segmt_1$, $segmt_2$, ... }]	filled curve with $segmt_1$ followed by $segmt_2$, etc.

Example: hypocycloids

Hypocycloids are curves generated by following a fixed point on a smaller circle rolling around the inside of a larger circle. In what follows, we will combine graphics primitives and directives together with a built-in graphics function to create a visualization of hypocycloids.

FIGURE 10.2. *Hypocycloid generated by rolling a smaller circle inside a larger circle.*

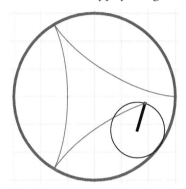

The formula for a hypocycloid is given parametrically by the following, where r is the radius of the smaller circle and R is the radius of the larger circle

In[49]:= **Hypocycloid[{a_, b_}, θ_] :=**
$$\left\{ (a - b) \, \text{Cos}[\theta] + b \, \text{Cos}\left[\theta \, \frac{a - b}{b}\right], \; (a - b) \, \text{Sin}[\theta] - b \, \text{Sin}\left[\theta \, \frac{a - b}{b}\right] \right\}$$

In[50]:= **Hypocycloid[{R, r}, θ] // TraditionalForm**

Out[50]//TraditionalForm=
$$\left\{ \cos(\theta)\,(R - r) + r\cos\left(\frac{\theta\,(R - r)}{r}\right), \; \sin(\theta)\,(R - r) - r\sin\left(\frac{\theta\,(R - r)}{r}\right) \right\}$$

Here is a plot of the curve for various values of the two radii R and r where their ratio R/r is an integer.

In[51]:= **Table[**
    ParametricPlot[
      Hypocycloid[{R, 1}, θ], {θ, 0, 2 π}, Axes → None],
      {R, 3, 7, 1}]

Out[51]= {, , , , }

And here are some curves for rational, but noninteger values of R/r.

```
In[52]:= Table[ParametricPlot[Hypocycloid[{R, 1}, θ],
          {θ, 0, 2 Denominator[R] π}, Axes → None],
          {R, {3/2, 5/3, 7/2, 13/5, 21/13}}]
```

Out[52]= { }

In fact, the curve only "closes up" when the ratio R/r is an integer or a rational number. Interested readers should consult Maor (1998) or visit the *MathWorld* page on hypocycloids (Weisstein 2011).

To start putting the graphics pieces together in our scene, we will fix the two radii for purposes of developing the code and then make them parameters that can be set by the user when our code is ready. Here is the outer circle, blue and thick.

```
In[53]:= With[{R = 3, r = 1},
          Graphics[{
            Blue, Thick, Circle[{0, 0}, R]
          }]]
```

Out[53]=

To draw the smaller inner circle, we first need to know its center. This will change as the smaller circle rotates around. In fact it is dependent upon the parameter $θ$. It is given by the following (left to the reader to verify).

```
In[54]:= center[θ_, R_, r_] := (R - r) {Cos[θ], Sin[θ]}
```

Here then are the two circles together, with the smaller circle given with a fixed (for now) center set by the angle $θ$.

```
In[55]:= With[{θ = π / 6, R = 3, r = 1},
         Graphics[{
           {Blue, Thick, Circle[{0, 0}, R]},
           {Circle[center[θ, R, r], r]}
         }]]
```

Out[55]=

We know where the center of the smaller circle is so let us draw a large point there together with a thick line from the center to the hypocycloid. Also we include a red point that shows the fixed point on the smaller circle that will trace out the hypocycloid as the angle θ changes.

```
In[56]:= With[{θ = π/6, R = 3, r = 1}, Graphics[{
           {Blue, Thick, Circle[{0, 0}, R]},
           {Circle[center[θ, R, r], r]},
           {PointSize[.015], Point[center[θ, R, r]]},
           {Thick, Line[{center[θ, R, r], Hypocycloid[{R, r}, θ]}]},
           {Red, PointSize[.02], Point[Hypocycloid[{R, r}, θ]]}
         }]]
```

Out[56]=

Of course we want to include the hypocycloid itself, from 0 to θ. We will combine a parametric plot of the curve with the graphics primitives we have developed so far. Because the plot ranges are quite different for the `ParametricPlot[...]` and the `Graphics[...]` pieces of the code, we need to add `PlotRange → All` as an option to the entire graphic, that is, as part of `Show`.

```
In[57]:=  With[{θ = π / 6, R = 3, r = 1},
            Show[{
              ParametricPlot[Hypocycloid[{R, r}, t],
               {t, 0, θ}, PlotStyle → Red, Axes → None],
              Graphics[{
                {Blue, Thick, Circle[{0, 0}, R]},
                {Circle[center[θ, R, r], r]},
                {PointSize[.015], Point[center[θ, R, r]]},
                {Thick,
                 Line[{center[θ, R, r], Hypocycloid[{R, r}, θ]}]},
                {Red, PointSize[.015], Point[Hypocycloid[{R, r}, θ]]}
                }]
              }, PlotRange → All, GridLines → Automatic]];
```

Finally, we sketch out the entire curve by having θ go from 0 to 2π.

```
In[58]:=  With[{θ = 2 π, R = 3, r = 1},
            Show[{
              ParametricPlot[Hypocycloid[{R, r}, t],
               {t, 0, θ}, PlotStyle → Red, Axes → None],
              Graphics[{
                {Blue, Thick, Circle[{0, 0}, R]},
                {Circle[center[θ, R, r], r]},
                {PointSize[.015], Point[center[θ, R, r]]},
                {Thick,
                 Line[{center[θ, R, r], Hypocycloid[{R, r}, θ]}]},
                {Red, PointSize[.015], Point[Hypocycloid[{R, r}, θ]]}
                }]
              }, PlotRange → All, GridLines → Automatic]]
```

Out[58]=

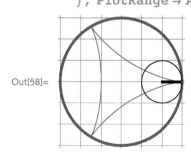

In Section 11.1 we will go a bit further and create several dynamic interfaces so that we can see the curve sketched out in real time while also providing controls to change the radii of each circle.

Exercises

1. Create a primitive color wheel by coloring successive sectors of a disk according to the `Hue` directive.

2. Create a graphic that contains a circle, a triangle, and a rectangle. Your graphic should include an identifying label for each object.

3. Create a three-dimensional graphic containing six `Cuboid` graphics primitives, randomly placed in the unit cube. Add an opacity directive to make them transparent.

4. Create a graphic consisting of a unit cube together with a rotation of 45° about the vertical axis through the center of that cube. Then create a dynamically rotating cube using `Manipulate`.

5. Create a graphic that consists of 500 points randomly distributed about the origin with standard deviation 1. Then, set the points to have random-size radii between 0.01 and 0.1 units and are colored randomly according to a `Hue` function.

6. Create a graphic that represents the solution to the following algebraic problem that appeared in the Calculus&*Mathematica* courseware (Porta, Davis, and Uhl 1994). Find the positive numbers r such that the following system has exactly one solution in x and y.

$$(x - 1)^2 + (y - 1)^2 = 2$$
$$(x + 3)^2 + (y - 4)^2 = r^2$$

Once you have found the right number r, then plot the resulting circles in true scale on the same axes, plotting the first circle with solid lines and the two solutions with dashed lines together in one graphic.

7. Create a graphic of the sine function over the interval $(0, 2\pi)$ that displays vertical lines at each point calculated by the `Plot` function to produce its plot.

8. Using options to the `Plot` function, create a plot showing the probability density function (pdf) of a normal distribution together with vertical lines at the first and second standard deviations. Your plot should look something like the following for a normal distribution with $\mu = 0$ and $\sigma = 1$:

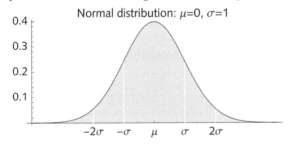

9. Modify `ProteinDotPlot` from the introduction to this chapter to accept options from `ArrayPlot`.

10. Modify the `Hypocycloid` code to create *epicycloids*, which are like hypocycloids except the smaller circle rotates on the *outside* of the larger circle. Then create an animation showing the epicycloid being sketched out as the smaller circle rotates around the larger circle. If your animation includes a way to select different radii for the circles, you will need to deal with the plot range as the size of the smaller circle changes.

10.2 Efficient structures

The built-in graphics functions are optimized for the tasks for which they are designed. What this means is that for a broad set of possible arguments, these function construct and display the graphics scene quickly and efficiently, keeping the size of the resulting graphic manageable. When creating visualizations of sizable datasets you can find yourself with very large graphical objects that are not optimal in terms of memory usage, storage on disk, and interactivity. In this section we will look at several approaches to optimizing graphical expressions introducing multi-objects and `GraphicsComplex` as two efficient structures for working with larger objects. Lastly, we will look at the use of numeric vs. symbolic expressions in the internal representation of graphical expressions.

Multi-objects

Visualizations that involve many graphics primitives often contain large data structures containing many instances of a single primitive object. For example, mapping `Point` across a set of pairs of coordinates is one way to create a graphic.

```
In[1]:= data = RandomReal[NormalDistribution[0, 1], {5, 2}];
        gr1 = Graphics[Map[Point, data]];
        FullForm[gr1]
```

```
Out[3]//FullForm=
        Graphics[
         List[Point[List[1.3587408177258289`, 1.0129471456926376`]],
           Point[List[-0.7139297202638747`, -0.08647150174959149`]],
           Point[List[1.0899030510218575`, -0.5685559001434687`]],
           Point[List[0.22032467637820483`, 1.1101331398563001`]],
           Point[List[-0.16904296153230453`, 0.22391875152064022`]]]]
```

Note that `Point` occurs five times in the above expression, once for each point created. On the other hand, simply wrapping `Point` around the entire list of coordinate pairs creates the same image, but note that `Point` is only used once in the underlying expression.

```
In[4]:= gr2 = Graphics[Point[data]];
        FullForm[gr2]
```

Out[5]//FullForm=

```
Graphics[
 Point[List[List[1.3587408177258289`, 1.0129471456926376`],
  List[-0.7139297202638747`, -0.08647150174959149`],
  List[1.0899030510218575`, -0.5685559001434687`],
  List[0.22032467637820483`, 1.1101331398563001`],
  List[-0.16904296153230453`, 0.22391875152064022`]]]]
```

The form in this latter case is referred to as a *multi-point expression,* and is treated differently than expressions with numerous primitives. The internal representation of multi-element objects is more compact and the *Mathematica* front end is able to render these objects much more quickly. Scaling up the size of the previous examples, this becomes quite apparent.

```
In[6]:= data = RandomVariate[NormalDistribution[0, 1], {5000, 3}];
```

```
In[7]:= AbsoluteTiming[
        gr1 = Graphics3D[{PointSize[.005], Map[Point, data]}]]
```

Out[7]= 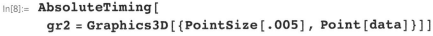$\left\{0.003957,\right.$

```
In[8]:= AbsoluteTiming[
        gr2 = Graphics3D[{PointSize[.005], Point[data]}]]
```

Out[8]= 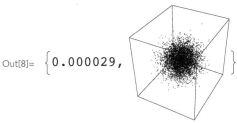$\left\{0.000029,\right.$

```
In[9]:= First[%%]
        ─────────
        First[%]
```

Out[9]= 1.4×10^2

Although the differences in kernel timings are impressive (two to three orders of magnitude in this example), the time it takes the front end to render these two objects is vastly different, with the first expression taking much much longer.

Since `Timing` and `AbsoluteTiming` measure kernel times, you will have to use a different function, `SessionTime`, to measure total wall clock time for a computation including the time it takes the front end to format and render the resulting expression.

```
In[10]:= t1 = SessionTime[];
         gr1 = Graphics3D[{PointSize[.005], Map[Point, data]}]
         t2 = SessionTime[];
         (t2 - t1) Seconds
```

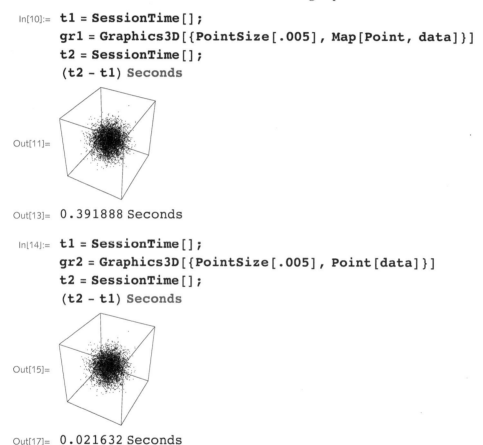

Out[11]=

Out[13]= 0.391888 Seconds

```
In[14]:= t1 = SessionTime[];
         gr2 = Graphics3D[{PointSize[.005], Point[data]}]
         t2 = SessionTime[];
         (t2 - t1) Seconds
```

Out[15]=

Out[17]= 0.021632 Seconds

Moreover, the memory needed to represent these objects is also vastly different with that for the multi-point expression being some 10 to 12 times smaller.

$$In[18]:= \left\{\texttt{ByteCount[gr1], ByteCount[gr2], N}\left[\frac{\texttt{ByteCount[gr1]}}{\texttt{ByteCount[gr2]}}\right]\right\}$$

Out[18]= {1 240 216, 120 392, 10.3015}

`Point`, `Line`, `Polygon`, `Arrow` are the only graphics primitives that have multi-element forms. The exercises at the end of this section and several applications at the end of this chapter explore other examples of multi-objects.

GraphicsComplex

Graphical expressions often contain repetitions of the coordinate points used in the graphic. For example, a coordinate triple $\{x, y, z\}$ might have several polygons that share that vertex and so it would be repeated for each of those polygons. A GraphicsComplex is an expression that you can use to compress the representation of such objects. It works by specifying each coordinate once, and then only referring to the coordinate by an index, given by its position in the coordinate list.

Many of the three-dimensional and region plotting functions use GraphicsComplex to represent the graphical expression that would otherwise be quite a bit larger.

In[19]:= **plt = Plot3D$\left[\sqrt{1 - x^2 - y^2}\,,\ \{x,\ -1,\ 1\},\ \{y,\ -1,\ 1\}\right]$**

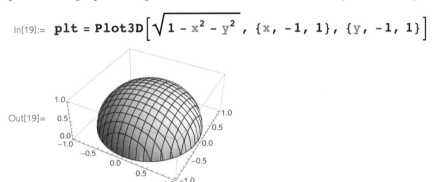

Out[19]=

In[20]:= **Short[InputForm[plt], 2]**

Out[20]//Short=

```
Graphics3D[GraphicsComplex[{{0.00027901781728316324,
   -0.9999998571428571, 0.00045559203033409366},
   {-0.42857136734693874, << 2 >>}, {<< 3 >>},
   << 2198 >>, {-0.4999999285714286, 0.6249999107142856,
   0.5979028111234589}}, << 2 >>], {<< 6 >>}]
```

GraphicsComplex takes two arguments: a list of coordinate points in 2- or 3-space, followed by a list of graphics primitives where each point is referenced by its position within the coordinate point list.

GraphicsComplex$[\,\{pt_1,\ pt_2,\ ...\},\ primitives\,]$

For example, here is a simple expression consisting of five points on the unit circle with the first point repeated at the end to close up the polygon.

In[21]:= **vertices[$n\_$] := Table$\left[\left\{\text{Cos}\left[\dfrac{2\,\pi\,\alpha}{n}\right],\ \text{Sin}\left[\dfrac{2\,\pi\,\alpha}{n}\right]\right\},\ \{\alpha,\ 0,\ n\}\right]$**

In[22]:= **coords = vertices[5]**

Out[22]= $\left\{\{1, 0\}, \left\{\frac{1}{4}\left(-1+\sqrt{5}\right), \sqrt{\frac{5}{8}+\frac{\sqrt{5}}{8}}\right\}, \left\{\frac{1}{4}\left(-1-\sqrt{5}\right), \sqrt{\frac{5}{8}-\frac{\sqrt{5}}{8}}\right\},\right.$

$\left\{\frac{1}{4}\left(-1-\sqrt{5}\right), -\sqrt{\frac{5}{8}-\frac{\sqrt{5}}{8}}\right\}, \left\{\frac{1}{4}\left(-1+\sqrt{5}\right), -\sqrt{\frac{5}{8}+\frac{\sqrt{5}}{8}}\right\}, \{1, 0\}\right\}$

The following creates a line connecting the points in order. The explicit coordinates are given as the first argument. The second argument contains the primitives, in this case, a single Line object. In the Line primitive, the points are referred to by their position in the list coords.

In[23]:= **GraphicsComplex[coords, Line[{1, 2, 3, 4, 5, 6}]]**

Out[23]= $\text{GraphicsComplex}\left[\left\{\{1, 0\}, \left\{\frac{1}{4}\left(-1+\sqrt{5}\right), \sqrt{\frac{5}{8}+\frac{\sqrt{5}}{8}}\right\},\right.\right.$

$\left\{\frac{1}{4}\left(-1-\sqrt{5}\right), \sqrt{\frac{5}{8}-\frac{\sqrt{5}}{8}}\right\}, \left\{\frac{1}{4}\left(-1-\sqrt{5}\right), -\sqrt{\frac{5}{8}-\frac{\sqrt{5}}{8}}\right\},$

$\left\{\frac{1}{4}\left(-1+\sqrt{5}\right), -\sqrt{\frac{5}{8}+\frac{\sqrt{5}}{8}}\right\}, \{1, 0\}\right\}, \text{Line}[\{1, 2, 3, 4, 5, 6\}]\right]$

Wrapping Graphics (or Graphics3D) around a GraphicsComplex displays the expression.

In[24]:= **Graphics[GraphicsComplex[coords, Line[{1, 2, 3, 4, 5, 6}]]]**

Out[24]=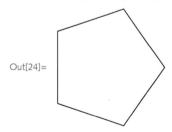

Changing the indices used in the second argument results in lines connecting the same coordinates but in a different order.

In[25]:= **Graphics[GraphicsComplex[coords, Line[{1, 3, 5, 2, 4, 6}]]]**

Out[25]=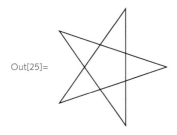

If you wanted to add points at each coordinate, do so in the second argument to GraphicsComplex.

In[26]:= **Graphics[GraphicsComplex[coords, {**
    Line[{1, 3, 5, 2, 4, 6}],
    Blue, PointSize[.05], Point[{1, 2, 3, 4, 5, 6}]
    }]]

Out[26]=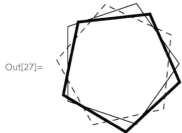

Once the list of coordinate points is specified (first argument of GraphicsComplex), the points can be referenced as many times as needed. In the following example, the same set of points is referred to in the first line segment as well as in the following two rotated line segments.

In[27]:= **Graphics[{**
    GraphicsComplex[coords, {
      {Line[{1, 2, 3, 4, 5, 6}]},
      {Dashed, Rotate[Line[{1, 2, 3, 4, 5, 6}], 30 Degree]},
      {Thick, Rotate[Line[{1, 2, 3, 4, 5, 6}], 60 Degree]}
    }]
    }]

Out[27]=

Numeric vs. symbolic expressions

One of the great strengths of *Mathematica* is that you generally do not need to worry about what type of numbers you are working with when performing many operations. This is true of graphical work as well as other kinds of computation. You can work with approximate numbers or symbolic/exact expressions and your graphics will just work. But for large graphical expressions, you may want to think about the types of numbers used.

For example, here is a graphics primitive – a polygon – generated from a list of exact coordinates.

In[28]:= `tri = Graphics[Polygon[{{0, 0}, {1, 0}, {`$\frac{1}{2}$`, `$\frac{\sqrt{3}}{2}$`}}]]`

Out[28]=

The front end, which renders the graphic, converts this list of exact coordinates into a numeric representation and maintains this in a cached form for purposes of efficiency. You can see this by converting to the internal box structure.

In[29]:= `ToBoxes[tri]`

Out[29]= `GraphicsBox[PolygonBox[NCache[{{0, 0}, {1, 0}, {`$\frac{1}{2}$`, `$\frac{\sqrt{3}}{2}$`}},`

`{{0, 0}, {1, 0}, {0.5, 0.866025}}]]]`

The exact coordinates as well as the numeric approximations are both part of this internal representation. Although this allows the front end to render the graphic quickly, it comes at a cost. Here is the size of this little graphic expression.

In[30]:= `ByteCount[tri]`

Out[30]= `872`

Turning off this cache results in a simpler internal representation, one in which the symbolic expression is not stored.

In[31]:= **tri2 = Graphics$\left[\text{Polygon}\left[\left\{\{0, 0\}, \{1, 0\}, \left\{\frac{1}{2}, \frac{\sqrt{3}}{2}\right\}\right\}\right]\right.$,**

Method → {"CacheSymbolicGraphics" → False}$\Big]$;

In[32]:= **ToBoxes[tri2]**

Out[32]= GraphicsBox[PolygonBox[{{0, 0}, {1, 0}, {0.5, 0.866025}}],
    Method → {CacheSymbolicGraphics → False}]

Fortunately, there is an easier way to get around this issue and that is simply to give the coordinates as numeric values rather than symbolic expressions.

In[33]:= **ntri = Graphics[Polygon[{{0, 0}, {1, 0}, {0.5, 0.866}}]]**

Out[33]=

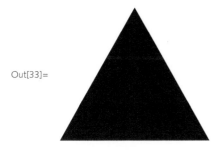

In[34]:= **ToBoxes[ntri]**

Out[34]= GraphicsBox[PolygonBox[{{0, 0}, {1, 0}, {0.5, 0.866}}]]

The resulting expression is about half the size of the cached version.

In[35]:= **ByteCount[ntri]**

Out[35]= 472

This becomes more important as the size and complexity of your graphics increases. Here is a random collection of lines in 3-space, first using symbolic coordinates.

In[36]:= **pairs = RandomChoice$\Big[$**

Join$\left[\text{Range}[8], \left\{\frac{1}{2}, \frac{\sqrt{2}}{2}, \frac{\sqrt{3}}{2}, \frac{1}{2}\left(1 - \sqrt{5}\right)\right\}\right]$, {2000, 3}$\Big]$;

```
In[37]:= lines3D = Graphics3D[
            {Opacity[.2], Line[Partition[pairs, 2]]}] // Timing
```

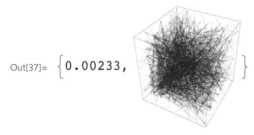

```
Out[37]= {0.00233,                }
```

```
In[38]:= ByteCount[lines3D]
```

```
Out[38]= 833 624
```

Here is the same graphic but using numerical coordinates only.

```
In[39]:= npairs = N[pairs];
         nlines3D = Graphics3D[
            {Opacity[.2], Line[Partition[npairs, 2]]}] // Timing
```

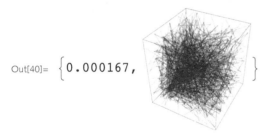

```
Out[40]= {0.000167,               }
```

```
In[41]:= ByteCount[nlines3D]
```

```
Out[41]= 336 344
```

The version using numerical approximations for the coordinates is about 2.5 times smaller in size. Also, the time to render the graphic is almost an order of magnitude faster from the kernel's perspective, and about twice as fast for the front end (you could use a similar approach to that in the previous section where we used `SessionTime`). This is mostly a result of not having to carry around all that extra information. Of course, if your graphical expression is highly dependent upon exact/symbolic expressions, then these suggestions might be moot. In that case, using either `GraphicsComplex` and/or multi-objects should make the representation more efficient.

Exercises

1. Create a hexagonal grid of polygons like the one below.

   First create the grid by performing appropriate translations using either **Translate** or the geometric transformation **TranslationTransform**. Compare this approach with a multi-polygon approach.

2. Create a graphic consisting of a three-dimensional lattice, that is, lines on the integer coordinates in 3-space. Compare approaches that use multi-lines as opposed to those that do not.

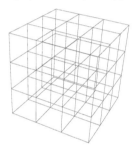

3. A common problem in computational geometry is finding the boundary of a given set of points. One way to think about this is to imagine the points as nails in a board and then to stretch a rubber band around all the nails. The stretched rubber band lies on a convex polygon commonly called the *convex hull* of the point set. The problem of determining the convex hull of a set of points has application in computer vision, pattern recognition, image processing, and many other areas. Using the **ConvexHull** function defined in the Computational Geometry package, create a function **ConvexHullPlot** for visualizing the convex hull together with its point set. The resulting graphic should include the points labeled with text as well as the convex polygon drawn as a line around the point set.

```
In[1]:= pts = RandomReal[1, {20, 2}];
In[2]:= Needs["ComputationalGeometry`"]
In[3]:= ConvexHull[pts]
Out[3]= {12, 19, 2, 1, 9, 6, 4, 10, 7, 8}
```

In[4]:= **ConvexHullPlot[pts]**

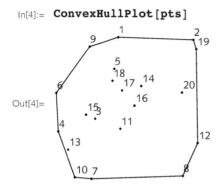

Out[4]=

4. Extend Exercise 9 from Section 8.4 to random walks on the base *n* digits of *π*. For example, in base 3, a 1 corresponds to an angle of 120° from the current position, 2 corresponds to 240°, and 0 to 360°. In base 4 the step angles will be multiples of 90° and in general, for base *n*, the step angles will be multiples of 360°/*n*. Use **GraphicsComplex** to visualize the walks. Include a color function that depends upon the length of the walk. For more on random walks on digits of *π* in various bases, see Bailey et al. (2012).

10.3 Sound

Although it might seem odd to include a section on sound in a chapter on graphics, there is much similarity between these two objects from both an experiential as well as computational and programmatic points of view. Graphics and sound are both used to visualize phenomena and to convey information, and both can be used to analyze data.

The syntax of the functions for sound in *Mathematica* follows that for graphics expressions. There are top-level functions that provide a basic interface for working with sounds together with options built in for modifying their default behaviors. And, like graphics, there are lower-level primitive objects for constructing sounds from scratch.

In this section we will introduce the symbolic sound language in *Mathematica* and, in Section 10.4, use it to construct several example sound expressions – compositions.

The sound of mathematics

We hear sound when the air around our ears compresses and expands the air near the eardrum. Depending upon how the eardrum vibrates, different signals are sent to the brain via the auditory nerves after the cochlea in the inner ear does some signal processing to convert the mechanical sound waves into electrochemical impulses. These signals are then interpreted in the brain as various sounds. Musical tones compress and expand the air periodically according to sine waves. The human ear is able to hear these waves when the frequency is between approximately 20 and 20 000 oscillations per second, or hertz.

One oscillation of sin(*x*) occurs between 0 and 2π; sin (4 *x*) oscillates four times in the same interval.

In[1]:= **Plot[{Sin[x], Sin[4 x]}, {x, 0, 2 π}]**

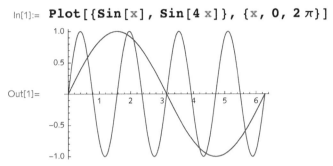

Out[1]=

Mathematica is able to take a function such as sine and sample its amplitudes roughly 8000 times per second, and then send corresponding voltages to the speaker on your computer to produce the sound of the sine wave. The function that accomplishes this is **Play**, which has the same syntax as the **Plot** command.

In[2]:= **? Play**

Play$\left[f, \{t, t_{min}, t_{max}\} \right]$ creates an object that plays as a sound whose amplitude is given by *f* as a function of time *t* in seconds between t_{min} and t_{max}. ≫

The function **Sin[256 t]** oscillates 256 times each 2π units, so, if we want to "play" a function that oscillates 256 times per second, we want **Sin[256 t (2 π)]**. This plays the function for one second.

In[3]:= **Play[Sin[256 t (2 π)], {t, 0, 1}]**

Out[3]=

Pressing the play button in the lower-left corner of the generated interface should play a note close to middle C played for one second. The graphic that *Mathematica* outputs with the sound object is a somewhat primitive attempt to display the waveform. You can suppress this graphical display and only play the sound by using **EmitSound**. This gives a slight saving in terms of the expressions that are stored with your notebook.

In[4]:= **Play[Sin[256 t (2 π)], {t, 0, 1}] // EmitSound**

The **Play** function encodes the sound amplitudes using eight bits and samples functions at a rate of about 8000 times per second, or hertz. This is good to keep in mind as anomalies can occur when playing a function whose periodicity is very close to the sample rate. Listen to the quite surprising result that follows (you will have to check the `SampleRate` on your computer and adjust the following code accordingly). Try other frequencies that are close to the sample rate on your computer.

```
In[5]:= Options[Play, {SampleDepth, SampleRate}]

Out[5]= {SampleDepth → 8, SampleRate → 8000}

In[6]:= Play[Sin[8000 × 2 π t], {t, 0, 1}]
```

```
Out[6]=
```

Although you would expect a tone at 8000 hertz, you get something quite different. `Play` is sampling the function 8000 times. Since the function itself oscillates 8000 times on this interval, the samples appear to be about the same and so `Play` misses the periodic nature of this function. If `Play` did adaptive sampling, much like `Plot` does, then it could avoid this particular problem. You could, of course, increase the sampling. This is analogous to increasing the value of `PlotPoints` in the initial sampling of points in such functions as `Plot`.

```
In[7]:= Play[Sin[8000 × 2 π t], {t, 0, 1}, SampleRate → 44 000]
```

```
Out[7]=
```

In addition to playing continuous functions with `Play`, you can also play lists of discrete amplitudes using `ListPlay`. For example, here are the digits of a rational number.

```
In[8]:= digits = First[RealDigits[N[1/19, 5000]]];
        Take[digits,50]

Out[9]= {5, 2, 6, 3, 1, 5, 7, 8, 9, 4, 7, 3, 6, 8, 4, 2,
         1, 0, 5, 2, 6, 3, 1, 5, 7, 8, 9, 4, 7, 3, 6, 8, 4,
         2, 1, 0, 5, 2, 6, 3, 1, 5, 7, 8, 9, 4, 7, 3, 6, 8}
```

The periodic nature of rational numbers should give a tone when played as a repeating set of amplitudes and it does. *Mathematica* scales the amplitudes to fit in a range that `ListPlay` can work with and that is audible.

In[10]:= **`ListPlay[digits]`**

Out[10]=

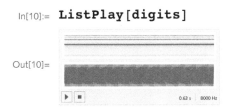

Contrast that with a nonperiodic list of digits, the digits of π – white noise.

In[11]:= **`irratdigits = First[RealDigits[N[π, 5000]]];`**
`ListPlay[irratdigits]`

Out[12]=

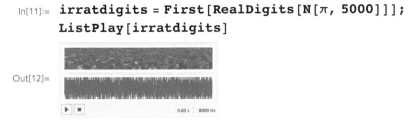

Sound primitives and directives

You can think of `Play` and `ListPlay` as audio analogues of `Plot` and `ListPlot`. They are top-level functions that provide a clean and easy-to-use interface for the user. But, as with graphics objects, you can create sound objects from scratch, building them up from primitives (Table 10.4) and styling them with directives.

TABLE 10.4. *Basic sound primitives*

Sound primitive	Usage
`SoundNote[`*pitch*`]`	music-like sound note
`SampledSoundFunction[`f`,` n`,`r`]`	amplitude levels given by a function
`SampledSoundList[{`a_1`,` a_2`,…},` r`]`	amplitude levels given as a list

`SoundNote` creates a sound primitive. Just as `Graphics` and `Graphics3D` are used to display graphics primitives, `Sound` is wrapped around sound primitives to play them on your computer. For example, this generates middle C, played for the default one second.

In[13]:= **`Sound[SoundNote["C"]]`**

Out[13]=

Given a numeric value n, SoundNote[n] will generate a note n semitones above middle C. The parameter n can also take on negative integer values to generate tones *below* middle C. For example, this plays a note five semitones below middle C, that is, G below middle C.

In[14]:= **Sound[SoundNote[-5]] // EmitSound**

Set the duration of each sound using a second argument to Sound. For example, this plays the note for two seconds.

In[15]:= **Sound[SoundNote[0], 2] // EmitSound**

To play several notes simultaneously as a chord, include them in a list as an argument to SoundNote. Here is an augmented ninth chord (think Jimi Hendrix's *Purple Haze*).

In[16]:= **Sound[SoundNote[{"E2", "G#", "B", "D", "G"}]] // EmitSound**

You can also specify a style which is essentially a MIDI instrument. Note how this syntax mirrors that for graphics directives. The style (directive) precedes the primitives which it modifies and is scoped in a manner similar to graphics.

In[17]:= **Sound[{**
            "GuitarDistorted", SoundNote[{"E2", "G#", "B", "D", "G"}]
          }] // EmitSound

In[18]:= **Sound[{"GuitarDistorted",**
            SoundNote[{"E2", "B2", "E2"}],
            SoundNote[{"E3", "G#3", "B3", "D3", "G3"}],
            SoundNote[{"E2", "B2", "E2"}],
            SoundNote[{"E3", "G#3", "B3", "D3", "G3"}]
          }]

Out[18]=

4 s

Alternatively, you can create sounds by sampling amplitude levels given by functions or lists. For example, this samples the sine function 8000 times per second (sample rate), by applying Sin to the integers 1 through 4000.

In[19]:= **Sound[SampledSoundFunction[Sin[#] &, 4000, 8000]]**

Out[19]=

0.5 s   8000 Hz

This creates a middle C tone from a list of amplitudes, sampled at 22 050 times per second, half the rate used by audio CDs.

```
In[20]:= rate = 22 050;
        lis = Table[Sin[261.626 × 2 π t], {t, 0, 0.5, 1 / rate}];
        Sound[SampledSoundList[lis, rate]]
```

Out[22]=

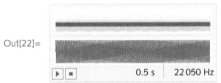

0.5 s　　22 050 Hz

Exercises

1. Evaluate `Play[Sin[1000 / x], {x, -2, 2}]`. Explain the dynamics of the sound generated from this function.

2. Experiment with the `Play` function by creating arithmetic combinations of sine functions. For example, you might try the following.

   ```
   In[1]:= Play[ Sin[440 × 2 π t]
                ───────────────── , {t, 0, 1}]
                 Sin[660 × 2 π t]
   ```

   Out[1]=

   1 s　8000 Hz

3. Create a tone that doubles in frequency each second.

4. Create a "composition" using the digits of π as representing notes on the C scale where a digit n is interpreted as a note n semitones from middle C. For example, the first few digits, 1, 4, 1, 5 would give the notes one, four, one, and five semitones from middle C.

5. A *square wave* consists of the addition of sine waves, each an odd multiple of a fundamental frequency, that is, it consists of the sum of sine waves having frequencies f_0, $3f_0$, $5f_0$, $7f_0$, etc. Create a square wave with a fundamental frequency f_0 of 440 hertz. The more overtones you include, the "squarer" the wave.

6. Create a square wave consisting of the sum of sine waves with frequencies f_0, $3f_0$, $5f_0$, $7f_0$, etc., and amplitudes 1, 1/3, 1/5, 1/7, respectively. This is actually a truer square wave than that produced in the previous exercise.

7. Create a square wave consisting of overtones that are randomly out of phase. How does this wave differ from the previous two?

8. A *sawtooth wave* consists of the sum of both odd- and even-numbered overtones: f_0, $2f_0$, $3f_0$, $4f_0$, etc. with amplitudes in the ratios 1, $1/2$, $1/3$, $1/4$, etc. Create a sawtooth wave and compare its tonal qualities with the square wave.

9. A wide variety of sounds can be generated using *frequency modulation (FM) synthesis*. The basic idea of FM synthesis is to use functions of the form,

    $$a \, \sin(2 \, \pi \, F_c \, t + \mathrm{mod} \, \sin(2 \, \pi \, F_m \, t)),$$

    where a is the peak amplitude, F_c is the carrier frequency in hertz, mod is the modulation index, and F_m is the modulating frequency in hertz.

    Determine what effect varying the parameters has on the resulting tones by creating a series of FM synthesized tones. First, create a function `FM[Amp, Fc, mod, Fm, time]` that implements the above formula and generates a tone using the `Play` function. Then you should try several examples to see what effect varying the parameters has on the resulting tones. For example, you can generate a tone with strong vibrato at a carrier frequency at middle A for one second by evaluating `FM[1, 440, 45, 5, 1]`.

10.4 Examples and applications

Up until this point, we have looked at the tools that are available to construct relatively simple graphics in *Mathematica* using the graphics building blocks – primitives, directives, and options. In this section we consider problems that are more involved or whose solution requires geometric insight as we construct our programs. We will not restrict our programs to those only constructed from graphics primitives but will also build upon and modify some of the built-in functions for our purposes here.

We will begin with four examples whose solutions involve building functions from primitive graphics elements: creating space-filling plots for proteins and other chemicals, plotting lines from data in three dimensions, finding simple closed paths through a set of data, and determining if a point lies inside or outside of a polygon. The next three problems use built-in functions in order to take advantage of established algorithms for computation and options for formatting and styling: visualizing the distribution of data including some statistical properties, root plotting, and trend plots. The last example uses sound primitives and directives to construct musical compositions tied to scaling functions.

Space-filling plots

Our first graphics example uses three-dimensional graphics primitives to construct a visualization of molecular structures. The built-in data collection `ChemicalData` contains a property for generating these plots – `"SpaceFillingMoleculePlot"` – but you cannot use this with other objects such as a protein or any object not in `ChemicalData`.

In[1]:= **ChemicalData["AceticAcid", "SpaceFillingMoleculePlot"]**

Out[1]=

The information needed to construct such a plot for any given molecule is:

- the list of atoms in the molecule;
- the positions in space of each atom;
- the radius of each atom;
- the color for each atom.

These data can come from a variety of sources. For our purposes, we will use some of the built-in data collections in *Mathematica* to gather the data.

The list of atoms for a known chemical is given by the "**VertexTypes**" property of **ChemicalData**.

In[2]:= **atoms = ChemicalData["AceticAcid", "VertexTypes"]**

Out[2]= {O, O, C, C, H, H, H, H}

Their positions in space are given by "**AtomPositions**".

In[3]:= **positions = ChemicalData["AceticAcid", "AtomPositions"]**

Out[3]= {{-140.19, -68.091, -9.3099}, {-43.767, 87.394, -133.26},
{87.692, 9.1899, 45.963}, {-36.804, 12.256, -38.892},
{159.89, 81.044, 7.1474}, {130.97, -90.809, 43.377},
{62.271, 35.133, 148.73}, {-220.07, -66.118, -63.757}}

The van der Waals radius of any atom is the radius of an imaginary, circumscribed sphere about the atom. It has been computed for many atoms (not all) and is also built into *Mathematica*.

In[4]:= **radii = Map[ElementData[#, "VanDerWaalsRadius"] &, atoms]**

Out[4]= {152., 152., 170., 170., 120., 120., 120., 120.}

The units are picometers, where $1\,pm = 10^{-12}\,m = 10^{-2}$ Å (ångströms). Atoms typically have radii in the range 60–520 pm, or, 0.6–5.2 Å.

```
In[5]:= Map[ElementData["C", "VanDerWaalsRadius", #] &,
          {"Value", "Units"}]
```

```
Out[5]= {170., Picometers}
```

A commonly-used color scheme for atoms was developed in the 1950s and 1960s by Corey, Pauling, and later Koltun, known as the CPK model. It is built into *Mathematica* via `ColorData`.

```
In[6]:= colors = Map[ColorData["Atoms", #] &, atoms]
```

```
Out[6]= {RGBColor[0.800498, 0.201504, 0.192061],
         RGBColor[0.800498, 0.201504, 0.192061],
         RGBColor[0.4, 0.4, 0.4], RGBColor[0.4, 0.4, 0.4],
         RGBColor[0.65, 0.7, 0.7], RGBColor[0.65, 0.7, 0.7],
         RGBColor[0.65, 0.7, 0.7], RGBColor[0.65, 0.7, 0.7]}
```

$\{color,\ \text{Sphere}[center,\ radius]\}$ is the graphics expression that we will use for each atom. The key observation here is that this list needs to be generated for *each* atom in a given molecule that we are visualizing. We have three lists: `colors`, `positions`, and `radii`. We want to slot them into a graphics list of the form $\{color,\ \text{Sphere}[pos,\ radius]\}$. We use `MapThread`, where #1 pulls an element from the first list, `colors`; #2 pulls an element from the second list, `positions`; and #3 pulls an element from the third list, `radii`.

```
In[7]:= Graphics3D[{
          MapThread[{#1, Sphere[#2, #3]} &, {colors, positions, radii}]
          }]
```

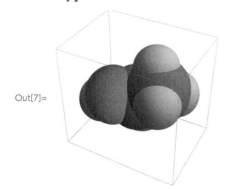

```
Out[7]=
```

This is the basic structure we need. We will next add some directives and options to get the effects in which we are interested. Using the `Specularity` directive gives control over the reflection of the lights. Setting the `Lighting` option to `"Neutral"` sets the light sources used to illuminate the object to be white in color.

In[8]:= `Graphics3D[{Specularity[White, 40],`
`  MapThread[{#1, Sphere[#2, #3]} &, {colors, positions, radii}]`
`}, Lighting → "Neutral"]`

Out[8]=

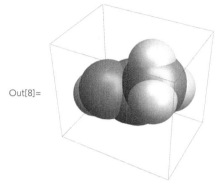

Putting all these pieces together, here is the function `ChemicalSpaceFillingPlot`. It is dependent upon `ChemicalData` and `ElementData` for all the atomic data. If you have other sources that you are drawing from, you will have to modify it accordingly.

In[9]:= `ChemicalSpaceFillingPlot[chem_] :=`
`  Module[{elements, pos, radii},`
`   elements = ChemicalData[chem, "VertexTypes"];`
`   pos = ChemicalData[chem, "AtomPositions"];`
`   radii =`
`    Map[ElementData[#, "VanDerWaalsRadius"] &, elements];`
`   Graphics3D[{Specularity[White, 50],`
`     MapThread[{ColorData["Atoms", #1], Sphere[#2, #3]} &,`
`      {elements, pos, radii}]`
`    }, Lighting → "Neutral"]]`

Try it out on an amino acid, l-tryptophan.

In[10]:= `ChemicalSpaceFillingPlot["LTryptophan"]`

Out[10]=

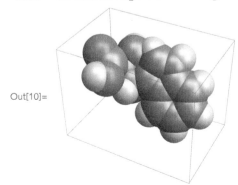

Using the legending functionality new to *Mathematica* 9, you can add a legend for each element.

(Mathematica 9) In[1]:=

```
ChemicalSpaceFillingPlot[chem_] :=
 Module[{elements, pos, radii},
  elements = ChemicalData[chem, "VertexTypes"];
  pos = ChemicalData[chem, "AtomPositions"];
  radii =
   Map[ElementData[#, "VanDerWaalsRadius"] &, elements];
  Legended[
   Graphics3D[{Specularity[White, 50],
     MapThread[{ColorData["Atoms", #1], Sphere[#2, #3]} &,
       {elements, pos, radii}]
    }, Lighting → "Neutral"],
   SwatchLegend[
    ColorData["Atoms", #1] & /@ DeleteDuplicates[elements],
    Map[ElementData[#, "StandardName"] &,
     DeleteDuplicates[elements]], LegendFunction → "Panel",
    LegendMarkers → "SphereBubble", LegendMarkerSize → 12]]]
```

(Mathematica 9) In[2]:=

```
ChemicalSpaceFillingPlot["LTryptophan"]
```

(Mathematica 9) Out[2]=

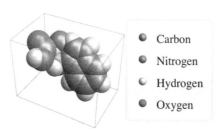

Let us go a few steps further and create a similar function for working with the proteins built into `ProteinData`. Whereas `ChemicalData` uses `"VertexTypes"` to get a list of the atoms, we need to use `"AtomTypes"` for `ProteinData`. Otherwise the code is similar.

In[11]:=
```
atoms = ProteinData["A2M", "AtomTypes"];
```

In[12]:=
```
colors = Map[ColorData["Atoms", #] &, atoms];
```

```
In[13]:= positions = ProteinData["A2M", "AtomPositions"];
        radii = Map[ElementData[#, "VanDerWaalsRadius"] &, atoms];
        Graphics3D[{Specularity[White, 40],
          MapThread[{#1, Sphere[#2, #3]} &, {colors, positions, radii}]
          }, Lighting → "Neutral"]
```

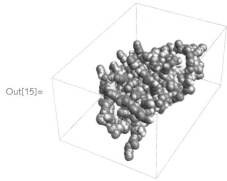

Out[15]=

Here is the bundled code for proteins.

```
In[16]:= ProteinSpaceFillingPlot[prot_] :=
        Module[{atoms, pos, radii, colors},
          atoms = ProteinData[prot, "AtomTypes"];
          colors = Map[ColorData["Atoms", #] &, atoms];
          pos = ProteinData[prot, "AtomPositions"];
          radii = Map[ElementData[#, "VanDerWaalsRadius"] &, atoms];
          Graphics3D[{Specularity[White, 50],
            MapThread[{#1, Sphere[#2, #3]} &, {colors, pos, radii}]
            }, Lighting → "Neutral"]]
```

It seems to work fine here on an enzyme involved in the regulation of cell motility and morphology.

```
In[17]:= ProteinSpaceFillingPlot["PAK1"]
```

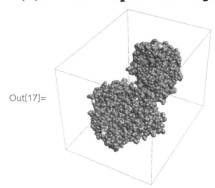

Out[17]=

But it fails when the database we are drawing from (`ProteinData`) has missing data.

```
In[18]:= ProteinSpaceFillingPlot["LOC100132316"]
```

ColorData::notprop : NotAvailable is not a known property
    for ColorData. Use ColorData["Properties"] for a list of properties. ≫

MapThread::mptd : Object Missing[ColorData[Atoms, NotAvailable]] at position {2, 1} in
    MapThread[{#1, Sphere[#2, #3]} &, {Missing[ColorData[Atoms, NotAvailable]], Missing[
        NotAvailable], Missing[ElementData[NotAvailable, VanDerWaalsRadius]]}]
    has only 0 of required 1 dimensions. ≫

```
In[19]:= pos = ProteinData["LOC100132316", "AtomPositions"]

Out[19]= Missing[NotAvailable]
```

We can pass on the "`Missing[...]`" output in such cases by adding a conditional that checks to see if the head `Missing` is part of the data.

```
In[20]:= MemberQ[Join[{atoms, pos}], _Missing]

Out[20]= True
```

Here is the updated code. We have also set things up so `ProteinSpaceFillingPlot` inherits the options from `Graphics3D`.

```
In[21]:= Clear[ProteinSpaceFillingPlot]
```

```
In[22]:= ProteinSpaceFillingPlot[prot_,
          opts : OptionsPattern[Graphics3D]] :=
        Module[{atoms, pos, radii},
          atoms = ProteinData[prot, "AtomTypes"];
          pos = ProteinData[prot, "AtomPositions"];
          If[MemberQ[Join[{atoms, pos}], _Missing],
            Missing["NotAvailable"],
            radii = Map[ElementData[#, "VanDerWaalsRadius"] &, atoms];
            Graphics3D[{Specularity[White, 50],
              MapThread[{ColorData["Atoms", #1], Sphere[#2, #3]} &,
                {atoms, pos, radii}]
            }, opts, Lighting → "Neutral"]]]
```

Let us exercise some of the graphics options.

```
In[23]:= ProteinSpaceFillingPlot["ABL1IsoformA",
           Boxed → False, FaceGrids → All]
```

Out[23]=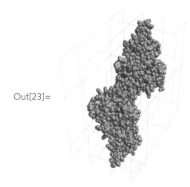

And here is what happens for a protein for which data are not available.

```
In[24]:= ProteinSpaceFillingPlot["ACR"]
```

Out[24]= Missing[NotAvailable]

Plotting lines in space

Mathematica has two basic functions for visualizing two-dimensional data: ListPlot and ListLinePlot. Although there is a function for scatter plots of points in three dimensions, there is no function for plotting three-dimensional data connected by lines; three-dimensional random walks are good examples of a phenomenon in need of such a visual tool. In this section we will create a new function, ListLinePlot3D that you can use to plot datasets consisting of triples of numbers (that is, coordinates of points in 3-space), connecting successive data points with lines.

Here are some data that we will use to prototype our function. It consists of twenty triples of random integers between −10 and 10.

```
In[25]:= data = RandomInteger[{-10, 10}, {20, 3}]
```

Out[25]= {{2, 7, 8}, {-2, 3, -7}, {5, -8, -7}, {-6, -3, -9}, {3, 3, -6},
          {2, -3, 1}, {-3, -7, 8}, {-3, -4, 1}, {-6, 9, -1}, {-10, 10, 7},
          {-2, 4, 4}, {5, 8, -10}, {4, 4, 6}, {-9, 7, 2}, {-9, -2, 1},
          {-10, 0, 9}, {8, 0, 1}, {-8, -7, 9}, {-3, -5, 0}, {-9, 0, -2}}

For a very basic first attempt, we simply connect each coordinate triple with a line.

In[26]:= **Graphics3D[Line[data]]**

Out[26]=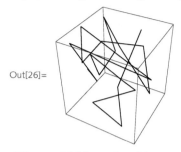

We would like to be able to use all the options for Graphics3D in our function, so we start to set up the options framework.

In[27]:= **Options[ListLinePlot3D] = Options[Graphics3D];**

In[28]:= **ListLinePlot3D[*lis_List*, *opts* : OptionsPattern[]] :=**
         Graphics3D[Line[*lis*], *opts*]

Let us exercise some of the Graphics3D options with our new function.

In[29]:= **ListLinePlot3D[data, Axes → True]**

Out[29]=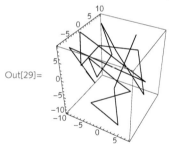

Our goal is to create a function that behaves much like the two-dimensional ListLinePlot. Here are the pieces that we will include:

- two rules for ListLinePlot3D: one for the case of a single dataset and another rule for plotting multiple datasets;
- the options inherited from Graphics3D;
- additional options that are not Graphics3D options: PlotStyle, Mesh, and MeshStyle;
- a usage message;
- a warning message for bad values of the Mesh option.

Let us set up the option structure first. As noted above, there are three options we are interested in using that are not options to `Graphics3D`.

```
In[30]:= MemberQ[First /@ Options[Graphics3D],
            PlotStyle | Mesh | MeshStyle]
```

```
Out[30]= False
```

We start by adding these, together with their default values, to the list of `Graphics3D` options. In the body of our function, we will need to define the behavior for each of the possible values of these options.

```
In[31]:= Remove[ListLinePlot3D]
```

```
In[32]:= Options[ListLinePlot3D] = Join[{
            Mesh → None,
            MeshStyle → Automatic,
            PlotStyle → ColorData[1][1]
            },
            Options[Graphics3D]];
```

The use of `ColorData` here warrants a note. Built-in functions such as `Plot` and `ListPlot` choose the default color for the `PlotStyle` using this construction. `ColorData[1]` is a color scheme consisting of a palette of colors. The first color in this list is the familiar dark blue style you see in plotting a function with `Plot` or `ListPlot`.

```
In[33]:= ColorData[1]
```

```
Out[33]= ColorDataFunction[{1, ∞, 1}, ▮▮▮▮▮▮▮▮▮▮▮▮▮ ]
```

```
In[34]:= ColorData[1][1]
```

```
Out[34]= RGBColor[0.2472, 0.24, 0.6]
```

Here is a first attempt at putting this function together. The first argument, `lis`, is checked to make sure it consists of a list of one or more triples; the plot style is picked up from the value of the `PlotStyle` option.

```
In[35]:= ListLinePlot3D[lis : {{_, _, _} ..},
            opts : OptionsPattern[]] :=
          Module[{plotStyle = OptionValue[PlotStyle]},
            Graphics3D[{plotStyle, Line[lis]}, opts]
          ]
```

In[36]:= **`ListLinePlot3D[data]`**

Out[36]=

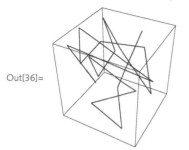

The rule that works with multiple datasets requires us to thread a list of colors over each dataset.

In[37]:= **`ListLinePlot3D[lis_List, opts : OptionsPattern[]] :=`**
`  Module[{colors = ColorData[1][#] & /@ Range[Length[lis]]},`
`    Graphics3D[Thread[{colors, Line /@ lis}], opts]]`

This is a very general rule that does no pattern matching on the first argument other than to check that it has head `List`. It would be better to give a more specific pattern that will be matched by lists of lists of the appropriate structure. The pattern `{{_, _, _} ..}` is matched by a list of one or more triples. Hence the pattern `{{{_, _, _} ..} ..}` is matched by one or more lists of lists of one or more triples, that is, multiple sets of three-dimensional data. Below we give this pattern a name, `lis`, so that we can refer to that pattern in the body of the function.

In[38]:= **`ListLinePlot3D[lis : {{{_, _, _} ..} ..},`**
`    opts : OptionsPattern[]] :=`
`  Module[{colors = ColorData[1][#] & /@ Range[Length[lis]]},`
`    Graphics3D[Thread[{colors, Line /@ lis}], opts]]`

Here are four datasets consisting of fifteen triples of random number each. Four different colors are automatically chosen from `ColorData` – one for each set of lines/data.

In[39]:= **`data = RandomReal[1, {4, 15, 3}];`**
`  ListLinePlot3D[data]`

Out[40]=

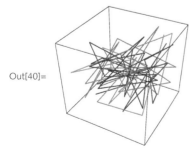

Next, we add the mesh and mesh style machinery. We will set things up so that the Mesh option can take only two different values, None or All. So, let us create an error message that will be issued if a different value is given to the Mesh option. We do this in the rule for a single dataset.

```
In[41]:= ListLinePlot3D::badmesh =
    "The value of the Mesh option should
       be either None or All";
```

We should also create a usage message for this function.

```
In[42]:= ListLinePlot3D::usage =
    "ListLinePlot3D[lis] creates a three-dimensional graphic of
       lines connecting the points given in lis which are
       assumed to be lists consisting of three coordinates.";
```

```
In[43]:= ? ListLinePlot3D
```

ListLinePlot3D[*lis*] creates a three–dimensional graphic of lines connecting the
points given in *lis* which are assumed to be lists consisting of three coordinates.

Here then is our function with all the pieces included.

```
In[44]:= ListLinePlot3D[lis : {{_, _, _} ..}, opts : OptionsPattern[]] :=
    Module[{plotStyle, mesh, meshStyle, gr3DOpts},
      mesh = OptionValue[Mesh];
      plotStyle = If[
        OptionValue[PlotStyle] === Automatic,
        ColorData[1][1],
        OptionValue[PlotStyle]];
      meshStyle = If[
        OptionValue[MeshStyle] === Automatic,
        {PointSize[Medium], ColorData[1][1]},
        OptionValue[MeshStyle]];
      gr3DOpts = FilterRules[{opts}, Options[Graphics3D]];
      Which[
        mesh === All, Graphics3D[{Flatten@{plotStyle, Line[lis]},
          Flatten@{meshStyle, Point[lis]}}, gr3DOpts],
        mesh === None, Graphics3D[Flatten@{plotStyle, Line[lis]},
          gr3DOpts],
        True, Message[ListLinePlot3D::badmesh]]]
```

Some comments on the code:

- Starting with `plotStyle`, the `If` statement will return `ColorData[1][1]` if the value of `PlotStyle` is `Automatic`. Otherwise, the user-supplied value is used. The same applies for `meshStyle`.

- `gr3DOpts` is used to filter only those options that are specific to `Graphics3D` and then those are passed into that function towards the end of the code.

- The `Which` statement determines what value of `Mesh` to use; if a value other than `All` or `None` is given, the warning message is issued.

- `Flatten` is used (three times) to insure the options are in the scope of the graphics primitives that they are modifying.

Let us try out the code on a list of triples of numbers generated from a three-dimensional random walk (the code for the `RandomWalk` function is developed in Section 13.1).

```
In[45]:=  << PwM`RandomWalks`
```

```
In[46]:=  RandomWalk[4, Dimension → 3, LatticeWalk → False]
```

```
Out[46]=  {{-0.331614, 0.7767, -0.535509}, {0.077708, 1.6684, -0.728714},
          {0.539855, 0.798301, -0.5574}, {-0.134958, 1.17306, 0.0783545}}
```

You could alternatively use any list of triples of numbers.

```
In[47]:=  RandomReal[{0, 1}, {4, 3}]
```

```
Out[47]=  {{0.391577, 0.379059, 0.645299}, {0.313523, 0.983738, 0.304593},
          {0.302268, 0.75095, 0.624754}, {0.340422, 0.626443, 0.90892}}
```

First, we generate a plot using the default option values.

```
In[48]:=  walk = RandomWalk[500, Dimension → 3, LatticeWalk → False];
          ListLinePlot3D[walk]
```

Out[48]=

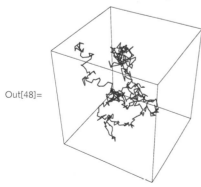

We then try out several options.

```
In[49]:= ListLinePlot3D[walk, Mesh→ All,
        MeshStyle → {PointSize[Small], Gray},
        PlotStyle → {Blue, Thickness[.001]}, FaceGrids → All]
```

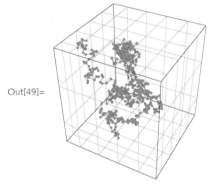

Out[49]=

There is, of course, much more we could add but this should give you a good idea of the kinds of things that should be included in such a function. In the exercises, you are asked to extend these ideas to make the function even more robust and useful, including incorporating these various options into the rule for multiple datasets.

Simple closed paths

Our next example of a graphical programming problem solves a very simplified variation of what are known as *traveling salesman problems*. For a given set of points, a *closed path* is one that travels to every point and returns to the starting point. The traveling salesman problem asks for the *shortest* closed path that connects an arbitrary set of points. The traveling salesman problem is one of great theoretical, as well as practical, importance. Airline routing and telephone cable wiring over large regions are examples of problems that could benefit from a solution to the traveling salesman problem.

From a theoretical point of view, the traveling salesman problem is part of a large class of problems that are known as *NP-complete* problems. These are problems that can be solved in polynomial time using nondeterministic algorithms. A *nondeterministic algorithm* has the ability to "choose" among many options when faced with numerous choices, and then to verify that the solution is correct. The outstanding problem in computer science at present is known as the $\mathcal{P} = \mathcal{NP}$ problem. This equation says that any problem that can be solved by a nondeterministic algorithm in polynomial time ($\mathcal{NP}$) can be solved by a deterministic algorithm in polynomial time ($\mathcal{P}$). It is widely believed that $\mathcal{P} \neq \mathcal{NP}$ and considerable effort has gone into solving this problem. See Cook (2000), Lawler et al. (1985) or Pemmaraju and Skiena (2003).

Our focus will be on a solvable problem that is a substantial simplification of the traveling salesman problem. We will find a *simple closed path* – a closed path that does not intersect itself –

through a set of *n* points. For example, Figure 10.3 displays a simple closed path through fifteen points chosen at random in the plane.

FIGURE 10.3.   *A simple closed path for fifteen points.*

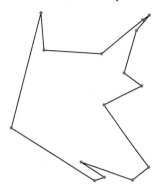

We will demonstrate a graphical solution to the problem by working with a small number of points and then generalizing to arbitrary numbers of points. Let us first create a set of ten pairs of points in the unit square.

```
In[50]:= SeedRandom[1234];
        coords = RandomReal[1, {10, 2}]
```

```
Out[51]= {{0.876608, 0.521964}, {0.0862234, 0.377913},
         {0.0116446, 0.927266}, {0.543757, 0.479332},
         {0.245349, 0.759896}, {0.984993, 0.217045},
         {0.459017, 0.884729}, {0.583854, 0.263973},
         {0.91956, 0.423835}, {0.98729, 0.587943}}
```

Next, we visualize the closed path through this set of points using `PathPlot`, developed in Section 4.2.

```
In[52]:= PathPlot[coords]
```

Out[52]=

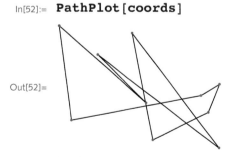

A simple closed path is one that does not cross itself. Simply taking the coordinates in the order in which they are given is not going to work here. Finding an ordering of the points such that a simple closed path results is geometric in nature. To develop an algorithm that insures our path does not cross itself for *any* set of points in the plane, we will first pick a point from our set at random and call this the *base* point.

```
In[53]:= base = RandomChoice[coords]
Out[53]= {0.0862234, 0.377913}
```

FIGURE 10.4. *Sorting points by polar angle.*

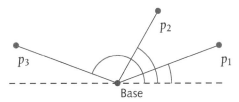

The path problem can be solved by first computing the counterclockwise (polar) angle between a horizontal line and each of the remaining points, using the base point as the vertex of the angle (Figure 10.4). Then, sorting the points according to this angle and connecting the points in this order should produce the desired result.

First we compute the polar angle between two points a and b (you should verify the trigonometry necessary to find this angle in the various cases).

```
In[54]:= angle[a_List, b_List] := Apply[ArcTan, (b - a)]
```

We can use this function to compute the polar angle between our base point and each of the points in the list coords. We need to make sure that we do not try to compute the angle between the base point and itself as this will evaluate to ArcTan[0, 0], which is undefined. This situation can be avoided by removing the base point from the list of coordinates when computing the angles.

```
In[55]:= remain = Complement[coords, {base}]
Out[55]= {{0.0116446, 0.927266}, {0.245349, 0.759896},
         {0.459017, 0.884729}, {0.543757, 0.479332},
         {0.583854, 0.263973}, {0.876608, 0.521964},
         {0.91956, 0.423835}, {0.984993, 0.217045}, {0.98729, 0.587943}}
```

```
In[56]:= Map[angle[base, #] &, remain]
Out[56]= {1.70573, 1.17608, 0.936601, 0.218137,
         -0.225085, 0.180276, 0.0550508, -0.177111, 0.229001}
```

The angle function gives an ordering on the list of coordinates. Sort[*list*, *orderFun*] sorts *list* according to the ordering function *orderFun*, which is a two-argument predicate. We wish to sort coords according to our ordering function on the angles between each point and the base point. The following code accomplishes this.

In[57]:= **s = Sort[remain, angle[base, *#1*] ≤ angle[base, *#2*] &]**

Out[57]= {{0.583854, 0.263973}, {0.984993, 0.217045},
         {0.91956, 0.423835}, {0.876608, 0.521964},
         {0.543757, 0.479332}, {0.98729, 0.587943}, {0.459017, 0.884729},
         {0.245349, 0.759896}, {0.0116446, 0.927266}}

This is our list of coordinates sorted according to the polar angle between each point and the base point. Put the base point at the beginning of the list and close the path by adding the base point to the end.

In[58]:= **path = Join[{base}, s, {base}]**

Out[58]= {{0.0862234, 0.377913}, {0.583854, 0.263973},
         {0.984993, 0.217045}, {0.91956, 0.423835},
         {0.876608, 0.521964}, {0.543757, 0.479332},
         {0.98729, 0.587943}, {0.459017, 0.884729}, {0.245349, 0.759896},
         {0.0116446, 0.927266}, {0.0862234, 0.377913}}

In[59]:= **PathPlot[path]**

Out[59]=

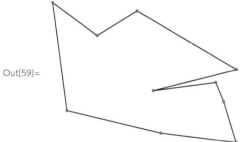

If we collect the above commands into a program `SimpleClosedPath`, then we can find such paths for arbitrary sets of coordinates.

In[60]:= **SimpleClosedPath[*lis_*] := Module[{base, angle, sorted},**
         base = RandomChoice[*lis*];
         angle[*a_*, *b_*] := Apply[ArcTan, *b* - *a*];
         sorted = Sort[Complement[*lis*, {base}],
            angle[base, *#1*] ≤ angle[base, *#2*] &];
         Join[{base}, sorted, {base}]]

Now we can create large sets of points and find the corresponding simple closed paths.

In[61]:= **data = RandomReal[1, {25, 2}];**

In[62]:= **PathPlot[SimpleClosedPath[data]]**

Out[62]=

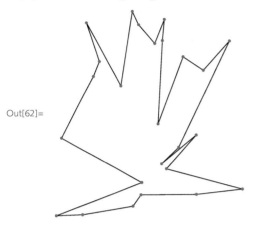

In[63]:= **data = RandomReal[1, {100, 2}];**

In[64]:= **PathPlot[SimpleClosedPath[data]]**

Out[64]=

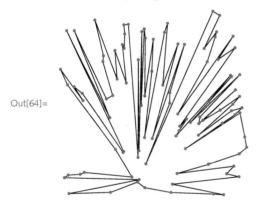

Although the algorithm we have developed in this section for computing simple closed paths seems to work fairly well, there are certain conditions under which it will still fail. The exercises at the end of this section investigate some of those conditions and walk you through how best to improve this algorithm.

Points in a polygon

Determining whether a point in the plane lies inside of a polygon is a common task in many computational areas. It has broad application in robot/computer vision, motion sensing, and geographic information systems (GIS), and is the basis of many algorithms in computational geometry. In this section we will solve this problem, first working with an idealized situation when the polygon is convex. The second implementation will be more general (and more involved) and solves the problem for nonconvex polygons.

There are two commonly used algorithms for solving point-in-polygon problems. One, ray crossing, involves drawing a ray from the point in question horizontally out to infinity and then asking how many times the ray crosses an edge of the polygon. If the number of crossings is even, you have entered the polygon as many times as you have exited it and so the point is outside. If the number of crossings is odd, then the point is inside the polygon. The ray crossing method is what we will use in the more general nonconvex case below.

Another commonly used algorithm for point-in-polygon problems involves winding numbers. This method computes the subtended angle from the point in question to each edge of the polygon and determines the number of turns the boundary of the polygon makes about the point. We will not implement this here; the interested reader is directed to O'Rourke (1998) or Heckbert (1994).

Convex polygons We start with a simplification of this problem, one in which the polygons are convex. A polygon is *convex* if any line segment connecting a pair of vertices is completely contained in the polygon; otherwise it is *concave*.

FIGURE 10.5. *Convex (left) and concave polygons.*

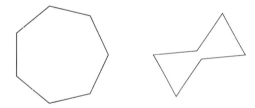

To solve the problem, we will need one important fact: given a line determined by two points, (x_1, y_1), (x_2, y_2), a third point (x_3, y_3) is to the left of the other two if the triangle formed by these three points has positive area, where the signed area of a triangle is given by the following determinant.

$$\text{Area}_\triangle = \frac{1}{2} \begin{vmatrix} x_1 & y_1 & 1 \\ x_2 & y_2 & 1 \\ x_3 & y_3 & 1 \end{vmatrix}$$

We can check this with a simple example.

```
In[65]:= pt1 = {0, 0};
         pt2 = {1, 1};
         ptL = {1 / 2, 1};
         ptR = {1 / 2, 0};
```

In[69]:= **Graphics[{**
Point[{pt1, pt2}], Line[{pt1, pt2}],
Red, Point[{ptL, ptR}]
}, Axes → Automatic]

Out[69]=

To construct the correct determinant, we need to embed the points in 3-space by padding them with 1s.

In[70]:= **Map[PadRight[#, 3, 1] &, {pt1, pt2, ptL}]**

Out[70]= $\left\{ \{0, 0, 1\}, \{1, 1, 1\}, \left\{ \frac{1}{2}, 1, 1 \right\} \right\}$

This gives the area of the triangle formed by these three points.

In[71]:= **TriangleArea[*tri* : {*v1_*, *v2_*, *v3_*}] :=**
Det[Map[PadRight[#, 3, 1] &, *tri*]] / 2

In[72]:= **TriangleArea[{pt1, pt2, ptL}]**

Out[72]= $\frac{1}{4}$

Note that this area is positive. Now use ptR instead of ptL.

In[73]:= **TriangleArea[{pt1, pt2, ptR}]**

Out[73]= $-\frac{1}{4}$

This negative quantity indicates that ptR is not to the left of the line formed by pt1 and pt2. The following predicate returns a value of True if the given point is to the left of the other two.

In[74]:= **leftOfQ[*line* : {{_, _}, {_, _}}, *pt* : {_, _}] :=**
TriangleArea[Join[{*pt*}, *line*]] ≥ 0

In[75]:= **leftOfQ[{pt1, pt2}, ptL]**

Out[75]= **True**

In[76]:= **leftOfQ[{pt1, pt2}, ptR]**

Out[76]= **False**

FIGURE 10.6. *One point inside and one point outside a polygon.*

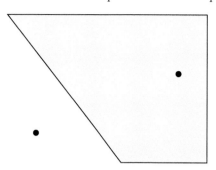

Now we are ready to answer the question posed at the beginning of this section: given a convex polygon and a point, how do you determine if that point is inside or outside the polygon? The basic idea is to take each line segment making up the polygon (its edges) and determine if the given point is to the left of *each* segment.

Partitioning that list of vertices of the polygon into pairs will give us the line segments we need. Note the need to use overlap in the partition so that the last line consists of the last point paired with the first.

```
In[77]:= poly = {{4, 0}, {7, 0}, {7, 5}, {0, 5}};
         pt1 = {6, 3}; pt2 = {1, 1};
```

```
In[79]:= lines = Partition[poly, 2, 1, 1]
```

```
Out[79]= {{{4, 0}, {7, 0}}, {{7, 0}, {7, 5}},
          {{7, 5}, {0, 5}}, {{0, 5}, {4, 0}}}
```

Now map leftOfQ with pt2 across these lines.

```
In[80]:= Map[leftOfQ[#, pt2] &, lines]
```

```
Out[80]= {True, True, True, False}
```

The given point is not to the left of all the lines. In fact, this test fails for the last line, the diagonal from the upper left to lower right. But the other point, pt1, is to the left of all lines of the polygon. This point is inside.

```
In[81]:= Map[leftOfQ[#, pt1] &, lines]
```

```
Out[81]= {True, True, True, True}
```

To check that leftOfQ returns True for *all* lines we take the conjunction of the list of Boolean values. If one or more are False, logical And will return False.

```
In[82]:= pointInPolygonQ[poly_, pt_] :=
            And @@ Map[leftOfQ[#, pt] &, Partition[poly, 2, 1, 1]]
```

```
In[83]:= pointInPolygonQ[poly, pt1]
```

```
Out[83]= True
```

```
In[84]:= pointInPolygonQ[poly, pt2]
```

```
Out[84]= False
```

Nonconvex polygons The case of nonconvex polygons is a bit more complicated. First, a moment's thought should convince you that the algorithm we used for convex polygons will fail for nonconvex polygons. The point inside the polygon in Figure 10.7 will give `False` for at least one of the edges of the polygon.

This more general scenario can be solved using a ray crossing algorithm. The idea is to draw a horizontal ray starting at the point in question, extending out to infinity (the restriction of the ray being horizontal can be relaxed with suitable adjustments to the algorithm). Then the point is in or out of the polygon if the number of crossings of edges is odd or even, respectively (try it with the two points and polygon in Figure 10.7).

FIGURE 10.7. *Point-in-polygon problem, nonconvex case.*

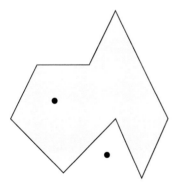

Below, we give the vertices of the polygon in Figure 10.7 together with the coordinates for the two points; `ptOut` is outside and `ptIn` is inside.

```
In[85]:= poly = {{-0.5, 0}, {0.5, -1}, {1.5, 0},
            {2., -1.1}, {2.5, 0}, {1.5, 2}, {1., 1}, {0., 1}};
        ptOut = {4 / 3, -2 / 3}; ptIn = {1 / 3, 1 / 3};
```

```
In[87]:= Show[{
           Graphics@{PointSize[.02], Point[{ptOut, ptIn}]},
           PathPlot[poly]
         }, Axes → Automatic]
```

Out[87]=

As before, here are the edges of the polygon.

```
In[88]:= edges = Partition[poly, 2, 1, 1]
```

```
Out[88]= {{{-0.5, 0}, {0.5, -1}}, {{0.5, -1}, {1.5, 0}},
         {{1.5, 0}, {2., -1.1}}, {{2., -1.1}, {2.5, 0}},
         {{2.5, 0}, {1.5, 2}}, {{1.5, 2}, {1., 1}},
         {{1., 1}, {0., 1}}, {{0., 1}, {-0.5, 0}}}
```

First, we do a little preprocessing. We can omit horizontal edges from consideration as the imaginary horizontal ray will never cross them.

```
In[89]:= edges2 = DeleteCases[edges, {{x1_, y1_}, {x2_, y2_}} /; y1 == y2]
```

```
Out[89]= {{{-0.5, 0}, {0.5, -1}}, {{0.5, -1}, {1.5, 0}},
         {{1.5, 0}, {2., -1.1}}, {{2., -1.1}, {2.5, 0}},
         {{2.5, 0}, {1.5, 2}}, {{1.5, 2}, {1., 1}}, {{0., 1}, {-0.5, 0}}}
```

We also delete edges where the edge is entirely above or entirely below the y-coordinate of the test point $\{x, y\}$.

```
In[90]:= {x, y} = ptIn;
         edges3 = DeleteCases[edges2, {{x1_, y1_}, {x2_, y2_}} /;
           (Min[y1, y2] ≥ y || Max[y1, y2] < y)]
```

```
Out[91]= {{{2.5, 0}, {1.5, 2}}, {{0., 1}, {-0.5, 0}}}
```

Next we orient these two line segments so that they extend from smallest y-coordinate to largest.

```
In[92]:= edges4 = Map[Reverse@SortBy[#, Last] &, edges3]
```

```
Out[92]= {{{1.5, 2}, {2.5, 0}}, {{0., 1}, {-0.5, 0}}}
```

Computing the area of the two triangles formed by these pairs of lines and the target point, we
see that one area is positive and one area is negative.

```
In[93]:= TriangleArea[Join[#, {{x, y}}]] & /@ edges4
Out[93]= {-2., 0.333333}
```

That is, there are an odd number of positive triangle areas and so we conclude that the target
point is inside the polygon.

```
In[94]:= Count[%, _?Positive]
Out[94]= 1
```

```
In[95]:= OddQ[Count[
          TriangleArea[Join[#, {{x, y}}]] & /@ edges4, _?Positive]]
Out[95]= True
```

Here is a function that puts all these pieces together.

```
In[96]:= PointInPolygonQ[poly : {{_, _} ..}, pt : {x_, y_}] :=
          Module[{edges, e2, e3, e4},
           edges = Partition[poly, 2, 1, 1];
           e2 = DeleteCases[edges, {{x1_, y1_}, {x2_, y2_}} /; y1 == y2];
           e3 = DeleteCases[e2, {{x1_, y1_}, {x2_, y2_}} /;
               (Min[y1, y2] ≥ y || Max[y1, y2] < y)];
           e4 = Map[Reverse@SortBy[#, Last] &, e3]; OddQ[
            Count[TriangleArea[Join[#, {pt}]] & /@ e4, _?Positive]]]
```

```
In[97]:= Map[PointInPolygonQ[poly, #] &, {ptIn, ptOut}]
Out[97]= {True, False}
```

Let us try this function out with some other examples. First, a set of five points and our concave polygon.

```
In[98]:= pts = Table[{i, 0}, {i, -1, 3}];
          Graphics[{PointSize[Medium], Point[pts], LightYellow,
            Opacity[.6], EdgeForm[Black], Polygon[poly]}, Axes → True]
```

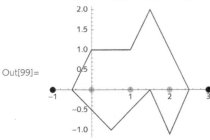

Out[99]=

The first and last points are outside and the other points are inside the polygon.

In[100]:= **Map[PointInPolygonQ[poly, #] &, pts]**

Out[100]= {False, True, True, True, False}

And here is a much larger example, one that will begin to give us a sense of the efficiency of this algorithm.

In[101]:= **pts = RandomReal[{-1, 3}, {7500, 2}];**

In[102]:= **Timing[Map[PointInPolygonQ[poly, #] &, pts];]**

Out[102]= {1.16082, Null}

Although this is really quite fast at determining if 7500 points are inside the given polygon, the computation can be sped up significantly by running in parallel. This is addressed in Section 12.3.

Finally, here is a graphic coloring those points inside the polygon black and those outside light gray. The key here is to use GatherBy on the set of points, pts. The second argument to GatherBy is the specification for how points should be gathered. In this case, all those points that return True for PointInPolygonQ[poly, #] & will be in one list returned by GatherBy and those that fail this test will be in another list. We are naming these two lists in and out for points that are inside and outside the polygon, respectively.

In[103]:= **Graphics[{**
         {PointSize[Tiny], GatherBy[pts,
            PointInPolygonQ[poly, #] &] /. {in_List, out_List} :>
            {{Black, Point@in}, {LightGray, Point@out}}},
         Thick, Line[poly /. {a_, b__} :> {a, b, a}],
         PointSize[Medium], Point[poly]
         }]

Out[103]=

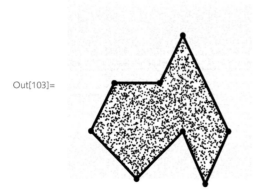

There is one wrinkle in the use of GatherBy to separate all those points that pass the PointInPolygonQ test from those that do not. If the first point in the list of points checked passes the test, then the first group of points will be gathered by all having passed the test. But if the first point fails the test, then all such failures will be grouped first and this will incorrectly be identified as the `in` list and colored and styled accordingly. Exercise 11 asks you to correct this problem.

Visualizing standard deviations

In Exercise 8 of Section 10.1, we created a visualization of standard deviation for a parametric distribution – in that case, a normal distribution. Suppose instead that you have some data and you are interested in seeing which data points live within one or two standard deviations of the mean. A box-and-whisker chart gives you an overview of the spread of the data, including the mean, confidence intervals, the data within various quantiles, and some sense of the outliers, if any. Figure 10.8 shows a screenshot of a `BoxWhiskerChart` for some normally distributed data.

In this section we will create a different visualization showing a scatter plot of some two-dimensional data together with dashed lines bounding the area that is within one (or two) standard deviations of the mean. The key observation is that we want to separate the data into those points that are within the range of one or two standard deviations from the mean and format them accordingly. Points outside the desired range will be formatted differently. In the previous example, `PointInPolygonQ`, we used `GatherBy` to group the two sets of points. We will use a different approach here; using `Pick`, we operate on the indices of the points rather than the coordinates directly.

FIGURE 10.8. *Box-and-whisker chart with descriptive statistics in tooltip.*

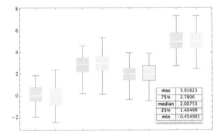

Let us start with a small dataset as we prototype.

```
In[104]:= data = RandomVariate[NormalDistribution[0, 1], {12}]
```

```
Out[104]= {0.100989, -0.368311, 0.204546, -1.75602, 0.236539, 0.61813,
          -0.301258, 0.250047, 0.015467, -0.917397, 0.558073, 1.3482}
```

We will use `Pick` to select the indices of those data points that are within one standard deviation of the mean. First, here is a list of all indices, from 1 through the length of the data.

```
In[105]:= lenrange = Range[Length[data]]
```

```
Out[105]= {1, 2, 3, 4, 5, 6, 7, 8, 9, 10, 11, 12}
```

Here are those indices for which the corresponding data point is within one ($n = 1$) standard deviation of the mean. Note that several are outside this threshold.

```
In[106]:= n = 1;
         μ = Mean[data];
         σ = StandardDeviation[data];
         in = Pick[lenrange, Thread[Abs[(data - μ) / σ] < n]]
```

```
Out[109]= {3, 4, 7, 8, 9, 10, 11, 12}
```

Using `Complement`, we have the indices of those points that are outside the threshold.

```
In[110]:= out = Complement[lenrange, in]
```

```
Out[110]= {1, 2, 5, 6}
```

We will use these two sets of indices to create points of the form $\{index,\ value\}$.

```
In[111]:= in = Transpose[{in, data[[in]]}]
```

```
Out[111]= {{3, -0.657262}, {4, -0.767936},
          {7, -0.317394}, {8, 0.482023}, {9, -0.415365},
          {10, -0.0952418}, {11, 0.436777}, {12, 0.259615}}
```

```
In[112]:= out = Transpose[{out, data[[out]]}]
```

```
Out[112]= {{1, 1.14664}, {2, -0.933961}, {5, -1.03752}, {6, 1.16042}}
```

Now we use `ListPlot` to visualize, setting different plot styles for the two sets of data `in` and `out`. We also add horizontal lines at one standard deviation from the mean.

```
In[113]:= len = Length[data];
         ListPlot[{in, out}, PlotStyle → {Blue, Pink}, PlotRange → All,
           Epilog → {Dashed, Line[{{0, μ + n σ}, {len, μ + n σ}}],
             Line[{{0, μ - n σ}, {len, μ - n σ}}]}]
```

This puts all the pieces together, checking that the data are one-dimensional vectors, inheriting options from `ListPlot`, doing some checking to make sure that the partitions of the data are both nonempty and returning `Missing[]` if they are.

```
In[115]:= StandardDeviationPlot[data_?VectorQ,
        n_ : 1, opts : OptionsPattern[ListPlot]] :=
     Module[{in, out, len = Length[data], lenrange,
       μ = Mean[data], σ = StandardDeviation[data]},
      lenrange = Range[Length[data]];
      in = Pick[lenrange, Thread[Abs[(data - μ) / σ] < n]];
      out = Complement[lenrange, in];
      in = If[Length[in] === 0,
        {Missing[]}, Transpose[{in, data[[in]]}]];
      out = If[Length[out] === 0, {Missing[]},
        Transpose[{out, data[[out]]}]];
      ListPlot[{in, out},
       opts,
       PlotStyle → {Blue, Pink},
       PlotRange → All,
       Epilog → {Dashed,
         Line[{{0, μ + n σ}, {len, μ + n σ}}],
         Line[{{0, μ - n σ}, {len, μ - n σ}}]}]]
```

Using a larger dataset with mean 5 and standard deviation 8, here is a plot highlighting all those points within two standard deviations of the mean.

```
In[116]:= data = RandomVariate[NormalDistribution[5, 8], {600}];
     StandardDeviationPlot[data, 2]
```

Out[117]=

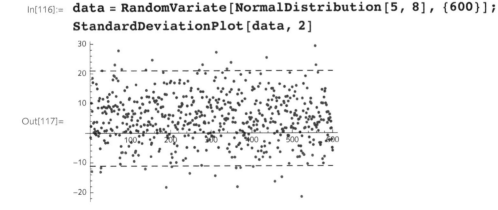

Root plotting

In this section we will use our knowledge of built-in graphics functions together with various programming techniques from previous chapters to write a program that plots a function together with all its roots in a given interval. Finding all the roots of a real-valued function on a given interval is made straightforward by NSolve, which can be given bounded regions within which roots are to be found. A second approach uses the meshing algorithms in Plot to extract and plot those roots on the horizontal axis.

Let us use a sinc function to prototype our work, as it has numerous roots in the interval below.

In[118]:= **Plot[Sinc[x], {x, -10, 10}]**

Out[118]=

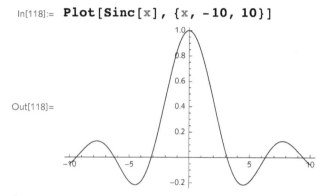

The roots are easily computed using NSolve with the domain specification $-10 < z < 10$ restricting the solutions to that interval.

In[119]:= **soln = NSolve[Sinc[z] == 0 && -10 < z < 10, z]**

Out[119]= $\{\{z \rightarrow -9.42478\}, \{z \rightarrow -6.28319\}, \{z \rightarrow -3.14159\},$
$\{z \rightarrow 3.14159\}, \{z \rightarrow 6.28319\}, \{z \rightarrow 9.42478\}\}$

To display these roots as points overlaid on the plot of the original function, we need to create point objects for each root and then use them in the graphic.

In[120]:= **pts = Map[Point[{#, 0}] &, z /. soln]**

Out[120]= $\{\text{Point}[\{-9.42478, 0\}], \text{Point}[\{-6.28319, 0\}],$
$\text{Point}[\{-3.14159, 0\}], \text{Point}[\{3.14159, 0\}],$
$\text{Point}[\{6.28319, 0\}], \text{Point}[\{9.42478, 0\}]\}$

In[121]:= `Plot[Sinc[z], {z, -10, 10}, Epilog → {`
`Red, PointSize[Medium], pts}]`

Out[121]=

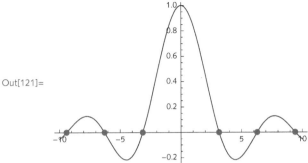

Here then is our first implementation, combining the above steps. Note that we have created a local variable f, which is a pure function that is then used throughout the body of `RootPlot`. One other change uses multi-points to give a slightly more efficient graphics structure (see Section 10.3).

In[122]:= `RootPlot[fun_, {var_, varmin_, varmax_}] :=`
`Module[{f = Function[z, fun]},`
`Plot[f[var], {var, varmin, varmax}, Epilog → {`
`Red, PointSize[Medium], Point@Map[{#, 0} &, var /.`
`NSolve[f[var] == 0 && varmin < var < varmax, var]]}]]`

In[123]:= `RootPlot[Sinc[z], {z, -10, 10}]`

Out[123]=

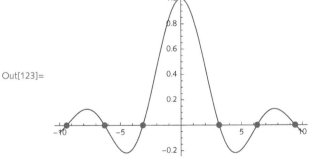

Let us try some more ambitious computations.

In[124]:= **RootPlot**$\left[\texttt{z Sin}\left[\texttt{z + }\sqrt{\texttt{2}}\texttt{ Sin[z]}\right]\texttt{, \{z, -5, 10\}}\right]$

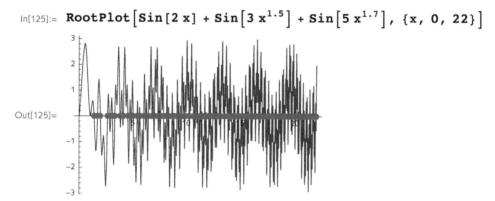

Out[124]=

In[125]:= **RootPlot**$\left[\texttt{Sin[2 x] + Sin}\left[\texttt{3 x}^{1.5}\right]\texttt{ + Sin}\left[\texttt{5 x}^{1.7}\right]\texttt{, \{x, 0, 22\}}\right]$

Out[125]=

For functions with many roots on the given interval, the large points might obscure other features of the graphic as seen in the plot above. Also, in the first example above, the default plotting range missed several key features of the function. It would be ideal if we could modify these plots as needed. Before we add options to RootPlot, note that there are two built-in functions here that can take options, Plot and NSolve. And we could also add some directives and options to the graphics primitives that are part of the Epilog.

The key to passing the options to the appropriate function inside RootPlot is to use FilterRules. So first we set up RootPlot to inherit the options of both NSolve and Plot.

In[126]:= **ClearAll[RootPlot]**

In[127]:= **Options[RootPlot] = Join[Options[NSolve], Options[Plot]];**
RandomSample[Options[RootPlot], 8]

Out[128]= {MaxRecursion → Automatic, ContentSelectable → Automatic,
          Filling → None, Evaluated → Automatic,
          PlotRangePadding → Automatic, ImageSizeRaw → Automatic,
          MeshShading → None, Ticks → Automatic}

Next we set up the argument structure to accept options by putting `OptionsPattern[]` immediately following the required arguments and giving the set of options a name, `opts`. Note the need to put the optional argument placeholder `opts` before any options that are hard-coded, in this case, `Epilog`. That way you can override any hard-coded option as *Mathematica* only pays attention to the first of multiple instances of an option.

The syntax for extracting the options for a particular function, say `Plot`, is given below; but remember that `Plot` has the `HoldAll` attribute and so you need to wrap `FilterRules` in `Evaluate` to force the evaluation here.

This puts all the pieces together.

```
In[129]:= RootPlot[fun_, {var_, varmin_, varmax_},
            opts : OptionsPattern[]] := Module[{f = Function[z, fun]},
           Plot[f[var], {var, varmin, varmax},
            Evaluate[FilterRules[{opts}, Options[Plot]]],
            Epilog → {
              Red, PointSize[Medium], Point@Map[{#, 0} &,
                var /. NSolve[f[var] == 0 && varmin < var < varmax,
                  var, FilterRules[{opts}, Options[NSolve]]]]
             }
           ]
          ]
```

```
In[130]:= RootPlot[z Sin[z + √2 Sin[z]], {z, -4, 10}, PlotRange → All]
```

In[131]:= **RootPlot$\left[\text{Sin}[2\ x]\ +\ \text{Sin}\left[3\ x^{3/2}\right]\ +\ \text{Sin}\left[5\ x^{3/2}\right]\right]$, {x, 0, 18},**
WorkingPrecision $\rightarrow$ 24, GridLines $\rightarrow$ Automatic$\Big]$

Out[131]=

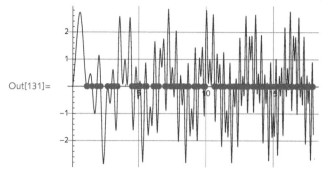

There is certainly much more we could do to improve this function, such as providing options to modify the style of the points. But instead, we will turn to a different approach that takes advantage of much of the built-in machinery in the plotting functions. Our second implementation will make use of Mesh and MeshFunctions as these options do a lot of computational work that we can harness for our purposes here. As a side note, it will also help to avoid problems with certain analytic functions:

In[132]:= **TimeConstrained[**
RootPlot[RiemannSiegelZ[z], {z, 1000, 1100}],
15]

Out[132]= **$Aborted**

The key observation is: setting Mesh to {{0.0}} creates only mesh points at height o.o, that is, on the horizontal axis. MeshFunctions should have a value that places the mesh points on the curve.

In[133]:= **Plot[Sinc[z], {z, -10, 10}, Mesh $\rightarrow$ {{0.0}},**
MeshFunctions $\rightarrow$ {Sinc[x] /. x $\rightarrow$ # &},
MeshStyle $\rightarrow$ {Red, PointSize[Medium]}]

Out[133]=

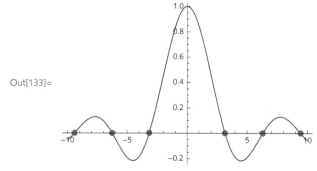

Here then is our second implementation of `RootPlot`. First we set the `RootPlot` options to inherit all those from `Plot`.

In[134]:= **ClearAll[RootPlot]**

In[135]:= **Options[RootPlot] = Options[Plot];**

Using `OptionsPattern` after the required arguments says that the argument structure of `RootPlot` may include options following the required arguments. The set of options is given a name, `opts`, and used inside of `Plot` where we want any optional arguments to be. As noted previously, it is important to put `opts` before any explicitly given options as *Mathematica* will only honor the first occurrence of an option if it occurs more than once.

In[136]:= **RootPlot[*fun_*, {*var_*, *varmin_*, *varmax_*},**
        ***opts* : OptionsPattern[]] := Module[{f = *fun*},**
        Plot[f, {*var*, *varmin*, *varmax*},
         ***opts*,**
         Mesh → {{0}}, MeshFunctions → {f /. *var* → # &},
         MeshStyle → {Red, PointSize[Medium]}]]

Let us now exercise some of the options. Note in this example that the adaptive routines built into the `Plot` function are quite efficient, especially compared with the difficulty that `NSolve` had with this particular function.

In[137]:= **RootPlot[RiemannSiegelZ[z], {z, 1000, 1100},**
        PlotStyle → Gray,
        MeshStyle → {Pink, PointSize[.015]}] // Timing

Out[137]=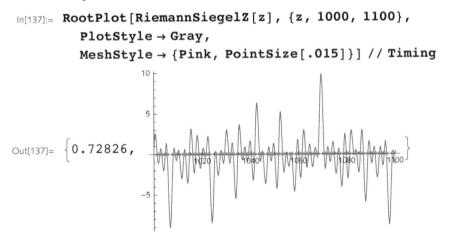

In[138]:= **RootPlot$\left[z\ Sin\left[z + \sqrt{2}\ Sin[z]\right]\right]$, {z, -4, 20},**
    PlotRange → All,
    MeshStyle → Directive[Opacity[0.5], PointSize[Medium]],
    GridLines → Automatic$\Big]$

Out[138]=

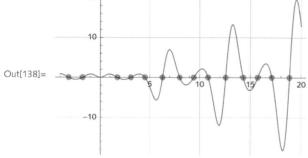

Exercise 9 asks you to use Mesh in a manner similar to how we used it here in RootPlot but to find and display curves of intersection for two surfaces in 3-space.

Trend plots

Trend plots provide a visual representation of trends in data. They are used throughout the financial world to give a quick visual indication of the magnitude of growth or loss over a specified time period. For example, a simple ten-day moving average shows a smoothed trend line.

In[139]:= **TradingChart[{"AAPL", DatePlus[-180]},**
    {FinancialIndicator["SimpleMovingAverage", 10]}]

Out[139]=

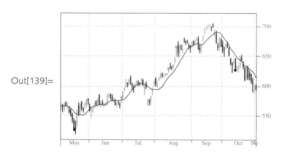

Or you could use a linear regression model for the trend lines where the standard error of the fit is allowed to vary ± 5%. In this example the trend line ranges over the past ten time periods (days).

In[140]:= **TradingChart[{"AAPL", DatePlus[-180]},**
            {FinancialIndicator["LinearRegressionTrendlines", 10]}]

Out[140]=
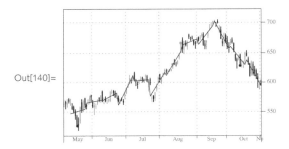

In this section we will develop a different visualization that overlays trend lines on a plot of time-series data (Figure 10.9). Our trend lines will show user-specified growth rates $\{r_1, r_2, ..., r_n\}$ measured from some starting value and projecting out for the time period covered by the data.

FIGURE 10.9. *Trend plot of financial data over 180-day time period.*

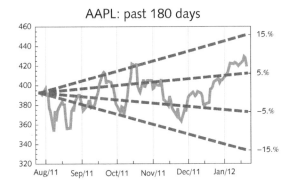

In addition to giving the time-series data and the rates to be displayed, the user should have a mechanism to supply options to adjust the plot range and modify style and formatting information. We will use **DateListPlot** as our base function and modify it accordingly for our needs in this visualization.

Let us start with some data we can use to start prototyping.

In[141]:= **data = FinancialData["SP500",**
            {"August 30 2011", "December 30 2011"}];

In[142]:= **Length[data]**

Out[142]= 86

In[143]:= **DateListPlot[data]**

Out[143]=

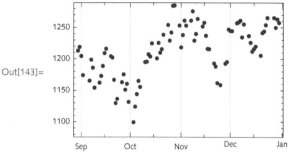

To construct the trend lines, we will essentially make lines of a given slope/growth rate starting at the first point in the dataset.

In[144]:= **pt1 = First[data]**

Out[144]= **{{2011, 8, 30}, 1212.92}**

The following rule constructs a line starting at this point with a growth rate of 5%. Note that we are attaching this new value to the date given by the last point in our dataset. This way we are keeping our data in a form that can continue to be used by **DateListPlot** which expects data of the form {*date*, *value*}.

In[145]:= **pt2 = Last[data] /.**
        {date_List, val_?NumberQ} :> {date, 1.05 pt1[[2]]}

Out[145]= **{{2011, 12, 30}, 1273.57}**

Given a set of time-series data and a growth rate *r*, here is a utility function to create a line starting at the first point in the data and growing at a rate *r*.

In[146]:= **tline[data_, r_] := {Dashed, Gray,**
        Line[{First[data], Last[data] /. {date_List, val_?NumberQ} :>
            {date, (1 + r) data[[1, 2]]}}]}

The trend lines at growth rates of ±5%, ±10% are given as part of **Epilog** to **DateListPlot**. In this example, we had to tinker manually with the plot range values in order for the trend lines and data all to be included in the plot properly. We will try to automate some of that later.

```
In[147]:= DateListPlot[data, Joined → True,
            Epilog :→ {
              tline[data, 0.05], tline[data, 0.10],
              tline[data, -0.05], tline[data, -0.10]
            }, PlotRange → {1080, 1340}]
```

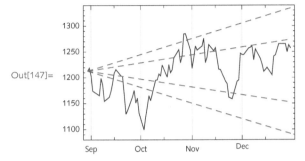

Out[147]=

We can simplify the `tline` part of this code by noting that each call to `tline` uses `data` and a different rate. This is a good candidate for `Map`.

```
In[148]:= DateListPlot[data, Joined → True,
            Epilog :→ Map[tline[data, #] &, {-0.05, -0.10, 0.05, 0.10}],
            PlotRange → {1080, 1340}]
```

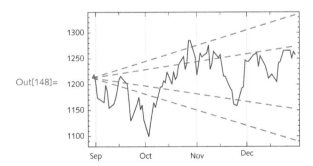

Out[148]=

We now have all the pieces to start putting together our function, `TrendPlot`. It will inherit the options from `DateListPlot` and take two required arguments: the time-series data and a list of growth rates. We have added the `FrameTicks` option here with some values that will suppress ticks on the top and right of the frame. Our plan is to add a custom tick specification to the right-hand side of the frame giving the rates of the trend lines.

```
In[149]:= Options[TrendPlot] = Options[DateListPlot];
```

```
In[150]:= TrendPlot[data_, rates_List, opts : OptionsPattern[]] :=
            Module[{tline},
              tline[r_] := {Dashed, Gray,
                 Line[{First[data], Last[data] /.
                    {d_List, val_?NumberQ} :> {d, (1 + r) data[[1, 2]]}}]};
              DateListPlot[data, Joined → True,
                FrameTicks → {{Automatic, None}, {Automatic, None}},
                Epilog :> Map[tline, rates], opts]]
```

```
In[151]:= TrendPlot[data, {0.05, 0.10, -0.05, -0.10},
            PlotRange → {1080, 1340}]
```

Out[151]=

The tick specification that we will use for the right-hand side of the plot will display the rates next to their corresponding trend line. The custom tick specification is of the form {*value*, *label*}, where *value* gives the location on the vertical axis and *label* is a string that will display the rate. The MapThread code below is a bit cryptic, but essentially what it is doing is taking a rate (a number between −1 and 1) and multiplying by that initial value to get the location. The second argument is slotted into a string using StringForm.

```
In[152]:= rates = {0.05, 0.10, -0.05, -0.10};
```

```
In[153]:= init = data[[1, 2]]
```

Out[153]= 1212.92

```
In[154]:= MapThread[{(1 + #1) init, StringForm[" `1`%", #2]} &,
            {rates, 100 rates}]
```

Out[154]= {{1273.57,   5.`%}, {1334.21,   10.`%},
           {1152.27, -5.%}, {1091.63, -10.%}}

Putting these pieces together, we have this updated version of TrendPlot.

```
In[155]:= ClearAll[TrendPlot];
```

```
In[156]:= Options[TrendPlot] = Options[DateListPlot];
```

```
In[157]:= TrendPlot[data_, rates_List, opts : OptionsPattern[]] :=
          Module[{tLine, rtTicks, init = data[[1, 2]]},

            tLine[r_] := {Dashed, Gray,
              Line[{First[data], Last[data] /.
                {d_List, val_ ?NumberQ} :> {d, (1 + r) init}}]};

            rtTicks = MapThread[{(1 + #) init, StringForm[" `1`%", #2]} &,
              {rates, 100 rates}];

            DateListPlot[data, Joined → True,
              Epilog :> Map[tLine, rates], opts,
              FrameTicks → {{Automatic, rtTicks}, {Automatic, None}}]
          ]
```

```
In[158]:= TrendPlot[data, rates, PlotRange → {1080, 1340}]
```

Finally, let us add several more features: the option `TrendlineStyle` gives the user the chance to modify the style of the trend lines themselves, somewhat similar to `PlotStyle` for many visualization functions. Also we add usage messages for the function `TrendPlot` as well as its new option `TrendlineStyle`.

```
In[159]:= ClearAll[TrendPlot]
          TrendPlot::usage =
            "TrendPlot[data,{r1,r2,…}] plots data with
              trend lines showing growth rates over time.";
```

```
In[161]:= TrendlineStyle::usage =
            "TrendlineStyle is an option for TrendPlot that
              specifies the style of the trend lines.";
```

```
In[162]:= Options[TrendPlot] =
            Join[{TrendlineStyle → Automatic}, Options[DateListPlot]];
```

```
In[163]:= TrendPlot[data_, rates_List,
            opts : OptionsPattern[]] := Module[
           {min, max, tlStyle, tLine, rtTicks, init = data[[1, 2]]},

           {min, max} = {Min[data[[All, 2]]], Max[data[[All, 2]]]};

           tlStyle = If[OptionValue[TrendlineStyle] === Automatic,
             {Dashed, Gray}, OptionValue[TrendlineStyle]];

           tLine[r_] := Flatten@{tlStyle,
             Line[{First[data], Last[data] /.
               {d_List, val_?NumberQ} :> {d, (1 + r) init}}]};

           rtTicks = MapThread[{(1 + #) init, StringForm[" `1`%", #2]} &,
             {rates, 100 rates}];

           DateListPlot[data, Joined -> True,
            Epilog :> Map[tLine, rates],
            FilterRules[{opts}, Options[DateListPlot]],
            PlotRange -> {0.97 min, 1.04 max},
            FrameTicks -> {{Automatic, rtTicks}, {Automatic, None}}]]
```

Let us try out the code together with various options, some of which are options to
DateListPlot and one option specific to TrendPlot.

```
In[164]:= TrendPlot[data, rates,
            PlotStyle -> {Thick, Blue},
            TrendlineStyle -> {Thick, Dashed, Lighter@Gray}]
```

The above code contains a very primitive attempt at choosing a sensible plot range. The
exercises ask you to make this a bit more rigorous by incorporating the maximum and minimum
values of the data together with the user-specified rates to find a better plot range.

Brownian music

Imagine playing an audio sample at different speeds. Normally you would expect the character of the resulting sound to be quite different than the original. Speeding up a recording of your voice makes it sound cartoon-like, and if sped up enough, unintelligible. Slowing down a recording of the first few bars of Gershwin's *Rhapsody in Blue* would make the clarinet solo sound like a rumble.

There are some sounds though that sound roughly the same when played at different speeds. Benoît Mandelbrot described these sounds as "scaling noises" (Mandelbrot 1982). White noise is probably the most common example of a scaling noise. If you tuned a radio in between stations, recorded the noise, and then played the recording at different speeds, you would hear roughly the same sound, although you would have to adjust the volume to get this effect.

Mandelbrot additionally characterized white noise as having zero *autocorrelation*. This means that the fluctuations in such a sound at any moment are completely unrelated to any previous fluctuations. In this section we will implement an algorithm for composing tunes with zero autocorrelation. We will then see how to generate tunes that have varying degrees of correlation among the notes.

A simple "melody" with no correlation can be generated by randomly selecting notes from a scale. First we generate the frequencies of the 12 semitones from a C major scale. This is just a chromatic scale beginning with middle C.

```
In[165]:= cmajor = Table[SoundNote[i], {i, 0, 11}]

Out[165]= {SoundNote[0], SoundNote[1], SoundNote[2], SoundNote[3],
          SoundNote[4], SoundNote[5], SoundNote[6], SoundNote[7],
          SoundNote[8], SoundNote[9], SoundNote[10], SoundNote[11]}
```

This plays the entire scale.

```
In[166]:= Sound[cmajor]
```

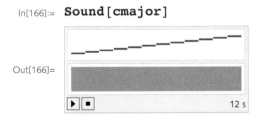

```
Out[166]=
```

Here is a list of twenty notes randomly selected from the C major scale.

```
In[167]:= Sound[RandomChoice[cmajor, 20]]
```

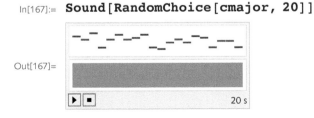

```
Out[167]=
```

Going a little further, we can add some rests and randomize the durations of each note. The symbol None is interpreted by Sound as a rest.

```
In[168]:= notes = Join[{None}, Range[0, 11]]
Out[168]= {None, 0, 1, 2, 3, 4, 5, 6, 7, 8, 9, 10, 11}
```

```
In[169]:= durations = Range[1 / 8, 1, 1 / 8]
```
$$Out[169]= \left\{\frac{1}{8}, \frac{1}{4}, \frac{3}{8}, \frac{1}{2}, \frac{5}{8}, \frac{3}{4}, \frac{7}{8}, 1\right\}$$

```
In[170]:= MapThread[SoundNote[#1, #2] &,
            {RandomChoice[notes, 8], RandomChoice[durations, 8]}]
```
$$Out[170]= \left\{\text{SoundNote}\left[\text{None}, \frac{7}{8}\right], \text{SoundNote}\left[11, \frac{1}{4}\right],\right.$$
$$\text{SoundNote}\left[11, \frac{3}{4}\right], \text{SoundNote}\left[2, \frac{1}{4}\right], \text{SoundNote}\left[11, \frac{5}{8}\right],$$
$$\left.\text{SoundNote}\left[3, \frac{1}{8}\right], \text{SoundNote}\left[1, \frac{1}{4}\right], \text{SoundNote}[10, 1]\right\}$$

```
In[171]:= Sound[%]
```

Out[171]=

4.13 s

Let us turn this into a reusable function that takes the number of notes and the instrument as arguments.

```
In[172]:= RandomCompose[n_Integer, instrument_: "Piano"] :=
            With[{notes = Join[{None}, Range[0, 11]],
              durations = Range[1 / 8, 1, 1 / 8]},
             Sound[{instrument,
               MapThread[SoundNote[#1, #2] &,
                {RandomChoice[notes, n], RandomChoice[durations, n]}]}]]
```

In[173]:= **RandomCompose[20, "Vibraphone"]**

Out[173]=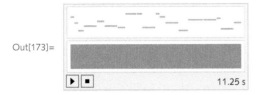

11.25 s

A listener would be hard pressed to find a pattern or any autocorrelation in this "tune" and the music is quite uninteresting as a result. Melodies generated using this scaling are referred to as $1/f^0$, where the 0 loosely refers to the level of correlation.

We leave as an exercise the writing of more sophisticated $1/f^0$ melodies, where the likelihood of a note being chosen obeys a certain probability distribution.

We now move in the other direction and generate melodies that are overly correlated. The randomness will be applied to the distance between notes, essentially performing a "random walk" through the C major scale. Music generated in such a way is called *Brownian* because it behaves much like the movement of particles suspended in liquid – Brownian motion.

Here is our random walk function, essentially borrowed from Section 13.1. We will limit the "distance" any step can take to the range -4 to 4.

In[174]:= **Accumulate[RandomChoice[Range[-4, 4], 12]]**

Out[174]= {0, 3, 1, -1, -1, -3, -2, 1, 4, 2, 5, 1}

This puts all the pieces together, plus one additional piece to create random durations.

In[175]:= **BrownianCompose[*steps_Integer*, *instr_* : "Vibraphone"] :=**
    Module[{walk, durs},
      walk[*n_*] := Accumulate[RandomChoice[Range[-4, 4], *n*]];
      durs = RandomChoice[Range[1/16, 1, 1/16], {*steps*}];
      Sound@
        MapThread[SoundNote[*#1*, *#2*, *instr*] &, {walk[*steps*], durs}]]

In[176]:= **BrownianCompose[18, "Marimba"]**

Out[176]=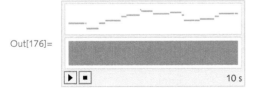

10 s

This melody has a different character from the $1/f^0$ melody produced above. In fact, it is quite overcorrelated and it is often referred to as $1/f^2$ music as a result of a computed spectral density. Although different in character from $1/f^0$ music, it is just as monotonous. The melody meanders up and down the scale aimlessly without any central theme. The exercises contain a discussion of $1/f$ music (or noise), that is, music that is moderately correlated. $1/f$ noise is quite widespread in nature and is intimately tied to areas of science that study fractal behavior; see Casti (1992) or Mandelbrot (1982).

Exercises

1. Create a function `ComplexListPlot` that plots a list of complex numbers in the complex plane using `ListPlot`. Set initial options so that the `PlotStyle` is red, the `PointSize` is a little larger than the default, and the horizontal and vertical axes are labeled "Re" and "Im," respectively. Set it up so that options to `ComplexListPlot` are inherited from `ListPlot`.

2. Create a function `ComplexRootPlot` that plots the complex solutions to a polynomial in the plane. Use your implementation of `ComplexListPlot` that you developed in the previous exercise.

3. Modify `PathPlot` so that it inherits options from `Graphics` as well as having its own option, `PathClosed`, that can take on values of `True` or `False` and closes the path accordingly by appending the first point to the end of the list of coordinate points.

4. Extend the code for `ListLinePlot3D` so that the rule for multiple datasets incorporates the options that were used for the single dataset rule in the text.

5. Although the program `SimpleClosedPath` works well, there are conditions under which it will occasionally fail. Experiment by repeatedly computing `SimpleClosedPath` for a set of ten points until you see the failure. Determine the conditions that must be imposed on the selection of the base point for the program to work consistently.

6. Modify `SimpleClosedPath` so that the point with the smallest x-coordinate of the list of data is chosen as the `base` point; repeat but with the largest y-coordinate.

7. Another way of finding a simple closed path is to start with any closed path and progressively make it simpler by finding intersections and changing the path to avoid them. Prove that this process ends, and that it ends with a closed path. Write a program to implement this procedure and then compare the paths given by your function with those of `SimpleClosedPath` given in the text.

8. Following on the framework of the `RootPlot` example in this section, create a function `ShowWalk [walk]` that takes the coordinates of a random walk and plots them in one, two, or three dimensions, depending upon the structure of the argument *walk*. For example:

```
In[1]:= << PwM`RandomWalks`
```

In[2]:= **ShowWalk[RandomWalk[500, Dimension → 1],**
Frame → True, GridLines → Automatic]

Out[2]=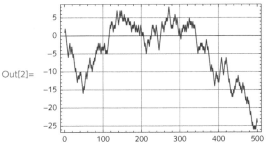

In[3]:= **ShowWalk[RandomWalk[500, Dimension → 2],**
Mesh → All, MeshStyle → Directive[Brown, PointSize[Small]]]

Out[3]=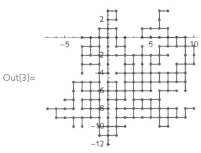

In[4]:= **ShowWalk[RandomWalk[2500, Dimension → 3],**
Background → LightGray, BoxRatios → {1, 1, 1}]

Out[4]=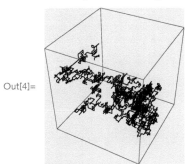

9. Use `Mesh` in a manner similar to its use in the `RootPlot` function to highlight the *intersection* of two surfaces, say $\sin(2x - \cos(y))$ and $\sin(x - \cos(2y))$. You may need to increase the value of `MaxRecursion` to get the sampling just right.

10. Rewrite `TrendPlot` to compute a more robust plot range, one based on the minimum and maximum values of the data together with the minimum and maximum user-specified rates.

11. Modify the graphics code at the end of the `PointInPolygonQ` example so that `GatherBy` always orders the two lists so that the list of points that pass occurs before the list of points that fail the test.

12. Write a function `pentatonic` that generates $1/f^2$ music choosing notes from a five-tone scale. A pentatonic scale can be played on a piano by beginning with C♯, and then playing only the black keys: C♯, E♭, F♯, A♭, C♯. The pentatonic scale is common to Chinese, Celtic, and Native American music.

13. Modify the routine for generating $1/f^0$ music so that frequencies are chosen according to a specified probability distribution. For example, you might use the following distribution that indicates a note and its probability of being chosen: C – 5%, C♯ – 5%, D – 5%, E♭ – 10%, E – 10%, F – 10%, F♯ – 10%, G – 10%, A♭ – 10%, A – 10%, B♭ – 5%, B – 5%, C – 5%.

14. Modify the routine for generating $1/f^0$ music so that the *durations* of the notes obey $1/f^0$ scaling.

15. If you read musical notation, take a musical composition such as one of Bach's *Brandenburg Concertos* and write down a list of the frequency intervals x between successive notes. Then find a function that interpolates the power spectrum of these frequency intervals and determine if this function is of the form $f(x) = c/x$ for some constant c. (*Hint*: To get the power spectrum, you will need to square the magnitude of the Fourier transform: take `Abs [Fourier [...] ]`^{2} of your data.) Compute the power spectra of different types of music using this procedure.

II

Dynamic expressions

Manipulating expressions · Control objects · Setter bars · Popup menus · Sliders · Locators · Input fields · Control · Viewers · Animating the hypocycloid · Visualizing logical operators · Structure of dynamic expressions · Dynamic · DynamicModule · Dynamic tips · Examples and applications · Creating interfaces for visualizing data · File openers · Dynamic random walks · Apollonius' circle

Up to this point, all the programming we have discussed has involved the creation of expressions that produce static output. Changing the value of a symbol does not change the value of a previously computed expression. But you can set things up so that *Mathematica* automatically updates symbols and expressions throughout your notebooks. This is done through a symbolic dynamic language. At its heart is the `Dynamic` construct that is used to update an arbitrary expression essentially in real time. This primitive dynamic building block, together with numerous control objects, provides a dynamic language that you can use to construct arbitrary dynamic expressions. And, like the graphics language, high-level functions are available that provide a clean and simple interface to many of these dynamic features.

We start by giving a brief overview of several top-level functions such as `Manipulate` and `Animate` that are designed to make it easy for you to create and control dynamic processes. Very little programming is needed to get started with these objects. But to go further, we will look at the underlying primitive objects, `Dynamic` and `DynamicModule`, to get a better understanding of this dynamic language and how you can use it to create your own interactive and dynamic interfaces.

11.1 Manipulating expressions

The `Table` function evaluates its argument over the range of values specified by its iterator list; it returns a *static* list of values.

In[1]:= **Table$\left[\texttt{i}^2, \{\texttt{i}, \texttt{1}, \texttt{100}, \texttt{2}\}\right]$**

Out[1]= {1, 9, 25, 49, 81, 121, 169, 225, 289, 361, 441, 529, 625, 729, 841, 961, 1089, 1225, 1369, 1521, 1681, 1849, 2025, 2209, 2401, 2601, 2809, 3025, 3249, 3481, 3721, 3969, 4225, 4489, 4761, 5041, 5329, 5625, 5929, 6241, 6561, 6889, 7225, 7569, 7921, 8281, 8649, 9025, 9409, 9801}

Manipulate, using the same syntax as Table, displays its output *dynamically*.

In[2]:= **Manipulate$\left[\texttt{i}^2, \{\texttt{i}, \texttt{1}, \texttt{100}, \texttt{2}\}\right]$**

Out[2]=

Manipulate automatically creates a user interface to display the output together with controls such as sliders to dynamically change the value of the parameter i. As you move the slider with your mouse, the value of i changes as does the value of the output expression i^2.

Animate creates a similar interface as Manipulate but provides less control over the details of the interaction. For example, this animates the function sinc ($b\,x$) as b varies from 1 to 5.

In[3]:= **Animate[**
        Plot[Sinc[b x], {x, -2 π, 2 π}, PlotRange $\rightarrow$ 1],
        {b, 1, 5}]

Out[3]=

In fact, Animate just creates a Manipulate object that displays a running animation when you evaluate the Animate expression. Both functions provide similar display, layout, and management of the output but Manipulate gives a bit more flexibility and control of several details. For our purposes here, we will mostly use Manipulate for the remainder of this chapter.

To begin expanding the kinds of things you can do with Manipulate, let us first manipulate multiple parameters. This is done by adding a new parameter list. In the following example, we have added a new parameter c that essentially gives a phase shift.

```
In[4]:=  Manipulate[
           Plot[Sinc[b x + c], {x, -2 π, 2 π}, PlotRange → 1],
           {b, 1, 5},
           {c, -2 π, 2 π}]
```

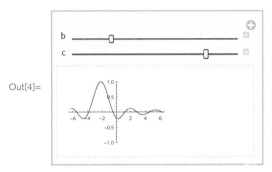

Out[4]=

By default, the initial value of the parameter is given by the first value following the parameter itself in the parameter list. So, for the parameter list {b, 1, 5}, the value 1 is the starting value for b; and for the second parameter list, −2 π is the starting value for c.

You can give different starting values by modifying the parameter list. For example, the following specifies that b should start at 3 while taking values between 1 and 5. Similarly, c is set to start at 0 below.

```
In[5]:=  Manipulate[
           Plot[Sinc[b x + c], {x, -2 π, 2 π}, PlotRange → 1],
           {{b, 3}, 1, 5},
           {{c, 0}, -2 π, 2 π}]
```

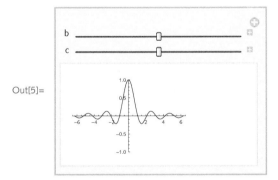

Out[5]=

One more useful variation is to label the control for each parameter using a different expression than the symbol itself. The syntax for this is: {{*param*, *init*, *label*}, *min*, *max*}, where *label* typically is a descriptive string, but can be any expression. For example, we have pasted an arbitrary graphic for the label for c below.

In[6]:= **Manipulate**[

   Plot[Sinc[b x + c], {x, -2 π, 2 π}, PlotRange → 1],
   {{b, 3, "Frequency"}, 1, 5},

   $\left\{\left\{c, 0, \blacksquare\right\}, -2\,\pi,\, 2\,\pi\right\}\right]$

Out[6]=

The basic idea behind the creation of these dynamic interfaces is to take some static output or visualization and to make it dynamic by adding a parameter that you can change using an interface element such as a slider. The next three sections introduce different control objects such as pulldown menus, locators, and viewers. Following that we combine several of the programming principles developed elsewhere in this book to create two dynamic interfaces: a dynamic Venn diagram to visualize expressions in propositional logic and also a reworking of the hypocycloid code developed in Section 10.1 to animate the sketching out of the curve.

Control objects

The objects created above with **Animate** and **Manipulate** all used sliders to control the parameters that were being manipulated. The slider is a convenient and easy-to-use control object that should be familiar to most computer users. But other controls are commonly used for various purposes: checkboxes to toggle values on and off, pulldown menus to select from a list of values, two-dimensional sliders to manipulate two parameters at once, input fields to enter expressions from the keyboard, and much more. In this section we will introduce some of these control objects. A complete listing and links to documentation can be found in the guide page on Control Objects (WMDC).

Setter bars and popup menus In the previous examples the parameters were controlled by a slider. Moving the slider changed the value of the parameter and any expression dependent upon that parameter inside the **Manipulate**. But sometimes you want to choose values for your parameter from a list of discrete values. A setter bar is a convenient control object for this. There are two ways of specifying the setter bar as the controller. One way is to use a different syntax for the parameter list. Specifically, something of the form $\{param, \{val_1, val_2, ..., val_n\}\}$ will cause `Manipulate` to automatically use a setter bar instead of a slider.

```
In[7]:= Manipulate[
          Plot[f[x], {x, 0, 2 π}],
          {f, {Sin, Cos, Tan}}]
```

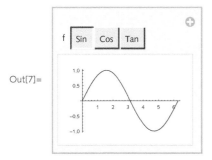

Out[7]=

Alternatively, you can explicitly set the `ControlType` inside the parameter list. Here we override the default specified by the syntax of the parameter list and explicitly specify that a `PopupMenu` should be used instead.

```
In[8]:= Manipulate[
          Plot[f[x], {x, 0, 2 π}],
          {f, {Sin, Cos, Tan}, ControlType → PopupMenu}]
```

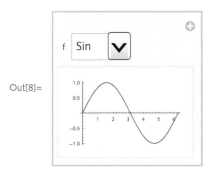

Out[8]=

Two-dimensional sliders When two different parameters need to be controlled simultaneously, a two-dimensional slider, `Slider2D`, can be used. The syntax for this control object is $\{param, \{x_1, y_1\}, \{x_2, y_2\}\}$. where $\{x_1, y_1\}$ are the smallest x and y values that the parameter can take on and $\{x_2, y_2\}$ are the maximum values.

In the following example, the parameter `center` is controlled by a two-dimensional slider because the parameter list is of the form that generates a `Slider2D` control object. The value of the `center` parameter is a list of two numbers that are passed dynamically to the first argument, the `center`, of the larger, red disk. As you move the slider, the vertical and horizontal values change as does the location of the red disk in the output.

```
In[9]:= Manipulate[
         Graphics[{Opacity[.5],
           {Red, Disk[center, 1.5]},
           {Blue, Disk[{1.5, 0}, 1]}
          }, PlotRange → {{-3, 3}, {-3, 2}}],
         {center, {-1, -1}, {2, 2}}]
```

Out[9]=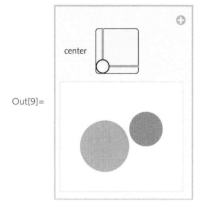

The following graphic contains four fixed control points, one dynamic point controlled by the slider, and a Bézier curve determined by these points. Moving the slider horizontally or vertically changes the *x*- or *y*-coordinate of the dynamic point `pt`. This parameter has a default starting value of {-3, -1}, while it can range over the values {-3, -3} to {2, 2}.

```
In[10]:= Manipulate[
          Graphics[{
            BezierCurve[Join[{pt}, controlPts]],
            Dashed, Line[Join[{pt}, controlPts]],
            Red, Point[controlPts], PointSize[Large],
            Blue, Point[pt]},
           PlotRange → 3.1, ImageSize → Small],
          {{pt, {-3, -1}}, {-3, -3}, {2, 2}},
          Initialization ⧴
          {controlPts = {{-2, 1}, {0, -1}, {1, 1}, {2, 0}}}]
```

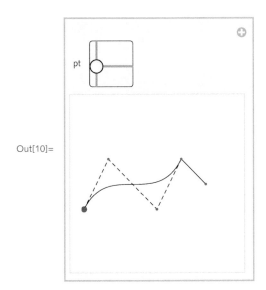

We have used an `Initialization` option to `Manipulate` in which the `controlPts` are defined. This option provides a way for you to include any needed definitions with the interface itself. This is particularly useful if you send your notebook to a colleague or student and you want the interface to be self-contained; in other words, the user can work with it without having to search for and evaluate any dependent definitions, such as `controlPts`, prior to using the interface.

Locators In the examples above involving 2D sliders, it would be much more convenient to be able to grab and manipulate objects in the graphic scene directly rather than using an intermediary like the `Slider2D` control object. This is what locators are for – they give you direct control over some object in the dynamic output.

For example, here is a static graphic: three points wrapped in `Polygon`, that is, a triangle.

```
In[11]:= Graphics[{EdgeForm[Black],
            LightGray, Polygon[{{0, 0}, {2, 0}, {1, 1}}]}]
```

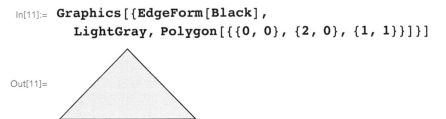

You could make one of the points dynamic with the `Slider2D` control but instead we will use the `Locator` control object to manipulate the point directly. In fact, one of the advantages of locators is that you can have as many of them as you wish. So let us turn all the vertices of this polygon into locators.

In[12]:= **Manipulate[**
 Graphics[{EdgeForm[Black], LightGray, Polygon[pts]}],
 {{pts, {{0, 0}, {2, 0}, {1, 1}}}, Locator}]

Out[12]=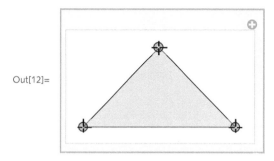

After moving some of the vertices around with your mouse, here is how the graphic might look.

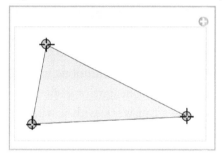

New locators can be added by clicking your mouse; this requires setting the option LocatorAutoCreate. Wherever you click, a new locator will be created in that position and added to the list of existing locators.

In[13]:= **Manipulate[**
 Graphics[{EdgeForm[Black], LightGray, Polygon[pts]}],
 {{pts, {{0, 0}, {2, 0}, {1, 1}}},
 Locator, LocatorAutoCreate → True}]

Out[13]=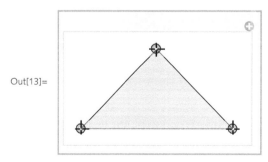

Returning to the example of the Bézier curve from the previous section, here we turn *all* the control points into locators.

In[14]:=
```
Manipulate[
    Graphics[{
        {Thick, BezierCurve[controlPts]},
        {Dashed, Line[controlPts], Point[controlPts]}
    }],
    {{controlPts, {{-2, 1}, {0, -1}, {1, 1}, {2, 0}}}, Locator}]
```

Out[14]=

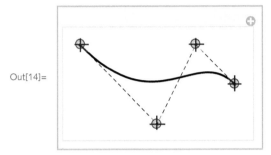

InputField In all the examples up to this point, the parameter was controlled with a mouse action: pulldown menus, sliders, locators, and so on. If instead, you need to interact with the dynamic object through the keyboard, then you need to use the `InputField` control object.

The following example uses three parameters: f, xmin, and xmax. All are `InputField` controls. To change the value of any one, type in the input field and press Enter to evaluate with the new values.

In[15]:=
```
Manipulate[Plot[f[x], {x, xmin, xmax}],
    {f, Sin}, {xmin, 0}, {xmax, 2 π}, ControlType → InputField]
```

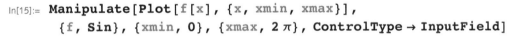

Out[15]=

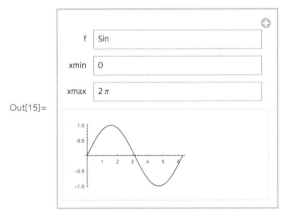

Let us try something a bit more ambitious – a dynamic table of weather information, one in which a user types in a city name to get the information for that city. Start by creating a static grid with the meteorological information. We have added several options to `Grid` to format the output.

In[16]:= `conditions =`
        `{"Elevation", "Humidity", "Pressure", "StationName",`
        `"Temperature", "WindChill", "WindDirection", "WindSpeed"};`

In[17]:= `Grid[`
        `Map[{#, WeatherData["Chicago", #]`
        `WeatherData["Chicago", #, "Units"]} &, conditions] /.`
        `_Missing :> "", Frame → All, Alignment → Left,`
        `Background → LightYellow]`

Out[17]=

Elevation	190. Meters
Humidity	0.7
Pressure	1019.64 Millibars
StationName	KMDW
Temperature	2. DegreesCelsius
WindChill	14.37 DegreesCelsius
WindDirection	Degrees
WindSpeed	0.

Finally, instead of the static value "Chicago" we use a parameter City, giving it an initial value Copenhagen; also set ControlType → InputField.

In[18]:= `Manipulate[`
        `Grid[Map[{#1, WeatherData[ToString[City], #] WeatherData[`
        `ToString[City], #, "Units"]} &, conditions] /.`
        `_Missing :> "", Frame → All, Alignment → Left,`
        `Background → LightYellow], {City, Copenhagen},`
        `ControlType → InputField]`

Out[18]=

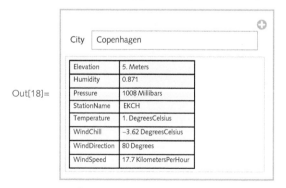

In this particular example, it was not necessary to explicitly specify the ControlType as the syntax of the parameter list would cause Manipulate to automatically use an input field as the controller.

Control wrapper

The control objects that we have looked at so far were all specified by the parameter syntax or by explicitly using `ControlType`. You can get greater control (pardon the pun) over these objects by using the `Control` wrapper. Hence, the following two expressions are equivalent.

```
In[19]:= Manipulate[
         Plot[Sin[b (t - c)], {t, -2 π, 2 π}],
         {{b, 2}, 1, 8},
         {{c, 4}, 1, 8}
         ]
```

Out[19]=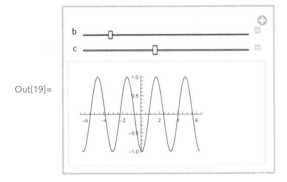

```
In[20]:= Manipulate[
         Plot[Sin[b (t - c)], {t, -2 π, 2 π}],
         Control[{{b, 2}, 1, 8}],
         Control[{{c, 4}, 1, 8}]
         ]
```

Out[20]=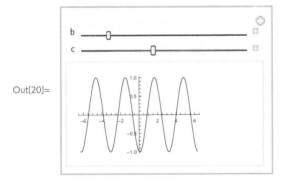

The advantage of using the `Control` wrapper is that it can give you greater flexibility in the placement and formatting of your dynamic interfaces. For example, the following puts the controls inside a `Grid` so that we can arrange them precisely how we want. The labels `"freq"` and `"phase"` make up one row of the grid, while the controls for the parameters b and c make up the next row of the grid. Within each `Control`, we have used `ControlType` to specify a `VerticalSlider` rather than the default horizontal slider. Lastly, `ControlPlacement` is used to put the controls on the left-hand side of the pane.

```
In[21]:= Manipulate[Plot[Sin[b (t - c)], {t, -2 π, 2 π}, PlotRange → 1],
           Grid[{{"freq", "phase"},
               {Control[{{b, 2, Null}, 1, 8, VerticalSlider}],
                 Control[{{c, 4, Null}, 1, 8, VerticalSlider}]}
             }], ControlPlacement → Left]
```

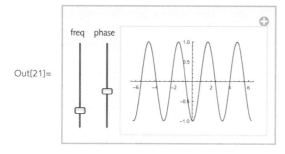

Out[21]=

Viewers

In addition to `Animate` and `Manipulate` many other functions are available for dynamic interaction using your mouse or other pointing devices to control the changing parameters. In this section we will look at various viewers that give you the ability to display different output by clicking a button (or tab).

For example, the following `TabView` contains a list of three expressions. Clicking the tabs causes the corresponding expression to be evaluated and displayed in the `TabView` pane.

```
In[22]:= TabView[{2³¹ - 1, PrimeQ[2³¹ - 1], BaseForm[2³¹ - 1, 2]}]
```

Out[22]=

```
1 | 2 | 3
2 147 483 647
```

Because `TabView` does not have any `Hold` attributes, its arguments are evaluated first, before being passed up to `TabView` itself. You can see this by repeatedly clicking any of the tabs below. The random numbers are generated when the `TabView` itself is first evaluated.

```
In[23]:= TabView[{RandomInteger[], RandomReal[], RandomComplex[]}]
```

Out[23]=

```
1 | 2 | 3
0.844099 + 0.756196 i
```

In[24]:= **Attributes[TabView]**

Out[24]= {Protected, ReadProtected}

A variation of the syntax for TabView gives labels to the tabs that you can customize with a string or any arbitrary expression. The syntax is:

$$\{label_1 \rightarrow expr_1,\ label_2 \rightarrow expr_2,\ ...,\ label_n \rightarrow expr_n\}.$$

In[25]:= **TabView[{"sin(x)" → Plot[Sin[x], {x, 0, 2 π}],**
       "sin(2x)" → Plot[Sin[2 x], {x, 0, 2 π}]}]

Out[25]=
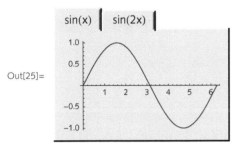

This is another good candidate for Map.

In[26]:= **TabView[Map[TraditionalForm[#] → Plot[#, {x, 0, 2 π}] &,**
       {Sin[x], Sin[2 x], Sin[3 x]}]]

Out[26]=
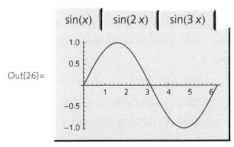

In addition to TabView, there are several other viewers with similar characteristics. Their behavior is suggested by their name: FlipView, MenuView, OpenerView, PopupView, and SlideView. For example, OpenerView provides a convenient interface for hiding and opening expressions. The syntax is OpenerView[{*label, expr*}].

```
In[27]:= OpenerView[
            {"Info on OpenerView", "OpenerView[{expr₁,expr₂}] represents
                an object which displays as an opener,
                together with expr₁ if the opener is closed,
                and both expr₁ and expr₂ if it is open."}]
```

Out[27]= ▶ Info on OpenerView

A second argument set to `True` will display the opener open, that is, with *expr* visible.

```
In[28]:= OpenerView[{"Chapter 11", Column[{"\tSection 11.1",
            "\tSection 11.2", "\tSection 11.3"}]}, True]
```

Out[28]= ▼ Chapter 11
                Section 11.1
                Section 11.2
                Section 11.3

In Section 11.3 we will put together a nontrivial application of `OpenerView`, an enhancement of the palette for opening files from a project directory introduced in Section 5.8.

Animating the hypocycloid

The hypocycloid example developed in Section 10.1 is a good candidate for a dynamic visualization; the phenomenon it describes involves varying a parameter (the angle θ) that causes more and more of the curve to be sketched out. Below is the static code from that section, incorporated into one function to generate a plot for given radii and angle θ.

Inside the `Manipulate` interface, we would like a control for each of the two radii. The syntax of the parameter list `{R, {3, 4, 5, 6, 7, 8}, Setter}` specifies `R` as the parameter that can take on the values `{3, 4, 5, 6, 7, 8}` with a control consisting of a setter button to select the different radii. Also with a little mathematics, you should find that the number of rotations until the curve closes up is given by `2 π Denominator[(R - r) / r]`, although you may need to be careful if `R / r` is irrational as the curve will never close up in that case!

```
In[29]:= HypocycloidPlot[R_, r_, θ_] := Module[{hypocycloid, center},
```

$$\text{hypocycloid}[\{a\_, b\_\}, t\_] := \left\{ (a - b) \, \text{Cos}[t] + b \, \text{Cos}\left[\frac{t\,(a - b)}{b}\right], \right.$$

$$\left. (a - b) \, \text{Sin}[t] - b \, \text{Sin}\left[\frac{t\,(a - b)}{b}\right]\right\};$$

```
    center[th_, R1_, r2_] := (R1 - r2) {Cos[th], Sin[th]};

    Show[{ParametricPlot[hypocycloid[{R, r}, t],
      {t, 0, θ}, PlotStyle → Red, Axes → None],

      Graphics[{{Blue, Thick, Circle[{0, 0}, R]},
        {Circle[center[θ, R, r], r]},
        {PointSize[.02], Point[center[θ, R, r]]}, {Thick,
        Line[{center[θ, R, r], hypocycloid[{R, r}, θ]}]}, {Red,
        PointSize[.02], Point[hypocycloid[{R, r}, θ]]}}}],

      PlotRange → All, GridLines → Automatic]
    ]

In[30]:= HypocycloidPlot[3, 1, 2 π - π / 3]
```

Out[30]=

```
In[31]:= Manipulate[
           HypocycloidPlot[R, r, θ],
           {{θ, 1}, 0, 2 π Denominator[(R - r) / r]},
           {R, {3, 4, 5, 6, 7, 8}, Setter},
           {r, {1, 2, 3, 4, 5}, Setter}]
```

Out[31]=

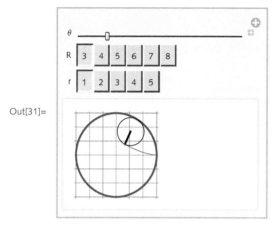

It might not be obvious, but there is a small problem: at $\theta = 0$ the `ParametricPlot` starts off ranging from 0 to 0, which returns an error. It might be easiest to have the animation start just a little past 0, say at 0.01.

```
In[32]:= Manipulate[
           HypocycloidPlot[R, r, θ],
           {θ, 0 + 0.01, 2 π Denominator[(R - r) / r]},
           {R, {3, 4, 5, 6, 7, 8}, Setter},
           {r, {1, 2, 3, 4, 5}, Setter}]
```

Out[32]=

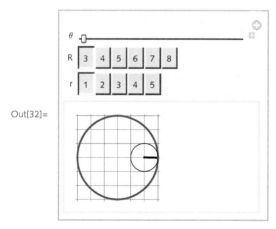

We include the definition of `HypocycloidPlot` by using the `SaveDefinitions` option so that the interface becomes self-contained; alternatively, you could include the entire definition of `HypocycloidPlot` as part of the `Initialization` option to `Manipulate`. Here then is our final version of this hypocycloid sketcher.

```
In[33]:= Manipulate[
        HypocycloidPlot[R, r, θ],
        {θ, 0 + 0.01, 2 π Denominator[(R - r) / r]},
        {R, {3, 4, 5, 6, 7, 8}, Setter},
        {r, {1, 2, 3, 4, 5}, Setter},
        SaveDefinitions → True]
```

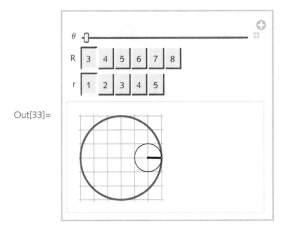

There is one issue that will arise when the radius, r, of the "inner" circle is larger than the radius, R, of the "outer" circle. In this case, the graphic will bounce around a bit as *Mathematica* computes a different plot range for these values. In Exercise 7 you are asked to correct this problem. Exercise 8 asks you to create a similar dynamic interface for epicycloids, curves that are generated by rolling a smaller circle around the *outside* of a larger circle.

Visualizing logical operators

In this example we will create a dynamic visualization of the basic logical operators `And`, `Or`, `Implies` and so on, using two-circle Venn diagrams. First we will create a static image for the `And` operator, and then extend this to the other operators in the dynamic interface.

Given their centers, this creates two circles A and B (the default radius for `Circle` is 1).

```
In[34]:= c1 = {-1 / 2, 0};
        c2 = {1 / 2, 0};
```

In[36]:= `Graphics[{Circle[c1], Circle[c2],`
`    Text["A", {-.5, .75}], Text["B", {.5, .75}]}]`

Out[36]=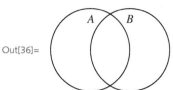

The region representing $A \wedge B$ (that is, "*A* and *B*") consists of all those points common to *A* and *B*. We will display this using `RegionPlot`. First we describe the regions as inequalities that can be used by `RegionPlot`.

In[37]:= `eqns = Apply[(#1 + x)² + (#2 + y)² < 1 &, {c1, c2}, {1}]`

Out[37]= $\left\{ \left(-\dfrac{1}{2} + x \right)^2 + y^2 < 1, \ \left(\dfrac{1}{2} + x \right)^2 + y^2 < 1 \right\}$

In[38]:= `RegionPlot[Apply[And, eqns],`
`    {x, -1, 1}, {y, -1, 1}, Frame → False]`

Out[38]=

Putting the two graphics together, adjusting for plot ranges, and adding some labels, we have the following:

In[39]:= `Show[RegionPlot[Apply[And, eqns], {x, -2, 2},`
`    {y, -2, 2}, Frame → None, PlotLabel → A && B,`
`    PlotRange → {{-2, 2}, {-1.2, 1.2}}, AspectRatio → Automatic,`
`    MaxRecursion → 5], Graphics[{Circle[c1], Circle[c2],`
`    Text["A", {-.5, .75}], Text["B", {.5, .75}]}]]`

Out[39]=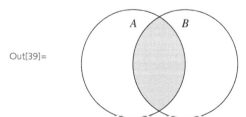

For the dynamic visualization, we want to be able to use any logical function, not just `And`. So we replace And everywhere by a parameter, say f, and set the values this parameter can take on as the list {And, Or, …}.

```
In[40]:= Manipulate[Show[
          RegionPlot[Apply[f, eqns], {x, -2, 2},
           {y, -2, 2}, Frame → None, PlotLabel → f[A, B],
           PlotRange → {{-2, 2}, {-1.2, 1.2}},
           AspectRatio → Automatic, MaxRecursion → 5],
          Graphics[{Circle[{-1/2, 0}], Circle[{1/2, 0}],
            Text["A", {-.5, .75}], Text["B", {.5, .75}]}]
         ], {{f, Xor, "Logical function"},
          {And, Or, Xor, Implies, Nand, Nor}}]
```

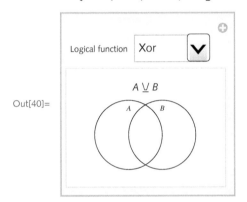

Out[40]=

See Ruskey and Weston (2005) for an excellent survey of work on Venn diagrams.

Exercises

1. Create a dynamic interface that displays various diagrams and plots of the amino acids. A list of the amino acids is given by:

```
In[1]:= ChemicalData["AminoAcids"]
```

```
Out[1]= {Glycine, LAlanine, LSerine, LProline, LValine, LThreonine,
         LCysteine, LIsoleucine, LLeucine, LAsparagine, LAsparticAcid,
         LGlutamine, LLysine, LGlutamicAcid, LMethionine, LHistidine,
         LPhenylalanine, LArginine, LTyrosine, LTryptophan}
```

The diagrams and plots that should be included are built into ChemicalData:

```
In[2]:= StringCases[ChemicalData["Properties"],
         __ ~~ "Diagram" | (__ ~~ "Plot")] // Flatten
```

```
Out[2]= {CHColorStructureDiagram, CHStructureDiagram,
         ColorStructureDiagram, MoleculePlot,
         SpaceFillingMoleculePlot, StructureDiagram}
```

2. Create a dynamic interface that applies several built-in effects to an image. The effects are given by `ImageEffect` and include `"Charcoal"`, `"Solarization"`, `"GaussianNoise"` and many others. See the documentation for `ImageEffect` for a complete list.

3. Modify the dynamic Venn diagram created in this section to display a truth table like that developed in Exercise 9 from Section 5.8. Include the truth table side-by-side with the Venn diagram, like in the following:

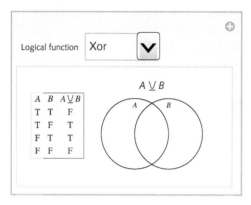

4. Create a dynamic interface that displays some sample text using two different fonts from your system's list of fonts. Set it up so that you can select which two fonts to compare by using a pull-down menu. The list of fonts on your system is given by the following:

```
In[3]:= fonts = FE`Evaluate[FEPrivate`GetPopupList["MenuListFonts"]];
In[4]:= RandomSample[fonts, 3]
Out[4]= {Gurmukhi Sangam MN → Gurmukhi Sangam MN, Impact → Impact,
            DTL Albertina TOT Italic → DTL Albertina TOT Italic}
```

5. Take one of the two-dimensional random walk programs developed elsewhere in this book (for example, Sections 8.1 and 13.1) and create an animation that displays successive steps of the random walk.

6. Create a plot of $\sin(\theta)$ side-by-side with a circle and a dynamic point that moves along the curve and the circle as θ varies from 0 to 2π.

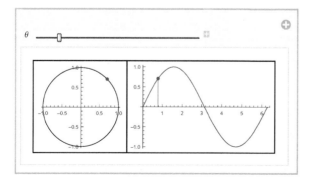

7. Modify the `Manipulate` expression that animates the hypocycloid so that the plot range deals with the situation when the radius of the inner circle is larger than the radius of the outer circle.

8. An *epicycloid* is a curve that can be generated by tracing out a fixed point on a circle that rolls around the outside of a second circle. The formula for an epicycloid is quite similar to that for the hypocycloid. The epicycloid is given parametrically by the following:

$$x = (a + b)\cos(\theta) - b\cos\left(\frac{a+b}{b}\,\theta\right),$$

$$y = (a + b)\sin(\theta) - b\sin\left(\frac{a+b}{b}\,\theta\right).$$

Create a dynamic interface to animate the epicycloid similar to that for the hypocycloid in this section.

9. In the 1920s and 1930s the artist Marcel Duchamp created what he termed *rotoreliefs*, spinning concentric circles (and variants thereof) giving a three-dimensional illusion of depth (Duchamp 1926). Create you own rotoreliefs by starting with several concentric circles of different radii, then varying their centers around a path given by another circle, and animating.

10. Create a dynamic table that displays the temperature of several cities around the world. Include a control (pulldown menu or setter bar) to switch the display between Celsius and Fahrenheit.

11. Looking forward to Chapter 13 where we develop a full application for computing and visualizing random walks, create a dynamic interface that displays random walks, adding controls to select the number of steps from a pulldown menu, the dimension from a setter bar, and a checkbox to turn on and off lattice walks.

12. Create a visualization of two-dimensional vector addition. The interface should include either a 2D slider for each of two vectors in the plane or locators to change the position of each vector; the display should show the two vectors as well as their vector sum. Extend the solution to three dimensions. (The solution of this vector arithmetic interface is due to Harry Calkins of Wolfram Research.)

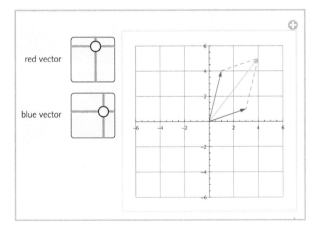

13. Create a dynamic interface to display information about a word drawn from `WordData`. The interface should include an input field for the word and use tabs to display either a definition, the Porter stem, or synonyms (try other word properties in `WordData`).

11.2 The structure of dynamic expressions

The interactive tools we have looked at in this chapter, `Manipulate`, `TabView`, `OpenerView`, and so on, provide a convenient and relatively easy-to-use interface for generating interactive expressions in *Mathematica*. But sometimes you will find that you need finer control over the expressions you are working with or you simply need to work on a more primitive level. This is quite similar to the situation with graphics in *Mathematica*. There are dozens of built-in, higher-level functions such as `Plot`, `DateListPlot`, `ArrayPlot`, and so on that are designed to handle a wide set of inputs and to return output that has high fidelity and accuracy, and are also aesthetically attractive. But, as discussed in Section 10.1, primitive objects are also available to create graphics using basic building blocks known as graphics primitives.

For dynamic interfaces, the primitive elements that are used to construct the higher-level functions such as `Manipulate` are `Dynamic` and `DynamicModule`. Similarly to graphics, you can build dynamic interfaces from these primitive elements directly. That is the subject of this section.

Before going further we should note that discussing dynamic objects in a static book is a bit problematic. Dynamic objects, as their name suggests, change dynamically and when updated, their values change wherever they occur. This is quite different from the situation with static symbols. For this reason, this section is best "read" by evaluating the examples in order in your own *Mathematica* notebooks and observing changes to previous computations as subsequent expressions are evaluated.

Dynamic

Whenever you make an assignment, you are fixing the value of a symbol at the time the definition is made. For example, the symbol `t` is given the value 10 here.

```
In[1]:= t = 10
```

```
Out[1]= 10
```

Whenever you use `t`, its (static) value will be automatically substituted.

```
In[2]:= 4 t - 1
```

```
Out[2]= 39
```

Change the value associated with `t` and all *subsequent* evaluations will use the new value.

```
In[3]:= t = 5;
        4 t - 1
```

Out[4]= 19

The outputs of previous computations involving t all retain the history, essentially showing you the value *when the assignment was evaluated*. The rule, t = 10, is stored in memory by the kernel. Close the kernel and that rule is no longer known, that is, you will need to reevaluate the rule in a new session to give the symbol t that value again.

Another kind of output is possible: a dynamic output which is automatically updated to reflect the current value of the symbol.

```
In[5]:= t + 1
```

Out[5]= 6

```
In[6]:= Dynamic[t + 1]
```

Out[6]= 1 + Bobby

Change the value of t and any dynamic outputs will change immediately.

```
In[7]:= t = Bobby
```

Out[7]= Bobby

The value of the expression t + 1 above is 6, reflecting that the symbol t in that expression is static: it gets its value from the last assigned value for t, which in this case was 5. But note that the expression Dynamic[t + 1] has a different value. The dynamic expression has automatically updated to reflect the current value of its argument. Even though we evaluated t = Bobby later in the session, it is that value that is used inside of Dynamic.

It is important to note that Dynamic[*expr*] displays as *expr* but internally it is represented as a dynamic object.

```
In[8]:= Dynamic[3 + w]
```

Out[8]= 3 + w

```
In[9]:= InputForm[%]
```

Out[9]//InputForm=
```
Dynamic[3 + w]
```

Any expression can be dynamic. For example, running ImageConvolve with an appropriate kernel on this image returns a static object. When it was evaluated immediately following the evaluation of img, it used that current value to perform the operation.

In[10]:= **img =** 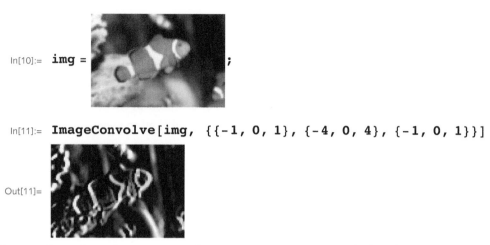 **;**

In[11]:= **ImageConvolve[img, {{-1, 0, 1}, {-4, 0, 4}, {-1, 0, 1}}]**

Out[11]=

Change the value of `img` in a subsequent computation and the above expression does not change, but any dynamic version does.

In[12]:= **img =**  **;**

In[13]:= **Dynamic[**
        ImageConvolve[img, {{-1, 0, 1}, {-12, 0, 12}, {-1, 0, 1}}]]

Out[13]=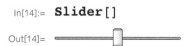

Let us start to build up interactive expressions using this dynamic building block. First, here is a slider object; by default it moves between values 0 and 1. You can move the slider with your mouse, but with no argument, it is not connected to anything.

In[14]:= **Slider[]**

Out[14]= ⊏━━━━━━━━━━▯━━━━━━━━━⊐

Let us give it a dynamic variable z, and display the value of z to the right of the slider.

In[15]:= `{Slider[Dynamic[z]], z}`

Out[15]=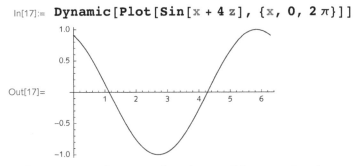

If you move the above slider, you will see that the value of z displayed to the right of the slider is *not* updating, it remains at 0. The reason is that the symbol z is not dynamic so it does not update. To make it dynamic, wrap it in `Dynamic`.

In[16]:= `{Slider[Dynamic[z]], Dynamic[z]}`

Out[16]=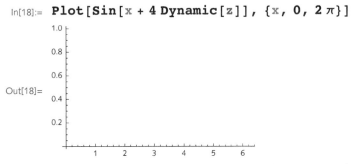

Now moving this latest slider causes the value of z to update dynamically. As you move the slider you will notice that the previous slider also moves! This is because it too has a dynamic z as argument. The plot below will also automatically update as you change the value of z in the slider above.

In[17]:= `Dynamic[Plot[Sin[x + 4 z], {x, 0, 2 π}]]`

Out[17]=

When creating dynamic plots, be careful to not simply wrap the variable z in `Dynamic` as this will not create a dynamic plot.

In[18]:= `Plot[Sin[x + 4 Dynamic[z]], {x, 0, 2 π}]`

Out[18]=

In fact no curve is generated because `Plot` needs specific values to create the curve. It is the plot itself that we want to update dynamically, so `Plot` should be wrapped in `Dynamic`.

Putting the slider together with the dynamic plot, you can essentially build up a scene much like `Manipulate`. `Manipulate` uses these very objects to construct its interfaces.

```
In[19]:= Panel[Column[{
            Slider[Dynamic[z]],
            Dynamic[Plot[Sin[x + 4 z], {x, 0, 2 π}]]
          }]
        ]
```

Out[19]=

This use of `Dynamic` inside of a slider is entirely general and can be applied to any control object, not just sliders.

```
In[20]:= {InputField[Dynamic[var]], Dynamic[var]}
```

Out[20]= { [var   ] , var }

Normally, `Dynamic[expr]` only updates when the value of *expr* changes. You can force dynamic expressions to update after a fixed interval by using the option `UpdateInterval`. For example, this creates a display of the current date and time, updating every second.

```
In[21]:= Dynamic[DateString[], UpdateInterval → 1]
```

Out[21]= Sat 1 Dec 2012 15:45:44

DynamicModule

As noted above, having several dynamic instances of a variable in a notebook will cause all of them to be updated whenever any of them are. For example, as you move one of the sliders below, the other moves in sync. This is because both sliders are tied to the same global variable, x.

```
In[22]:= {Slider[Dynamic[x]], Slider[Dynamic[x]]}
```

Out[22]= { ————◻————— , ————◻————— }

This behavior might cause problems if a global symbol interferes with a dynamic version of that symbol inadvertently. Much like `Module` is used to localize symbols in functions, `DynamicModule` is used to localize variables in dynamic interfaces. For example, assigning the global symbol x the value zero affects the two sliders above. Change its value and the sliders will update accordingly.

In[23]:= **x = 0;**

On the other hand, the following expression localizes x and initializes it to 0.5. You can still move the sliders below but changing this local x will have no affect on any global x such as those in the sliders above.

In[24]:= **DynamicModule[{x = 0.5},**
{Slider[Dynamic[x]], Slider[Dynamic[x]]}
]

Out[24]=

Use additional dynamic modules if you want the two local variables to be independent.

In[25]:= **{DynamicModule[{x = 0.25}, Slider[Dynamic[x]]],**
DynamicModule[{x = 0.75}, Slider[Dynamic[x]]]}

Out[25]=

In the following example we build a graphics scene consisting of a tube passing through some points. A slider is displayed that controls the radius of the tube. In this example we have simply put the graphic and the slider side-by-side by placing them in a list inside the DynamicModule.

In[26]:= **pts = Table[{Sin[t], Cos[t], t/5}, {t, 0, 20, .25}];**

In[27]:= **DynamicModule[{r = 0.1}, {**
Graphics3D[{EdgeForm[], Red, Tube[pts, Dynamic[r]]}],
Slider[Dynamic[r], {0.05, 1}]
}]

Out[27]=

Going a bit further, this puts the graphic in a panel and places a vertical slider to its left. We have added an **Appearance** option to the slider to give it a different "thumb."

```
In[28]:= DynamicModule[{r = 0.1},
           Panel[
             Graphics3D[{EdgeForm[], Red, Tube[pts, Dynamic[r]]}],
             VerticalSlider[Dynamic[r],
               {0.05, 1}, Appearance → "RightArrow"],
             Left],
           Initialization :→
             {pts = Table[{Sin[t], Cos[t], t / 5}, {t, 0, 20, .25}]}]
```

Out[28]=

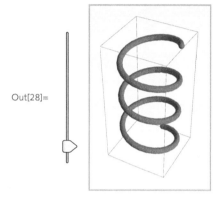

One of the advantages of DynamicModule is that it saves state. What this means is that you can end your *Mathematica* session, close the notebook, restart *Mathematica* and reopen the notebook and any output created with a DynamicModule will be in the same state as when you closed the notebook. This is because the output of a DynamicModule includes an expression embedded in the output that is initialized when it is displayed again. That expression includes values of the local variables created with DynamicModule. Another way of thinking about this is that global variables are known to (and in a sense, owned by) the kernel; variables created by DynamicModule, on the other hand, live in the front end.

Let us recreate some of the objects from earlier in this chapter that used the top-level Manipulate, but instead, we will put them together using these dynamic building blocks. First, here is the dynamic triangle from Section 11.1. The variable pts is localized inside DynamicModule and initialized with three points. LocatorPane[*pos, expr*] is a low-level object that creates a pane with locators given at the positions specified by *pos* and a background given by the expression *expr*. So, in this example, Dynamic[pts] gives the (dynamic) locator positions and Graphics[...] is displayed in the background.

```
In[29]:= DynamicModule[{pts = {{-1, 0}, {1, 0}, {0, 1}}},
        LocatorPane[Dynamic[pts], Graphics[{
            LightGray, EdgeForm[Black], Dynamic[Polygon[pts]]}]]]
```

Out[29]=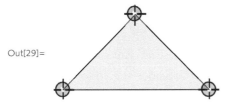

As another example of the use of `LocatorPane`, here is a dynamic Bézier curve as defined by several control points.

```
In[30]:= DynamicModule[{pts = {{0, 0}, {1, 1}, {2, 1}}},
        LocatorPane[Dynamic[pts],
          Graphics[Dynamic@BezierCurve[pts]]]]
```

Out[30]=

One very useful thing that can be done with locators is to constrain them to a defined region. This is done by giving `LocatorPane` a third argument that defines the constrained area. For example, this constrains the locator to the square with lower left vertex at $\{-1, -1\}$ and upper right vertex at $\{1, 1\}$. The background consists of an ellipse. There is no interaction between the background and the locator in this example. We have added a rectangle to identify the area in which the locator is constrained.

```
In[31]:= LocatorPane[{0, 0}, Graphics[{
          Circle[{0, 0}, {3, 2}],
          EdgeForm[Dashed],
          Opacity[.25], Rectangle[{-1, -1}, {1, 1}]}],
        {{-1, -1}, {1, 1}}]
```

Out[31]=

Dynamic tips

Because dynamic expressions update frequently, such as whenever you move a locator with the mouse, they can trigger a lot of evaluation during the updates. This can be the main cause of slow dynamics. In this section we will look at several things to consider to make your dynamic expressions as efficient as possible.

First, think about where you use `Dynamic`. You might think that you only need to wrap variables with it, but this may not produce what you want. Consider the following dynamic integration. Moving the slider you will see that only the value of a updates, not the value of the entire integral.

```
In[32]:= DynamicModule[{a}, {
            Slider[Dynamic[a], {0, 1}],
            Integrate[Exp[Dynamic[a] v], {v, 0, 1}]
          }]
```

Out[32]= $\left\{ \rule{3cm}{0pt} , \dfrac{-1 + e^{0.}}{0.} \right\}$

It is the integration that you want to be dynamic here. So wrap `Integrate` in `Dynamic`.

```
In[33]:= DynamicModule[{a}, {
            Slider[Dynamic[a], {0, 1}],
            Dynamic[Integrate[Exp[a v], {v, 0, 1}]]
          }]
```

Out[33]= $\left\{ \rule{3cm}{0pt} , 1. \right\}$

Similarly for a dynamic plot label.

```
In[34]:= DynamicModule[{a}, {
            Slider[Dynamic[a], {1, 5}],
            Plot[Sin[Dynamic[a] v], {v, 0, 2 π},
              PlotLabel → StringForm["Frequency = `1`", Dynamic[a]]]
          }]
```

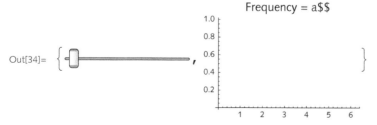

Since both the plot and the plot label need to be updated dynamically, it is probably a bit cleaner to wrap the entire plot in `Dynamic`.

```
In[35]:= DynamicModule[{a}, {
          Slider[Dynamic[a], {1, 5}],
          Dynamic[Plot[Sin[a v], {v, 0, 2 π},
            PlotLabel → StringForm["Frequency = `1`", a]]]
        }]
```

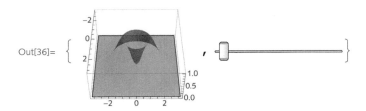

Out[35]=

This last example might lead you to conclude that it is generally a good idea to wrap larger and larger expressions in `Dynamic`. But this can lead to inefficiencies in that the entire plot will update frequently. For a simple two-dimensional plot such as the sine function above, this is not too expensive. But for a three-dimensional, high-resolution surface with transparency this inefficiency might slow things down to an unacceptable level.

The following three-dimensional plot includes an opacity directive, increased adaptive sampling through `MaxRecursion`, and a dynamic view point, all of which add up to a computationally intensive object that is a bit slow to manipulate.

```
In[36]:= DynamicModule[{θ = 0}, {
            Dynamic@Plot3D[ (x² + y²) Exp[1 - x² - y²], {x, -π, π},
              {y, -π, π}, PlotStyle → {Purple, Opacity[0.5]},
              Mesh → None, MaxRecursion → 5,
              SphericalRegion → True,
              ViewPoint → RotationTransform[θ, {0, 0, 1}][{3, 0, 3}]],
            Slider[Dynamic[θ], {0, 2 π}]}]
```

Out[36]=

It is not necessary to redraw the entire plot when the viewpoint changes. By wrapping just the value of the `ViewPoint` option in `Dynamic`, the entire plot is not recomputed every time the viewpoint changes thus making the manipulation with the mouse much quicker.

```
In[37]:= DynamicModule[{θ = 0}, {
            Plot3D[ (x² + y²) Exp[1 - x² - y²], {x, -π, π},
             {y, -π, π}, PlotStyle → {Purple, Opacity[0.5]},
             Mesh → None, MaxRecursion → 5,
             SphericalRegion → True,
             ViewPoint →
              Dynamic[RotationTransform[θ, {0, 0, 1}][{3, 0, 3}]]],
            Slider[Dynamic[θ], {0, 2 π}]}]
```

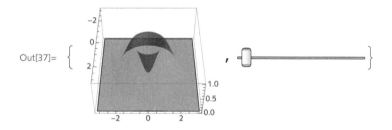

This is not a hard-and-fast rule. There are some situations where you need to be careful about wrapping expressions in `Dynamic`. The following does not work because `PlotPoints` needs to pass an explicit numeric value to `Plot` to generate the graphic. Wrapping `Dynamic` around an expression causes that expression to remain unevaluated until the front end receives it, typically when you display it in your notebook. But the kernel is where `Plot` lives and the kernel is unable to do the computation to generate the plot at this point.

```
In[38]:= DynamicModule[{pp = 5}, {
            Plot[Sin[x], {x, 0, 2 π},
             PlotPoints → Dynamic[pp], MaxRecursion → 0],
            Slider[Dynamic[pp], {5, 30}]
            }]
```

The reason the examples above with `ViewPoint` worked is that `ViewPoint` is an option that does its computations in the front end, which is where `Dynamic` lives.

Exercises

1. Display a random word from the dictionary (`DictionaryLookup`) that changes every second.

2. Create a dynamic interface consisting of a locator constrained to the unit circle.

3. Create a dynamic interface that controls one sphere rotating about another.

11.3 Examples and applications

Creating interfaces for visualizing data

Analyzing and visualizing large sets of data is made easier by interfaces that allow you to quickly select the data you are interested in and make comparisons. For example, consider trying to interpret some data that lists energy used by type (coal, natural gas, nuclear, renewables, etc.) over the years. One large spreadsheet covering say thirty years of such data can be difficult to parse. An interface in which you can see a time-series plot for any chosen energy source and compare it with any other would be a very useful visualization of such a large dataset.

In this section, we will import data from the US National Bureau of Economic Research that gives industrial production by sector from 1790–1915 (Davis 2004). The industrial sectors for this historical data are: food, textiles, wood/paper, leather, chemicals/fuels, machinery, and metals. The data uses 1850 as a benchmark, that is, the index for that year is 100.

Let us start by importing the data from the internet, and displaying the first few rows of the spreadsheet.

```
In[1]:= data = Import[
          "http://www.nber.org/data/industrial-production-index/ip-
            sectors.xls", {"XLS", "Data", 1}];
        Take[data, 3]
```

```
Out[2]= {{Year, Food, Textiles, Wood_Paper,
          Leather, Chemicals_Fuels, Machinery, Metals},
         {1827., 28.6996, 18.4986, 16.7097, 15.8894, 22.221,
          28.5287, 22.6592}, {1828., 29.5944, 15.8334,
          20.2374, 16.7859, 21.6499, 29.7857, 21.2395}}
```

The first row consists of column headers which we can use to label the categories that will be displayed in our interface.

```
In[3]:= categories = Rest@data[[1]]
```

```
Out[3]= {Food, Textiles, Wood_Paper,
         Leather, Chemicals_Fuels, Machinery, Metals}
```

Our visualization will use `DateListPlot`, so we need to transform the data into a form suitable for that function. It expects the time-series data in the form $\{date,\ value\}$. The first two columns are the year and food sectors. So let us prototype the transformation with just that subset of data.

```
In[4]:= food = data[[2 ;; -1, {1, 2}]] /.
          {year_, val_} :> {{Round@year}, val};
```

```
In[5]:= Take[food, 8]
```

```
Out[5]= {{{1827}, 28.6996}, {{1828}, 29.5944},
          {{1829}, 26.2247}, {{1830}, 32.7878}, {{1831}, 33.6961},
          {{1832}, 31.9668}, {{1833}, 34.8419}, {{1834}, 33.6196}}
```

Let's do the same for textiles, that is, columns 1 and 3.

```
In[6]:= textiles = data[[2 ;; -1, {1, 3}]] /.
          {year_, val_} :> {{Round@year}, val};
```

```
In[7]:= Take[textiles, 8]
```

```
Out[7]= {{{1827}, 18.4986}, {{1828}, 15.8334},
          {{1829}, 15.3377}, {{1830}, 16.1311}, {{1831}, 23.0132},
          {{1832}, 23.1964}, {{1833}, 25.2582}, {{1834}, 26.4568}}
```

With just these two sectors, we can try out the syntax for `TabView`.

```
In[8]:= TabView[{
          "Food" -> DateListPlot[food],
          "Textiles" -> DateListPlot[textiles]
        }]
```

For the full dataset we need to extend these computations to all columns (sectors). Mapping the rule above across the range of columns 2 through 8 does this.

```
In[9]:= ipData = Map[data[[2 ;; -1, {1, #}]] /.
            {year_, val_} :> {{Round@year}, val} &, Range[2, 8]];
```

TabView is expecting a list of rules of the form *label → expression*. Our labels will come from the categories list and the expressions will be the plots. Threading across these two lists puts all the pieces together. We have also added some options to DateListPlot.

```
In[10]:= allData = MapThread[
           #1 → DateListPlot[Tooltip[#2], {1827}, Joined → True,
             Mesh → All, ImageSize → 220, AspectRatio → 1 / 2] &,
           {categories, ipData}];
```

Here is the rule for the second sector, the textiles.

```
In[11]:= allData[[2]]
```

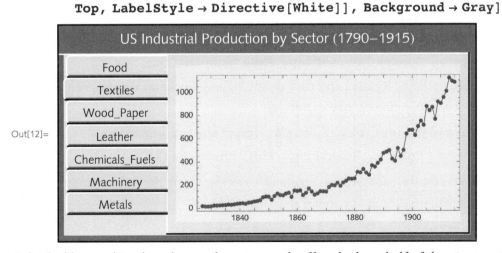

Out[11]= Textiles →

Finally, pass allData to TabView and add a frame and a label for the entire interface.

```
In[12]:= Framed[Labeled[
           TabView[allData,
             ControlPlacement → Left, Background → LightGray],
           "US Industrial Production by Sector (1790-1915)",
           Top, LabelStyle → Directive[White]], Background → Gray]
```

Out[12]=

It looks like machine-based manufacturing took off in the later half of the nineteenth century (due to the Industrial Revolution no doubt) and this is reflected in most of these sectors.

File openers

In Section 5.8 we created a basic palette consisting of buttons that, when clicked, open a file in a project directory. Let us take that a few steps further and create a palette that has different sections that can be opened and closed using `OpenerView`. For our purposes, we will create one opener for all notebooks in a given directory and another opener for packages. You can organize your openers in whatever manner is most sensible for your working environment.

The notebooks (.nb) and packages (.m) are located in the following directory:

In[13]:= **dir = FileNameJoin[{$BaseDirectory, "Applications", "PwM"}]**

Out[13]= /Library/Mathematica/Applications/PwM

The buttons on the palette are hyperlinks of the form `Hyperlink[`*label, url*`]`. So we need to create labels and URLs (uniform resource locators) for each file that will be listed in the palette. First, here are the full pathnames for each of the files. We only display the packages here.

In[14]:= **notebooks = FileNames["*.nb", dir];**
packages = FileNames["*.m", dir]

Out[15]= {/Library/Mathematica/Applications/PwM/Collatz.m,
         /Library/Mathematica/Applications/PwM/Common.m,
         /Library/Mathematica/Applications/PwM/PrintPrep.m,
         /Library/Mathematica/Applications/PwM/PWM.m,
         /Library/Mathematica/Applications/PwM/RandomWalks.m}

Second, we create the labels using each file's base name.

In[16]:= **nblabels = Map[FileBaseName, notebooks];**
paclabels = Map[FileBaseName, packages]

Out[17]= {Collatz, Common, PrintPrep, PWM, RandomWalks}

As before, we need to thread `Hyperlink` over these two lists. Clicking on any of the links in the output opens the corresponding file in the front end.

In[18]:= **MapThread[Hyperlink[#1, #2] &, {paclabels, packages}]**

Out[18]= {Collatz, Common, PrintPrep, PWM, RandomWalks}

Here are the openers for the packages and notebooks. Note, we wrap the links in `Column` to get a vertical list rather than the default horizontal arrangement.

In[19]:= **OpenerView[{"Packages", Column@**
MapThread[Hyperlink[#1, #2] &, {paclabels, packages}]}]

Out[19]= ▶ Packages

```
In[20]:=  OpenerView[{"Notebooks", Column@
            MapThread[Hyperlink[#1, #2] &, {nblabels, notebooks}]]}]
```

Out[20]= ▶ Notebooks

Next we put these two openers inside a column and then wrap that in `CreatePalette`.

```
In[21]:=  CreatePalette[Column[{

            OpenerView[{"Notebooks", Column@MapThread[
                Hyperlink[#1, #2] &, {nblabels, notebooks}]}],

            OpenerView[{"Packages", Column@MapThread[
                Hyperlink[#1, #2] &, {paclabels, packages}]}]
            }]
        ];
```

Here is a screenshot of the palette just created after having clicked the Packages opener label.

The default settings for `CreatePalette`, `Column`, and `Hyperlink` create a fairly plain palette so let us add several options to format it nicely.

```
In[22]:=  openerStyles = {FontSize → 12, FontColor → White};
        linkStyles = {FontSize → 9, FontColor → Red};

In[24]:=  colOpts = {Background → Darker@Gray, Dividers → All};
        linkOpts = {ImageSize → {Automatic, 15}};
        palOpts = {WindowTitle → "File Palette",
            WindowElements → "MagnificationPopUp"};
```

Here then is the polished palette.

```
In[27]:= CreatePalette[
          Column[{
            OpenerView[{Style["Notebooks", openerStyles],
              Column@MapThread[Hyperlink[Style[#1, linkStyles],
                #2, linkOpts] &, {nblabels, notebooks}]}],
            OpenerView[{Style["Packages", openerStyles],
              Column@MapThread[Hyperlink[Style[#1, linkStyles],
                #2, linkOpts] &, {paclabels, packages}]}]
          }, colOpts],
          palOpts];
```

Dynamic random walks

The random walk functions that are developed throughout this book are good candidates for dynamic interfaces allowing you to watch the evolution of a random walk by varying the number of steps displayed in a graphic. The `PwM`RandomWalks` package is fully developed in Section 13.4 so we will simply use the main function, `RandomWalk`, here by loading the package that accompanies this book.

```
In[28]:= << PwM`RandomWalks`
```

The first interface we will create is a basic animation of a two-dimensional lattice walk. To prevent the graphics frame from bouncing around as *Mathematica* recomputes the plot range for each frame, we precompute the walk and find the minimum and maximum values in both the horizontal and vertical directions. These are `xran` and `yran` used below. The rest of the `Manipulate` is straightforward including a nested list as the second argument to `Manipulate` to generate a pulldown list for values of n, allowing the user to select the size of the random walk. We use `DynamicModule` here to initialize and localize the symbols `rw`, `xran`, and `yran`.

In[29]:= `Manipulate[DynamicModule[{rw, xran, yran},`
        `rw = RandomWalk[n, Dimension → 2, LatticeWalk → True];`
        `{xran, yran} = Map[{Min[#], Max[#]} &, Transpose[rw]];`
        `Animate[Graphics[Line[Take[rw, i]],`
    `PlotRange → {xran, yran}], {{i, 100}, 2, n, 1}]],`
        `{{n, 500, "total steps"}, {100, 500, 1500, 2500}}]`

Out[29]=

Another control that can be incorporated with dynamic interfaces is `EventHandler`. The "events" that this function works with are mouse or keyboard events, that is, clicks, drags, use of the up arrow key, and so on. The first argument to `EventHandler` is typically a dynamic expression. The second argument identifies the "event" that will trigger an update and an action that should be performed when that occurs. So, the following displays a random number to high precision in a frame; when the mouse is clicked while the cursor hovers over that expression, a new random number will be generated and displayed. The variable `rand` is initialized in the `DynamicModule`.

In[30]:= `DynamicModule[{rand = RandomReal[1, WorkingPrecision → 20]},`
        `EventHandler[Framed[Dynamic[rand]], {"MouseClicked" :→`
            `(rand = RandomReal[1, WorkingPrecision → 20])}`
        `]]`

Out[30]= `0.25563842007137634608`

The action that is triggered by an event can be given by any expression. So let us use `EventHandler` to create a graphic that displays a new random walk each time the graphic is clicked; the right-hand side of the rule with `MouseClicked` is the event that will be triggered when the mouse is clicked. That event is a reevaluation of the random walk, rw, for 2500 steps.

```
In[31]:= DynamicModule[{rw = RandomWalk[2500, LatticeWalk → False]},
           EventHandler[
            Dynamic[Graphics[{{Thin, Line[rw]}}]],
            {"MouseClicked" :→
              (rw = RandomWalk[2500, LatticeWalk → False])}]]
```

Out[31]=

Every time you click on the above graphics, a new 2500-step random walk is generated and displayed.

To add a setter bar for setting the length of the walk as well as a checkbox for lattice/off-lattice walks, we put the entire object inside of a `Manipulate`. Fixing the `ContentSize` forces *Mathematica* to fit the graphic inside of a fixed graphics box.

```
In[32]:= Manipulate[DynamicModule[
           {rw = RandomWalk[len, LatticeWalk → lw]}, EventHandler[
            Dynamic[Graphics[{{Thin, Line[rw]}}]], {"MouseClicked" :→
              (rw = RandomWalk[len, LatticeWalk → lw])}]],
         {len, {100, 1000, 10 000, 25 000}},
         {{lw, False, "Lattice walk"}, {True, False}},
         ContentSize → {200, 100}]
```

Out[32]=

Apollonius' circle

Our final dynamic example is a demonstration of an ancient bit of geometry. Circles are typically defined as the set of points some fixed distance (radius) from a given point (the center). Another definition, due to the Greek astronomer Apollonius of Perga (*ca.* 262 BC – *ca.* 190 BC), defines a circle as the locus of points *P*, such that the ratio of the distances of two fixed points *A* and *B* to point *P* is a constant, different from one (Figure 11.1).

FIGURE 11.1. *Circle defined as the locus of points such that PA / PB is a constant.*

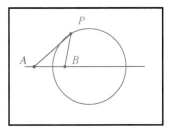

In this section we will create a graphic including the following dynamic elements: a point *P*, lines *PA* and *PB*, and a display of the ratio of the two distances. Point *P* will be a locator restricted to a circle. This restriction is accomplished by using a second argument to `Dynamic`. `Normalize` takes a vector as input and returns a unit vector, thus restricting point *P* to the unit circle.

```
Dynamic[ptP, (ptP = Normalize[#1]) &]
```

The two lines connecting point *P* to points *A* and *B* are dynamic, as is point *P* itself. Here then is our initial interface with point *P* initialized to start at $\theta = 2\pi / 3$.

In[33]:= `DynamicModule[`

$$\left\{\text{ptP} = \left\{\text{Cos}\left[\frac{2\pi}{3}\right], \text{Sin}\left[\frac{2\pi}{3}\right]\right\}, \text{ptA} = \left\{-\frac{3}{2}, 0\right\}, \text{ptB} = \left\{-\frac{2}{3}, 0\right\}\right\},$$

```
  LocatorPane[Dynamic[ptP, (ptP = Normalize[#]) &], Graphics[
    {Gray, Circle[{0, 0}, 1], Line[{{-1.75, 0}, {1.5, 0}}],
     Green, PointSize[0.025], Point[Dynamic[ptP]],
     Blue, Point[ptA], Dynamic[Line[{ptA, ptP}]],
     Red, Point[ptB], Dynamic[Line[{ptB, ptP}]]},
    PlotRange → {{-1.75, 1.5}, {-1.1, 1.1}}]]
```

Out[33]=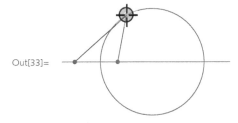

Let us add some text identifying the two fixed points and also a plot label with a dynamic string that shows the ratio *PA* / *PB* of the distances.

In[34]:= **DynamicModule[**

$$\left\{ptP = \left\{Cos\left[\frac{2\pi}{3}\right], Sin\left[\frac{2\pi}{3}\right]\right\}, ptA = \left\{-\frac{3}{2}, 0\right\}, ptB = \left\{-\frac{2}{3}, 0\right\}\right\},$$

```
   LocatorPane[Dynamic[ptP, (ptP = Normalize[#1]) &], Graphics[
      {Gray, Circle[{0, 0}, 1], Line[{{-1.75, 0}, {1.5, 0}}],
       Green, PointSize[0.025], Point[Dynamic[ptP]],
       Blue, Point[ptA], Dynamic[Line[{ptA, ptP}]],
       Text["A", ptA, {2, -1}], Red, Point[ptB],
       Dynamic[Line[{ptB, ptP}]], Text["B", ptB, {-3, -1}]},
      PlotRange → {{-1.75, 1.5}, {-1.1, 1.1}}, PlotLabel →
       Dynamic[StringForm["Ratio = `1`", EuclideanDistance[
          ptA, ptP] / EuclideanDistance[ptB, ptP]]]]]
```

Out[34]=

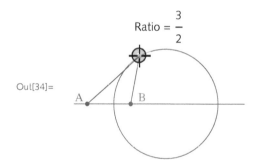

Exercises

1. Here are data on Nobel prizes in the fields of chemistry, medicine, and physics, available from the National Bureau of Economic Research.

In[1]:= **data =**
   Import["http://www.nber.org/nobel/Jones_Weinberg_2011_PNAS.xlsx",
      {"XLSX", "Data", 1}];

In[2]:= **Take[data, 4]**

Out[2]= {{name, field, year_birth, year_prize, year_research_mid,
   year_death, TheoryOrTheoryAndEmpirical, age_highdegree},
   {Van'T Hoff, Jacobus Henricus, Chemistry, 1852., 1901., 1885.,
   1911., 1., 22.}, {Fischer, Hermann Emil, Chemistry, 1852.,
   1902., 1895., 1919., 0., 22.}, {Arrhenius, Svante August,
   Chemistry, 1859., 1903., 1884., 1927., 1., 25.}}

Create a `TabView` visualization showing the age of each prize recipient vs. the year of prize award. Include one tab for each of the three fields given in the data and also include a plot label that displays the mean age at award for each field.

2. Using `FunctionsWithAttribute` developed in Section 5.6, create a paneled interface that displays all built-in functions with a specified attribute. Include an input field control to allow the user to type in an attribute. Do likewise for `FunctionsWithOption` also developed in Section 5.6.

3. Create a dynamic interface that displays twenty random points in the unit square whose locations are randomized each time you click your mouse on the graphic display of these points. Add a checkbox to toggle the display of the shortest path (`FindShortestTour`) through the points.

4. Create a similar dynamic interface to that in the industrial production index problem in this section but comparing industrial production with unemployment rates with retail sales data over the last twenty years or some other suitable time period. Annual and historical retail sales data are available at the US Census Bureau (www.census.gov/retail); unemployment data are available at the US Bureau of Labor Statistics (www.bls.gov/cps/cpsatabs.htm); industrial production indices are available at the US Federal Reserve System (www.federalreserve.gov/releases/g17/download.htm).

12

Optimizing *Mathematica* programs

Measuring evaluation time · Memory storage · Low-level vs. high-level functions · Pattern matching · Reducing size of computation · Symbolic vs. numeric computation · Listability · Pure functions · Packed arrays · Parallel processing · Distributing definitions across subkernels · Profiling · Compiling · Compiling to C

We should forget about small efficiencies, say about 97% of the time: premature optimization is the root of all evil.

— Donald E. Knuth (Knuth 1992)

When you are first learning to program in a language your emphasis is usually on correctness, that is, getting your programs to run and return accurate and error-free results – and rightly so. There is little point in trying to speed up a program that returns incorrect answers! You develop your programs, prototyping with simple inputs so that you can see at a glance how things are progressing. At some point in the development process you start to increase the size or complexity of the inputs to your program and, if all goes well, the program scales well. But commonly, there are bottlenecks at various stages of the computation that slow things down. Some of these may be unavoidable, but often you can find optimizations that improve the efficiency and running time of your programs. This chapter introduces some of the optimization principles to think about both during the development process and after they are complete and you are satisfied that they produce the desired output.

There are two measures we will focus on – timing and memory footprint. Sometimes one plays a more prominent role than the other. But ultimately, squeezing another tenth of a second out of a computation that is only going to be run once or twice does not make a lot of sense. On the other hand, if that computation is part of a loop that is going to be evaluated thousands of times, little things really start to add up. You will be the best judge of where you need to focus your efforts. We will start by creating some auxiliary functions that can help measure timing. The rest of the chapter is designed to provide some case studies and tips to guide you in your efforts to improve your *Mathematica* programs. It includes an introduction to parallel processing and also compilation in *Mathematica*.

12.1 Measuring efficiency

Evaluation time

Two built-in functions, `Timing` and `AbsoluteTiming`, are commonly used to measure evaluation time. Both functions give the time to evaluate an expression in the kernel. The main difference between them is that `Timing` is a bit system-dependent. On computers with multiple processors, threads may be dealt with differently from one multi-core system to another; `Timing` will include time spent on all threads on one system but ignore some of them on others. `AbsoluteTiming` should be more consistent across systems.

One of the problems with measuring timing is that computers are often doing many things simultaneously: checking mail, running system scripts in the background, and so on. To give an accurate measure of the time spent on a computational task and to take into account these background tasks, we will run several trials and then average the results. `AverageTiming`, defined below, does this. Note that it is set up to return only the average time; the result itself is not returned. You should modify the function accordingly if you want both the result and the timing returned, similar to what `Timing` and `AbsoluteTiming` return.

First, we set things up so that `AverageTiming` has the `HoldAll` attribute. This way its argument, the expression to be measured, does not evaluate before it is used inside the body of the `AverageTiming` function itself.

```
In[1]:= SetAttributes[AverageTiming, HoldAll]
```

```
In[2]:= AverageTiming[expr_, trials_] :=
          Mean[Table[First[AbsoluteTiming[expr]], {trials}]]
```

As a simple test, here we compute the time needed to invert a large matrix.

```
In[3]:= mat = RandomReal[1, {1000, 1000}];
        AbsoluteTiming[mat.mat;]
```

```
Out[4]= {0.146887, Null}
```

And for five trials, the average time is given by the following.

```
In[5]:= AverageTiming[mat.mat, 5]
```

```
Out[5]= 0.137580
```

For a compound expression, you could either enclose the subexpressions in a list or separate them with semicolons.

```
In[6]:= AverageTiming[{
           mat.mat,
           Inverse[mat],
           Det[mat]
         }, 3]
```

```
Out[6]= 0.436309
```

```
In[7]:= AverageTiming[
           mat.mat;
           Inverse[mat];
           Det[mat];,
           3]
```

```
Out[7]= 0.425944
```

Memory storage

`ByteCount` gives the number of bytes needed to store an expression. For example, in Section 10.2, we saw the vast difference in storage of a multi-point graphics object compared with a graphics object that does not use multi-points.

```
In[8]:= pts = RandomReal[1, {100, 2}];
        gr = Graphics[Map[Point, pts]];
        grMulti = Graphics[Point[pts]];
```

```
In[11]:= {ByteCount[gr], ByteCount[grMulti]}
```

```
Out[11]= {24 088, 1864}
```

Different computer systems may store expressions differently and so it is possible that `ByteCount` could give slightly different results from one system to another.

One additional function we should point out is `MemoryInUse`. This gives the current amount of memory used by the kernel. It will change after each computation, but because the internals of *Mathematica*'s memory management are fairly complicated, it may not be ideal to use systematically for our purposes here.

```
In[12]:=  start = MemoryInUse[]
```
```
Out[12]=  436 963 112
```
```
In[13]:=  vec = RandomReal[1, {10^6}];
```
```
In[14]:=  end = MemoryInUse[]
```
```
Out[14]=  444 965 728
```
```
In[15]:=  end - start
```
```
Out[15]=  8 002 616
```
```
In[16]:=  ByteCount[vec]
```
```
Out[16]=  8 000 168
```

If you clear the value of **vec**, the amount of memory in use should go down but it will depend upon the current state of your session and so is not a simple way to track memory usage.

```
In[17]:=  vec =.
```
```
In[18]:=  MemoryInUse[]
```
```
Out[18]=  444 965 992
```

12.2 Efficient programs

Low-level vs. high-level functions

Many computational tasks are first programmed as procedures that loop through an expression, extracting and operating on various pieces, and then putting the transformed pieces into a temporary list or array. Typical examples include adding lists of numbers, operating on rows or columns from a matrix, and so on. This low-level approach to a common task is typical of procedural languages, but a modern language such as *Mathematica* provides many functions that are optimized for these tasks. Using such tools can save time and effort in many common tasks, not just in coding and debugging but in the running of your programs.

As an example, consider the task of reversing pairs of elements in a matrix. The standard procedural approach starts by setting up a temporary list of the same size as the input. Then, inside a Do loop, parts are extracted and put in a list in the order we want and assigned to the appropriate element in the temporary list.

```
In[1]:=  mat = {{a, b}, {c, d}, {d, e}};
```

```
In[2]:= temp = Table[0, {Length[mat]}];
     Do[temp[[i]] = {mat[[i, 2]], mat[[i, 1]]},
       {i, 1, Length[mat]}];
     temp

Out[4]= {{b, a}, {d, c}, {e, d}}
```

Reversing the elements in a list is a fairly common task and a functional construct is available for just this.

```
In[5]:= Map[Reverse, mat]

Out[5]= {{b, a}, {d, c}, {e, d}}
```

Not only is the code compact and quite readable, but this functional approach is much faster in practice. Here is a matrix consisting of one million pairs of numbers.

```
In[6]:= mat = RandomReal[1, {10^6, 2}];
```

Reversing each pair with a procedural approach takes about two to three seconds whereas the functional approach speeds this up by over an order of magnitude.

```
In[7]:= AverageTiming[
       temp = Table[0, {Length[mat]}];
       Do[temp[[i]] = {mat[[i, 2]], mat[[i, 1]]},
         {i, 1, Length[mat]}],
       3]

Out[7]= 2.361527
```

```
In[8]:= AbsoluteTiming[Map[Reverse, mat];]

Out[8]= {0.127700, Null}
```

The point is that although you *can* program in a procedural manner in *Mathematica*, there often are some good reasons not to, the main ones being ease of coding and the efficiency of running your programs. The built-in *Mathematica* functions are optimized to be as fast as possible for the types of input and computations for which they are designed. And with the thousands of functions that are built in, you have at your fingertips a vast set of tools that are designed for many specialized tasks.

As a second example, consider summing a list of numbers. Several different implementations are possible.

```
In[9]:= sumDo[n_] := Module[{i = 0, result = 0},
       Do[result = result + i, {i, 1.0, n}];
       result]
```

```
In[10]:= AverageTiming[sumDo[10^6], 3]

Out[10]= 0.868591

In[11]:= sumTable[n_] := Module[{result= 0.0},
           Table[result = result + i, {i, 1.0, n}];
           result]

In[12]:= AverageTiming[sumTable[10^6], 3]

Out[12]= 0.883381

In[13]:= AverageTiming[Sum[i, {i, 1.0, 10^6}], 3]

Out[13]= 0.313786

In[14]:= sumApply[n_] := Apply[Plus, N@Range[n]]

In[15]:= AverageTiming[sumApply[10^6], 3]

Out[15]= 0.261534
```

Of all these approaches (and there are many more!), using Total is optimal. It is designed expressly for the task of adding lists of numbers.

```
In[16]:= sumTotal[n_] := Total[N@Range[n]]

In[17]:= AverageTiming[sumTotal[10^6], 3]

Out[17]= 0.007976
```

You might wonder why Sum, which is also designed for this task, is slower than both the functional approach with Apply and the approach with Total. The Sum function contains hundreds of rules for the various expressions it can handle and also has to keep track of an iterator i. Although these constructs are necessary for complicated summations, this extra overhead comes at a cost that is reflected in the timings here.

As an aside, some mathematical knowledge goes a long way in this particular case. The sum of the integers 1 through n is given by the binomial expression $\binom{n+1}{2}$.

```
In[18]:= Binomial[10^6 + 1, 2] // Timing

Out[18]= {0.000024, 500 000 500 000}

In[19]:= Binomial[10^6 + 1, 2] == Total[Range[10^6]]

Out[19]= True
```

Pattern matching

As we have seen throughout this book, pattern matching is one of the key features of *Mathematica* and distinguishes it from many other programming languages. It provides a natural mechanism to identify classes of expressions that you want to operate on or transform based on some criteria of interest. But for computations where speed is at a premium, the convenience of pattern matching can be overshadowed by slower overall evaluation. In this section we will look at some larger examples that highlight this issue and discuss other approaches that you might want to consider.

A fairly common task is counting the number of elements in an expression that meet some criteria. For example, suppose you want to count the positive numbers in a vector. You could use Count with the appropriate pattern.

```
In[20]:= vec = RandomReal[{-1, 1}, {10}]

Out[20]= {-0.517127, 0.999706, 0.838879, -0.948481, 0.152518,
          0.314375, -0.475982, -0.855164, 0.451484, 0.679374}
```

```
In[21]:= Count[vec, _?Positive]

Out[21]= 6
```

For a more arithmetic approach, you could use Sign which returns −1 for negative numbers and 1 for positive numbers; then add 1 to each element, turning the −1s into 0s and the 1s into 2s.

```
In[22]:= Sign[vec]

Out[22]= {-1, 1, 1, -1, 1, 1, -1, -1, 1, 1}
```

```
In[23]:= Sign[vec] + 1

Out[23]= {0, 2, 2, 0, 2, 2, 0, 0, 2, 2}
```

Lastly, add up the numbers and divide by 2.

```
In[24]:= Total[Sign[vec] + 1] / 2

Out[24]= 6
```

The first approach using Count seems much more natural and easier to code and read, while the second approach involves a lot of steps to get the same result. You might think that the more natural, compact approach using Count would be faster. But, for large vectors, this is not the case.

```
In[25]:= vec = RandomReal[{-1, 1}, {10^6}];
```

```
In[26]:= Count[vec, _?Positive] // Timing

Out[26]= {0.532912, 500 310}
```

In[27]:= **Total[Sign[vec] + 1] / 2 // Timing**

Out[27]= {0.017079, 500 310}

Why is this? The pattern matcher can work with many different kinds of expressions – numbers, strings, functions, images, and so on. One of the things it must do in order to maintain this generality is work with arbitrary arrays of numbers so that it can identify different types that may be present in that array. `Total` and `Sign`, on the other hand, are purely arithmetic functions and they can and do operate on packed arrays of numbers whenever possible, thus taking advantage of compiled code. You can see that this is the case by turning on the display of a message that is issued whenever an array is unpacked internally.

In[28]:= **SetSystemOptions[**
        "PackedArrayOptions" → "UnpackMessage" → True]

Out[28]= PackedArrayOptions → {ListableAutoPackLength → 250,
        PackedArrayMathLinkRead → True, PackedArrayPatterns → True,
        PackedRange → True, UnpackMessage → True}

In[29]:= **Count[vec, _?Positive]**

        Developer`FromPackedArray::unpack : Unpacking array in call to Count. ≫

Out[29]= 500 310

In[30]:= **Total[Sign[vec] + 1] / 2**

Out[30]= 500 310

The call to `Count` caused the packed vector to be unpacked. This was not the case with `Total` and `Sign`. Although not prohibitively expensive here, pattern matching comes at a cost. We will have more to say about packed arrays later in this section.

Reset the packed array message option to its default value.

In[31]:= **SetSystemOptions[**
        "PackedArrayOptions" → "UnpackMessage" → False]

Out[31]= PackedArrayOptions → {ListableAutoPackLength → 250,
        PackedArrayMathLinkRead → True, PackedArrayPatterns → True,
        PackedRange → True, UnpackMessage → False}

As another, less trivial, example, we will look at two approaches for generating upper triangular matrices – matrices with 0s below the diagonal and, in this case, 1s everywhere else. We will start by using `SparseArray`. The pattern matcher is invoked to determine the value of the nonzero elements.

```
In[32]:= With[{n = 5},
            SparseArray[{i_, j_} /; i ≤ j → 1, {n, n}]
        ] // MatrixForm
```

Out[32]//MatrixForm=

$$\begin{pmatrix} 1 & 1 & 1 & 1 & 1 \\ 0 & 1 & 1 & 1 & 1 \\ 0 & 0 & 1 & 1 & 1 \\ 0 & 0 & 0 & 1 & 1 \\ 0 & 0 & 0 & 0 & 1 \end{pmatrix}$$

```
In[33]:= With[{n = 500},
            matSA = SparseArray[{i_, j_} /; i ≤ j → 1, {n, n}]
        ] // Timing
```

Out[33]= {0.36844, SparseArray[<125 250>, {500, 500}]}

Using a procedural approach is significantly faster.

```
In[34]:= With[{n = 5},
            Table[If[j ≥ i, 1, 0], {i, n}, {j, n}]
        ] // MatrixForm
```

Out[34]//MatrixForm=

$$\begin{pmatrix} 1 & 1 & 1 & 1 & 1 \\ 0 & 1 & 1 & 1 & 1 \\ 0 & 0 & 1 & 1 & 1 \\ 0 & 0 & 0 & 1 & 1 \\ 0 & 0 & 0 & 0 & 1 \end{pmatrix}$$

```
In[35]:= With[{n = 500},
            matT = Table[If[j ≥ i, 1, 0], {i, n}, {j, n}];
        ] // Timing
```

Out[35]= {0.010477, Null}

That is over thirty times faster using If to determine the nonzero elements. The comparison is a bit unfair since we are not accounting for the internals of Table compared with SparseArray. But you could check that, in general, creating sparse array objects is quite fast compared with using Table for similarly-sized expressions.

```
In[36]:= matT = Table[0, {i, 10^4}, {j, 10^4}]; // Timing
```

Out[36]= {2.65011, Null}

```
In[37]:= matSA = SparseArray[{_, _} → 0, {10^4, 10^4}]; // Timing
```

Out[37]= {0.000062, Null}

Only one rule was necessary to create this sparse array of os.

In[38]:= **ArrayRules[matSA]**

Out[38]= $\{\{\_, \_\} \to 0\}$

For the upper triangular matrix above, the position index for *every* element had to be compared with the pattern to determine its value. The approach using **Table** had just as many comparisons to make but it did not invoke the pattern matcher to do so.

We should check to make sure that the matrices produced by these two approaches are the same.

In[39]:= **matSA == matT**

Out[39]= **True**

As an aside, the two matrices are not identical as one has the structure of a sparse array and the other is a list. **SameQ** (===) tests if they have identical structures and elements.

In[40]:= **matSA === matT**

Out[40]= **False**

Reducing size of computation

Although it may seem obvious, you should look to reduce the raw number of computations performed when trying to optimize your programs. Usually, such inefficiencies are not apparent on a first look. As an example, consider the following two loops used to add up the first one million integers.

In[41]:= (
    For$\left[\text{i} = 0; \text{result} = 0, \text{i} \le 10^6, \text{i} + +, \text{result} = \text{result} + \text{i}\right]$;
    result
) // **Timing**

Out[41]= $\{2.25038, 500\,000\,500\,000\}$

In[42]:= (
    result = 0;
    Do$\left[\text{result} = \text{result} + \text{i}, \{\text{i}, 1, 10^6\}\right]$;
    result
) // **Timing**

Out[42]= $\{0.888957, 500\,000\,500\,000\}$

Why is the **Do** loop faster? Think about how many computations are done in each loop. With the **For** loop, there is a comparison of i with 10^6, an increment of i, the addition **result + i**, and an assignment to `result`. That is essentially four computations each time through the loop. Inside the `Do` loop, there is the addition `result + i`, the assignment, and the increment of the iterator `i`. There are at least 25% fewer raw computations with the `Do` loop for this computation.

As a more applied example, consider the Sieve of Eratosthenes we implemented in Section 6.3. For each value of p inside the `For` loop, the `Do` loop runs for `i = 2 p` to `i = n` in increments of p. In the code below, we have made a slight modification to `Sieve` to add a counter that gives the number of iterations of the inner `Do` loop.

```
In[43]:= SieveCnt[n_Integer] := Module[{ints = Range[n], p, cnt = 0},
           For[p = 2,
             p ≠ 1 && p ≤ Floor[Sqrt[n]],
             p++,
             Do[ints[[i]] = 1; cnt++, {i, 2 p, n, p}]];
           DeleteCases[ints, 1];
           cnt
         ]
```

For this computation, 532 988 iterations of the inner `Do` loop were performed.

```
In[44]:= SieveCnt[10^5] // Timing
```

```
Out[44]= {1.13214, 532 988}
```

So how could we reduce the overall number of computations? We will use list component assignment, discussed in Section 3.3. We do this by having the `Do` loop cross out values (assign a value of 1) to multiples of p in the list `ints`, but instead of using the `For` loop to get those values of p, use the `Part` function with the `Span` shorthand `2 p ;; -1 ;; p` indicating that we extract parts 2 p through the end in steps of p, that is, the multiples of p.

```
In[45]:= Sieve2[n_Integer] := Module[{ints = Range[n]},
           Do[ints[[2 p ;; -1 ;; p]] = 1,
             {p, 2, √n}];
           DeleteCases[ints, 1]]
```

First let us do a few basic checks for correctness.

```
In[46]:= Sieve2[100]
```

```
Out[46]= {2, 3, 5, 7, 11, 13, 17, 19, 23, 29, 31, 37,
          41, 43, 47, 53, 59, 61, 67, 71, 73, 79, 83, 89, 97}
```

In[47]:= **Length[Sieve2[1000]]**

Out[47]= 168

In[48]:= **PrimePi[1000]**

Out[48]= 168

Next we check the speed of this function.

In[49]:= **Sieve2$\left[10^5\right]$; // Timing**

Out[49]= {0.02608, Null}

That is almost two orders of magnitude faster! Let us count the number of iterations inside the Do loop in Sieve2.

In[50]:= **Sieve2Cnt[*n_Integer*] := Module$\Big[${ints = Range[*n*], cnt = 0},**

Do$\Big[$ints[[2 p ;; -1 ;; p]] = 1;

cnt++,

$\left\{p, 2, \sqrt{n}\right\}\Big]$;

DeleteCases[ints, 1];

cnt

$\Big]$

In[51]:= **Sieve2Cnt$\left[10^5\right]$ // Timing**

Out[51]= {0.025143, 315}

Although it appears as if we have reduced the sheer number of computations from over 500 000 to about 300, that is not quite accurate – it is a bit subtle as to why things have in fact been sped up. For Sieve2, there is an implicit iteration given by ints[[2 p ;; -1 ;; p]] = 1 that is, in fact, handled in compiled C code. So what we are seeing is the difference between explicit iteration in *Mathematica* and implicit iteration that is being done at the level of compiled C code. The list component assignment transfers that iteration to compiled code and this is what has caused the significant speedup.

A different example of superfluous computation occurs when you are passing a table to a function that has one of the Hold attributes. In the following example, the HoldAll attribute of Plot keeps the Table from being evaluated initially. In fact, the Table is evaluated over and over as each value of x is used to construct the plot. The first value returned below is the timing, the second number (45080) is the value of the counter, cnt.

```
In[52]:=  Block[{cnt = 0},
            Plot[Table[cnt++; LegendreP[n, x], {n, 1, 10}], {x, 0, 1}];
            cnt] // Timing
```

Out[52]= {0.299285, 45 080}

Forcing the evaluation of the `Table` before it is passed to `Plot` results in far fewer evaluations there which is reflected in the speedup as well.

```
In[53]:=  Block[{cnt = 0},
            Plot[Table[cnt++; LegendreP[n, x], {n, 1, 10}],
              {x, 0, 1}, Evaluated → True];
            cnt] // Timing
```

Out[53]= {0.048092, 10}

Many of the plotting functions have the attribute `Evaluated`. For those that do not, you can wrap the function to be plotted in `Evaluate` to the same effect.

Symbolic vs. numeric computation

Another issue to think about in trying to improve the speed and efficiency of your programs is the contrast between numeric and symbolic computation. In general, numeric-based computation can be quite fast as much of it is done on the hardware of your machine rather than in software (see the discussion in Section 8.2). This is not a hard-and-fast rule; many of the linear algebra operations take advantage of numeric libraries such as Basic Linear Algebra Subprograms (BLAS) that are optimized for the hardware of your machine. As a result, differences in evaluation time amongst different computers will inevitably occur.

To get a sense of some of the differences between numeric and symbolic computation, let us revisit the radius of gyration tensor computation from Section 8.4. Here is the code developed in that section.

```
RadiusOfGyrationTensor[lis_] :=
  Module[{cmx, cmy, xcoords, ycoords, xy},
    {cmx, cmy} = Mean[lis];
    {xcoords, ycoords} = Transpose[lis];
    xy = (xcoords - cmx).(ycoords - cmy) / Length[lis];
    {{Mean[(xcoords - cmx)^2], xy}, {xy, Mean[(ycoords - cmy)^2]}}]
```

First, let us compute the tensor for an exact matrix (a lattice walk) and also for a matrix consisting of approximate numbers (off-lattice walk).

```
In[54]:=  << PwM`RandomWalks`
```

```
In[55]:=  walkLat = RandomWalk[10^6, LatticeWalk → True];
```

In[56]:= **RadiusOfGyrationTensor[walkLat] // Timing**

Out[56]= $\left\{12.8358, \left\{\left\{\dfrac{3\,726\,499\,413\,459\,191}{62\,500\,000\,000}, \dfrac{2\,620\,753\,801\,968\,301}{125\,000\,000\,000}\right\}, \right.\right.$

$\left.\left.\left\{\dfrac{2\,620\,753\,801\,968\,301}{125\,000\,000\,000}, \dfrac{5\,331\,861\,173\,105\,511}{250\,000\,000\,000}\right\}\right\}\right\}$

In[57]:= **walkOffLat = RandomWalk$\left[10^6,\ \text{LatticeWalk} \to \text{False}\right]$;**

In[58]:= **RadiusOfGyrationTensor[walkOffLat] // Timing**

Out[58]= $\{0.439694, \{\{30\,542.9, 16\,265.8\}, \{16\,265.8, 141\,897.\}\}\}$

That is almost one-and-a-half orders of magnitude faster compared with the exact input. So what is causing this difference? We will focus on the three computations at the heart of this function: computing column means, a transpose operation, and a dot product. This process of *profiling* code to isolate the parts in which the most time is spent is something that can be done using integrated development environments (IDEs) such as Wolfram *Workbench*. We will adopt a very basic approach here since our function is fairly simple to deconstruct. Section 12.3 discusses profiling in more detail.

First, here is the column mean computation for the two walks.

In[59]:= **{cmxL, cmyL} = Mean[walkLat]; // Timing**

Out[59]= $\{0.012443, \text{Null}\}$

In[60]:= **{cmxOL, cmyOL} = Mean[walkOffLat]; // Timing**

Out[60]= $\{0.004598, \text{Null}\}$

Second, this is the transpose computation.

In[61]:= **{xcoordsL, ycoordsL} = Transpose[walkLat]; // Timing**

Out[61]= $\{0.025509, \text{Null}\}$

In[62]:= **{xcoordsOL, ycoordsOL} = Transpose[walkOffLat]; // Timing**

Out[62]= $\{0.09116, \text{Null}\}$

And finally, this is the dot product step.

In[63]:= **(xcoordsL - cmxL).(ycoordsL - cmyL) // Timing**

Out[63]= $\left\{4.0323, \dfrac{2\,620\,753\,801\,968\,301}{125\,000}\right\}$

In[64]:= **(xcoordsOL - cmxOL).(ycoordsOL - cmyOL) // Timing**

Out[64]= $\{0.054526, 1.62658 \times 10^{10}\}$

The transpose operation is several times faster for symbolic (integer) input but the absolute time for the transpose operation is small relative to the overall time for the entire computation; a large difference in timing occurs for the dot product. We can verify these operations by abstracting them out of the context of the radius of gyration computation. First, we compute the dot product on an exact 1000×1000 matrix, followed by the same computation on a matrix consisting of floating point numbers.

```
In[65]:= matInt = RandomInteger[100, {1000, 1000}];
```

```
In[66]:= AbsoluteTiming[matInt.matInt;]
```
Out[66]= {0.697565, Null}

```
In[67]:= matRe = RandomReal[100, {1000, 1000}];
```

```
In[68]:= AbsoluteTiming[matRe.matRe;]
```
Out[68]= {0.159191, Null}

A naive interpretation of this result is that using approximate numbers for the dot product provides a significant speedup compared with the same operation using integers. But there are two caveats. First, the linear algebra libraries that are optimized for your computer may contain slightly slower or faster implementations for integer or floating point computation than those for another machine. Second, because *Mathematica* automatically threads such linear algebra computations over any multiple cores that are available, some of these operations will see significant speedups on machines with larger numbers of cores.

In fact, the difference in timings for many linear algebra operations scales. Behind the scenes, so to speak, multi-threading is happening automatically. You can get a hint of this by comparing `Timing` and `AbsoluteTiming` for these operations.

```
In[69]:= AbsoluteTiming[matRe.matRe;]
```
Out[69]= {0.158654, Null}

```
In[70]:= Timing[matRe.matRe;]
```
Out[70]= {0.301283, Null}

On the machine on which these computations were run, `Timing` is adding the total time spent on all threads that were launched to do this computation.

So what can you take away from this discussion? If you have a program that you need to speed up, profiling is a sensible way to find those computations to optimize. Once you find the bottlenecks, try to see if you can replace an exact computation with one using approximate numbers. Of course, if you need an exact result for some reason, then simply switching to approximate arithmetic is not an option and you will have to consider one of the other approaches discussed in this chapter.

Listability

Many *Mathematica* functions have the `Listable` attribute. Functions with this attribute automatically thread across lists element-wise. We have seen examples of this in many places in this book, for example, with vector and matrix operations:

```
In[71]:= {1, 2, 3, 4} + {10, 20, 30, 40}
Out[71]= {11, 22, 33, 44}
```

```
In[72]:= 10 {1, 2, 3, 4, 5}
Out[72]= {10, 20, 30, 40, 50}
```

But there is much more to listable functions. For large inputs, they can automatically take advantage of multi-threading on vector operations for machines whose hardware supports this. Most of the elementary functions call specialized code that performs this multi-threading behind the scenes. The way to best take advantage of this behavior is to use these functions directly on the vectors or matrices with which you are working.

Mapping elementary functions like `Sin` across a vector is fast, but does not take direct advantage of the listability attribute.

```
In[73]:= vec = RandomReal[{-100, 100}, 10^6];
```

```
In[74]:= AbsoluteTiming[Map[Sin, vec];]
Out[74]= {0.071676, Null}
```

Simply wrapping `Sin` around the input `vec` causes a vectorized version of `Sin` to be called and this is the fastest way to perform the computation, essentially working at the speeds of compiled code.

```
In[75]:= AbsoluteTiming[Sin[vec];]
Out[75]= {0.006034, Null}
```

User-defined functions can inherit the `Listable` attribute.

```
In[76]:= SetAttributes[fun, Listable];
         fun[x_] := If[-1 < x < 1, Exp[x], x^2]
```

```
In[78]:= AbsoluteTiming[fun[vec];]
Out[78]= {1.918452, Null}
```

You can squeeze even more speed out of this function by defining it as a pure function that is listable. This is done by giving `Function` a third argument, `Listable`.

In[79]:= **purefun = Function$\left[\{x\}, \text{If}\left[-1 < x < 1, \text{Exp}[x], x^2\right], \text{Listable}\right]$;**

In[80]:= **AbsoluteTiming[purefun[vec];]**

Out[80]= $\{0.107282, \text{Null}\}$

To generate a list of all built-in functions that have the listable attribute you can use FunctionsWithAttributes defined in Section 5.6.

In[81]:= **lis = FunctionsWithAttribute[Listable];**
Length[lis]

Out[82]= 275

In[83]:= **RandomSample[lis, 25]**

Out[83]= {NonPositive, ExtendedGCD, Negative, BesselJ,
  SpheroidalS2Prime, Sqrt, Ceiling, MakeExpression,
  FactorialPower, ChebyshevT, Log, Log10, BesselK,
  InverseGudermannian, BetaRegularized, PolyGamma, QBinomial,
  ParabolicCylinderD, BitSet, BitAnd, IntegerLength,
  StruveL, NumberFieldRootsOfUnity, Together, Factorial2}

Pure functions

The last example in the previous section raises another efficiency issue: the use of pure functions vs. formally-defined functions. As a simple example, consider two functions, one defined using pure functions and a second defined using a formal function assignment.

In[84]:= **vec = RandomReal$\left[\{-100, 100\}, 10^6\right]$;**

In[85]:= **fun1 = Function$\left[\{x\}, x^2 + 1\right]$;**

In[86]:= **fun2[x_] := $x^2 + 1$**

In[87]:= **AbsoluteTiming[Map[fun1, vec];]**

Out[87]= $\{0.065884, \text{Null}\}$

In[88]:= **AbsoluteTiming[Map[fun2, vec];]**

Out[88]= $\{1.301795, \text{Null}\}$

What accounts for this substantial difference in timing? For expressions above a certain size, Map will automatically try to compile that expression. Below is a list of the system options that are involved with internal compilation.

```
In[89]:= SystemOptions["CompileOptions"]

Out[89]= {CompileOptions → {ApplyCompileLength → ∞,
            ArrayCompileLength → 250, AutoCompileAllowCoercion → False,
            AutoCompileProtectValues → False, AutomaticCompile → False,
            BinaryTensorArithmetic → False, CompileAllowCoercion → True,
            CompileConfirmInitializedVariables → True,
            CompiledFunctionArgumentCoercionTolerance → 2.10721,
            CompiledFunctionMaxFailures → 3,
            CompileDynamicScoping → False, CompileEvaluateConstants →
             True, CompileOptimizeRegisters → False,
            CompileReportCoercion → False, CompileReportExternal → False,
            CompileReportFailure → False, CompileValuesLast → True,
            FoldCompileLength → 100, InternalCompileMessages → False,
            ListableFunctionCompileLength → 250,
            MapCompileLength → 100, NestCompileLength → 100,
            NumericalAllowExternal → False, ProductCompileLength → 250,
            ReuseTensorRegisters → True, SumCompileLength → 250,
            SystemCompileOptimizations → All, TableCompileLength → 250}}
```

For expressions whose size is below the threshold of `MapCompileLength` little absolute difference in timing results.

```
In[90]:= vecSmall = RandomReal[{-100, 100}, {99}];
```

```
In[91]:= AbsoluteTiming[Map[fun1, vecSmall];]

Out[91]= {0.000398, Null}
```

```
In[92]:= AbsoluteTiming[Map[fun2, vecSmall];]

Out[92]= {0.000197, Null}
```

Turning off the auto-compile feature by setting the threshold to ∞ shows nearly identical timings for the computations on the large arrays.

```
In[93]:= SetSystemOptions["CompileOptions" → "MapCompileLength" → ∞];
```

```
In[94]:= AbsoluteTiming[Map[fun1, vec];]

Out[94]= {1.833040, Null}
```

```
In[95]:= AbsoluteTiming[Map[fun2, vec];]

Out[95]= {1.397250, Null}
```

For programs that call functions within loops in particular, this discussion would suggest that you will see speed improvements by using pure functions on larger arrays whenever possible.

Reset the system option to its default value.

In[96]:= **SetSystemOptions["CompileOptions" → "MapCompileLength" → 100];**

Packed arrays

As indicated in Section 8.3, large arrays are operated on very quickly and efficiently when they are packed. Many functions automatically pack arrays.

In[97]:= **Range[1000] // Developer`PackedArrayQ**

Out[97]= **True**

In[98]:= **RandomInteger[{0, 2}, 10³] // Developer`PackedArrayQ**

Out[98]= **True**

In[99]:= **Fourier[RandomInteger[{0, 2}, 10³]] // Developer`PackedArrayQ**

Out[99]= **True**

But some functions do not, and in particular, many expressions created from scratch are not packed. For example, the compass directions used in the random walk example developed in Section 13.1, are not packed.

In[100]:= **NSEW = {{0, 1}, {0, -1}, {1, 0}, {-1, 0}};**
Developer`PackedArrayQ[NSEW]

Out[101]= **False**

In[102]:= **ByteCount[NSEW]**

Out[102]= **488**

The walk function using `Accumulate` and `RandomChoice` is already quite fast. It only takes a few seconds to perform a two-dimensional lattice walk of ten million steps.

In[103]:= **Accumulate[RandomChoice[NSEW, 10⁷]]; // AbsoluteTiming**

Out[103]= **{3.385123, Null}**

For this function, it is not speed that is a constraint, it is memory use. The output of walk2D is an array of dimensions 10 000 000 × 2. Its memory footprint is quite large, over 1 GB!

In[104]:= **Accumulate[RandomChoice[NSEW, 10⁷]] // ByteCount**

Out[104]= **1 120 000 040**

It turns out that `RandomChoice` is the culprit. When choosing from a set of alternatives it does not produce a packed array automatically.

In[105]:= **RandomChoice[NSEW, 1000] // Developer`PackedArrayQ**

Out[105]= **False**

Because the original array NSEW was not itself packed, RandomChoice did not create a packed array as output. If we force NSEW to become packed, then RandomChoice will generate a packed array.

In[106]:= **NSEWpacked =**
    Developer`ToPackedArray[{{0, 1}, {0, -1}, {1, 0}, {-1, 0}}];
    RandomChoice[NSEWpacked, 1000] // Developer`PackedArrayQ

Out[107]= **True**

With this new definition, the random walk code produces a packed array result. The computation also runs about four to eight times faster than before and consumes less than one-tenth of the memory.

In[108]:= **packedResult = Accumulate$\left[\text{RandomChoice}\left[\text{NSEWpacked, }10^7\right]\right]$; //**
    AbsoluteTiming

Out[108]= **{0.360374, Null}**

In[109]:= **Developer`PackedArrayQ[packedResult]**

Out[109]= **True**

In[110]:= **ByteCount[packedResult]**

Out[110]= **80 000 168**

Note that the Accumulate function was given a packed array from RandomChoice and it produced a result that was also packed. Many *Mathematica* functions, but not all, will produce packed results when given packed input. It is not difficult to inadvertently trigger unpacking of an array, so a useful debugging technique is to ask *Mathematica* to issue a message whenever an array is forced to unpack.

In[111]:= **SetSystemOptions[**
    "PackedArrayOptions" → "UnpackMessage" → True]

Out[111]= PackedArrayOptions → {ListableAutoPackLength → 250,
    PackedArrayMathLinkRead → True, PackedArrayPatterns → True,
    PackedRange → True, UnpackMessage → True}

To see the warning message in action, map a function with no definition over the packed array returned by RandomChoice.

In[112]:= **foo /@ RandomChoice[NSEWpacked, {1000}];**
During evaluation of In[112]:=
       Developer`FromPackedArray::punpackl1 :
         Unpacking array with dimensions {1000, 2} to level 1. ≫

You probably will not want this message turned on all the time, but it can be quite handy if you are trying to understand where in your program an array is being unpacked.

In[113]:= **SetSystemOptions[**
    "PackedArrayOptions" → "UnpackMessage" → False]

Out[113]= PackedArrayOptions → {ListableAutoPackLength → 250,
    PackedArrayMathLinkRead → True, PackedArrayPatterns → True,
    PackedRange → True, UnpackMessage → False}

Other functions in `SystemOptions` are worth exploring; for example, note the value of `TableCompileLength`, 250. This is the threshold above which `Table` will automatically pack its output.

In[114]:= **vec = Table[RandomReal[], {249}];**
    Developer`PackedArrayQ[vec]

Out[115]= False

In[116]:= **vec = Table[RandomReal[], {250}];**
    Developer`PackedArrayQ[vec]

Out[117]= True

Below this threshold, the input is small enough that it can be operated on directly without a significant loss of speed. A balance is struck between the speed gained from working with packed arrays and the extra overhead to convert between unpacked and packed expressions.

One last note about manual packing: you can only pack arrays consisting of machine-size integers, reals, or complex numbers. A machine-real can be tested with `MachineNumberQ`.

In[118]:= **MachineNumberQ[N[1, 100]]**

Out[118]= False

For integers, machine numbers are typically in the range $[-2^{31} + 1, 2^{31} - 1]$.

In[119]:= **Map[Developer`MachineIntegerQ, $\{-2^{31}, -2^{31} + 1, 2^{31} - 1, 2^{31}\}$]**

Out[119]= {False, True, True, False}

In[120]:= **smallInts = RandomInteger[$\{2^0, 2^{31}\}$, {100}];**

In[121]:= **Developer`PackedArrayQ[smallInts]**

Out[121]= True

In[122]:= **longInts = RandomInteger$\left[\left\{2^{31},\ 2^{63}\right\},\ \{100\}\right]$;**

In[123]:= **Developer`PackedArrayQ[longInts]**

Out[123]= **False**

One final point: machine numbers and *Mathematica*'s support for them are evolving concepts – as machines become more powerful and the libraries that support them are extended, these definitions will change. *Mathematica* 9 (not released when this book went to print) will support machine numbers on 64-bit machines that are larger than those discussed here and so numbers in the range $[-2^{63} + 1,\ 2^{63} - 1]$ will be considered machine numbers.

(Mathematica 9) In[1]:=

$$\mathrm{Map}\left[\text{Developer`MachineIntegerQ},\ \left\{-2^{63},\ -2^{63} + 1,\ 2^{63} - 1,\ 2^{63}\right\}\right]$$

(Mathematica 9) Out[1]=

{False, True, True, False}

Exercises

1. Modify `AverageTiming` to return both the average time and the result of evaluating its argument, mirroring the behavior of `Timing` and `AbsoluteTiming`.

2. The *n*th triangular number is defined as the sum of the integers 1 through *n*. They are so named because they can be represented visually by arranging rows of dots in a triangular manner (Figure 12.1). Program several different approaches to computing triangular numbers and compare their efficiency.

FIGURE 12.1. *Pictorial representation of the first five triangular numbers.*

3. Several different implementations of the Hamming distance computation were given in Section 5.8; some run much faster than others. For example, the version with bit operators runs about one-and-a-half orders of magnitude faster than the version using `Count` and `MapThread`. Using some of the concepts from this section, determine what is causing these differences.

In[1]:= **HammingDistance1[*lis1_*, *lis2_*] :=**
   Count[MapThread[SameQ, {*lis1*, *lis2*}], False]

In[2]:= **HammingDistance2[*lis1_*, *lis2_*] := Total[BitXor[*lis1*, *lis2*]]**

In[3]:= **sig1 = RandomInteger$\left[1,\ \left\{10^{6}\right\}\right]$;**

In[4]:= **sig2 = RandomInteger$\left[1,\ \left\{10^{6}\right\}\right]$;**

In[5]:= **Timing[HammingDistance1[sig1, sig2]]**

Out[5]= {0.459499, 498 955}

In[6]:= **Timing[HammingDistance2[sig1, sig2]]**

Out[6]= {0.00906, 498 955}

12.3 Parallel processing

Most modern computers now come with multiple core processors enabling many tasks to be performed in parallel. Many system operations are automatically distributed across multiple processors and *Mathematica* also does some automatic parallelization, particularly for many linear algebra operations. But there are plenty of computations that can be done in parallel that are not otherwise automatically threaded or parallelized. In this section we will see how you can use *Mathematica*'s parallel processing framework to speed up many kinds of computation.

Depending upon your licensing, *Mathematica* can be launched and run on each available core on your computer. In general, it will handle the communication between the master kernel and the subkernels automatically and when the computation is done, it will also gather the results from the subprocesses. Although there are tools for getting fine control over many of these aspects of parallel computation, in this section we will introduce the basic functionality only and point you at other resources for further study.

Basic examples

Let us start with a straightforward example – factoring a list of large integers. (These integers were created by multiplying several large prime numbers together, giving numbers that are generally more difficult to factor than a random integer of the same size.)

In[1]:= **ints = {6 816 621 442 891 306 800 904 744 383 119 905 653 635 103 851,**
73 388 383 728 563 244 425 930 590 337 481 080 121 879 717 077,
52 013 328 811 529 395 666 589 446 962 910 372 930 994 642 737,
505 513 202 541 467 917 512 749 204 086 148 326 575 935 117 323};

Doing the computation on one processor takes about eight seconds.

In[2]:= **AbsoluteTiming[Map[FactorInteger, ints]]**

Out[2]= {7.460074, {{{322 901 609 390 167, 1}, {3 515 118 683 942 573, 1},
{6 005 635 550 849 761, 1}}, {{2 294 373 045 611 351, 1},
{3 323 461 128 609 971, 1}, {9 624 378 352 212 737, 1}},
{{1 570 432 314 085 519, 1}, {5 086 852 194 050 141, 1},
{6 510 979 192 425 803, 1}}, {{7 415 796 267 244 853, 1},
{7 673 045 464 769 561, 1}, {8 883 967 089 924 631, 1}}}}

The machine on which this computation was performed has two processors on which *Mathematica* can run kernels. (Actually, the machine has two physical processors and two virtual ones and so $ProcessorCount returns 4.)

In[3]:= **$ProcessorCount**

Out[3]= **4**

This launches *Mathematica* on each of the available processors.

In[4]:= **LaunchKernels[]**

Out[4]= {KernelObject[1, local], KernelObject[2, local],
        KernelObject[3, local], KernelObject[4, local]}

To do the factorization in parallel, use `ParallelMap` instead of `Map`. *Mathematica* will automatically distribute the computations across the subkernels and return the result of each.

In[5]:= **AbsoluteTiming[ParallelMap[FactorInteger, ints]]**

Out[5]= {3.935546, {{{322 901 609 390 167, 1}, {3 515 118 683 942 573, 1},
        {6 005 635 550 849 761, 1}}, {{2 294 373 045 611 351, 1},
        {3 323 461 128 609 971, 1}, {9 624 378 352 212 737, 1}}},
        {{1 570 432 314 085 519, 1}, {5 086 852 194 050 141, 1},
        {6 510 979 192 425 803, 1}}, {{7 415 796 267 244 853, 1},
        {7 673 045 464 769 561, 1}, {8 883 967 089 924 631, 1}}}}}

When finished, you can terminate the *Mathematica* processes on the subkernels by evaluating `CloseKernels`.

In[6]:= **CloseKernels[]**

Out[6]= {KernelObject[1, local, <defunct>],
        KernelObject[2, local, <defunct>],
        KernelObject[3, local, <defunct>],
        KernelObject[4, local, <defunct>]}

If you prefer, launching and closing kernels can be managed using a graphical user interface by selecting Parallel Kernel Configuration or Parallel Kernel Status from the Evaluation menu (Figure 12.2). From this interface you can set the properties that you want to monitor as well as set various configuration parameters for your kernels.

FIGURE 12.2. *Parallel kernel user interface.*

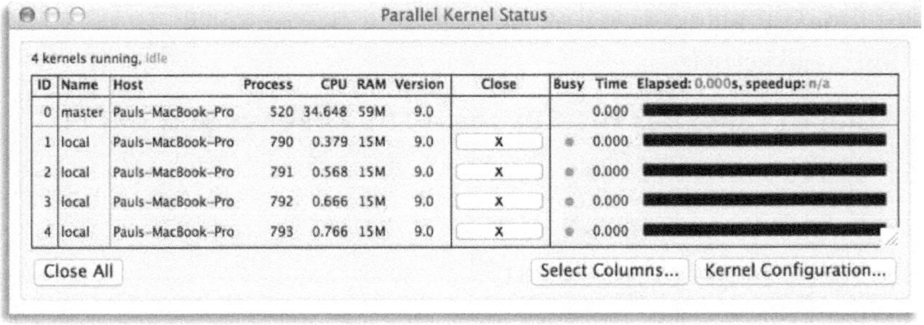

Let us look at another example, this time drawn from Section 5.2 where we computed Mersenne primes.

In[7]:= **Select$\left[$Table$\left[2^{\text{Prime}[n]} - 1, \{n, 1, 1000\}\right]$, PrimeQ$\right]$; //**
       AbsoluteTiming

Out[7]= {58.590406, Null}

Although there is a parallel version of **Table**, we will use another function, **Parallelize**, that automatically handles much of the parallelization.

In[8]:= **LaunchKernels[]**

Out[8]= {KernelObject[5, local], KernelObject[6, local],
         KernelObject[7, local], KernelObject[8, local]}

In[9]:= **Parallelize$\left[$Select$\left[$Table$\left[2^{\text{Prime}[n]} - 1, \{n, 1, 1000\}\right]$,**
       PrimeQ$\right]\right]$; // AbsoluteTiming

Out[9]= {32.961034, Null}

A **Method** option is available for **Parallelize** with which you can set the size of the pieces that are sent to the kernels to give you some additional control of overhead and load balancing amongst the kernels. Setting the method to **"FinestGrained"** breaks ups the computation into the smallest possible chunks. **"CoarsestGrained"** on the other hand, breaks up the computation into as many pieces as there are kernels and is more appropriate when all the computational chunks take the same amount of time.

In[10]:= **Parallelize$\left[$Select$\left[$Table$\left[2^{\text{Prime}[n]} - 1, \{n, 1, 1000\}\right]$, PrimeQ$\right]$,**
        Method → "FinestGrained"$\right]$; // AbsoluteTiming

Out[10]= {34.440888, Null}

Another function for parallel computation is **ParallelEvaluate**. With it, you can evaluate any expression on all subkernels or some subset of the subkernels if you wish. The key difference between `ParallelEvaluate` and other functions is that functions such as `Parallelize` or `ParallelMap` distribute the computation across subkernels, whereas `ParallelEvaluate` does the same computation on all kernels.

In[11]:= `ParallelEvaluate[{$KernelID, $ProcessID, AbsoluteTime[]}]`

Out[11]= $\{\{5, 11\,906, 3.548690244467625 \times 10^9\},$
$\{6, 11\,907, 3.548690244467849 \times 10^9\},$
$\{7, 11\,908, 3.548690244468009 \times 10^9\},$
$\{8, 11\,909, 3.548690244468174 \times 10^9\}\}$

Of course, some computations do not parallelize neatly. For example, any computation that depends upon previous values is generally not a good candidate for parallel computation as the overhead of communicating between subkernels would often erase any gains that might be made by splitting the computation.

In[12]:= `Parallelize[Accumulate[Range[40]]]`

Parallelize::nopar1 :
Accumulate[Range[40]] cannot be parallelized; proceeding with sequential evaluation. ≫

Out[12]= $\{1, 3, 6, 10, 15, 21, 28, 36, 45, 55, 66, 78, 91, 105, 120, 136,$
$153, 171, 190, 210, 231, 253, 276, 300, 325, 351, 378, 406,$
$435, 465, 496, 528, 561, 595, 630, 666, 703, 741, 780, 820\}$

It is important also to note that many of the built-in functions automatically multi-thread, thus gaining a significant degree of parallelism. What this means is that trying to run some of these functions using the parallel framework will not give any further speedup as they already are running in parallel, but behind the scenes so to speak. This is true of the linear algebra functions in particular.

In[13]:= `mat = RandomReal[1, {500, 500}];`

In[14]:= `Do[Inverse[mat], {100}] // AbsoluteTiming`

Out[14]= $\{3.325530, \text{Null}\}$

In[15]:= `ParallelDo[Inverse[mat], {100}] // AbsoluteTiming`

Out[15]= $\{2.947143, \text{Null}\}$

Distributing definitions across subkernels

Let us now apply these ideas to some more substantial computations where the use of parallel processing provides a real boost.

Recall the functions developed in Section 10.4 for determining if a point is inside or outside of a polygon.

In[16]:= **Needs["PwM`Chap10Visualization`"]**

In[17]:= **? PointInPolygonQ**

PointInPolygonQ[*poly*,*pt*] returns True if the
point *pt* is inside the polygon specified by the set of vertices *poly*.

Given a large list of points and a polygon, it takes some time to determine which points are inside the polygon.

In[18]:= **pts = RandomReal[{-1, 3}, {10 000, 2}];**
poly = {{-0.5, 0}, {0.5, -1}, {1.5, 0}, {2., -1.1},
**   {2.5, 0}, {1.5, 2}, {1., 1}, {0., 1}, {-0.5, 0}};**

In[20]:= **gbPts = GatherBy[pts, PointInPolygonQ[poly, #] &];**
Graphics[{
**   {PointSize[Tiny], If[PointInPolygonQ[poly, gbPts[[1, 1]]],**
**   gbPts, Reverse[gbPts]] /. {in_List, out_List} :>**
**   {{Black, Point@in}, {LightGray, Point@out}}},**
**   Thick, Line[poly /. {a_, b__} :> {a, b, a}],**
**   PointSize[Medium], Point[poly]}]**

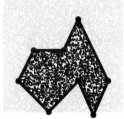

In[22]:= **AbsoluteTiming[Map[PointInPolygonQ[poly, #] &, pts];]**
Out[22]= {1.713795, Null}

This is a good candidate for a parallel computation since the large set of points can be distributed across the subkernels and each checked against the polygon using the PointInPolygonQ code.

In[23]:= **AbsoluteTiming[ParallelMap[PointInPolygonQ[poly, #] &, pts];]**
Out[23]= {3.558163, Null}

Using ParallelMap gave us no speedup here. What happened is that the subkernels knew nothing of PointInPolygonQ nor any of the other code that was given as user-defined functions. In such situations, you will need to distribute these dependent definitions across the subkernels before running the parallel computation.

```
In[24]:= DistributeDefinitions[
            PointInPolygonQ, TriangleArea, pts, poly]

Out[24]= {PointInPolygonQ, TriangleArea, pts}
```

Now the speedup is quite pronounced – about four times the serial computation – which is all that we can expect on a system with four subkernels.

```
In[25]:= Timing[ParallelMap[PointInPolygonQ[poly, #] & , pts];]

Out[25]= {0.293113, Null}

In[26]:= CloseKernels[];
```

Profiling

When you are developing programs it is not always obvious where speed bottlenecks may live. Especially with longer programs, there are numerous steps where the evaluation can bog down. If you are trying to determine which steps will benefit from running in parallel you need to get some sense of where most of the time is being spent. One way to help locate the computational bottlenecks is to profile the code. Integrated development environments such as Wolfram *Workbench* have built-in profilers, but here we will create a simple set of profiling steps to determine where we should focus our efforts in improving the running time of our code.

Recall the `Blanagrams` function from Section 9.5.

```
In[27]:= Blanagrams[word_String] := Module[{blana},
            blana = Table[Map[StringReplacePart[word, ch, {#, #}] & ,
              Range[StringLength[word]]],
             {ch, CharacterRange["a", "z"]}];
            DeleteDuplicates[Flatten[Map[Anagrams, blana, {2}]]]]
```

Although the nested functions might obscure the numerous computations being done here, we will break things down into three parts:

- using `Table` to create a list of alternate "words" by sequentially replacing each letter in word with one of the twenty-six letters *a* through *z*;

- mapping `Anagrams` across the list produced by `Table`;

- flattening and deleting duplicates.

To do the profiling of the steps in this code, we first create a small auxiliary function that wraps `AbsoluteTiming` around an expression and adds a tag to make it easy to identify the various steps of the computation. The `timing` function is given the `HoldAll` attribute to prevent `AbsoluteTiming` from evaluating before its argument is passed to it.

```
In[28]:= timing[expr_, tag_] :=
            Print[{NumberForm[First@AbsoluteTiming[expr], 10], tag}]
          SetAttributes[timing, HoldAll];
```

For the test word, "string", here are the three steps pulled out of the Blanagrams function. First, load the package containing the definition of Anagrams.

```
In[30]:= Needs["PwM`Chap09Strings`"]
```

```
In[31]:= word = "string";
          timing[tmp = Table[
              Map[StringReplacePart[word, ch, {#, #}] &,
                Range[StringLength[word]]],
              {ch, CharacterRange["a", "z"]}];, "table"];

          timing[Flatten[tmp2 = Map[Anagrams, tmp, {2}]];,
            "map Anagrams"];

          timing[DeleteDuplicates[Flatten[tmp2]];,
            "flatten and delete duplicates"]
```

{0.001996, table}

{7.357115, map Anagrams}

{0.000043, flatten and delete duplicates}

Creating the many possible letter combinations is very quick. Similarly, flattening and deleting duplicates at the end is not too expensive. The greatest part of this computation is spent mapping Anagrams across the many word combinations. So we can simply try to parallelize that using ParallelMap.

```
In[35]:= BlanagramsParallel[word_String] := Module[{blana},
            blana = Table[
              Map[StringReplacePart[word, ch, {#, #}] &,
                Range[StringLength[word]]],
              {ch, CharacterRange["a", "z"]}];
            DeleteDuplicates@
              Flatten[ParallelMap[Anagrams, blana, {2}]]
          ]
```

There is no need to distribute BlanagramsParallel across the subkernels as the only parallel piece in it is ParallelMap. But ParallelMap is mapping Anagrams which is not a built-in function, so we need to distribute that definition across the subkernels.

```
In[36]:= LaunchKernels[]
```

```
Out[36]= {KernelObject[5, local], KernelObject[6, local],
          KernelObject[7, local], KernelObject[8, local]}
```

```
In[37]:= DistributeDefinitions[Anagrams]
```

```
Out[37]= {Anagrams}
```

```
In[38]:= BlanagramsParallel["strands"] // AbsoluteTiming
```

```
Out[38]= {19.959044, {strands, stander,
             sanders, dristan, strains, rostand, tundras}}
```

For comparison, here is the computation done serially on one kernel.

```
In[39]:= Blanagrams["strands"] // AbsoluteTiming
```

```
Out[39]= {33.712342, {strands, stander,
             sanders, dristan, strains, rostand, tundras}}
```

On the machine on which this computation was run, we are getting almost a 2× speedup. Recall that each evaluation of Anagrams makes a call to DictionaryLookup to check that the string is in fact a word appearing in the dictionary. This bit of extra overhead is a further bottleneck in this particular code. We could next look to Anagrams as another source of code to optimize and speed up, but we will leave that as an exercise to the interested reader.

Note: There is a mechanism to automatically launch packages on all parallel kernels. ParallelNeeds[" *package*` "] evaluates Needs[" *package*` "] on each of the available subkernels.

```
In[40]:= ParallelNeeds["PwM`Chap09Strings`"]
```

You can then see that the package has been added to the context path of each subkernel.

```
In[41]:= ParallelEvaluate[$ContextPath, Kernels[]]
```

```
Out[41]= {{PwM`Chap09Strings`, PacletManager`,
            WebServices`, System`, Global`}, {PwM`Chap09Strings`,
            PacletManager`, WebServices`, System`, Global`},
          {PwM`Chap09Strings`, PacletManager`, WebServices`,
            System`, Global`}, {PwM`Chap09Strings`,
            PacletManager`, WebServices`, System`, Global`}}
```

```
In[42]:= ParallelEvaluate[Anagrams["float"]]
```

```
Out[42]= {{float, aloft}, {float, aloft},
          {float, aloft}, {float, aloft}}
```

```
In[43]:= CloseKernels[];
```

Exercises

1. In the eighteenth century, Leonhard Euler proved that all even perfect numbers must be of the form $2^{p-1}(2^p - 1)$ for $2^p - 1$ prime. (No one has yet proved that any odd perfect numbers exist.) Use this fact to find all even perfect numbers for $p < 10^4$.

2. The following code can be used to create a plot of the Mandelbrot set. It uses `Table` to compute the value for each point in the complex plane on a small grid. We have deliberately chosen a relatively coarse grid ($n = 100$) as this is an intensive and time-consuming computation. The last argument to `NestWhileList`, 250 here, sets a limit on the number of iterations that can be performed for each input.

```
In[1]:= Mandelbrot[c_] :=
          Length[NestWhileList[#^2 + c &, 0, Abs[#] < 2 &, 1, 250]]
```

```
In[2]:= data = With[{n = 100}, Table[Mandelbrot[x + I y],
          {y, -0.5, 0.5, 1/n}, {x, -1.75, -0.75, 1/n}]];
```

```
In[3]:= ArrayPlot[data, ColorFunction → "GreenPinkTones"]
```

Out[3]=

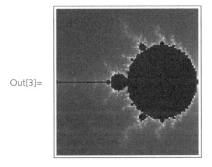

Increase the resolution of the graphic by running the computation in parallel.

12.4 Compiling

In addition to the techniques outlined earlier in this chapter, you can also create compiled functions in *Mathematica* in a variety of ways. Compiled functions are objects that can be executed quickly by being close to the machine code of your computer. The great advantage of working with compiled functions is that they are very fast. Part of the reason they are fast is that they do not need to worry about all the possible kinds of expressions on which they might be called to operate. For example, the built-in `Plus` function has to handle any kind of argument it might be given.

In[1]:= **{1 / 3 + 2, 2 – 4 I + 5.1, 2 + 7}**

Out[1]= $\left\{\dfrac{7}{3},\ 7.1 - 4.\ \dot{\imath},\ 9\right\}$

This kind of generality comes at a cost: *Mathematica* needs to keep track of the kinds of numbers you are passing to arithmetic functions so that the correct internal rule is applied, precision and accuracy are tracked and maintained, and so on. A compiled function, on the other hand, has its argument type explicitly specified so that it only operates on arguments of that type.

Compile

Let us start with a simple example, creating a compiled function called **cfun**. It is expecting an argument **x**, that must match the pattern **_Real**, that is, the argument must have head **Real**.

In[2]:= **cfun = Compile[{{x, _Real}}, x^2 + 1]**

Out[2]= $\text{CompiledFunction}\Big[\{x\},\ x^2 + 1,\ -\text{CompiledCode}-\Big]$

Mathematica creates a **CompiledFunction** object using something called the *Mathematica* virtual machine. Essentially *Mathematica* contains a compiler that can be used for this purpose. The advantage is that it is easy to use and does not require you to have a C compiler installed on your computer. On the other hand, it is not going to compete in optimized code with a commercial C compiler. We will look at compiling to C in the next section.

You use a compiled function like any other, for example, you can evaluate it at an argument or plot it, or integrate it.

In[3]:= **cfun[2.0]**

Out[3]= **5.**

In[4]:= **Plot[cfun[x], {x, –1, 1}]**

Out[4]=
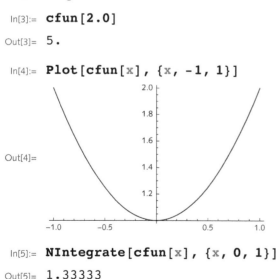

In[5]:= **NIntegrate[cfun[x], {x, 0, 1}]**

Out[5]= **1.33333**

The point of creating and working with compiled functions is that they can speed up computations. This is most pronounced with expressions that have to be evaluated many times. For example, let us return to the function created in Section 12.1.

In[6]:= **fun[x_] := If$\left[-1 < x < 1, \text{Exp}[x], x^2\right]$**

In[7]:= **vec = RandomReal$\left[\{-100, 100\}, 10^6\right]$;**

In[8]:= **AbsoluteTiming[Map[fun, vec];]**

Out[8]= {1.948716, Null}

In[9]:= **purefun = Function$\left[\{x\}, \text{If}\left[-1 < x < 1, \text{Exp}[x], x^2\right], \text{Listable}\right]$;**

In[10]:= **AbsoluteTiming[purefun[vec];]**

Out[10]= {0.107674, Null}

Here is the compiled version.

In[11]:= **compfun = Compile$\left[\{\{x, \_Real\}\}, \text{If}\left[-1 < x < 1, \text{Exp}[x], x^2\right]\right]$**

Out[11]= CompiledFunction$\Big[\{x\},$
  If$\left[-1 < x < 1, \text{Exp}[x], x^2\right], -\text{CompiledCode}-\Big]$

In[12]:= **AbsoluteTiming[Map[compfun, vec];]**

Out[12]= {0.205933, Null}

Not bad, but we can go a bit further and add a runtime attribute to the compiled function that makes it listable.

In[13]:= **compfunListable = Compile$\left[\{\{x, \_Real\}\},\right.$**
  If$\left[-1 < x < 1, \text{Exp}[x], x^2\right], \text{RuntimeAttributes} \rightarrow \{\text{Listable}\}\Big]$

Out[13]= CompiledFunction$\Big[\{x\},$
  If$\left[-1 < x < 1, \text{Exp}[x], x^2\right], -\text{CompiledCode}-\Big]$

In[14]:= **AbsoluteTiming[compfunListable[vec];]**

Out[14]= {0.098877, Null}

Another option, **Parallelization → True**, sets the function to run in parallel if run on a multi-core machine.

```
In[15]:= compfunParallel =
           Compile[{{x, _Real}}, If[-1 < x < 1, Exp[x], x²],
             RuntimeAttributes → {Listable}, Parallelization → True]

Out[15]= CompiledFunction[{x},
           If[-1 < x < 1, Exp[x], x²], -CompiledCode-]

In[16]:= AbsoluteTiming[compfunParallel[vec];]

Out[16]= {0.098661, Null}
```

An additional option can be specified to optimize for speed: `"RuntimeOptions"` with the value `"Speed"`. The caveat here is that this turns off checks and warning messages that might be issued if underflow or overflow errors were caught. Use it with caution.

```
In[17]:= compfunSpeed = Compile[{{x, _Real}},
             If[-1 < x < 1, Exp[x], x²], RuntimeAttributes → {Listable},
             Parallelization → True, "RuntimeOptions" → "Speed"]

Out[17]= CompiledFunction[{x},
           If[-1 < x < 1, Exp[x], x²], -CompiledCode-]

In[18]:= AbsoluteTiming[compfunSpeed[vec];]

Out[18]= {0.088693, Null}
```

If you want to see some of the internals of what `Compile` produces and operates on, use `CompilePrint` which is defined in the CompiledFunctionTools package (we only show a short fragment of the code).

```
In[19]:= << CompiledFunctionTools`

In[20]:= CompilePrint[compfunSpeed] // Short
Out[20]//Short=
                  1 argument
                  1 Boolean register
                  2 In … 0
              8    R2 = Square[ R0]
              9    R4 = R2
             10    Return
```

Compiling to C

If you have a third-party C compiler installed on your computer, you can compile your functions to C, thus taking advantage of any optimizations inherent in your C compiler. If you are not sure if your system has a C compiler installed, you can evaluate `SystemInformation[]` and look under the section External Compilers ▸ Available C Compilers. Alternatively, you can list any C compilers that are installed on your computer as follows:

```
In[21]:= Needs["CCompilerDriver`"]
```

```
In[22]:= CCompilers[]
```

```
Out[22]= {{Name → GCC,
          Compiler → CCompilerDriver`GCCCompiler`GCCCompiler,
          CompilerInstallation → /usr/bin, CompilerName → Automatic}}
```

The syntax to compile to C code is `Compile[…, CompilationTarget → "C"]`. For example, the following code compiles the function from the last section to C.

```
In[23]:= compfunC = Compile[{{x, _Real}},
          If[-1 < x < 1, Exp[x], x^2], CompilationTarget → "C"]
```

```
Out[23]= CompiledFunction[{x},
          If[-1 < x < 1, Exp[x], x^2], -CompiledCode-]
```

For this example, the C compiler provides a speedup over using `Compile` using *Mathematica*'s virtual machine as we did in the previous section.

```
In[24]:= AbsoluteTiming[Map[compfunC, vec];]
```

```
Out[24]= {0.073675, Null}
```

Finally, let us combine several of the optimization suggestions in this chapter in one nontrivial computation. We will create a compiled function that computes the points in the Julia set. The Julia set is the set of points in the complex plane that remain unbounded under iteration of a function such as $z^2 + c$. For most values of $c \in \mathbb{C}$ (the set of complex numbers), this iteration generates fractals. The basic idea is to fix a value of c in the complex plane and then iterate the function for points z on a fine grid in the complex plane. Since there are many points and many iterations for each point, this is very computationally intensive and so it is a good candidate for some of the techniques we have been discussing in this chapter.

First, here is the compiled version of the Julia set function. `Length` returns the length of the list of iterates. We will iterate each point until the iterate is a certain distance from the origin.

```
In[25]:= cJulia = Compile[{{z, _Complex}, {c, _Complex}},
           Length@FixedPointList[(#^2 + c &),
             z, 100, SameTest → (Abs[#2] > 2.0 &)],
           CompilationTarget → "C", RuntimeAttributes → {Listable},
           Parallelization → True, "RuntimeOptions" → "Speed"]
```

$$Out[25]= \text{CompiledFunction}\Big[\{z, c\},$$
$$\text{Length}\Big[\text{FixedPointList}\Big[\#1^2 + c \&, z, 100,$$
$$\text{SameTest} → (\text{Abs}[\#2] > 2. \&)\Big]\Big], -\text{CompiledCode}-\Big]$$

The grid of values that the function will evaluate is given by `ParallelTable` below. The result is passed to `ArrayPlot` which colors each point in the grid according to its iteration length as given by `cJulia`.

```
In[26]:= LaunchKernels[]
```

$$Out[26]= \{\text{KernelObject}[5, \text{local}], \text{KernelObject}[6, \text{local}],$$
$$\text{KernelObject}[7, \text{local}], \text{KernelObject}[8, \text{local}]\}$$

```
In[27]:= DistributeDefinitions[cJulia]
```

$$Out[27]= \{\text{cJulia}, z\}$$

Different Julia sets are generated for different complex numbers c. Here is the Julia set for the complex number, $c = -0.8 - 0.156\,i$.

```
In[28]:= With[{res = 250},
           ArrayPlot[ParallelTable[-cJulia[x + y i, -0.8 - 0.156 i],
```
$$\Big\{y, -1.5, 1.5, \frac{1}{\text{res}}\Big\}, \Big\{x, -1.5, 1.5, \frac{1}{\text{res}}\Big\}\Big],$$
```
           ColorFunction → "Pastel"]] // AbsoluteTiming
```

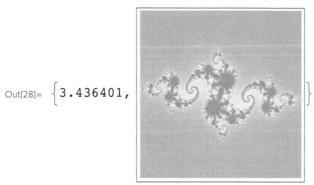

$$Out[28]= \Big\{3.436401,$$

Changing c means changing both its real and imaginary parts so this is a good candidate for a 2D slider. Two modifications are needed here: the value of c from the parameter list will be a list of two numbers that need to be converted into a complex number for the second argument of `cJulia`; and we have reduced the resolution of the grid of points used to make quick updating easier. We also have included a setter bar to select different grid resolutions. The default value for the resolution is set low so that you can quickly move the 2D slider to find an interesting result and then click one of the higher-resolution buttons to see it in full fidelity.

```
In[29]:= Manipulate[
          With[{res1 = res},
            ArrayPlot[Table[cJulia[x + y I, Apply[#1 + #2 I &, c]],
              {y, -1.5, 1.5, 1/res1}, {x, -1.5, 1.5, 1/res1}],
              ColorFunction → "Pastel",
              PlotLabel → Style[StringForm["c = `1`",
                Dynamic[(#1 + #2 I &) @@ c]], 10]]],
          Row[{
            Control[
              {{c, {-0.123, 0.745}, "c"}, {-1.5, -1.5}, {1.5, 1.5}}],
            Spacer[40],
            Control[{{res, 20, "resolution"}, {20, 50, 100}}]
          }], Bookmarks → {
            "Siegel disk" :→ (c = {-0.391, -0.587}),
            "Douady's Rabbit" :→ (c = {-0.123, 0.745})},
          SaveDefinitions → True]
```

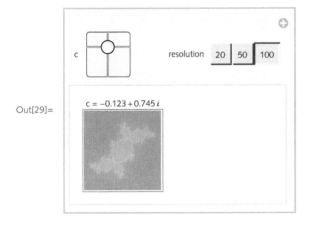

Out[29]=

One way to deal with the tug between quick interactivity and high resolution is to use the function `ControlActive`[*act, norm*] that returns the value *act* when the controller is active (for example, when you are moving a slider) and returns the value *norm* when the controller is not active (for example, when you release the slider). In this way, dynamically changing the value of the parameter will result in quick updates since the low-resolution value will be used during that update, but the graphic will snap to a high-resolution image soon after you release the mouse. Which actual values to choose for `ControlActive` will depend a bit on the speed of your hardware and some other factors, so you will have to experiment to find appropriate values.

```
In[30]:=  Manipulate[
            ArrayPlot[
              Table[-cJulia[x + y i, Apply[Complex, c]],
                {y, -1.5, 1.5, 1 / ControlActive[30, 1000]},
                {x, -1.5, 1.5, 1 / ControlActive[30, 1000]}
              ], ColorFunction → "GreenPinkTones"
            ],
            {{c, {-0.8, -0.156}}, {-1, -1}, {1, 1}}
          ]
```

Out[30]=

As we saw in Section 11.1, it is a bit more convenient to use a locator instead of a 2D slider so that you can manipulate the point *c* directly. Below, we also include a different implementation of the Julia function as part of the initialization as well as a dynamic plot label to display the value of the parameter *c* as the locator is moved.

```
In[31]:= Manipulate[
    Graphics[{
        PointSize[Tiny], Point[Transpose[{Re[#], Im[#]}] &@
            Nest[julia[Apply[Complex, loc], #] &, {0.0}, 12]]
    },
    PlotLabel → StringForm["c = `1`", Apply[Complex, loc]]],
    {{loc, {-0.4, 0.6}}, {-2, -2}, {2, 2}, Locator},
    Initialization :> {
        julia = Compile[{{c, _Complex}, {z, _Complex, 1}},
            Flatten[{√(z - c), -(√(z - c))}]]
    },
    SaveDefinitions → True
]
```

Out[31]=

$c = -0.4 + 0.6\,i$

Exercises

1. Create a compiled function that computes the distance to the origin of a two-dimensional point. Then compare it to some of the built-in functions such as `Norm` and `EuclideanDistance` for a large set of points. If you have a C compiler installed on your computer, use the `Compile` option, `CompilationTarget → "C"` and compare the results.

2. Modify the previous exercise under the assumption that complex numbers are given as input to your compiled function.

3. Many other iteration functions can be used for the Julia set computation. Experiment with some other functions such as $c \sin(z)$, $c \, e^z$, or Gaston Julia's original function:

$$z^4 + z^3/(z-1) + z^2/(z^3 + 4z^2 + 5) + c.$$

For these functions, you will have to adjust the test to determine if a point is unbounded upon iteration. Try `(Abs[Im[#]] > 50 &)`.

13

Applications and packages

Random walk application · Lattice walks · Off-lattice walks · RandomWalk · Error and usage messages · Visualization · Animation · Working with packages · Package location · Contexts · Package framework · Creating and installing the package · RandomWalks package · Running the package

When you have developed several programs for some related tasks, you will find it convenient to group them together and make them available as a cohesive application that can easily be used and incorporated in your work. Packages and applications are part of the framework in *Mathematica* that makes this possible. A package is simply a text file containing *Mathematica* code. Typically you put related functions in a package. So there might be a computational geometry package or a random walks package that includes functions in support of those tasks. An application, in *Mathematica*, is a set of packages together with various user-interface elements such as documentation, palettes, and perhaps stylesheets.

When you develop an application, it is important to think about how your functions work with each other as well as how well they integrate with the rest of *Mathematica*. The user's interface to your programs should be as close as possible to that of the built-in functions in *Mathematica* so that users can more easily pick up the syntax and usage. Packages provide the framework to do this. In this chapter, features such as options, argument checking, messaging, and documentation are all discussed in the context of a larger application – random walks. We will gather much of the code fragments from earlier chapters and add an options framework, error and usage messages, and some new interactive visualization tools as we develop the RandomWalks package in this chapter.

13.1 Random walk application

Random walks are widely used to represent random processes in nature: physicists use them to model the transport of molecules, biologists work with models of the locomotion of organisms, engineers use random walks to model heat conduction, and economists model time behavior of financial markets with them. This model can be envisioned by thinking of a person taking a succession of steps that are randomly oriented with respect to one another. It provides a good application of *Mathematica* to a problem that involves a diverse set of computational tasks: modeling, simulation, statistical analysis, visualization, and interface construction.

In this section, we will gather many of the random walk programs from earlier sections and exercises in this book and create an application for working with random walks in one, two, and three dimensions. Our application will include options for setting the dimension and whether the random walk is on or off the lattice. We will add error and usage messages as well as functions for visualization and animation. Finally, we will introduce contexts and the package framework and pour our application into a package that can be distributed to others and used like any other *Mathematica* package. The contents of the RandomWalks package are included with the materials that accompany this book (see Preface).

Lattice walks

One-dimensional lattice walks The simplest random walk model consists of a number of steps of equal length, back-and-forth along a line. A step in the direction of the positive horizontal axis corresponds to a value of 1 and a step in the direction of the negative horizontal axis corresponds to a value of -1. A list of the successive step directions of a t-step random walk in one dimension is therefore a list of t randomly selected 1s and -1s. For example, here are five step directions, randomly selected from the list $\{-1, 1\}$.

```
In[1]:= dirs = RandomChoice[{-1, 1}, 5]
```

```
Out[1]= {-1, -1, -1, 1, 1}
```

From these step directions how do we create the random walk? A moment's thought should convince you that we can add one step direction to the previous location to generate the "walk". `Accumulate` essentially computes partial sums, which is perhaps clearer with an example using symbolic input.

```
In[2]:= Accumulate[{a, b, c, d, e}]
```

```
Out[2]= {a, a + b, a + b + c, a + b + c + d, a + b + c + d + e}
```

So if we accumulate the list `dirs` above, this generates a list of the locations of a one-dimensional five-step walk starting at the origin.

In[3]:= **Accumulate[dirs]**

Out[3]= $\{-1, -2, -3, -2, -1\}$

Here then is a function, `walk1D`, that generates a list of the step locations of a *t*-step random walk.

In[4]:= **walk1D[*t*_] := Accumulate[RandomChoice[{-1, 1}, *t*]]**

Here is a small run of the `walk1D` program for ten steps.

In[5]:= **walk1D[10]**

Out[5]= $\{-1, -2, -1, -2, -1, -2, -1, -2, -3, -4\}$

To visualize such a random walk quickly we use `ListLinePlot`. The heights of the graph represent distances from the starting point and the number of steps is given along the horizontal axis.

In[6]:= **ListLinePlot[walk1D[1000]]**

Out[6]=

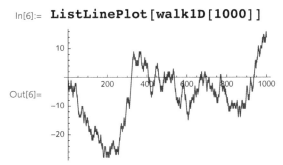

Here is a picture of twelve random walks, each of length 1000.

In[7]:= **ListLinePlot[Table[walk1D[1000], {12}]]**

Out[7]=

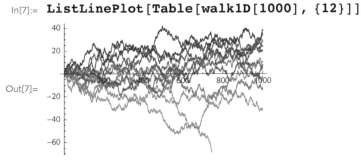

One property that starts to become apparent with these plots is the fact that as the length of the random walk increases, so does the average distance to the origin, as seen by the vertical height from the curves to the horizontal axis. A plot comparing walk length with distance to the origin shows those distances growing ever wider.

In[8]:= `ListLinePlot[Table[{len, Abs@Last@walk1D[len]},`
     `{len, 1000, 500 000, 1000}], AspectRatio → .3]`

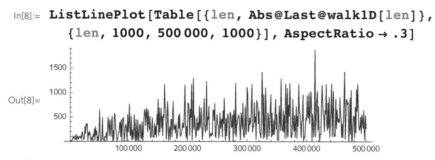

Out[8]=

Before we go further, there is one minor wrinkle in this implementation of `walk1D`. The use of `Accumulate` does not give the origin as the first element in its output. For purposes of analyzing these random walks numerically, it is often convenient to have the list of locations start at the origin. This can be accomplished by using `FoldList` instead of `Accumulate`, joining 0 to the output of `Accumulate`.

In[9]:= `SeedRandom[0];`
     `FoldList[Plus, 0, RandomChoice[{-1, 1}, 10]]`

Out[10]= $\{0, 1, 0, 1, 0, -1, 0, 1, 2, 1, 0\}$

In[11]:= `SeedRandom[0];`
      `Join[{0}, walk1D[10]]`

Out[12]= $\{0, 1, 0, 1, 0, -1, 0, 1, 2, 1, 0\}$

In the next section we will implement a slightly different approach using identity matrices. We will use the simpler code here in the text to aid in readability but either implementation could be altered to start at the origin using a construct like `Join` above.

Two-dimensional lattice walks   The random walk model in higher dimensions is a bit more complicated than the random walk in one dimension. In one dimension, each step of the walk is either a forward step represented by 1 or a backwards step represented by − 1. In higher dimensions, a step can take a range of orientations with respect to previous steps.

FIGURE 13.1.   *Two-dimensional rectangular lattice.*

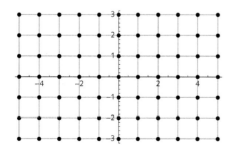

We will consider a random walk on a lattice, appropriately referred to as a *lattice walk*. Specifically, we will look at a lattice walk on the two-dimensional rectangular lattice (Figure 13.1). This walk consists of steps of uniform length, randomly taken in the north, south, east, or west direction – the *compass directions*. Essentially, we are working with the following four vectors in the Cartesian plane. These four points are often referred to as the *von Neumann neighborhood* of the central point (Figure 13.2).

In[13]:= **NSEW = {{0, 1}, {0, -1}, {1, 0}, {-1, 0}};**

FIGURE 13.2.   *A site with its four nearest (von Neumann) neighbors.*

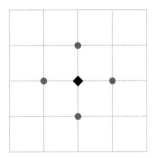

A list of *t* step increments is created by randomly selecting one of the four directions and then adding that vector to the existing site. For example, this chooses two step directions from NSEW.

In[14]:= **RandomChoice[NSEW, 2]**

Out[14]= {{1, 0}, {0, -1}}

If the current site had coordinates {2, 3}, then adding the first step location to that site gives the new position.

In[15]:= **{2, 3} + {1, 0}**

Out[15]= {3, 3}

Adding the second step location to {3, 3} gives the next position.

In[16]:= **% + {0, -1}**

Out[16]= {3, 2}

Using Accumulate as we did in the case of the one-dimensional random walk, we iterate this process for an arbitrary number of steps. Here is a program to generate a list of the step locations of a *t*-step, two-dimensional lattice walk.

In[17]:= **walk2D[t_] := Accumulate[RandomChoice[NSEW, t]]**

Try this out on a ten-step walk, that is, for $t = 10$.

In[18]:= **walk2D[10]**

Out[18]= {{-1, 0}, {0, 0}, {0, 1}, {0, 2},
        {0, 3}, {1, 3}, {2, 3}, {2, 2}, {2, 1}, {2, 2}}

There is more than a little similarity between the two functions walk1D and walk2D. Both use Accumulate, randomly choosing *t* elements from some list. In the case of one-dimensional walks, that list is simply {-1, 1}; for two-dimensional walks it is the list NSEW. Let us try a slightly different approach, one that uses these similarities to simplify the lattice walk code.

The key observation is to think about this as a vector problem. In two dimensions, the vectors that RandomChoice is choosing are essentially the two orthogonal vectors {1, 0} and {0, 1} together with the opposite of each of these. Both these vectors are given by the identity matrix of the appropriate dimension.

In[19]:= **Join[IdentityMatrix[1], -IdentityMatrix[1]]**

Out[19]= {{1}, {-1}}

In[20]:= **Join[IdentityMatrix[2], -IdentityMatrix[2]]**

Out[20]= {{1, 0}, {0, 1}, {-1, 0}, {0, -1}}

In[21]:= **Join[IdentityMatrix[3], -IdentityMatrix[3]]**

Out[21]= {{1, 0, 0}, {0, 1, 0}, {0, 0, 1},
        {-1, 0, 0}, {0, -1, 0}, {0, 0, -1}}

This makes the code for the random walks consistent but it also generalizes to *n*-dimensional space. We will pursue this approach for the lattice walks.

Before we write the code for the *n*-dimensional lattice walk, we need to make one adjustment in the case of one-dimensional walks. IdentityMatrix[1] returns the list {1} so we will need to flatten that list for this case only.

Here then is the code for an *n*-dimensional lattice walk.

In[22]:= **latticeWalk[steps_, dim_] := Module[{w},**
    w = Accumulate[RandomChoice[Join[
        IdentityMatrix[dim], -IdentityMatrix[dim]], steps]];
    If[dim == 1, Flatten[w], w]]

In[23]:= **latticeWalk[5, 2]**

Out[23]= {{0, -1}, {-1, -1}, {-2, -1}, {-2, -2}, {-2, -1}}

We visualize the path these steps take in the plane by connecting each of these points with a line. This displays a 2500-step random walk. We have set the AspectRatio so that our plot has a more natural ratio of height to width.

In[24]:= **ListLinePlot[latticeWalk[2500, 2], AspectRatio → Automatic]**

Out[24]=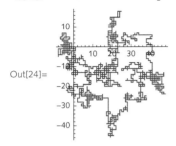

And here is a one-dimensional lattice walk.

In[25]:= **ListLinePlot[latticeWalk[2500, 1]]**

Out[25]=

Three-dimensional lattice walks In three dimensions, there are six different directions that can be taken at any given step (Figure 13.3).

FIGURE 13.3. *A site (cube) with its six nearest neighbors in a three-dimensional rectangular lattice.*

We have seen above that steps along the direction given by the nearest neighbors can be represented by joining the identity matrix with its opposite; this is already built into the `lat-ticeWalk` function.

In[26]:= `Join[IdentityMatrix[3], -IdentityMatrix[3]]`

Out[26]= `{{1, 0, 0}, {0, 1, 0}, {0, 0, 1},`
`{-1, 0, 0}, {0, -1, 0}, {0, 0, -1}}`

The visualization of these points in 3-space is straightforward – connect each point with a line (or tube) and then convert to a graphical object to display.

In[27]:= `Graphics3D[Tube[latticeWalk[2500, 3]]]`

Out[27]=
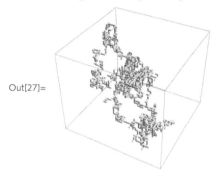

As an aside, the `latticeWalk` function can be used to create *n*-dimensional walks for any positive integer *n* > 0. Although visualizing such objects is difficult, we can still ask questions about the nature of such walks similar to the discussion in Section 8.4. For example, here are five steps in a nine-dimensional random walk.

In[28]:= `latticeWalk[5, 9]`

Out[28]= `{{0, 0, 1, 0, 0, 0, 0, 0, 0},`
`{0, 0, 1, 1, 0, 0, 0, 0, 0}, {0, -1, 1, 1, 0, 0, 0, 0, 0},`
`{0, -1, 1, 1, 1, 0, 0, 0, 0}, {-1, -1, 1, 1, 1, 0, 0, 0, 0}}`

This computes the distance to the origin of the last step in this nine-dimensional walk.

In[29]:= `Norm[Last[%]]`

Out[29]= $\sqrt{5}$

Off-lattice walks

Although lattice walks are fairly easy to visualize and program, there are many physical phenomena, such as Brownian motion, for which walks off the lattice are more appropriate models. In this section, we will create off-lattice versions of the random walk functions from the previous section. They are similar to the lattice walk code except that the step directions are real numbers in a certain range instead of integers from the lattice. Once they are developed, we will create a function, `offLatticeWalk`, that will call the appropriate function for a given dimension. For two and three dimensions, we have chosen to use walks in which each step is of unit length. You are encouraged to modify these programs to allow other step lengths.

One-dimensional off-lattice walk In the one-dimensional case, steps of unit length give the lattice walk described above. For our off-lattice walk, we will take step directions chosen to be any real number between -1 and 1. Of course, this means that for this case, steps are not of length 1.

In[30]:= **walk1DOffLattice[t_] := Accumulate[RandomReal[{-1, 1}, t]]**

In[31]:= **walk1DOffLattice[5]**

Out[31]= {0.187697, 0.0873112, 0.0752274, -0.906305, -1.896}

Two-dimensional off-lattice walk In the two-dimensional case, we essentially compute polar points and so the directions are polar angles between 0 and 2π; the coordinates of the points are given by the pair $(\cos\theta, \sin\theta)$, which gives steps of unit length.

In[32]:= **walk2DOffLattice[t_] :=**
       Accumulate[Map[{Cos[#], Sin[#]} &, RandomReal[{0, 2 π}, t]]]

In[33]:= **walk2DOffLattice[5]**

Out[33]= {{-0.993598, -0.112978},
      {-0.900142, -1.1086}, {-1.81362, -0.701705},
      {-2.08523, -1.66411}, {-1.12155, -1.93117}}

Let us quickly check that each step is of length 1.

In[34]:= **Partition[%, 2, 1]**

Out[34]= {{{-0.993598, -0.112978}, {-0.900142, -1.1086}},
      {{-0.900142, -1.1086}, {-1.81362, -0.701705}},
      {{-1.81362, -0.701705}, {-2.08523, -1.66411}},
      {{-2.08523, -1.66411}, {-1.12155, -1.93117}}}

In[35]:= **Apply[EuclideanDistance, %, 1]**

Out[35]= {1., 1., 1., 1.}

Three-dimensional off-lattice walk There are several different ways to approach the three-dimensional off-lattice walk. Using a spherical coordinate system, a point uniformly distributed on the sphere can be obtained from the following equations (Weisstein, Sphere point picking):

$$x = \cos(\theta) \sqrt{1 - u^2},$$
$$y = \sin(\theta) \sqrt{1 - u^2},$$
$$z = u.$$

We need to produce *pairs* of random numbers θ and u with θ in the interval $[0, 2\pi)$ and u in the interval $[-1, 1]$. Here then is the function to generate t steps of an off-lattice random walk in three dimensions.

```
In[36]:= walk3DOffLattice[t_] := Accumulate[Table[

            Function[{θ, u}, {Cos[θ] √(1 - u²) , Sin[θ] √(1 - u²) , u}] @@

              {RandomReal[{0, 2 π}], RandomReal[{-1, 1}]}, {t}]

          ]
```

```
In[37]:= walk3DOffLattice[4]
```

```
Out[37]= {{0.487841, -0.240428, -0.83917},
           {1.14515, 0.153194, -1.48183},
           {0.686236, 1.00981, -1.24599}, {1.13357, 0.93944, -0.354398}}
```

Again, check that each step is of unit length.

```
In[38]:= Apply[EuclideanDistance, Partition[%, 2, 1], 1]
```

```
Out[38]= {1., 1., 1.}
```

The offLatticeWalk function We now use the common elements to simplify our code, similarly to what we did earlier with the lattice walk code. The only difference amongst these three cases is the function that we are accumulating. We will use Which to slot in the appropriate function to Accumulate, based on the value of the dimension argument, dim.

```
In[39]:= offLatticeWalk[t_, dim_] := Module[{f1, f2, f3},

            f1:= RandomReal[{-1, 1}, t];
            f2:= Map[{Cos[#], Sin[#]} &, RandomReal[{0, 2π}, t]];
            f3:= Table[

                Function[{θ, u}, {Cos[θ] √(1 - u²) , Sin[θ] √(1 - u²) , u}] @@

                  {RandomReal[{0, 2 π}], RandomReal[{-1, 1}]}, {t}];
            Which[
              dim == 1, Accumulate[f1],
              dim == 2, Accumulate[f2],
              dim == 3, Accumulate[f3]
            ]
          ]
```

Try out the code for dimensions one through three.

In[40]:= `ListLinePlot[offLatticeWalk[10 000, 1]]`

Out[40]=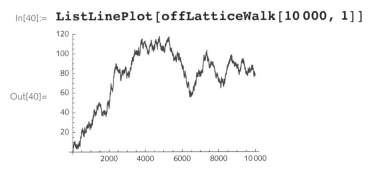

In[41]:= `ListLinePlot[offLatticeWalk[10 000, 2],`
`  AspectRatio → Automatic]`

Out[41]=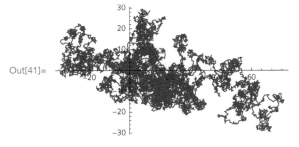

In[42]:= `Graphics3D[Line@offLatticeWalk[10 000, 3]]`

Out[42]=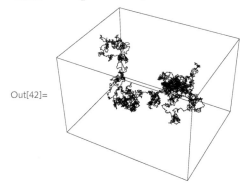

RandomWalk

We have now developed two separate functions, `latticeWalk` and `offLatticeWalk`. Our intention is that these will be auxiliary functions that the user should not have to remember. It is preferable to have one function, `RandomWalk`, that has a simple, easy-to-remember interface that calls the appropriate function when needed. In computer languages, the `RandomWalk` function is often called the *public* function, the user's interface to the underlying code. The two auxiliary functions `latticeWalk` and `offLatticeWalk` are referred to as *private* functions and are kept hidden from the user interface. The developer of such code is then free to change these underlying private constructs as the need arises and the user does not need to worry about them as the public interface remains unchanged.

Following on from the discussion of options in Section 5.7, we start by creating two optional arguments (options) to our `RandomWalk` function – `LatticeWalk` and `Dimension` – and give their default values. These are the values that will be used whenever explicit options to `RandomWalk` are not given. The idea is that if `LatticeWalk` has a value of `True`, `RandomWalk` will call the `latticeWalk` function. Similarly, if the `Dimension` option has a value of 3 say, that will be passed to the appropriate function automatically.

```
In[43]:=  Options[RandomWalk] = {LatticeWalk → True, Dimension → 2}

Out[43]=  {LatticeWalk → True, Dimension → 2}
```

Here is the `RandomWalk` function with the option structure in place.

```
In[44]:=  RandomWalk[t_, OptionsPattern[]] := Module[{dim, latticeQ},
            {latticeQ, dim} = OptionValue[{LatticeWalk, Dimension}];
            If[latticeQ, latticeWalk[t, dim], offLatticeWalk[t, dim]]
          ]
```

Some comments on this code are in order:

- To pass the options into the `RandomWalk` function, we use `OptionsPattern` on the left-hand side of the function definition.

- To extract the values from the options, we use `OptionValue`. We can use the syntax `OptionValue[{LatticeWalk, Dimension}]` to extract the values of these options since, in this case, `OptionValue` will assume the function to which the options are referring is the head of the left-hand side of the rule.

- We assign the values of the options to local symbols `latticeQ` and `dim` inside the body of the `RandomWalk` function.

- Note the use of `If` to check the value of the `LatticeWalk` option and then call the appropriate auxiliary (private) function. If the `LatticeWalk` option has been set to `True`, then the first branch of the `If` statement is followed, giving the lattice walk. If `LatticeWalk` has any other value (`False`, for example), then the off-lattice definition is used.

This will be the user-interface to the random walk machinery we are building. The two functions `latticeWalk` and `offLatticeWalk` will be private, meaning the user does not need to know anything about them to use `RandomWalk`.

Let us exercise the options and check that each of the six possible walks produces a sensible result. First, we compute the lattice walks.

In[45]:= **RandomWalk[5, Dimension → 1]**

Out[45]= {-1, 0, -1, 0, 1}

In[46]:= **RandomWalk[5]**

Out[46]= {{1, 0}, {2, 0}, {3, 0}, {4, 0}, {5, 0}}

In[47]:= **RandomWalk[5, Dimension → 3]**

Out[47]= {{0, 0, -1}, {-1, 0, -1}, {-1, 0, -2}, {-1, 0, -1}, {0, 0, -1}}

And here are some off-lattice walks in one, two, and three dimensions.

In[48]:= **RandomWalk[5, Dimension → 1, LatticeWalk → False]**

Out[48]= {0.197714, 0.337862, -0.32516, -0.80017, 0.0871163}

In[49]:= **RandomWalk[5, Dimension → 2, LatticeWalk → False]**

Out[49]= {{-0.960645, 0.277779},
        {-1.65285, -0.443924}, {-2.64838, -0.538359},
        {-1.7695, -0.0613185}, {-2.62799, 0.451512}}

In[50]:= **RandomWalk[5, Dimension → 3, LatticeWalk → False]**

Out[50]= {{0.715746, -0.465297, -0.520775},
        {0.327593, -0.724388, -1.4052},
        {0.032606, -0.0297681, -2.06131},
        {1.00896, -0.0818691, -2.27113},
        {1.79858, -0.658968, -2.47958}}

Error and usage messages

While developing programs, it is a good idea to anticipate how a user of your programs will interact with them. In particular, it is good programming style to try to catch any errors the user may make and respond with an appropriate message. It is also a good idea to make your functions, as much as possible, behave like built-in functions in terms of these error and warning messages. A user that has already become familiar with these elements in *Mathematica* does not need to learn new elements and this makes it that much easier for anyone to adopt and use your code.

One of the conditions we might want to check for with our **RandomWalk** function is that the user enters a positive integer as the first argument. Let us first write the warning message.

In[52]:= **RandomWalk::rwn = "Argument `1` is not a positive integer.";**

And here is a simple trap for this condition that will be placed in the body of RandomWalk:

$$\text{If}[!\,(\text{IntegerQ}[t]\,\&\&\,t > 0)\,,\,\text{Message}[\text{RandomWalk::rwn, } t]\,,\,\ldots]$$

If the first argument, *t* (the number of steps), to RandomWalk passes the test inside this If statement – if it fails to be an integer or fails to be greater than zero – then a message will be generated substituting the argument t for `` `1` `` in the rwn message above.

In[53]:= **Message[RandomWalk::rwn, -42]**

> RandomWalk::rwn : Argument –42 is not a positive integer.

Let us also create a warning message to be issued if the value of the Dimension option is anything but the integers 1, 2, or 3.

In[54]:= **RandomWalk::baddim =**
   "The value `1` of the option Dimension is
   not an integer between 1 and 3.";

In[55]:= **Message[RandomWalk::baddim, 0]**

> RandomWalk::baddim : The value 0 of the option Dimension is not an integer between 1 and 3.

The usage message for RandomWalk begins with a function template.

In[56]:= **RandomWalk::usage =**
   "RandomWalk[*t*] generates a *t*-step random walk.
   The default behavior gives a two-dimensional
   lattice walk with steps in one of the four
   compass directions. The option LatticeWalk
   takes values True or False. The value of the
   option Dimension can be any of 1, 2, or 3.";

Below is the rewritten RandomWalk function with the messaging included. Which is used here so that if the either of the first two conditions pass, then the corresponding warning message is issued. If the two conditions fail – if the argument is a positive integer – then the last condition, True, passes and the If statement is evaluated generating a lattice or off-lattice walk depending upon the value of latticeQ. We clear out any previous definitions for RandomWalk. Clear does not remove messages and options. If you need to remove messages, attributes, or options, use ClearAll or Remove.

In[57]:= **Clear[RandomWalk]**

```
In[58]:= RandomWalk[t_, OptionsPattern[]] := Module[{dim, latticeQ},
         {latticeQ, dim} = OptionValue[{LatticeWalk, Dimension}];
         Which[
           ! (IntegerQ[t] && t > 0), Message[RandomWalk::"rwn", t],
           ! (IntegerQ[dim] && 1 ≤ dim ≤ 3),
           Message[RandomWalk::baddim, dim],
           True, If[latticeQ, latticeWalk[t, dim],
             offLatticeWalk[t, dim]]]]
```

If we pass a noninteger or negative argument to `RandomWalk`, the warning will be triggered.

```
In[59]:= RandomWalk[-6]
```

RandomWalk::rwn : Argument −6 is not a positive integer.

If the value of the `Dimension` option is invalid, another warning is issued.

```
In[60]:= RandomWalk[12, Dimension → 4]
```

RandomWalk::baddim : The value 4 of the option Dimension is not an integer between 1 and 3.

Visualization

Since our random walks can be represented by points (and possibly lines) in the plane or in 3-space, we can use built-in visualization functions or graphics primitives that are designed to work with these objects. There are two advantages to this approach: once implemented, computations are very fast and the resulting graphics objects are as compact as possible. Both of these facts are quite important when working with very large graphical objects, objects that can have over a million components, for example.

We will prototype the visualization functions by first creating simplified functions without options or messaging. Once that framework is in place, we will then flesh out the full versions by adding in these other components.

For one-dimensional random walks we simply connect the coordinates with a line using the built-in function `ListLinePlot`.

$$\texttt{ListLinePlot}\big[\textit{coords}\big]$$

If our list of coordinates consists of pairs of numbers, `ListLinePlot` will plot each pair in the coordinate plane using the usual association of first coordinate of each pair along the horizontal axis and the second coordinate of each pair along the vertical axis.

Since there is no provision for `ListLinePlot` to take coordinate triples, we will have to manually construct the graphics from primitive elements in the three-dimensional case. Alternatively, you could call `ListLinePlot3D` developed in Section 10.4.

$$\texttt{Graphics3D}\big[\texttt{Line}\big[\textit{coords}\big]\big]$$

Here is the code for `ShowWalk`. The patterns `{{_, _} ..}` and `{{_, _, _} ..}` match the cases of one or more pairs or triples of coordinates, respectively. In each case, the pattern is given a name, `coords`, to be used in the body of each function.

```
In[61]:= ShowWalk[coords_?VectorQ] := ListLinePlot[coords]
```

```
In[62]:= ShowWalk[coords : {{_, _} ..}] :=
             ListLinePlot[coords, AspectRatio → Automatic]
```

```
In[63]:= ShowWalk[coords : {{_, _, _} ..}] := Graphics3D[Line[coords]]
```

This displays a 100 000-step one-dimensional random walk.

```
In[64]:= ShowWalk[RandomWalk[10^5, Dimension → 1]]
```

Here is a 100 000-step, two-dimensional, off-lattice walk.

```
In[65]:= ShowWalk[RandomWalk[10^5, Dimension → 2, LatticeWalk → False]]
```

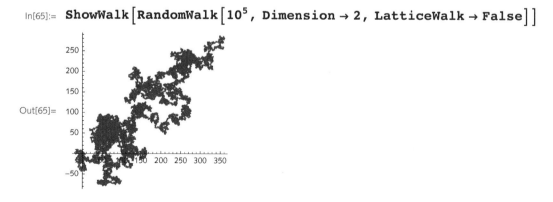

And here is a three-dimensional lattice walk.

In[66]:= `ShowWalk[RandomWalk[10⁴, Dimension → 3, LatticeWalk → True]]`

Out[66]=

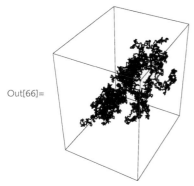

Next, we want to use the many built-in graphics options with our `ShowWalk` function but some options are only valid for `ListLinePlot` (one and two dimensions) and other options are specific to `Graphics3D`. By filtering the appropriate options, we ensure that `Graphics3D` options are passed to the `Graphics3D` function and `ListLinePlot` options are passed to `ListLinePlot`. This is done by using `FilterRules`. For example, the expression below will return only those options that are specific to `ListLinePlot`.

```
FilterRules[{opts}, Options[ListLinePlot]]
```

Here are the rewritten rules for `ShowWalk`, including the options structure.

In[67]:= `Clear[ShowWalk]`

In[68]:= `Options[ShowWalk] =`
`    Join[Options[ListLinePlot], Options[Graphics3D]];`

In[69]:= `ShowWalk[coords_?VectorQ, opts : OptionsPattern[]] :=`
`        ListLinePlot[coords,`
`    FilterRules[{opts}, Options[ListLinePlot]]]`

In[70]:= `ShowWalk[coords : {{_, _} ..}, opts : OptionsPattern[]] :=`
`        ListLinePlot[coords,`
`    Append[FilterRules[{opts}, Options[ListLinePlot]],`
`    AspectRatio → Automatic]]`

In[71]:= `ShowWalk[coords : {{_, _, _} ..}, opts : OptionsPattern[]] :=`
`    Graphics3D[Line[coords],`
`    FilterRules[{opts}, Options[Graphics3D]]]`

Alternatively, you could put all the different patterns inside a `Switch` and choose the appropriate function based on the pattern match inside `Switch`. That approach may be a bit more compact, but it comes at the cost of readability and greater difficulty modifying the code later.

Here is a 500-step off-lattice walk in two dimensions for which we have passed options to `ListLinePlot` to set the aspect ratio and also to display all coordinates visited as points.

```
In[72]:= ShowWalk[RandomWalk[500, LatticeWalk → False],
           Mesh → All, AspectRatio → Automatic]
```

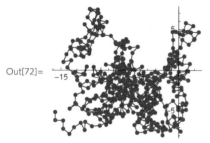

Out[72]=

This exercises some of the three-dimensional graphics options for `ShowWalk`.

```
In[73]:= ShowWalk[RandomWalk[2500, Dimension → 3, LatticeWalk → False],
           FaceGrids → {{-1, 0, 0}, {0, 1, 0}, {0, 0, -1}},
           BoxStyle → {Thin, Gray}, AspectRatio → Automatic]
```

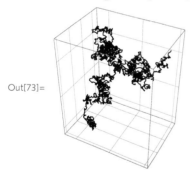

Out[73]=

There are several alternative approaches that could be used to visualize random walks. Other approaches (for example, one using `GraphicsComplex` and another using graphs) have their advantages; we will find that graphics primitives and the built-in `ListLinePlot`, as we have done here, is extremely fast and is the most efficient in terms of the size of the objects that we will be generating. These issues and alternative approaches are explored in some detail in the exercises at the end of this chapter.

Animation

Looking at the visualizations of random walks, it is clear that a lattice walk repeatedly revisits sites in the course of its meandering. As a result, it is difficult to discern the history of the walk from a snapshot of the path. The best way to see the entire evolution of the walk in an unobscured fashion is to create an animation.

Animations are created by successively displaying graphical expressions, one frame at a time. This is most easily accomplished with `Animate`, passing it one additional step in each frame.

You might try to animate a random walk by wrapping `Animate` around `ListLinePlot`, making the length, n, the parameter to be manipulated by `Animate`.

```
In[74]:= Animate[
            ListLinePlot[RandomWalk[n]], {n, 1, 500, 1}]
```

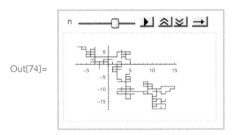

Out[74]=

But a moment's thought should convince you that this is not the correct approach. For *each* value of n, the expression `ListLinePlot[RandomWalk[...]]` is reevaluated and a new walk is created so there is no correlation between successive "steps." A second problem is that the bounding box of each plot is jumping around quite a bit as *Mathematica* computes a new plot range for *each* frame.

To tackle the first problem, we will pregenerate the entire walk and then take successive steps using $\text{Take}\left[\text{walk, } n\right]$ and pass the first n steps of the walk to $\text{Graphics}\left[\text{Line}[...]\right]$.

```
In[75]:= walk = RandomWalk[8]
```
```
Out[75]= {{1, 0}, {1, -1}, {1, -2},
            {0, -2}, {0, -1}, {0, 0}, {0, 1}, {1, 1}}
```

```
In[76]:= Take[walk, 1]
```
```
Out[76]= {{1, 0}}
```

```
In[77]:= Take[walk, 2]
```
```
Out[77]= {{1, 0}, {1, -1}}
```

```
In[78]:= Take[walk, 3]
```
```
Out[78]= {{1, 0}, {1, -1}, {1, -2}}
```

Here is a sample 2000-step random walk that we will use for our animation.

```
In[79]:= rw = RandomWalk[2000, Dimension → 2, LatticeWalk → False];
```

For the second problem, the plot range issue, we need to find the minimum and maximum values in the horizontal and vertical directions from our walk so that we can pass their values to the `PlotRange` option. Otherwise *Mathematica* would set the plot range for each graphic frame using a heuristic that only looks at the values of the coordinates for that particular frame and not the entire set of graphics frames in the animation. This would create a different size frame for each graphic, causing quite a bit of jumpiness in the animation.

We first transpose the matrix of coordinates from $\{\{x_1, y_1\}, \{x_2, y_2\}, ..., \{x_n, y_n\}\}$ to $\{\{x_1, x_2, ..., x_n\}, \{y_1, y_2, ..., y_n\}\}$; this generalizes to three-dimensional lists as well. Then we get the minimum and maximum values from each using `Map`.

```
In[80]:= Map[{Min[#], Max[#]} &, Transpose[rw]]

Out[80]= {{-28.5516, 23.1099}, {-18.4443, 25.678}}
```

This output, by design, is precisely of the form needed by `PlotRange`.

Here is the code to create an animation of the random walk `rw`. In print, we can only show a representative snapshot of the animation. We have set `DisplayAllSteps` to `True` to override the default behavior of `Animate` to skip some of the frames. You will have to balance the need for speed with the need to see the entire sequence.

```
In[81]:= Animate[
         Graphics[Line[Take[rw, steps]],
           PlotRange -> Map[{Min[#], Max[#]} &, Transpose[rw]]],
         {steps, 2, Length[rw], 1},
         DisplayAllSteps -> True]
```

Out[81]=

Here are the similar computations for the three-dimensional walk.

```
In[82]:= rw3 = RandomWalk[10 000, Dimension -> 3, LatticeWalk -> True];
```

```
In[83]:= Map[{Min[#], Max[#]} &, Transpose[rw3]]

Out[83]= {{-103, 0}, {-128, 1}, {-39, 14}}
```

And this creates the animation using these range of values for *x*, *y*, and *z* as the `PlotRange`.

In[84]:= **Animate[**
Graphics3D[Line[Take[rw3, steps]],
PlotRange → Map[{Min[#], Max[#]} &, Transpose[rw3]]],
{steps, 2, Length[rw3], 1}]

Out[84]=

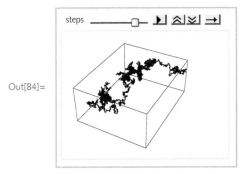

The code for two and three dimensions is bundled up in the `AnimateWalk` function.

In[85]:= **AnimateWalk[*coords*_List, *opts* : OptionsPattern[Animate]] :=**
Module[{range, dim = Last[Dimensions[*coords*]]},
range = ({Min[#], Max[#]} &) /@ Transpose[*coords*];
Animate[If[dim == 2, Graphics, Graphics3D] @@
{Line[Take[*coords*, steps]], PlotRange → range},
{steps, 2, Length[*coords*], 1}, *opts*]]

In[86]:= **rw4 = RandomWalk[2500, Dimension → 3, LatticeWalk → False];**
AnimateWalk[rw4, DisplayAllSteps → True]

Out[87]=

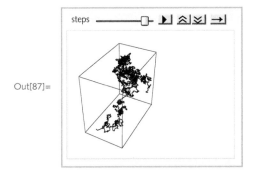

Some additional user interface elements could include checkboxes to toggle lattice/off-lattice walks, a pulldown menu to select the size of the walk, other elements such as buttons to let the user set the dimension, and so on. Section 11.3 discussed several different dynamic interfaces for random walks including one to generate new walks by simply clicking your mouse on the graphic (using `EventHandler`).

Exercises

1. Although all the lattice walks in this chapter were done on the square lattice, we could also implement the walks on lattices with different geometries. For example, the hexagonal lattice in two dimensions can be used as the grid on which our random walkers move.

    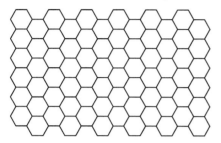

    Create a two-dimensional random walk that can move in one of six directions each separated by 60 degrees.

2. Generate random walks where the step length t occurs with a probability proportional to $1/t^2$. These walks are sometimes referred to as Lévy flights.

3. Create a version of `ShowWalk` that uses `GraphicsComplex` directly. The first argument to `GraphicsComplex` is the coordinate information as given by `RandomWalk`; the second argument should be graphics primitives (`Line`, `Point`) that indicate how the coordinates should be displayed.

4. Create a visualization of random walks that takes advantage of the efficiency of `Graph` to store and represent large amounts of graphical data. The first argument to `Graph` can be a list of rules that represents the connectivity information. For example, 2 $\mapsto$ 3 indicates that the second vertex is connected to the third vertex with a directed edge. Use the option `VertexCoordinates` to pass the explicit coordinate information from `RandomWalk` to `Graph`. Run some tests to determine the efficiency (in terms of running time and memory) of this approach as compared to the `ShowWalk` function that was developed in this chapter.

5. Create a function that generates random walks with random step length. Advanced: Do the same but allow for arbitrary distributions.

6. Create a random walk that is bounded by a region in the Cartesian plane, for example, a circle centered at the origin of radius 2.

7. Create a one-dimensional random walk over the digits of π – if the digit is even, take a step to the right; if the digit is odd, take a step to the left.

13.2 Overview of packages

When you begin a *Mathematica* session, the built-in functions are immediately available for you to use. There are, however, many more functions that you can access that reside in files supplied with *Mathematica*. In principle, the only difference between those files and the ones you create is that those were written by professional programmers. There is another difference: the definitions in those files are placed in special structures called *packages*. Indeed, these files themselves are often called "packages" instead of "files."

Packages are text files that contain *Mathematica* commands. They are designed to make it easy to distribute your programs to others, but they also provide a framework for you to write programs that integrate with *Mathematica* in a seamless manner. That framework includes a *name localizing* construct, analogous to **Module**, but for entire files of definitions. The idea is to allow you, the programmer, to define a collection of functions for *export*. These exported functions are for the users of your package to work with and are often referred to as *public* functions. Other functions, those that are *not for export*, are auxiliary, or *private* functions, and are not intended to be accessible to users. The package framework, and contexts specifically, provide a convenient way to declare some functions public and others private. Contexts will be introduced in Section 13.3. Finally, in Section 13.4, we will put all these ideas together, using the random walk code developed earlier in this chapter.

Working with packages

Mathematica packages have been written for a great variety of problem domains. Many are provided with each version of *Mathematica* and are referred to as the Standard Extra Packages. Their documentation is available in the Documentation Center (under the Help menu).

For example, one of the packages listed under the Standard Extra Packages is the Computational Geometry package. It provides functionality for computing and visualizing such things as Delaunay triangulations, Voronoi diagrams, and convex hulls of lists of points.

Once you know which package you want to use, you load it using either **Get** or **Needs**.

- `<< ComputationalGeometry`` will read the file and evaluate each expression and definition as if it had been typed in. Actually, the argument of `<<` is a string, but the quotation marks can be omitted. `<< package`` is shorthand for `Get[" package` "]`.

In[1]:= **<< ComputationalGeometry``**

- `Needs["ComputationalGeometry``"]` will read the package, just like `<<`, but only if it has not already been read.

In[2]:= **Needs["ComputationalGeometry``"]**

Once a package has been loaded into the *Mathematica* kernel, you can access and use the functions defined in that package just like any built-in function. For example, you can use ? to get the usage message for any of those functions.

In[3]:= **? ConvexHull**

> ConvexHull$[\{\{x_1, y_1\}, \{x_2, y_2\}, \ldots\}]$ yields the planar convex hull of the points $\{\{x_1, y_1\}, \ldots\}$, represented as a list of point indices arranged in counterclockwise order. ≫

Using a function from a package is just like using a built-in function. For example, this computes the convex hull of a small set of points in the plane using the `ConvexHull` function.

In[4]:= **ConvexHull[RandomInteger[100, {10, 2}]]**

Out[4]= {1, 9, 4, 7, 8, 5}

Here a list of hyperlinks to the documentation for each of the functions defined in this package.

In[5]:= **? ComputationalGeometry`***

▼ ComputationalGeometry`

AllPoints	DelaunayTriangulationQ	Ray
BoundedDiagram	DiagramPlot	TileAreas
ConvexHull	Hull	TriangularSurfacePlot
ConvexHullArea	LabelPoints	TrimPoints
ConvexHullMedian	NearestNeighbor	VoronoiDiagram
DelaunayTriangulation	PlanarGraphPlot	

Clicking any of the above links will display the usage message associated with that function. You can also display a list of the names defined in the package using `Names`.

In[6]:= **Names["ComputationalGeometry`*"]**

Out[6]= {AllPoints, BoundedDiagram, ConvexHull,
    ConvexHullArea, ConvexHullMedian, DelaunayTriangulation,
    DelaunayTriangulationQ, DiagramPlot, Hull, LabelPoints,
    NearestNeighbor, PlanarGraphPlot, Ray, TileAreas,
    TriangularSurfacePlot, TrimPoints, VoronoiDiagram}

If you forget the name of the package, you can easily browse through the Documentation Center which lists all packages, names, and usage messages of the functions defined in these packages. Alternatively, you locate where the directory of packages is stored on your system and browse through it using your operating system's interface.

Package location

All the built-in *Mathematica* packages are located in one of several directories on *Mathematica*'s search path. If you put your package in one of these special directories, it will be found quickly when you try to load it with `Get` or `Needs`. This search path is given by `$Path`. Here we display only some of these locations.

In[7]:= **Take[$Path, 8] // TableForm**

Out[7]//TableForm=
```
/Applications/Mathematica.app/SystemFiles/Links
/Users/wellin/Library/Mathematica/Kernel
/Users/wellin/Library/Mathematica/Autoload
/Users/wellin/Library/Mathematica/Applications
/Library/Mathematica/Kernel
/Library/Mathematica/Autoload
/Library/Mathematica/Applications
.
```

Typically, packages are put in one of the Applications directories on that path.

In[8]:= **Select[$Path, MatchQ[FileNameTake[#], "Applications"] &] //**
      TableForm

Out[8]//TableForm=
```
/Users/wellin/Library/Mathematica/Applications
/Library/Mathematica/Applications
/Applications/Mathematica.app/AddOns/Applications
```

Certain special directories are identified on your system using one of the $ functions below.

In[9]:= **$UserBaseDirectory**

Out[9]= `/Users/wellin/Library/Mathematica`

In[10]:= **$BaseDirectory**

Out[10]= `/Library/Mathematica`

In[11]:= **$InstallationDirectory**

Out[11]= `/Applications/Mathematica.app`

These directories will be different on different operating systems but putting a package in one of them will work across systems consistently. For example, the instructions to install the packages that accompany this book specify that you should put them in one of the directories given by the following:

In[12]:= **FileNameJoin[{$BaseDirectory, "Applications"}]**

Out[12]= `/Library/Mathematica/Applications`

In[13]:= **FileNameJoin[{$UserBaseDirectory, "Applications"}]**

Out[13]= /Users/wellin/Library/Mathematica/Applications

Alternatively, you could use the Install item in the File menu to be guided through the process somewhat automatically. This is described for the RandomWalks package in Section 13.4.

If you know the name of your package, you can use FindFile to see precisely where the package is located. Specifically, using the package name as an argument returns the location of the Kernel/init.m file. This works whether your package has been loaded or not.

In[14]:= **FindFile["PwM`"]**

Out[14]= /Library/Mathematica/Applications/PwM/Kernel/init.m

13.3 Contexts

Every symbol you use in a computation in *Mathematica* has a *full name* consisting of the symbol preceded by the *context* in which the name was first mentioned. The context is a means for organizing symbols. You can think of the context like a namespace – different symbols are in different contexts just like different files on your computer live in different directories.

When you first start your session, the *current context* is Global` (note the back quote), and any symbol you mention now has full name Global`*symbol*. $Context gives the current context.

In[1]:= **$Context**

Out[1]= Global`

Here is a function created, by default, in the Global` context.

In[2]:= **f[x_] := x + 1**

Context[*sym*] gives the context of the symbol *sym*.

In[3]:= **Context[f]**

Out[3]= Global`

You can use the function by specifying its full name.

In[4]:= **Global`f[3]**

Out[4]= 4

But, of course, it is much more convenient to use the regular, short form.

In[5]:= **f[3]**

Out[5]= 4

Mathematica first searches the current context for definitions associated with any symbols; by default, this is the Global` context. To see a list of the contexts that *Mathematica* uses to search for symbols, use `$ContextPath`. Note that the `ComputationalGeometry`` context is included as we loaded that package in the previous section.

```
In[6]:= $ContextPath
```

```
Out[6]= {ComputationalGeometry`,
        PacletManager`, WebServices`, System`, Global`}
```

As we saw above, any symbols defined when your session begins have context `Global``. Built-in functions have context `System``. Symbols defined in packages have their context set by the package (discussed below).

```
In[7]:= Map[Context, {Integrate, f, ConvexHull}]
```

```
Out[7]= {System`, Global`, ComputationalGeometry`}
```

To use a different context for any new symbols you mention, use the function `Begin`.

```
In[8]:= Begin["ContextA`"]
```

```
Out[8]= ContextA`
```

```
In[9]:= g[x_] := x + 2
```

This uses g by specifying its full name.

```
In[10]:= ContextA`g[3]
```

```
Out[10]= 5
```

Or, since we are currently in the `ContextA`` context, use the short name. In this new context, the name g is an abbreviation for `ContextA`g`.

```
In[11]:= g[3]
```

```
Out[11]= 5
```

Here is the current context.

```
In[12]:= $Context
```

```
Out[12]= ContextA`
```

Note that we can still refer to f, even though it was not defined in this context. This is because f lives in the `Global`` context which is searched as part of `$ContextPath`.

```
In[13]:= Map[Global`f, {5, 7, 9}]
```

```
Out[13]= {6, 8, 10}
```

```
In[14]:= Map[f, {5, 7, 9}]
```

```
Out[14]= {6, 8, 10}
```

After exiting the context using `End`, you may define a different g, having context `Global``.

In[15]:= **End[]**

Out[15]= ContextA`

In[16]:= **g[x_] := x + 3**

In[17]:= **g[3]**

Out[17]= 6

In[18]:= **Context[g]**

Out[18]= Global`

We now have two definitions of g: one definition of Global`g and one of ContextA`g. Since our current context is Global`, when we just say g we get Global`g; but we can still refer to ContextA`g by its full name.

In[19]:= **g[3]**

Out[19]= 6

In[20]:= **ContextA`g[3]**

Out[20]= 5

The question arises: when you enter a symbol *sym*, how does *Mathematica* decide which version of *sym* to use? And how can you tell which one it has chosen? As we saw above, the function Context gives the context of a symbol.

In[21]:= **Context[Map]**

Out[21]= System`

In[22]:= **Context[ContextA`g]**

Out[22]= ContextA`

You can also use ?.

In[23]:= **?g**

Global`g

g[x_] := x + 3

How does *Mathematica* decide which definition to use? It maintains two variables, $Context and $ContextPath. $Context contains the current context; $ContextPath contains a list of contexts. *Mathematica* looks in $Context first, then in the contexts in $ContextPath in the order in which they appear there; if it does not find the symbol at all, then it creates it in context $Context. Of course, none of this applies if you give the symbol's full name.

In[24]:= **$Context**

Out[24]= Global`

In[25]:= **$ContextPath**

Out[25]= {ComputationalGeometry`,
        PacletManager`, WebServices`, System`, Global`}

In[26]:= **Begin["ContextA`"]**

Out[26]= ContextA`

In[27]:= **$Context**

Out[27]= ContextA`

In[28]:= **$ContextPath**

Out[28]= {ComputationalGeometry`,
        PacletManager`, WebServices`, System`, Global`}

In[29]:= **End[]**

Out[29]= ContextA`

In[30]:= **$Context**

Out[30]= Global`

So the effect of entering a new context using Begin is simply to change the value of $Context; End[] changes it back. In either case, $ContextPath is not changed.

In[31]:= **$ContextPath**

Out[31]= {ComputationalGeometry`,
        PacletManager`, WebServices`, System`, Global`}

One final point about contexts: contexts can be nested within contexts, that is, you can have context names like A`B`C`.

In[32]:= **Begin["A`"]**      (* enter context A` *)

Out[32]= A`

In[33]:= **Begin["`B`"]**   (* enter context A`B` *)

Out[33]= A`B`

In[34]:= **Begin["`C`"]**   (* enter context A`B`C` *)

Out[34]= A`B`C`

In[35]:= **End[]**   (* back in context A`B` *)

Out[35]= A`B`C`

In[36]:= **End[]**   (* back in context A` *)

Out[36]= A`B`

In[37]:= **End[]**   (* back in context Global` *)

Out[37]= A`

Note the back quote *before* the context name in the second and third `Begin`. This is used to indicate that the new context should be a subcontext of the current context. We could have also indicated this as follows:

In[38]:= **Begin["A`"]**

Out[38]= A`

In[39]:= **Begin["A`B`"]**

Out[39]= A`B`

In[40]:= **Begin["A`B`C`"]**

Out[40]= A`B`C`

Nested contexts are a way of managing the multiplicity of contexts. In fact, package names are contexts. When you load a package using `Needs` or `<<`, *Mathematica* translates the package name directly into a path name in the hierarchical file system on your computer.

For example, you can load the package `RandomWalks.m` that lives in a directory PwM according to the commands given in Table 13.1.

TABLE 13.1. *Commands to load packages on different systems*

Operating System	Input
Windows	`<< PwM\RandomWalks.m`
Unix X/Linux	`<< PwM/RandomWalks.m`

Since *Mathematica* provides a system-independent means of loading packages, you can simply use `Get` with the following syntax and *Mathematica* will automatically translate this into a path name appropriate for your computer.

       `<< PwM`RandomWalks` `

13.4 Creating packages

Packages provide a framework to organize a collection of related functions. With them, you can identify private functions and constants that the user, or client, of the package will not ordinarily see. Usage and warning messages for the public functions, those that the user of your package will interact with, are also defined in the package. When set up properly using contexts, packages help to avoid naming collisions, or shadowing, with other definitions of those names.

In this section, we will lay out the package framework that you can use as a template for developing all your packages. We will briefly show some ways that you can easily deploy your packages. All of these components are demonstrated using the random walk application developed earlier in this chapter.

Package framework

Every package uses a framework containing several common elements. Let us start by outlining each of those pieces that you need to include in your package (Program Listing 13.1). You can create these in a new *Mathematica* notebook or use the PackageTemplate.nb notebook that accompanies this book's support materials (see Preface).

PROGRAM LISTING 13.1. *Package template*

```
BeginPackage["package`"]

(* usage messages *)
package::usage = "usage message here…";

(* options *)
Options[package] = {opt1 → value1, opt2 → value2, …}

(* private context *)
Begin["`Private`"]

(* function definitions *)
fun[x_] := …
fun2[x_, y_] := …

(* end private context *)
End[]

EndPackage[]
```

BeginPackage and EndPackage Packages start with a `BeginPackage` statement and end with an `EndPackage`. Evaluating `BeginPackage["`*package*`` `"]` sets `$Context` to *package*``, and `$ContextPath` to {*package*`, `System``}. `EndPackage[]` resets both variables to their values prior to the evaluation of `BeginPackage[]`, and then prepends *package*`` to `$ContextPath`.

As an example, suppose you are in a *Mathematica* session, with current context `Global``, and you read in a file containing the following:

```
BeginPackage["package`"]

  f[x_] := …

  g[y_] := …

EndPackage[]
```

After it is read, the functions `f` and `g`, with full names `package`f` and `package`g`, will be defined, and the context `package`` will be in `$ContextPath`. If you do not have any other definitions of `f`, you can refer to it as just `f`; if there are other definitions for a symbol `f` in other contexts, then use `package`f`; and similarly for the function `g`.

In[1]:= **$ContextPath**

Out[1]= {ComputationalGeometry`,
          PacletManager`, WebServices`, System`, Global`}

In[2]:= **BeginPackage["myPackage`"]**

Out[2]= myPackage`

In[3]:= **$ContextPath**

Out[3]= {myPackage`, System`}

It is important to realize, too, that *Mathematica* determines the full name of any symbol when it reads it in. Thus, if `g` calls `f`, then the occurrence of `f` in the body of `g` becomes *package*`*f* when *package* is loaded. `g` will always call this `f`, even if there is a different `f` defined in the context in which the call to `g` is made.

The `BeginPackage` function can be given multiple arguments. The second and subsequent arguments are the names of other packages that this one uses. They are treated as if they were arguments to the `Needs` function, that is, they are loaded if they have not already been. Furthermore, they are included in `$ContextPath` *during the loading* of this package, so its functions can refer to their functions by their short names.

`EndPackage[]` resets `$Context` and `$ContextPath` to their prior values, except that *package*`` is added to the front of `$ContextPath`.

In[4]:= **EndPackage[]**

In[5]:= **$ContextPath**

Out[5]= {myPackage`, ComputationalGeometry`,
      PacletManager`, WebServices`, System`, Global`}

Usage and warning messages Put usage messages for all public functions immediately after the **BeginPackage**. Defining usage messages for the functions in your packages creates symbols for the functions in the current context. Each of the functions for which you define a usage message will be exported for public use, that is, those functions are visible and usable immediately after loading the package. This is in contrast to any functions that are defined in your package for which you do not have usage messages (or, more precisely, for those functions that you have not explicitly exported by mentioning that symbol before the **Begin** statement). Those functions will be private, unavailable for the user of your package to access.

Making your functions behave much like the built-in functions will make it easier for users of your packages, since they will expect usage messages and general functionality similar to that of *Mathematica*'s functions. It is also a good way for you to document your programs. You might even consider writing your usage messages *before* you write the function definitions in *Mathematica*. This will help you to understand clearly what it is you want your functions to do.

As discussed earlier (Section 5.7), usage messages have the following syntax:

In[6]:= **funName::usage =**
      "funName[x,y] computes something using x and y.";

In[7]:= **? funName**

---

funName[x,y] computes something using x and y.

The message itself starts with a template for that function. This template is used by *Mathematica* to provide a convenient user-interface feature: function templates. For any built-in function, you can get a template by entering the function name and then selecting Make Template from the Edit menu, or use the appropriate keyboard shortcut. When you do, this is the kind of thing you will see:

Plot3D$\left[\, f\, ,\, \left\{\, x\, ,\, x_{min}\, ,\, x_{max}\,\right\}\, ,\, \left\{\, y\, ,\, y_{min}\, ,\, y_{max}\,\right\}\right]$

By starting your usage message with the template for your function, you automatically inherit this user interface element.

funName$\left[\, x\, ,\, y\,\right]$

Options Options for each public function should follow next. Options for private functions should follow the `Begin` statement, that is, options for private functions should themselves be private.

$$\texttt{Options}\left[\textit{functionName}\right] = \left\{\textit{opt}_1 \to \textit{value}_1,\ \textit{opt}_2 \to \textit{value}_2\right\}$$

Begin private context The `Begin` command changes the current context without affecting the context path. By starting the argument `` `Private` `` with a context mark `` ` ``, we change to a subcontext of the current context.

Function definitions Definitions for both public and private functions follow next. Only those functions that have been declared public (typically via usage messages before the `Begin` statement) will be available to the user of your package.

End private context The `End[]` command closes the `Begin[]` and puts you back in the package context *package`*. Any symbols that were defined in the subcontext *package`*`Private`` can no longer be accessed.

EndPackage The `EndPackage[]` command puts you back in the context you were in prior to the `BeginPackage[]` command, typically `Global``.

Creating and installing the package

Since a package is simply a text file, you could create and develop it in a text editor if you preferred. But there are much more convenient environments in which you can do package development. One such application is an IDE such as Wolfram *Workbench*. In these IDEs, you can develop your code, debug it, profile (look for bottlenecks), and create and deploy documentation. Working with IDEs is beyond the scope of this book and there are excellent resources available for learning about them. Instead, we will focus on package development using an environment you should already be familiar with: the *Mathematica* notebook interface.

Using a *Mathematica* notebook as your programming environment provides several useful tools for package development that we will outline here. In particular, converting your notebook into a package and installing it in a location that will make it instantly available are both straightforward using the front end. Probably the most useful aspect of using *Mathematica* notebooks as your programming environment is the fact that you can experiment and try out code snippets or large-scale programs all in the same environment in which you are used to working.

As you are creating your package, keep each function definition, each option statement, and so on in a separate cell. This is generally a good practice whether you are developing packages or not. This way, if a problem arises, an error or warning message will be issued immediately after the cell that triggers that message. If you had dozens of definitions in one cell, warning messages would still be issued after that input cell, but you would have a difficult time trying to determine which part of your code was causing the problem.

Once you have completed the code development in your notebook, select all Input cells (option-click on Mac OS X or Alt-click on Windows) and then convert them to initialization cells by selecting Cell Properties ▶ Initialization Cell from the Cell menu. This marks those cells that will be included in the package. Saving your notebook at this point should trigger a dialog that asks if you would like to create an autogenerated package from this notebook. Answering yes will cause a package (a text file with the .m extension instead of .nb) to be saved in the same location as your notebook. Furthermore, that package will be automatically updated whenever you save any changes to the corresponding notebook.

Finally, to install the package, select Install from the File menu. This will bring up a dialog in which you can identify the type of item to install (Package), the source (point to your newly created and saved notebook containing initialization cells), the install name (typically the name of your package), and whether the package should be made available to all users of your computer or just you (Figure 13.4).

FIGURE 13.4. *Deploying packages through the* File ▶ Install *menu item.*

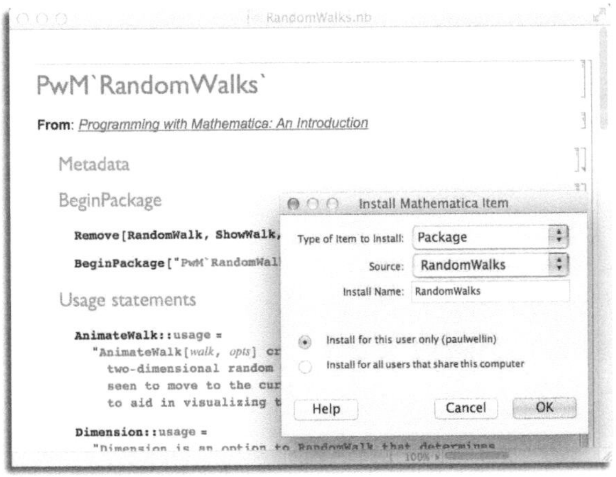

RandomWalks package

In this section, we list the RandomWalks package, elements of which were developed in earlier chapters. We will add several important user interface elements, such as additional usage statements. The full package is included in the PwM archive that accompanies this book (see Preface).

Because we have worked with several `RandomWalk` implementations in this chapter, it is a good idea to clear all definitions, attributes, and options in the `Global`` context before proceeding.

In[8]:= **ClearAll**["Global`"]

BeginPackage The RandomWalks package lives in a directory, PwM, which itself lives inside one of the Applications directories that are on *Mathematica*'s path. This is reflected in the argument to BeginPackage. This expression sets the value of Context`, which causes $ContextPath to be set to {PwM`RandomWalks`, System`}.

In[9]:= **BeginPackage**["PwM`RandomWalks`"]

Out[9]= PwM`RandomWalks`

As mentioned above, you could import one or more packages by using an optional argument to BeginPackage. In that case, you would have:

$$\text{BeginPackage}\left[\text{"PwM`RandomWalks`"}, \{package_1, package_2, ...\}\right]$$

Usage statements Usage statements for each of the public functions are given next. We also provide a usage message for each option to RandomWalk.

In[10]:= **RandomWalk**::usage =
```
"RandomWalk[t] generates a t-step random walk.
   The default behavior gives a two-dimensional
   lattice walk with steps in one of the four
   compass directions. The option LatticeWalk
   takes values True or False. The value of the
   option Dimension can be any of 1, 2, or 3.";
```

In[11]:= **Dimension**::usage =
```
"Dimension is an option to RandomWalk that
   determines whether the random walk will
   be a one-, two-, or three-dimensional
   walk. Possible values are 1, 2, or 3.";
```

In[12]:= **LatticeWalk**::usage =
```
"LatticeWalk is an option to RandomWalk that
   determines whether the random walk will
   be a lattice walk or an off-lattice walk.
   Possible values are True and False.";
```

In[13]:= **ShowWalk::usage =**
"ShowWalk[*walk*] displays a one, two, or three-dimensional
random walk connecting each site with a line.
Graphics options can be passed to ShowWalk.
E.g., ShowWalk[*walk*, Background→GrayLevel[0]]
to produce a black background.";

Warning messages One message is for a bad value for the argument that specifies the number of steps, and another message is for a bad value given to the Dimension option.

In[14]:= **RandomWalk::rwn = "Argument `1` is not a positive integer.";**

In[15]:= **RandomWalk::baddim =**
"The value `1` of the option Dimension is
not an integer between 1 and 3.";

Options Next we list options for public functions. This declares RandomWalk to have two options and sets their default values.

In[16]:= **Options[RandomWalk] = {LatticeWalk → True, Dimension → 2};**

Begin private context The argument `Private` changes the current context to a subcontext of the current context. This new subcontext is PwM`RandomWalks`Private`.

In[17]:= **Begin["`Private`"]**

Out[17]= PwM`RandomWalks`Private`

Function definitions Public and private function definitions are given below. RandomWalk and ShowWalk are the main public functions in this package. Note that latticeWalk and offLatticeWalk are both private. The user has no need to worry about them, let alone be aware of them.

We have not included all the definitions here that are included in the RandomWalks package. The full package includes definitions for animating random walks, computing radius of gyration tensor, and several others.

In[18]:= **latticeWalk[*steps_*, *dim_*] := Module[{w},**
w = Accumulate[RandomChoice[Join[
IdentityMatrix[*dim*], -IdentityMatrix[*dim*]], *steps*]];
If[*dim* == 1, Flatten[w], w]]

```
In[19]:= offLatticeWalk[t_, dim_] := Module[{f1, f2, f3},
    f1 := RandomReal[{-1, 1}, t];
    f2 := Map[{Cos[#], Sin[#]} &, RandomReal[{0, 2π}, t]];
    f3 := Function[{ϕ, θ}, {Sin[ϕ] Cos[θ], Sin[ϕ] Sin[θ],
        Cos[ϕ]}] @@@ RandomReal[{0, 2 π}, {t, 2}];
    Which[
     dim == 1, Accumulate[f1],
     dim == 2, Accumulate[f2],
     dim == 3, Accumulate[f3]
    ]]

In[20]:= RandomWalk[t_, OptionsPattern[]] := Module[{dim, latticeQ},
    {latticeQ, dim} = OptionValue[{LatticeWalk, Dimension}];
    Which[
     ! (IntegerQ[t] && t > 0), Message[RandomWalk::"rwn", t],
     ! (IntegerQ[dim] && 1 ≤ dim ≤ 3),
     Message[RandomWalk::baddim, dim],
     True, If[latticeQ, latticeWalk[t, dim],
      offLatticeWalk[t, dim]]
    ]
   ]

In[21]:= RandomWalk[x__] /; Message[RandomWalk::rwn, x] := Null
   RandomWalk[] /; Message[General::argx, RandomWalk, 0] := Null;

In[23]:= ShowWalk[coords_?VectorQ, opts : OptionsPattern[]] :=
       ListLinePlot[coords,
     FilterRules[{opts}, Options[ListLinePlot]]]

In[24]:= ShowWalk[coords : {{_, _} ..}, opts : OptionsPattern[]] :=
       ListLinePlot[coords,
     Append[FilterRules[{opts}, Options[ListLinePlot]],
      AspectRatio → Automatic]]

In[25]:= ShowWalk[coords : {{_, _, _} ..}, opts : OptionsPattern[]] :=
       Graphics3D[Line[coords],
     FilterRules[{opts}, Options[Graphics3D]]]
```

End private context The End[] command closes the matching Begin[] and returns us to the context RandomWalks`. Symbols that were defined in PwM`RandomWalks`Private` can no longer be accessed.

In[26]:= **End[]**

Out[26]= PwM`RandomWalks`Private`

EndPackage End the package and reset $Context and $ContextPath.

In[27]:= **EndPackage[]**

Running the package

It is a good idea, when doing package development, to start with a new session before testing out your package. This way you can avoid some issues with contexts that might arise if you evaluated some context-changing commands in one context and then loaded a package in another.

In[28]:= **Quit[]**

Assuming that the RandomWalks package has been installed in a directory/folder where *Mathematica* can find it, this loads the package.

In[1]:= **<< PwM`RandomWalks`**

Here is the usage message for the RandomWalk function.

In[2]:= **? RandomWalk**

> RandomWalk[*t*] generates a *t*–step random walk. The default behavior gives a two–dimensional lattice walk with steps in one of the four compass directions. The option LatticeWalk takes values True or False. The value of the option Dimension can be any of 1, 2, or 3.

This gives a random walk of length 10 in two dimensions.

In[3]:= **RandomWalk[10, Dimension → 2]**

Out[3]= {{0, -1}, {1, -1}, {2, -1}, {1, -1}, {1, -2}, {2, -2}, {1, -2}, {1, -1}, {0, -1}, {1, -1}}

Check that RandomWalk does the right thing when passed a bad argument or given a value for the Dimension option that the function is not set up to handle.

In[4]:= **RandomWalk[-5]**

> RandomWalk::rwn : Argument -5 is not a positive integer.

In[5]:= **RandomWalk[100, Dimension → 5]**

> RandomWalk::baddim : The value 5 of the option Dimension is not an integer between 1 and 3.

This shows a 2500-step off-lattice random walk using the default of two dimensions.

In[6]:= **ShowWalk[RandomWalk[2500, LatticeWalk → False]]**

Out[6]=

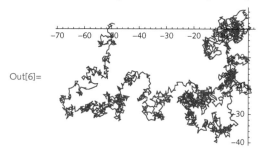

Here is a 5000-step two-dimensional random walk with some graphics options.

In[7]:= **ShowWalk[RandomWalk[5000], Frame → True]**

Out[7]=

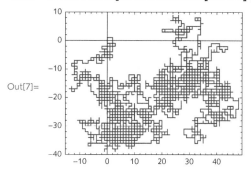

And here is a 2500 step off-lattice random walk in three dimensions followed by an animation.

In[8]:= **ShowWalk[RandomWalk[2500, Dimension → 3, LatticeWalk → False]]**

Out[8]=

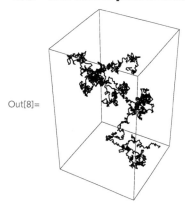

```
In[9]:=  AnimateWalk[
           RandomWalk[2500, Dimension → 3, LatticeWalk → False]]
```

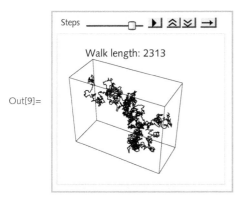

Out[9]=

Exercises

1. The following set of exercises will walk you through the creation of a package `Collatz`, a package
    of functions for performing various operations related to the Collatz problem that we investigated
    earlier (Exercises 3 and 4 of Section 4.1, Exercise 6 of Section 6.2, and Exercise 4 of Section 7.3).
    Recall that the Collatz function, for any integer n, returns $3n + 1$ for odd n, and $n/2$ for even n. The
    (as yet unproven) Collatz Conjecture is the statement that, for any initial positive integer n, the
    iterates of the Collatz function always reach the cycle 4, 2, 1,…. Start by creating an auxiliary
    function `collatz[n]` that returns $3n + 1$ for n odd and $n/2$ for n even.

    a. Create the function `CollatzSequence[n]` that lists the iterates of the auxiliary function
        `collatz[n]`. Here is some sample output of the `CollatzSequence` function.

        ```
        In[1]:=  CollatzSequence[7]
        Out[1]=  {7, 22, 11, 34, 17, 52, 26, 13, 40, 20, 10, 5, 16, 8, 4, 2, 1}
        ```

    b. Create a usage message for `CollatzSequence` and warning messages for each of the following
        situations:

        `notint`: the argument to `CollatzSequence` is not a positive integer

        `argx`: `CollatzSequence` was called with the wrong number of arguments

    c. Modify the definition of `CollatzSequence` that you created in part a. above so that it does
        some error trapping and issues the appropriate warning message that you created in part b.

    d. Finally, put all the pieces together and write a package `Collatz`` that includes the appropriate
        `BeginPackage` and `Begin` statements, usage messages, warning messages, and function
        definitions. Make `CollatzSequence` a public function and `collatz` a private function. Put
        your package in a directory where *Mathematica* can find it on its search path and then test it to see
        that it returns correct output such as in the examples below.

In[11]:= **Quit[];**

In[1]:= **<< PwM`Collatz`**

In[2]:= **? CollatzSequence**

CollatzSequence[*n*] computes the sequence of Collatz iterates starting with
initial value *n*. The sequence terminates as soon as it reaches the value 1.

Here are various cases in which `CollatzSequence` is given bad input.

In[3]:= **CollatzSequence[-5]**

CollatzSequence::notint : First argument, −5, to CollatzSequence must be a positive integer.

In[4]:= **CollatzSequence[4, 6]**

CollatzSequence::argx : CollatzSequence called with 2 arguments; 1 argument is expected. ≫

Out[4]= CollatzSequence[4, 6]

And this computes the sequence for starting value 27.

In[5]:= **CollatzSequence[27]**

Out[5]= {27, 82, 41, 124, 62, 31, 94, 47, 142, 71, 214, 107, 322, 161, 484,
242, 121, 364, 182, 91, 274, 137, 412, 206, 103, 310, 155, 466,
233, 700, 350, 175, 526, 263, 790, 395, 1186, 593, 1780, 890,
445, 1336, 668, 334, 167, 502, 251, 754, 377, 1132, 566, 283,
850, 425, 1276, 638, 319, 958, 479, 1438, 719, 2158, 1079,
3238, 1619, 4858, 2429, 7288, 3644, 1822, 911, 2734, 1367,
4102, 2051, 6154, 3077, 9232, 4616, 2308, 1154, 577, 1732,
866, 433, 1300, 650, 325, 976, 488, 244, 122, 61, 184, 92, 46,
23, 70, 35, 106, 53, 160, 80, 40, 20, 10, 5, 16, 8, 4, 2, 1}

2. The square end-to-end distance of a two-dimensional walk is defined as $(x_f - x_i)^2 + (y_f - y_i)^2$, where $\{x_i, y_i\}$ and $\{x_f, y_f\}$ are the initial and final locations of the walk, respectively. Assuming the initial point is the origin, then this simplifies to $x_f^2 + y_f^2$. Write a function `SquareDistance` that takes a two-dimensional walk as an argument and computes the square end-to-end distance. Write a usage message and include this function as a publicly exported function in the RandomWalks package.

Solutions to exercises

Below we give solutions to many of the exercises in this book. Space does not allow the inclusion of every solution in print, but all solutions are provided online both as a PDF file and in notebook form at www.cambridge.org/wellin.

2   The *Mathematica* language

2.1   Expressions

1. The expression $a (b + c)$ is given in full form as `Times[a, Plus[b, c]]`.

3. There are three elements in the expression, with the term `b x` being the second.

    ```
    In[1]:= expr = a x^2 + b x + c;
    ```

    ```
    In[2]:= FullForm[expr]
    ```

    ```
    Out[2]//FullForm=
            Plus[c, Times[b, x], Times[a, Power[x, 2]]]
    ```

    The first element of `Times[b, x]` is b, so the part specification is `2, 1`.

    ```
    In[3]:= expr[[2]]
    ```

    ```
    Out[3]= b x
    ```

    ```
    In[4]:= expr[[2, 1]]
    ```

    ```
    Out[4]= b
    ```

2.2   Definitions

1. This exercise focuses on the difference between immediate and delayed assignments.

    a. This will generate a list of *n* random numbers.

    ```
    In[1]:= randLis1[n_] := RandomReal[1, {n}]
    ```

    ```
    In[2]:= randLis1[3]
    ```

    ```
    Out[2]= {0.251941, 0.214991, 0.615347}
    ```

    b. Since the definition for x is an immediate assignment, its value does not change in the body of `randLis2`. But each time `randLis2` is called, a new value is assigned to x.

    ```
    In[3]:= randLis2[n_] := (x = RandomReal[]; Table[x, {n}])
    ```

    ```
    In[4]:= randLis2[3]
    ```

    ```
    Out[4]= {0.225983, 0.225983, 0.225983}
    ```

In[5]:= **randLis2[3]**

Out[5]= {0.817911, 0.817911, 0.817911}

   c. Because the definition for x is a delayed assignment, the definition for randLis3 is functionally
      equivalent to randLis1.

In[6]:= **randLis3[$n\_$] := (x := RandomReal[]; Table[x, {n}])**

In[7]:= **randLis3[3]**

Out[7]= {0.395331, 0.652456, 0.243081}

   d. In an immediate assignment, the right-hand side of the definition is evaluated first. But in this case, n
      does not have a value, so Table is not able to evaluate properly.

In[8]:= **randLis4[$n\_$] = Table[RandomReal[], {n}]**

      Table::iterb : Iterator {n} does not have appropriate bounds. ≫

Out[8]= Table[RandomReal[], {n}]

In[9]:= **Clear[x]**

3.   The rules for the logarithm function are as follows. Note, there is no need to program the division rule
      separately. Do you see why? (Look at FullForm[x / y].)

In[10]:= **log[$a\_$ * $b\_$] := log[a] + log[b]**

In[11]:= **log[$a\_^{n}\_$] := n log[a]**

In[12]:= **log[$x\ y^2\ z^3$]**

Out[12]= log[x] + 2 log[y] + 3 log[z]

In[13]:= **log[x / y]**

Out[13]= log[x] − log[y]

2.3 Predicates and Boolean operations

1.   There are several ways to define this function, either using the relational operator for less than, or with the
      absolute value function.

In[1]:= **f[$x\_$] := −1 < x < 1**

In[2]:= **f[$x\_$] := Abs[x] < 1**

In[3]:= **f[4]**

Out[3]= False

In[4]:= **f[-0.35]**

Out[4]= True

3.   A number n can be considered a natural number if it is both an integer and greater than or equal to zero.
      There is some disagreement in the mathematics community about 0, but for our purposes, we will adopt
      the convention that 0 is a natural number.

In[5]:= **NaturalQ[$n\_$] := IntegerQ[n] && $n \geq 0$**

In[6]:= **NaturalQ[0]**

Out[6]= True

In[7]:= **NaturalQ[-4]**

Out[7]= False

5.   There are three tests that have to be satisfied: integer, greater than 1, not prime.

In[8]:= **CompositeQ[$n\_$] := IntegerQ[n] && n > 1 && Not[PrimeQ[n]]**

In[9]:= **CompositeQ$\left[2^{31} - 1\right]$**

Out[9]= False

In[10]:= **CompositeQ$\left[2^{31} + 1\right]$**

Out[10]= True

This is more neatly done using conditional pattern matching. See, for example, Section 4.1 on patterns.

2.4   Attributes

1.   First clear any definitions and attributes that might be associated with f.

In[1]:= **ClearAll[f]**

Then set the HoldAll attribute to prevent initial evaluation of the argument of this function.

In[2]:= **SetAttributes[f, HoldAll]**

In[3]:= **f[$x\_$ + $y\_$] := x^2 + y^2**

In[4]:= **f[a + b]**

Out[4]= $a^2 + b^2$

In[5]:= **f[2 + 3]**

Out[5]= 13

2.   Here is a small list of random numbers to use.

In[6]:= **vec = RandomReal[{-1, 1}, 10]**

Out[6]= {-0.847838, -0.241155, 0.318935, 0.711714, 0.427628,
          -0.342618, -0.601334, -0.733025, -0.58182, -0.985515}

The function could be set up to take two arguments, the number and the bound.

In[7]:= **fun[$x\_$? NumberQ, $bound\_$] := If$\left[-bound < x < bound, x, \sqrt{x}\right]$**

Make fun listable.

In[8]:= **SetAttributes[fun, Listable]**

In[9]:= **fun[vec, 0.5]**

Out[9]= {0. + 0.920781 i, -0.241155, 0.318935, 0.843631, 0.427628, -0.342618,
          0. + 0.775457 i, 0. + 0.856169 i, 0. + 0.762771 i, 0. + 0.992731 i}

3   Lists

3.1   Creating and displaying lists

1.   You can take every other element in the iterator list, or encode that in the expression 2 j.

In[1]:= **Table[j, {i, 0, 8, 2}, {j, 0, i, 2}]**

Out[1]= {{0}, {0, 2}, {0, 2, 4}, {0, 2, 4, 6}, {0, 2, 4, 6, 8}}

In[2]:= **Table[2 j, {i, 0, 4}, {j, 0, i}]**

Out[2]= {{0}, {0, 2}, {0, 2, 4}, {0, 2, 4, 6}, {0, 2, 4, 6, 8}}

3.   Here are three ways to generate the list.

In[3]:= **2 RandomInteger[1, {10}] - 1**

Out[3]= {1, -1, 1, -1, -1, 1, -1, 1, -1, -1}

In[4]:= **(-1)$^{\text{RandomInteger[1,\{10\}]}}$**

Out[4]= {-1, -1, -1, -1, 1, 1, 1, -1, -1, -1}

The most direct way to do this is to use RandomChoice.

In[5]:= **RandomChoice[{-1, 1}, {10}]**

Out[5]= {-1, 1, 1, 1, -1, -1, 1, 1, -1, 1}

5.   Some thought is needed to get the iterators right using Table.

In[6]:= **xmin = -2; xmax = 2; ymin = -1; ymax = 1;**
          hlines = Table[{{xmin, y}, {xmax, y}}, {y, ymin, ymax}]

Out[7]= {{{-2, -1}, {2, -1}}, {{-2, 0}, {2, 0}}, {{-2, 1}, {2, 1}}}

In[8]:= **vlines = Table[{{x, ymin}, {x, ymax}}, {x, xmin, xmax}]**

Out[8]= {{{-2, -1}, {-2, 1}}, {{-1, -1}, {-1, 1}},
          {{0, -1}, {0, 1}}, {{1, -1}, {1, 1}}, {{2, -1}, {2, 1}}}

Join the two sets of lines and then flatten to remove one set of braces.

In[9]:= **pairs = Flatten[{hlines, vlines}, 1]**

Out[9]= {{{-2, -1}, {2, -1}}, {{-2, 0}, {2, 0}},
          {{-2, 1}, {2, 1}}, {{-2, -1}, {-2, 1}}, {{-1, -1}, {-1, 1}},
          {{0, -1}, {0, 1}}, {{1, -1}, {1, 1}}, {{2, -1}, {2, 1}}}

In[10]:= **Graphics[Line[pairs]]**

Out[10]=

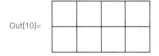

Here is a function that puts all this together:

In[11]:= **Lattice[{*xmin_*, *xmax_*}, {*ymin_*, *ymax_*}] :=**
          Module[{hlines, vlines, coords},
            hlines = Table[{{*xmin*, y}, {*xmax*, y}}, {y, *ymin*, *ymax*}];
            vlines = Table[{{x, *ymin*}, {x, *ymax*}}, {x, *xmin*, *xmax*}];
            coords = Flatten[{hlines, vlines}, 1];
            Graphics[Line[coords]]]

In[12]:= **Lattice[{-3, 3}, {-2, 2}]**

Out[12]=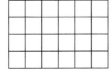

3.2   The structure of lists

1.   Here is the list of integers to use.

In[1]:= **ints = RandomInteger[{-5, 5}, 30]**

Out[1]= {2, 0, 0, -3, -3, 0, -1, 3, 0, 0, -4, 0, -3, 2,
         1, 5, -2, 4, 5, 1, 0, -5, -4, 4, -3, -4, 1, -3, 1, -3}

Count all elements that match 0.

In[2]:= **Count[ints, 0]**

Out[2]= 7

Count all integers in ints that do not match 1.

In[3]:= **Count[ints, Except[1]]**

Out[3]= 26

3.   The Position function tells us that the 9s are located in the second sublist, first position, and in the fourth sublist, third position.

In[4]:= **Position[{{2, 1, 10}, {9, 5, 7}, {2, 10, 4}, {10, 1, 9}, {6, 1, 6}}, 9]**

Out[4]= {{2, 1}, {4, 3}}

3.3   Working with lists

1.   This is a straightforward use of the Transpose function.

In[1]:= **Transpose[{{x_1, y_1}, {x_2, y_2}, {x_3, y_3}, {x_4, y_4}, {x_5, y_5}}]**

Out[1]= {{x_1, x_2, x_3, x_4, x_5}, {y_1, y_2, y_3, y_4, y_5}}

2.   Here is one way to do it. First create a list representing the directions.

In[2]:= **NSEW = {{0, 1}, {0, -1}, {1, 0}, {-1, 0}};**

RandomChoice chooses with replacement.

In[3]:= **RandomChoice[NSEW, {10}]**

Out[3]= {{0, 1}, {-1, 0}, {-1, 0}, {0, -1},
         {0, -1}, {-1, 0}, {0, 1}, {-1, 0}, {0, -1}, {0, -1}}

3.   Start by dropping the first element in the list, then create a nested list of every other element in the remaining list, and finally unnest the resulting list.

In[4]:= **Rest[{a, b, c, d, e, f, g}]**

Out[4]= {b, c, d, e, f, g}

In[5]:= **Partition[%, 1, 2]**

Out[5]= {{b}, {d}, {f}}

In[6]:= **Flatten[%]**

Out[6]= **{b, d, f}**

This can also be done directly in one step using `Part` with `Span`. The expression 2 ;; -1 ;; 2 indicates the range from the second element to the last element in increments of 2.

In[7]:= **Part[{a, b, c, d, e, f, g}, 2 ;; -1 ;; 2]**

Out[7]= **{b, d, f}**

4.   The standard procedural approach is to use a temporary variable to do the swapping.

In[8]:= **mat = RandomInteger[9, {4, 4}];**

MatrixForm[mat]

Out[9]//MatrixForm=

$$\begin{pmatrix} 6 & 7 & 6 & 5 \\ 8 & 2 & 7 & 1 \\ 9 & 4 & 4 & 7 \\ 4 & 4 & 0 & 7 \end{pmatrix}$$

In[10]:= **temp = mat[[1]];**

mat[[1]] = mat[[2]];

mat[[2]] = temp;

MatrixForm[mat]

Out[13]//MatrixForm=

$$\begin{pmatrix} 8 & 2 & 7 & 1 \\ 6 & 7 & 6 & 5 \\ 9 & 4 & 4 & 7 \\ 4 & 4 & 0 & 7 \end{pmatrix}$$

But you can use parallel assignments to avoid the temporary variable.

In[14]:= **mat = RandomInteger[9, {4, 4}];**

MatrixForm[mat]

Out[15]//MatrixForm=

$$\begin{pmatrix} 2 & 3 & 6 & 9 \\ 1 & 6 & 8 & 6 \\ 9 & 9 & 0 & 5 \\ 3 & 0 & 1 & 6 \end{pmatrix}$$

In[16]:= **{mat[[2]], mat[[1]]} = {mat[[1]], mat[[2]]};**

MatrixForm[mat]

Out[17]//MatrixForm=

$$\begin{pmatrix} 1 & 6 & 8 & 6 \\ 2 & 3 & 6 & 9 \\ 9 & 9 & 0 & 5 \\ 3 & 0 & 1 & 6 \end{pmatrix}$$

In fact you can make this a bit more compact.

```
In[18]:=  mat = RandomInteger[9, {4, 4}];
          MatrixForm[mat]
```
Out[19]//MatrixForm=
$$\begin{pmatrix} 8 & 9 & 0 & 6 \\ 8 & 5 & 9 & 5 \\ 0 & 5 & 4 & 4 \\ 8 & 2 & 3 & 5 \end{pmatrix}$$

```
In[20]:=  mat[[{2, 1}]] = mat[[{1, 2}]];
          MatrixForm[mat]
```
Out[21]//MatrixForm=
$$\begin{pmatrix} 8 & 5 & 9 & 5 \\ 8 & 9 & 0 & 6 \\ 0 & 5 & 4 & 4 \\ 8 & 2 & 3 & 5 \end{pmatrix}$$

A key point to notice is that in this exercise, the matrix mat was overwritten in each case; in other words, these were destructive operations. Section 5.5 discusses how to handle row and column swapping properly so that the original matrix remains untouched.

5. You need to first transpose the matrix to operate on the columns as rows.

```
In[22]:=  mat = RandomInteger[9, {4, 4}];
          MatrixForm[mat]
```
Out[23]//MatrixForm=
$$\begin{pmatrix} 0 & 7 & 5 & 1 \\ 5 & 5 & 4 & 7 \\ 2 & 6 & 2 & 4 \\ 7 & 4 & 8 & 3 \end{pmatrix}$$

```
In[24]:=  Transpose[mat]
```
Out[24]= {{0, 5, 2, 7}, {7, 5, 6, 4}, {5, 4, 2, 8}, {1, 7, 4, 3}}

Now insert the column vector at the desired position. Then transpose back.

```
In[25]:=  Insert[Transpose[mat], {a, b, c, d}, 3] // MatrixForm
```
Out[25]//MatrixForm=
$$\begin{pmatrix} 0 & 5 & 2 & 7 \\ 7 & 5 & 6 & 4 \\ a & b & c & d \\ 5 & 4 & 2 & 8 \\ 1 & 7 & 4 & 3 \end{pmatrix}$$

```
In[26]:=  Transpose@Insert[Transpose[mat], {a, b, c, d}, 3] // MatrixForm
```
Out[26]//MatrixForm=
$$\begin{pmatrix} 0 & 7 & a & 5 & 1 \\ 5 & 5 & b & 4 & 7 \\ 2 & 6 & c & 2 & 4 \\ 7 & 4 & d & 8 & 3 \end{pmatrix}$$

Here then is the function, with some basic argument checking to make sure the number of elements in the column vector is the same as the number of rows of the matrix.

```
In[27]:=  AddColumn[mat_, col_, pos_] /; Length[col] == Length[mat] :=
            Transpose[Insert[Transpose[mat], col, pos]]
```

8.   `Join` expects lists as arguments.

In[28]:= **Join[{z}, {x, y}]**

Out[28]= {z, x, y}

9.   Joining the two lists and then using `Part` with `Span` is the most direct way to do this.

In[29]:= **expr = Join[{1, 2, 3, 4}, {a, b, c, d}]**

Out[29]= {1, 2, 3, 4, a, b, c, d}

In[30]:= **expr[[2 ;; -1 ;; 2]]**

Out[30]= {2, 4, b, d}

11.   This is another way of asking for all those elements that are in the union but not the intersection of the two sets.

In[31]:= **A = {a, b, c, d};**

  B = {a, b, e, f};

In[33]:= **Complement[A ⋃ B, A ⋂ B]**

Out[33]= {c, d, e, f}

In[34]:= **Complement[Union[A, B], Intersection[A, B]]**

Out[34]= {c, d, e, f}

13.   This is a straightforward extension of the previous exercise.

In[35]:= **NGrams[*text_*, *n_*] := Partition[**
    StringSplit[*text*, RegularExpression["\\W+"]], *n*, 1]

In[36]:= **sentence = "Use StringSplit to split long strings into words.";**
  NGrams[sentence, 3]

Out[37]= {{Use, StringSplit, to}, {StringSplit, to, split}, {to, split, long},
    {split, long, strings}, {long, strings, into}, {strings, into, words}}

4   Patterns and rules

4.1   Patterns

1.   Start by creating a list of integers with which to work.

In[1]:= **lis = RandomInteger[1000, {20}]**

Out[1]= {775, 422, 36, 680, 264, 470, 794, 174, 619,
    584, 342, 345, 104, 997, 988, 576, 808, 958, 336, 551}

`IntegerQ` is a predicate; it returns `True` or `False`, so we need to use the logical OR to separate clauses here.

In[2]:= **Cases[lis, *n_* /; IntegerQ[*n* / 2] || IntegerQ[*n* / 3] || IntegerQ[*n* / 5]]**

Out[2]= {775, 422, 36, 680, 264, 470, 794, 174,
    584, 342, 345, 104, 988, 576, 808, 958, 336}

This is a bit more compact and direct.

In[3]:= `Cases[lis, n_ /; Mod[n, 2] == 0 || Mod[n, 3] == 0 || Mod[n, 5] == 0]`

Out[3]= {775, 422, 36, 680, 264, 470, 794, 174,
        584, 342, 345, 104, 988, 576, 808, 958, 336}

Once you are familiar with pure functions (Section 5.6), you can also do this with `Select`.

In[4]:= `Select[lis, Mod[#, 2] == 0 || Mod[#, 3] == 0 || Mod[#, 5] == 0 &]`

Out[4]= {775, 422, 36, 680, 264, 470, 794, 174,
        584, 342, 345, 104, 988, 576, 808, 958, 336}

3. The Collatz function has a direct implementation based on its definition. There is no need to check explicitly that the argument is an integer since `OddQ` and `EvenQ` handle that.

In[5]:= `Collatz[n_ ? OddQ] := 3 n + 1`

In[6]:= `Collatz[n_ ? EvenQ] :=` $\dfrac{n}{2}$

Here we iterate the Collatz function fifteen times starting with an initial value of 23.

In[7]:= `NestList[Collatz, 23, 15]`

Out[7]= {23, 70, 35, 106, 53, 160, 80, 40, 20, 10, 5, 16, 8, 4, 2, 1}

Check for arguments that do not match the patterns above.

In[8]:= `Collatz[24.0]`

Out[8]= Collatz[24.]

5. Using alternatives, this gives the definition for real, integer, or rational arguments.

In[9]:= `abs[x_Real | x_Integer | x_Rational] := If[x ≥ 0, x, -x]`

Here is the definition for complex arguments.

In[10]:= `abs[x_Complex] :=` $\sqrt{Re[x]^2 + Im[x]^2}$

Note that these rules are not invoked for symbolic arguments.

In[11]:= `Map[abs, {-3, 3 + 4 I,` $\dfrac{-4}{5}$`, a}]`

Out[11]= {3, 5, $\dfrac{4}{5}$, abs[a]}

4.2 Transformation rules

1. The problem here is that the pattern is too general and has been matched by the entire expression, which has the form {x_, y_}, where x is matched by {a, b} and y is matched by {c, d}. To fix this, use patterns to restrict the expressions that match.

In[1]:= `{{a, b}, {c, d}} /. {x_Symbol, y_Symbol} :> {y, x}`

Out[1]= {{b, a}, {d, c}}

In[2]:= `{{a, b}, {c, d}, {e, f}} /. {x_Symbol, y_Symbol} :> {y, x}`

Out[2]= {{b, a}, {d, c}, {f, e}}

3. The cross product is only defined for three dimensions, so first we need to embed the two-dimensional vectors in 3-space; in this case, in the plane $z = 0$.

In[3]:= `{x₁, y₁} /. {x_, y_} :> {x, y, 0}`

Out[3]= `{x₁, y₁, 0}`

We need to compute the cross product of two vectors that span the triangle.

In[4]:= `Cross[{x₂, y₂} - {x₁, y₁} /. {x_, y_} :> {x, y, 0},`
        `{x₃, y₃} - {x₁, y₁} /. {x_, y_} :> {x, y, 0}]`

Out[4]= `{0, 0, -x₂ y₁ + x₃ y₁ + x₁ y₂ - x₃ y₂ - x₁ y₃ + x₂ y₃}`

Here are the coordinates for a triangle.

In[5]:= `a = {0, 0};`
        `b = {5, 0};`
        `c = {3, 2};`

And here is the computation for the cross product.

In[8]:= `Cross[b - a /. {x_, y_} :> {x, y, 0}, c - a /. {x_, y_} :> {x, y, 0}]`

Out[8]= `{0, 0, 10}`

So the given area is then just half the magnitude of the cross product.

In[9]:= $\dfrac{\texttt{Norm[\%]}}{2}$

Out[9]= `5`

This is done more simply using determinants. Note the change here: each vector (edge of triangle) is embedded in the plane $z = 1$.

In[10]:= `TriangleArea[tri : {v1_, v2_, v3_}] :=` $\dfrac{1}{2}$ `Det[tri /. {x_, y_} :> {x, y, 1}]`

In[11]:= `TriangleArea[{a, b, c}]`

Out[11]= `5`

In[12]:= `Clear[a, b, c]`

4.   First, get the solutions to this polynomial.

In[13]:= `soln = Solve[x⁹ + 3.4 x⁶ - 25 x⁵ - 213 x⁴ - 477 x³ + 1012 x² + 111 x - 123 == 0, x]`

Out[13]= `{{x → -2.80961}, {x → -1.85186 - 2.15082 i}, {x → -1.85186 + 2.15082 i},`
          `{x → -0.376453}, {x → 0.323073}, {x → 1.06103 - 3.12709 i},`
          `{x → 1.06103 + 3.12709 i}, {x → 1.30533}, {x → 3.13931}}`

The pattern needs to match an expression consisting of a list with a rule inside where the value on the right-hand side of the rule should pass the `Negative` test.

In[14]:= `Cases[soln, {x_ → _?Negative}]`

Out[14]= `{{x → -2.80961}, {x → -0.376453}}`

Here are two solutions for the noncomplex roots.

In[15]:= `Cases[soln, {_ → _Real}]`

Out[15]= `{{x → -2.80961}, {x → -0.376453},`
          `{x → 0.323073}, {x → 1.30533}, {x → 3.13931}}`

```
In[16]:= DeleteCases[soln, {_ → _Complex}]
Out[16]= {{x → -2.80961}, {x → -0.376453},
          {x → 0.323073}, {x → 1.30533}, {x → 3.13931}}
```

6. Note the need to put y in a list on the right-hand side of the rule. Also, an immediate rule is required here.

```
In[17]:= sumList[lis_] := First[lis //.{x_, y___} → x + {y}]
In[18]:= sumList[{1, 5, 8, 3, 9, 3}]
Out[18]= 29
```

8. For an expression of the form `Power[a, b]`, the number of multiplies is $b - 1$.

```
In[19]:= Cases[{x^4}, Power[_, exp_] :→ exp - 1]
Out[19]= {3}
```

For an expression of the form `Times[a, b, c, …]`, the number of multiplications is given by one less then the number of arguments.

```
In[20]:= Cases[{a b c d e}, fac_Times :→ Length[fac] - 1]
Out[20]= {4}
```

For a mix of terms of these two cases, we will need to total up the counts from the respective terms. Here is a function that puts this all together. Use `Infinity` as a third argument to `Cases` to make sure the search goes all the way down the expression tree.

```
In[21]:= MultiplyCount[expr_ ? PolynomialQ] :=
           Total@Cases[{expr}, Power[_, exp_] :→ exp - 1, Infinity] +
             Total@Cases[{expr}, fac_Times :→ Length[fac] - 1, Infinity]
In[22]:= MultiplyCount[a b^2 c d^5]
Out[22]= 8
In[23]:= poly = Expand[(x + y - z)^3]
Out[23]= x^3 + 3 x^2 y + 3 x y^2 + y^3 - 3 x^2 z - 6 x y z - 3 y^2 z + 3 x z^2 + 3 y z^2 - z^3
In[24]:= MultiplyCount[poly]
Out[24]= 28
```

9. First, we create a grid of the nine locations on the die.

```
In[25]:= lis = Partition[Range[9], 3];
         Grid[lis]
         1 2 3
Out[26]= 4 5 6
         7 8 9
```

Next, use graphics primitives to indicate if a location on the grid is colored (on) or not (off).

```
In[27]:= off = {Red, Disk[]};
         on = {White, Disk[]};
```

Here are the rules for a five.

```
In[29]:= GraphicsGrid[Map[Graphics,
           lis /. {1 → on, 2 → off, 3 → on,
             4 → off, 5 → on, 6 → off, 7 → on, 8 → off, 9 → on},
           {2}], Background → Red, Spacings → 10, ImageSize → 50]
```

Out[29]=

The five other rules are straightforward. Here then is a function that wraps up the code. Note the use of the Background option to GraphicsGrid to pick up the color from the value of off.

```
In[30]:= Dice[n_] :=
         Module[{rules, off = {Darker@Blue, Disk[]}, on = {White, Disk[]}},
           rules = {
             {1 → off, 2 → off, 3 → off,
               4 → off, 5 → on, 6 → off, 7 → off, 8 → off, 9 → off},
             {1 → off, 2 → off, 3 → on, 4 → off, 5 → off,
               6 → off, 7 → on, 8 → off, 9 → off},
             {1 → off, 2 → off, 3 → on, 4 → off, 5 → on,
               6 → off, 7 → on, 8 → off, 9 → off},
             {1 → on, 2 → off, 3 → on, 4 → off, 5 → off,
               6 → off, 7 → on, 8 → off, 9 → on},
             {1 → on, 2 → off, 3 → on, 4 → off, 5 → on, 6 → off,
               7 → on, 8 → off, 9 → on},
             {1 → on, 2 → off, 3 → on, 4 → on, 5 → off, 6 → on,
               7 → on, 8 → off, 9 → on}
           };
           GraphicsGrid[Map[Graphics,
             Partition[Range[9], 3] /. rules[[n]],
             {2}], Background → First[off], Spacings → 10, ImageSize → 40]
         ]
In[31]:= Table[Dice[n], {n, 1, 6}]
```

Out[31]=

4.3 Examples and applications

1.   Here is the function FindSubsequence as given in the text.

```
In[1]:= FindSubsequence[lis_List, subseq_List] :=
        Module[{p, len = Length[subseq]},
          p = Partition[lis, len, 1];
          Position[p, subseq] /. {num_ ? IntegerQ} :→ {num, num + len - 1}]
```

This creates another rule associated with FindSubsequence that simply takes each integer argument, converts it to a list of integer digits, and then passes that off to the rule above.

```
In[2]:= FindSubsequence[n_Integer, subseq_Integer] :=
```

```
Module[{nlist = IntegerDigits[n], sublist = IntegerDigits[subseq]},
  FindSubsequence[nlist, sublist]
]
```

Create the list of the first 100 000 digits of π.

In[3]:= `pi = FromDigits[RealDigits[N[Pi, 10^5] - 3][[1]]];`

The subsequence 1415 occurs seven times at the following locations in this digit expansion of π.

In[4]:= `FindSubsequence[pi, 1415]`

Out[4]= `{{1, 4}, {6955, 6958}, {29 136, 29 139}, {45 234, 45 237},`
`{79 687, 79 690}, {85 880, 85 883}, {88 009, 88 012}}`

2. Here is the plot of the sine function.

In[5]:= `splot = Plot[Sin[x], {x, -2 π, 2 π}]`

Out[5]=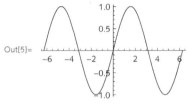

This replacement rule interchanges each ordered pair of numbers. Note the need to modify the plot range here.

In[6]:= `Show[splot /. {x_?NumberQ, y_?NumberQ} :> {y, x}, PlotRange → {-2 π, 2 π}]`

Out[6]=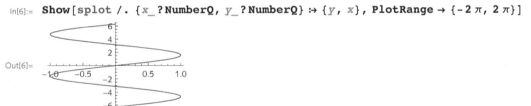

Although this particular example may have worked without the argument checking (_?NumberQ), it is a good idea to include it so that pairs of arbitrary expressions are not pattern matched here. We only want to interchange pairs of numbers, not pairs of options or other expressions that might be present in the underlying expression representing the graphic.

3. We are embedding the two-dimensional data into a three-dimensional array. The embedding function is written directly as a transformation rule.

In[7]:= `data = RandomReal[{0, 1}, {8, 2}]`

Out[7]= `{{0.925874, 0.136988}, {0.0928518, 0.895481},`
`{0.863376, 0.0878501}, {0.15219, 0.773304}, {0.10783, 0.0809593},`
`{0.374144, 0.880981}, {0.711271, 0.608961}, {0.208222, 0.329782}}`

```
In[8]:=  data /. {x_, y_} :> {x, y, Norm[{x, y}]} // MatrixForm
```
Out[8]//MatrixForm=

$$\begin{pmatrix} 0.925874 & 0.136988 & 0.935953 \\ 0.0928518 & 0.895481 & 0.900282 \\ 0.863376 & 0.0878501 & 0.867834 \\ 0.15219 & 0.773304 & 0.788137 \\ 0.10783 & 0.0809593 & 0.134839 \\ 0.374144 & 0.880981 & 0.957137 \\ 0.711271 & 0.608961 & 0.936344 \\ 0.208222 & 0.329782 & 0.390016 \end{pmatrix}$$

5 Functional programming

5.2 Functions for manipulating expressions

1. First, here is the definition given in Section 4.1.

```
In[1]:=  SquareMatrixQ[mat_ ?MatrixQ] :=
            Dimensions[mat][[1]] == Dimensions[mat][[2]]
```

For a matrix, `Dimensions` returns a list of two integers. Applying `Equal` to the list will return `True` if the two dimensions are identical, that is, if the matrix is square.

```
In[2]:=  SquareMatrixQ[mat_ ?MatrixQ] := Apply[Equal, Dimensions[mat]]
```

2. First create a set of points with which to work.

```
In[3]:=  points = RandomReal[1, {100, 2}];
```

The set of all two-element subsets is given by:

```
In[4]:=  pairs = Subsets[points, {2}];
```

Apply the distance function to `pairs`. Note the need to apply `EuclideanDistance` at level 1.

```
In[5]:=  Apply[EuclideanDistance, pairs, {1}];
```

The maximum distance (diameter) is given by `Max`.

```
In[6]:=  Max[%]
```
Out[6]= 1.2765

Here is a function that puts it all together.

```
In[7]:=  PointsetDiameter[pts_List] :=
            Max[Apply[EuclideanDistance, Subsets[pts, {2}], {1}]]
In[8]:=  PointsetDiameter[points]
```
Out[8]= 1.2765

In fact, this function works on *n*-dimensional point sets.

```
In[9]:= points3D = RandomReal[1, {5, 3}]
```

```
Out[9]= {{0.0776908, 0.260979, 0.796066},
        {0.707468, 0.453237, 0.155118}, {0.728849, 0.580631, 0.319354},
        {0.88149, 0.0464455, 0.0383026}, {0.238723, 0.844875, 0.0790128}}
```

```
In[10]:= PointsetDiameter[points3D]
```

```
Out[10]= 1.12531
```

3. Here is a test matrix.

```
In[11]:= mat = RandomInteger[1, {5, 5}];
        MatrixForm[mat]
```

Out[12]//MatrixForm=
$$\begin{pmatrix} 0 & 0 & 1 & 1 & 0 \\ 0 & 0 & 0 & 0 & 1 \\ 1 & 1 & 1 & 0 & 0 \\ 1 & 1 & 0 & 1 & 1 \\ 1 & 1 & 0 & 0 & 1 \end{pmatrix}$$

A bit of thought should convince you that adding the matrix to its transpose and then totaling all the 1s in each row will give the correct count.

```
In[13]:= Map[Total, mat + Transpose[mat]]
```

```
Out[13]= {5, 4, 5, 6, 6}
```

Using graphs you can accomplish the same thing.

```
In[14]:= gr = AdjacencyGraph[mat, VertexLabels → "Name"]
```

Out[14]=

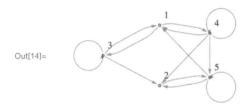

```
In[15]:= VertexDegree[gr]
```

```
Out[15]= {5, 4, 5, 6, 6}
```

4. Applying `DirectedEdge` at level 1 will do the trick.

```
In[16]:= ToGraph[lis : {{_, _} ..}] := Apply[DirectedEdge, lis, {1}]
```

```
In[17]:= lis = RandomInteger[9, {12, 2}];
        ToGraph[lis]
```

```
Out[18]= {0 ↔ 6, 7 ↔ 9, 5 ↔ 3, 8 → 0, 3 ↔ 6,
         0 ↔ 5, 9 ↔ 3, 1 ↔ 7, 0 ↔ 2, 2 ↔ 4, 4 ↔ 3, 4 ↔ 5}
```

This rule fails for the case when the argument is a single flat list of a pair of elements.

```
In[19]:= ToGraph[{3, 6}]
```

```
Out[19]= ToGraph[{3, 6}]
```

A second rule is needed for this case.

```
In[20]:= ToGraph[lis : {_, _}] := Apply[DirectedEdge, lis]
```

```
In[21]:= ToGraph[{3, 6}]
```

```
Out[21]= 3 ↦ 6
```

5. RGBColor takes a sequence of three values between 0 and 1. So you only need to apply RGBColor to this list.

```
In[22]:= RandomColor[] := Apply[RGBColor, RandomReal[1, {3}]]
```

A second rule uses pattern matching to make sure the argument, *n*, to RandomColor is a positive integer; then create a list of *n* triples of random reals before applying RGBColor at level 1.

```
In[23]:= RandomColor[n_Integer ? Positive] :=
            Apply[RGBColor, RandomReal[1, {n, 3}], {1}]
```

6. First, create the random centers and radii.

```
In[24]:= n = 12;
         centers = RandomReal[{-1, 1}, {n, 2}]
```

```
Out[25]= {{0.226222, -0.111298}, {0.462016, -0.845492}, {0.840404, 0.558368},
          {-0.989743, 0.633542}, {0.23714, -0.315888}, {0.476561, 0.873451},
          {0.65813, -0.916153}, {0.287248, -0.833235}, {-0.70788, 0.685656},
          {0.215158, -0.464512}, {0.65807, -0.925023}, {0.962352, 0.477038}}
```

```
In[26]:= radii = RandomReal[1, {n}]
```

```
Out[26]= {0.883751, 0.549666, 0.576343, 0.470191, 0.425309, 0.0544009,
          0.553858, 0.0168329, 0.940539, 0.669541, 0.755542, 0.865138}
```

MapThread is perfect for the task of grabbing one center, one radii, and wrapping Circle around them.

```
In[27]:= circles = MapThread[Circle, {centers, radii}] // Short
```

```
Out[27]//Short= {Circle[{0.226222, -0.111298}, 0.883751],
                 ≪10≫, Circle[{0.962352, ≪20≫}, ≪19≫]}
```

```
In[28]:= Graphics[circles]
```

Out[28]=

And here is a rule to transform each circle into a scoped list that includes Thick and RandomColor. Note the need for the delayed rule (:→).

In[29]:= `Graphics[circles /. Circle[x__] :> {Thick, RandomColor[], Circle[x]}]`

Out[29]=

7. Here is the `Inner` example from the text.

In[30]:= `Inner[f, {a, b, c}, {d, e, f}, g]`

Out[30]= `g[f[a, d], f[b, e], f[c, f]]`

Using `MapThread`, we zip together the two lists and wrap f around each pair. Then apply g.

In[31]:= `MapThread[f, {{a, b, c}, {d, e, f}}]`

Out[31]= `{f[a, d], f[b, e], f[c, f]}`

In[32]:= `Apply[g, %]`

Out[32]= `g[f[a, d], f[b, e], f[c, f]]`

9. To get down to the level of the nested lists, you have to use a second argument to `Apply`.

In[33]:= `facs = FactorInteger[3 628 800]`

Out[33]= `{{2, 8}, {3, 4}, {5, 2}, {7, 1}}`

In[34]:= `Apply[Power, facs, {1}]`

Out[34]= `{256, 81, 25, 7}`

One more use of `Apply` is needed to multiply these terms.

In[35]:= `Apply[Times, %]`

Out[35]= `3 628 800`

Here is a function that puts this all together.

In[36]:= `ExpandFactors[lis_] := Apply[Times, Apply[Power, lis, {1}]]`

In[37]:= `FactorInteger[295 232 799 039 604 140 847 618 609 643 520 000 000]`

Out[37]= `{{2, 32}, {3, 15}, {5, 7}, {7, 4}, {11, 3},`
`{13, 2}, {17, 2}, {19, 1}, {23, 1}, {29, 1}, {31, 1}}`

In[38]:= `ExpandFactors[%]`

Out[38]= `295 232 799 039 604 140 847 618 609 643 520 000 000`

11. First, here is the prime factorization of a test integer:

In[39]:= `lis = FactorInteger[10!]`

Out[39]= `{{2, 8}, {3, 4}, {5, 2}, {7, 1}}`

Apply `Superscript` at level 1 to each of the sublists:

In[40]:= `Apply[Superscript, lis, {1}]`

Out[40]= $\{2^8, 3^4, 5^2, 7^1\}$

Finally, apply `CenterDot` to this list.

In[41]:= **Apply[CenterDot, %]**

Out[41]= $2^8 \cdot 3^4 \cdot 5^2 \cdot 7^1$

Put it all together (using shorthand notation for Apply) and Apply at level 1.

In[42]:= **PrimeFactorForm[p_] := CenterDot @@ (Superscript @@@ FactorInteger[p])**

In[43]:= **PrimeFactorForm[20!]**

Out[43]= $2^{18} \cdot 3^8 \cdot 5^4 \cdot 7^2 \cdot 11^1 \cdot 13^1 \cdot 17^1 \cdot 19^1$

Unfortunately, this rule fails for numbers that have only one prime factor.

In[44]:= **PrimeFactorForm[9]**

Out[44]= $\text{CenterDot}\left[3^2\right]$

A second rule is needed for this special case.

In[45]:= **PrimeFactorForm[p_ ? PrimePowerQ] :=**
　　　　First[Superscript @@@ FactorInteger[p]]

In[46]:= **PrimeFactorForm[9]**

Out[46]= 3^2

A subtle point is that *Mathematica* has automatically ordered these two rules, putting the one involving prime powers first.

In[47]:= **? PrimeFactorForm**

```
Global`PrimeFactorForm


PrimeFactorForm[p_ ? PrimePowerQ] :=
 First[Apply[Superscript, FactorInteger[p], {1}]]


PrimeFactorForm[p_] :=
 CenterDot @@ Apply[Superscript, FactorInteger[p], {1}]
```

This reordering (we evaluated the rules in a different order) is essential for this function to work properly. If the general rule was checked first, it would apply to arguments that happen to be prime powers and it would give wrong answers.

One final point: the expressions returned by PrimeFactorForm will not evaluate like ordinary expressions due to the use of CenterDot which has no evaluation rules associated with it. You could add an "interpretation" to such expressions by using $\text{Interpretation}\left[disp, \ expr\right]$ as follows.

In[48]:= **PrimeFactorForm[p_Integer] := With[{fp = FactorInteger[p]},**
　　　　Interpretation[
　　　　　CenterDot @@ (Superscript @@@ fp),
　　　　　Times @@ (Power @@@ fp)]]

Now the output of the following expression can be evaluated directly to get an interpreted result.

In[49]:= **PrimeFactorForm[12!]**

Out[49]= $2^{10} \cdot 3^5 \cdot 5^2 \cdot 7^1 \cdot 11^1$

12. This is a straightforward application of the `Outer` function.

```
In[50]:= VandermondeMatrix[n_, x_] :=
           Outer[Power, Table[xᵢ, {i, 1, n}], Range[0, n - 1]]
```

```
In[51]:= VandermondeMatrix[4, x] // MatrixForm
```

Out[51]//MatrixForm=

$$\begin{pmatrix} 1 & x_1 & x_1^2 & x_1^3 \\ 1 & x_2 & x_2^2 & x_2^3 \\ 1 & x_3 & x_3^2 & x_3^3 \\ 1 & x_4 & x_4^2 & x_4^3 \end{pmatrix}$$

14. First create a table of primes and then use that list for values of p in the second table.

```
In[52]:= primes = Table[Prime[n], {n, 1, 50}]
```

Out[52]= {2, 3, 5, 7, 11, 13, 17, 19, 23, 29, 31, 37, 41, 43, 47, 53, 59, 61, 67, 71, 73, 79, 83, 89, 97, 101, 103, 107, 109, 113, 127, 131, 137, 139, 149, 151, 157, 163, 167, 173, 179, 181, 191, 193, 197, 199, 211, 223, 227, 229}

```
In[53]:= Select[Table[2^p - 1, {p, primes}], PrimeQ]
```

Out[53]= {3, 7, 31, 127, 8191, 131 071, 524 287, 2 147 483 647, 2 305 843 009 213 693 951, 618 970 019 642 690 137 449 562 111, 162 259 276 829 213 363 391 578 010 288 127, 170 141 183 460 469 231 731 687 303 715 884 105 727}

Or you could do the same thing more directly.

```
In[54]:= Select[Table[2^Prime[n] - 1, {n, 1, 50}], PrimeQ]
```

Out[54]= {3, 7, 31, 127, 8191, 131 071, 524 287, 2 147 483 647, 2 305 843 009 213 693 951, 618 970 019 642 690 137 449 562 111, 162 259 276 829 213 363 391 578 010 288 127, 170 141 183 460 469 231 731 687 303 715 884 105 727}

5.3 Iterating functions

1. First generate the step directions.

```
In[1]:= Table[(-1)^Random[Integer], {10}]
```

Out[1]= {1, 1, -1, 1, -1, 1, -1, -1, -1, 1}

Or the following also works.

```
In[2]:= steps = 2 RandomInteger[1, {10}] - 1
```

Out[2]= {-1, 1, -1, -1, -1, -1, -1, -1, -1, 1}

Then, starting at 0, the fold operation generates the locations.

```
In[3]:= FoldList[Plus, 0, steps]
```

Out[3]= {0, -1, 0, -1, -2, -3, -4, -5, -6, -7, -6}

3. Starting with 1, fold the `Times` function across the first *n* integers.

```
In[4]:= fac[n_] := Fold[Times, 1, Range[n]]
```

```
In[5]:= fac[10]
```

Out[5]= 3 628 800

4.   First create the vertices of the triangle. Wrapping them in N [...] helps to keep the graphical structures small
      (see Section 10.2 for more on this).

      In[6]:= **vertices = N[{{0, 0}, {1, 0}, {1 / 2, 1}}];**

      This gives the three different translation vectors.

      In[7]:= **translateVecs = 0.5 vertices**

      Out[7]= {{0., 0.}, {0.5, 0.}, {0.25, 0.5}}

      Here is the set of transformations of the triangle described by **vertices**, scaled by 0.5, and translated
      according to the translation vectors.

      In[8]:= **tri = Polygon[vertices];**
              Graphics[{
                 Blue, Translate[Scale[tri, 0.5, {0., 0.}], translateVecs]
                 }]

      Out[9]=

      Finally, iterate the transformations by wrapping them in **Nest**.

      In[10]:= **Graphics[**
               {Blue, Nest[{Blue, Translate[Scale[#, 0.5, {0., 0.}], translateVecs]} &,
                  Polygon[vertices], 3]}]

      Out[10]=

      Once you have been through the rest of this chapter, you should be able to turn this into a reusable
      function, scoping local variables, using pure functions, and adding options.

      In[11]:= **SierpinskiTriangle[*iter_*, *opts* : OptionsPattern[Graphics]] :=**
               Module[{vertices, vecs},
                 vertices = N[{{0, 0}, {1, 0}, {1 / 2, 1}}];
                 vecs = 0.5 vertices;
                 Graphics[
                  {Blue, Nest[{Blue, Translate[Scale[#, 0.5, {0., 0.}], vecs]} &,
                     Polygon[vertices], *iter*]}, *opts*]]

In[12]:= **SierpinskiTriangle[8, ImageSize → Tiny]**

Out[12]=

5.4 Programs as functions

1. Generate the list of integers 1 through *n*, then total that list.

    In[1]:= **sumInts[*n_*] := Total[Range[*n*]]**

    In[2]:= **sumInts[100]**

    Out[2]= 5050

    In[3]:= **sumInts[1000]**

    Out[3]= 500 500

    We have not been careful to check that the arguments are positive integers here. See Section 5.6 for a proper definition to check arguments.

2. Use MemberQ to check if any elements of the list pass the OddQ test. If they do, True is returned and so we take the Boolean negation of that. In other words, if the list contains an odd number, False is returned, indicating that the list does not consist of even numbers exclusively.

    In[4]:= **listEvenQ2[*lis_*] := Not[MemberQ[*lis*, _?OddQ]]**

    In[5]:= **listEvenQ2[{2, 4, 6, 4, 8}]**

    Out[5]= True

    In[6]:= **listEvenQ2[{2, 4, 6, 5, 8}]**

    Out[6]= False

    Alternatively, you could have FreeQ check to see if the list is free of numbers that are equal to 1 mod 2.

    In[7]:= **listEvenQ3[*lis_*] := FreeQ[*lis*, *p_* /; Mod[*p*, 2] == 1]**

    In[8]:= **listEvenQ3[{2, 4, 6, 4, 8}]**

    Out[8]= True

    In[9]:= **listEvenQ3[{2, 4, 6, 5, 8}]**

    Out[9]= False

3. Some simple experiments iterating the shuffle function shows that the number of shuffles to return the deck to its original state is dependent upon the number of cards in the deck. For a deck of 52 cards, eight such perfect (Faro) shuffles will return the deck to its original state.

    In[10]:= **shuffle[*lis_*] := Module[{len = Ceiling[Length[*lis*] / 2]},**
            Apply[Riffle, Partition[*lis*, len, len, 1, {}]]]

```
In[11]:=  Nest[shuffle, Range[52], 8]
Out[11]=  {1, 2, 3, 4, 5, 6, 7, 8, 9, 10, 11, 12, 13, 14, 15, 16, 17, 18, 19,
           20, 21, 22, 23, 24, 25, 26, 27, 28, 29, 30, 31, 32, 33, 34, 35,
           36, 37, 38, 39, 40, 41, 42, 43, 44, 45, 46, 47, 48, 49, 50, 51, 52}
```

4. The obvious way to do this is to take the list and simply pick out elements at random locations. The rightmost location in the list is given by Length[lis], using Part and RandomInteger.

```
In[12]:=  randomChoice[lis_, n_] := lis[[RandomInteger[{1, Length[lis]}, {n}]]]
In[13]:=  randomChoice[{a, b, c, d, e, f, g, h}, 12]
Out[13]=  {c, a, g, h, g, f, e, g, a, c, c, d}
```

6. Here is our user-defined stringInsert.

```
In[14]:=  stringInsert[str1_, str2_, pos_] := StringJoin@Join[
              Take[Characters[str1], pos - 1],
              Characters[str2],
              Drop[Characters[str1], pos - 1]
              ]
In[15]:=  stringInsert["Joy world", "to the ", 5]
Out[15]=  Joy to the world
In[16]:=  stringDrop[str_, pos_] := StringJoin[Drop[Characters[str], pos]]
In[17]:=  stringDrop["ABCDEF", -2]
Out[17]=  ABCD
```

The idea in these two examples is to convert a string to a list of characters, operate on that list using list manipulation functions like Join, Take, and Drop, then convert back to a string. More efficient approaches use string manipulation functions directly (see Chapter 9).

8. First, here is how we might write our own StringJoin.

```
In[18]:=  FromCharacterCode[Join[
              ToCharacterCode["To be, "], ToCharacterCode["or not to be"]
              ]]
Out[18]=  To be, or not to be
```

And here is a how we might implement a StringReverse.

```
In[19]:=  FromCharacterCode[Reverse[ToCharacterCode[%]]]
Out[19]=  eb ot ton ro ,eb oT
```

5.5 Scoping constructs

1. In the first definition, we only use one auxiliary function inside the Module.

```
In[1]:=  latticeWalk2D[n_] := Module[{NSEW = {{1, 0}, {-1, 0}, {0, 1}, {0, -1}}},
            Accumulate[RandomChoice[NSEW, n]]]
In[2]:=  latticeWalk2D[10]
Out[2]=  {{-1, 0}, {0, 0}, {0, 1}, {0, 2},
          {0, 3}, {0, 2}, {-1, 2}, {0, 2}, {0, 1}, {-1, 1}}
```

2. The following function creates a local function `perfectQ` using the `Module` construct. It then checks every other number between *n* and *m* by using a third argument to the `Range` function.

```
In[3]:= PerfectSearch[n_, m_] := Module[{perfectQ},
            perfectQ[j_] := Total[Divisors[j]] == 2 j;
            Select[Range[n, m, 2], perfectQ]]

In[4]:= PerfectSearch[2, 10000]

Out[4]= {6, 28, 496, 8128}
```

This function does not guard against the user supplying "bad" inputs. For example, if the user starts with an odd number, then this version of `PerfectSearch` will check every other odd number, and, since it is known that there are no odd perfect numbers below at least 10^{300}, none is reported.

```
In[5]:= PerfectSearch[1, 10000]

Out[5]= {}
```

You can fix this situation by using the (as yet unproved) assumption that there are *no* odd perfect numbers. This next version first checks that the first argument is an even number.

```
In[6]:= Clear[PerfectSearch]

In[7]:= PerfectSearch[n_?EvenQ, m_] := Module[{perfectQ},
            perfectQ[j_] := Total[Divisors[j]] == 2 j;
            Select[Range[n, m, 2], perfectQ]]
```

Now, the function only works if the first argument is even.

```
In[8]:= PerfectSearch[2, 10000]

Out[8]= {6, 28, 496, 8128}

In[9]:= PerfectSearch[1, 1000]

Out[9]= PerfectSearch[1, 1000]
```

3. This function requires a third argument.

```
In[10]:= Clear[PerfectSearch];
         PerfectSearch[n_, m_, k_] := Module[{perfectQ},
             perfectQ[j_] := Total[Divisors[j]] == k j;
             Select[Range[n, m], perfectQ]]
```

The following computation can be quite time consuming and requires a fair amount of memory to run to completion. If your computer's resources are limited, you should split up the search intervals into smaller units or try running this in parallel. See Section 12.3 for a discussion on how to set up parallel computation.

```
In[12]:= PerfectSearch[1, 2200000, 4] // AbsoluteTiming

Out[12]= {31.730753, {30240, 32760, 2178540}}
```

We also give a speed boost by using `DivisorSigma[1, j]` which gives the sum of the divisors of *j*.

```
In[13]:= PerfectSearchParallel[n_, m_, k_] :=
            Module[{perfectQ}, perfectQ[j_] := DivisorSigma[1, j] == k j;
            DistributeDefinitions[perfectQ];
            Parallelize[Select[Range[n, m, 2], perfectQ]]]
```

```
In[14]:= PerfectSearchParallel[2, 2 200 000, 4] // AbsoluteTiming
Out[14]= {4.435988, {30 240, 32 760, 2 178 540}}
```

4. Many implementations are possible for `convertToDate`. The task is made easier by observing that `DateList` handles this task directly if its argument is a string.

```
In[15]:= DateList["20120515"]
Out[15]= {2012, 5, 15, 0, 0, 0.}
```

The string is necessary otherwise `DateList` will interpret the integer as an absolute time (from Jan 1 1900).

```
In[16]:= DateList[20 120 515]
Out[16]= {1900, 8, 21, 21, 1, 55.}
```

So we need to convert the integer to a string first,

```
In[17]:= DateList[ToString[20 120 515]]
Out[17]= {2012, 5, 15, 0, 0, 0.}
```

and then take the first three elements.

```
In[18]:= Take[%, 3]
Out[18]= {2012, 5, 15}
```

Here is the function that puts these steps together.

```
In[19]:- convertToDate[n_Integer] := Take[DateList[ToString[n]], 3]

In[20]:= convertToDate[20 120 515]
Out[20]= {2012, 5, 15}
```

With a bit more manual work, you could also do this with `StringTake`.

```
In[21]:= convertToDate2[n_Integer /; Length[IntegerDigits[n]] == 8] :=
           Module[{str = ToString[n]},
             {StringTake[str, 4], StringTake[str, {5, 6}], StringTake[str, -2]}]

In[22]:= convertToDate2[20 120 515]
Out[22]= {2012, 05, 15}
```

You could avoid working with strings by making use of `FromDigits`. This uses `With` to create a local constant d, as this expression never changes throughout the body of the function.

```
In[23]:= convertToDate3[num_] := With[{d = IntegerDigits[num]},
           {FromDigits[Take[d, 4]],
            FromDigits[Take[d, {5, 6}]],
            FromDigits[Take[d, {7, 8}]]}]

In[24]:= convertToDate3[20 120 515]
Out[24]= {2012, 5, 15}
```

5. The computation of zeroing out one or more columns of a matrix can be handled with list component assignment. We need to use a local variable here to avoid changing the original matrix.

```
In[25]:= mat = RandomReal[1, {5, 5}];
         MatrixForm[mat]
```

Out[26]//MatrixForm=

$$\begin{pmatrix} 0.199196 & 0.763633 & 0.916951 & 0.254458 & 0.670371 \\ 0.831198 & 0.82132 & 0.351393 & 0.933563 & 0.431222 \\ 0.0868469 & 0.457891 & 0.299765 & 0.362697 & 0.462591 \\ 0.715115 & 0.780563 & 0.264595 & 0.445087 & 0.639657 \\ 0.306235 & 0.960085 & 0.151313 & 0.110208 & 0.809649 \end{pmatrix}$$

Here is a rule for zeroing out one column:

```
In[27]:= zeroColumns[mat_, n_Integer] := Module[{lmat = mat},
           lmat[[All, n]] = 0;
           lmat]
```

This next rule is for zeroing out a range of columns:

```
In[28]:= zeroColumns[mat_, Span[m_, n_]] := Module[{lmat = mat},
           lmat[[All, m ;; n]] = 0;
           lmat]
```

We also need a final rule for zeroing out a discrete set of columns whose positions are given by a list.

```
In[29]:= zeroColumns[mat_, lis : {__}] := Module[{lmat = mat},
           lmat[[All, lis]] = 0;
           lmat]
```

```
In[30]:= zeroColumns[mat, 3] // MatrixForm
```

Out[30]//MatrixForm=

$$\begin{pmatrix} 0.199196 & 0.763633 & 0 & 0.254458 & 0.670371 \\ 0.831198 & 0.82132 & 0 & 0.933563 & 0.431222 \\ 0.0868469 & 0.457891 & 0 & 0.362697 & 0.462591 \\ 0.715115 & 0.780563 & 0 & 0.445087 & 0.639657 \\ 0.306235 & 0.960085 & 0 & 0.110208 & 0.809649 \end{pmatrix}$$

```
In[31]:= zeroColumns[mat, 1 ;; 2] // MatrixForm
```

Out[31]//MatrixForm=

$$\begin{pmatrix} 0 & 0 & 0.916951 & 0.254458 & 0.670371 \\ 0 & 0 & 0.351393 & 0.933563 & 0.431222 \\ 0 & 0 & 0.299765 & 0.362697 & 0.462591 \\ 0 & 0 & 0.264595 & 0.445087 & 0.639657 \\ 0 & 0 & 0.151313 & 0.110208 & 0.809649 \end{pmatrix}$$

```
In[32]:= zeroColumns[mat, {1, 3, 5}] // MatrixForm
```

Out[32]//MatrixForm=

$$\begin{pmatrix} 0 & 0.763633 & 0 & 0.254458 & 0 \\ 0 & 0.82132 & 0 & 0.933563 & 0 \\ 0 & 0.457891 & 0 & 0.362697 & 0 \\ 0 & 0.780563 & 0 & 0.445087 & 0 \\ 0 & 0.960085 & 0 & 0.110208 & 0 \end{pmatrix}$$

5.6 Pure functions

1. This function adds the squares of the elements in a list.

    In[1]:= **elementsSquared[$lis\_$] := Total$\left[lis^2\right]$**

    In[2]:= **elementsSquared[{1, 3, 5, 7, 9}]**

    Out[2]= 165

    Using a pure function, this becomes:

    In[3]:= **Function$\left[lis,$ Total$\left[lis^2\right]\right]$[{1, 3, 5, 7, 9}]**

    Out[3]= 165

    or simply,

    In[4]:= **Total$\left[\#^2\right]$ &[{1, 3, 5, 7, 9}]**

    Out[4]= 165

2. To compute the distance between two points, use either **EuclideanDistance** or **Norm**.

    In[5]:= **pts = RandomReal[1, {4, 2}]**

    Out[5]= {{0.197291, 0.772739}, {0.125458, 0.9729},
        {0.674665, 0.105554}, {0.679087, 0.196272}}

    In[6]:= **Norm[pts[[1]] - pts[[2]]]**

    Out[6]= 0.21266

    In[7]:= **EuclideanDistance[pts[[1]], pts[[2]]]**

    Out[7]= 0.21266

    Now we need the distance between every pair of points. So we first create the set of pairs.

    In[8]:= **pairs = Subsets[pts, {2}]**

    Out[8]= {{{0.197291, 0.772739}, {0.125458, 0.9729}},
        {{0.197291, 0.772739}, {0.674665, 0.105554}},
        {{0.197291, 0.772739}, {0.679087, 0.196272}},
        {{0.125458, 0.9729}, {0.674665, 0.105554}},
        {{0.125458, 0.9729}, {0.679087, 0.196272}},
        {{0.674665, 0.105554}, {0.679087, 0.196272}}}

    Then we compute the distance between each pair and take the **Max**.

    In[9]:= **Apply[Norm[#1 - #2] &, pairs, {1}]**

    Out[9]= {0.21266, 0.820379, 0.751294, 1.02661, 0.953759, 0.0908256}

    In[10]:= **Max[%]**

    Out[10]= 1.02661

    Or, use **Outer** on the set of points directly, but note the need to get the level correct.

    In[11]:= **Max@Outer[Norm[#1 - #2] &, pts, pts, 1]**

    Out[11]= 1.02661

    Now put it all together using a pure function in place of the distance function. The **diameter** function operates on lists of pairs of numbers, so we need to specify them in our pure function as #1 and #2.

In[12]:= **diameter[*lis_*] := Max[Apply[Norm[*#1* - *#2*] &, Subsets[*lis*, {2}], {1}]]**

In[13]:= **diameter[pts]**

Out[13]= 1.02661

EuclideanDistance is a bit faster here, but for large datasets, the difference is more pronounced.

In[14]:= **Max[Apply[EuclideanDistance, Subsets[pts, {2}], {1}]]**

Out[14]= 1.02661

In[15]:= **pts = RandomReal[1, {1500, 2}];**
Max[Apply[Norm[*#1* - *#2*] &, Subsets[pts, {2}], {1}]] // Timing

Out[16]= {6.50623, 1.36706}

In[17]:= **Max[Apply[EuclideanDistance, Subsets[pts, {2}], {1}]] // Timing**

Out[17]= {1.60753, 1.36706}

3. Pure functions are needed to replace both addOne and CompositeQ:

In[18]:= **nextPrime[*n_Integer* /; *n* > 1] := NestWhile[*#* + 1 &, *n*, Not[PrimeQ[*#*]] &]**

Here is a quick check for correctness.

In[19]:= **nextPrime$\left[2^{123}\right]$ == NextPrime$\left[2^{123}\right]$**

Out[19]= True

Compare timing with the built-in function.

In[20]:= **Timing$\left[\text{nextPrime}\left[2^{2500}\right];\right]$**

Out[20]= {0.336794, Null}

In[21]:= **Timing$\left[\text{NextPrime}\left[2^{2500}\right];\right]$**

Out[21]= {0.312704, Null}

5. Here are some sample data taken from a normal distribution.

In[22]:= **data = RandomVariate[NormalDistribution[0, 1], {500}];**

Quickly visualize the data together with dashed lines drawn one standard deviation from the mean.

In[23]:= **mean = Mean[data];**
sd = StandardDeviation[data];
len = Length[data];
ListPlot[data,
  Epilog → {Dashed, Red,
    Line[{{0, mean + sd}, {len, mean + sd}}],
    Line[{{0, mean - sd}, {len, mean - sd}}]}
]

Out[26]=

Select those data elements whose distance to the mean is less than one standard deviation.

In[27]:= **filtered = Select[data, (Abs[(# - mean)] < sd &)];**

Here is a quick check that we get about the value we might expect (we would expect about 68% for normally distributed data).

In[28]:= $\mathbf{N}\left[\dfrac{\mathtt{Length[filtered]}}{\mathtt{Length[data]}}\right]$

Out[28]= **0.686**

In[29]:= **ListPlot[filtered, PlotRange → All,**
   Epilog → {Dashed, Red,
      Line[{{0, mean + sd}, {len, mean + sd}}],
      Line[{{0, mean - sd}, {len, mean - sd}}]}
   ]

Out[29]=

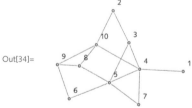

8. Using **Fold**, this pure function requires two arguments. The key is to start with an initial value of 0.

In[30]:= **Horner[*list_List*, *var_*] := Fold[*var* #1 + #2 &, 0, *list*]**

In[31]:= **Horner[{a, b, c, d, e}, x]**

Out[31]= $e + x (d + x (c + x (b + a x)))$

In[32]:= **Expand[%]**

Out[32]= $e + d x + c x^2 + b x^3 + a x^4$

9. Here is the prototype graph we will work with:

In[33]:= **SeedRandom[16];**
   gr = RandomGraph[{10, 15}, VertexLabels → "Name"]

Out[34]=

And here are its edges and its vertices:

In[35]:= **EdgeList[gr]**

Out[35]= $\{2 \leftrightarrow 10,\ 2 \leftrightarrow 3,\ 3 \leftrightarrow 5,\ 4 \leftrightarrow 5,\ 4 \leftrightarrow 1,\ 4 \leftrightarrow 7,\ 4 \leftrightarrow 3,$
   $5 \leftrightarrow 7,\ 5 \leftrightarrow 8,\ 6 \leftrightarrow 5,\ 9 \leftrightarrow 8,\ 9 \leftrightarrow 6,\ 10 \leftrightarrow 9,\ 10 \leftrightarrow 8,\ 10 \leftrightarrow 4\}$

In[36]:= **VertexList[gr]**

Out[36]= $\{1,\ 2,\ 3,\ 4,\ 5,\ 6,\ 7,\ 8,\ 9,\ 10\}$

Below are those edges from vertex 3 to any other vertex. In other words, this gives the adjacency list for vertex 3.

```
In[37]:= With[{u = 3},
         Select[VertexList[gr], (EdgeQ[gr, UndirectedEdge[u, #]] &)]
        ]
```
```
Out[37]= {2, 4, 5}
```

The case for directed graphs is similar. Here then is a function that returns the adjacency list for a given vertex u in graph gr.

```
In[38]:= adjacencyList[gr_, u_] := If[DirectedGraphQ[gr],
         Select[VertexList[gr], EdgeQ[gr, DirectedEdge[u, #]] &],
         Select[VertexList[gr], EdgeQ[gr, UndirectedEdge[u, #]] &]
        ]
```

The adjacency structure is then given by mapping the above function across the vertex list.

```
In[39]:= AdjacencyStructure[gr_Graph] :=
         Map[{#, adjacencyList[gr, #]} &, VertexList[gr]]
```
```
In[40]:= AdjacencyStructure[gr]
```
```
Out[40]= {{1, {4}}, {2, {3, 10}}, {3, {2, 4, 5}},
         {4, {1, 3, 5, 7, 10}}, {5, {3, 4, 6, 7, 8}}, {6, {5, 9}},
         {7, {4, 5}}, {8, {5, 9, 10}}, {9, {6, 8, 10}}, {10, {2, 4, 8, 9}}}
```

Check that it works for a directed graph also.

```
In[41]:= gr2 = Graph[{1 ⟶ 2, 2 ⟶ 1, 3 ⟶ 1, 3 ⟶ 2, 4 ⟶ 1, 4 ⟶ 2, 4 ⟶ 4},
         VertexLabels → "Name"]
```

Out[41]=
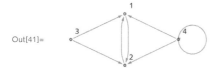

```
In[42]:= AdjacencyStructure[gr2]
```
```
Out[42]= {{1, {2}}, {2, {1}}, {3, {1, 2}}, {4, {1, 2, 4}}}
```

11. A first, naive implementation will use the fact that the factors are all less than 6. Here are the factors for a single integer.

```
In[43]:= facs = FactorInteger[126]
```
```
Out[43]= {{2, 1}, {3, 2}, {7, 1}}
```

This extracts only the prime factors.

```
In[44]:= Map[First, facs]
```
```
Out[44]= {2, 3, 7}
```

In this case, they are not all less than 6.

In[45]:= **Max[%] < 6**

Out[45]= False

Putting these pieces together, here are the Hamming numbers less than 1000.

In[46]:= **Select[Range[1000], Max[Map[First, FactorInteger[#]]] < 6 &]**

Out[46]= {1, 2, 3, 4, 5, 6, 8, 9, 10, 12, 15, 16, 18, 20, 24, 25, 27, 30, 32, 36, 40, 45, 48,
50, 54, 60, 64, 72, 75, 80, 81, 90, 96, 100, 108, 120, 125, 128, 135, 144, 150,
160, 162, 180, 192, 200, 216, 225, 240, 243, 250, 256, 270, 288, 300, 320,
324, 360, 375, 384, 400, 405, 432, 450, 480, 486, 500, 512, 540, 576, 600,
625, 640, 648, 675, 720, 729, 750, 768, 800, 810, 864, 900, 960, 972, 1000}

Factoring is slow for large integers and so this implementation does not scale well. This finds the 507 Hamming numbers less than 10^6.

In[47]:= $\textbf{With}\Big[\{n = 10^6\},$

   Select[Range[n], Max[Map[First, FactorInteger[#]]] < 6 &]

   $\Big]$; **// Timing**

Out[47]= {7.83722, Null}

See Dijkstra (1981) for a different implementation that starts with $h = \{1\}$, then builds lists $2\,h, 3\,h, 5\,h$, merges these lists, and iterates.

In[48]:= $\textbf{HammingNumberList}[n\_] := \textbf{Module}\Big[\{\text{lim}\},$

   $\text{lim} = \textbf{If}\Big[n < 100, \textbf{Ceiling}[\textbf{Log2}[n]], \textbf{Ceiling}\Big[\textbf{Log2}\Big[\dfrac{n}{2 \times 3 \times 5}\Big]\,\textbf{Log2}[n]\Big]\Big];$

   Join[{1}, Take[Union @@ NestList[

      Union @@ Outer[Times, {2, 3, 5}, #] &, {2, 3, 5}, lim], n - 1]

   $\Big]\Big]$

In[49]:= **HammingNumber[n_] := Part[HammingNumberList[n], n]**

In[50]:= **HammingNumberList[20]**

Out[50]= {1, 2, 3, 4, 5, 6, 8, 9, 10, 12, 15, 16, 18, 20, 24, 25, 27, 30, 32, 36}

In[51]:= **HammingNumber[1691] // Timing**

Out[51]= {0.122587, 2 125 764 000}

This gives the one-millionth Hamming number.

In[52]:= $\textbf{HammingNumber}\big[10^6\big]$ **// Timing**

Out[52]= {14.88,
519 312 780 448 388 736 089 589 843 750 000 000 000 000 000 000 000 000 000 000 000
000 000 000 000 000 000 000 000 000}

5.7 Options and messages

1. The message will slot in the values of the row indices being passed to the function switchRows, as well as the length of the matrix, that is, the number of matrix rows.

In[1]:= **switchRows::badargs =**

   "The absolute value of the row indices `1` and `2`

```
                 in switchRows[mat,`1`,`2`] must be between
                 1 and `3`, the size of the matrix.";
```

The message is issued if either of the row indices have absolute value greater than the length of the matrix or if either of these indices is equal to 0.

```
In[2]:= switchRows[mat_, {r1_Integer, r2_Integer}] :=
          Module[{lmat = mat, len = Length[mat]},
            If[Abs[r1] > len || Abs[r2] > len || r1 r2 == 0,
              Message[switchRows::badargs, r1, r2, len],
              lmat[[{r1, r2}]] = lmat[[{r2, r1}]]];
            lmat]
```

```
In[3]:= mat = RandomInteger[9, {4, 4}];
        MatrixForm[mat]
```

Out[4]//MatrixForm=

$$\begin{pmatrix} 0 & 0 & 8 & 5 \\ 4 & 6 & 9 & 9 \\ 0 & 0 & 0 & 3 \\ 2 & 7 & 0 & 8 \end{pmatrix}$$

```
In[5]:= switchRows[mat, {0, 4}]
```

switchRows::badargs : The absolute value of the row indices
            0 and 4 in switchRows[mat,0,4] must be between 1 and 4, the size of the matrix.

Out[5]= {{0, 0, 8, 5}, {4, 6, 9, 9}, {0, 0, 0, 3}, {2, 7, 0, 8}}

```
In[6]:= switchRows[mat, {2, 8}]
```

switchRows::badargs : The absolute value of the row indices
            2 and 8 in switchRows[mat,2,8] must be between 1 and 4, the size of the matrix.

Out[6]= {{0, 0, 8, 5}, {4, 6, 9, 9}, {0, 0, 0, 3}, {2, 7, 0, 8}}

2. If the first argument is not a list containing numbers, then issue a message.

```
In[7]:= MatchQ[{1, 2, a}, {__?NumericQ}]
```

Out[7]= False

Here is the message:

```
In[8]:= StemPlot::badarg =
          "The first argument to StemPlot must be a list of numbers.";
```

```
In[9]:= Options[StemPlot] = Options[ListPlot];
```

```
In[10]:= StemPlot[lis_, opts : OptionsPattern[]] :=
           If[MatchQ[lis, {__?NumericQ}],
             ListPlot[lis, opts, Filling → Axis],
             Message[StemPlot::badarg]
           ]
```

```
In[11]:= StemPlot[4]
```

StemPlot::badarg : The first argument to StemPlot must be a list of numbers.

```
In[12]:= StemPlot[{1, 2, c}]
```

StemPlot::badarg : The first argument to StemPlot must be a list of numbers.

In[13]:= `StemPlot[{1, 2, 3, 4, 5}]`

Out[13]=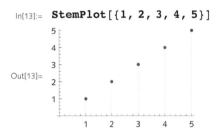

5.8 Examples and applications

1. Here are two sample lists.

In[1]:= `l1 = {1, 0, 0, 1, 1};`
`l2 = {0, 1, 0, 1, 0};`

First, pair them.

In[3]:= `ll = Transpose[{l1, l2}]`

Out[3]= `{{1, 0}, {0, 1}, {0, 0}, {1, 1}, {1, 0}}`

Here is the conditional pattern that matches any pair where the two elements are *not* identical. The Hamming distance is the number of such nonidentical pairs.

In[4]:= `Count[ll, {p_, q_} /; p ≠ q]`

Out[4]= `3`

Finally, here is a function that puts this all together.

In[5]:= `HammingDistance3[lis1_List, lis2_List] :=`
`    Count[Transpose[{lis1, lis2}], {p_, q_} /; p ≠ q]`

In[6]:= `HammingDistance3[l1, l2]`

Out[6]= `3`

The running times of this version of `HammingDistance` are quite a bit slower than those where we used bit operators. This is due to additional computation (`Transpose`) and the use of pattern matching and comparisons at every step.

In[7]:= `HammingDistance2[lis1_, lis2_] := Total[BitXor[lis1, lis2]]`

In[8]:= `data1 = RandomInteger[1, {10^6}];`

In[9]:= `data2 = RandomInteger[1, {10^6}];`

In[10]:= `Timing[HammingDistance2[data1, data2]]`

Out[10]= `{0.00861, 501 049}`

In[11]:= `Timing[HammingDistance3[data1, data2]]`

Out[11]= `{0.766642, 501 049}`

2. Using `Total`, which simply gives the sum of the elements in a list, Hamming distance can be computed as follows:

In[12]:= `HammingDistance4[lis1_, lis2_] := Total[Mod[lis1 + lis2, 2]]`

Timing tests show that the implementation with `Total` is quite a bit more efficient than the previous versions, although still slower than the version that uses bit operators.

```
In[13]:= sig1 = RandomInteger[1, {10^6}];
In[14]:= sig2 = RandomInteger[1, {10^6}];
In[15]:= HammingDistance1[lis1_, lis2_] :=
          Count[MapThread[SameQ, {lis1, lis2}], False]
In[16]:= Map[{#, Timing[#[sig1, sig2]]} &, {HammingDistance1,
          HammingDistance2, HammingDistance3, HammingDistance4}] // Grid
         HammingDistance1  {0.48052, 499991}
         HammingDistance2  {0.006952, 499991}
Out[16]=  HammingDistance3  {0.764652, 499991}
         HammingDistance4  {0.023833, 499991}
```

3. Just one change is needed here: add a second argument to `RotateLeft` that specifies the number of positions to rotate. We have used `NestList` to display the intermediate steps.

```
In[17]:= survivor[n_, m_] := NestList[Rest[RotateLeft[#, m-1]] &, Range[n], n-1]
In[18]:= survivor[11, 3]
Out[18]= {{1, 2, 3, 4, 5, 6, 7, 8, 9, 10, 11}, {4, 5, 6, 7, 8, 9, 10, 11, 1, 2},
          {7, 8, 9, 10, 11, 1, 2, 4, 5}, {10, 11, 1, 2, 4, 5, 7, 8},
          {2, 4, 5, 7, 8, 10, 11}, {7, 8, 10, 11, 2, 4},
          {11, 2, 4, 7, 8}, {7, 8, 11, 2}, {2, 7, 8}, {2, 7}, {7}}
```

4. The median of a list containing an odd number of elements is the middle element of the sorted list.

```
In[19]:= median[lis_List /; OddQ[Length[lis]]] :=
          Part[Sort[lis], Ceiling[Length[lis] / 2]]
```

When the list has an even number of elements, take the mean of the middle two.

```
In[20]:= median[lis_List /; EvenQ[Length[lis]]] :=
          Module[{len = Length[lis] / 2},
            Mean[Part[Sort[lis], len ;; len + 1]]
          ]
```

Check the two cases – an even number of elements, and an odd number of elements. Then compare with the built-in `Median`.

```
In[21]:= dataE = RandomInteger[10000, 100000];
In[22]:= dataO = RandomInteger[10000, 100001];
In[23]:= median[dataE] // Timing
Out[23]= {0.020506, 4977}
In[24]:= Median[dataE] // Timing
Out[24]= {0.020093, 4977}
In[25]:= median[dataO] // Timing
Out[25]= {0.018505, 4962}
In[26]:= Median[dataO] // Timing
Out[26]= {0.020531, 4962}
```

The two rules given here should be more careful about the input, using pattern matching to insure that these rules only apply to one-dimensional lists. The following modifications handle that more robustly.

```
In[27]:= Clear[median]

In[28]:= median[lis : {__} /; OddQ[Length[lis]]] :=
            Part[Sort[lis], Ceiling[Length[lis] / 2]]

In[29]:= median[lis : {__} /; EvenQ[Length[lis]]] :=
            Module[{len = Length[lis] / 2},
              Mean[Part[Sort[lis], len ;; len + 1]]]
```

6. Here is a list of coins (modify for other currencies).

```
In[30]:= coins = {p, p, q, n, d, d, p, q, q, p};
```

First count the occurrences of each.

```
In[31]:= Map[Count[coins, #] &, {p, n, d, q}]

Out[31]= {4, 1, 2, 3}
```

Then a dot product of this count vector with a value vector does the trick.

```
In[32]:= %.{.01, .05, .10, .25}

Out[32]= 1.04

In[33]:= CountChange[lis_] :=
            Dot[Map[Count[lis, #] &, {p, n, d, q}], {.01, .05, .10, .25}]

In[34]:= CountChange[coins]

Out[34]= 1.04

In[35]:= CountChange2[lis_] :=
            Inner[Times,
              Map[Count[lis, #] &, {p, n, d, q}], {.01, .05, .10, .25}, Plus]

In[36]:= CountChange2[coins]

Out[36]= 1.04
```

And here is a rule-based approach.

```
In[37]:= Tally[coins] /. {d → .10, n → .05, p → .01, q → .25}

Out[37]= {{0.01, 4}, {0.25, 3}, {0.05, 1}, {0.1, 2}}

In[38]:= Total[Apply[Times, %, {1}]]

Out[38]= 1.04

In[39]:= CountChange3[lis_] := Module[{freq},
            freq = Tally[lis] /. {p → .01, n → .05, d → .10, q → .25};
            Total[Apply[Times, freq, {1}]]]

In[40]:= CountChange3[coins]

Out[40]= 1.04
```

7. The two-dimensional implementation insures steps of unit length by mapping the pure function {Cos[#], Sin[#]} & over the angles.

```
In[41]:= walk1DOffLattice[steps_] := Accumulate[RandomReal[{-1, 1}, steps]]
```

In[42]:= **walk2DOffLattice[*steps_*] :=**
Accumulate[Map[{Cos[#], Sin[#]} &, RandomReal[{0, 2 π}, *steps*]]]

The three-dimensional walk requires two angles, θ in the interval $[0, 2\pi)$ and ϕ in the interval $[-1, 1]$. See Section 13.1 for a discussion of the three-dimensional off-lattice walk.

In[43]:= **walk3DOffLattice[*t_*] := Accumulate[**

Table[Function[{θ, φ}, {Cos[θ] $\sqrt{1 - \phi^2}$, Sin[θ] $\sqrt{1 - \phi^2}$, φ}] @@

{RandomReal[{0, 2 π}], RandomReal[{-1, 1}]}, {*t*}]]

With the one-dimensional walk, the vertical axis gives displacement from the origin and the horizontal axis shows the number of steps.

In[44]:= **ListLinePlot[walk1DOffLattice[1000]]**

Out[44]=

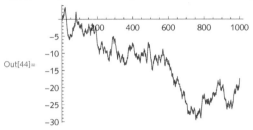

In[45]:= **ListLinePlot[walk2DOffLattice[5000]]**

Out[45]=

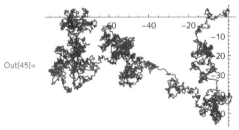

In[46]:= **Graphics3D[Line[walk3DOffLattice[5000]]]**

Out[46]=

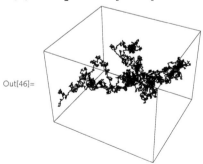

8. Column 4 of this matrix contains several different nonnumeric values.

    In[47]:= `mat3 = {{0.796495, "N/A", 0.070125, "nan", 0.806554},`
             `{"nn", -0.100365, 0.992736, -0.320560, -0.0805351},`
             `{0.473571, 0.460741, 0.030060, -0.412400, 0.788522},`
             `{0.614974, -0.503201, 0.615744, 0.966053, -0.011776},`
             `{-0.828415, 0.035514, 0.8911617, "N/A", -0.453926}};`
             `MatrixForm[col4 = mat3[[All, 4]]]`

    Out[48]//MatrixForm=
    $$\begin{pmatrix} \text{nan} \\ -0.32056 \\ -0.4124 \\ 0.966053 \\ \text{N/A} \end{pmatrix}$$

    To pattern match on either "N/A" or "nan", use `Alternatives` (|).

    In[49]:= `col4 /. "N/A" | "nan" → Mean[Cases[mat3[[All, 4]], _?NumberQ]] //`
             `MatrixForm`

    Out[49]//MatrixForm=
    $$\begin{pmatrix} 0.0776977 \\ -0.32056 \\ -0.4124 \\ 0.966053 \\ 0.0776977 \end{pmatrix}$$

    Convert the list of strings to a set of alternatives.

    In[50]:= `Apply[Alternatives, {"N/A", "nan", "nn"}]`

    Out[50]= `N/A | nan | nn`

    Here is a third set of definitions, including a new rule for `ReplaceElement` where the second argument is a list of strings. And another rule for `ReplaceElement` accommodates the new argument structure of `colMean`.

    In[51]:= `colMean[col_, {strings___String}] :=`
             `col /. Apply[Alternatives, {strings}] → Mean[Cases[col, _?NumberQ]]`
    In[52]:= `ReplaceElement[mat_, {strings__}] :=`
             `Transpose[Map[colMean[#, {strings}] &, Transpose[mat]]]`
    In[53]:= `ReplaceElement[mat3, {"N/A", "nan", "nn"}] // MatrixForm`

    Out[53]//MatrixForm=
    $$\begin{pmatrix} 0.796495 & -0.0268277 & 0.070125 & 0.0776977 & 0.806554 \\ 0.264156 & -0.100365 & 0.992736 & -0.32056 & -0.0805351 \\ 0.473571 & 0.460741 & 0.03006 & -0.4124 & 0.788522 \\ 0.614974 & -0.503201 & 0.615744 & 0.966053 & -0.011776 \\ -0.828415 & 0.035514 & 0.891162 & 0.0776977 & -0.453926 \end{pmatrix}$$

9. Start with a prototype logical expression.

    In[54]:= `Clear[A, B]`
    In[55]:= `expr = (A || B) ⟹ C;`
    In[56]:= `vars = {A, B, C};`

List all the possible truth value assignments for the variables.

```
In[57]:= tuples = Tuples[{True, False}, Length[vars]]
```

Out[57]= {{True, True, True}, {True, True, False},
 {True, False, True}, {True, False, False}, {False, True, True},
 {False, True, False}, {False, False, True}, {False, False, False}}

Next, create a list of rules, associating each of the triples of truth values with a triple of variables.

```
In[58]:= rules = Map[Thread[vars → #] &, tuples]
```

Out[58]= {{A → True, B → True, C → True}, {A → True, B → True, C → False},
 {A → True, B → False, C → True}, {A → True, B → False, C → False},
 {A → False, B → True, C → True}, {A → False, B → True, C → False},
 {A → False, B → False, C → True}, {A → False, B → False, C → False}}

Replace the logical expression with each set of rules.

```
In[59]:= expr /. rules
```

Out[59]= {True, False, True, False, True, False, True, True}

Put these last values at the end of each "row" of the tuples.

```
In[60]:= table = Transpose@Join[Transpose[tuples], {expr /. rules}]
```

Out[60]= {{True, True, True, True}, {True, True, False, False},
 {True, False, True, True}, {True, False, False, False},
 {False, True, True, True}, {False, True, False, False},
 {False, False, True, True}, {False, False, False, True}}

Create a header for `table`.

```
In[61]:= head = Append[vars, TraditionalForm[expr]]
```

Out[61]= {A, B, C, $A \lor B \Rightarrow C$}

Prepend `head` to `table`.

```
In[62]:= Prepend[table, head]
```

Out[62]= {{A, B, C, $A \lor B \Rightarrow C$}, {True, True, True, True}, {True, True, False, False},
 {True, False, True, True}, {True, False, False, False},
 {False, True, True, True}, {False, True, False, False},
 {False, False, True, True}, {False, False, False, True}}

Pour into a grid.

In[63]:= **Grid[Prepend[table, head]]**

	A	B	C	$A \lor B \Rightarrow C$
	True	True	True	True
	True	True	False	False
	True	False	True	True
Out[63]=	True	False	False	False
	False	True	True	True
	False	True	False	False
	False	False	True	True
	False	False	False	True

Replace True with "T" and False with "F".

In[64]:= **Grid[Prepend[table /. {True → "T", False → "F"}, head]]**

	A	B	C	$A \lor B \Rightarrow C$
	T	T	T	T
	T	T	F	F
	T	F	T	T
Out[64]=	T	F	F	F
	F	T	T	T
	F	T	F	F
	F	F	T	T
	F	F	F	T

Add formatting via options to Grid.

In[65]:= **Grid[Prepend[table /. {True → "T", False → "F"}, head],**
Dividers → {{1 → Black, -1 → Black, -2 → LightGray},
{1 → Black, 2 → LightGray, -1 → Black}},
BaseStyle → {FontFamily → "Times"}]

	A	B	C	$A \lor B \Rightarrow C$
	T	T	T	T
	T	T	F	F
	T	F	T	T
Out[65]=	T	F	F	F
	F	T	T	T
	F	T	F	F
	F	F	T	T
	F	F	F	T

Put the pieces together.

```
In[66]:= TruthTable[expr_, vars_] :=
           Module[{len = Length[vars], tuples, rules, table, head},
             tuples = Tuples[{True, False}, len];
             rules = Thread[vars → #1] & /@ tuples;
             table = Transpose@Join[Transpose[tuples], {expr /. rules}];
             head = Append[vars, TraditionalForm[expr]];
             Grid[Prepend[table /. {True → "T", False → "F"}, head],
               Dividers → {{1 → {Thin, Black},
                 -1 → {Thin, Black}, -2 → {Thin, LightGray}},
                {1 → {Thin, Black}, 2 → {Thin, LightGray}, -1 → {Thin, Black}}},
               BaseStyle → {FontFamily → "Times"}]]

In[67]:= TruthTable[A ∧ B ⇒ ¬ C, {A, B, C}]
```

A	B	C	$A \land B \Rightarrow \neg C$
T	T	T	F
T	T	F	T
T	F	T	T
T	F	F	T
F	T	T	T
F	T	F	T
F	F	T	T
F	F	F	T

Out[67]=

10. Position $\big[$*lis, elem*$\big]$ returns a list of positions at which *elem* occurs in *lis*. Extract $\big[$*lis, pos*$\big]$ returns those elements whose positions are specified by Position.

```
In[68]:= NearTo[lis_List, elem_, n_] :=
           Module[{pos = Position[lis, elem]}, Extract[lis, {pos - n, pos + n}]]

In[69]:= NearTo[lis_List, elem_, {n_}] := Module[
             {pos = Position[lis, elem]}, Extract[lis, Range[pos - n, pos + n]]]

In[70]:= chars = CharacterRange["a", "z"];

In[71]:= NearTo[chars, "q", 3]

Out[71]= {{n}, {t}}

In[72]:= NearTo[chars, "q", {4}]

Out[72]= {{m, n, o, p, q, r, s, t, u}}
```

The key to writing the distance function is to observe that it must be a function of two variables and return a numeric value (the distance metric). We are finding the difference of the positions of a target element in the list with the element in question, y and x, respectively in the pure function. The use of [[1, 1]] is to strip off extra braces returned by Position.

```
In[73]:= NearToN[lis_, elem_, n_] :=
           Nearest[lis, elem, {2 n + 1, n}, DistanceFunction →
             Function[{x, y}, Abs[(Position[lis, y] - Position[lis, x])[[1, 1]]]]]
```

In[74]:= **NearToN[chars, "q", 4]**

Out[74]= {q, p, r, o, s, n, t, m, u}

6   Procedural programming

6.1   Loops and iteration

1.   To compute the square root of a number *r*, iterate the following expression.

In[1]:= **fun[x_] := x^2 - r;**

Simplify$\left[x - \dfrac{fun[x]}{fun'[x]}\right]$

Out[2]= $\dfrac{r + x^2}{2\,x}$

This can be written as a pure function, with a second argument giving the initial guess. Here we iterate ten times, starting with a high-precision initial value, 2.0 to 30-digit precision.

In[3]:= **nestSqrt[r_, init_] := Nest$\left[\dfrac{r + \#^2}{2\,\#}\right.$ &, init, 10$\left.\right]$**

In[4]:= **nestSqrt[2, N[2, 30]]**

Out[4]= 1.41421356237309504880168872

2.   Here is a first basic attempt to replace the Do loop with Table.

In[5]:= **f[x_] := x^2 - 2**

In[6]:= **a = 2;**

Table$\left[a = N\left[a - \dfrac{f[a]}{f'[a]}\right], \{10\}\right]$

Out[7]= {1.5, 1.41667, 1.41422, 1.41421, 1.41421,
        1.41421, 1.41421, 1.41421, 1.41421, 1.41421}

In[8]:= **findRoot[fun_Symbol, {var_, init_}, iter_ : 10] := Module$\left[\{xi = init\},\right.$**

Table$\left[xi = N\left[xi - \dfrac{fun[xi]}{fun'[xi]}\right], \{iter\}\right];$

{var → xi}$\left.\right]$

In[9]:= **findRoot[f, {x, 2}]**

Out[9]= {x → 1.41421}

This runs the iteration only three times.

In[10]:= **findRoot[f, {x, 2}, 3]**

Out[10]= {x → 1.41422}

3.   Note that this version of the Fibonacci function is much more efficient than the simple recursive version given in Chapter 7, and is closer to the version there that uses dynamic programming.

```
In[11]:= fib[n_] := Module[{prev = 0, this = 1, next},
          Do[next = prev + this;
            prev = this;
            this = next,
            {n}];
          prev]
In[12]:= Table[fib[i], {i, 1, 10}]
Out[12]= {1, 1, 2, 3, 5, 8, 13, 21, 34, 55}
```

Actually, this code can be simplified a bit by using parallel assignments.

```
In[13]:= fib2[n_] := Module[{f1 = 0, f2 = 1},
          Do[{f1, f2} = {f2, f1 + f2},
            {n - 1}];
          f2]
In[14]:= Table[fib2[i], {i, 1, 10}]
Out[14]= {1, 1, 2, 3, 5, 8, 13, 21, 34, 55}
```

Both of these implementations are quite fast and avoid the deep recursion of the classical definition.

```
In[15]:= {Timing[fib[100 000];], Timing[fib2[100 000];]}
Out[15]= {{0.22523, Null}, {0.183665, Null}}
```

5. The variable b is the current approximation, and the variable a is the previous approximation.

$$
In[16]:= \text{findRoot}[fun\_, \{var\_, init\_\}, \epsilon\_] := \text{Module}\Big[\{a = init, b = fun[init]\},
$$
$$
\text{While}\Big[\text{Abs}[b - a] > \epsilon,
$$
$$
a = b;
$$
$$
b = N\Big[b - \frac{fun[b]}{fun'[b]}\Big]\Big];
$$
$$
\{var \to b\}\Big]
$$

```
In[17]:= f[x_] := x^2 - 50
In[18]:= findRoot[f, {x, 10}, 0.0001]
Out[18]= {x → 7.07107}
```

7. Based on a previous version of findRoot, the following adds multiple initial values.

$$
In[19]:= \text{findRootList}[fun\_, inits\_List, \epsilon\_] := \text{Module}\Big[\{a = inits\},
$$
$$
\text{While}\Big[\text{Min}[\text{Abs}[\text{Map}[fun, a]]] > \epsilon,
$$
$$
a = \text{Map}\Big[N\Big[\# - \frac{fun[\#]}{fun'[\#]}\Big] \&, a\Big]\Big];
$$
$$
\text{Select}[a, \text{Min}[\text{Abs}[\text{Map}[fun, a]]] == \text{Abs}[fun[\#]] \&]\Big]
$$

```
In[20]:= findRootList[(#^2 - 50) &, {-10, 1, 10}, .001]
Out[20]= {-7.07108, 7.07108}
```

8. A bit of variable swapping is needed here depending on whether or not a sign change occurs.

```
In[21]:= bisect[f_, {var_, a_, b_}, e_] :=
         Module[{midpt = N[a + b / 2], low = a, high = b},
           While[Abs[f[midpt]] > e,
             If[Sign[f[low]] == Sign[f[midpt]], low = midpt, high = midpt];
             midpt = low + high / 2];
           {var → midpt}]

In[22]:= f[x_] := x^2 - 2
         bisect[f, {x, 0, 2}, .0001]

Out[23]= {x → 1.41418}
```

9.   This is a direct implementation of the Euclidean algorithm.

```
In[24]:= gcd[m_, n_] := Module[{a = m, b = n, tmpa},
           While[b > 0,
             tmpa = a;
             a = b;
             b = Mod[tmpa, b]];
           a]

In[25]:= With[{m = 12 782, n = 5 531 207},
           gcd[m, n]]

Out[25]= 11
```

You can avoid the need for the temporary variable tmpa by performing a parallel assignment as in the following function. In addition, some argument checking insures that *m* and *n* are integers.

```
In[26]:= gcd[m_Integer, n_Integer] := Module[{a = m, b = n},
           While[b > 0,
             {a, b} = {b, Mod[a, b]}];
           a]

In[27]:= With[{m = 12 782, n = 5 531 207},
           gcd[m, n]]

Out[27]= 11
```

6.2 Flow control

1.   If, for element a_{ij}, i is bigger than j, then we are below the diagonal and should insert a 0, otherwise insert a

1.

```
In[1]:= UpperTriangularMatrix[{m_, n_}] := Table[If[i ≥ j, 0, 1], {i, m}, {j, n}]
```

A default value can be given for an optional argument that specifies the elements above the diagonal.

```
In[2]:= UpperTriangularMatrix[{m_, n_}, val_:1] :=
        Table[If[i ≥ j, 0, val], {i, m}, {j, n}]
```

```
In[3]:= UpperTriangularMatrix[{5, 5}, α] // MatrixForm
```
Out[3]//MatrixForm=

$$\begin{pmatrix} 0 & \alpha & \alpha & \alpha & \alpha \\ 0 & 0 & \alpha & \alpha & \alpha \\ 0 & 0 & 0 & \alpha & \alpha \\ 0 & 0 & 0 & 0 & \alpha \\ 0 & 0 & 0 & 0 & 0 \end{pmatrix}$$

3. The test as the first argument of If on the right-hand side checks to see if x is an element of the domain of complex numbers and, if it is, then $\sqrt{re(x)^2 + im(x)^2}$ is computed. If x is not complex, nothing is done, but then the other definitions for abs will be checked.

```
In[4]:= Clear[abs];
        abs[x_] := Sqrt[Re[x]² + Im[x]²] /; x ∈ Complexes;
        abs[x_] := x /; x ≥ 0
        abs[x_] := -x /; x < 0
In[8]:= abs[3 + 4 I]
Out[8]= 5
In[9]:= abs[-3]
Out[9]= 3
```

The condition itself can appear on the left-hand side of the function definition, as part of the pattern match. Here is a slight variation on the abs definition.

```
In[10]:= Clear[abs]
         abs[x_] := If[x ≥ 0, x, -x]
         abs[x_ /; x ∈ Complexes] := Sqrt[Re[x]² + Im[x]²]
In[13]:= abs[3 + 4 I]
Out[13]= 5
In[14]:= abs[-3]
Out[14]= 3
```

5. This is a straightforward conversion from the two rules given in Exercise 4 in Section 5.8 to an If statement.

```
In[15]:= medianP[lis : {__}] := Module[{len = Length[lis]},
           If[OddQ[len],
             Part[Sort[lis], Ceiling[len / 2]],
             Mean@Part[Sort[lis], len / 2 ;; len / 2 + 1]
           ]]
In[16]:= dataO = RandomInteger[10 000, 100 001];
         dataE = RandomInteger[10 000, 100 000];
In[18]:= medianP[dataO] // Timing
Out[18]= {0.01935, 5005}
In[19]:= Median[dataO] // Timing
Out[19]= {0.018673, 5005}
```

In[20]:= **medianP[dataE] // Timing**

Out[20]= $\left\{0.019162, \dfrac{10\,019}{2}\right\}$

In[21]:= **Median[dataE] // Timing**

Out[21]= $\left\{0.019867, \dfrac{10\,019}{2}\right\}$

6. First, define the auxiliary function using conditional statements.

In[22]:= **collatz[$n\_$] := $\dfrac{n}{2}$ /; EvenQ[n]**

In[23]:= **collatz[$n\_$] := 3 n + 1 /; OddQ[n]**

Alternatively, use If.

In[24]:= **collatz[$n\_Integer$? Positive] := If[EvenQ[n], n / 2, 3 n + 1]**

Then iterate Collatz, starting with n, and continue while n is not equal to 1.

In[25]:= **CollatzSequence[$n\_$] := NestWhileList[collatz, n, # ≠ 1 &]**

In[26]:= **CollatzSequence[17]**

Out[26]= {17, 52, 26, 13, 40, 20, 10, 5, 16, 8, 4, 2, 1}

6.3 Examples and applications

1. Here is the gcd function implemented using an If structure.

In[1]:= **Clear[gcd]**

In[2]:= **gcd[$m\_Integer$, $n\_Integer$] := If[m > 0, gcd[Mod[n, m], m], gcd[m, n] = n]**

In[3]:= **With[{m = 12 782, n = 5 531 207},
      gcd[m, n]]**

Out[3]= 11

2. Given an integer, this totals the list of its digits.

In[4]:= **Total[IntegerDigits[7763]]**

Out[4]= 23

To repeat this process until the resulting integer has only one digit, use While.

In[5]:= **digitRoot[$n\_Integer$? Positive] := Module[{locn = n, lis},
      While[
        Length[lis = IntegerDigits@locn] > 1,
        locn = Total[lis]];
      locn]**

In[6]:= **digitRoot[7763]**

Out[6]= 5

This can also be accomplished without iteration as follows:

In[7]:= **digitRoot2[$n\_Integer$? Positive] := If[Mod[n, 9] == 0, 9, Mod[n, 9]]**

```
In[8]:= digitRoot2[1000!]

Out[8]= 9
```

4. The alternatives we need to check for are 0 | 0.0 for both *x* and *y*.

```
In[9]:= quadrant[{0 | 0.0, 0 | 0.0}] := 0
        quadrant[{x_, 0 | 0.0}] := -1
        quadrant[{0 | 0.0, y_}] := -2
        quadrant[{x_, y_}] := If[x < 0, 2, 1] /; y > 0
        quadrant[{x_, y_}] := If[x < 0, 3, 4]

In[14]:= quadrant[{0.0, 0}]

Out[14]= 0

In[15]:= quadrant[{1, 0}]

Out[15]= -1
```

6. Start with a small list of odd numbers.

```
In[16]:= ints = Range[1, 100, 2]

Out[16]= {1, 3, 5, 7, 9, 11, 13, 15, 17, 19, 21, 23, 25, 27, 29, 31, 33, 35,
         37, 39, 41, 43, 45, 47, 49, 51, 53, 55, 57, 59, 61, 63, 65, 67,
         69, 71, 73, 75, 77, 79, 81, 83, 85, 87, 89, 91, 93, 95, 97, 99}
```

On the first iteration, drop every third number, that is, drop 5, 11, 17, and so on.

```
In[17]:= p = ints[[2]];
         ints = Drop[ints, p ;; -1 ;; p]

Out[18]= {1, 3, 7, 9, 13, 15, 19, 21, 25, 27, 31, 33, 37, 39, 43, 45, 49,
         51, 55, 57, 61, 63, 67, 69, 73, 75, 79, 81, 85, 87, 91, 93, 97, 99}
```

Get the next number, 7, in the list `ints`; then drop every seventh number.

```
In[19]:= p = ints[[3]];
         ints = Drop[ints, p ;; -1 ;; p]

Out[20]= {1, 3, 7, 9, 13, 15, 21, 25, 27, 31, 33, 37, 43, 45, 49,
         51, 55, 57, 63, 67, 69, 73, 75, 79, 85, 87, 91, 93, 97, 99}
```

Iterate. You will need to be careful about the upper limit of the iterator i.

```
In[21]:= ints = Range[1, 1000, 2];
         Do[
          p = ints[[i]];
          ints = Drop[ints, p ;; -1 ;; p],
          {i, 2, 32}]
         ints

Out[23]= {1, 3, 7, 9, 13, 15, 21, 25, 31, 33, 37, 43, 49, 51, 63, 67, 69, 73, 75, 79, 87, 93,
         99, 105, 111, 115, 127, 129, 133, 135, 141, 151, 159, 163, 169, 171, 189, 193, 195,
         201, 205, 211, 219, 223, 231, 235, 237, 241, 259, 261, 267, 273, 283, 285, 289, 297,
         303, 307, 319, 321, 327, 331, 339, 349, 357, 361, 367, 385, 391, 393, 399, 409, 415,
         421, 427, 429, 433, 451, 463, 475, 477, 483, 487, 489, 495, 511, 517, 519, 529,
         535, 537, 541, 553, 559, 577, 579, 583, 591, 601, 613, 615, 619, 621, 631, 639,
         643, 645, 651, 655, 673, 679, 685, 693, 699, 717, 723, 727, 729, 735, 739, 741,
         745, 769, 777, 781, 787, 801, 805, 819, 823, 831, 841, 855, 867, 873, 883, 885,
         895, 897, 903, 925, 927, 931, 933, 937, 957, 961, 975, 979, 981, 991, 993, 997}
```

It would be more efficient if you did not need to manually determine the upper limit of the iteration. A `While` loop is better for this task. The test checks that the value of the iterator has not gone past the length of the successively shortened lists.

```
In[24]:= LuckyNumbers[n_Integer?Positive] :=
          Module[{p, i = 2, ints = Range[1, n, 2]},
            While[ints[[i]] < Length[ints],
              p = ints[[i]];
              ints = Drop[ints, p ;; -1 ;; p];
              i++];
            ints]
```

```
In[25]:= LuckyNumbers[1000]
```

```
Out[25]= {1, 3, 7, 9, 13, 15, 21, 25, 31, 33, 37, 43, 49, 51, 63, 67, 69, 73, 75, 79, 87, 93,
          99, 105, 111, 115, 127, 129, 133, 135, 141, 151, 159, 163, 169, 171, 189, 193, 195,
          201, 205, 211, 219, 223, 231, 235, 237, 241, 259, 261, 267, 273, 283, 285, 289, 297,
          303, 307, 319, 321, 327, 331, 339, 349, 357, 361, 367, 385, 391, 393, 399, 409, 415,
          421, 427, 429, 433, 451, 463, 475, 477, 483, 487, 489, 495, 511, 517, 519, 529,
          535, 537, 541, 553, 559, 577, 579, 583, 591, 601, 613, 615, 619, 621, 631, 639,
          643, 645, 651, 655, 673, 679, 685, 693, 699, 717, 723, 727, 729, 735, 739, 741,
          745, 769, 777, 781, 787, 801, 805, 819, 823, 831, 841, 855, 867, 873, 883, 885,
          895, 897, 903, 925, 927, 931, 933, 937, 957, 961, 975, 979, 981, 991, 993, 997}
```

This latter approach is also reasonably fast. Here is the time it takes to compute all lucky numbers less than one million; there are 71918 of them.

```
In[26]:= Length[LuckyNumbers[10^6]] // Timing
```

```
Out[26]= {0.313757, 71 918}
```

7.   Use the same constructs as were used in the text for selection sort.

```
In[27]:= bubbleSortList[lis_] :=
          Module[{slist = lis, len = Length[lis], tmp = {}},
            For[i = len, i > 0, i--,
              AppendTo[tmp, slist];
              For[j = 2, j ≤ i, j++,
                If[slist[[j - 1]] > slist[[j]],
                  slist[[{j - 1, j}]] = slist[[{j, j - 1}]]]]];
            tmp]
```

```
In[28]:= data = RandomReal[1, 500];
         sort = bubbleSortList[data];
         ListAnimate[ListPlot /@ sort];
```

7 Recursion

7.1 Fibonacci numbers

1. The key here is to get the stopping conditions right in each case.

   a. This is a straightforward recursion, multiplying the previous two values to get the next.

   In[1]:= `a[1] := 2`
   `a[2] := 3`
   `a[i_] := a[i - 1] a[i - 2]`

   In[4]:= `Table[a[i], {i, 1, 8}]`

   Out[4]= {2, 3, 6, 18, 108, 1944, 209 952, 408 146 688}

   b. The sequence is obtained by taking the difference of the previous two values.

   In[5]:= `b[1] := 0`
   `b[2] := 1`
   `b[i_] := b[i - 2] - b[i - 1]`

   In[8]:= `Table[b[i], {i, 1, 9}]`

   Out[8]= {0, 1, -1, 2, -3, 5, -8, 13, -21}

   c. Here we add the previous three values.

   In[9]:= `c[1] := 0`
   `c[2] := 1`
   `c[3] := 2`
   `c[i_] := c[i - 3] + c[i - 2] + c[i - 1]`

   In[13]:= `Table[c[i], {i, 1, 9}]`

   Out[13]= {0, 1, 2, 3, 6, 11, 20, 37, 68}

2. It is important to get the two base cases right here.

   In[14]:= `FA[1] := 0`
   `FA[2] := 0`
   `FA[i_] := FA[i - 2] + FA[i - 1] + 1`

   In[17]:= `Map[FA, Range[9]]`

   Out[17]= {0, 0, 1, 2, 4, 7, 12, 20, 33}

   It is interesting to note that the number of additions needed to compute the nth Fibonacci number is one less than the nth Fibonacci number itself. As the Fibonacci numbers grow, so too does the computation!

   In[18]:= `Fibonacci /@ Range[9]`

   Out[18]= {1, 1, 2, 3, 5, 8, 13, 21, 34}

3. This is a direct implementation of the traditional mathematical notation given in the exercise. Avoiding the double recursion of the naive implementation reduces the memory required and speeds things up significantly, although it is still too slow for large numbers.

   In[19]:= `Clear[fib, f];`
   `fib[0] = 0;`
   `fib[1] = 1;`

```
In[22]:= fib[n_Integer?Positive] := With[{k = IntegerPart[n / 2]},
          Which[
            EvenQ[n], fib[k] (fib[k] + 2 fib[k - 1]),
            Mod[n, 4] == 1, (2 fib[k] + fib[k - 1]) (2 fib[k] - fib[k - 1]) + 2,
            True, (2 fib[k] + fib[k - 1]) (2 fib[k] - fib[k - 1]) - 2
          ]]
In[23]:= Timing@Table[fib[i], {i, 1, 40}]
Out[23]= {0.024248, {1, 1, 2, 3, 5, 8, 13, 21, 34, 55, 89, 144, 233, 377, 610, 987,
            1597, 2584, 4181, 6765, 10 946, 17 711, 28 657, 46 368, 75 025, 121 393,
            196 418, 317 811, 514 229, 832 040, 1 346 269, 2 178 309, 3 524 578, 5 702 887,
            9 227 465, 14 930 352, 24 157 817, 39 088 169, 63 245 986, 102 334 155}}
```

4. You can use your earlier definition of the Fibonacci numbers, or use the built-in `Fibonacci`.

```
In[24]:= f[n_Integer?NonPositive] := (-1)^{n-1} Fibonacci[-n]
In[25]:= f[0] = 0;
          f[-1] = 1;
In[27]:= Table[f[i], {i, 0, -8, -1}]
Out[27]= {f[i], f[i], f[i], f[i], f[i], f[i], f[i], f[i], f[i]}
```

7.2 Thinking recursively

1. This is similar to the `length` function in the text – recursion is on the tail. The base case is a list consisting of a single element.

```
In[1]:= reverse[{x_, y__}] := Join[reverse[{y}], {x}]
In[2]:= reverse[{x_}] := {x}
In[3]:= reverse[{1, β, 3 / 4, "practice makes perfect"}]
Out[3]= {practice makes perfect, 3/4, β, 1}
```

3. Recursion is on the tail.

```
In[4]:= sumOddElements[{}] := 0
          sumOddElements[{x_, r___}] := x + sumOddElements[{r}] /; OddQ[x]
          sumOddElements[{x_, r___}] := sumOddElements[{r}]
In[7]:= sumOddElements[{2, 3, 5, 6, 7, 9, 12, 13}]
Out[7]= 37
```

4. Again, recursion is on the tail.

```
In[8]:= sumEveryOtherElement[{}] := 0
          sumEveryOtherElement[{x_}] := x
          sumEveryOtherElement[{x_, y_, r___}] := x + sumEveryOtherElement[{r}]
In[11]:= sumEveryOtherElement[{1, 2, 3, 4, 5, 6, 7, 8, 9}]
Out[11]= 25
```

5. This is a direct extension of the `addPairs` function discussed in this section.

```
In[12]:= addTriples[{}, {}, {}] := {}
          addTriples[{x1_, y1___}, {x2_, y2___}, {x3_, y3___}] :=
```

```
        Join[{x1 + x2 + x3}, addTriples[{y1}, {y2}, {y3}]]
In[14]:= addTriples[{w₁, x₁, y₁, z₁}, {w₂, x₂, y₂, z₂}, {w₃, x₃, y₃, z₃}]

Out[14]= {w₁ + w₂ + w₃, x₁ + x₂ + x₃, y₁ + y₂ + y₃, z₁ + z₂ + z₃}
```

7. Recursion is on the tails of each of the two lists.

```
In[15]:= maxPairs[{}, {}] := {}
        maxPairs[{x_, r___}, {y_, s___}] :=
        Join[{Max[x, y]}, maxPairs[{r}, {s}]]
In[17]:= maxPairs[{1, 2, 4}, {2, 7, 2}]

Out[17]= {2, 7, 4}
```

8. Again, we do recursion on the tails of the two lists.

```
In[18]:= riffle[{}, {}] := {}
        riffle[{x_, r___}, {y_, s___}] := Join[{x, y}, riffle[{r}, {s}]]
In[20]:= riffle[{a, b, c}, {x, y, z}]

Out[20]= {a, x, b, y, c, z}
```

Here is the built-in function that does this.

```
In[21]:= Riffle[{a, b, c}, {x, y, z}]

Out[21]= {a, x, b, y, c, z}
```

9. Here is maxima using an auxiliary function.

```
In[22]:= maxima[{}] := {}
        maxima[{x_, r___}] := maxima[x, {r}]
In[24]:= maxima[x_, {}] := {x}
        maxima[x_, {y_, r___}] := maxima[x, {r}] /; x ≥ y
        maxima[x_, {y_, r___}] := Join[{x}, maxima[y, {r}]]
```

7.3 Dynamic programming

1. Here are the rules translated directly from the formulas given in the exercise.

```
In[1]:= EulerianNumber[0, k_] = 0;
       EulerianNumber[n_Integer, 0] = 1;
       EulerianNumber[n_Integer, k_Integer] /; k ≥ n = 0;
In[4]:= EulerianNumber[n_Integer, k_Integer] :=
          (k + 1) EulerianNumber[n - 1, k] + (n - k) EulerianNumber[n - 1, k - 1]
In[5]:= Table[EulerianNumber[n, k], {n, 0, 7}, {k, 0, 7}] // TableForm
```

Out[5]//TableForm=

0	0	0	0	0	0	0	0
1	0	0	0	0	0	0	0
1	1	0	0	0	0	0	0
1	4	1	0	0	0	0	0
1	11	11	1	0	0	0	0
1	26	66	26	1	0	0	0
1	57	302	302	57	1	0	0
1	120	1191	2416	1191	120	1	0

Because of the triple recursion, computing larger values is not only time and memory intensive but also bumps up against the built-in recursion limit.

In[6]:= `EulerianNumber[25, 15] // Timing`

Out[6]= `{18.7849, 531 714 261 368 950 897 339 996}`

This is a good candidate for dynamic programming. In the following implementation we have temporarily reset the value of `$RecursionLimit` using `Block`.

In[7]:= `Clear[EulerianNumber];`

In[8]:= `EulerianNumber[0, k_] = 0;`
`EulerianNumber[n_Integer, 0] = 1;`
`EulerianNumber[n_Integer, k_Integer] /; k ≥ n = 0;`

In[11]:= `EulerianNumber[n_Integer, k_Integer] :=`
`  Block[{$RecursionLimit = Infinity},`
`    EulerianNumber[n, k] =`
`      (k + 1) EulerianNumber[n - 1, k] + (n - k) EulerianNumber[n - 1, k - 1]]`

In[12]:= `EulerianNumber[25, 15] // Timing`

Out[12]= `{0.002171, 531 714 261 368 950 897 339 996}`

In[13]:= `EulerianNumber[600, 65]; // Timing`

Out[13]= `{0.411056, Null}`

In[14]:= `N[EulerianNumber[600, 65]]`

Out[14]= $4.998147102049161 \times 10^{1091}$

2. This implementation uses the identities given in the exercise together with some pattern matching for the even and odd cases.

In[15]:= `F[1] := 1`
`F[2] := 1`

In[17]:= $F[n\_ ?\text{EvenQ}] := 2\, F\!\left[\dfrac{n}{2} - 1\right] F\!\left[\dfrac{n}{2}\right] + F\!\left[\dfrac{n}{2}\right]^2$

$F[n\_ ?\text{OddQ}] := F\!\left[\dfrac{n-1}{2} + 1\right]^2 + F\!\left[\dfrac{n-1}{2}\right]^2$

In[19]:= `Map[F, Range[10]]`

Out[19]= `{1, 1, 2, 3, 5, 8, 13, 21, 34, 55}`

In[20]:= $\text{Timing}\!\left[F\!\left[10^4\right];\right]$

Out[20]= `{0.410249, Null}`

3. The use of dynamic programming speeds up the computation by several orders of magnitude.

In[21]:= `FF[1] := 1`
`FF[2] := 1`

In[23]:= $FF[n\_ ?\text{EvenQ}] := FF[n] = 2\, FF\!\left[\dfrac{n}{2} - 1\right] FF\!\left[\dfrac{n}{2}\right] + FF\!\left[\dfrac{n}{2}\right]^2$

$FF[n\_ ?\text{OddQ}] := FF[n] = FF\!\left[\dfrac{n-1}{2} + 1\right]^2 + FF\!\left[\dfrac{n-1}{2}\right]^2$

```
In[25]:= Map[FF, Range[10]]
```
```
Out[25]= {1, 1, 2, 3, 5, 8, 13, 21, 34, 55}
```
```
In[26]:= Timing[FF[10^5];]
```
```
Out[26]= {0.00133, Null}
```

This is fairly fast, even compared with the built-in `Fibonacci` which uses a method based on the binary digits of *n*.

```
In[27]:= Timing[Fibonacci[10^5];]
```
```
Out[27]= {0.002, Null}
```

7.4 Classical examples

1. Perhaps the most straightforward way to do this is to write an auxiliary function that takes the output from `runEncode` and produces output such as `Split` would generate.

```
In[1]:= runEncode[{}] := {}
        runEncode[{x_}] := {{x, 1}}
In[3]:= runEncode[{x_, res___}] := Module[{R = runEncode[{res}], p},
           p = First[R];
           If[x == First[p],
             Join[{{x, p[[2]] + 1}}, Rest[R]],
             Join[{{x, 1}}, R]]]
```

Then our `split` simply operates on the output of `runEncode`. The iterator for the `Table` is the second element in each sublist, that is, the frequency.

```
In[4]:= sp[lis_] := Map[Table[#[[1]], {#[[2]]}] &, lis]
In[5]:= sp[{{3, 2}, {4, 1}, {2, 5}}]
```
```
Out[5]= {{3, 3}, {4}, {2, 2, 2, 2, 2}}
```
```
In[6]:= split[lis_] := sp[runEncode[lis]]
In[7]:= split[{9, 9, 9, 9, 9, 4, 3, 3, 3, 3, 5, 5, 5, 5, 5, 5}]
```
```
Out[7]= {{9, 9, 9, 9, 9}, {4}, {3, 3, 3, 3}, {5, 5, 5, 5, 5, 5}}
```

Check against the built-in function.

```
In[8]:= Split[{9, 9, 9, 9, 9, 4, 3, 3, 3, 3, 5, 5, 5, 5, 5, 5}]
```
```
Out[8]= {{9, 9, 9, 9, 9}, {4}, {3, 3, 3, 3}, {5, 5, 5, 5, 5, 5}}
```

2. The order of this list of rules is the order in which the *Mathematica* evaluator will search for a pattern match.

```
In[9]:= runEncode[{}] := {}
        runEncode[{x_, r___}] := runEncode[x, 1, {r}]
        runEncode[x_, k_, {}] := {{x, k}}
        runEncode[x_, k_, {x_, r___}] := runEncode[x, k + 1, {r}]
        runEncode[x_, k_, {y_, r___}] := Join[{{x, k}}, runEncode[y, 1, {r}]]
```

3. Recursion is on the tail.

```
In[14]:= runDecode[{}] := {}
         runDecode[{{x_, k_}, r___}] := Join[Table[x, {k}], runDecode[{r}]]
```

```
In[16]:= runDecode[{{9, 5}, {4, 1}, {3, 4}, {5, 6}}]
Out[16]= {9, 9, 9, 9, 9, 4, 3, 3, 3, 3, 5, 5, 5, 5, 5, 5}
```

8   Numerics

8.1   Numbers

1.   This function gives the polar form as a list consisting of the magnitude and the polar angle.

```
In[1]:= complexToPolar[z_] := {Abs[z], Arg[z]}
```

```
In[2]:= complexToPolar[3 + 3 i]
```

$$Out[2]= \left\{ 3\sqrt{2}, \frac{\pi}{4} \right\}$$

```
In[3]:= complexToPolar[e^{\frac{\pi i}{3}}]
```

$$Out[3]= \left\{ 1, \frac{\pi}{3} \right\}$$

2.   This function uses a default value of 2 for the base. (Try replacing `Fold` with `FoldList` to see more clearly what this function is doing.)

```
In[4]:= convert[digits_List, base_ : 2] := Fold[(base #1 + #2) &, 0, digits]
```

Here are the digits for 9 in base 2:

```
In[5]:= IntegerDigits[9, 2]
Out[5]= {1, 0, 0, 1}
```

This converts them back to the base 10 representation.

```
In[6]:= convert[%]
Out[6]= 9
```

Note, this functionality is built into the function `FromDigits[lis, base]`.

```
In[7]:= FromDigits[{1, 0, 0, 1}, 2]
Out[7]= 9
```

This function is essentially an implementation of Horner's method for fast polynomial multiplication.

```
In[8]:= convert[{a, b, c, d, e}, x]
Out[8]= e + x (d + x (c + x (b + a x)))
```

```
In[9]:= Expand[%]
Out[9]= e + d x + c x^2 + b x^3 + a x^4
```

3.   One rule can cover both parts of this exercise, using a default value of 10 for the base.

```
In[10]:= DigitSum[n_, base_ : 10] := Total[IntegerDigits[n, base]]
```

```
In[11]:= DigitSum[10!]
Out[11]= 27
```

The Hamming weight of a number is the number of 1s in its binary representation.

In[12]:= **DigitSum$\left[2^{31} - 1, 2\right]$**

Out[12]= 31

Here is a comparison with a built-in function:

In[13]:= **DigitCount$\left[2^{31} - 1, 2, 1\right]$**

Out[13]= 31

8. Mapping Dice (from Exercise 9 in Section 4.2) over a list of two random integers between 1 and 6 simulates a roll of a pair of dice.

In[14]:= **Map[Dice, RandomInteger[{1, 6}, {2}]]**

Out[14]= { , }

Here is a function to do that.

In[15]:= **RollDice[] := GraphicsRow[Map[Dice, RandomInteger[{1, 6}, {2}]]]**

In[16]:= **RollDice[]**

Out[16]=

And here is the rule for rolling the pair of dice n times.

In[17]:= **RollDice[$n\_$] := Table[RollDice[], {n}]**

In[18]:= **RollDice[4]**

Out[18]= { , 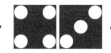 , , }

9. Using the hint in the exercise, here are the directions for the two- and three-dimensional cases.

In[19]:= **NSEW = {{0, 1}, {0, -1}, {1, 0}, {-1, 0}};**

In[20]:= **NSEW3 = {{1, 0, 0}, {0, 1, 0}, {0, 0, 1}, {-1, 0, 0}, {0, -1, 0}, {0, 0, -1}};**

The walk functions follow directly from the one-dimensional case given in the text.

In[21]:= **walk2D[$t\_$] := Accumulate[RandomChoice[NSEW, t]]**

In[22]:= **walk3D[$t\_$] := Accumulate[RandomChoice[NSEW3, t]]**

Exercise the functions and visualize.

In[23]:= **ListLinePlot[walk2D[1500], AspectRatio → Automatic]**

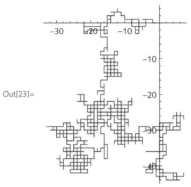

Out[23]=

In[24]:= **Graphics3D[Line[walk3D[2500]]]**

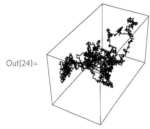

Out[24]=

For a more complete discussion of these functions, see Section 13.1.

10. Here is the linear congruential generator.

In[25]:= **linearCongruential[x_, mod_, mult_, incr_] := Mod[*mult x + incr*, *mod*]**

With modulus 100 and multiplier 15, this generator quickly gets into a cycle.

In[26]:= **NestList[linearCongruential[#, 100, 15, 1] &, 5, 10]**

Out[26]= {5, 76, 41, 16, 41, 16, 41, 16, 41, 16, 41}

With a larger modulus and multiplier, it appears as if this generator is doing better.

Here are the first 60 terms starting with a seed of 0.

In[27]:= **data = NestList[linearCongruential[#, 381, 15, 1] &, 0, 5000];**
Take[data, 60]

Out[28]= {0, 1, 16, 241, 187, 139, 181, 49, 355, 373, 262, 121, 292, 190, 184, 94,
         268, 211, 118, 247, 277, 346, 238, 142, 226, 343, 193, 229, 7, 106,
         67, 244, 232, 52, 19, 286, 100, 358, 37, 175, 340, 148, 316, 169, 250,
         322, 259, 76, 379, 352, 328, 349, 283, 55, 64, 199, 319, 214, 163, 160}

Sometimes it is hard to see if your generator is doing a poor job. Graphical analysis can help by allowing you to see patterns over larger domains. Here is a ListPlot of this sequence taken out to 5000 terms.

In[29]:= **ListPlot[data, PlotStyle → PointSize[.005]]**

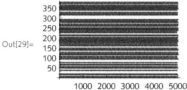

Out[29]=

It appears as if certain numbers are repeating. Looking at the plot of the Fourier data shows peaks at certain frequencies, indicating a periodic nature to the data.

In[30]:= **ListPlot[Abs[Fourier[data]], PlotStyle → PointSize[.005]]**

Out[30]=

Using a much larger modulus and multiplier and an increment of zero (actually, these are the default values for *Mathematica*'s built-in "Congruential" method for SeedRandom), you can keep your generator from getting into such short loops.

In[31]:= **ListPlot[data = NestList[linearCongruential[#1, 2 305 843 009 213 693 951,**
      1 283 839 219 676 404 755, 0] &, 1, 5000], PlotStyle → PointSize[.005]]

Out[31]=

In[32]:= **ListPlot[Abs[Fourier[data]], PlotStyle → PointSize[.005]]**

Out[32]=

12. Here is a simple implementation of the middle square method. It assumes a ten-digit seed. To work with arbitrary-length seeds, modify the number of middle digits that are extracted with the Part function.

In[33]:= **middleSquareGenerator[n_, seed_ : 1 234 567 890] :=**
     Module[{tmp = {seed}, s2, len, s = seed},
       Do[
         s2 = IntegerDigits[s^2];
         len = Length[s2];
         s = FromDigits[If[len < 20, PadLeft[s2, 20, 0], s2][[6 ;; 15]]];
         AppendTo[tmp, s],
         {n}];
       tmp
     ]

In[34]:= **middleSquareGenerator[3]**

Out[34]= {1 234 567 890, 1 578 750 190, 4 521 624 250, 858 581 880}

In[35]:= **data = middleSquareGenerator[1000];**
Take[data, 12]

Out[36]= {1 234 567 890, 1 578 750 190, 4 521 624 250, 858 581 880,
1 628 446 643, 8 384 690 979, 428 133 239, 2 980 703 366,
5 925 560 837, 2 712 329 881, 7 333 833 654, 1 160 645 429}

13.   Run 10 000 trials with a range of probabilities from 0 to 1 in increments of .001.

In[37]:= **incr = 0.001;**
trials = 10 000;
lis = Table[
RandomVariate[BernoulliDistribution[p], trials], {p, 0, 1, incr}];

Pair up the probabilities with the entropies (in base 2) for each trial.

In[40]:= **info = Transpose[{Range[0, 1, incr], Map[Entropy[2, #] &, lis]}];**

Make a plot.

In[41]:= **ListPlot[info, AspectRatio → 1,**
GridLines → Automatic, PlotStyle → PointSize[Small]]

Out[41]=
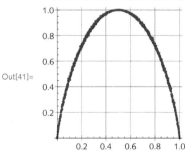

8.2 Working with numbers

1.   The number 1.23 has machine precision.

In[1]:= **Precision[1.23]**

Out[1]= MachinePrecision

Asking *Mathematica* to generate 100 digits of precision from a number that only contains about 16 digits of precision would require it to produce 84 digits without any information about where those digits should come from.

2.   This generates a table showing the number of digits of precision needed in the input compared with the accuracy of the result.

In[2]:= `Table[{x, Accuracy[N[√2, x]^200 - (√2)^200]}, {x, 100, 140, 5}] //`
`TableForm`

Out[2]//TableForm=

100	67.596
105	72.596
110	77.596
115	82.596
120	87.596
125	92.596
130	97.596
135	102.596
140	107.596

8.3 Arrays of numbers

1. Note the need for a delayed rule in this function.

In[1]:= `RandomSparseArray[n_Integer] :=`
`SparseArray[{Band[{1, 1}] :> RandomReal[]}, {n, n}]`

In[2]:= `Normal[RandomSparseArray[5]] // MatrixForm`

Out[2]//MatrixForm=

$$\begin{pmatrix} 0.778393 & 0 & 0 & 0 & 0 \\ 0 & 0.685614 & 0 & 0 & 0 \\ 0 & 0 & 0.639995 & 0 & 0 \\ 0 & 0 & 0 & 0.79101 & 0 \\ 0 & 0 & 0 & 0 & 0.427544 \end{pmatrix}$$

2. Here is the definition of `TridiagonalMatrix`.

In[3]:= `TridiagonalMatrix[n_, p_, q_] := SparseArray[`
`{Band[{1, 1}] → p, Band[{1, 2}] → q, Band[{2, 1}] → q}, {n, n}]`

In[4]:= `TridiagonalMatrix[5, α, β]`

Out[4]= `SparseArray[<13>, {5, 5}]`

In[5]:= `Normal[%] // MatrixForm`

Out[5]//MatrixForm=

$$\begin{pmatrix} \alpha & \beta & 0 & 0 & 0 \\ \beta & \alpha & \beta & 0 & 0 \\ 0 & \beta & \alpha & \beta & 0 \\ 0 & 0 & \beta & \alpha & \beta \\ 0 & 0 & 0 & \beta & \alpha \end{pmatrix}$$

3. First we create the packed array vector.

In[6]:= `vec = RandomVariate[NormalDistribution[1, 3], {10^5}];`

In[7]:= `Developer`PackedArrayQ[vec]`

Out[7]= `True`

Replacing the first element in vec with a 1 gives an expression that is not packed.

In[8]:= `newvec = ReplacePart[vec, 1, 1];`

In[9]:= `Developer`PackedArrayQ[newvec]`

Out[9]= `False`

The size of the unpacked object is about four times larger than the packed array.

In[10]:= **Map[ByteCount, {vec, newvec}]**

Out[10]= {800 168, 3 200 040}

Sorting the packed object is about three times faster than sorting the unpacked object.

In[11]:= **Timing[Do[Sort[vec], {5}]]**

Out[11]= {0.094712, Null}

In[12]:= **Timing[Do[Sort[newvec], {5}]]**

Out[12]= {0.243469, Null}

Finding the minimum element is about one order of magnitude faster with the packed array.

In[13]:= **Timing[Min[vec];]**

Out[13]= {0.000213, Null}

In[14]:= **Timing[Min[newvec];]**

Out[14]= {0.002076, Null}

4. Since the definition involving determinants only makes sense for $n > 2$, we include a condition on the left-hand side of that definition and also specific rules for the cases $n = 1, 2$.

In[15]:= **fibMat[n_ /; n > 2] := Det@SparseArray[**
        {Band[{1, 1}] → 1, Band[{2, 1}] → i, Band[{1, 2}] → i}, {n - 1, n - 1}]

In[16]:= **fibMat[1] = fibMat[2] = 1;**

In[17]:= **Table[fibMat[i], {i, 1, 20}]**

Out[17]= {1, 1, 2, 3, 5, 8, 13, 21, 34, 55, 89,
         144, 233, 377, 610, 987, 1597, 2584, 4181, 6765}

The computation of determinants using decomposition methods is on the order of $O(n^3)$ computational complexity. So this computation tends to slow down considerably for large n.

In[18]:= **Timing[fibMat[10³]]**

Out[18]= {6.7663,
          43 466 557 686 937 456 435 688 527 675 040 625 802 564 660 517 371 780 402 481 729 089 536 ⋮
          555 417 949 051 890 403 879 840 079 255 169 295 922 593 080 322 634 775 209 689 623 239 873 ⋮
          322 471 161 642 996 440 906 533 187 938 298 969 649 928 516 003 704 476 137 795 166 849 228 ⋮
          875}

In[19]:= **Fibonacci[10³] == fibMat[10³]**

Out[19]= True

5. The sparse array needs only one rule {2, 2} → 0 together with a third argument that specifies the default values should be set to 1. Then pick off the nth Fibonacci number in the first row, second column.

In[20]:= **fibMat2[n_] := Module[{mat},**
        mat = SparseArray[{{2, 2} → 0}, {2, 2}, 1];
        MatrixPower[mat, n][[1, 2]]
        ]

Quick check of the first few numbers.

In[21]:= **Table[fibMat2[n], {n, 1, 10}]**

Out[21]= {1, 1, 2, 3, 5, 8, 13, 21, 34, 55}

The time to compute a large number is quite fast.

In[22]:= **Timing[fibMat2[10³]]**

Out[22]= {0.000216,
    43 466 557 686 937 456 435 688 527 675 040 625 802 564 660 517 371 780 402 481 729 089 536 ⸜
    555 417 949 051 890 403 879 840 079 255 169 295 922 593 080 322 634 775 209 689 623 239 873 ⸜
    322 471 161 642 996 440 906 533 187 938 298 969 649 928 516 003 704 476 137 795 166 849 228 ⸜
    875}

Check correctness against the built-in function, using a large random integer *n*.

In[23]:= **With[{n = RandomInteger[10⁶]},**
    fibMat2[n] == Fibonacci[n]
    ]

Out[23]= True

8.4 Examples and applications

I.   We will overload findRoot to invoke the secant method when given a list of two numbers as the second argument.

In[1]:= **Options[findRoot] = {**
    MaxIterations :→ $RecursionLimit,
    PrecisionGoal → Automatic,
    WorkingPrecision → Automatic
    };

In[2]:= **findRoot[*fun_*, {*var_*, *x1_*?NumericQ, *x2_*?NumericQ}, OptionsPattern[]] :=**
    Module[{maxIterations, precisionGoal,
      workingPrecision, initx, df, next, result},
      {maxIterations, precisionGoal, workingPrecision} =
      OptionValue[{MaxIterations, PrecisionGoal, WorkingPrecision}];
      If[precisionGoal === Automatic,
      precisionGoal = Min[{Precision[*x1*], Precision[*x2*]}]];
      If[workingPrecision === Automatic,
      workingPrecision = precisionGoal + 10];
      initx = SetPrecision[{*x1*, *x2*}, workingPrecision];
      df[*a_*, *b_*] := (*fun*[*b*] - *fun*[*a*]) / (*b* - *a*);
      next[{*a_*, *b_*}] := {*a*, *b* - $\dfrac{fun[b]}{df[a, b]}$};
      result = SetPrecision[
      FixedPoint[next, initx, maxIterations][[2]], precisionGoal];
      {*var* → result}]

In[3]:= **f[*x_*] := *x*² - 2**

In[4]:= **findRoot[f, {x, 1., 2.}]**

Out[4]= {x → 1.41421}

In[5]:= **findRoot[f, {x, 1.0`60, 2.0`50}]**

Out[5]= {x → 1.4142135623730950488016887242096980785696740946953}

In[6]:= **Precision[%]**

Out[6]= 50.

5. Here is a three-dimensional vector.

In[7]:= **vec = {1, -3, 2};**

This computes the l_∞ norm of the vector.

In[8]:= **norm[v_?VectorQ, l_: Infinity] := Max[Abs[v]]**

In[9]:= **norm[vec]**

Out[9]= 3

Compare this with the built-in Norm function.

In[10]:= **Norm[vec, Infinity]**

Out[10]= 3

Here is a 3×3 matrix.

In[11]:= **mat = {{1, 2, 3}, {1, 0, 2}, {2, -3, 2}};**

Here, then, is the matrix norm.

In[12]:= **norm[m_?MatrixQ, l_: Infinity] :=**
      norm[Total[Abs[Transpose[m]]], Infinity]

In[13]:= **norm[mat]**

Out[13]= 7

Again, here is a comparison with the built-in Norm function.

In[14]:= **Norm[mat, Infinity]**

Out[14]= 7

Notice how we *overloaded* the definition of the function norm so that it would act differently depending upon what type of argument it was given. This is a particularly powerful feature of *Mathematica*. The expression _?MatrixQ on the left-hand side of the definition causes the function norm to use the definition on the right-hand side *only if* the argument is in fact a matrix (if it passes the MatrixQ test). If that argument is a vector (if it passes the VectorQ test), then the previous definition is used.

6. Here is the function to compute the condition number of a matrix (using the l_2 norm).

In[15]:= **conditionNumber[m_?MatrixQ] := Norm[m, 2] Norm[Inverse[m], 2]**

In[16]:= **conditionNumber[HilbertMatrix[3]] // N**

Out[16]= 524.057

Compare this with the condition number of a random matrix.

In[17]:= **mat = RandomInteger[5, {3, 3}];**
        conditionNumber[mat] // N

Out[18]= 2.31709

An alternative definition for the condition number of a matrix is the ratio of largest to smallest singular value.

In[19]:= **N@SingularValueList[mat]**

Out[19]= {6.37231, 4.22261, 2.75013}

In[20]:= **First[%] / Last[%]**

Out[20]= 2.31709

In[21]:= **conditionNumber2[*mat_* ? MatrixQ] :=**
        Module[{sv = SingularValueList[*mat*]},
        First[sv] / Last[sv]]

In[22]:= **conditionNumber2[mat] // N**

Out[22]= 2.31709

7. Pairing up values with preceding values is accomplished by transposing the appropriate lists.

$$\text{Transpose}\big[\big\{\text{Drop}\big[data,\ lag\big],\ \text{Drop}\big[data,\ -lag\big]\big\}\big]$$

Here then is the code for LagPlot.

In[23]:= **LagPlot[*data_*, *lag_* : 1, *opts* : OptionsPattern[ListPlot]] :=**
        ListPlot[Transpose[{Drop[*data*, *lag*], Drop[*data*, -*lag*]}], *opts*]

Trying it out on a sequence of "random" numbers generated using a linear congruential generator shows patterns that indicate a very low likelihood of randomness in the sequence.

In[24]:= **data = BlockRandom[SeedRandom[1, Method → {"Congruential",**
        "Multiplier" → 11, "Increment" → 0, "Modulus" → 17}];
        RandomReal[1, {1000}]];

In[25]:= **Table[LagPlot[data, i, ImageSize → Small], {i, 1, 4}]**

Out[25]=

NIST describes the data in lew.dat as originating "from an underlying single-cycle sinusoidal model."

In[26]:= **lewdata = Import[**
        FileNameJoin[{NotebookDirectory[], "Data", "lew.dat"}], "List"];

In[27]:= **LagPlot[lewdata, 1, ImageSize → Small]**

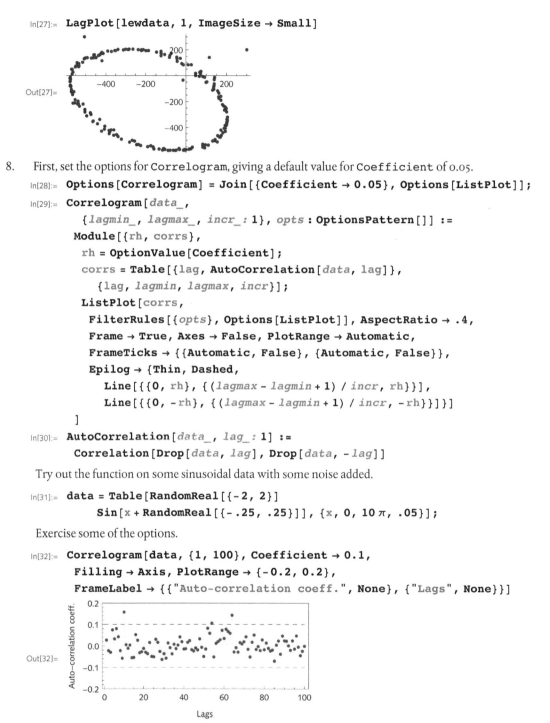

Out[27]=

8.   First, set the options for Correlogram, giving a default value for Coefficient of 0.05.

In[28]:= **Options[Correlogram] = Join[{Coefficient → 0.05}, Options[ListPlot]];**

In[29]:= **Correlogram[*data_*,**
            {*lagmin_*, *lagmax_*, *incr_* : 1}, *opts* : OptionsPattern[]] :=
            Module[{rh, corrs},
              rh = OptionValue[Coefficient];
              corrs = Table[{lag, AutoCorrelation[*data*, lag]},
                {lag, *lagmin*, *lagmax*, *incr*}];
              ListPlot[corrs,
                FilterRules[{*opts*}, Options[ListPlot]], AspectRatio → .4,
                Frame → True, Axes → False, PlotRange → Automatic,
                FrameTicks → {{Automatic, False}, {Automatic, False}},
                Epilog → {Thin, Dashed,
                  Line[{{0, rh}, {(*lagmax* - *lagmin* + 1) / *incr*, rh}}],
                  Line[{{0, -rh}, {(*lagmax* - *lagmin* + 1) / *incr*, -rh}}]}]
            ]

In[30]:= **AutoCorrelation[*data_*, *lag_* : 1] :=**
            Correlation[Drop[*data*, *lag*], Drop[*data*, -*lag*]]

Try out the function on some sinusoidal data with some noise added.

In[31]:= **data = Table[RandomReal[{-2, 2}]**
                Sin[x + RandomReal[{-.25, .25}]], {x, 0, 10 π, .05}];

Exercise some of the options.

In[32]:= **Correlogram[data, {1, 100}, Coefficient → 0.1,**
            Filling → Axis, PlotRange → {-0.2, 0.2},
            FrameLabel → {{"Auto-correlation coeff.", None}, {"Lags", None}}]

Out[32]=

9.   Here are the binary digits of π. First is used to get only the digits from RealDigits.

In[33]:= **First[RealDigits[N[Pi, 12], 2]]**

Out[33]= {1, 1, 0, 0, 1, 0, 0, 1, 0, 0, 0, 0, 1, 1, 1, 1, 1, 1, 0,
        1, 1, 0, 1, 0, 1, 0, 1, 0, 0, 0, 1, 0, 0, 0, 1, 0, 0, 0, 1, 0}

Convert 0s to −1s.

In[34]:= **2 % − 1**

Out[34]= {1, 1, −1, −1, 1, −1, −1, 1, −1, −1, −1, −1, 1, 1, 1, 1, 1, 1, −1, 1, 1,
        −1, 1, −1, 1, −1, 1, −1, −1, −1, 1, −1, −1, −1, 1, −1, −1, −1, 1, −1}

Here then is a plot for the first fifty thousand digits.

In[35]:= **ListLinePlot[**
        With[{digits = 50 000},
          Accumulate[2 First[RealDigits[N[Pi, digits], 2]] − 1]
        ]]

Out[35]=

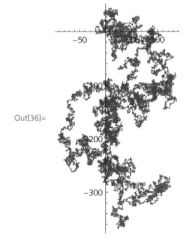

For the two-dimensional case, use `Partition` to pair up the binary digits, then a transformation rule to convert them to compass directions.

In[36]:= **With[{digs = First[RealDigits[N[Pi, 50 000], 2]]},**
        ListLinePlot[Accumulate[
          Partition[digs, 2, 2] /. {{0, 0} → {−1, 0}, {1, 1} → {0, −1}}],
        AspectRatio → Automatic]]

Out[36]=

9   Strings

9.1   Structure and syntax

1.   Here is a test string we will use for this exercise.

In[1]:= **str = "this is a test string"**

Out[1]= this is a test string

This extracts the first character from str.

In[2]:= **StringTake[str, 1]**

Out[2]= t

Here is its character code.

In[3]:= **ToCharacterCode[%]**

Out[3]= {116}

For each lowercase letter of the English alphabet, subtracting 32 gives the corresponding uppercase character.

In[4]:= **% - 32**

Out[4]= {84}

Convert back to a character.

In[5]:= **FromCharacterCode[%]**

Out[5]= T

Take the original string minus its first character.

In[6]:= **StringDrop[str, 1]**

Out[6]= his is a test string

Finally, join the previous string with the capital T.

In[7]:= **StringJoin[%%, %]**

Out[7]= This is a test string

You can do this more efficiently using ToUpperCase and StringTake. This approach is more general in that it does not assume that the first character in your string is lower case.

In[8]:= **ToUpperCase[StringTake[str, 1]]**

Out[8]= T

In[9]:= **StringTake[str, 2 ;; -1]**

Out[9]= his is a test string

In[10]:= **ToUpperCase[StringTake[str, 1]] <> StringTake[str, 2 ;; -1]**

Out[10]= This is a test string

3.   Start by extracting the individual characters in a string.

In[11]:= **str = "Mississippi";**
       Characters[str]

Out[12]= {M, i, s, s, i, s, s, i, p, p, i}

This gives the set of unique characters in this string.

`In[13]:=` **Union[Characters[str]]**

`Out[13]=` {i, M, p, s}

`Union` sorts the list whereas `DeleteDuplicates` does not.

`In[14]:=` **DeleteDuplicates[Characters[str]]**

`Out[14]=` {M, i, s, p}

Here then is the function.

`In[15]:=` **UniqueCharacters[*str_String*] := DeleteDuplicates[Characters[*str*]]**

Try it out on a more interesting example.

`In[16]:=` **protein = ProteinData["PP2672"]**

`Out[16]=` MKSSEELQCLKQMEEELLFLKAGQGSQRARLTPPLPRALQGNFGAPALCGIWFAEHLHPAVGMPPNYNSSMLSLSPER ‹
TILSGGWSGKQTQQPVPPLRTLLLRSPFSLHKSSQPGSPKASQRIHPLFHSIPRSQLHSVLLGLPLLFIQTRPS ‹
PPAQYGAQMPLRYICFGPNIFWGSKKPQKE

`In[17]:=` **UniqueCharacters[protein]**

`Out[17]=` {M, K, S, E, L, Q, C, F, A, G, R, T, P, N, I, W, H, V, Y}

It even works in the degenerate case.

`In[18]:=` **UniqueCharacters[""]**

`Out[18]=` {}

9.2 Operating with strings

1. Here is the function that checks if a string is a palindrome.

   `In[1]:=` **PalindromeQ[*str_String*] := StringReverse[*str*] == *str***

   `In[2]:=` **PalindromeQ["mood"]**

   `Out[2]=` False

   `In[3]:=` **PalindromeQ["PoP"]**

   `Out[3]=` True

   An argument that is a number is converted to a string and then the previous rule is called.

   `In[4]:=` **PalindromeQ[*num_Integer*] := PalindromeQ[ToString[*num*]]**

   `In[5]:=` **PalindromeQ[12 522 521]**

   `Out[5]=` True

   Get all words in the dictionary that comes with *Mathematica*.

   `In[6]:=` **words = DictionaryLookup[];**

   Select those that pass the `PalindromeQ` test.

```
In[7]:=  Select[words, PalindromeQ]
```
```
Out[7]= {a, aha, aka, bib, bob, boob, bub, CFC, civic, dad, deed, deified, did, dud, DVD,
          eke, ere, eve, ewe, eye, gag, gig, huh, I, kayak, kook, level, ma'am, madam, mam,
          MGM, minim, mom, mum, nan, non, noon, nun, oho, pap, peep, pep, pip, poop, pop,
          pup, radar, redder, refer, repaper, reviver, rotor, sagas, sees, seres, sexes,
          shahs, sis, solos, SOS, stats, stets, tat, tenet, TNT, toot, tot, tut, wow, WWW}
```

2. Use the argument structure of RotateLeft.

```
In[8]:=  StringRotateLeft[str_, n_ : 1] :=
           StringJoin[RotateLeft[Characters[str], n]]
```
```
In[9]:=  StringRotateLeft["squeamish ossifrage", 5]
```
```
Out[9]= mish ossifragesquea
```

4. First, using StringJoin, put *n* spaces at the end of the string.

```
In[10]:=  StringPad[str_String, {n_}] := StringJoin[str, Table[" ", {n}]]
```
```
In[11]:=  StringPad["ciao", {5}] // FullForm
```
```
Out[11]//FullForm=
          "ciao     "
```

For the second rule, first create a message that will be issued if the string is longer than *n*.

```
In[12]:=  StringPad::badlen =
            "Pad length `1` must be greater than the length of string `2`.";
```
```
In[13]:=  StringPad[str_String, n_] := With[{len = StringLength[str]}, If[len > n,
             Message[StringPad::badlen, n, str], StringPad[str, {n - len}]]]
```
```
In[14]:=  StringPad["ciao", 8] // FullForm
```
```
Out[14]//FullForm=
          "ciao    "
```

```
In[15]:=  StringPad["ciao", 3]
```
```
          StringPad::badlen : Pad length 3 must be greater than the length of string ciao.
```

Finally, here is a rule for padding at the beginning and end of the string.

```
In[16]:=  StringPad[str_String, n_, m_] :=
            StringJoin[Table[" ", {n}], str, Table[" ", {m}]]
```
```
In[17]:=  StringPad["ciao", 3, 8] // FullForm
```
```
Out[17]//FullForm=
          "   ciao        "
```

Note, StringInsert could also be used.

```
In[18]:=  StringInsert["ciao", " ", {1, -1}] // FullForm
```
```
Out[18]//FullForm=
          " ciao "
```

```
In[19]:=  StringPad2[str_String, n_, m_] :=
            StringInsert[str, " ", Join[Table[1, {n}], Table[-1, {m}]]]
```
```
In[20]:=  StringPad2["ciao", 3, 8] // FullForm
```
```
Out[20]//FullForm=
          "   ciao        "
```

5.   This is a simple modification of the code given in the text. But first we add the space character to the alphabet.

```
In[21]:= ToCharacterCode[" "]

Out[21]= {32}

In[22]:= alphabet = Join[{FromCharacterCode[32]}, CharacterRange["a", "z"]]

Out[22]= { , a, b, c, d, e, f, g, h, i, j, k, l, m, n, o, p, q, r, s, t, u, v, w, x, y, z}

In[23]:= coderules = Thread[alphabet → RotateRight[alphabet, 5]]

Out[23]= { → v, a → w, b → x, c → y, d → z, e → , f → a, g → b, h → c,
         i → d, j → e, k → f, l → g, m → h, n → i, o → j, p → k, q → l,
         r → m, s → n, t → o, u → p, v → q, w → r, x → s, y → t, z → u}

In[24]:= decoderules = Map[Reverse, coderules]

Out[24]= {v → , w → a, x → b, y → c, z → d, → e, a → f, b → g, c → h,
         d → i, e → j, f → k, g → l, h → m, i → n, j → o, k → p, l → q,
         m → r, n → s, o → t, p → u, q → v, r → w, s → x, t → y, u → z}

In[25]:= code[str_String] := Apply[StringJoin, Characters[str] /. coderules]

In[26]:= decode[str_String] := Apply[StringJoin, Characters[str] /. decoderules]

In[27]:= code["squeamish ossifrage"]

Out[27]= nlp whdncvjnndamwb

In[28]:= decode[%]

Out[28]= squeamish ossifrage
```

6.   First, here is the list of characters from the plaintext alphabet.

```
In[29]:= PlainAlphabet = CharacterRange["a", "z"]

Out[29]= {a, b, c, d, e, f, g, h, i, j, k, l, m, n, o, p, q, r, s, t, u, v, w, x, y, z}
```

Here is our key, *django*:

```
In[30]:= key = "django"

Out[30]= django
```

And here is the cipher text alphabet, prepending the key:

```
In[31]:= StringJoin[Characters@key, Complement[PlainAlphabet, Characters@key]]

Out[31]= djangobcefhiklmpqrstuvwxyz
```

Make a reusable function.

```
In[32]:= CipherAlphabet[key_String] := With[{k = Characters[key]},
            StringJoin[k, Complement[CharacterRange["a", "z"], k]]]
```

Generate the coding rules:

```
In[33]:= codeRules = Thread[PlainAlphabet → Characters@CipherAlphabet["django"]]

Out[33]= {a → d, b → j, c → a, d → n, e → g, f → o, g → b, h → c,
         i → e, j → f, k → h, l → i, m → k, n → l, o → m, p → p, q → q,
         r → r, s → s, t → t, u → u, v → v, w → w, x → x, y → y, z → z}
```

The encoding function follows that in the text of this section.

```
In[34]:= encode[str_String] := StringJoin[Characters[str] /. codeRules]

In[35]:= encode["the sheik of araby"]

Out[35]= tcg scgeh mo drdjy
```

Omit spaces and punctuation and output in blocks of length 5 (using `StringPartition` from Section 9.5).

```
In[36]:= StringPartition[str_String, seq__] :=
          Map[StringJoin, Partition[Characters[str], seq]]

In[37]:= StringSplit[encode["the sheik of araby"], RegularExpression["\\W+"]]

Out[37]= {tcg, scgeh, mo, drdjy}

In[38]:= StringJoin[Riffle[StringPartition[StringJoin[%], 5, 5, 1, ""], " "]]

Out[38]= tcgsc gehmo drdjy
```

Finally, this puts all these pieces together.

```
In[39]:= Clear[encode];
         encode[str_String, key_String, blocksize_ : 5] :=
           Module[{CipherAlphabet, codeRules, s1, s2, s3},
             CipherAlphabet[k_] :=
               StringJoin[Characters[k],
                 Complement[CharacterRange["a", "z"], Characters[k]]];

             codeRules =
               Thread[CharacterRange["a", "z"] → Characters@CipherAlphabet[key]];

             s1 = StringJoin[Characters[str] /. codeRules];
             s2 = StringSplit[s1, RegularExpression["\\W+"]];
             s3 = StringPartition[StringJoin[s2], blocksize, blocksize, 1, ""];
             StringJoin[Riffle[s3, " "]]]

In[41]:= encode["the sheik of araby", "django", 3]

Out[41]= tcg scg ehm odr djy
```

9.3 String patterns

1. First, recall the predicate created in Section 9.1.

```
In[1]:= OrderedWordQ[word_String] := OrderedQ[ToCharacterCode[word]]
```

`DictionaryLookup` can be given a pattern as its argument and it will return only those words that match the pattern. Using `StringJoin`, test the first character with `LowerCaseQ`; the remainder of the word (zero or more characters) has no conditions.

```
In[2]:= words = DictionaryLookup[f_?LowerCaseQ ~~ r___];
        Short[words, 4]

Out[3]//Short= {a, aah, aardvark, aardvarks, abaci, aback, abacus,
          ≪81 804≫, zwieback, zydeco, zygote, zygotes, zygotic, zymurgy}
```

```
In[4]:=  Select[words, OrderedWordQ];
         RandomSample[%, 20]
Out[5]=  {now, coop, ills, firs, chops, ass, chin, ells, go, clops,
           lox, sty, beep, alp, dims, befit, any, accost, aims, amp}
```

2. We will work with a small sample of words from the dictionary.

```
In[9]:=  words = DictionaryLookup[];
         sample = RandomSample[words, 12]
Out[10]= {habitually, aborting, remote, bean, dinned, clothes,
           sine, quail, resolutely, hiya, dreamers, hearings}
```

`StringReplace` operates on any words that match the pattern and leave those that do not match unchanged.

```
In[11]:= StringReplace[sample, f_?UpperCaseQ ~~ r___ :> ToLowerCase[f] ~~ r]
Out[11]= {habitually, aborting, remote, bean, dinned, clothes,
           sine, quail, resolutely, hiya, dreamers, hearings}
```

3. You can do a dictionary lookup with a pattern that tests whether the word is palindromic. Then find all palindromic words of a given length. Note the need for `BlankSequence` (`__`) as the simple pattern `_` would only find words consisting of one character.

```
In[12]:= Palindromes[len_Integer] := DictionaryLookup[
           w__ /; (w == StringReverse[w] && StringLength[w] == len)]
```

We also add a rule to return all palindromes of any length.

```
In[13]:= Palindromes[] := DictionaryLookup[w__ /; (w == StringReverse[w] )]
In[14]:= Palindromes[7]
Out[14]= {deified, repaper, reviver}
In[15]:= Palindromes[]
Out[15]= {a, aha, aka, bib, bob, boob, bub, CFC, civic, dad, deed, deified, did,
           dud, DVD, eke, ere, eve, ewe, eye, gag, gig, huh, I, kayak, kook,
           level, ma'am, madam, mam, MGM, minim, mom, mum, nan, non, noon,
           nun, oho, pap, peep, pep, pip, poop, pop, pup, radar, redder, refer,
           repaper, reviver, rotor, sagas, sees, seres, sexes, shahs, sis,
           solos, SOS, stats, stets, tat, tenet, TNT, toot, tot, tut, wow, WWW}
```

4. First import some sample text.

```
In[16]:= text = ExampleData[{"Text", "AliceInWonderland"}];
```

To split into words, use a similar construction to that in this section.

```
In[17]:= words = StringSplit[text, Characters[":;\"',.?/\-` *"] ..];
         Short[words, 4]
Out[18]//Short= {I, DOWN, THE, RABBIT, HOLE, Alice, was, beginning,
           ≪9955≫, might, what, a, wonderful, dream, it, had, been}
```

Get the total number of (nonunique) words.

```
In[19]:= Length[words]
Out[19]= 9971
```

Convert uppercase to lowercase.

In[20]:= **lcwords = ToLowerCase[words];**
Short[lcwords, 4]

Out[21]//Short= {i, down, the, rabbit, hole, alice, was, beginning,
    ≪9955≫, might, what, a, wonderful, dream, it, had, been}

Finally, count the number of unique words.

In[22]:= **DeleteDuplicates[lcwords] // Length**

Out[22]= 1643

In fact, splitting words using a list of characters as we have done here is not terribly robust. A better approach uses regular expressions (introduced in Section 9.4):

In[23]:= **words = StringSplit[text, RegularExpression["\\W+"]];**
Length[words]

Out[24]= 9970

In[25]:= **lcwords = StringReplace[words,**
        RegularExpression["([A-Z])"] :> ToLowerCase["$1"]];
DeleteDuplicates[lcwords] // Length

Out[26]= 1528

9.4 Regular expressions

1. The pattern used earlier in the chapter was "AA" ~~ _ ~~ "T". In a regular expression, we want the character *A* repeated exactly once. Use the expression "A{2,2}" for this. The regular expression "." stands for any character.

    In[1]:= **gene = GenomeData["IGHV357"];**

    In[2]:= **StringCases[gene, RegularExpression["A{2,2}.T"]]**

    Out[2]= {AAGT, AAGT, AAAT, AAGT, AAAT, AAAT}

2. First, read in the web page.

    In[3]:= **webpage =**
            Import["http://www.wolfram.com/company/contact.cgi", "HTML"];

    In the original example in Section 9.3, we used the pattern NumberString, to represent arbitrary strings of numbers. The regular expression "\\d+" accomplishes a similar thing but it will also match strings of numbers that may not be in a phone number format (try it!). Instead, use "\\d{3}" to match a list of exactly three digits, and so on.

    In[4]:= **StringCases[webpage,**
            RegularExpression["\\d{3}.\\d{3}.\\d{4}"]] // DeleteDuplicates

    Out[4]= {217-398-0700, 217-398-0747, 617-764-0094}

3. First, here is the function using regular expressions. (.) will be matched by any single character; the parentheses are used to refer to this expression on the right-hand side of the rule as "$1". Similarly, parentheses surround [a - z] + which is matched by any sequence of lowercase characters; this expression is referred to on the right as "$2".

```
In[5]:= UcLc[word_String] := StringReplace[word,
           RegularExpression["(.)([a-z]+)"] :> ToUpperCase["$1"] ~~ "$2"]
In[6]:= UcLc["hello"]
Out[6]= Hello
```

You can also do this with string patterns.

```
In[7]:= UcLc[word_String] := StringReplace[word,
           WordBoundary ~~ x_ ~~ y__ :> ToUpperCase[x] ~~ ToLowerCase[y]]
In[8]:= UcLc["ciao"]
Out[8]= Ciao
```

4. The first solution uses regular expressions. The second uses string patterns and alternatives.

```
In[9]:= DictionaryLookup[RegularExpression["[aeiouy]+"], IgnoreCase → True]
Out[9]= {a, aye, eye, I, IOU, oi, ya, ye, yea, yo, you}
In[10]:= DictionaryLookup[("a" | "e" | "i" | "o" | "u" | "y") .., IgnoreCase → True]
Out[10]= {a, aye, eye, I, IOU, oi, ya, ye, yea, yo, you}
```

5. Here is the short list of words with which we will work.

```
In[11]:= words = {"building", "finch", "fix", "ratio",
           "envy", "boy", "baby", "faculty", "honorarium"};
```

Using regular expressions, these rules encapsulate those given in the exercise.

```
In[12]:= rules = {
           (RegularExpression["(\\w+)x"] :> "$1" ~~ "x" ~~ "es"),
           (RegularExpression["(\\w+)(ch)"] :> "$1" ~~ "$2" ~~ "es"),
           (RegularExpression["(\\w+)([aeiou])(y)"] :>
             "$1" ~~ "$2" ~~ "$3" ~~ "s"),
           (RegularExpression["(\\w+)(y)"] :> "$1" ~~ "ies"),
           (RegularExpression["(\\w+)(i)um"] :> "$1" ~~ "$2" ~~ "a"),
           (RegularExpression["(\\w+)(.)"] :> "$1" ~~ "$2" ~~ "s")
           };
In[13]:= StringReplace[words, rules]
Out[13]= {buildings, finches, fixes, ratios,
           envies, boys, babies, faculties, honoraria}
```

Of course, lots of exceptions exist:

```
In[14]:= StringReplace[{"man", "cattle"}, rules]
Out[14]= {mans, cattles}
```

7. Start by importing a somewhat lengthy text, Charles Darwin's *On the Origin of Species*.

```
In[16]:= text = ExampleData[{"Text", "OriginOfSpecies"}];
```

There are numerous instances of "Mr." and "Dr.", words that end in a period that would trigger a sentence-ending detector such as StringSplit.

```
In[17]:= StringCount[text, "Mr." | "Dr."]
Out[17]= 119
```

To keep our sentence count accurate, we will replace such words (and a few others in this particular text) with words that will not cause errors in our sentence count. This step of cleaning text based on identified issues is a common one in textual analysis.

```
In[18]:= cleanText =
           StringReplace[text, {"Mr." → "Mr", "Dr." → "Dr", "H.M.S." → "HMS"}];
```

```
In[19]:= t = StringTake[cleanText, 200]
```

```
Out[19]= INTRODUCTION. When on board HMS 'Beagle,' as naturalist, I was much
             struck with certain facts in the distribution of the inhabitants
                of South America, and in the geological relations of the present to
```

Now split on a small set of delimiters.

```
In[20]:= s = StringSplit[cleanText, Characters[".!?"] ..];
         Short[s, 5]
```

```
Out[21]//Short= {INTRODUCTION, ≪4225≫,
                    There is grandeur in this view of life, with
                        its several powers, hav … s most beautiful and
                        most wonderful have been, and are being, evolved}
```

The same thing can be accomplished with a regular expression.

```
In[22]:= s = StringSplit[cleanText, RegularExpression["[.!?]+"]];
```

Using a regular expression, this counts the number of words in each sentence.

```
In[23]:= sentenceLens = StringCount[s, RegularExpression["\\w+"]];
```

Finally, here is a histogram displaying the distribution of sentence lengths.

```
In[24]:= Histogram[sentenceLens]
```

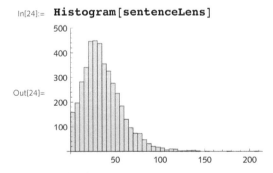

It looks like there are some very long sentences!

In[25]:= `Select[s, StringCount[#, RegularExpression["\\w+"]] > 200 &]`

Out[25]= { I have attempted to show that the geological record is extremely imperfect; that only a small portion of the globe has been geologically explored with care; that only certain classes of organic beings have been largely preserved in a fossil state; that the number both of specimens and of species, preserved in our museums, is absolutely as nothing compared with the incalculable number of generations which must have passed away even during a single formation; that, owing to subsidence being necessary for the accumulation of fossiliferous deposits thick enough to resist future degradation, enormous intervals of time have elapsed between the successive formations; that there has probably been more extinction during the periods of subsidence, and more variation during the periods of elevation, and during the latter the record will have been least perfectly kept; that each single formation has not been continuously deposited; that the duration of each formation is, perhaps, short compared with the average duration of specific forms; that migration has played an important part in the first appearance of new forms in any one area and formation; that widely ranging species are those which have varied most, and have oftenest given rise to new species; and that varieties have at first often been local}

8. First read in some sample phrases.

In[25]:= `searchPhrases = {"Find my favorite phone",`
`      "How deep is the ocean?", "What is the meaning of life?"};`

There are several ways to approach this problem. We will break it up into two steps: first eliminating punctuation, then a sample set of stop words.

In[26]:= `tmp = StringSplit["How deep is the ocean?", Characters[":,;.!? "] ..]`

Out[26]= {How, deep, is, the, ocean}

In[27]:= `stopwords = {"how", "the", "is", "an"};`

In[28]:= `Apply[Alternatives, stopwords]`

Out[28]= how | the | is | an

Note the need for WordBoundary in what follows; otherwise, *ocean* would be split leaving *oce* because *an* is a stop word.

In[29]:= `StringSplit[tmp, WordBoundary ~~ Apply[Alternatives, stopwords] ~~`
`      WordBoundary, IgnoreCase → True] // Flatten`

Out[29]= {deep, ocean}

In[30]:= `FilterText[str_String, stopwords_List] := Module[{tmp},`
`      tmp = StringSplit[str, Characters[":,;.!? "] ..];`
`      Flatten@StringSplit[tmp, WordBoundary ~~`
`          Apply[Alternatives, stopwords] ~~ WordBoundary, IgnoreCase → True]`
`      ]`

In[31]:= `stopwords = Rest@Import["StopWords.dat", "List"];`

In[32]:= `FilterText["What is the meaning of life?", stopwords]`

Out[32]= {meaning, life}

9.5 Examples and applications

1. One rule is needed for one-dimensional output and another for multi-dimensional output.

In[1]:= `ClearAll[RandomString]`

In[2]:= `Options[RandomString] = {Weights → {}};`

In[3]:= `RandomString::badwt =`
`      "The length of the list of weights must be the same`

```
                    as the length of the list of characters.";
In[4]:=  RandomString[{c__String}, n_Integer: 1, OptionsPattern[]] :=
          Module[{wts = OptionValue[Weights]},
            Which[
              Length[wts] == 0, StringJoin[RandomChoice[{c}, n]],
              Length[wts] == Length[{c}],
              StringJoin[RandomChoice[wts → {c}, n]],
              True, Message[RandomString::badwt]
            ]]
In[5]:=  RandomString[{c__String}, {n_Integer, len_Integer},
            OptionsPattern[]] := Module[{wts = OptionValue[Weights]},
            Which[
              Length[wts] == 0, Map[StringJoin, RandomChoice[{c}, {n, len}]],
              Length[wts] == Length[{c}],
              Map[StringJoin, RandomChoice[wts → {c}, {n, len}]],
              True, Message[RandomString::badwt]
            ]]
In[6]:=  RandomString[{"A", "C", "T"}]
Out[6]=  A
In[7]:=  RandomString[{"A", "C", "T"}, 10]
Out[7]=  TCCTCACCCC
In[8]:=  RandomString[{"A", "C", "T"}, {4, 10}]
Out[8]=  {ACATCTCATC, TCCCACTATC, AAACCCTCTC, CAATATAATC}
In[9]:=  RandomString[{"A", "C", "T"}, {4, 10}, Weights → {.2, .7, .1}]
Out[9]=  {CAAAACCCCC, CCCCACCCTC, CACCCCCACC, CAACCCCCCT}
In[10]:= RandomString[{"A", "C", "T"}, {4, 10}, Weights → {.2, .7}]
```
RandomString::badwt : The length of the list of weights must be the same as the length of the list of characters.

2. Two words are anagrams if they contain the same letters but in a different order. This function is fairly slow as it sorts and compares every word in the dictionary with the sorted characters of the input word.

```
In[11]:= Anagrams2[word_String] := Module[{chars = Sort[Characters[word]]},
            DictionaryLookup[x__ /; Sort[Characters[x]] == chars]]
In[12]:= Anagrams2["parsley"] // Timing
Out[12]= {2.1535, {parleys, parsley, players, replays, sparely}}
```

You can speed things up a bit by only working with those words in the dictionary of the same length as the source word.

```
In[13]:= Anagrams3[word_String] := Module[{len = StringLength[word], words},
            words = DictionaryLookup[w__ /; StringLength[w] == len];
            Select[words, Sort[Characters[#]] == Sort[Characters[word]] &]
         ]
```

```
In[14]:=  Anagrams3["parsley"] // Timing

Out[14]=  {0.890161, {parleys, parsley, players, replays, sparely}}
```

In fact, you can speed this up a bit further by using regular expressions even though the construction of the regular expression in this case is a bit clumsy looking. The lesson here is that conditional string patterns tend to be slower.

```
In[15]:=  Anagrams4[word_String] := Module[{len = StringLength[word], words},
            words =
              DictionaryLookup[RegularExpression["\\w{" <> ToString[len] <> "}"]];
            Select[words, Sort[Characters[#]] == Sort[Characters[word]] &]
          ]

In[16]:=  Anagrams4["parsley"] // Timing

Out[16]=  {0.098408, {parleys, parsley, players, replays, sparely}}
```

3. The pattern `"\\bcite.*\\b"` matches any string starting with a word boundary followed by the string *cite*, followed by characters repeated one or more times, followed by a word boundary.

```
In[17]:=  DictionaryLookup[RegularExpression["\\bcite.*\\b"]]

Out[17]=  {cite, cited, cites}
```

With suitable modifications to the above for the target string occurring in the middle, end, or anywhere, here is the rewritten function. Note the need for StringJoin here to properly pass the argument str, as a string, into the body of the regular expression.

```
In[18]:=  Options[FindWordsContaining] = {WordPosition → "Start"};

In[19]:=  FindWordsContaining[str_String, OptionsPattern[]] :=
            Module[{wp = OptionValue[WordPosition]},
              Which[
                wp == "Start", DictionaryLookup[
                  RegularExpression[StringJoin["\\b", str, ".*\\b"]]],
                wp == "Middle", DictionaryLookup[
                  RegularExpression[StringJoin["\\b.+", str, ".+\\b"]]],
                wp == "End", DictionaryLookup[RegularExpression[
                  StringJoin["\\b.*", str, "\\b"]]],
                wp == "Anywhere", DictionaryLookup[
                  RegularExpression[StringJoin["\\b.*", str, ".*\\b"]]]
              ]]

In[20]:=  FindWordsContaining["cite"]

Out[20]=  {cite, cited, cites}

In[21]:=  FindWordsContaining["cite", WordPosition → "End"]

Out[21]=  {anthracite, calcite, cite, excite,
            incite, Lucite, overexcite, plebiscite, recite}

In[22]:=  FindWordsContaining["cite", WordPosition → "Middle"]

Out[22]=  {elicited, excited, excitedly, excitement, excitements, exciter,
            exciters, excites, incited, incitement, incitements, inciter, inciters,
            incites, Lucites, overexcited, overexcites, plebiscites, recited,
            reciter, reciters, recites, solicited, unexcited, unsolicited}
```

In[23]:= **FindWordsContaining["cite", WordPosition → "Anywhere"]**

Out[23]= {anthracite, calcite, cite, cited, cites, elicited, excite, excited, excitedly, excitement, excitements, exciter, exciters, excites, incite, incited, incitement, incitements, inciter, inciters, incites, Lucite, Lucites, overexcite, overexcited, overexcites, plebiscite, plebiscites, recite, recited, reciter, reciters, recites, solicited, unexcited, unsolicited}

5. Here is the function as developed in the text.

In[24]:= **StringPartition[*str_String*, *blocksize_*] := Map[StringJoin, Partition[Characters[*str*], *blocksize*, *blocksize*, 1, {}]]**

This passes the argument structure directly to Partition.

In[25]:= **Clear[StringPartition]**

In[26]:= **StringPartition[*str_String*, *seq__*] := Map[StringJoin, Partition[Characters[*str*], *seq*]]**

In[27]:= **str = RandomString[{"A", "C", "G", "T"}, 20]**

Out[27]= ATCTGTTCCAAGGTACGATT

Try out some of the argument structures commonly used with Partition. For example, this partitions the string into blocks of length 3 with offset 1, with no padding.

In[28]:= **StringPartition[str, 3, 3, 1, {}]**

Out[28]= {ATC, TGT, TCC, AAG, GTA, CGA, TT}

6. Start by creating a substitution cipher by simply shifting the alphabet three characters to the left.

In[29]:= **keyRL3 = Transpose[
        {CharacterRange["a", "z"], RotateLeft[CharacterRange["a", "z"], 3]}]**

Out[29]= {{a, d}, {b, e}, {c, f}, {d, g}, {e, h}, {f, i}, {g, j}, {h, k}, {i, l}, {j, m}, {k, n}, {l, o}, {m, p}, {n, q}, {o, r}, {p, s}, {q, t}, {r, u}, {s, v}, {t, w}, {u, x}, {v, y}, {w, z}, {x, a}, {y, b}, {z, c}}

Next, encode a single character using a designated key.

In[30]:= **encodeChar[*char_String*, *key_List*] :=
        First@Cases[*key*, {*char*, *next_*} :> *next*]**

In[31]:= **encodeChar["z", keyRL3]**

Out[31]= c

Finally, here is the encoding function. Recall the "$1" on the right-hand side of the rule refers to the first (and only in this case) regular expression on the left that is enclosed in parentheses.

In[32]:= **encode[*str_String*, *key_List*] := StringReplace[*str*,
        RegularExpression["([a-z])"] :> encodeChar["$1", *key*]]**

The decoding uses the same key, but reverses the pairs.

In[33]:= **decode[*str_String*, *key_List*] := encode[*str*, Map[Reverse, *key*]]**

In[34]:= **encode["squeamish ossifrage", keyRL3]**

Out[34]= vtxhdplvk rvvliudjh

In[35]:= **decode[%, keyRL3]**

Out[35]= squeamish ossifrage

You might want to modify the encoding rule to deal with uppercase letters. One solution is simply to convert them to lowercase.

```
In[36]:= encode[str_String, key_List] := StringReplace[ToLowerCase[str],
           RegularExpression["([a-z])"] :> encodeChar["$1", key]]
In[37]:= encode["Squeamish Ossifrage", keyRL3]
Out[37]= vtxhdplvk rvvliudjh
```

10   Graphics and visualization

10.1 Structure of graphics

1.   The color wheel can be generated by mapping the `Hue` directive over successive sectors of a disk. Note that the argument to `Hue` must be scaled so that it falls within the range 0 to 1.

```
In[1]:= colorWheel[n_] :=
         Graphics[({Hue[Rescale[#, {0, 2 π}]], Disk[{0, 0}, 1, {#, # + n}]} &) /@
           Range[0, 2 π, n]]
```

Here is a color wheel created from 256 separate sectors (hues).

```
In[2]:= colorWheel[π/256]
```

Out[2]=

3.   `Cuboid` takes a list of three numbers as the coordinates of its lower-left corner. This maps the object across two such lists.

```
In[3]:= Map[Cuboid, RandomReal[1, {2, 3}]]
Out[3]= {Cuboid[{0.989389, 0.262121, 0.446654}],
         Cuboid[{0.712346, 0.910876, 0.329548}]}
```

Below is a list of six cuboids and the resulting graphic. Notice the large amount of overlap of the cubes. You can reduce the large overlap by specifying minimum *and* maximum values of the cuboid.

```
In[4]:= cubes = Map[Cuboid, RandomReal[1, {6, 3}]];
In[5]:= Graphics3D[{Opacity[.5], cubes}]
```

Out[5]=

4.   Start by creating a unit cube centered on the origin. An opacity directive adds transparency.

In[6]:= **Graphics3D[{Opacity[.25], Cuboid[{-0.5, -0.5, -0.5}]},
        Boxed → False, Axes → Automatic]**

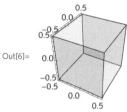

Out[6]=

Next rotate 45°. Note the third argument of Rotate used to specify the axis about which the rotation should occur.

In[7]:= **Graphics3D[{Opacity[.25], Cuboid[{-.5, -.5, -.5}],
        Rotate[Cuboid[{-.5, -.5, -.5}], 45°, {0, 0, 1}]}]**

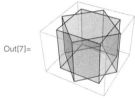

Out[7]=

Here is the dynamic version. The angle θ is the parameter that is manipulated here.

In[8]:= **Manipulate[
        Graphics3D[
          Rotate[Cuboid[{-.5, -.5, -.5}], θ, {0, 0, 1}], PlotRange → 1],
        {θ, 0, 2π}]**

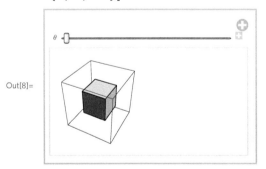

Out[8]=

5. First we create the Point graphics primitives using a normal distribution with mean 0 and standard deviation 1.

    In[9]:= **randomcoords := Point[RandomVariate[NormalDistribution[0, 1], {1, 2}]]**

    This creates the point sizes according to the specification given in the statement of the problem.

    In[10]:= **randomsize := PointSize[RandomReal[{.01, .1}]]**

    This will assign a random color to each primitive. The four-argument form of Hue specifies hue, saturation, brightness, opacity.

    In[11]:= **randomcolor := Hue[RandomReal[], 1, 1, .4]**

Here then are 500 points. (You may find it instructive to look at just one of these points.)

In[12]:= **pts = Table[{randomcolor, randomsize, randomcoords}, {500}];**

And here is the graphic.

In[13]:= **Graphics[pts]**

Out[13]=

6. The algebraic solution is given by the following steps. First solve the equations for *x* and *y*.

In[14]:= **Clear[x, y, r]**

In[15]:= **soln = Solve[{(x − 1)² + (y − 1)² == 2, (x + 3)² + (y − 4)² == r²}, {x, y}]**

Out[15]= $\left\{\left\{x \to \frac{1}{50}\left(-58 + 4\,r^2 - 3\sqrt{-529 + 54\,r^2 - r^4}\right),\ y \to \frac{1}{50}\left(131 - 3\,r^2 - 4\sqrt{-529 + 54\,r^2 - r^4}\right)\right\},\right.$
$\left.\left\{x \to \frac{1}{50}\left(-58 + 4\,r^2 + 3\sqrt{-529 + 54\,r^2 - r^4}\right),\ y \to \frac{1}{50}\left(131 - 3\,r^2 + 4\sqrt{-529 + 54\,r^2 - r^4}\right)\right\}\right\}$

Then find those values of *r* for which the *x* and *y* coordinates are identical.

In[16]:= **Solve[{**
        (x /. soln⟦1⟧) == (x /. soln⟦2⟧),
        (y /. soln⟦1⟧) == (y /. soln⟦2⟧)},
      r]

Out[16]= $\left\{\left\{r \to -5 - \sqrt{2}\right\},\ \left\{r \to 5 - \sqrt{2}\right\},\ \left\{r \to -5 + \sqrt{2}\right\},\ \left\{r \to 5 + \sqrt{2}\right\}\right\}$

Here then are those values of *r* that are positive.

In[17]:= **Cases[%, {r → _?Positive}]**

Out[17]= $\left\{\left\{r \to 5 - \sqrt{2}\right\},\ \left\{r \to 5 + \sqrt{2}\right\}\right\}$

To display the solution, we will plot the first circle with solid lines and the two solutions with dashed lines together in one graphic. Here is the first circle centered at (1, 1).

In[18]:= **circ = Circle[{1, 1}, $\sqrt{2}$];**

Here are the circles that represent the solution to the problem.

In[19]:= **r1 = 5 − $\sqrt{2}$;**
      r2 = 5 + $\sqrt{2}$;

In[21]:= **Graphics[{circ, Circle[{-3, 4}, r1], Circle[{-3, 4}, r2]},**
              Axes → Automatic]

Out[21]=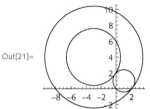

We wanted to display the solutions (two circles) using dashed lines. The graphics directive
Dashing[{x, y}] directs all subsequent lines to be plotted as dashed, alternating the dash x units and
the space y units. We use it as a graphics directive on the two circles c1 and c2. The circles inherit only
those directives in whose scope they appear.

In[22]:= **dashc1 = {Dashing[{.025, .025}], Circle[{-3, 4}, r1]};**
          dashc2 = {Dashing[{.05, .05}], Circle[{-3, 4}, r2]};

In[24]:= **Graphics[{circ, dashc1, dashc2}, Axes → Automatic]**

Out[24]=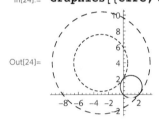

7.   Here is a plot of the sine function.

In[25]:= **sinplot = Plot[Sin[x], {x, 0, 2 π}]**

Out[25]=

Using pattern matching, here are the coordinates.

In[26]:= **Short[coords = Cases[sinplot, Line[{x__}] :→ x, Infinity], 2]**

Out[26]//Short= $\{\{1.28228 \times 10^{-7}, 1.28228 \times 10^{-7}\}, \ll 429\gg, \{\ll 1\gg\}\}$

Create vertical lines from each coordinate.

In[27]:= **Short[lines = Map[Line[{{#[[1]], 0}, #}] &, coords], 2]**

Out[27]//Short= $\{Line[\{\{1.28228 \times 10^{-7}, 0\}, \{\ll 23\gg, \ll 23\gg\}\}], \ll 430\gg\}$

Here then is the final graphic.

In[28]:= **Show[sinplot, Graphics[{Thickness[.001], lines}]]**

Out[28]=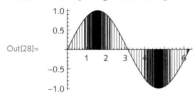

8. First set the distribution and compute the mean and standard deviation.

In[29]:= $\mathcal{D}$ **= NormalDistribution[0, 1];**
        σ **= StandardDeviation[$\mathcal{D}$];**
        μ **= Mean[$\mathcal{D}$];**

Next we manually construct four vertical lines at the standard deviations going from the horizontal axis to the pdf curve.

In[32]:= **Plot[PDF[$\mathcal{D}$, x], {x, -4, 4}, Filling → Axis,**
        Epilog → {White, Line[{{{μ + σ, 0}, {μ + σ, PDF[$\mathcal{D}$, μ + σ]}}, {{μ - σ, 0},
        {μ - σ, PDF[$\mathcal{D}$, μ - σ]}}, {{μ + 2 σ, 0}, {μ + 2 σ, PDF[$\mathcal{D}$, μ + 2 σ]}},
        {{μ - 2 σ, 0}, {μ - 2 σ, PDF[$\mathcal{D}$, μ - 2 σ]}}}]}, AxesOrigin → {-4, 0},
        Ticks → {{{-2 σ, "-2σ"}, {-σ, "-σ"}, {μ, "μ"}, {σ, "σ"}, {2 σ, "2σ"}},
        Automatic}, AspectRatio → 0.4,
        PlotLabel → StringForm["Normal distribution: μ=`1`, σ=`2` ", μ, σ]]

Out[32]=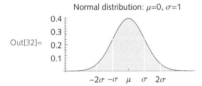

And here is a little utility function to make the code a bit more readable and easier to use.

In[33]:= **sdLine[$\mathcal{D}$_, μ_, σ_] := Line[{{{μ + σ, 0}, {σ + μ, PDF[$\mathcal{D}$, μ + σ]}},**
        {{μ - σ, 0}, {-σ + μ, PDF[$\mathcal{D}$, μ - σ]}}}]

In[34]:= **Plot[PDF[$\mathcal{D}$, x], {x, -4, 4}, Filling → Axis,**
        Epilog → {White, Thickness[.0035], sdLine[$\mathcal{D}$, μ, σ], sdLine[$\mathcal{D}$, μ, 2 σ]},
        AxesOrigin → {-4, 0},
        Ticks → {{{-2 σ, "-2σ"}, {-σ, "-σ"}, {μ, "μ"}, {σ, "σ"}, {2 σ, "2σ"}},
        Automatic}, AspectRatio → 0.4,
        PlotLabel → StringForm["Normal distribution: μ=`1`, σ=`2` ", μ, σ]]

Out[34]=

9. Following the discussion of options in Section 5.7, we use OptionsPattern to inherit options from ArrayPlot.

In[35]:= ```
ProteinDotPlot[p1_, p2_, opts : OptionsPattern[ArrayPlot]] :=
   ArrayPlot[Outer[Boole[#1 == #2] &, Characters[p1], Characters[p2]],
     opts, Frame → True]
```

In[36]:= ```
seq1 = ProteinData["SCNN1A"];
seq2 = ProteinData["SCNN1G"];
```

In[38]:= ```
ProteinDotPlot[seq1, seq2,
   FrameLabel → {"SCNN1A", "SCNN1G"},
   LabelStyle → {FontFamily → "Times", 11}]
```

Out[38]=

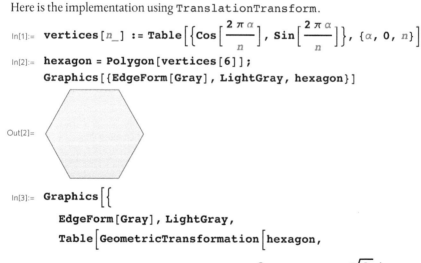

## 10.2 Efficient structures

1. Here is the implementation using TranslationTransform.

In[1]:= $\texttt{vertices}[n\_] := \texttt{Table}\left[\left\{\texttt{Cos}\left[\dfrac{2\,\pi\,\alpha}{n}\right],\ \texttt{Sin}\left[\dfrac{2\,\pi\,\alpha}{n}\right]\right\},\ \{\alpha,\ 0,\ n\}\right]$

In[2]:= ```
hexagon = Polygon[vertices[6]];
Graphics[{EdgeForm[Gray], LightGray, hexagon}]
```

Out[2]=

In[3]:= $\texttt{Graphics}\Big[\Big\{$

$\quad\texttt{EdgeForm[Gray], LightGray,}$

$\quad\texttt{Table}\Big[\texttt{GeometricTransformation}\Big[\texttt{hexagon,}$

$\qquad\texttt{TranslationTransform}\Big[\Big\{3\ i + \dfrac{3}{4}\left((-1)^{j} + 1\right),\ \dfrac{\sqrt{3}\ j}{2}\Big\}\Big]$

$\quad\Big],\ \{i,\ 5\},\ \{j,\ 8\}\Big]$

$\Big\}\Big]$

Out[3]=

Or use `Translate` directly.

```
In[4]:= gr1 = Graphics[{
          EdgeForm[Gray], LightGray,
          Table[
            Translate[hexagon, {3 i + 3/4 ((-1)^j + 1), √3 j/2}], {i, 5}, {j, 8}]
        }]
```

Out[4]=

This implementation contains one `Polygon` per hexagon.

```
In[5]:= Count[gr1, _Polygon, Infinity]
Out[5]= 40
```

Now use multi-polygons. The following version of `hexagon` is defined so that it can take a pair of translation coordinates. Note also the need to flatten the table of vertices so that `Polygon` can be applied to the correct list structure.

```
In[6]:= Clear[hexagon];
        hexagon[{x_, y_}] := Table[{Cos[2 π i/6] + x, Sin[2 π i/6] + y}, {i, 1, 6}]

In[8]:= gr2 = Graphics[{EdgeForm[Gray], LightGray, Polygon[Flatten[
            Table[hexagon[{3 i + 3/4 ((-1)^j + 1), √3 j/2}], {i, 5}, {j, 8}], 1]]}
        }]
```

Out[8]=

```
In[9]:= Count[gr2, _Polygon, Infinity]
Out[9]= 1
```

2. One approach to creating the lattice is to manually specify the coordinates for the lines and then map the `Line` primitive across these coordinates. We will work with a small lattice.

```
In[10]:= xmin = 0; xmax = 3;
         ymin = 0; ymax = 3;
         zmin = 0; zmax = 3;
         Table[{{x, ymin, zmin}, {x, ymax, zmin}}, {x, xmin, xmax}]
Out[13]= {{{0, 0, 0}, {0, 3, 0}}, {{1, 0, 0}, {1, 3, 0}},
          {{2, 0, 0}, {2, 3, 0}}, {{3, 0, 0}, {3, 3, 0}}}
```

Here are the three grids.

```
In[14]:= gridX =
    Table[{{xmin, y, z}, {xmax, y, z}}, {y, ymin, ymax}, {z, zmin, zmax}];
    gridY = Table[{{x, ymin, z}, {x, ymax, z}},
        {x, xmin, xmax}, {z, zmin, zmax}];
    gridZ = Table[{{x, y, zmin}, {x, y, zmax}},
        {x, xmin, xmax}, {y, ymin, ymax}];
```

Finally, map `Line` across these grids and display as a `Graphics3D` object.

```
In[17]:= gr1 = Graphics3D[{
        Map[Line, gridX, {2}],
        Map[Line, gridY, {2}],
        Map[Line, gridZ, {2}]
        }, Boxed → False]
```

Out[17]=
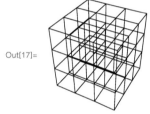

```
In[18]:= Count[gr1, _Line, Infinity]
```

Out[18]= 48

Using multi-lines reduces the number of `Line` objects substantially.

```
In[19]:= gr2 = Graphics3D[{
        Map[Line, gridX],
        Map[Line, gridY],
        Map[Line, gridZ]
        }, Boxed → False]
```

Out[19]=
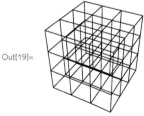

```
In[20]:= Count[gr2, _Line, Infinity]
```

Out[20]= 12

3. The Computational Geometry package contains a function for computing the convex hull.
   `ConvexHull[pts]` returns a list of the indices of the points on the convex hull.

```
In[21]:= Needs["ComputationalGeometry`"]
```

```
In[22]:= pts = RandomReal[1, {12, 2}];
         ch = ConvexHull[pts]
Out[23]= {10, 1, 2, 9, 11, 7, 8}
```

Use those indices as the positions in `pts` through which we wish to pass a line. Note the need to close up the polygon, connecting the last point with the first.

```
In[24]:= Graphics[GraphicsComplex[pts, Line[ch /. {a_, b__} :> {a, b, a}]]]
```

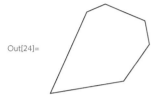

```
Out[24]=
```

Now add the text.

```
In[25]:= ran = Range[Length[pts]];
         Graphics[GraphicsComplex[pts,
             {Line[ch /. {a_, b__} :> {a, b, a}], PointSize[.015], Point[ran],
              Map[Text[StringForm["`1`", #], pts[[#]], {-1.25, -1.25}] &, ran]}]]
```

```
Out[26]=
```

Putting everything together, note that because `Module` is a scoping construct, you need to give full context names for any function that is defined in a package loaded inside `Module`.

```
In[27]:= Clear[ConvexHullPlot]
```

```
In[28]:= ConvexHullPlot[pts_, opts : OptionsPattern[Graphics]] :=
         Module[{ch, ran = Range[Length[pts]]},
           Needs["ComputationalGeometry`"];
           ch = ComputationalGeometry`ConvexHull[pts];
           Graphics[{GraphicsComplex[
               pts,
               {Line[ch /. {a_, b__} :> {a, b, a}],
                PointSize[.015], Point[ran],
                Map[
                  Text[StringForm["`1`", #], pts[[#]], {-1.25, -1.25}] &, ran]
               }
             ]}, opts]]
```

In[29]:= **ConvexHullPlot[pts]**

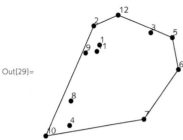

Out[29]=

4.   Here is the random walk on the digits of π in bases given by the second argument.

In[30]:= **RandomWalkPi[$d\_$, $base\_$ /; $base$ > 2] := Module[{digits, angles, rules},**
         digits = First[RealDigits[N[π, d], $base$]];
         angles = Rest@Range[0., 2 π, 2 π / ($base$)];
         rules = MapThread[$\#1 \rightarrow \#2$ &, {Range[0, $base$ - 1], angles}];
         Accumulate[Map[{Cos[$\#$], Sin[$\#$]} &, digits /. rules]]
         ]

Using `ListPlot`, here is a quick visualization on base 5 digits:

In[31]:= **ListLinePlot[RandomWalkPi[10 000, 5], AspectRatio $\rightarrow$ Automatic]**

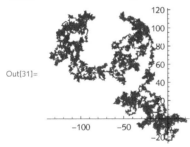

Out[31]=

Here is the `GraphicsComplex`.

In[32]:= **walk = RandomWalkPi[10 000, 5];**
         len = Length[walk];

In[34]:= **Graphics[GraphicsComplex[walk,**
         {AbsoluteThickness[.2], Line[Range[len]]}], AspectRatio $\rightarrow$ Automatic]

Out[34]=

And here it is with color mapped to the distance from the origin.

```
In[35]:=  Graphics[GraphicsComplex[walk,

              Map[{Hue[#[[1]]/len], AbsoluteThickness[.25], Line[#]} &,

              Partition[Range[2, len], 2, 1]]], AspectRatio → Automatic]
```

Out[35]=

10.3 Sound

1. When x is close to -2, the frequency is quite low. As x increases, the fraction $1000/x$ increases, making the frequency of the sine function bigger. This in turn makes the tone much higher in pitch. As x approaches 0, the function is oscillating more and more, and at 0, the function can be thought of as oscillating infinitely often. In fact, it is oscillating so much that the sampling routine is not able to compute amplitudes effectively and, hence, we hear noise near $x = 0$.

```
In[1]:=  Play[Sin[1000/x], {x, -2, 2}]
```

3. To generate a tone whose rate increases one octave per second, you need the sine of a function whose derivative doubles each second (frequency is a rate). That function is 2^t. You need to carefully choose values for t that generates tones in a reasonable range.

```
In[2]:=  Play[Sin[2^t], {t, 10, 14}] // EmitSound
```

4. First generate 100 digits for a 100-note "composition".

```
In[3]:=  digs = First[RealDigits[N[π, 100]]];
```

Fix note duration at 0.5 seconds.

```
In[4]:=  Sound[SoundNote[#, 0.5] & /@ digs] // EmitSound
```

Change the duration to be dependent upon the digit. Also change the MIDI instrument.

```
In[5]:=  Sound[SoundNote[#, 1 / (# + 1), "Vibraphone"] & /@ digs] // EmitSound
```

Go a bit further, expanding the range of notes that will be played.

```
In[6]:=  Sound[SoundNote[1 + 2 #, 1 / (# + 1), "Vibraphone"] & /@ digs] // EmitSound
```

5. Here is a function that creates a square wave with decreasing amplitudes for higher overtones.

```
In[7]:=  squareWave[freq_, n_] := Sum[Sin[freq i 2 π t]/i, {i, 1, n, 2}]
```

In[8]:= `Plot[squareWave[440, 17], {t, 0, .01}]`

Out[8]=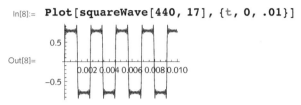

Here then, is an example of playing a square wave.

In[9]:= `Play[squareWave[440, 17], {t, 0, .5}] // EmitSound`

8. This function creates a sawtooth wave. The user specifies the fundamental frequency and the number of terms in the approximation.

In[10]:= `sawtoothWave[freq_, n_] := Sum[` $\dfrac{\text{Sin}[\text{freq i } 2\,\pi\,\text{t}]}{\text{i}}$ `, {i, 1, n}]`

In[11]:= `Plot[sawtoothWave[440, 17], {t, 0, .01}]`

Out[11]=

This plays the wave for a half-second duration.

In[12]:= `Play[sawtoothWave[440, 17], {t, 0, .5}] // EmitSound`

10.4 Examples and applications

1. The function `ComplexListPlot` plots a list of numbers in the complex plane – the real part is identified with the horizontal axis and the imaginary part is identified with the vertical axis. Start by setting the options for `ComplexListPlot` to inherit those for `ListPlot`.

In[1]:= `Options[ComplexListPlot] = Options[ListPlot];`

In[2]:= `ComplexListPlot[points_, opts : OptionsPattern[]] :=`
    `ListPlot[Map[{Re[#], Im[#]} &, points],`
      `opts, PlotStyle → {Red, PointSize[.025]},`
      `AxesLabel → {Style["Re", 10], Style["Im", 10]},`
      `LabelStyle → Directive["Menu", 7]]`

This plots four complex numbers in the plane and uses some options, inherited from `ListPlot`.

In[3]:= `ComplexListPlot[{-1 + I, 2 + I, 1 - 2 I, 0, 1},`
    `PlotStyle → {Blue, PointSize[Medium]}]`

Out[3]=

2. The function `ComplexRootPlot` takes a polynomial, solves for its roots, and then uses
    `ComplexListPlot` from the previous exercise to plot these roots in the complex plane.

    In[4]:= `ComplexRootPlot[poly_, z_, opts : OptionsPattern[]] := ComplexListPlot[`
    `    z /. NSolve[poly == 0, z], opts, AspectRatio → Automatic]`

    In[5]:= `ComplexRootPlot[Cyclotomic[17, z], z, GridLines → Automatic]`

    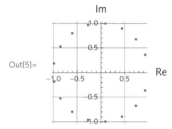

    Out[5]=

3. First, set up the options structure.

    In[6]:= `Options[PathPlot] = Join[{ClosedPath → True}, Options[Graphics]];`

    Make two changes to the original `PathPlot`: add an `If` statement that checks the value of `ClosedPath`
    and if `True`, appends the first point to the end of the list; if `False`, it leaves the coordinate list as is. The
    second change is to filter those options that are specific to `Graphics` and insert them in the appropriate
    place.

    In[7]:= `PathPlot[lis_List, opts : OptionsPattern[]] := Module[{coords = lis},`
    `    If[OptionValue[ClosedPath], coords = coords /. {a_, b__} :> {a, b, a}];`
    `    Graphics[{Line[coords], PointSize[Medium], Red, Point[coords]},`
    `     FilterRules[{opts}, Options[Graphics]]]]`

    In[8]:= `SeedRandom[424];`
    `coords = RandomReal[1, {10, 2}];`

    In[10]:= `PathPlot[coords, ClosedPath → True, GridLines → Automatic]`

    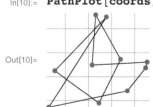

    Out[10]=

5. Choosing a base point randomly and then sorting according to the arc tangent could cause a number of
    things to go wrong with the algorithm. The default branch cut for `ArcTan` gives values between $-\pi/2$ and
    $\pi/2$. (You are encouraged to think about why this could occasionally cause the algorithm in the text to
    fail.) By choosing the base point so that it lies at some extreme of the diameter of the set of points, the polar
    angle algorithm given in the text will work consistently. If you choose the base point so that it is lowest and
    left-most, then all the angles will be in the range $(0, \pi)$.

    In[11]:= `SimpleClosedPath1[lis_List] := Module[{base, angle, sorted},`
    `    base = First[SortBy[lis, Last]];`
    `    angle[a_, b_] := ArcTan @@ (b - a);`
    `    sorted = Sort[Complement[lis, {base}],`
    `      angle[base, #1] ≤ angle[base, #2] &]; Join[{base}, sorted, {base}]]`

```
In[12]:= pts = RandomReal[1, {20, 2}];

In[13]:= PathPlot[coords_List] :=
           Show[Graphics[{Line[coords], PointSize[Medium],
               RGBColor[1, 0, 0], Point /@ coords}]]

In[14]:= PathPlot[SimpleClosedPath1[pts]]
```

Out[14]=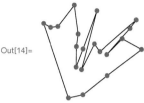

8.　Create three rules, one for each of the three dimensions of random walk that will be passed to `ShowWalk`. Some pattern matching will help to identify the rule to use for the one-, two-, and three-dimensional cases.

```
In[15]:= MatchQ[{1, 2, 3}, _?VectorQ]

Out[15]= True

In[16]:= MatchQ[{{1, 1}, {1, 2}, {0, 2}}, {{_, _} ..}]

Out[16]= True

In[17]:= MatchQ[{{1, 1, 0}, {1, 2, 0}, {0, 2, 0}}, {{_, _, _} ..}]

Out[17]= True
```

The first rule uses a pattern that will be matched by a one-dimensional vector.

```
In[18]:= ShowWalk[coords_?VectorQ, opts : OptionsPattern[]] :=
            ListLinePlot[coords, FilterRules[{opts}, Options[ListLinePlot]]]
```

The second rule uses a pattern that will be matched by a list of one or more pairs of numbers.

```
In[19]:= ShowWalk[coords : {{_?NumberQ, _?NumberQ} ..},
            opts : OptionsPattern[]] :=
              ListLinePlot[coords, Append[FilterRules[{opts},
              Options[ListLinePlot]], AspectRatio → Automatic]]
```

The third rule uses a pattern that will be matched by one or more triples of numbers.

```
In[20]:= ShowWalk[coords : {{_?NumberQ, _?NumberQ, _?NumberQ} ..},
            opts : OptionsPattern[]] :=
              Graphics3D[Line[coords],
              FilterRules[{opts}, Options[Graphics3D]]]
```

9.　Use `PlotStyle` to highlight the two different surfaces and `MeshStyle` and `Mesh` to highlight their intersection.

```
In[21]:= f[x_, y_] := Sin[2 x - Cos[y]];
         g[x_, y_] := Sin[x - Cos[2 y]];
```

In[23]:= `Plot3D[{f[x, y], g[x, y]}, {x, -π, π}, {y, -π, π}, Mesh → {{0.}},`
`MaxRecursion → 4, MeshFunctions → (f[#1, #2] - g[#1, #2] &),`
`MeshStyle → {Thick, Red}, PlotStyle → {Cyan, Yellow}]`

Out[23]=

11. If the first point returned by GatherBy fails the PointInPolygonQ test, then reverse the two lists (out and in), otherwise, leave it alone.

In[24]:= `poly = {{-0.5, 0}, {0.5, -1}, {1.5, 0},`
`        {2., -1.1}, {2.5, 0}, {1.5, 2}, {1., 1}, {0., 1}};`
`pts = RandomReal[{-1, 3}, {7500, 2}];`

In[26]:= `TriangleArea[tri : {v1_, v2_, v3_}] :=`
`  Det[Map[PadRight[#, 3, 1] &, tri]] / 2`

In[27]:= `PointInPolygonQ[poly : {{_, _} ..}, pt : {x_, y_}] :=`
`  Module[{edges, e2, e3, e4},`
`    edges = Partition[poly /. {a_, b__} ⧴ {a, b, a}, 2, 1];`
`    e2 = DeleteCases[edges, {{x1_, y1_}, {x2_, y2_}} /; y1 == y2];`
`    e3 = DeleteCases[e2,`
`       {{x1_, y1_}, {x2_, y2_}} /; (Min[y1, y2] ≥ y || Max[y1, y2] < y)];`
`    e4 = Map[Reverse@SortBy[#, Last] &, e3];`
`    OddQ[Count[TriangleArea[Join[#, {pt}]] & /@ e4, _?Positive]]`
`  ]`

In[28]:= `gbPts = GatherBy[pts, PointInPolygonQ[poly, #] &];`
`Graphics[{`
`  {PointSize[Small],`
`   If[PointInPolygonQ[poly, gbPts[[1, 1]]], gbPts, Reverse[gbPts]] /.`
`    {in_List, out_List} ⧴ {{Black, Point@in}, {LightGray, Point@out}}},`
`  Thick, Line[poly /. {a_, b__} ⧴ {a, b, a}],`
`  PointSize[Large], Point[poly]`
`  }]`

Out[29]=

14. First set up the options structure.

```
In[30]:= Options[BrownianCompose] = {Weights -> Automatic};
```

```
In[31]:= BrownianCompose[steps_Integer, instr_ : "Vibraphone",
           OptionsPattern[]] := Module[{walk, durs, weights},
           weights = If[OptionValue[Weights] === Automatic,
             Table[1 / 9, {9}], OptionValue[Weights]];
           walk[n_] := Accumulate[RandomChoice[weights -> Range[-4, 4], n]];
           durs = RandomChoice[Range[1 / 16, 1, 1 / 16], {steps}];
           Sound@MapThread[SoundNote[#1, #2, instr] &, {walk[steps], durs}]
           ]
```

```
In[32]:= BrownianCompose[18, "Marimba"] // EmitSound
```

```
In[33]:= BrownianCompose[18, "Marimba",
           Weights -> Abs@RandomVariate[NormalDistribution[0, 4], 9]] // EmitSound
```

11   Dynamic expressions

11.1   Manipulating expressions

1. We will put this together in two parts: first create a function to display any amino acid using one of the various diagrams; then pour it into a `Manipulate`. Note, this function is dependent upon `ChemicalData` to create the displays. You could modify it to use you own visualizations, such as the space-filling plots in Section 10.4.

```
In[1]:= AminoAcidPlot[aa_String, diagram_ : "ColorStructureDiagram"] :=
           Labeled[Framed[ChemicalData[aa, diagram], ImageSize -> All],
             ChemicalData[aa, "Name"], LabelStyle -> Directive["Menu", 9]]
```

```
In[2]:= AminoAcidPlot["Glycine"]
```

Out[2]=

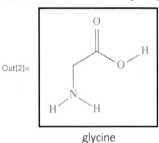

glycine

In[3]:= `Manipulate[`
`  AminoAcidPlot[aminoacid, diagram],`
`  {{aminoacid, "LAlanine", "Amino acid"}, aa},`
`  {diagram, {"StructureDiagram", "CHColorStructureDiagram",`
`    "CHStructureDiagram", "ColorStructureDiagram",`
`    "MoleculePlot", "SpaceFillingMoleculePlot"}},`
`  Initialization :> {aa = ChemicalData["AminoAcids"]}]`

Out[3]=

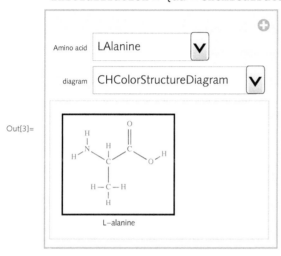

2. This is a straightforward use of `Manipulate`. The lengthy parameter list forces a pulldown menu to be used as the control.

In[4]:= `Manipulate[`

`  ImageEffect[`  `, effect],`

`  {effect, {"Charcoal", "Embossing", "OilPainting",`
`    "Posterization", "Solarization", "MotionBlur", "Noise",`
`    "GaussianNoise", "SaltPepperNoise", "PoissonNoise"}}]`

Out[4]=

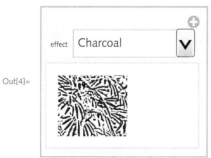

3. Here is the code for the `TruthTable` function from Exercise 9 in Section 5.8:

```
In[5]:= TruthTable[expr_, vars_] :=
    Module[{len = Length[vars], tuples, rules, table, head},
      tuples = Tuples[{True, False}, len];
      rules = (Thread[vars → #1] &) /@ tuples;
      table = Transpose[Join[Transpose[tuples], {expr /. rules}]];
      head = Append[vars, TraditionalForm[expr]];
      Grid[Prepend[table /. {True → "T", False → "F"}, head], Dividers →
        {{1 → {Thin, Black}, -1 → {Thin, Black}, -2 → {Thin, LightGray}},
          {1 → {Thin, Black}, 2 → {Thin, LightGray}, -1 → {Thin, Black}}}]]
```

This puts the truth table together with the Venn diagram using Row.

```
In[6]:= Manipulate[Row[{TruthTable[f[A, B], {A, B}],
      Show[RegionPlot[f @@ eqns, {x, -2, 2}, {y, -2, 2}, Frame → None,
        PlotLabel → f[A, B], PlotRange → {{-2, 2}, {-1.2, 1.2}},
        AspectRatio → Automatic, MaxRecursion → 5], Graphics[{Circle[c1],
          Circle[c2], Text[Style["A", FontSlant → "Italic"], {-.5, .8}],
          Text[Style["B", FontSlant → "Italic"], {.5, .8}]}],
        ImageSize → Small]}], {{f, Xor, "Logical function"},
      {And, Or, Xor, Implies, Nand, Nor}},
    Initialization :> {c1 = {-1/2, 0}; c2 = {1/2, 0};
      eqns = Apply[(#1 + x)^2 + (#2 + y)^2 < 1 &, {c1, c2}, {1}]},
    SaveDefinitions → True]
```

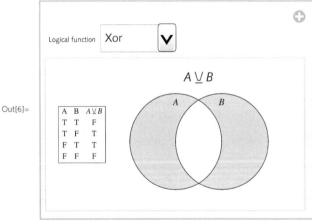

Out[6]=

5.   First load the package that contains the random walk code. You could use you own implementation as well.

```
In[7]:= << PwM`RandomWalks`
```

Create a 1000-step, two-dimensional, lattice walk.

```
In[8]:= rw = RandomWalk[1000, Dimension → 2, LatticeWalk → True];
```

This is a basic start. `Take` is used to display successive increments. Note the need for the 1 in the parameter list to insure that steps only take on integer values.

In[9]:= `Animate[`
        `Graphics[Line[Take[rw, n]]],`
        `{n, 2, Length[rw], 1}]`

Out[9]=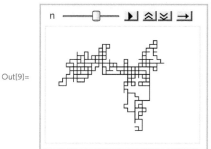

The output above suffers from the fact that the display jumps around a lot as *Mathematica* tries to figure out a sensible plot range for *each* frame. Instead, we should fix the plot range for *all* frames to avoid this jumpiness. This is done in the definitions for `xran` and `yran` in the `Initialization` below.

In[10]:= `Manipulate[`
        `Graphics[Line[Take[rw, n]], PlotRange → {xran, yran}],`
        `{n, 2, Length[rw], 1},`
        `Initialization ⧴ {`
        `    rw = RandomWalk[1000, Dimension → 2, LatticeWalk → True];`
        `    {xran, yran} = Map[{Min[#1], Max[#1]} &, Transpose[rw]]}]`

Out[10]=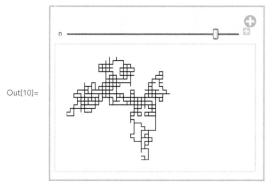

6. Putting the two graphics pieces (`Graphics[...]` and `Plot[...]`) in a grid gives you finer control over their placement and formatting.

```
In[12]:= Manipulate[Grid[
           {{Graphics[{Circle[], Blue, PointSize[.04], Point[{Cos[θ], Sin[θ]}]},
              Axes → True], Plot[Sin[x], {x, 0, 2 π}, ImageSize → 300,
              Epilog → {Blue, Line[{{θ, 0}, {θ, Sin[θ]}}], PointSize[.025],
                Point[{θ, Sin[θ]}]}]}}], Frame → All], {θ, 0, 2 π}]
```

Out[12]=

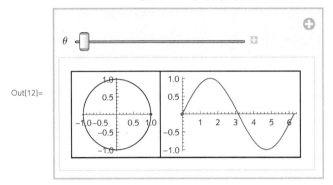

8. Just a few modifications to the code for the hypocycloid are needed: use the formula for the epicycloid; change the center of the rotating circle so that its radius is $R + r$, not $R - r$; and modify the plot range.

```
In[12]:= EpicycloidPlot[R_, r_, θ_] := Module[{epicycloid, center},
           epicycloid[{a_, b_}, t_] :=
             {(a + b) Cos[t] - b Cos[t (a + b)/b], (a + b) Sin[t] + b Sin[t (a + b)/b]};
           center[th_, R1_, r2_] := (R1 + r2) {Cos[th], Sin[th]};
           Show[{
             ParametricPlot[epicycloid[{R, r}, t],
               {t, 0, θ}, PlotStyle → Red, Axes → None],
             Graphics[{
               {Blue, Thick, Circle[{0, 0}, R]},
               {Circle[center[θ, R, r], r]},
               {PointSize[.015], Point[center[θ, R, r]]},
               {Thick, Line[{center[θ, R, r], epicycloid[{R, r}, θ]}]},
               {Red, PointSize[.015], Point[epicycloid[{R, r}, θ]]}
             }]}, PlotRange → 1.5 (R + r), GridLines → Automatic]]
```

First, create a static image.

```
In[13]:= EpicycloidPlot[3, 1, 2 π]
```

Out[13]=

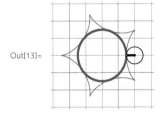

And here is the dynamic version.

```
In[14]:= Manipulate[EpicycloidPlot[R, r, θ],
            {θ, 0 + 0.01, 2 Denominator[(R - r) / r] π},
            {R, {3, 4, 5, 6, 7, 8}, Setter},
            {r, {1, 2, 3, 4, 5}, Setter}, SaveDefinitions → True]
```

Out[14]=

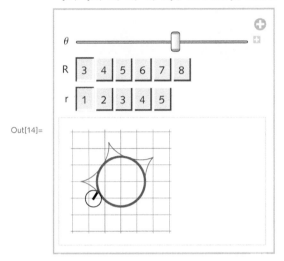

9.   Modify the radii and the centers to get different effects. Try using transparent disks instead of circles.

```
In[15]:= Manipulate[
            Graphics[
              Table[Circle[r / 4 {Cos[t], Sin[t]}, 1.1 - r], {r, .2, 1, .05}],
              PlotRange → 1],
            {t, 0, 2 π, .1},
            TrackedSymbols :> {t}]
```

Out[15]=

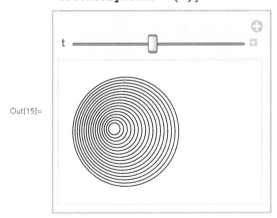

11. Using the programs developed in Section 13.1, here is the code, including a pulldown menu for the steps
     parameter, a setter bar for the dimension parameter, and a checkbox for the lattice parameter.

In[16]:= **Manipulate[**
    ShowWalk@RandomWalk[steps, Dimension → dim, LatticeWalk → latticeQ],
    {steps, {100, 250, 500, 750, 1000, 10 000}},
    {{dim, 1, "Dimension"}, {1, 2, 3}},
    {{latticeQ, True, "Lattice walk"}, {True, False}},
    Initialization ⧴ Needs["PWM`RandomWalks`"], SaveDefinitions → True]

Out[16]=

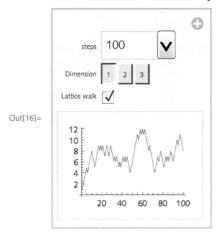

12.   Here is the solution using Slider2D. Using Locator instead is left for the reader.

In[17]:= **Manipulate[**
    Graphics[{
      Red, Arrow[{{0, 0}, pt1}],
      Blue, Arrow[{{0, 0}, pt2}],
      Green, Arrow[{{0, 0}, pt1 + pt2}],
      Dashed, Orange, Line[{pt1, pt1 + pt2, pt2}]},
     PlotRange → 6, Axes → True, GridLines → Automatic],
    {{pt1, {1, 4}, "Red vector"}, {-5, -5}, {5, 5}},
    {{pt2, {3, 1}, "Blue vector"}, {-5, -5}, {5, 5}},
    ControlPlacement → Left]

Out[17]=

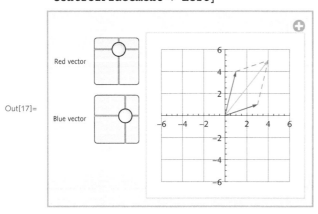

11.2 The structure of dynamic expressions

1. Use the `UpdateInterval` option to `Dynamic`.

   In[1]:= `Dynamic[RandomChoice[DictionaryLookup[]], UpdateInterval → 5]`

   Out[1]= goners

2. `Normalize` takes a vector as input and returns a unit vector.

   In[2]:= `DynamicModule[{pt = {1, 0}}, Graphics[{`
   `    Circle[],`
   `    Locator[Dynamic[pt, (pt = Normalize[#]) &]]`
   `  }]]`

   Out[2]=

11.3 Examples and applications

1. Import the data only; the first four columns give name, field, birth year, award year.

   In[1]:= `data =`
   `    Import["http://www.nber.org/nobel/Jones_Weinberg_2011_PNAS.xlsx",`
   `      {"XLSX", "Data", 1, All, {1, 2, 3, 4}}];`

   In[2]:= `data[[{1, -1}]]`

   Out[2]= `{{name, field, year_birth, year_prize},`
   `  {Nambu, Yoichiro, Physics, 1921., 2008.}}`

   In[3]:= `data[[-1]] /.`
   `    {a__String, birth_Real, award_Real} :→ {a, birth, award, award - birth}`

   Out[3]= `{Nambu, Yoichiro, Physics, 1921., 2008., 87.}`

   In[4]:= `nobelData = data[[2 ;; -1]] /. {a__String, birth_Real, award_Real} :→`
   `      {a, birth, award, award - birth};`

   In[5]:= `chem = Cases[nobelData, {name_String, "Chemistry", rest__}];`
   `med = Cases[nobelData, {name_String, "Medicine", rest__}];`
   `physics = Cases[nobelData, {name_String, "Physics", rest__}];`

   In[8]:= `timeChem = chem[[All, {4, 5}]];`
   `timeMed = med[[All, {4, 5}]];`
   `timePhysics = physics[[All, {4, 5}]];`

In[9]:= **DateListPlot[Tooltip[timeChem /. {*a_*, *b_*} :→ {{Round@*a*}, *b*}],**
 Joined → True, Mesh → All,
 PlotLabel → StringForm["Average age for chemistry Nobel award = `1`",
 Mean[timeChem[[All, 2]]]]]

Average age for chemistry Nobel award = 56.5556

Out[9]=

In[10]:= **TabView[**
 MapThread[#1 → DateListPlot[
 Tooltip[#2 /. {*a_*, *b_*} :→ {{Round@*a*}, *b*}], Joined → True, Mesh → All,
 PlotLabel → StringForm["Average age for `1` Nobel award = `2`",
 #1, Mean[#2[[All, 2]]]]] &,
 {{"Chemistry", "Medicine", "Physics"},
 {timeChem, timeMed, timePhysics}}]]

Out[10]=

3. Create a static version of the problem; we use `GraphicsComplex` to display the points and the tour.

In[13]:= **pts = RandomReal[1, {20, 2}];**

In[14]:= **Graphics[GraphicsComplex[pts, Point@Range[Length[pts]]],**
 Axes → Automatic]

Out[14]=

```
In[15]:= tour = Last[FindShortestTour[pts]];
        Graphics[GraphicsComplex[pts,
          {Line[tour], Red, PointSize[.015], Point[tour]}], Axes → Automatic]
```

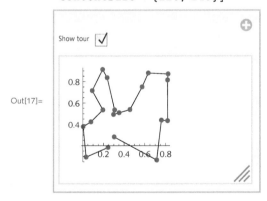

Out[16]=

Here is the dynamic interface using `EventHandler` to choose a new set of random points with each mouse click.

```
In[17]:= Manipulate[
        DynamicModule[{pts = RandomReal[1, {20, 2}], tour},
          tour = Dynamic[Last[FindShortestTour[pts]]];
          EventHandler[
            Dynamic[Graphics[GraphicsComplex[pts,
              If[Not[showtour], Point@Range[Length[pts]], {Line[tour], Red,
                PointSize[Medium], Point[tour]}], Axes → Automatic]],
            {"MouseClicked" :> (pts = RandomReal[1, {20, 2}])}
          ]],
        {{showtour, False, "Show tour"}, {True, False}},
        ContentSize → {220, 140}]
```

Out[17]=

A suggested addition would be to add a control to change the number of points that are used. But be careful: traveling salesman type problems are notoriously hard; in fact they are known to be NP-hard, meaning they cannot be computed in polynomial time. See Lawler et al. (1985) for more on traveling salesman problems.

12 Optimizing *Mathematica* programs

12.2 Efficient programs

1. Collect the results of the `Table` and pull out the parts needed – the timings and the result.

```
In[1]:= SetAttributes[AverageTiming, HoldAll]

In[2]:= AverageTiming[expr_, trials_] := Module[{lis},
            lis = Table[AbsoluteTiming[expr], {trials}];
            {Mean[lis[[All, 1]]], lis[[1, 2]]}
        ]

In[3]:= AverageTiming[FactorInteger[50! + 1], 5 ]

Out[3]= {1.355980, {{149, 1}, {3989, 1}, {74 195 127 103, 1},
            {6 854 870 037 011, 1}, {100 612 041 036 938 568 804 690 996 722 352 077, 1}}}
```

2. A first attempt, using a brute force approach, is to total the list $\{1, 2, ..., n\}$ for each n.

```
In[4]:= TriangularNumber[n_] := Total[Range[n]]

In[5]:= Table[TriangularNumber[i], {i, 1 , 1 0 0 }]

Out[5]= {1, 3, 6, 10, 15, 21, 28, 36, 45, 55, 66, 78, 91, 105, 120, 136, 153, 171, 190, 210,
            231, 253, 276, 300, 325, 351, 378, 406, 435, 465, 496, 528, 561, 595, 630,
            666, 703, 741, 780, 820, 861, 903, 946, 990, 1035, 1081, 1128, 1176, 1225,
            1275, 1326, 1378, 1431, 1485, 1540, 1596, 1653, 1711, 1770, 1830, 1891, 1953,
            2016, 2080, 2145, 2211, 2278, 2346, 2415, 2485, 2556, 2628, 2701, 2775, 2850,
            2926, 3003, 3081, 3160, 3240, 3321, 3403, 3486, 3570, 3655, 3741, 3828, 3916,
            4005, 4095, 4186, 4278, 4371, 4465, 4560, 4656, 4753, 4851, 4950, 5050}

In[6]:= Timing[TriangularNumber[10^7]]

Out[6]= {3.21174, 50 000 005 000 000}
```

A second approach uses iteration. As might be expected, this is the slowest of the approaches here.

```
In[7]:= TriangularNumber2[n_] := Fold[#1+ #2 &, 0, Range[n]]

In[8]:= Timing[TriangularNumber2[10^7]]

Out[8]= {7.26054, 50 000 005 000 000}
```

This is a situation where some mathematical knowledge is useful. The nth triangular numbers is just the $(n + 1)$th binomial coefficient $\binom{n + 1}{2}$.

```
In[9]:= TriangularNumber3[n_] := Binomial[n+ 1, 2]

In[10]:= Timing[TriangularNumber3[10^7]]

Out[10]= {0.000133, 50 000 005 000 000}
```

3. The first implementation essentially performs a transpose of the two lists, wrapping `SameQ` around each corresponding pair of numbers. It then does a pattern match (`Count`) to determine which expressions of the form $SameQ[expr_1, expr_2]$ return `False`.

```
In[11]:= HammingDistance1[lis1_, lis2_] :=
            Count[MapThread[SameQ, {lis1, lis2}], False]

In[12]:= HammingDistance2[lis1_, lis2_] := Total[BitXor[lis1, lis2]]

In[13]:= sig1 = RandomInteger[1, {10^6}];
```

In[14]:= **sig2 = RandomInteger$\left[1, \left\{10^6\right\}\right]$;**

In this case, it is the threading that is expensive rather than the pattern matching with Count.

In[15]:= **res = MapThread[SameQ, {sig1, sig2}]; // Timing**

Out[15]= {0.44688, Null}

In[16]:= **Count[res, False] // Timing**

Out[16]= {0.054779, 499 587}

The reason the threading is expensive can be seen by turning on the packing message as discussed in this section.

In[17]:= **SetSystemOptions["PackedArrayOptions" → "UnpackMessage" → True]**

Out[17]= PackedArrayOptions →
    {ListableAutoPackLength → 250, PackedArrayMathLinkRead → True,
     PackedArrayPatterns → True, PackedRange → True, UnpackMessage → True}

In[18]:= **res = MapThread[SameQ, {sig1, sig2}];**

Developer`FromPackedArray::punpack1 : Unpacking array with dimensions {1000000}. ≫

The other factors contributing to the significant timing differences have to do with the fact that BitXor has the Listable attribute. MapThread does not. And so, BitXor can take advantage of specialized (compiled) codes internally to speed up its computations.

In[19]:= **Attributes[BitXor]**

Out[19]= {Flat, Listable, OneIdentity, Orderless, Protected}

In[20]:= **Attributes[MapThread]**

Out[20]= {Protected}

In[21]:= **Timing[temp = BitXor[sig1, sig2];]**

Out[21]= {0.004166, Null}

And finally, compute the number of 1s using Total which is extremely fast at adding lists of numbers.

In[22]:= **Timing[Total[temp];]**

Out[22]= {0.003537, Null}

Return the packed array messaging to its default value.

In[23]:= **SetSystemOptions["PackedArrayOptions" → "UnpackMessage" → False];**

12.3 Parallel processing

1. First we find those values of p for which $2^p - 1$ is prime. This first step is quite compute-intensive; fortunately, it parallelizes well.

In[1]:= **LaunchKernels[]**

Out[1]= {KernelObject[1, local], KernelObject[2, local],
     KernelObject[3, local], KernelObject[4, local]}

In[2]:= `primes = Parallelize[Select[Range[10 000], PrimeQ[2^# - 1] &]]`

Out[2]= `{2, 3, 5, 7, 13, 17, 19, 31, 61, 89, 107, 127, 521,`
`607, 1279, 2203, 2281, 3217, 4253, 4423, 9689, 9941}`

So for each of the above values of the list `primes`, $2^{p-1}(2^p - 1)$ will be perfect (thanks to Euler).

In[3]:= `perfectLis = Map[2^#-1 (2^# - 1) &, primes];`

And finally, a check.

In[4]:= `perfectQ[j_] := Total[Divisors[j]] == 2 j;`

In[5]:= `Map[perfectQ, perfectLis]`

Out[5]= `{True, True, True, True, True, True, True, True, True, True, True,`
`True, True, True, True, True, True, True, True, True, True}`

In[6]:= `CloseKernels[];`

These are very large numbers indeed.

In[7]:= `2^#-1 (2^# - 1) &[9941] // N`

Out[7]= $5.988854963873362 \times 10^{5984}$

2. Only two changes are required to run this in parallel – distribute the definition for `Mandelbrot` and change `Table` to `ParallelTable`. Of course, to increase the resolution, the grid now has many more divisions in each direction ($n = 500$).

In[8]:= `Mandelbrot[c_] :=`
`    Length[NestWhileList[#^2 + c &, 0, Abs[#] < 2 &, 1, 250]]`

In[9]:= `LaunchKernels[]`

Out[9]= `{KernelObject[5, local], KernelObject[6, local],`
`KernelObject[7, local], KernelObject[8, local]}`

In[10]:= `DistributeDefinitions[Mandelbrot]`

Out[10]= `{Mandelbrot}`

In[11]:= `data = With[{n = 500}, ParallelTable[`
`    Mandelbrot[x + i y], {y, -0.5, 0.5, `$\frac{1}{n}$`}, {x, -1.75, -0.75, `$\frac{1}{n}$`}]];`

In[12]:= `ArrayPlot[data, ColorFunction -> "CMYKColors"]`

Out[12]=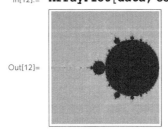

12.4 Compiling

1. First, create a test point with which to work.

In[1]:= `pt = RandomReal[1, {2}]`

Out[1]= `{0.333881, 0.135321}`

The following does not quite work because the default pattern is expected to be a flat expression.

In[2]:= `distReal = Compile[{{p, _Real}}, Sqrt[First[p]^2 + Last[p]^2],`
`RuntimeAttributes -> {Listable}, Parallelization -> True]`

Compile::part : Part specification p[[1]] cannot be compiled since the argument
is not a tensor of sufficient rank. Evaluation will use the uncompiled function. >>

Out[2]= $\text{CompiledFunction}\left[\{p\}, \sqrt{\text{First}[p]^2 + \text{Last}[p]^2}, \text{-CompiledCode-}\right]$

Give a third argument to the pattern specification to deal with this: `{p, _Real, 1}`.

In[3]:= `ArrayDepth[pt]`

Out[3]= `1`

In[4]:= `distReal = Compile[{{p, _Real, 1}}, Sqrt[First[p]^2 + Last[p]^2],`
`RuntimeAttributes -> {Listable}, Parallelization -> True]`

Out[4]= $\text{CompiledFunction}\left[\{p\}, \sqrt{\text{First}[p]^2 + \text{Last}[p]^2}, \text{-CompiledCode-}\right]$

In[5]:= `distReal[pt]`

Out[5]= `0.360261`

Check it against the built-in function:

In[6]:= `Norm[pt]`

Out[6]= `0.360261`

Check that it threads properly over a list of points.

In[7]:= `pts = RandomReal[1, {3, 2}]`

Out[7]= `{{0.223743, 0.810299}, {0.873595, 0.72168}, {0.951892, 0.547475}}`

In[8]:= `distReal[pts]`

Out[8]= `{0.840622, 1.13313, 1.0981}`

`Norm` does not have the `Listable` attribute so it must be mapped over the list.

In[9]:= `Map[Norm, pts]`

Out[9]= `{0.840622, 1.13313, 1.0981}`

In[10]:= `distReal[pts] == Map[Norm, pts]`

Out[10]= `True`

Now scale up the size of the list of points and check efficiency.

In[11]:= `pts = RandomReal[1, {10^6, 2}];`

In[12]:= `AbsoluteTiming[distReal[pts];]`

Out[12]= `{0.109824, Null}`

```
In[13]:= AbsoluteTiming[Map[Norm, pts];]
```

```
Out[13]= {0.113652, Null}
```

```
In[14]:= distReal[pts] == Map[Norm, pts]
```

```
Out[14]= True
```

Compiling to C (assuming you have a C compiler installed), speeds things up even more.

```
In[15]:= distReal = Compile[{{p, _Real, 1}},
           Sqrt[First[p]^2 + Last[p]^2], RuntimeAttributes -> {Listable},
           Parallelization -> True, CompilationTarget -> "C"]
```

$$Out[15]= \text{CompiledFunction}\left[\{p\}, \sqrt{\text{First}[p]^2 + \text{Last}[p]^2}, -\text{CompiledCode-}\right]$$

You can squeeze a little more speed out of these functions by using `Part` instead of `First` and `Last`.

```
In[16]:= distReal2 = Compile[{{p, _Real, 1}},
           Sqrt[p[[1]]^2 + p[[2]]^2], RuntimeAttributes -> {Listable},
           Parallelization -> True, CompilationTarget -> "C"]
```

$$Out[16]= \text{CompiledFunction}\left[\{p\}, \sqrt{p[\![1]\!]^2 + p[\![2]\!]^2}, -\text{CompiledCode-}\right]$$

```
In[17]:= AbsoluteTiming[distReal2[pts];]
```

```
Out[17]= {0.059632, Null}
```

As an aside, the mean distance to the origin for random points in the unit square approaches the following, asymptotically.

```
In[18]:= NIntegrate[Sqrt[x^2 + y^2], {x, 0, 1}, {y, 0, 1}]
```

```
Out[18]= 0.765196
```

```
In[19]:= Mean@distReal[pts]
```

```
Out[19]= 0.765452
```

2.   We need to make just three slight modifications to the code from the previous exercise: remove the rank specification; specify `Complex` as the type; extract the real and imaginary parts to do the norm computation.

```
In[20]:= Clear[distComplex];
         distComplex = Compile[{{z, _Complex}}, Sqrt[Re[z]^2 + Im[z]^2],
           RuntimeAttributes -> {Listable}, Parallelization -> True]
```

$$Out[21]= \text{CompiledFunction}\left[\{z\}, \sqrt{\text{Re}[z]^2 + \text{Im}[z]^2}, -\text{CompiledCode-}\right]$$

```
In[22]:= pts = RandomComplex[1, {3}]
```

```
Out[22]= {0.349519 + 0. i, 0.506776 + 0. i, 0.153516 + 0. i}
```

```
In[23]:= distComplex[pts]
```

```
Out[23]= {0.349519, 0.506776, 0.153516}
```

```
In[24]:= distComplex[pts] == Map[Norm, pts]
```

```
Out[24]= True
```

3.   Here is the computation for the iteration function $c \sin(z)$ using $c = 1 + 0.4\,i$.

```
In[25]:= cJulia2 = Compile[{{z, _Complex}, {c, _Complex}}, Module[{cnt = 1},
             FixedPoint[(cnt++; c Sin[#]) &,
               z, 100, SameTest → (Abs[Im[#2]] > 50 &)]; cnt],
             CompilationTarget → "C", RuntimeAttributes → {Listable},
             Parallelization → True, "RuntimeOptions" → "Speed"]
```

```
Out[25]= CompiledFunction[{z, c},
           Module[{cnt = 1}, FixedPoint[(cnt++; c Sin[#1]) &, z, 100,
             SameTest → (Abs[Im[#2]] > 50 &)]; cnt], -CompiledCode-]
```

```
In[26]:= With[{res = 100},
           ArrayPlot[ParallelTable[-cJulia2[x + y I, 1 + 0.4 I], {y, -2 π, 2 π, 1/res},
             {x, -2 π, 2 π, 1/res}], ColorFunction → ColorData["CMYKColors"]]]
```

Out[26]=

13   Applications and packages

13.1   Random walk application

3.   Here is the usage message for `GraphicsComplex`,

```
In[1]:= ? GraphicsComplex
```

GraphicsComplex$[\{pt_1, pt_2, \ldots\}, data]$ represents a graphics complex in which
coordinates given as integers i in graphics primitives in *data* are taken to be pt_i. ≫

The first argument to `GraphicsComplex` is a list of coordinate points, such as the output from
`RandomWalk`. The second argument is a set of graphics primitives indexed by the positions of the points
in the list of coordinates. Here are two examples, one in two dimensions and the other in three.

```
In[2]:= Needs["PWM`RandomWalks`"]
```

In[3]:= **Graphics[GraphicsComplex[**
  RandomWalk[500, LatticeWalk → False], Line[Range[500]]]]

Out[3]=

In[4]:= **Graphics3D[GraphicsComplex[RandomWalk[500,**
  Dimension → 3, LatticeWalk → False], Line[Range[500]]]]

Out[4]=

We can quickly modify the code for ShowWalk developed in the chapter to use GraphicsComplex instead.

In[5]:= **ShowWalkGC[*walk*_] :=**
  Module[{dim = Dimensions[*walk*], ran = Range[Length[*walk*]]},
   If[Length[dim] == 1 || dim[[2]] == 2,
    Graphics[GraphicsComplex[*walk*, Line[ran]]],
    Graphics3D[GraphicsComplex[*walk*, Line[ran]]]]]

In[6]:= **ShowWalkGC[RandomWalk[2500]]**

Out[10]=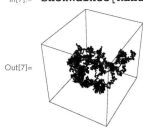

In[7]:= **ShowWalkGC[RandomWalk[2500, Dimension → 3, LatticeWalk → False]]**

Out[7]=

Here are some comparisons of running times for this approach and the ShowWalk function developed in the chapter.

In[8]:= **rw = RandomWalk[1 000 000, Dimension → 3, LatticeWalk → False];**

In[9]:= **Timing[gc = ShowWalkGC[rw];]**

Out[9]= {0.003836, Null}

In[10]:= **Timing[sw = ShowWalk[rw];]**

Out[10]= {0.12881, Null}

4. Start by creating a list of rules that indicate the first point is connected to the second, the second point is connected to the third, and so on. If you have ten points, partition them as follows.

In[11]:= `Partition[Range[10], 2, 1]`

Out[11]= `{{1, 2}, {2, 3}, {3, 4}, {4, 5}, {5, 6}, {6, 7}, {7, 8}, {8, 9}, {9, 10}}`

The graph rules are created by applying `DirectedEdge` at level 1.

In[12]:= `Apply[DirectedEdge, %, {1}]`

Out[12]= `{1 ⟷ 2, 2 ⟷ 3, 3 ⟷ 4, 4 ⟷ 5, 5 ⟷ 6, 6 ⟷ 7, 7 ⟷ 8, 8 ⟷ 9, 9 ⟷ 10}`

Here is a little function that puts these pieces together.

In[13]:= `Clear[bonds];`
`bonds[n_] := Apply[DirectedEdge, Partition[Range[n], 2, 1], {1}]`

The bond information is the first argument to `Graph`; the coordinates given by `RandomWalk` are the value of the option `VertexCoordinates`.

In[15]:= `<< PWM`RandomWalks``

In[16]:= `With[{steps = 1500}, Graph[bonds[steps],`
`    VertexCoordinates → RandomWalk[steps, LatticeWalk → True]]]`

Out[16]=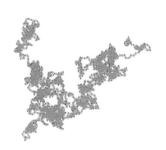

One of the advantages of representing these random walks as graphs is that you have all the graph formatting and styling functions available to quickly modify your graph.

In[17]:= `With[{steps = 1500},`
`    Graph[bonds[steps], DirectedEdges → False, EdgeStyle → Gray,`
`    VertexSize → {1 → {"Scaled", .025}, steps → {"Scaled", .025}},`
`    VertexStyle → {1 → {Opacity[0.4], Green}, steps → {Opacity[0.4], Red}},`
`    VertexCoordinates → RandomWalk[steps, LatticeWalk → False]]]`

Out[17]=

The disadvantage of this approach is that it is limited to two-dimensional walks. `Graph` does not support three-dimensional objects and it does not make much sense in one dimension.

13.4 Creating packages

1.   Here are the definitions for the auxiliary `collatz` function.

In[1]:= **collatz[*n_* ?EvenQ] := *n* / 2**

In[2]:= **collatz[*n_* ?OddQ] := 3 *n* + 1**

a. This is essentially the definition given in the solution to Exercise 5 from Section 6.2.

In[3]:= **CollatzSequence[*n_*] := NestWhileList[collatz, *n*, # ≠ 1 &]**

In[4]:= **CollatzSequence[7]**

Out[4]= {7, 22, 11, 34, 17, 52, 26, 13, 40, 20, 10, 5, 16, 8, 4, 2, 1}

b. First we write the usage message for `CollatzSequence`, our public function. Notice that we write no usage message for the private `collatz` function.

In[5]:= **CollatzSequence::usage =**
          "CollatzSequence[n] computes the sequence of Collatz
              iterates starting with initial value n. The sequence
              terminates as soon as it reaches the value 1.";

Here is the warning message that will be issued whenever `CollatzSequence` is passed an argument that is not a positive integer.

In[6]:= **CollatzSequence::notint =**
          "First argument, `1`, to CollatzSequence must
              be a positive integer.";

c. Here is the modified definition which now issues the warning message created above whenever the argument *n* is not a positive integer.

In[7]:= **CollatzSequence[*n_*] :=**
          If[IntegerQ[*n*] && *n* ≥ 0, NestWhileList[collatz, *n*, # ≠ 1 &],
              Message[CollatzSequence::notint, *n*]]

The following case covers the situation when `CollatzSequence` is passed two or more arguments. Note that it uses the built-in `argx` message, which is issued whenever built-in functions are passed the wrong number of arguments.

In[8]:= **CollatzSequence[_, *args__*] /; Message[CollatzSequence::argx,**
          CollatzSequence, Length[{*args*}] + 1] := Null

d. The package begins by giving *usage messages* for every exported function. The functions to be exported are *mentioned* here – *before* the subcontext `Private`` is entered – so that the symbol `CollatzSequence` has context `Collatz``. Notice that `collatz` is *not* mentioned here and hence will not be accessible to the user of this package.

In[9]:= **Quit[]**

In[1]:= **BeginPackage["PwM`Collatz`"];**

In[2]:= **CollatzSequence::usage =**
          "CollatzSequence[n] computes the sequence of Collatz
              iterates starting with initial value n. The sequence
              terminates as soon as it reaches the value 1.";

In[3]:= **CollatzSequence::notint =**

```
"First argument, `1`, to CollatzSequence must
    be a positive integer.";
```

A new context PwM`Collatz`Private` is then begun *within* PwM`Collatz`. All the definitions of this package are given within this new context. The context PwM`Collatz`CollatzSequence is defined within the System` context. The context of collatz, on the other hand, is PwM`Collatz`Private`.

In[4]:= **Begin["`Private`"];**

In[5]:= **collatz[*n_* ? EvenQ] := *n* / 2**

In[6]:= **collatz[*n_* ? OddQ] := 3 *n* + 1**

In[7]:= **CollatzSequence[*n_*] :=**
    If[IntegerQ[*n*] && *n* ≥ 0, NestWhileList[collatz, *n*, # ≠ 1 &],
      Message[CollatzSequence::notint, *n*]]

In[8]:= **CollatzSequence[_, *args__*] /; Message[CollatzSequence::argx,**
      CollatzSequence, Length[{*args*}] + 1] := Null

In[9]:= **End[];**

In[10]:= **EndPackage[]**

After the End[] and EndPackage[] functions are evaluated, $Context and $ContextPath revert to whatever they were before, except that PwM`Collatz` is added to $ContextPath. Users can refer to CollatzSequence using its short name, but they can only refer to the auxiliary function collatz by its full name. The intent is to discourage clients from using collatz at all, and doing so should definitely be avoided, since the author of the package may change or remove auxiliary definitions at a later time.

Bibliography

In addition to those items explicitly tied to the material in the book's chapters, tutorials and other reference materials from the *Mathematica* documentation are listed here. These are available both in *Mathematica* proper through the Documentation Center under the Help menu and also online. References in the text to the documentation are labeled WMDC, for Wolfram *Mathematica* Documentation Center. Some general references on the topics in this book are also listed here. As the list of *Mathematica* titles is an ever-expanding one, this listing is, by nature, incomplete.

1. Introduction

CALLAWAY, DUNCAN S., MARK E.J. NEWMAN, STEVEN H. STROGATZ, and DUNCAN J. WATTS. 2000. Network robustness and fragility: percolation on random graphs. *Physical Review Letters*, **5**, 355–360.

GRIMMETT, GEOFFREY. 1999. *Percolation*, second edition. Springer.

MOORE, CRISTOPHER and MARK E.J. NEWMAN. 2000. Exact solution of bond percolation on small-world networks. *Physical Review E*, **62**, 7059–7064.

NATIONAL ELEVATION DATASET. US Geological Survey, http://ned.usgs.gov/downloads.asp.

PADMANABHAN, THANU. 1998. *After the First Three Minutes: The Story of our Universe*. Cambridge University Press.

STAUFFER, DIETRICH and AMMON AHARONY. 1994. *Introduction to Percolation Theory*, second edition. Taylor & Francis.

Tutorials and guides

C/C++ LANGUAGE INTERFACE. Wolfram *Mathematica* Documentation Center, http://reference.wolfram.com/mathematica/guide/CLanguageInterface.html.

DATABASE CONNECTIVITY. Wolfram *Mathematica* Documentation Center, http://reference.wolfram.com/mathematica/guide/DatabaseConnectivity.html.

ENTERING TWO-DIMENSIONAL INPUT. Wolfram *Mathematica* Documentation Center, http://reference.wolfram.com/mathematica/tutorial/EnteringTwoDimensionalInput.html.

J/LINK USER GUIDE. Wolfram *Mathematica* Documentation Center, http://reference.wolfram.com/mathematica/JLink/tutorial/Overview.html.

.NET/LINK USER GUIDE. Wolfram *Mathematica* Documentation Center, http://reference.wolfram.com/mathematica/NETLink/tutorial/Overview.html.

TWO-DIMENSIONAL EXPRESSION INPUT. Wolfram *Mathematica* Documentation Center, http://reference.wolfram.com/mathematica/tutorial/TwoDimensionalExpressionInputOverview.html.

USING A NOTEBOOK INTERFACE. Wolfram *Mathematica* Documentation Center, http://reference.wolfram.com/mathematica/tutorial/UsingANotebookInterface.html.

WORKING WITH CELLS. Wolfram *Mathematica* Documentation Center, http://reference.wolfram.com/mathematica/tutorial/WorkingWithCells.html.

2. The *Mathematica* language

ENDERTON, HERBERT B. 1972. *A Mathematical Introduction to Logic.* Academic Press.

MAEDER, ROMAN E. 1992. The design of the *Mathematica* programming language. *Dr. Dobb's Journal,* **17**(4), 86.

MAEDER, ROMAN E. 1997. *Programming in Mathematica,* third edition. Addison-Wesley.

MAEDER, ROMAN E. 2000. *Computer Science with Mathematica: Theory and Practice for Science, Mathematics, and Engineering.* Cambridge University Press.

Tutorials and guides

ATTRIBUTES. Wolfram *Mathematica* Documentation Center, http://reference.wolfram.com/mathematica/tutorial/Attributes.html.

EVALUATION OF EXPRESSIONS. Wolfram *Mathematica* Documentation Center, http://reference.wolfram.com/mathematica/tutorial/EvaluationOfExpressionsOverview.html.

EVALUATION: THE STANDARD EVALUATION SEQUENCE. Wolfram *Mathematica* Documentation Center, http://reference.wolfram.com/mathematica/tutorial/Evaluation.html.

OPERATOR INPUT FORMS. Wolfram *Mathematica* Documentation Center, http://reference.wolfram.com/mathematica/tutorial/OperatorInputForms.html.

3. Lists

DAVIS, TIMOTHY A. and YIFAN HU. 2011. The University of Florida sparse matrix collection. *ACM Transactions on Mathematical Software,* **38**(1), 1–25.

DUFF, IAIN S., ROGER G. GRIMES, and JOHN G. LEWIS. 1989. Sparse matrix test problems. *ACM Transactions on Mathematical Software,* **15**(1), 1–14. doi.acm.org/10.1145/62038.62043.

WATTS, DUNCAN J. and STEVEN H. STROGATZ. 1998. Collective dynamics of small-world networks. *Nature,* **393**, 440–442.

4. Patterns and rules

LAGARIAS, JEFFREY. 1985. The $3x + 1$ problem. *American Mathematical Monthly,* **92**, 3–23.

MAEDER, ROMAN E. 1994. Animated algorithms. *The Mathematica Journal,* **4**(4), 86, www.mathematica-journal.com/issue/v4i4/columns/maeder.

SEDGEWICK, ROBERT and KEVIN WAYNE. 2011. *Algorithms,* fourth edition. Addison-Wesley.

WAGON, STAN. 1999. *Mathematica in Action,* second edition. TELOS/Springer-Verlag.

5. Functional programming

BRENT, RICHARD P. 1980. An improved Monte Carlo factorization algorithm. *BIT,* **20**(2), 176–184, http://mathspeople.anu.edu.au/~brent/pd/rpb051a.pdf.

CRANDALL, RICHARD E. and CARL POMERANCE. 2005. *Prime Numbers: A Computational Perspective,* second edition. Springer.

DIACONIS, PERSI and DAVE BAYER. 1992. Trailing the dovetail shuffle to its lair. *Annals of Applied Probability*, **2**(2), 294–313, http://projecteuclid.org/euclid.aoap/1177005705.

DIACONIS, PERSI, RON L. GRAHAM, and WILLIAM M. KANTOR. 1983. The mathematics of perfect shuffles. *Advances in Applied Mathematics*, **4**(2), 175–196, www-stat.stanford.edu/~cgates/PERSI/papers/83_05_shuffles.pdf.

DIJKSTRA, EDSGER W. 1981. Hamming's exercise in SASL. Report EWD792, www.cs.utexas.edu/users/EWD/ewd07xx/EWD792.PDF.

FLOYD, ROBERT W. 1962. Algorithm 97: shortest path. *Communications of the ACM*, **5**(6).

GRAHAM, RONALD, DONALD E. KNUTH, and OREN PATASHNIK. 1994. *Concrete Mathematics: A Foundation for Computer Science*, second edition. Addison-Wesley.

HAMMING, RICHARD W. 1950. Error detecting and error correcting codes. *Bell System Technical Journal*, **29**(2), 147–160.

HERSTEIN, ISRAEL N. and IRVING KAPLANSKY. 1978. *Matters Mathematical*. AMS Chelsea Publishing.

HOFFMAN, PAUL. 1998. *The Man Who Loved Only Numbers: The Story of Paul Erdös and the Search for Mathematical Truth*. Hyperion.

KNUTH, DONALD E. 1993. *The Stanford GraphBase: A Platform for Combinatorial Computing*. ACM Press.

MERINGER, MARKUS and ERIC W. WEISSTEIN. Regular graph. *MathWorld*, http://mathworld.wolfram.com/RegularGraph.html.

DE LAS RIVAS, J. and C. FONTANILLO. 2010. Protein–protein interactions essentials: key concepts to building and analyzing interactome networks. *PLoS Computational Biology*, **6**(6): E1000807. doi:10.1371/journal.pcbi.1000807.

SEDGEWICK, ROBERT and KEVIN WAYNE. 2011. *Algorithms*, fourth edition. Addison-Wesley.

WORM INTERACTOME DATABASE. Center for Cancer Systems Biology, http://interactome.dfci.harvard.edu/C_elegans.

6. Procedural programming

KNUTH, DONALD E. 1998. *The Art of Computer Programming, Volume 3: Sorting and Searching*, second edition. Addison-Wesley.

LAGARIAS, JEFFREY C., VICTOR S. MILLER, and ANDREW M. ODLYZKO. 1985. Computing $\pi(x)$: the Meissel–Lehmer method. *Mathematics of Computation*, **44**, 537–560.

LAGARIAS, JEFFREY C. and ANDREW M. ODLYZKO. 1987. Computing $\pi(x)$: an analytic method. *Journal of Algorithms*, **8**, 173–191.

PRESS, WILLIAM H., SAUL A. TEUKOLSKY, WILLIAM T. VETTERLING, and BRIAN P. FLANNERY. 2007. *Numerical Recipes: The Art of Scientific Computing*, third edition. Cambridge University Press.

RUST, BERT W. and WALTER R. BURRUS. 1972. *Mathematical Programming and the Numerical Solution of Linear Equations*. American Elsevier.

WEISSTEIN, ERIC W. Lucky number. *MathWorld*, http://mathworld.wolfram.com/LuckyNumber.html.

7. Recursion

GRAHAM, RONALD, DONALD E. KNUTH, and OREN PATASHNIK. 1994. *Concrete Mathematics: A Foundation for Computer Science*, second edition. Addison-Wesley.

HASKELLWIKI. *The Fibonacci sequence*. The Haskell Programming Language, www.haskell.org/haskellwiki/The_Fibonacci_sequence.

KNUTH, DONALD E. 1997. *The Art of Computer Programming, Volume 1: Fundamental Algorithms*, third edition. Addison-Wesley.

KNUTH, DONALD E. 2001. Textbook examples of recursion, in *Selected Papers on Analysis of Algorithms*. Center for the Study of Language and Information, http://arxiv.org/abs/cs/9301113.

PEMMARAJU, SRIRAM V. and STEVEN S. SKIENA. 2003. *Computational Discrete Mathematics: Combinatorics and Graph Theory with Mathematica*. Cambridge University Press.

8. Numerics

BAILEY, DAVID H., JONATHAN M. BORWEIN, CRISTIAN S. CALUDE, ET AL. 2012. Normality and the digits of π, www.davidhbailey.com/dhbpapers/normality-digits-pi.pdf.

BOX, GEORGE E.P., GWILYM M. JENKINS, and GREGORY C. REINSEL. 2008. *Time Series Analysis: Forecasting and Control*, fourth edition. John Wiley & Sons.

BURDEN, RICHARD L. and J. DOUGLAS FAIRES. 2001. *Numerical Analysis*, seventh edition. Brooks/Cole.

CHATFIELD, CHRISTOPHER. 2004. *The Analysis of Time Series: An Introduction*, fourth edition. Chapman & Hall/CRC Press.

COSTA, LUCIANO DA FONTOURA and ROBERTO MARCONDES CESAR. 2001. *Shape Analysis and Classification: Theory and Practice*. CRC Press.

COVER, THOMAS M. and JOY A. THOMAS. 2006. *Elements of Information Theory*, second edition. Wiley Interscience.

GOLDBERG, DAVID. 1991. What every computer scientist should know about floating-point arithmetic. *ACM Computing Surveys*, **23**(1), 5–47. Reprint available online at www.validlab.com/goldberg/paper.pdf.

HAYES, ALLAN. 1992. Sum of cubes of digits, driven to abstraction. *Mathematica in Education*, **1**(4), 3–11.

KENNY, CHARMAINE. Random number generators: an evaluation and comparison of random.org and some commonly used generators. Management Science and Information Systems Studies, Trinity College Dublin, www.random.org/analysis/Analysis2005.pdf.

KNAPP, ROB. 2001. *Numerical Mathematica*. 2001 International *Mathematica* Symposium, http://library.wolfram.com/infocenter/Conferences/4044.

KNUTH, DONALD E. 1997. *The Art of Computer Programming, Volume 2: Seminumerical Algorithms*, third edition. Addison-Wesley.

MANNING, CHRISTOPHER D. and HINRICH SCHÜTZE. 1999. *Foundations of Statistical Natural Language Processing*. The MIT Press.

MULLER, JEAN-MICHEL, NICOLAS BRISEBARRE, FLORENT DE DINECHIN, ET AL. 2010. *Handbook of Floating-Point Arithmetic*. Birkhäuser.

NATIONAL INSTITUTE OF STANDARDS AND TECHNOLOGY. *Nist/Sematech e-handbook of statistical methods*, www.itl.nist.gov/div898/handbook.

NATIONAL INSTITUTE OF STANDARDS AND TECHNOLOGY. *Sparse matrix collection*, http://math.nist.gov/MatrixMarket/collections/hb.html.

RUDNICK, JOSEPH and GEORGE GASPARI. 2004. *Elements of the Random Walk: An Introduction for Advanced Students and Researchers.* Cambridge University Press.

RUKHIN, ANDREW, JUAN SOTO, JAMES NECHVATAL, ET AL. 2010. *A Statistical Test Suite for Random and Pseudorandom Number Generators for Cryptographic Applications.* National Institute of Standards and Technology. Special publication 800–22, Rev. 1a.

SHANNON, CLAUDE E. 1948. A mathematical theory of computation. *Bell System Technical Journal,* **27**, 379–423 and 623–656. Reprint available online at http://cm.bell-labs.com/cm/ms/what/shannonday/shannon1948.pdf.

SKEEL, ROBERT D. and JERRY B. KEIPER. 1993. *Elementary Numerical Computing with Mathematica.* McGraw-Hill.

SOTO, JUAN. Statistical testing of random number generators. National Institute of Standards and Technology, http://csrc.nist.gov/groups/ST/toolkit/rng/documents/nissc-paper.pdf.

9. Strings

BORGES, JORGE LUIS. 1983. The Library of Babel, in *Labyrinths: Selected Short Stories & Other Writings.* Modern Library.

BRITISH ACADEMIC SPOKEN ENGLISH (BASE) and BASE PLUS COLLECTIONS. Centre for Applied Linguistics, University of Warwick. www2.warwick.ac.uk/fac/soc/al/research/collect/base.

CHOMSKY, NOAM. 2002. *Syntactic Structures,* second edition. Mouton de Gruyter.

CRISTIANINI, NELLO and MATTHEW W. HAHN. 2007. *Introduction to Computational Genomics: A Case Studies Approach.* Cambridge University Press.

DNA DATA BANK OF JAPAN. Center for Information Biology, National Institute of Genetics, www.ddbj.nig.ac.jp.

FRIEDL, JEFFREY E.F. 2006. *Mastering Regular Expressions,* third edition. O'Reilly Media.

GENOME COMPOSITION DATABASE. Research Organization of Information and Systems, National Institute of Genetics, http://esper.lab.nig.ac.jp/study/genome.

JOYCE, JAMES. 1939. *Finnegans Wake.* Viking Penguin Inc.

JURAFSKY, DANIEL and JAMES H. MARTIN. 2009. *Speech and Language Processing: An Introduction to Natural Language Processing, Computational Linguistics, and Speech Recognition,* second edition. Pearson Prentice Hall.

MANNING, CHRISTOPHER D. and HINRICH SCHÜTZE. 1999. *Foundations of Statistical Natural Language Processing.* The MIT Press.

MANNING, CHRISTOPHER D., PRABHAKAR RAGHAVAN, and HINRICH SCHÜTZE. 2008. *Introduction to Information Retrieval.* Cambridge University Press.

NUCLEOTIDE DATABASE. National Center for Biotechnology Information, www.ncbi.nlm.nih.gov/nuccore.

PAAR, CHRISTOF and JAN PELZL. 2010. *Understanding Cryptography: A Textbook for Students and Practitioners.* Springer.

PROJECT GUTENBERG. www.gutenberg.org.

SCHWARTZ, RANDAL L., BRIAN D FOY, and TOM PHOENIX. 2011. *Learning Perl,* sixth edition. O'Reilly & Associates.

SINKOV, ABRAHAM. 1966. *Elementary Cryptanalysis: A Mathematical Approach.* The Mathematical Association of America.

TEETOR, PAUL. 2011. *R Cookbook.* O'Reilly Media.

UNICODE 6.1 CHARACTER CODE CHARTS. The Unicode Consortium. www.unicode.org/charts.

UNIVERSITY OF CHICAGO PRESS. 2010. *The Chicago Manual of Style*, sixteenth edition. University of Chicago Press.

WALL, LARRY, TOM CHRISTIANSEN, and JON ORWANT. 2000. *Programming Perl*, third edition. O'Reilly Media.

WIKIBOOKS. *Python programming/strings*, www.wikibooks.org/wiki/Python_Programming/Strings.

Tutorials and guides

REGULAR EXPRESSIONS. Wolfram *Mathematica* Documentation Center, http://reference.wolfram.com/mathematica/tutorial/RegularExpressions.html.

WORKING WITH STRING PATTERNS. Wolfram *Mathematica* Documentation Center, http://reference.wolfram.com/mathematica/tutorial/WorkingWithStringPatternsOverview.html.

10. Visualization

ABBOTT, PAUL. 1998. Finding roots in an interval. *The Mathematica Journal*, **7**(2), 108–112.

BAILEY, DAVID H., JONATHAN M. BORWEIN, CRISTIAN S. CALUDE, ET AL. 2012. Normality and the digits of π, www.davidhbailey.com/dhbpapers/normality-digits-pi.pdf.

BOWERMAN, BRUCE L., RICHARD T. O'CONNELL, and ANNE B. KOEHLER. 2005. *Forecasting, Time Series, and Regression: An Applied Approach*. Thomson Brooks/Cole.

CASTI, JOHN L. 1992. *Reality Rules I, Picturing the World in Mathematics – The Fundamentals*. John Wiley & Sons.

COOK, STEPHEN A. 2000. *The P versus NP Problem*. Manuscript prepared for the Clay Mathematics Institute for the Millennium Prize Problems, www.claymath.org/millennium/P_vs_NP.

GARDNER, MARTIN. 1992. *Fractal Music, Hypercards, and More…Mathematical Recreations from Scientific American Magazine*. W.H. Freeman.

GOLDREICH, ODED. 2010. *P, NP, and NP-Completeness: The Basics of Computational Complexity*. Cambridge University Press.

GOLIN, MORDECAI and ROBERT SEDGEWICK. 1988. Analysis of a simple yet efficient convex hull algorithm. *Proceedings of the Fourth Annual Symposium on Computational Geometry*, 153–163, ACM.

GRAHAM, RONALD. 1994. An efficient algorithm for determining the convex hull of a finite planar set. *Information Processing Letters*, **1**, 1972.

HECKBERT, PAUL S., ED. 1994. *Graphics Gems IV*. Academic Press.

JARVIS, RAY A. 1973. On the identification of the convex hull of a finite set of points in the plane. *Information Processing Letters*, **2**, 18–21.

LAWLER, EUGENE L., JAN KAREL LENSTRA, A.H.G. RINNOOY KAN, and D.B. SHMOYS. 1985. *The Traveling Salesman Problem: A Guided Tour of Combinatorial Optimization*. John Wiley & Sons.

LIMA, MANUEL. 2011. *Visual Complexity: Mapping Patterns of Information*. Princeton Architectural Press.

LIN, SHEN 1965. Computer solutions of the traveling salesman problem. *Bell System Technical Journal*, **44**, 2245–2269.

MANDELBROT, BENOÎT. 1982. *The Fractal Geometry of Nature*. W.H. Freeman.

MAOR, ELI. 1998. *Trigonometric Delights*. Princeton University Press.

MATHEWS, MAX V., JOAN E. MILLER, F. RICHARD MOORE, ET AL. 1969. *The Technology of Computer Music*. The MIT Press.

O'ROURKE, JOSEPH. 1998. *Computational Geometry in C*, second edition. Cambridge University Press.

PEMMARAJU, SRIRAM V. and STEVEN S. SKIENA. 2003. *Computational Discrete Mathematics: Combinatorics and Graph Theory with Mathematica*. Cambridge University Press.

PIERCE, JOHN R. 1983. *The Science of Musical Sound*. W.H. Freeman.

PLATZMAN, LOREN K. and JOHN J. BARTHOLDI III. 1989. Spacefilling curves and the planar traveling salesman problem. *Journal of the ACM*, **36**, 719–737.

PORTA, HORACIO, WILLIAM DAVIS, and JERRY UHL. 1994. *Calculus&Mathematica*. Addison-Wesley.

PREPARATA, FRANCO P. and MICHAEL IAN SHAMOS. 1985. *Computational Geometry: An Introduction*. Springer-Verlag.

ROSENKRANTZ, DANIEL J., RICHARD E. STEARNS, and PHILIP M. LEWIS. 1977. An analysis of several heuristics for the traveling salesman problem. *SIAM Journal of Computing*, **6**(3), 563–581, http://dx.doi.org/10.1137/0206041.

ROSSING, THOMAS D. 1990. *The Science of Sound*, second edition. Addison-Wesley.

SHAMOS, MICHAEL I. and DAN HOEY. 1975. Closest-point problems. In *16th Annual Symposium on Foundations of Computer Science*. IEEE.

SHEPARD, ROGER. 1962. The analysis of proximities: multidimensional scaling with an unknown distance factor. *Psychometrika*, **27**, 125–140.

THOMSEN, DIETRICH E. 1980. Making music – fractally. *Science News*, **117**, 187.

VOSS, RICHARD F. and JOHN CLARKE. 1978. $1/f$ noise in music and speech. *Journal of the Acoustical Society of America*, **63**, 258–263.

WEISSTEIN, ERIC W. Hypocycloid. *MathWorld*, http://mathworld.wolfram.com/Hypocycloid.html.

Tutorials and guides

THREE-DIMENSIONAL GRAPHICS DIRECTIVES (tutorial). Wolfram *Mathematica* Documentation Center, http://reference.wolfram.com/mathematica/tutorial/ThreeDimensionalGraphicsDirectives.html.

THREE-DIMENSIONAL GRAPHICS PRIMITIVES (tutorial). Wolfram *Mathematica* Documentation Center, http://reference.wolfram.com/mathematica/tutorial/ThreeDimensionalGraphicsPrimitives.html.

11. Dynamic expressions

BOYER, CARL B. 1985. *A History of Mathematics*. Princeton University Press.

DAVIS, JOSEPH, H. 2004. An annual index of US industrial production, 1790–1915. *Quarterly Journal of Economics*, **119**(4): 1177–1215. Data available online at www.nber.org/data/industrial-production-index/.

DUCHAMP, MARCEL. 1926. *Anémic Cinéma*. Video available online at www.ubu.com/film/duchamp_anemic.html.

GRÜNBAUM, BRANKO. 1984. On Venn diagrams and the counting of regions. *The College Mathematics Journal*, **15**, 433–435.

LAWLER, EUGENE L., JAN KAREL LENSTRA, A.H.G. RINNOOY KAN, and D.B. SHMOYS. 1985. *The Traveling Salesman Problem: A Guided Tour of Combinatorial Optimization*. John Wiley & Sons.

RUSKEY, FRANK and MARK WESTON. 2005. A survey of Venn diagrams. *The Electronic Journal of Combinatorics*, **DS5**, www.combinatorics.org/files/Surveys/ds5/VennEJC.html.

Tutorials and guides

ADVANCED DYNAMIC FUNCTIONALITY. Wolfram *Mathematica* Documentation Center, http://reference.wolfram.com/-mathematica/tutorial/AdvancedDynamicFunctionality.html.

CONTROL OBJECTS. Wolfram *Mathematica* Documentation Center, http://reference.wolfram.com/mathematica/guide/-ControlObjects.html.

INTRODUCTION TO DYNAMIC. Wolfram *Mathematica* Documentation Center, http://reference.wolfram.com/mathematica/tutorial/IntroductionToDynamic.html.

12. Optimizing *Mathematica* programs

BOURKE, PAUL. 2001. *Julia Set Fractal (2D)*, www.paulbourke.net/fractals/juliaset.

KNUTH, DONALD E. 1992. *Literate Programming*. Center for the Study of Language and Information.

PEITGEN, HEINZ-OTTO, HARTMUT JÜRGENS, and DIETMAR SAUPE. 1992. *Chaos and Fractals: New Frontiers of Science*. Springer-Verlag.

13. Applications and packages

BARBER, MICHAEL N. and BARRY W. NINHAM. 1970. *Random and Restricted Walks: Theory and Applications*. Gordon and Breach.

FELLER, WILLIAM. 1968. *An Introduction to Probability Theory and its Applications*, Volume 1, third edition. John Wiley & Sons.

GAYLORD, RICHARD J. and PAUL R. WELLIN. 1995. *Computer Simulations with Mathematica, Explorations in Complex Physical and Biological Systems*. TELOS/Springer-Verlag.

MADRAS, NEAL and GORDON SLADE. 1996. *The Self-Avoiding Walk*. Birkhäuser.

PEARSON, KARL. 1905. The problem of the random walk, *Nature*, **72**, 294.

WEISS, GEORGE H. 1983. Random walks and their applications. *American Scientist*, **71**, 65–71.

WEISS, GEORGE H. 1994. *Aspects and Applications of the Random Walk*. North-Holland.

WEISSTEIN, ERIC W. Sphere point picking. *MathWorld*, http://mathworld.wolfram.com/SpherePointPicking.html.

WOLFRAM WORKBENCH. *Mathematica* development user guide, http://reference.wolfram.com/workbench.

General reference

CRANDALL, RICHARD E. 1994. *Projects in Scientific Computation*. TELOS/Springer-Verlag.

CRANDALL, RICHARD E. 1996. *Topics in Advanced Scientific Computation*. TELOS/Springer-Verlag.

FLOYD, ROBERT W. 1979. The paradigms of programming. *Communications of the ACM*, **22**(8).

MANGANO, SALVATORE. 2010. *Mathematica Cookbook*. O'Reilly Media.

THE *MATHEMATICA* JOURNAL. Wolfram Media, www.mathematica-journal.com.

TROTT, MICHAEL. 2004. *The Mathematica Guidebook for Programming*. Springer-Verlag.

TROTT, MICHAEL. 2004. *The Mathematica Guidebook for Graphics*. Springer-Verlag.

WICKHAM-JONES, TOM. 1994. *Computer Graphics with Mathematica*. TELOS/Springer-Verlag.

Index